CONCISE
DUTCH AND ENGLISH
DICTIONARY

. . . this work can be recommended for those about to buy
their first Dutch dictionary or those wishing to bridge the
gap between a "pocket" dictionary and an advanced work.

Modern Languages

D1386645

TEACH YOURSELF BOOKS

CONCISE DUTCH AND ENGLISH DICTIONARY

Dutch–English/English–Dutch

Peter and Margaretha King

TEACH YOURSELF BOOKS
Hodder and Stoughton

First printed 1958
Seventh impression 1976

This volume is published in the U.S.A.
by David McKay Company Inc.,
750 Third Avenue, New York, N.Y. 10017.

ISBN 0 340 05779 3

Printed in Great Britain
for Teach Yourself Books, Hodder and Stoughton, London
by Richard Clay (The Chaucer Press), Ltd., Bungay, Suffolk

INTRODUCTION

ABOUT 17,000 words are given in the Dutch–English section, and about 14,000 in the English–Dutch, though the actual number of equivalents is really far greater than this, and certainly enough for everyday use.

Condensation was essential if the maximum amount of information was to be given, and this has been effected by the use of brackets and punctuation.

Brackets. Where brackets occur in a word and its translation, two separate equivalents can be obtained by the inclusion or rejection of the parts in the brackets on both sides :

peril(ous), ge'vaar(lijk) (*n*)

Here, *the symbol "n", used throughout for neuter nouns,* is also placed in brackets, since, of course, it cannot apply to the adjective. Hence

peril, het ge'vaar
perilous, ge'vaarlijk

Similarly, **washing,** was(goed *n*) gives the two renderings : *de was* or *het wasgoed.*

Hyphens placed after Dutch words signify that they can be used as adjectives in composites :

autumn(al), herfst(–)

i.e., the autumn, *de herfst* ; autumn (*or* autumnal) weather, *herfstweer.* Likewise foster(-mother), *pleeg(moeder)* implies that the Dutch *pleeg* can be used to form a composite equivalent to any of the English foster-relations (*pleegkind* = foster-child, etc.).

Punctuation between two or more translations is intended to assist in deciding which one is required. Commas have been used between two words that are more or less synonymous ; semi-colons separate literal from metaphorical meanings, the literal being given first, even where that is far less common, and they also separate words of entirely different meaning but the same origin ; colons are used between words of different origin and between different parts of speech. Finally, where an English word can be used as a noun or adjective as well as a verb, the verbal meaning is always given last. Hence in the example—

lead, leiding ; eerste plaats, voorsprong ; riem ; voorbeeld *n* :
    lood *n* : leiden, ertoe brengen ; voor('op)gaan ; aanvoeren

the commonest literal noun form is given first (*guidance*), followed by other literal meanings, *first place* (cf. " in the lead ") and the extent of this advance (" a lead of two lengths "), another quite different literal meaning, riem (*the dog's lead*) and then the metaphorical application (*example*). After the first colon the translation of the other English noun of the same spelling, the metal *lead*, is given, followed by the various equivalents of the verb *to lead* (with a condensation, by the use of brackets, of the two verbs *voorgaan*, to lead the way and *voor'opgaan*, to go in front of).

Obviously the final selection from a number of alternative translations must be made by the reader himself, and this can be done with reasonable accuracy only by cross-reference. *Where there is any doubt about the correct Dutch equivalent for an English word, the only safe check is to refer to the Dutch–English section in order to eliminate those Dutch words which do not correspond with the sense of the English word.*

Adverbs have the same form as adjectives in Dutch, so that these are shown separately only where an adverb has no corresponding adjectival form.

Stress marks, denoted by ' immediately preceding the stressed syllable in Dutch words, are given only where the main stress does *not* fall on the first syllable.

Spelling. Inconsistencies in the spelling of Dutch words in the two parts of the dictionary may be encountered. The reason for this is that the official spelling list recently published (1954) introduces a number of changes, chiefly in the spelling of loan-words. Since many of the older spellings are more common than the revised forms in the official list, these commoner spellings are given in the Dutch–English section (though the new spelling may be given too), while the English–Dutch section gives only the revised forms. Further reference to this, and the earlier spelling reform of 1947, is made on p. 13.

CONTENTS

ACKNOWLEDGEMENTS

The authors wish to record their deep regret that illness prevented Mr H. Koolhoven from completing this work, which owes so much to his guidance in the earlier stages, and they are grateful to him too for the use they have made of his Teach Yourself Dutch in the Teach Yourself series:

They also express their appreciation to the publishers of Mrs Annie Holch Justesen's Hollandsk Grammatik, which they strongly recommend for advanced students of the language, for permission to use this work in the preparation of the section on grammar.

A special word of gratitude is due to Miss A. Huysinga for her extensive advice and reading of the manuscript.

SOUNDS AND SPELLING

THE way in which the vowel sounds in Dutch influence the spelling can be explained much more easily if a distinction is made between open and checked vowels, instead of between long and short. A long vowel is called open (or free), since it can occur anywhere, and in particular at the end of an open syllable. A short vowel can never occur at the end of a syllable, since it is checked by the consonant that follows it, with which it stands in close contact.

Consequently in a word like *poten*, the *o* is open [po·tə], since the two syllables are split between the *o* and the *t*, whereas in *potten* [pɔtə] the *o* is checked because though only one *t* is pronounced, the division between the syllables falls within this *t*, as is shown in the spelling *pot-ten*.

All the diphthongs, whether consisting of long or short elements, are open.

All vowels, whether open or checked, are lengthened by a following *r*.

Open Vowels

[a·]   More open and further forward in the mouth than Eng. *father*. (cf. first element in Eng. *eye*).
Spelt **aa** in closed syllables, **a** in open syllables.

[o·]   A rounded vowel as in Fr. *beau*. It is particularly affected by a following *r* (as in *oor*, *toren*), when it tends towards [u·r].
Spelt **oo** in closed syllables, **o** in open syllables.

[y·]   A high front vowel with strong lip-rounding, as in Fr. *lu*.
Spelt **uu** in closed syllables, **u** in open syllables.

[e·]   Between Fr. *é* (as in *été*) and Eng. *face*. It is strongly affected by a following *r* when it tends towards [i·r].
Spelt **ee** in closed syllables, **e** in open syllables, except at the end of a word, when it is spelt **ee** to distinguish it from final *e*, which is pronounced [ə].

[i·]   As in Eng. *see*, but a little shorter (except before *r*).
Spelt **ie** in closed syllables. In open syllables it is generally spelt **ie**, though in a number of loan words it is spelt **i**. The ending *-isch* is always pronounced [i·s].

[u·]   As in Eng. *cool* but shorter (except when followed by *r*).
Always spelt **oe**.

[ø]   Like Fr. *feu* (i.e., with the tongue as for [e·] and the lips tightly rounded).
Always spelt **eu**.

Checked Vowels

These always occur in closed syllables.

[ɑ]   Between *hut* and *hot*, or like Eng. [ɑ:] (as in *father*) shortened.
Always spelt **a**.

[ɔ]   Between *cot* and *caught*.
Always spelt **o**.

[œ]   As in *away*, but with the lips slightly rounded.
Always spelt **u**.

11

[ɛ]   Between *wet* and *hat* (see below).

Always spelt **e**, except in a few words loaned from English, when it is spelt **a** (*jam, tram, shag*, etc.).

[ɪ]   Between *pit* and *pet* (see below).

Always spelt **i**.

The Dutch sounds [ɪ] and [ɛ] fall about half-way between the alternative words in the following descending scale:

pit (Eng.)
pit (Du.)
pet (Eng.)
pet (Du.)
pat (Eng.)

The Neutral Vowel

[ə]   Like the indistinct sound in *away*, and, as in English, always unstressed. It can occur in closed or open syllables (hence also finally), and is generally spelt *e*, though it also occurs in the suffixes *-ig, -lijk*: *enig* [eˑnəx], *lelijk* [leˑlək].

Diphthongs

[aːi] When the diphthongs [aːi], [oːi], [uˑi] are followed by a vowel,
[oːi] the second element is replaced by a [j]-glide, becoming re-
[uˑi] spectively: [aːj], [oːj], [uˑj].

They are always spelt **aai, ooi, oei**.

[ɪˑu] When followed by a vowel, these diphthongs, which are
[eːu] always spelt **ieuw, eeuw, uw**, become [iˑʋ], [eːʋ], [yˑʋ].
[yˑu]

[ɛi]   Between *rite* and *rate*.

It is spelt **ij** or **ei** according to the origin of the word.

[œy] This is probably the most difficult Dutch sound for the English-man. It falls between the [ʌ] in Eng. *hut* followed by Dutch [y] (as in *nu*) and the French diphthong in *feuille*.

It is always spelt **ui**.

[ɔu] The first element is more open than [ɔ], tending towards [ɑ].

The spelling is either **ou** or **au**, depending on the origin of the word.

Consonants and Semi-vowels

Final consonants are never voiced; i.e., [b, d; v, g, z] become [p, t; f, x, s] and this has partially affected the spelling, so that *v, z* never appear at the end of a word.

The plosives **p, t, k ; b, d** are pronounced as in English but with-out any aspiration. Intervocalic **d** is often dropped in normal speech, particularly in the West of the country, and replaced by a [j]-glide (*goede* [guˑjə]) or [ʋ]-glide after u (*oude* [ɔuʋə]).

The fricatives **f, v** are pronounced as in English, except that **v** initially passes from unvoiced to voiced or even remains entirely unvoiced. [ʋ] (spelt **w**) is pronounced like [v] but with no friction. It is always entirely voiced. When followed by **r** it is pronounced [v].

[z]   Pronounced like Eng. **z**, except that initial **z**, like initial **v**, starts slightly unvoiced.

13

[x]	This is the sound in the Scottish *loch*. It is represented by **ch** and also, at the end of a word, by **g**. The combination *schr* is rarely pronounced [sxr]; the [x] is reduced or dropped altogether, but where this sound [sr] is heard, the spelling will always be *schr*.
[g]	This consonant (written **g**) starts unvoiced [x] and then becomes voiced (cf. initial **v** and **z**), though it is often entirely unvoiced.
[j]	As in *yes*, and often with distinct friction. Always spelt **j**.
[ŋ]	Written **ng** and pronounced as in *long*, never [ŋg] as in *finger*.
[n]	Written **n** and pronounced as in English, except in the ending **-en**, where in spoken standard (i.e., Holland) Dutch it is dropped: *even kijken* [eˑvə kɛikə].
[l]	**l** has the same pronunciation as in English, but where it is followed by **f, g, k, m, p** in the same syllable a short [ə] separates the two consonants: *elf* [ɛləf].
[r]	The *r* is always trilled in Dutch except at the end of a word, where it is audible only as a weak fricative.

The remaining consonants are pronounced in Dutch as they are in English.

Assimilation

Assimilation plays a very important part in Dutch pronunciation, where any combination of fricatives and plosives must be either voiced or voiceless, so that such a combination as in Eng. *width* is impossible.

The following rules apply where consonants fall together within a word or at the end and beginning of two adjacent words:

1. In combinations of a plosive (in which the air stream is emitted in a staccato explosion) and a fricative (in which the air stream is constant), the plosive decides whether the combination shall be voiced or voiceless:

   opvegen [ɔpfeˑɡə]   *niet zo* [niˑt soˑ]

2. A combination of two fricatives is always voiceless:

   grasveld [ɡrɑsfɛlt]   *droog zand* [droˑx sɑnt]

3. An unvoiced next to a voiced plosive becomes voiced:

   uitbarsten [œydbɑrstə]   *op de tafel* [ɔb də taˑfəl]

Spelling

In the older spelling, which was officially revised in 1947, double vowels will frequently be found in open syllables, and *sch* may occur medially and finally even where the *ch* is not pronounced. A further attempt to remove anomalies, particularly in the use of such foreign digraphs as *th* and *ph*, and the plural endings in such composites as *paardenhaar* (horsehair), has been made by the Dutch and Belgian Governments' publication of a *Woordenlijst van de Nederlandse Taal* in 1954. Further reference is made to this list in the Introduction.

The rules of pronunciation which affect spelling can be summarized as follows:

1. Final consonants are always voiceless.
2. Assimilation may change the voicing of two adjacent consonants.

14

3. Whether an open (long) vowel is written with a double or single letter will depend on whether it falls in a closed or open syllable, and conversely, the consonant after a checked (short) vowel must be doubled if another syllable be added (*man, mannen*; man, men).

4. In words ending in *-isch* the *ch* is not pronounced and the *i* is long [i·s]. The suffixes *-lijk, -ig* are pronounced with the neutral vowel-sound [ə], i.e., [lək], [əx].

GRAMMAR
Articles

1. There are two forms of the definite article:

de for the common gender (formed by the coalescence of the older masculine and feminine genders) in the singular and plural.

het for neuter nouns in the singular and *de* in the plural.

de tuin, the garden	*het huis*, the house
de tuinen, the gardens	*de huizen*, the houses

There is one form only of the indefinite article:

een peer, a pear   *een appel*, an apple

het is sometimes written '*t* [ət], indicating its normal pronunciation. *een* is similarly sometimes written (and always pronounced) '*n* [ən].

2. Relicts of the inflected forms of the articles are still used in some names and phrases, e.g.:

Den Haag (The Hague, *meaning* at-the-Hedge)

'*s nachts* (from *des nachts*, of a night, i.e., at night *or* every night)

Nouns

3. The *gender* of nouns is indicated in the dictionary by denoting neuter nouns by the symbol *n*; the remainder may be assumed to be common gender. (See further the Introduction.)

4. There are three plural endings: *-en, -s, -eren*. *-en* is the normal ending:

hand, handen; *huis, huizen*; *man, mannen*; *naam, namen* (for changes in spelling see pp. 12, 14 above)

and

getuige, getuigen (witness(es)), where only *-n* is added.

A number of plurals do not undergo the spelling changes we should expect, with a resultant change in vowel-sound:

dag, dagen (days); *gat, gaten* (holes); *pad, paden* (paths); *spel, spelen* (games); *weg, wegen* (ways); *oorlog, oorlogen* (wars)

and where the vowel itself changes:

lid, leden (members); *schip, schepen* (ships); *stad, steden* (towns) and the suffix *-heid*, plur. *-heden*: *moeilijkheid, moeilijkheden* (difficulties)

Note also:

    koe, koeien (cows); *zee, zeeën* (seas); *knie, knieën* (knees)

-*s* is used for the plural of:

    all diminutives: *huisjes* (cottages), etc.
    all words ending in -*el*, -*em*, -*en*, -*er*, -*aar*(*d*), -*erd*.
    loan-words ending in vowels: *drama's*; *studies*; *piano's*; *cadeaus*
    and a number of other foreign words: *details*; *romans*; *trams*, etc.

-*eren* is added to the following words, all of which are neuter, to form their plurals:

    ei(*eren*), egg(s); *lam*(*meren*), lamb(s); *rund*(*eren*), cow(s),
    bull(s); *kind*(*eren*), child(ren); *lied*(*eren*), song(s); *goed*(*eren*),
    stuff, goods; *kalf, kalveren*; *hoen*(*deren*), hen(s); *rad*(*eren*),
    wheel(s); *gemoed*(*eren*), mind(s); *gelid, gelederen*, joint(s)

also

    been (bone, leg), *benen* (legs), *beenderen* (bones)
    blad (leaf, page, tray), *bladen* (pages, trays), *bladeren, blaren*
    (leaves)
    kleed (cloth), *kleden* (cloths), *kleren* (clothes)

5. Composites ending in -*man* form their plurals with the formal suffix -*lieden* or the less formal -*lui*:

    werkman, werklui (workmen); *staatsman, staatslieden* (statesmen)

but

    Engelsman, Engelsen; *Fransman, Fransen*

6. *Singular* forms are used for measures after definite numerals and *een paar* (a few):

    drie meter; *anderhalve liter* (one and a half litres); *vier maal* (four
    times); *een paar keer* (a few times, once or twice); *tien jaar*
    (ten years); *zes uur* (six o'clock)

But the plural is used after adjectives:

    twee lange jaren (two long years)

and the plural is always used for:

    seconden, minuten, dagen, weken, maanden (months), *eeuwen*
    (centuries, ages)

The following have no plural forms:

    hoop (hope); *dank* (thank(s)); *arbeid* (labour); *doel* (aim);
    lof (praise); *dood* (death)

7. There are no *case-endings*, except -*s*, (-'*s* after *a, o, u*) for the genitives of names and titles:

    Jans broer (John's brother); *Anna's jurk* (Anne's dress); *tantes
    bril* (auntie's glasses)

Otherwise the written genitive uses the preposition *van*, while the use of the possessive pronoun is common in everyday speech:

    de naam van de man, de man z'n (= *zijn*) *naam* (the man's name);
    de man van de vrouw, de vrouw d'r (= *haar*) *man* (the woman's
    husband)

The genitive in -*s* is also used for days, periods of the day and seasons, with the meaning *every* or *during*:

('*s*) *Vrijdags* (on Fridays); *'s avonds* (in the evening); *'s zomers* (in the summer) (cf. § 2)

and in the formation of many compounds:

stadsmens (townsman); *veiligheidshalve* (for safety's sake)

Relicts of a dative case occur in a few expressions, the commonest of which are given in the dictionary, e.g.:

ten dele (in part); *ter wille van* (for the sake of)

Adjectives

8. These take the ending -*e* before singular and plural nouns of both genders:

de laatste tijd (the last time); *het oude huis* (the old house); *de betere scholen* (the better schools)

They remain uninflected when they follow their nouns or when preceding a singular neuter noun, by itself, with the indefinite article, or with an indefinite pronoun:

moederlief (dear mother); *de zon is warm*; *vorig jaar* (last year); *een oud huis*; *zulk mooi weer* (such lovely weather)

Attributive adjectives are also uninflected when they describe the quality of a person:

een groot dichter (a great poet); *een oud vriend* (i.e., a friend of long standing rather than a person of great age)

Adjectives ending in -*en* are never inflected:

de Gouden Eeuw (the Golden Age); *mijn eigen tijd* (my own time); *verleden week* (last week)

9. Final *f* or *s* after open vowels or diphthongs in adjectives become *v* or *z* when they are inflected:

doof, dove (deaf); *lief, lieve* (dear); *wijs, wijze* (wise)

also

half, halve

but

kies(e) (delicate); *kuis(e)* (chaste); *heus(e)* courteous

10. *Comparatives* are formed by the addition of -*er*. *Superlatives* by the addition of -*st*. They are inflected in the normal way and are used more extensively than in English.

trouweloos, trouwelozer, trouweloost (faithless)

Where adjectives end in -*r*, a *d* is inserted before the comparative ending:

ver, verder, verst (far)

Irregularities:

goed, beter, best (good)
veel, meer, meest (much)
weinig, minder, minst (little, few)

When comparing two persons or things, Dutch uses the superlative:

Dit is het langste van de twee. This is the longer of the two.

11. Adjectives used substantivally take the inflection -*e*, and -*en* when referring to more than one person:

het beste (the best thing); *de blinden* (the blind)

Adverbs

12. These have exactly the same form as adjectives:

Om goed te zijn moet een boek goed geschreven zijn. To be good, a book must be written well.

Peculiar to Dutch are the diminutive forms *zachtjes* (softly) and *netjes* (nicely), comparable with the predicative adjectives *netjes*, *frisjes* and others.

The comparison of adverbs is also the same as of adjectives except that *graag, gaarne* (gladly, willingly) borrow from *lief* (dear) for their comparative and superlative forms:

liever (rather) and *liefst* (by preference)

Similarly *dikwijls* borrows from *vaak* (often), *vaker, vaakst*.

The superlative adverb is formed with *het* and the superlative adjective:

wat ik het liefst zou willen, what I should like most

or the simple adjectival form is used adverbially with a qualifying adverb to express the superlative sense:

uiterst zelden, very seldom
hoogst waarschijnlijk, most probably

Pronouns

13. *Personal pronouns.*

AS SUBJECTS	AS OBJECTS AND AFTER PREPOSITIONS
Singular	Singular
1. *ik*	*mij, me*
2. *jij, je*	*jou, je*
u	*u*
gij, ge	*u*
3. *hij* } *die* *zij, ze*	*hem, 'm* } *die* *haar, ze*
het, 't	**het, 't*
Plural	Plural
1. *wij, we*	*ons*
2. *jullie*	*jullie*
u	*u*
gij	*u*
3. *zij, ze*	*hen, hun, *ze*

* *het, ze* (when referring to things) are never used after a preposition:

of it (them), to it (them), with it (them), etc.; *ervan, ertoe* (or *eraan*), *ermee*, etc. (cf. thereof, thereto, therewith)

The written forms are named first; the alternatives are used in speech or quoted speech.

The three forms of the second person express ascending degrees of formality:

> *jij* *(je)*, *jullie* are used in addressing animals and between (intimate) friends, by adults to children and by seniors to juniors (in rank or relationship).
>
> *u* is used otherwise (i.e., where the surname or some title, *dokter, tante*, etc., is used), and in correspondence the capital *U* is normal.
>
> *gij* (thou, ye) and *u* (thee, you) are used in the Bible, prayer, poetry, ceremonial occasions or formal speeches and in some dialects.

The third person subject-case *die* is frequently used when referring to things which are not neuter:

> *Waar is je fiets?—Die staat thuis.*
> Where is your bicycle?—It's at home.

Otherwise *hij* is used or, where the writer is familiar with the one-time feminine gender of the noun referred to, *zij*.
But *hem* (pronounced [əm]) is generally used in the object case:

> *Waar is je fiets?—Ik heb 'm verkocht.*
> Where is your bicycle?—I've sold it.

14. *Possessive pronouns.*

Singular	Plural
1. *mijn, m'n*	*ons* (inflected form *onze*)
2. *jouw, je*	*jullie, je*
uw	*uw*
3. *zijn, z'n* (his *or* its)	*hun*
haar, d'r	

ons *huis heeft* **zijn** *(z'n) achterdeur in* **onze** *tuin*
our house has its back door in our garden

Independent possessives are formed with the definite article (*de* or *het* according to the gender of the noun referred to), followed by the possessive pronoun ending in *-e* (or *-ne* after *hun*):

> *Dit huis is het onze.* This house is ours.
> *Is deze wagen de hunne of die van jullie?* Is this car theirs or yours?
> (There is no independent possessive of *jullie*.)

15. *Demonstrative pronouns.*

Singular (common gender)	*deze* (this)	*die* (that)
(neuter)	*dit* (this)	*dat* (that)
Plural (both genders)	*deze* (these)	*die* (those)

The genitive *dezer* (occasionally *dier*, of those) is used in certain expressions and to avoid cumbersome constructions:

> *één dezer dagen*, one of these days, in the near future

and the neuter genitives *dezes, dies* and datives *dezen, dien* (from *dit, dat,* respectively) may be encountered in literary writing and a few expressions:

> *en wat dies meer zij,* and so on (*literally*: and whatever more
> there may be of that)

Note:

> *dit (dat) zijn vrienden van me,* these (those) are friends of mine

Independent demonstrative pronouns are not used with prepositions. *With* (etc.) *this, these* is rendered by *hiermee* (etc.); *with* (etc.), *that, those* is *daarmee* (etc.) (cf. bottom of §§ 13, 16).

The other demonstrative pronouns are inflected like adjectives, except *zo'n* (*zo'n man,* such a man):

> *dat zijn degenen die ik bedoel,* those are the ones I mean

16. *Interrogative pronouns.*

> *wie,* who; *wat,* what; *welk,* which; *wat voor (een),* what sort
> of (a)

Since the genitive *wiens* is formal, the form *wie* + possessive pronoun is sometimes used:

> *Wiens boek bedoelt u?* Whose book do you mean?
> *Wie z'n boek bedoelt u?* (cf. §§ 7, 17)

wat and *wat 'n* are also used in exclamations:

> *Wat idioot!* How ridiculous!
> *Wat is die veranderd!* Hasn't he changed!
> *Wat 'n mensen!* What a lot of people!

As with *het* (§ 12 *passim*), *wat* can never follow a preposition, the forms *waarmee,* etc., being used instead. *Waar* and its propositional suffixes are generally split up:

> *waar denk je aan?* What are you thinking of?

welk is inflected:

> *welk huis; welke tuin; welke huizen*

wat voor (een) is frequently used where there is no parallel in English:

> *Wat voor een dokter is hij?*
> or *Wat is hij voor een doktor?* } What is he like as a doctor?

> *Wat voor boek heb je gekocht?* What did you buy in the way of a
> book?

It is often used with the partitive genitive:

> *Wat heb je daar voor lekkers?* That looks nice; what is it?

17. *Relative pronouns.*

> *die, dat; wie; wat; welk*

dat (that, which) is used when the noun to which it refers is singular and neuter; *die* (who, that, which) is used in all other cases.

waaraan, waarmee, waarvan, etc., are used instead of *die, dat, wat* + preposition (cf. §§ 12, 13, 16), but *wie* can be used after a preposition when referring to persons:

> *Het boek waarvoor ik een gulden betaalde.*
> or *Het boek waar ik een gulden voor betaalde.*
>
> The book for which I paid a guilder.
>
> *Waar ik voor gekomen ben is dit.* What I've come for (*or* about) is this.
>
> *De jongen waarmee hij naar school gaat.*
> *De jongen met wie hij naar school gaat.*
> The boy he goes to school with.*

wat is used after the indefinite pronouns *alles, iets,* the demonstrative *dat* and in constructions where any of these is implied:

> *Ik doe alles wat ik kan.* I'm doing everything I can.
> *Dat is precies wat ik bedoelde.* That is just what I meant.

welk (which) is used adjectivally, in more formal writing.

18. *Indefinite pronouns.*

The possessive forms of *men* (one), *iemand* (someone, anyone), *niemand* (nobody), *ieder* (everyone) are *zijn, iemands, niemands, ieders.*

Plurals take *-e* when referring to things and *-en* for persons:

> *alle(n),* all; *enige(n),* a few, any; *enkele(n),* a few; *sommige(n),* some; *andere(n),* others; *verscheidene(n),* and *verschillende(n),* various, several; *vele(n),* many; *weinige(n),* (a) few

When used as adjectives all indefinite pronouns except *wat* and *geen* are inflected like other adjectives:

> *elke dag; ieder jaar; enkele weken*

As in English, *al* precedes the definite article or pronoun:

> *al het water; al mijn boeken*

though *alle* is the normal form of *al de*:

> *alle lucht,* all the air
> *alle huizen,* all the houses

These pronouns are so much a part of Dutch idiom that it is not possible to do more than name a few commoner instances of their application.

men (one) is frequently used where English requires the passive voice:

> *naar men weet,* as far as is known

iemand is used for some *or* any unspecified person:

> *Iemand vroeg of iemand hem ook kon helpen.* Somebody asked whether there was anyone who could help him.

---

* Note that the pronoun can never be omitted in Dutch as it is in English.

out where *anyone* is used with emphasis in English, the Dutch requires *iedereen*, which also means each one, everyone (cf. *ieder* below) :

> *Iedereen zal je de weg kunnen wijzen.* Anyone will show you the way.
> *Iedereen weet dat.* Anyone (everyone) knows that.

iets and *wat* are interchangeable, and can be used with a partitive genitive :

> *Heb je iets gekocht?—Ja ik heb wat lekkers voor je.*
> Did you buy anything?—Yes, I've got something nice for you.

They can also be used in the sense of *somewhat, a bit* :

> *Dit is iets te veel, mag ik wat minder hebben?* This is a bit too much, may I have a little less?

allemaal is used in everyday language to replace *alle* (all, referring to things), *allen* (all, of people) and *alles* (everything) :

> *Zij zijn alle (allemaal) te koop,* they are all for sale
> *Wij fietsen allen (allemaal) graag,* we all like cycling
> *Alles moet weg, het moet allemaal weg,* everything must go

A preposition followed by *iets, niets* or *alles* is often rendered by *ergens, nergens* or *overal* + the preposition (*met* and *tot* becoming *mee* and *toe*) :

> *Dat herinnert me ergens aan.* } That reminds me of something.
> *Dat herinnert me aan iets.* }

> *Ik weet nergens van.* } I know nothing about it.
> *Ik weet van niets.* }

wie and (less commonly) *alwie* are really relative pronouns used indefinitely :

> *(Al)wie dit zag zal het nooit vergeten.* Anyone who saw this will never forget it.

ieder and *elk* can both mean *each* or *every* as adjectives or nouns :

> *ieder (elk) op zijn buurt,* each in turn
> *iedere (elke) keer,* every (or each) time

and as stressed adjectives they also have the sense of *any (at all)*

> *Ieder (elk) huis is better dan helemaal geen huis.* A house of any sort is better than no house at all.

sommige(n) means *some* in the sense of a certain number of individual things or persons :

> *Sommigen aanvaardden het, anderen weigerden.* Some accepted, others refused.

enig(e) is more restrictive, i.e., it means *some* only in the sense of *a few* or *a little*, hence *any* :

> *Is er enige kans op herstel?* Is there any chance of recovery?
> *Ja, er is wel enige kans.* Yes, there is some chance (but not a great deal).
> *Enigen waren zeeziek.* A few people were seasick.

enkel(e) could have been used in the last example, as also:

enkele (or *enige*) *weken geleden*, some (i.e., a few) weeks ago

enig and *enkel* also mean *only* and *single* resp.:

  het enige wat ik kon doen, the only thing possible
  Er was maar één enkele mogelijkheid. There was only one (single) possibility.

enkel is also used adverbially, meaning *only*:

  enkel en alleen, simply and solely

ander is frequently used in conjunction with *een* [e·n]:

  een of andere dokter, some doctor or other
  Ik moet 't een en ander doen. I've one or two things to do.

but *met het een en het ander*, with one thing and another.

As a noun referring to a person it means *someone else*:

  Ik gaf het aan een ander. I gave it to someone else.

and as a partitive genitive it means *else*:

  niemand (iets) anders, no one (something) else

19. **er.** As we have seen (§ 13), English *it, them* (of things) after a preposition is rendered by *er* with the preposition in Dutch. But it is also used as a pronoun meaning *of it, of them* without a preposition when qualified by an indefinite pronoun or a numeral:

  Zal ik er één nemen? Shall I take one (of them)?

It can also be used adverbially:

  Er is iemand voor u. There is someone to see you.

frequently in passive, impersonal constructions:

  Er wordt gebeld. There is a ring at the door.
  Er is mij gezegd dat . . . I was told that . . .

er is sometimes omitted when it has already been used in the sentence:

  Er is wat voor te zeggen. There is something to be said in its favour.

Numerals

20. *Cardinals.* Units precede tens (e.g., as in English *five and twenty past two*):

  vierenveertig, 44
  honderdzesendertig, 136

honderd and *duizend* are never preceded by *een* or followed by *en*. An old dative ending -*en* has survived in the use of cardinals:

  (*a*) after prepositions—
      voor zessen, before six (o'clock)
      hij sneed het touw in tweeën, he cut the string in half
  (*b*) in constructions *met* + poss. pronoun + cardinal—
      wij waren met z'n drieën, there were three of us
  (*c*) after *wij, jullie*—
      jullie vieren, you four

ongeveer, meaning *roughly* or *about*, (*approx.* is written as *circa* or
±, i.e., *plusminus*) is often replaced by *'n* (*stuk*) *of* in conversation:

> *ik heb er een stuk of drie*, I've got about three of them
> *een week of vijf geleden*, about five weeks ago

Ordinals. With the exception of *eerste*, *derde* and *achtste*, all cardinals from 1 to 19 form their ordinals by the addition of -*de*. The
remainder are formed by adding -*ste*, as are also the indefinite ordinals:

> *De hoeveelste is het vandaag?—De tweede* (*Juli*).
> What is the date today?—The second (of July).

Verbs

21. Dutch verbs fall into three groups: weak, strong and auxiliary
verbs. The same parts of the verbs are used in Dutch as in English,
i.e., the present and preterite tenses, the present and past participles,
the imperative and, of course, the infinitive. The perfect and pluperfect are formed with the auxiliaries *hebben* (to have) and *zijn* (to be),
and the future tense with *zullen* (shall, will). The passive mood is
formed in conjunction with *worden* (to become) and *zijn*. There is
no equivalent of the English progressive tenses.

22. *The infinitive* ends in -*en* or -*n*. The stem is found by taking
away the ending.
When the ending is -*en* preceded by a double consonant, or -*n*
preceded by a double vowel, one consonant or one vowel is dropped
with the ending: the stems of *hebben* and *gaan* are *heb* and *ga*.
When the ending -*en* is preceded by *v* or *z*, the stem ends in *f* or *s*:

> *leven*, to live—stem: *leef*
> *lezen*, to read—stem: *lees*

23. *The present tense* of weak and strong verbs is formed from the
stem, the stem + *t* and the form of the infinitive:

staan, stem: *sta*	*geloven*, stem: *geloof*
ik sta (I stand)	*ik geloof* (I believe)
je, u, gij staat	*je, u, gij gelooft*
hij staat	*hij gelooft*
wij staan	*wij geloven*
jullie staan	*jullie geloven*
u, gij staat	*u, gij gelooft*
zij staan	*zij geloven*

When the stem ends in *t* no second *t* is added. (No Dutch word
ends in a double consonant): *je, u, gij, hij vecht* (*vechten*, to fight).
The interrogative form is obtained by a straightforward inversion,
sta ik, etc., except that final -*t* is omitted before *je*. Note also:

> *Houd je* (pronounced *hou' je*) *d'r niet van?* Don't you like it?

24. *The preterite or past tense* of weak verbs only (strong verbs are
dealt with in § 28) is formed by the addition of -*de* or -*den* to the

stem unless the consonant preceding the ending *-en* in the infinitive is unvoiced, when the ending is *-te, -ten*:

ik geloofde	*ik praatte* (I talked)
je, u, gij geloofde	*je, u, gij praatte*
hij geloofde	*hij praatte*
wij geloofden	*wij praatten*
jullie geloofden	*jullie praatten*
u, gij geloofde	*u, gij praatte*
zij geloofden	*zij praatten*

25. *The participles*. The present participle of weak and strong verbs and the auxiliaries is formed by the addition of *-d(e)* to the infinitive:

> *Al huilend(e) viel hij in slaap,* Still crying he fell asleep
> *stromend water,* running water
> *bestaande methoden,* existing methods

The past participle of weak verbs only (for strong verbs and auxiliaries see §§ 27, 29) is formed by adding the prefix *ge-* to the stem and *d* or *t*, after it, according to whether the past tense takes *-de* or *-te*. But (see note to § 23) no *d* or *t* is added when the stem ends in *d* or *t*:

> *gestudeerd; gereisd; gehoopt; gepraat*

Verbs with an unstressed prefix do not take *ge-* in the past participle:

> (*ge'loven*), *ge'loofd*; (*be'duiden*), *be'duid*; (*veront'rusten*), *veront'-rust*

Verbs with a stressed prefix place *ge-* between the prefix and the verb to form the past participle:

> ('*aanhalen*), '*aangehaald*: (*voor'opstellen*), *voor'opgesteld*;
> but ('*voorbereiden*), '*voorbereid* (because of the second, unstressed, prefix *be-*)

26. *The imperative* singular is the same as the stem; the plural is formed by adding *t* to the stem (unless this ends in a *t*);

> *lach niet, lacht niet,* do not laugh
> *sta, staat,* stand

27. *The strong verbs*. Strong verbs differ from weak verbs primarily in that the vowel of the stem itself changes in the preterite and past participles and the past participle always has the ending *-en*.

There are seven classes of strong verbs which are given below, each group having the same vowels in the preterite and past participle as the example given at the head of the group. Composites are not normally shown, since they follow the same pattern as the simple verbs.

I. Type: **bijten—beet—gebeten**

> belijden, bezwijken, blijken, blijven, drijven, glijden, grijpen, hijsen, knijpen, kijken, kijven, krijgen, zich kwijten van, lijden, (ge)lijken, nijgen, overlijden, prijzen, rijden, rijgen, rijzen, schrijden, schrijven, schijnen, slijpen, slijten, smijten, snijden, spijten, splijten, stijgen, stijven, strijden, strijken, verdwijnen, (ver)mijden, verwijten, wijken, wijzen, wrijven, zwijgen.

II(*a*). Type: **bieden—bood—geboden** *verbeten verbot verbten*

bedriegen, gieten, genieten, kiezen, liegen, schieten, verbieden,
verdrieten, vliegen; verliezen (verloor—verloren), vriezen
(vroor—gevroren).

II(*b*). Type: **buigen—boog—gebogen** *schliessen schloss geschlossen*

druipen, duiken, fluiten, kluiven, kruipen, ruiken, schuilen,
schuiven, sluipen, sluiten, snuiten, snuiven, spruiten, spuiten,
stuiven, zuigen, zuipen; *also* spugen, tijgen

III. Type: **binden—bond—gebonden** *finden fand gefunden*

beginnen, blinken, dingen, dringen, drinken, dwingen, glimmen,
klimmen, klinken, krimpen, ontginnen, slinken, spinnen,
springen, stinken, verslinden, vinden, winden, winnen, wringen,
zingen, zinken, zinnen

IV. Type: **bergen—borg—geborgen**

delven, gelden, melken, schelden, schenden, schenken, smelten,
treffen, trekken, vechten, vlechten, zenden, (ver)zwelgen,
zwellen, zwemmen; *also* schrikken

V. Type: **nemen—nam, namen—genomen** *nehmen nahm genommen*

bevelen, breken, spreken, steken, stelen; *also* komen (kwam,
kwamen—gekomen)

VI. Type: **geven—gaf, gaven—gegeven** *geben gab gegeben*

genezen, lezen, meten, treden, vergeten, vreten; *also* eten (at,
aten—gegeten) *and* bidden, (bad, baden—gebeden) liggen,
zitten

VII(*a*). Type: **laten—liet—gelaten** *lassen liess gelassen*

blazen, slapen, vallen; lopen (liep—gelopen), roepen (riep—
geroepen), houden (hield—gehouden), houwen (hieuw, gehou-
wen), wassen (wies—gewassen) (to grow); *also* gaan, hangen,
vangen *with preterites in* -i- (ging—gegaan, *etc.*)

VII(*b*). Type: **sterven—stierf—gestorven** *sterben starb gestorben*

bederven, helpen, verwerven, werpen, zwerven; *also* heffen
(hief—geheven), scheppen (schiep—geschapen) (to create)

In addition there are three more like **dragen—droeg—gedragen** :

graven, slaan (sloeg—geslagen), varen

and like **scheren—schoor—geschoren** are :

bewegen, wegen, zweren (to fester) *and* zweren (to swear)
(zwoer—gezworen)

The following are irregular:

doen—deed—gedaan	to do
staan—stond—gestaan	to stand
weten—wist—geweten	to know
zien—zag—gezien	to see

A number of verbs have regular weak preterites and regular strong past participles formed by adding *ge-* to the infinitive:

bakken (bakte—gebakken), bannen, barsten, brouwen, heten, lachen, laden, malen, raden, scheiden, spannen, stoten, vouwen, wassen (to wash), weven, zouten; *also* wreken (wreekte—gewroken)

Finally there are some irregular weak verbs:

brengen—bracht—gebracht	to bring
denken—dacht—gedacht	to think
zoeken—zocht—gezocht	to seek
kopen—kocht—gekocht	to buy
plegen—placht (no p.p.)	* to be in the habit of
durven—durfde or *dorst—gedurfd*	to dare
vragen—vroeg—gevraagd	to ask
jagen—joeg or *jaagde—gejaagd*	to hunt, to chase
waaien—woei or *waaide—gewaaid*	to blow
zeggen—zei, zeiden—gezegd	to say

28. *Strong preterites* are conjugated in this way:

blijven, to remain	*nemen*, to take
ik bleef, I remained	*ik nam*, I took
je, u bleef	*je, u nam*
gij bleeft	*gij naamt*
hij bleef	*hij nam*
wij bleven	*wij namen*
jullie bleven	*jullie namen*
u bleef	*u nam*
gij bleeft	*gij naamt*
zij bleven	*zij namen*

29. *Auxiliary verbs:—zijn, hebben, worden, zullen, kunnen, mogen, willen, moeten.* Note that there is no equivalent of the English auxiliary *do* used

(*a*) in negative constructions—
I do not smoke. *Ik rook niet*

(*b*) in questions—
Do you smoke? *Rookt u?*

(*c*) to emphasize the main verb—
Do take care. *Pas toch op.*

---

* The regular weak verb *plegen, pleegde, gepleegd* means to commit: *hij pleegde een moord,* he committed murder.
Verplegen (to nurse) is also regular

zijn, to be.

An alternative form, *wezen*, is always used where the infinitive is used instead of the past participle:

Ik ben wezen kijken. I have been to have a look. (See § 31.)

Present	Preterite	Subjunctive
ik ben	*ik was*	*hij zij*, may he be
je bent	*je was*	*hij ware*, he were
u bent, (*is*)	*u was*	
gij zijt	*gij waart*	Imperative
hij is	*hij was*	sing. *wees*
wij zijn	*wij waren*	plur. *weest*
jullie zijn	*jullie waren*	
u bent	*u was*	Participles
gij zijt	*gij waart*	pres. *zijnde*
zij zijn	*zij waren*	past *geweest*

hebben, to have

Present	Preterite	Imperative
ik heb	*ik had*	sing. *heb*
je, gij hebt	*je, u had*	plur. *hebt*
u hebt, (*heeft*)	*gij hadt*	
hij heeft	*hij had*	
wij hebben	*wij hadden*	Participles
jullie hebben	*jullie hadden*	pres. *hebbende*
u hebt, (*heeft*)	*u had*	past *gehad*
gij hebt	*gij hadt*	
zij hebben	*zij hadden*	

worden—werd, werden—geworden (to become) is conjugated in the same way as other strong verbs.

The remaining auxiliary verbs are conjugated in the same way as strong verbs except in the present tense.

zullen—zou, zouden (no past participle)
kunnen—kon, konden—gekund
mogen—mocht, mochten—gemogen
willen—wilde, wilden—gewild (but, *gij woudt*, cf. would; and in speech, *wou, wou'en*)
moeten—moest, moesten—gemoeten

ik zal, I shall, will	*kan*, can	*mag*, may	*wil*, want	*moet*, must
je, zult, (zal)	*kunt, (kan)*	*mag*	*wil(t)*	*moet*
gij zult	*kunt*	*moogt*	*wilt*	*moet*
hij zal	*kan*	*mag*	*wil*	*moet*
wij zullen	*kunnen*	*mogen*	*willen*	*moeten*
jullie zullen	*kunnen*	*mogen*	*willen*	*moeten*
u, gij zult	*kunt*	*mag, moogt*	*wilt*	*moet*
zij zullen	*kunnen*	*mogen*	*willen*	*moeten*

30. *Compound forms of the verb.*

The perfect tense is formed with the present tense of *hebben* or *zijn* and the past participle of the main verb.

The pluperfect is obtained from the preterite of *hebben* or *zijn* in conjunction with the past participle.

zijn and *blijven* always take *zijn* in the perfect and pluperfect. Otherwise the rule for the auxiliaries is that all transitive verbs take *hebben*. Intransitive verbs take *hebben* when they express a continued action or state; they take *zijn* when they denote a passing from one position or state to another, e.g.:

> *ik heb geslapen,* I have slept; *ik heb gestaan,* I have stood; *de prijzen zijn gestegen,* prices have risen; *hij is vroeg vertrokken,* he left early; *ik ben thuis geweest,* I have been home

cf. also:

> *Wij hebben uren gelopen.* We have walked for hours (continued action).
>
> *Wij zijn naar huis gelopen.* We walked home (from one position to another).

Accordingly we should expect the transitive verb *vergeten* (to forget) to take *hebben*, whereas it often takes *zijn*, since to **have** forgotten something can imply a condition in the present, cf. *ik ben het kwijt,* (literally) I am without it, i.e., I **have** mislaid it.

> *Ik heb mijn bril vergeten.* I've forgotten my glasses.
>
> *Ik ben uw naam vergeten.* I've forgotten your name *or* I **forget** your name.

The future is rendered by the auxiliary *zullen* and the infinitive of the main verb:

> *Hij zal het morgen doen.* He will do it tomorrow.

The present *conditional* is rendered by *zouden* and the infinitive; the past conditional by *zouden + hebben* (or *zijn*) and the past participle or, in normal speech, by the pluperfect:

> *Dat zou ik nooit doen.* I would never do that.
>
> *Dat zou ik geweigerd hebben.* } I would have refused.
> *Dat had ik geweigerd.*

The *passive voice* uses the auxiliary *worden* in the present and preterite and *zijn* in the perfect tenses, both with the past participle. Similarly, the future passives use *zullen + worden or zijn* and the past participle.

The complete paradigm of *halen*.

Active	Indicative	
present	*ik haal*	I fetch
preterite	*ik haalde*	I fetched
perfect	*ik heb gehaald*	I have fetched
pluperfect	*ik had gehaald*	I had fetched
future	*ik zal halen*	I shall fetch
future perfect	*ik zal gehaald hebben*	I shall have fetched
present conditional	*ik zou halen*	I would fetch
past conditional	*ik zou gehaald hebben* }	I would have fetched
	ik had gehaald	

Imperative
sing. *haal*.   plur. *haalt* (*u*), fetch

Infinitive

present	(*te*) *halen*	to fetch
perfect	*gehaald* (*te*) *hebben*	to have fetched

Participle

present	*halend*(*e*)	fetching

Passive	Indicative	
present	*ih word gehaald*	I am fetched
preterite	*ik werd gehaald*	I was fetched
perfect	*ik ben gehaald*	I have been fetched
pluperfect	*ik was gehaald*	I had been fetched
future	*ik zal gehaald worden*	I shall be fetched
future perfect	*ik zal gehaald zijn*	I shall have been fetched
present conditional	*ih zou gehaald worden*	I would be fetched
past conditional	*ik zou gehaald zijn* } *ik was gehaald*	I would have been fetched

Infinitive

present	*gehaald* (*te*) *worden*	to be fetched
perfect	*gehaald* (*te*) *zijn*	to have been fetched

Participle

perfect	*gehaald*	fetched

The Use of the Verb

31. *The infinitive* is used without *te* after the auxiliary verbs *zullen, kunnen, mogen, willen, moeten* and also after *blijven, doen, gaan, helpen, horen, komen, laten, leren, voelen, zien :*

Hij wil helpen afwassen.	He wants to help with the washing up.
Dat doet me denken.	That reminds me.
Het gaat regenen.	It is going to rain.
Ik moet het laten repareren.	I must have it repaired.

It will be seen in the first and last examples above that an accumulation of infinitives is possible in sentences where the main verb (or a compound future tense) governs an infinitive which is itself followed by another infinitive. The same thing occurs in the perfect tenses, where the past participle is replaced by the infinitive if it governs an infinitive:

Ik had het moeten laten repareren.   I ought to have had it repaired.

The infinitive without *te* is also very frequently used instead of the (singular and plural) imperative:

Niet doen (pron. *nie'doen*) !   Don't do it ! *or* Stop it !
Niet Roken, No Smoking

The infinitive can always be used as a (neuter) noun, often equivalent to the English gerund:

Ik houd (pron. *hou'*) *van zwemmen.* I like swimming.
Specialisten in het fabriceren van beddegoed. Specialists in the manufacture of bedding.

The infinitive with *te* is used after the following verbs where English uses the present participle, the gerund or the infinitive: *komen* (when it implies futurity); *liggen, lopen, hangen, staan, zitten*; *(be)hoeven, (be)horen, dienen* (ought), *plegen, weten* (to know how), *zien* (when it implies to manage); *beginnen, denken, durven, menen,* and a number of others which take the same construction in English (expect, hope, refuse, etc.).

Dat moet ik zien te weten te komen. I must find out about that (somehow).
Hij stond met zijn vrouw te praten. He was (*or* stood) talking to his wife (see § 32).

But *te* is omitted between the infinitives in the group *liggen—zitten* above and a following infinitive:

Wij hoorden hier niet te staan praten. We ought not to be standing talking here.

The infinitive with *te* can be used as a passive attributive adjective:

het door ons te betalen bedrag, the amount payable (to be paid) by us

The infinitive after *om te* is used to express purpose:

Zij is naar de stad (gegaan) om boodschappen te doen. She has gone into town to do some shopping.
een doek om mijn fiets (mee) schoon te maken, a cloth for cleaning my bicycle

and also where some quality or quantity is defined, sometimes implicitly:

Het was om te gillen, It was screamingly funny (literally : it was enough to make anyone scream with laughter)
te weinig om te gebruiken, too little to use
iets om te onthouden, something worth remembering

32. *The use of the present participle.* The present participle can be used as an adjective or as an adverb:

drukkend weer, oppressive weather
verbazend snel, amazingly quick(ly)

It cannot be used to form progressive tenses as in English. These can be rendered in a number of ways:

I have (had) been living there for years. *Ik woon (woonde) daar al jaren.*
He was talking to his wife when I entered the room. *Hij stond (zat) met zijn vrouw te praten toen ik de kamer binnenkwam.*
He was waiting for the train. *Hij wachtte op de trein.*
She is cooking. *Zij is aan het koken* or *zij is bezig met koken.*
I shall be going away next week. *Volgende week denk ik uit te gaan.*

Nor can it be used independently:

> Finding it was cold, he put on a coat. *Toen hij merkte dat het koud was, trok hij een jas aan.*

33. *The past participle* can also be used as an adjective or adverb.

34. *The present tense* is used for the present, sometimes for the future, and for expressing continuity from the past to the present time (cf. § 32).

> *Ziet u hem morgen?* Will you be seeing him tomorrow?
> *Hij is al lang dood.* He has been dead for a long time.

35. *The perfect tense* is used when an isolated action is completed, even when the time of the action is stated and English requires the preterite :

> *Vanochtend ben ik vroeg wakker geworden.* I woke up early this morning.

Otherwise the past tenses are used in the same way in both languages, except, of course, that the English imperfect (*I was living, etc.*) is rendered by the Dutch preterite tense (cf. § 32).

Prepositions

36. These are small but fearful hazards in any language, witness the frequent errors by Englishmen in their own language. To give all the equivalents for every Dutch preposition would be no more helpful than to give none at all, and as with all idiom, a dictionary can help only with making a start. The rest must come through familiarity with Dutch usage.

A number of prepositions, e.g., *binnen, door, in, langs, om, op, over, uit, voor, voorbij,* are used adverbially after the object as the prefix of a separable verb of which the main part has either occurred earlier or is omitted as self-evident:

> *zij kwamen de kamer binnen,* they came into the room

but *binnen de kamer,* inside the room

> *hij is de stad in(gegaan),* he has gone into town

but *in de stad,* in the town

> *de straat langs,* past or along the street

but *langs de straat,* along the street

> *de heuvel op,* up the hill

but *op de heuvel,* on the hill

> *de stad uit,* out of town

but *uit de stad,* from the town

> *het huis voorbij,* past the house

but *voorbij het huis,* beyond the house

Conjunctions

37. *dat* can never be omitted as *that* often is in English; and it is normally preceded by a comma:

> *Ik wist, dat ik gelijk had.* I knew I was right.

Unlike English, *after, before* and *until* are rendered in Dutch by the preposition + *dat*, whereas *now that* is just *nu*:

> after (before, until) I had seen him, *nadat (voordat, totdat) ik hem gezien had*
> now that I've met you, *nu ik U ontmoet heb*

Syntax

If a sentence begins with some word that is not the subject, the subject is placed immediately behind the verb:

> *Ik ga morgen naar kantoor.*
> or *Morgen ga ik naar kantoor.* } I am going to the office to-morrow.

niet normally comes immediately after the direct object:

> *Ik gaf hem het boek niet,* I did not give him the book.

When compound verbs are used, the participle or infinitive always comes at the end:

> *Morgen zal ik haar opzoeken.* I will go and see her tomorrow.

Similarly where the main verb governs an infinitive (with or without *te*):

> *Hij heeft geweigerd mij geld te geven.* He has refused to give me money.
> *Wij kunnen de kinderen op straat horen spelen.* We can hear the children playing in the street.

In subordinate clauses the verb always comes at the end:

> *Hij zei, dat hij het niet gedaan had* (or *had gedaan*). He said that he had not done it.

Prepositions used adverbially (i.e., as prefixes of separable verbs and with *er-, daar-, waar-*) come as late as possible in the sentence compatible with the above rules for the end position of verbs:

> *Daar wist ik niets van.* I knew nothing about that.
> *Denk er eens over na.* Just think it over a while. (Cf. § 19.)
> *iets waar ik heel weinig van af kon weten* (cf. § 16), something which I could only know very little about

A DUTCH-ENGLISH DICTIONARY

For notes on the use of this dictionary see the Introduction

A

aaien, to stroke
aak, (Rhine) barge
aal, eel
aalbes, red, black or white currant
aalmoes, (an) alms
aalmoeze'nier, almoner, chaplain to the forces
aambeeld n, anvil
aambeien, piles
aam'borstig, short-winded
aan, at; on; to
aanbeeld n, anvil
aanbellen, to ring the bell
aanbesteden, to put out to contract
aanbevelen, to recommend
aanbevelens'waardig, recommendable
aanbeveling, recommendation
aan'biddelijk, adorable
aan'bidden, to worship, to adore
aanbieden, to offer
aanbieding, offer
aanbinden, to tie on
 de strijd aanbinden, to join issue
aanblik, sight, spectacle
aanbod n, offer
aanbouw: in —, under construction
aanbranden, to burn (in cooking)
aanbreken, to dawn; to open (a bottle); to broach (a cask)
aandacht, attention
aan'dachtig, attentive
aandeel n, share, portion
aandeelhouder, shareholder

aandenken n, memory; memento
aandienen, to announce
 zich laten aandienen, to send up one's name
aandikken, to lay additional stress on
aandoen, to put on; to move; to affect; to call at a place
 hoe kun je me dat aandoen? how can you do such a thing to me?
aandoening, emotion; affection (of the throat, etc.)
aan'doenlijk, moving
aandrang, insistence; urgency; impulse
aandringen op, to press for; to insist on
 op aandringen van, at the instance of
aanduiden, to indicate
aan'een, together; consecutively
aanfluiting, mockery, byword
aangaan, to begin; to enter into (an arrangement); to concern
 wat gaat U dat aan? what concern is it of yours?
aan'gaande, concerning
aangapen, to gape at
aangeboren, innate
aangedaan, moved, affected
aangelegen, adjacent
aange'legenheid, affair, concern
aangenaam, agreeable, pleasant
 aangenaam! pleased to meet you!
aangenomen, adopted; assumed
aangeschoten, tipsy
aangetrouwd, connected by marriage

aangeven, to give; to hand; to indicate; to register (luggage); to notify; to inform the police

aangezicht *n,* countenance

aangezien, seeing that, since

aangifte, notification, declaration

aangorden, to gird on

aan'grenzend, adjacent

aangrijnzen, to grin at

aangrijpen, to grasp, to seize; to assail

aan'grijpend, moving, touching

aangroeien, to increase, to grow

aanhalen, to tighten; to quote; to fondle, to paw

aan'halig, physically demonstrative

aanhalingstekens *n,* inverted commas

aanhang, followers; favour

aanhangen, to adhere to

aanhanger, adherent

aan'hangig, pending, *sub judice*

aanhangmotor, outboard motor

aanhangsel *n,* appendix

aanhangwagen, trailer

aan'hankelijk, affectionate

aanhebben, to have on

aanhechten, to affix

aanhef, opening words

aanheffen, to start, to strike up

aanhitsen, to incite, to set on

aanhoren, to listen to, to hear out

aan'horig, appertaining

aanhouden, to keep on; to persist; to arrest

aanhouden op, to make for

aan'houdend, constant; persistent

aanhouding, arrest, detention

aanjagen : schrik —, to give a fright

aankijken, to look at

aanklacht, charge, accusation

aanklagen, to charge, to accuse

aanklager, plaintiff, prosecutor

aanklampen, to buttonhole, to accost

aankleden, to dress

aankleven, to adhere

aankloppen, to knock at the door; to appeal

aanknopen, to enter into

aanknopingspunt *n,* point of contact

aankomen, to arrive

daar komt het juist op aan, that is just the point

aankomst, arrival

aankondigen, to announce

aankondiging, announcement

aankoop, purchase

aankopen, to purchase

aankoppelen, to couple

aankunnen, to be a match for, to cope (with)

aankweek, cultivation

aankweken, to cultivate

aanleg, lay-out; (natural) aptitude

in aanleg, in course of construction

aanleggen, to lay out; to build; to moor; to manage

aanlegplaats, berth (at a wharf)

aanlegsteiger, landing-stage

aanleiding, occasion

naar aanleiding van, with reference to

aanlengen, to dilute

aanleren, to learn, to acquire

aanleunen, to lean against

aanliggend, adjacent

aan'lokkelijk, tempting, attractive

aanlokken, to allure

aanloop, preliminary run; preamble

veel aanloop, many callers

aanloophaven, port of call

aanlopen bij, to drop in on

aanlopen tegen, to collide with; to come across

aanmaak, manufacture

aanmaken, to manufacture; to light (a fire)

aanmanen, to urge, to exhort, to press

aanmatigen : zich —, to presume

aan'matigend, arrogant, presumptuous

aanmelden : zich —, to present oneself

aan'merkelijk, considerable

aanmerken op, to find fault with
aanmerking, critical remark
 in aanmerking nemen, to take
 into consideration
aangemeten, made to measure
aan'minnig, charming
aanmoedigen, to encourage
aanmoediging, encouragement
aanmonsteren, to sign on
aanmunten, to coin
aan'nemelijk, acceptable, plausible
aannemen, to accept; to assume;
 to adopt; to contract for
aannemer, contractor
aanpakken, to take hold of; to
 tackle
aanpappen, to chum up
aanpassen, to try on
 zich aanpassen bij, to adapt
 oneself to
aanpassingsvermogen n, adaptability
aanplakbiljet n, poster
aanplakbord n, hoarding
aanplakken, to post up
aanplakker, bill-sticker
aanplant, plantation
aanplanten, to plant
aanporren, to stir up, to prod
aanpraten, to talk (a person)
 into
aanprijzen, to recommend
 strongly
aanraden, to advise
aanraken, to touch
aanraking, contact
aanranden, to assault
aanrander, assailant
aanrecht, draining-board
aanreiken, to hand
aanrekenen, to account
 iemand iets aanrekenen, to
 hold something against a person
aanrichten, to cause, to do
aanrijden, to run into
 komen aanrijden, to drive up
aanrijding, collision, crash
aanroepen, to hail, to invoke
aanroeren, to touch (upon); to
 mix
aanschaffen, to procure, to purchase

aanschijn n, appearance; countenance
aan'schouwelijk, clear, graphic
aan'schouwen, to behold
aanschrijven, to notify officially
 hij staat goed aangeschreven,
 he is well thought of
aanschrijving, notification
aanslaan, to strike (a note); to
 affix; to give tongue; to
 assess; to fur up; to start (up)
 hoog aanslaan, to think highly
 of
aanslag, touch (of a piano);
 attempt (on one's life); (tax)
 assessment; moisture, fur, scale
aanslibben, to silt (up)
aansluiten, to connect, to link up
 zich aansluiten bij, to join
 verkeerd aangesloten! wrong
 number!
aansluiting, connection
aansmeren, to foist on
aansnijden, to start cutting; to
 broach
aanspannen, to put (the horses)
 to; to tighten up
aanspoelen, to drift ashore
aansporen, to urge on
aansporing, incentive
aanspraak, claim
aan'sprakelijk, answerable
aanspreken, to address
aanspreker, undertaker's man
aanstaan, to please; to be ajar
aanstaande, next; prospective
 mijn aan'staande, my fiancé(e)
aanstalten maken, to get ready
aan'stekelijk, infectious
aansteken, to light; to infect
aansteker, (cigarette) lighter
aanstellen, to appoint
 zich aanstellen, to put on airs
aan'stellerig, affected
aanstelle'rij, affectation
aanstelling, appointment
aansterken, to recuperate
aanstevenen op, to bear down
 upon
aanstichten, to instigate
aanstichting, instigation
aanstippen, to touch (on)
aanstonds, by and by

aanstoot, offence
aan'stotelijk, offensive
aanstrepen, to mark, to tick off
aansturen op, to head for, to aim at
aantal n, number
aantasten, to attack; to impair
aantekenen, to note; to register
aantekening, note
aantijgen, to impute
aantocht : in —, approaching
aantonen, to demonstrate
aan'toonbaar, demonstrable
aantreden, to fall in
aantreffen, to meet, to find
aan'trekkelijk, attractive
aantrekken, to attract; to put on
  trek je daar maar niets van aan! forget it!
aan'vaarden, to begin; to assume, to accept
aanval(len), (to) attack
aanvaller, assailant
aan'vallig, charming
aanvang(en), (to) start
aanvangssnelheid, initial speed
aan'vankelijk, initial
aanvaren, to collide
  aanvaren op, to make for
aanvatten, to take hold of
aan'vechtbaar, debatable
aanvechting, sudden impulse
aanvoelen, to feel; to sense
aanvoer, supply
aanvoerder, leader
aanvoeren, to supply; to adduce; to command
aanvraag, application
aanvragen, to apply for
aanvullen, to supplement
aanvuren, to spur on
aanwakkeren, to rouse; to fan
aanwas, increase
aanwenden, to apply
aanwennen: zich —, to acquire (a habit)
aanwensel n, mannerism
aanwerven, to recruit
aan'wezig, present
aanwijzen, to point out
aangewezen, obvious; dependent

aan'wijzend voornaamwoord n, demonstrative pronoun
aanwijzing, indication
aanwinst, acquisition, asset
aanwippen, to drop in
aanwrijven, to impute
aanzeggen, to notify
  men zou hem zijn leeftijd niet aanzeggen, he doesn't look his age
aanzetten, to put on; to hone; to tighten up; to egg on
aanzien, to look at: n, distinction, reputation
  aanzien voor, to (mis)take for
aan'zienlijk, notable; considerable
aanzijn n, existence
aanzoek n, request, proposal
aanzuiveren, to pay off arrears
aanzwellen, to swell
aap, monkey
  de aap uit de mouw, the cat out of the bag
aar, ear (of corn)
aard, kind; nature, character
  uit de aard der zaak, naturally
  van allerlei aard, of all kinds
aardappel, potato
aardas, earth's axis
aardbei, strawberry
aardbeving, earthquake
aardbol, globe
aarde, earth; soil
aarden, to thrive
  aarden naar, to take after
aardewerk n, earthenware
aardgas n, natural gas
aardgeest, gnome
aardig, nice, pleasant
  aardig wat, a fair amount
aardigheid, joke, fun
aardkunde, geology
aardlaag, stratum
aardrijk n, earth
aardrijkskunde, geography
aardrijks'kundig, geographical
aards, earthly
aardschok, earth tremor
aard(ver)schuiving, landslide
aarts-, arch-
aarts'bisschop, archbishop

aarts'deugniet, arrant knave
aarts'lui, bone idle
aartsvader, patriarch
aarzelen, to hesitate
aarzeling, hesitation
aas *n,* ace; bait; carrion
aasvlieg, blue-bottle
ab'ces *n,* abscess
ab'dij, abbey
ab'dis, abbess
abnor'maal, abnormal
abomi'nabel, abominable
abon'nee, subscriber
abonne'ment *n,* subscription;
  season-ticket
abon'neren : zich — op, to
  subscribe to
abri'koos, apricot
ab'sent, absent(-minded)
ab'sentie, absence
absor'beren, to absorb
ab'sorptie, absorption
ab'stract, abstract(ed)
abstra'heren, to abstract
absurdi'teit, absurdity
abt, abbot
a'buis *n,* (in) error
abu'sievelijk, erroneously
aca'demie, university; academy
aca'demisch, academic
accentu'eren, to accent(uate)
accep'teren, to accept
ac'cijns, excise duty
ac'coord *n,* agreement; chord:
  agreed!
accor'deren, to come to an agreement
ac'countant, chartered accountant, auditor
accu, accumulator, battery
accu'raat, accurate
accura'tesse, accuracy
ach ! ah!, oh!, alas
acht, eight: attention
  acht slaan op, to heed
  in acht nemen, to observe
achtbaar, honourable
achteloos, negligent
achten, to consider; to esteem
achtens'waardig, estimable
achter, behind, aft, behindhand
  van achteren, from behind
achter'aan, last, in the rear

achter'af, on second thoughts
  zich achteraf houden, to keep
  in the background
achteras, back-axle
achter'baks, underhand
achterblijven, to stay *or* lag
  behind
achterblijver, straggler
achterbuurt, back-street, slums
achterdek *n,* quarterdeck
achterdocht, suspicion
achter'dochtig, suspicious
achter'een, at a stretch
achtereen'volgend, consecutive
achtereen'volgens, successively
achtergrond, background
achter'halen, to overtake; to
  recover
achterhoede, rear-guard
achterhouden, to keep back
achter'in, at *or* in the back
achterklap, slander
achterkleinkind *n,* great-grandchild
achterlaten, to leave behind
achterlijf *n,* abdomen
achterlijk, backward
achter'nalopen, to run after
achternaam, surname
achterneef(-nicht), great-
  nephew(-niece), second cousin
achter'om, round the back
achter'op, behind(hand)
achter'over, back(wards)
achterschip *n,* aft(er end)
achterstaan bij, to be inferior to
achter'stallig, in arrear
achterstand, arrears
achterste *n,* posterior(s); hind-
  most
achterstellen bij, to discriminate
  against
achtersteven, stern(post)
achter'uit, backwards; aft
achter'uitgaan, to move backwards; to fall (off); to deteriorate
achter'uitgang, decline; deterioration
achtervoegsel *n,* suffix
achter'volgen, to pursue
achter'volging, pursuit
achterwaarts, backward(s)

achter'wege laten, to omit
achthoek, octagon
achting, esteem
achtste, eighth; quaver
achttien(de), eighteen(th)
ac'quit n, discharge
acro'baat, acrobat
acroba'tiek, acrobatics
ac'teren, to act
ac'teur, actor
actie, action, campaign
ac'tief, active
actieradius, range
ac'tiva, assets
activi'teit, activity
ac'trice, actress
actuali'teit, topic(ality)
actu'eel, topical
adder, viper
adel, nobility
adelaar, eagle
adelborst, midshipman
adeldom, nobility
adelen, to ennoble
adellijk, noble; high, gamy
adelstand, peerage
adem(loos), breath(less)
 buiten adem, out of breath
 op adem komen, to recover
 one's breath
ademen, ademhalen, to breathe
ademtocht, breath
ader, vein
aderlaten, to let blood
aderontsteking, phlebitis
aderverkalking, hardening of the
 arteries
adju'dant, adjutant; warrant-
 officer
ad'junct, assistant
administra'teur, manager; pur-
 ser
admini'stratie, bookkeeping;
 management
administra'tief, administrative
admini'streren, to keep the
 books; to manage
admi'raal, admiral
admirali'teit, admiralty
a'dres n, address; petition
 je bent aan het goede adres,
 you've come to the right place
a'dresboek n, directory

adres'sant, petitioner
adres'seren, to address
adver'tentie, advertisement
adver'teren, to advertise
ad'vies n, advice
advi'seren, to advise
advi'seur, adviser
advo'caat, barrister: egg-flip
af, off; down; finished
 af en aan, to and fro
 af en toe, now and then
afbakenen, to buoy; to stake
 out; to define
afbeelden, to depict
afbeelding, picture
afbellen, to ring off
afbestellen, to cancel
afbetalen, to pay off
afbetaling, hire purchase
afbeulen, to work to death
afbinden, to untie; to ligate
afboeken, to write off
afbraak, demolition, rubble
afbreken, to demolish; to break
 off
afbrengen, to dissuade
 het er afbrengen, to come
 through
afbreuk doen aan, to injure; to
 detract from
afbrokkelen, to crumble (away)
afdak n, penthouse
afdalen, to descend
afdammen, to dam
afdanken, to discard; to dismiss,
 to disband
afdekken, to cover (up)
afdeling, division, section, detachment, department
afdingen, to haggle
afdoen, to take off; to settle
 die theorie heeft afgedaan,
 that theory is quite exploded
afdoend, conclusive
afdragen, to hand over (money)
 vaders kleren afdragen, to
 wear father's old clothes
afdreigen, to extort
afdreiging, blackmail
afdrijven, to drift away, to float
 down; to cause abortion
afdrijving, leeway; abortion
afdrogen, to dry (up)

afdruipen, to drip off; to slink off

afdruk, copy, print; imprint

afdrukken, to print (off)

afdwalen, to stray; to digress

afdwaling, digression; aberration

afdwingen, to extort; to compel

af'fiche *n,* poster

af'freus, horrible

af'fuit, gun-carriage

afgaan, to go down; to go off

  van school afgaan, to leave school

  het gaat hem goed af, it comes easy to him

  op iemand afgaan, to go up to a person

  afgaande op de feiten, judging by the facts

afgelasten, to countermand

afgeleefd, decrepit

afgelegen, remote

afgemeten, measured; formal

afgescheiden van, apart from

afge'scheidene, dissenter

afgetobd, worn, jaded

afgetrokken, absent-minded

afgevaardigde, deputy

afgeven, to hand over; to hand in; to emit

  de verf geeft af, the paint comes off

afgezaagd, hackneyed

afgezant, envoy

afgezien van, apart from

afgieten, to strain off

afgietsel *n,* (plaster) cast

afgifte, delivery; issue

afgod, idol

afgodendienaar, idolater

afgode'rij, idolatry

afgodsbeeld *n,* idol

af'grijselijk, horrible

afgrijzen *n,* horror

afgrissen, to snatch from

afgrond, abyss

afgunst, jealousy

af'gunstig op, jealous of

afhalen, to take down; to collect; to strip; to string (beans)

afhandelen, to settle (business)

af'handig maken, to filch

afhangen, to hang down; to depend

af'hankelijk van, dependent on

afhaspelen, to reel off

afhebben, to have finished

afhechten, to cast off

afhellen, to slope down

afhelpen, to help off; to help down

afhouden, to keep off; to deduct

afkammen, to disparage

afkapen, to filch

afkappen, to chop off

afkeer, aversion

afkeren, to avert; to turn away

af'kerig van, averse to

afketsen, to glance off; to reject; to come to naught

afkeuren, to disapprove of; to reject as unfit, to condemn

afkeurens'waardig, reprehensible

afkijken, to crib; to look down

afkloppen, to beat off; to "touch wood"

afknippen, to trim, to cut off

afknotten, to truncate

afkomen, to come down

 er afkomen, to get off

 ergens van afkomen, to get rid of a thing

afkomst, origin, birth

af'komstig van, originating from

afkondigen, to proclaim

afkondiging, proclamation

afkooksel *n,* decoction

afkoopsom, ransom

afkopen, to buy off

afkorten, to abbreviate

afkrijgen, to get off; to get finished

afkunnen, to be able to manage

aflaat, indulgence

afleggen, to cover (a distance); to pay (a call); to take (an oath); to sit for (an examination)

afleiden, to distract; to deduce; to derive

afleiding, distraction; derivation

afleren, to unlearn; to break of a habit

afleveren, to deliver

aflevering, delivery; number, instalment

afloop, end, outcome; expiry

aflopen, to run down; to slope; to end; to expire

ik heb alle winkels afgelopen, I have been to every shop in town

af'losbaar, redeemable

aflossen, to redeem; to relieve

afluisteren, to eavesdrop

afmaken, to finish; to kill; to break off

afmatten, to tire out

af'mattend, exhausting

afmatting, exhaustion

afmeten, to measure (off)

afmeting, dimension

afmonsteren, to sign off; to pay off

afnemen, to take off; to take down; to clear away; to decrease

afnemer, customer

afpakken, to snatch out of one's hand

afpassen, to measure

afpersen, to extort

afpersing, extortion

afpingelen, to haggle

afpoeieren, to send packing

afraden, to dissuade

afranselen, to thrash

afrastering, (wire) fence

afreageren, to work off (one's emotions)

afreis, departure

het land afreizen, to travel all over the country

afrekenen, to settle accounts

afrekening, settlement

africhten, to train

afrissen, afristen, to string

afroepen, to call

afrollen, to roll down; to unroll

afronden, to round off

afrossen, to thrash

afruimen, to clear away

afrukken, to tear off

afschaffen, to abolish

afschaffing, abolition

afscheid *n,* parting

afscheid nemen, to take one's leave

afscheiden, to separate; to secrete

afschepen, to fob off

afschieten, to fire; to shoot off; to partition

afschieten op, to rush up to

afschilderen, to depict

afschrift *n,* copy

afschrijven, to copy; to write off; to cancel

afschrijving, depreciation

afschrik, horror

afschrikken, to frighten away

afschuw, loathing

af'schuwelijk, horrible, hideous

afslaan, to beat off; to decline

rechts afslaan, to turn to the right

afslachten, to butcher

afslag, Dutch auction

afslager, auctioneer

afsloven : (zich) —, to wear (oneself) out

afsluitboom, boom

afsluitdijk, dam; causeway

afsluiten, to lock; to close; to turn off; to cut off; to balance; to conclude

afsnauwen, to snap at

afsnijden, to cut off

afsnoepen, to snatch from; to forestall

afspannen, to unharness

afspelen : zich —, to be enacted

afspiegelen, to reflect

afspoelen, to rinse (off)

afspraak, appointment, date, arrangement

afspreken, to agree, to arrange

afstaan, to cede

afstammeling, descendant

afstammen, to descend

afstamming, descent

afstand, distance; cession

afstandsmars, route march

afstandsmeter, range finder

afstappen, to get down; to put up

afsteken, to push off; to let off; to deliver

afsteken bij, to contrast with

afstemmen, to negative; to reject; to attune

afstempelen, to stamp

afsterven, to die off

afstijgen, to dismount

afstoffen, to dust

afstompen, to blunt

afstormen op, to rush at

afstoten, to push off; to repel

af'stotelijk, repellent

afstraffen, to punish; to reprimand

afstraffing, dressing-down

afstropen, to skin

afstuiten op, to rebound from; to be frustrated by

afsturen, to dispatch

 afsturen op, to head for

aftakelen, to dismantle; to age badly

af'tands, long in the tooth

aftappen, to tap; to draw off

aftekenen, to sign

 zich aftekenen tegen, to stand out against

aftocht, retreat

aftrap, kick-off

aftrappen, to kick off; to kick down

aftreden, to resign

aftrek, deduction; demand

aftrekken, to deduct, to subtract; to distract

aftrekking, subtraction

aftreksel *n,* infusion

aftroeven, to trump

aftroggelen, to wheedle out of

aftuigen, to unharness; to give a hiding

afvaardigen, to delegate

afvaart, departure, sailing

afval, refuse; apostasy

afvallen, to fall down, to fall away; to lose weight

af'vallig, disloyal

af'vallige, renegade

afvaren, to (set) sail

afvegen, to wipe (off)

afvloeien, to flow down; to be discharged

afvoer, removal; discharge; waste(-pipe)

afvoeren, to carry away

afvoerkanaal *n,* drainage channel

afvragen : zich —, to wonder

afwachten, to await, to wait and see (about)

afwachting, expectation

afwasbak, washing-up bowl

afwassen, to wash up *or* off

afwateren, to drain

afwatering, drainage

afweer, defence

afweergeschut *n,* anti-aircraft guns

afwegen, to weigh out

afwenden, to avert

 zich afwenden, to turn away

afwennen, to break of a habit

afwentelen, to roll away

afweren, to ward off

afwerken, to finish off

afwerking, finish

afwerpen, to throw off; to yield

af'wezig, absent

af'wezigheid, absence

afwijken, to deviate

afwijking, deviation

afwijzen, to turn down *or* away, to reject

afwikkelen, to unroll; to wind up

afwisselen, to alternate, to vary

 elkaar afwisselen, to take turns

af'wisselend, alternating; varied

afwisseling, variation; change

afzakken, to come down

afzeggen, to cancel

afzenden, to dispatch

afzet, sale

afzetgebied *n,* market

afzetten, to take off; to depose; to amputate; to trim; to cordon off; to cheat

 een ge'voel van zich afzetten, to shake off a feeling

afzetter, cheat

afzette'rij, swindle

af'zichtelijk, hideous

afzien van, to give up

 afgezien van, apart from

 binnen af'zienbare tijd, within the not too distant future

af'zijdig, aloof

afzonderen, to isolate, to segregate

afzondering, seclusion
af'zonderlijk, separate—
afzweren, to abjure
a'gaat, agate
a'genda, agenda; diary
a'gent, agent; policeman
a'gentschap n, agency, branch (bank)
agen'tuur n, agency
a'geren, to agitate
a'horn, maple
air n, appearance
a'jour, open-worked
akelig, nasty, unpleasant; unwell
akker, (arable) field
akkermaalshout n, copse
ak'koord n, agreement; chord: agreed!
akoes'tiek, acoustics
akte, diploma, deed; act
aktentas, brief-case
al, all: already: even though .
al te, too
alar'meren, to give the alarm
al'bast n, alabaster
alcoholhoudend, alcoholic
alco'holica, intoxicants
al'daar, there
aldoor, all the time
al'dra, ere long
al'dus, thus
alge'meen, general, common
over het algemeen, in general
al'hier, here
alhoe'wel, although
a'linea, paragraph
al'koof, (bedroom) recess
alle'bei, both
alle'daags, commonplace,of daily occurrence
al'leen, alone; only
al'leenheerser, absolute ruler
al'leenspraak, soliloquy
alle'gaartje n, hotchpotch
alle'maal, all; altogether
allemaal tegelijk, all together
alle'machtig, devilish: good lor'!
allemansvriend, friend to everybody
allen, all
al'lengs, gradually

aller'liefst, most charming
aller'eerst, first of all
Aller'heiligen, All Saints' Day
allerlei, allerhande, all sorts of
aller'minst, (the) very least; not in the least
allerwegen, everywhere
allerzijds, on all sides
alles, everything
van alles, all sorts of things
alles en nog wat, anything and everything
al'licht, quite likely: I should think so!
we kunnen het allicht proberen, no harm in trying!
al'looi n, alloy
al'lures, airs
almacht, omnipotence
al'machtig, almighty
al'om, everywhere
alomtegen'woordig, ubiquitous
als, as; like; if; when
als'dan, then
alsem, wormwood
alsje'blieft, please; here you are; there now—what did I tell you!
als'mede, as well as
als'nog, as yet
als'nu, now
als'of, as if
alstu'blieft (see alsje'blieft)
alt, alto; contralto
altaar n, altar
al'thans, at least
altijd, altoos, always
altsleutel, tenor clef
altviool, viola
a'luin, alum
al'vast, meanwhile
al'vorens, before
al'waar, where
al'weer, again
al'wetend, omniscient
al'wetendheid, omniscience
al'zijdig, versatile, all-round
al'zo, thus
a'mandel, almond
a'mandelen, tonsils
amanu'ensis, laboratory assistant
ama'ril, emery
ambacht n, trade

ambachtsheer, lord of the manor
ambachtsman, artisan
ambas'sade, embassy
ambassa'deur, ambassador
ambi'eren, to aspire to
am'bitie, zest; ambition
ambiti'eus, ambitious
ambt *n*, function; office
ambtelijk, official
ambteloos burger, private citizen
ambtenaar, official, civil servant
ambtena'rij, red tape
a'mechtig, out of breath
ameuble'ment *n*, (suite of) furniture
amfi'bie, amphibian
am'fibisch, amphibious
ami'caal, pally
ampel, ample
amper, scarcely
amu'sant, amusing
amu'seren, to amuse
ana'loog, analogous
ana'lyse, analysis
analy'seren, to analyse
ana'lytisch, analytical
ana'nas, pine-apple
ana'toom, anatomist
anciënni'teit, seniority
ander, different; other
 des anderen daags, the next day
 om de andere dag, every other day
 onder andere (o.a.), *inter alia*
anderdeels, on the other hand; partly
anderhalf, one and a half
anders, different; else
 net als anders, just as usual
anders'denkend, andersge'zind, dissentient
anders'om, the other way round
anderzijds, on the other hand
an'dijvie, endive
ane'moon, anemone
angel, sting; fish-hook
angst, fear, terror
angstig, afraid, fearful
angst'vallig, scrupulous, timid
angst'wekkend, alarming
angstzweet *n*, cold sweat

a'nijszaad *n*, aniseed
ani'meren, to encourage
 geanimeerd, animated
animo, zest
anje'lier, anjer, carnation
anker *n*, anchor; wall-brace; armature
ankeren, to anchor
ankergrond, anchorage
ankerhand, fluke
ankerlicht *n*, riding light
an'nex, annexe: enclosed; attached
an'nonce, advertisement, announcement
anno'teren, to annotate
annuï'teit, annuity
ano'niem, anonymous
ansicht, picture postcard
an'sjovis, anchovy
an'tenne, aerial
anti'chambre, anteroom
anticham'breren, to wait outside
an'tiek, antique(s)
anti'monium *n*, antimony
antipa'thiek, antipathetic
anti'quaar, antique dealer
antiquari'aat *n*, secondhand bookshop, antique shop
antiqui'teiten, antiques
antwoord(en) (*n*), (to) answer
a'part, apart; separate
 iets zeer a'parts, something very special
a'pathisch, apathetic
apegapen: op — liggen, to be at one's last gasp
apekool, rubbish
apekuur, monkey trick
apeliefde, molly-coddling
apolo'geet, apologist
apenootje *n*, monkey-nut
a'postel, apostle
apo'theek, (dispensing) chemist('s)
apo'theker, pharmacist
appa'raat *n*, apparatus
ap'pel *n*, appeal; roll-call
appel, apple
appelbol, apple dumpling
appelflauwte, swoon, fit
appel'leren, to appeal

appelmoes, apple *purée*
appelsap, cydrax
appe'tijtelijk, appetizing
ap'plaus *n*, applause
applaudi'sseren, to applaud
appreci'ëren, to appreciate
approvian'deren, to provision
apro'pos, by the way
aqua'rel, water-colour
ar(reslee), horse-drawn sleigh
arbeid(en), (to) labour
arbeider, labourer
arbeidersklasse, working classes
arbeidsbeurs, arbeidsbureau *n*,
  labour exchange
ar'beidzaam, industrious
arbi'trair, arbitrary
ar'chief *n*, archives; record office
archi'varis, archivist; keeper of
  the records
are, 100 square metres
arend, eagle
arendsjong *n*, eaglet
arendsneus, aquiline nose
argeloos, unsuspecting
arglist, guile
arg'listig, crafty
argwaan, suspicion
arg'wanend, suspicious
arm, arm; branch: poor
armband, bracelet, armlet
armenzorg, poor relief
armhuis *n*, workhouse
arm'lastig, in receipt of poor-
  relief
armleuning, elbow-rest
armoe(de), poverty
ar'moedig, needy; shabby
armoedzaaier, poor devil
armsgat *n*, arm-hole
arm'zalig, pitiful
armslag, elbow-room
arres'tant, prisoner
arres'teren, to arrest
ar'senicum *n*, arsenic
ar'tesisch, artesian
ar'tiest, variety artist
artille'rie, artillery
artille'rist, gunner
arti'sjok, artichoke
arts, doctor
artse'nij, physic
artse'nijkunde, pharmacology

as, ash(es): axle; axis
asbakje *n*, ash-tray
as'best *n*, asbestos
as'ceet, ascetic
asem, breath
as'perge, asparagus
aspi'rant, candidate
Assepoes(ter), Cinderella
assura'deur, insurer; under-
  writer
assu'rantie, insurance
assu'reren, to insure
as'trant, cocky
astro'loog, astrologer
astro'noom, astronomer
a'syl, asylum; refuge
ate'lier *n*, studio, workshop
aterling, miscreant
at'leet, athlete
atle'tiek, athletics
a'toomsplitsing, nuclear fission
at'tent, attentive; considerate
at'tentie, attention; act of courtesy
at'test *n*, certificate, testimonial
attes'teren, to attest, to certify
attra'peren, to catch in the act
audi'ëntie, audience; formal
  interview
au'gurk, gherkin
augustus, August
aula, auditorium
au'teur, author
au'teursrecht *n*, copyright
auto, (motor-)car
autodi'dact, self-taught (person)
auto'maat, automaton; slot-
  machine
auto'noom, autonomous
autori'seren, to authorize
autori'tair, high-handed; authoritarian
averechts, wrong
  een recht, een averecht, knit
  one, purl one
ave'rij, average; damage
avond, evening
avondeten *n*, **avondmaal** *n*, supper
avondschemering, dusk
avontu'rier, adventurer
avon'tuur *n*, adventure
avon'tuurlijk, adventurous

azen op, to prey on
a'zijn, vinegar
a'zijnzuur *n*, acetic acid
a'zuur (*n*), azure

B

baai, bay
baak, beacon
baal, bale, bag
baan, way, track; orbit; (tennis) court; job
  dat is van de baan, that's shelved
baanbreker, pioneer
baar, billow: bier: ingot
baar geld, ready cash
baard, beard
  hij heeft de baard in de keel, his voice is breaking
baarmoeder, womb
baars, perch
baas, master, boss
  iets de baas worden, to get the better of a thing
baat, benefit
  ten bate van, for the benefit of
baatzucht, selfishness
babbelen, to chatter; to gossip
baby oppas, baby-sitter
bad *n*, bath
baden, to bath, to bathe
  zich in weelde baden, to wallow in luxury
badhuis *n*, public baths
ba'gage, luggage
baga'tel *n*, trifle
bagger, mud
baggeren, to dredge; to squelch
baggermolen, dredger
bak, tray; bin; pan
bakbeest *n*, huge thing
bakboord *n*, port
baken *n*, beacon
baker, maternity nurse
bakeren, to dry-nurse
bakermat, birthplace
bakerpraat, old wives' tale
bakfiets, carrier-cycle
bakkebaarden, side-whiskers
bakke'leien, to scrap
bakken, to bake, to fry
  iemand een poets bakken, to play a trick on somebody

bakker, baker
bakke'rij, bakery
bakmeel *n*, flour
baksel *n*, batch (of cakes, *etc.*)
baksteen, brick
  het regent bakstenen, it is raining cats and dogs
bakvis, teen-ager
bal, ball: *n*, dance, ball
  elkaar de bal toewerpen, to play into one another's hands
ba'lans, balance(-sheet), scales
bal'dadig, wanton, destructive
ba'lein, whalebone; rib of umbrella
balie, railing, counter
  tot de balie toelaten, to call to the bar
baliekluiver, loafer
baljuw, bailiff
balk, beam, rafter
  over de balk gooien, to squander
balken, to bray
bal'kon *n*, balcony
balling(schap), exile
bal'lon, balloon
ballo'tage, ballot
bal'orig, refractory; truculent
balsem, balm
balsemen, to embalm
ban, excommunication, ban
  in de ban doen, to excommunicate
ba'naal, banal
ba'naan, banana
band, band, tape; ligament; waveband; tyre; bond
  aan banden leggen, to put under restraint
  uit de band springen, to get out of hand
bande'lier, shoulder-belt
bandeloos, lawless
bandepech, tyre-trouble
ban'diet, bandit
banen: de weg—voor, to pave the way for
  zich een weg banen, to force one's way (through)
bang, afraid
bangmake'rij, intimidation
ba'nier, banner

bank, bench, settee; bank
bankbiljet *n*, bank-note
ban'ket *n*, banquet; fancy cakes
ban'ketbakker, pastry-cook
ban'kier, banker
bankpapier *n*, bank-notes
bank'roet (*n*), bankrupt(cy)
bankschuld, overdraught
bankstel *n*, sitting-room suite
bankwezen *n*, banking
banneling, exile
bannen, to banish
banvloek, anathema
bar, inclement: bar
  bar slecht, very bad
  hij maakt het al te bar, he is
  going too far
ba'rak, hut(ment)
bar'baar, barbarian
bar'baars, barbaric
bar'bier, barber
baren, to give birth to; to engender
barensnood, labour (pains)
ba'ret, cap, beret, biretta
bar'goens *n*, jargon
barm'hartig, merciful
barnsteen *n*, amber
barrevoets, barefoot
bars, gruff, stern
barst, crack
barsten, to burst, to crack; to
  explode
bas, bass
bas'cule, weigh-bridge, kitchen-
  scales
ba'seren, to base
basi'liek, basilica
basis, basis, base; footing
bassen, to bay
bassleutel, bass clef
bast, bark
basta! enough!
bastaard, bastard; mongrel
basterdsuiker, moist (brown)
  sugar
baten, to avail
batig saldo *n*, credit balance
batte'rij, battery
bavi'aan, baboon
ba'za(a)r, bazaar; sale of work
bazelen, to talk nonsense
bazig, bossy

ba'zin, mistress
ba'zuin, trumpet, trombone
be'ambte, official; employee
be'amen, to assent
be'angst, uneasy
be'angstigen, to alarm
be'antwoorden, to answer; to
  return; to correspond
be'bloed, bloody
be'boeten, to fine
be'bossen, to afforest
be'bouwen, to cultivate; to
  build on (*or* up)
becriti'seren, to criticize
bed *n*, bed
be'daard, calm, composed
be'dacht op, alive to, mindful of
be'dachtzaam, circumspect
be'danken, to thank; to decline;
  to resign
  wel bedankt! thanks very
  much!
be'dankje *n*, bread-and-butter
  letter
be'daren, to calm down
beddegoed *n*, bedding
bedding, river-bed
bede, prayer, request
be'deesd, timid; coy
bedehuis *n*, place of worship
be'dekken, to cover
bedeklok, angelus
bedelaar, beggar
bedela'rij, begging, mendicity
bedelen, to beg
be'delen, to endow; to distribute
  relief
be'deling, poor-relief
bedelmonnik, mendicant friar
be'delven, to bury
be'denkelijk, grave; precarious;
  questionable
be'denken, to recollect; to consider; to think up
  zich bedenken, to change one's
  mind
be'denking, objection; consideration
be'derf *n*, corruption; decay
be'derven, to spoil; to go bad
bedevaart, pilgrimage
bedevaartganger, pilgrim
be'diende, servant; employee

be'dienen, to serve; to (ad)minister (to)
be'diening, service
be'dilal, fault-finder
be'dillen, to find fault with
be'ding *n* : onder geen —, not in any circumstances
be'dingen, to stipulate
be'disselen, to see to
bed'legerig, bed-ridden
be'doelen, to mean
be'doeling, intention
be'dompt, close; stuffy
be'donderen, to bamboozle
ben je bedonderd? are you crazy?
be'dotten, to diddle
be'drag *n*, amount
be'dragen, to amount to
be'dreigen, to threaten
be'dremmeld, shy, confused
be'dreven, proficient
be'driegen, to deceive
bedriege'rij, deception
be'drieg(e)lijk, deceptive, deceitful
be'drijf *n*, industry, business, undertaking; act
be'drijven, to commit
be'drijvigheid, bustle, activity
be'drinken: zich —, to get drunk
be'droefd, sad
be'droefd weinig, precious little
be'droeven, to grieve
be'drog *n*, deceit, trickery
be'druipen, to baste
zichzelf bedruipen, to pay one's (*or* its) way
be'drukt, depressed; printed
be'ducht, apprehensive
be'duiden, to signify, to indicate
be'duvelen, to fool
be'duusd, abashed, taken aback
be'dwang *n*, restraint
zich in bedwang houden, to restrain oneself
be'dwelmen, to stun; to drug; to intoxicate
be'dwelming, stupor; narcosis
be'dwingen, to suppress, to curb
be'ëdigen, to swear in
be'ëindigen, to terminate
beek, brook

beeld *n*, image; picture, statue; beauty
zich een beeld vormen van, to visualize
beeldenaar, effigy
beeld(er)ig, charming, very pretty
beeldhouwen, to sculpture
beeldhouwer, sculptor
beeldrijk, ornate
beeldspraak, metaphor
beeltenis, image
beemd, (lush) meadow
been *n*, leg; bone
beenbreuk, fracture
beer, bear; boar; buttress
beerput, cesspit
beest *n*, animal, beast
beestachtig, beastly
beestenboel, filthy mess, pig-sty
beestenspel *n*, menagerie
beet, bite, sting
beet hebben, to have got hold of
beetje *n*, (little) bit
beetnemen, to take in
beetpakken, to take hold of
be'faamd, famous, notorious
be'gaafd, gifted
be'gaan, to tread; to commit
begaan met, sorry for
een flater begaan, to drop a brick
begane grond, ground level
be'geerlijk, desirable
be'geerte, desire
bege'leiden, to accompany
bege'nadigen, to pardon, to bless
be'geren, to desire, to covet
be'gerig, desirous, covetous
be'gerigheid, greed
be'geven, to give way; to bestow
zich begeven, to go, to proceed
be'gieten, to water
be'giftigen, to endow
be'gin *n*, beginning
be'ginneling, beginner
be'ginnen, to start, to begin
wat moet ik nu beginnen? whatever shall I do now?
er is niets met hem te beginnen, there is no doing anything with him
be'ginsel *n*, principle

be'ginstadium *n,* initial stage
be'graafplaats, cemetery
be'grafenis, funeral
be'graven, to bury
be'grenzen, to bound, to limit
be'grijpelijk, understandable
be'grijpelijkerwijze, understandably
be'grijpen, to understand; include
be'grip *n,* concept(ion); notion; comprehension
  kort begrip, abstract
  vlug van begrip, quick in the uptake
be'groeid, overgrown
be'groeten, to greet; to hail
be'groten, to estimate
be'groting, estimate, budget
be'gunstigen, to favour
be'haaglijk, pleasant, comfortable
be'haagziek, coquettish
be'haard, hairy
be'hagen, to please
  behagen scheppen, to take pleasure
be'halen, to gain, to win
be'halve, except, apart from
be'handelen, to treat, to deal with
be'handeling, treatment
be'hang(sel) *n,* wall-paper
be'hangen, to paper, to drape
be'hanger, paper-hanger
be'hartigen, to have at heart, to look after
be'hartiging, care
be'heer *n,* management
be'heerder, manager, administrator
be'heersen, to rule; to control; to command (a language); to dominate
be'heksen, to bewitch
be'helpen: zich —, to make do, to rough it
be'helzen, to contain
be'hendig, dexterous
be'hept met, afflicted with
be'heren, to manage, to administer
be'hoeden voor, to protect from

be'hoedzaam, cautious
be'hoefte, need
be'hoeftig, needy
be'hoeve: ten — van, for the sake of, in aid of
be'hoeven, to need
be'hoorlijk, proper; decent
be'horen, to belong; to be fitting
  naar behoren, properly
be'houd *n,* preservation; retention
be'houden, to retain; to preserve
  behouden terugkeer, safe return
be'houdend, conservative
be'houdens, except for; subject to
be'huild, tear-stained
be'huisd: klein —, cramped for room
be'huizing, housing
be'hulp: met — van, with the aid of
be'hulpzaam, helpful
be'huwd (zuster), *etc.,* (sister-)in-law, *etc.*
beiaard, carillon
beide(n), both; two
  geen van beide(n), neither (of them)
beiderlei, of both sorts
beiderzijds, on both sides
be'ijveren: zich —, to do one's utmost
be'invloeden, to influence
beitel, chisel
beits, (wood) stain
beitsen, to stain (wood)
be'jaard, aged
be'jag naar *n,* pursuit of
be'jammeren, to lament
be'jegenen, to treat
bek, mouth, beak
be'kaaid: er — afkomen, to come off badly
bekaf, dog-tired
be'keerling, convert
be'kend, (well-)known; acquainted
  ik ben hier niet bekend, I'm a stranger here
be'kende, acquaintance

be'kendheid, acquaintance; reputation, notoriety

van algemene bekendheid, generally known

be'kendmaking, announcement

be'kennen, to admit, to confess; to follow suit

be'kentenis, admission, confession

beker, cup, mug

be'keren, to convert

be'kering, conversion

be'keuren, to charge

be'keuring, charge, fine

be'kijken, to look at; to look into

be'kijk(s) hebben, to attract attention

bekken *n,* basin; pelvis

be'klaagde, accused

be'kladden, to besmirch

be'klag *n,* complaint

be'klagen, to pity

zich beklagen, to complain

beklagens'waardig, pitiable

be'kleden, to cover; to upholster

een ambt bekleden, to hold an office

be'kleding, be'kleedsel *n,* covering, upholstery; lagging

be'klemd, oppressed; stressed

be'klemdheid, oppression; constriction

be'klimmen, to climb

be'klinken, to rivet; to settle

be'kneld, locked, jammed

be'knibbelen, to beat down; to stint

be'knopt, concise

be'knorren, to scold

be'knotten, to curtail

be'kocht, cheated

be'koelen, to cool down

be'kogelen, to pelt

be'kokstoven, to wangle

be'komen, to recover; to agree with

be'kommeren: zich — om, to bother about

be'komst *n:* **zijn — eten,** to eat one's fill

ik heb er mijn bekomst van, I've had more than enough of it

be'konkelen, to scheme

be'koorlijk, charming

be'kopen (met de dood), to pay (with one's life)

be'koren, to charm, to appeal to

be'koring, charm; temptation

be'korten, to curtail

be'kostigen, to pay for

be'krachtigen, to confirm, to ratify

be'krassen, to cover with scratches

be'krimpen: zich —, to retrench

be'krompen, narrow-minded; restricted

be'kronen, to crown, to award a prize

be'kruipen, to take by surprise

het gevoel bekroop me, the feeling came over me

be'kruisen: zich —, to make the sign of the cross

bekvechten, to wrangle noisily

be'kwaam, capable

be'kwaamheid, ability

be'kwamen, to qualify, to fit

bel, bell; bubble

be'labberd, rotten

be'lachelijk, ridiculous

be'laden, to load

be'lagen, to waylay

be'landen, to land (up)

be'lang *n,* interest; importance

be'langeloos, disinterested

be'langrijk, important

belang'stellend, interested

be'langstelling, interest

belang'wekkend, interesting

be'lastbaar, taxable, dutiable

be'lasten, to burden; to tax; to charge; to debit

zich belasten met, to take upon oneself

be'lasteren, to slander; to libel

be'lasting, tax(ation); load

be'lazeren, to bamboozle

ben je belazerd? are you barmy?

be'ledigen, to insult

be'lediging, insult

be'leefd(heid), polite(ness)

beleefdheids'halve, out of politeness

be'leg *n*, siege
be'legen, matured
be'legeren, to besiege
be'leggen, to cover; to call (a meeting); to invest
be'legsel *n*, trimming(s); facing
be'leid *n*, administration; prudence
be'leidvol, tactful
be'lemmeren, to hamper
be'lendend, adjacent
be'lenen, to pawn, to raise a loan on
be'let *n*: — vragen, to ask for an appointment
be'letsel *n*, obstacle, hindrance
be'letten, to prevent
be'leven, to experience, to live through
    dat had hij moeten beleven! if only he could have lived to see this!
be'lezen, well-read
belhamel, ringleader, rascal
be'lichamen, to embody
be'lichten, to throw light upon; to expose
be'lieven, to please
    naar believen, as one pleases
be'lijden, to confess; to profess
be'lijdenis, confession, creed; confirmation
belknop, bell-pull, bell-push
bellen, to ring (the bell)
belle'trie, *belles-lettres*
be'loeren, to spy upon
be'lofte, promise
be'lonen, to reward
be'loop *n*, course
be'lopen, to amount to
    met bloed belopen ogen, blood-shot eyes
be'loven, to promise
be'luisteren, to listen to
be'lust op, eager for
be'machtigen, to secure
be'malen, to drain
be'mannen, to man
be'manning, crew; garrison
be'merken, to perceive
be'mesten, to manure
be'middelaar, intermediary
be'middeld, well-to-do

be'middelen, to mediate
be'middeling, mediation
be'minnelijk, charming, lovable
be'minnen, to love
be'moedigen, to encourage
be'moeial, busy-body
be'moeien: zich — met, to concern oneself with, to meddle with
be'moeienis, concern
be'moeilijken, to hinder
be'moeiziek, meddlesome
be'nadelen, to harm
be'naderen, to estimate; to get near
be'nadering: bij —, approximately
be'naming, name
be'nard, critical; perilous
be'nauwd, close, stuffy; constricted; afraid
    ik heb het benauwd, I can't breathe
be'nauwdheid, closeness; constriction; fear
bende, gang; mess
be'neden, below, downstairs; under, beneath
be'nedenhuis *n*, bottom flat
be'nedenverdieping, ground-floor
be'nedenwaarts, downwards
be'nemen, to take away
    de moed benemen, to discourage
be'nepen, cramped; narrow-minded; timid
be'nevelen, to befog, to fuddle
be'nevens, together with
bengel, bell-clapper; young rascal
bengelen, to dangle
be'nieuwen: het zal me —, I wonder
be'nieuwd, curious to know
benig, bony
be'nijden, to envy
benijdens'waard(ig), enviable
be'nodigd, required
be'nodigdheden, requisites
be'noemen, to appoint; to nominate
be'noorden, to the north of

be'nul *n*, notion
be'nutten, to make use of
ben'zine, petrol
be'oefenaar, student, votary
be'oefenen, to study, to practise
be'ogen, to have in view
be'oordelen, to judge, to review
be'oorlogen, to wage war against
be'oosten, to the east of
bepaald, positive; definite; appointed
   in een bepaald geval, in a given case
   niet bepaald beleefd, not exactly polite
be'pakken, to pack
be'palen, to determine, to define
   zich bepalen tot, to confine oneself to
be'paling, definition; regulation; stipulation
be'peinzen, to muse on
be'perken, to limit, to confine
be'plakken, to plaster
be'planten, to plant
be'pleiten, to plead
be'praten, to talk over
   zich laten bepraten, to be persuaded
be'proefd, well-tried
be'proeven, to try, to put to the test; to afflict
be'raad *n*, deliberation, consideration
be'raadslagen, to deliberate
be'raden: zich — (op), to consider
be'ramen, to devise
berde: te — brengen, to broach
be'rechten, to adjudicate
be'redderen, to arrange
be'reden, mounted
berede'neren, to reason out
be'reid, ready, prepared
be'reiden, to prepare
be'reids, already
bereid'vaardig, bereid'willig, ready to help
be'reik *n*, reach; range
be'reiken, to reach, to achieve
be'reikbaar, attainable
be'reisd, (much-)travelled
be'reizen, to travel (all over)

be'rekenen, to calculate; to charge
   niet berekend voor het werk, not equal to the work
be'rekening, calculation
beremuts, busby
berg, mountain
   de haren rezen mij te berge, it was a hair-raising experience
bergachtig, mountainous
bergen, to store; to salvage; to accommodate
   hij is geborgen, he is a made man
bergengte, defile
bergingswerk *n*, salvage-operations
bergkam, bergrug, mountain-ridge
bergkloof, ravine, gorge
bergloon *n*, salvage-money
bergplaats, store, depository
bergruimte, storage space
bergzout *n*, rock-salt
be'richt *n*, news, report; notice
be'richten, to inform
be'rijden, to ride
be'rispen, to rebuke, to reprimand
berk, birch
berm, (grass) verge
be'roemd, famous
be'roemdheid, fame, celebrity
be'roemen: zich — op, to pride oneself on
be'roep *n*, profession; appeal
   in hoger beroep gaan, to appeal
beroepen: zich — op, to appeal to, to plead, to refer to
be'roeps-, professional
be'roepsleger *n*, regular army
be'roerd, rotten
be'roeren, to stir, to disturb
be'roering, disturbance, turmoil
be'roerte, stroke, fit
be'rokkenen, to cause
be'rooid, penniless
be'rookt, smoky
be'rouw *n*, repentance
be'rouwen: het zal je —, you will be sorry (for it)
be'rouwvol, repentant

be'roven, to rob, to deprive
be'rucht, notorious
be'rusten bij, to be in the safe keeping of
  be'rusten in, to be resigned to
  be'rusten op, to rest on; to be due to
bes, berry, (red-)currant
be'schaafd, well-bred; civilized
be'schaamd, ashamed
be'schadigen, to damage
be'schamen, to shame; to dash (hope); to betray (confidence)
  beschamend, humiliating
be'schaven, to civilize
be'schaving, culture, civilization
be'scheid *n*, reply; document
be'scheiden, modest, retiring
be'schermeling, protégé(e)
be'schermen, to protect
be'schermheer, patron
be'scherming, protection, patronage
be'schieten, to fire on
be'schijnen, to shine on
be'schikbaar, available
be'schikken over, to have at one's disposal
be'schikking: ter —, available
be'schilderde ramen, stained glass windows
be'schimmelen, to go mouldy
be'schimpen, to abuse
be'schonken, tipsy
be'schoren: hem was een ander lot —, a different fate was in store for him
be'schot *n*, partition
be'schouwen, to regard, to contemplate
  wel beschouwd, all things considered
be'schrijven, to describe; to cover with writing
be'schroomd, timid
be'schuit, tea-rusk
be'schuldigen, to accuse
be'schutten, to shelter
be'sef *n*, realization; notion
be'seffen, to realize, to be aware of
besje *n*, old woman

be'slaan, to take up (space); to mount (with silver, etc.); to shoe; to get blurred; to tarnish
be'slag *n*, (metal) fitting(s), mounting(s) *or* ornament(s); batter; seizure
  beslag leggen op, to distrain on; to take up
be'slapen, to sleep on *or* in
be'slissen, to decide
  be'slist, decided, for certain
be'slommeringen, cares, worries
be'sloten, private; close
be'sluipen, to steal up on
be'sluit *n*, conclusion; decision
be'sluiteloos, irresolute
be'sluiten, to conclude; to decide
be'smettelijk, contagious, infectious
be'smetten, to infect, to contaminate
be'smeuren, to besmirch
be'sneeuwd, snow-covered
be'snijden, to circumcise
be'snoeien, to lop, to prune; to cut down
be'snuffelen, to sniff at
be'spannen, to span; to string
  een met paarden bespannen wagen, a horse-drawn cart
be'sparen, to save
be'spatten, to bespatter
be'spelen, to play
be'speuren, to perceive
be'spieden, to spy on
be'spiegelend, contemplative
be'spiegeling, contemplation
be'spoedigen, to speed up
be'spottelijk, ridiculous
be'spotten, to ridicule
be'spraakt, never at a loss for a word
be'spreken, to book, to reserve; to discuss, to review
be'sprenkelen, to sprinkle
be'springen, to pounce upon
be'sproeien, to water
be'spuiten, to spray
best, best; very good; dear: very well
  het is mij best, it is all right by me
  ten beste geven, to contribute

be'staan *n*, existence, livelihood; to exist

bestaan uit, to consist of

bestaan van, to subsist on

be'staanbaar, possible; compatible

be'staansmiddel *n*, means of support

be'stand *n*, truce

be'stand tegen, proof against

be'standdeel *n*, ingredient, component

be'steden, to spend; to devote

be'stek *n*, compass; specification; spoon and fork

het bestek opmaken, to calculate a ship's position

be'stelen, to rob

be'stellen, to order; to deliver

be'stelwagen, (delivery) van

be'stemmen, to destine; to intend

be'stempelen, to stamp; to designate

be'stendig, constant; lasting; steady

be'stendigen, to perpetuate

be'sterven: hij bestierf het van schrik, he nearly died of fright

dat woord ligt in zijn mond bestorven, he is always using that word

be'stijgen, to mount, to ascend

be'stoken, to harass

be'stormen, to storm

be'straffen, to punish

be'stralen, to shine upon, to give X-ray treatment to

be'straten, to pave

be'strijden, to combat; to defray

be'strijken, to cover

be'strooien, to strew, to sprinkle

bestu'deren, to study

be'stuiven, to (cover with) dust; to pollinate

be'sturen, to govern; to drive; to steer

be'stuur *n*, government, administration; committee

bestwil: om uw eigen —, for your own good

been leugen om bestwil, a white lie

be'talen, to pay (for)

ik zal het hem betaald zetten, I'll get even with him

be'tamelijk, seemly

be'tamen, to behove

be'tasten, to feel

bete, morsel

be'tegelen, to tile

be'tekenen, to mean

het heeft niets te betekenen, it is of no consequence

be'tekenis, meaning; significance

beter, better

beterhand: aan de — —, on the road to recovery

beterschap, recovery

be'teugelen, to curb

be'teuterd, taken aback

be'tichten, to accuse

be'timmeren, to face with wood, to panel

be'titelen, to style

be'togen, to argue

be'ton *n*, concrete

be'tonen, to accent; to show

be'tonmolen, concrete mixer

be'toog *n*, argument; exposition

be'toon *n*, demonstration

be'toveren, to bewitch, to fascinate

betovergrootmoeder, great-grandmother

be'traand, tear-stained

be'trachten, to do, to show

be'trappen, to catch (out)

be'treden, to tread; to set foot on

be'treffen, to concern

wat mij betreft, as far as I am concerned

be'trekkelijk, relative

be'trekken, to move into; to involve; to cloud over

be'trekking, post, job; relation-(ship)

met betrekking tot, with reference to

be'treuren, to deplore

betreurens'waardig, deplorable

be'trokken, overcast

be'trokken bij, concerned in

be'trouwbaar, reliable

betten, to dab

be'tuigen, to express; to protest; to profess
betweter, know-all
be'twijfelen, to doubt
be'twistbaar, contestable
be'twisten, to dispute, to contest
beu, fed up
beuk, beech
beukehout *n*, beechwood
beuken, to beat, to pound
beul, executioner; brute
beunhaas, bungler
beunhazen, to dabble
beuren, to lift; to receive
beurs, purse; scholarship; exchange: over-ripe; bruised
beurt, turn
  een flinke beurt, a thorough cleaning-up
beurtelings, in turn
beurtvaart, waterway transport service
beuzelachtig, trivial
be'vallen, to please; to be confined
be'vallig, graceful
be'valling, confinement
be'vangen, to overcome
be'varen, to navigate
be'vattelijk, intelligent, intelligible
be'vatten, to contain; to comprehend
be'vechten, to fight (against)
be'veiligen, to safeguard
be'vel *n*, order, command
be'velen, to command
be'velhebber, be'velvoerder, commander
beven, to tremble
bever, beaver
beverig, shaky
be'vestigen, to fasten; to consolidate; to confirm; to induct
be'vinden, to find
  zich bevinden, to be (situated)
be'vlekken, to stain
be'vlieging, sudden impulse, whim
be'vloeien, to irrigate
be'vochtigen, to moisten
be'voegd, competent, qualified
be'volken, to populate

be'volking, population
be'voordelen, to benefit
bevoor'oordeeld, prejudiced
be'voorrechten, to privilege
be'vorderen, to promote
be'vorderlijk voor, conducive to
be'vrachten, to load; to charter
be'vragen: hier te —, inquire within
be'vredigen, to satisfy; to appease
be'vreemden, to surprise
be'vreesd voor, afraid of
be'vriend, on friendly terms
be'vriezen, to freeze, to get frostbitten
be'vrijden, to liberate, to release
be'vroeden, to surmise
be'vruchten, to fertilize
be'vuilen, to soil
be'waarheiden, to confirm
be'waken, to guard
be'wandelen, to walk in *or* on
be'wapenen, to arm
be'waren, to keep, to preserve
be'waring, keeping, custody
  in bewaring geven, to deposit
be'weegbaar, movable
be'weeglijk, mobile; fidgety
be'weegreden, motive
be'wegen, to move; to induce
be'weging, movement, motion
  uit eigen beweging, of one's own accord
be'wenen, to weep for
be'weren, to assert, to contend
be'werkelijk, unmanageable
be'werken, to till; to work on *or* up; to adapt; to bring about
bewerk'stelligen, to bring about
be'westen, to the west of
be'wieroken, to incense; to praise to the skies
be'wijs *n*, proof; certificate; evidence
be'wijsgrond, argument
be'wijzen, to prove, to show
be'wind *n*, government, rule
be'wolken, to cloud over
be'wonderen, to admire
be'wonen, to inhabit
be'woner, resident, occupant, inhabitant

be'woordingen, terms
be'wust, conscious
  zich bewust zijn van, to be aware of
  de bewuste brief, the letter in question
be'wusteloos, unconscious
be'wustheid, awareness
be'wustzijn *n*, consciousness
  buiten bewustzijn, unconscious
be'zaaien, to sow; to litter
be'zadigd, sober-minded
be'zegelen, to seal
be'zeilen, to sail
  er is geen land met hem te bezeilen, you cannot do a thing with him
bezem, broom
be'zending, consignment
  de hele bezending, the whole lot
be'zeren, to hurt
be'zet, occupied, engaged; set
be'zeten, possessed
be'zetten, to occupy; to set
be'zetting, garrison; occupation; cast (of a play)
be'zichtigen, to view
be'zielen, to inspire
  wat bezielt je? what has come over you?
be'zien, to look at
  dat staat nog te bezien, that remains to be seen
bezig, occupied, busy
  druk bezig, hard at work
bezigen, to use
bezigheid, occupation
bezighouden, to keep occupied
be'zijden, beside
be'zingen, to sing (the praises of)
be'zinken, to settle (down); to sink in
be'zinksel *n*, sediment
be'zinnen: zich —, to reflect; to change one's mind
bezinning: tot — komen, to come to one's senses
be'zit *n*, possession(s), estate
be'zittelijk voornaamwoord *n*, possessive pronoun
be'zitten, to possess

be'zittingen, property, possessions
be'zoedelen, to defile
be'zoek, *n*, visit
  we krijgen bezoek, we are expecting visitors
be'zoeken, to visit; to afflict
be'zoldigen, to pay a salary
be'zoldiging, salary, pay
be'zondigen: zich — aan, to perpetrate
be'zonken, considered
be'zonnen, level-headed
be'zopen, tipsy; crazy
be'zorgd, anxious; provided for
be'zorgen, to procure; to give; to deliver
be'zuiden, to the south of
be'zuinigen, to economize
be'zuren, to suffer for
be'zwaar *n*, objection; drawback
be'zwaard, weighted; burdened, oppressed
be'zwaarlijk, scarcely
  bezwaarlijk vinden, to object to
be'zwaarschrift, *n*, petition
be'zwangeren, to impregnate
be'zwarende omstandigheden, aggravating circumstances
be'zweet, sweating
be'zweren, to adjure; to exorcise
be'zwijken, to succumb, to collapse
be'zwijmen, to faint
bibberen, to shiver
bibliothe'caris, librarian
biblio'theek, library
bidden, to pray, to say grace
bidstond, prayer-meeting
biecht, confession
biechten, to confess; to go to confession
biechtvader, confessor
bieden, to offer; to bid
biefstuk, rump-steak
bier *n*, ale, beer
biet, beet
  rode biet, beetroot
biezen, (made of) rushes
big, piglet
biggelen, to trickle
biggen, to farrow

bij, near, at, with, by; present; in addition: bee

bij zijn leven, during his lifetime

hij is goed bij, he is all there

er ligt me iets van bij, I seem to remember something of it

bij-, secondary, in addition

bijbedoeling, ulterior motive

Bijbel, Bible

bijblijven, to keep pace with; to stick in the memory

bijbrengen, to adduce (reasons); to bring round; to inculcate

bijde'hand, smart; "all there"

bijde'handje n, bright child

bijdraaien, to heave to; to come round

bijdrage, contribution

bijdragen, to contribute; to tend

bij'een, together

bij'eenkomen, to come together

bij'eenkomst, meeting, gathering

bij'eengenomen: alles —, all things considered

bijenkorf, bee-hive

bijenstal, apiary

bijgaand, enclosed

bijgebouw n, outhouse

bijgedachte, implication; association

bijgeloof n, superstition

bijge'lovig, superstitious

bijgenaamd, nicknamed

bijge'val, by any chance; in case

bijge'volg, in consequence

bijhouden, to keep (the books); to keep up with

bijkantoor n, branch-office

bijkeuken, scullery

bijknippen, to-trim

bijkomen, to come to, to revive

er komt nog bij, what is more

bijkomend, bij'komstig, attendant; incidental

bijl, hatchet, axe

het bijltje erbij neerleggen, to down tools

bijlage, enclosure; appendix

bijleggen, to make up (a quarrel); to add (money) to

bijlichten, to give (a person) some light

bijltjesdag, day of reckoning

bijna, almost

bijna niet, hardly

bijnaam, nickname

bijoorzaak, contributory cause

bijpassen, to pay the difference

bijpassend, matching

bijschenken, to fill up

bijschrift n, caption

bijslaap, cohabitation; bedfellow

bijslag, additional payment

bijsmaak, trace, tang

bijspringen, to help

bijstaan, to assist

bijstand, assistance

bijstelling, apposition

bijster: het spoor—zijn, to have lost one's way

niet bijster, not particularly

bijt, hole cut in the ice.

bijten, to bite

van zich af bijten, to show fight

bijtend, caustic; cutting; corrosive

bij'tijds, in good time

bijtrekken, to pull up; to improve

bijvak n, subsidiary subject

bijval, approbation; applause

bijvallen, to back up

bijvoegen, to add

bij'voeglijk naamwoord n, adjective

bijvoegsel n, supplement

bij'voorbeeld, for instance

bijwerken, to touch up; to bring up to date; to give extra coaching

bijwijf n, concubine

bijwonen, to attend

bijwoord n, adverb

bijzaak, matter of secondary importance

bijzettafeltje n, occasional table

bijzetten, to inter; to add

bijzetting, interment

bij'ziend(e), short-sighted

bijzijn n, presence

bijzin, subordinate clause

bijzit, concubine

bijzitter, assessor
bij'zonder, special, particular; private
niets bijzonders, nothing out of the ordinary
bij'zonderheden, particulars
bil, buttock
bil'jart *n*, billiard-table, billiards
bil'jet *n*, (bank)note; ticket
billijk, fair
billijken, to justify; to approve of
binden, to bind, to tie (up); to thicken
binnen, within, inside, in
het schoot me te binnen, it (suddenly) struck me
binnen'door gaan, to take a short cut
binnengaan, to go in
binnenhuis *n*, interior
binnenkomen, to come in
binnen'kort, shortly
binnenlands, internal, home . . .
Ministerie van Binnenlandse Zaken, Home Office
binnens'huis, indoors
binnens'monds, under one's broath, indistinctly
binnenste'buiten, inside out
binnenvaart, inland navigation
binnenwaarts, inward(s)
bint, tie-beam
bio'loog, biologist
bios'coop, cinema
bisdom *n*, diocese
bisschop, bishop
bis'schoppelijk, episcopal
bisschopszetel, (episcopal) see
bis'seren, to encore
bits, snappish
bitter, bitter
bitter weinig, next to nothing
bitterkoekje *n*, macaroon
bittertje *n*, gin and bitters
bivak *n*, bivouac
blaadje *n*, petal; leaflet; tray
ik sta bij hem in een goed blaadje, I am in his good books
blaag, whipper-snapper
blaam, blame
blaar, blister
blaas, bladder; bubble

blaasbalg, pair of bellows
blaasinstrument, wind-instrument
blaaskaak, gasbag
blad *n*, (*pl.* bladen), leaf; sheet of paper; newspaper; tray: (*pl.* bladeren), leaf of a tree
hij neemt geen blad voor de mond, he does not mince his words
van het blad spelen, to play at sight
bladgroente(n), greens
bladzij(de), page
blaffen, to bark
blaken, to blaze, to glow
in blakende welstand, in the pink of health
blakeren, to scorch
blanco, blank
blank, white; pure; naked (sword); flooded
blaten, to bleat
blauw (*n*), blue
blauwe'regen, wistaria
blauwtje: een—lopen, to be turned down
blauwsel *n*, washing-blue
blauwzuur *n*, prussic acid
blazen, to blow; to spit (cat)
hoog van de toren blazen, to brag
bleek, pale
bleekheid, pallor
bleken, to bleach
bleren, to shout, to bawl
bles'seren, to wound
bles'suur, wound
bleu, bashful
blieven, (cf. *believen*): wat blieft u? what can I do for you? I beg your pardon?
ik blief het niet, I don't like it
blij(de), glad
blijdschap, gladness
blijk *n* geven van, to show signs of
blijkbaar, apparently
blijken, to appear, to transpire
't moet nog blijken, it remains to be seen
blijkens, as appears from
blij'moedig, cheerful

blijspel *n*, comedy

blijven, to stay, to remain

blijvend, lasting, permanent

blik, glance, look; eyes: *n*, tin (-plate); dustpan

blikken: zonder — of blozen, without turning a hair

bliksem, lightning; blazes

  handige bliksem! smart fellow!

blind, blind: *n*, shutter

  zich blind staren op, to be obsessed by

  de blinde, dummy (at bridge)

blinddoeken, to blindfold

blinde'darmontsteking, appendicitis

blindelings, blindly

blindheid, blindness

blinken, to shine, to gleam

bloed *n*, blood

bloedarmoede, anæmia

bloedbad *n*, carnage

bloedeigen, of one's own (flesh and) blood

bloeden, to bleed

bloederig, bloody

bloedig, bloody; bitter

bloedlichaampje *n*, blood-corpuscle

bloedneus, nose-bleed

bloedschande, incest

bloedsomloop, circulation (of the blood)

bloedwraak, vendetta

bloei, bloom, blossom(ing); prosperity

bloeien, to bloom; to flourish

bloeitijd, blossom-time; heyday

bloem, flower; flour

  de bloemetjes buiten zetten, to paint the town red

bloemig, floury

bloe'mist, florist

bloemkool, cauliflower

bloemlezing, anthology

bloempjesdag, flag-day

bloemrijk, florid

bloemstuk *n*, bouquet

bloesem, blossom

blok *n*, block; log

blokfluit, recorder

blok'kade, blockade

blokken, to swot

blok'keren, to block; to blockade

blokwachter, signalman

blond, fair

blon'dine, blonde

bloodaard, coward

bloot, bare, naked; sheer

blootgeven: zich —, to lay oneself open (to attack)

blootleggen, to reveal

blootshoofds, bareheaded

blootstaan aan, to be exposed to

blootstellen, to expose

blos, blush; bloom

blozen, to blush

bluffen, to brag

blussen, to extinguish; to quell

blut, broke

bobbel(ig), lump(y)

bochel, hump; hunchback

bocht, bend: *n*, awful stuff

bochtig, winding

bod *n*, bid

bode, messenger; carrier

bodem, bottom; soil; territory

  de bodem inslaan, to frustrate

bodemloos, bottomless

boedel, household goods; personal estate

boef, rogue

boefje *n*, guttersnipe

boeg, bow(s)

  het over een andere boeg gooien, to try another tack

  veel werk voor de boeg, a lot of work on hand

boegspriet, bowsprit

boei, buoy

boeien, fetters: to fetter; to hold the attention

boeiend, fascinating

boek *n*, book

  te boek staan als, to have the reputation of

  je gaat buiten je boekje, you are overstepping the mark

boekdeel *n*, volume

boekelegger, book-mark(er)

boeken, to book

boekenkast, bookcase

boekenwijsheid, book-learning

boeke'rij, library

boekhandel, bookshop

boekhouden (*n*), book-keeping: to keep accounts

boekjaar *n*, financial year

boel: een —, a lot

  een armoedig boeltje, a shoddy outfit

  je boeltje *n,* your goods and chattels

boemelen, to be on the spree

boemeltrein, slow train

boender, scrubbing-brush

boenen, to scrub

boenwas, wax polish

boer, peasant, farmer; knave (at cards); **boor:** belch

boerde'rij, farm

boeren, to belch

boeren'jongens, brandy and raisins

boeren'kool, kale

boe'rin, peasant woman, farmer's wife

boers, boorish

boertig, slapstick

boete, penalty, fine; penance

boeten voor, to atone for

boet'seren, to model

boet'vaardig, penitent

boezelaar, apron

boezem, bosom

bof, stroke of luck: mumps

boffen, to be lucky

bogen op, to boast (of)

bok, buck; billy-goat

  een bok schieten, to make a blunder

bo'kaal, goblet

bokkesprong, caper

bokkig, churlish

bokking, bloater

boksen, to box

bol, globe, sphere; crown (of hat); bulb; head: convex, bulging

bolhoed, bowler hat

bolleboos, adept

bollen, to bulge

bolster, shell, husk

bolwerk *n,* bulwark

bolwerken: hij kon het niet—, he could not manage it

bom, bomb

bombar'deren, to shell; to bomb(ard)

bom'barie, fuss and bother

bomen, to punt; to chat

bomgat *n,* bung-hole

bon, voucher; coupon

bond, alliance, union

bondgenoot, ally

bondig, terse

bonk, chunk, lump

bonken, to thump

bonkig, bony

bons, bump, thud

  de bons geven, to sack, to throw over

bont, many-coloured; gaudy; piebald; varied; motley: *n,* fur

  je maakt het te bont, you are going too far

bonzen, to throb; to pound; to bump

boodschap, message, errand

  boodschappen doen, to go shopping

boog, arch, arc; bow

boom, tree; boom; barrier; pole

boomgaard, orchard

boomstam, tree-trunk

boon, bean

boor, drill, gimlet

boord *n,* collar; (ship)board

  aan boord, on board

boordevol, brim-full

boos, angry; evil

boos'aardig, malicious

boosheid, anger

booswicht, villain

boot, boat

bootsman, bo'sun

bootwerker, dock labourer

bord *n,* plate; board

bor'deel *n,* brothel

bor'des *n,* (flight of) steps

bor'duren, to embroider

boren, to drill, to bore

borg, surety, security, bail

borgstelling, borgtocht, security; bail

borrel, short drink

borrelen, to (have a) drink; to bubble

borst, breast, chest: lad
  tegen de borst stuiten, to go against the grain
borstbeeld *n*, bust
borstel, brush; bristle
borstelen, to brush
borstelig, bristly
borstkas, chest
borstplaat, fondant
borstvliesontsteking, pleurisy
borstwering, parapet
bos, bunch, bundle, tuft: *n*, wood
bosachtig, wooded
bosbes, bilberry
bosbouw, forestry
bosgrond, woodland
bosje *n*, spinney
boskat, wild cat
bosrijk, wooded
bos'schage *n*, grove
boswachter, (forest)-keeper
bot, blunt: flounder: *n*, bone
  bot vangen, to meet with a curt refusal
botvieren, to give rein to
boter, butter
boterbloem, buttercup
boterham, slice of bread and butter
botsen, to collide, to bump
botsing, collision
botte'lier, butler, steward
botweg, flatly
boud, bold
bou'gie, sparking plug
bouil'lon, beef-tea, stock
bout, bolt; wooden pin; leg cut of meat
bouw, build, construction; cultivation; structure
bouwen, to build
bouw'kundig, architectural
bouwkunst, architecture
bouw'vallig, tumble-down, dilapidated
boven, above, over
  te boven gaan, to exceed
  te boven komen, to get over
bovenaan, at the top
boven'dien, moreover
bovenhuis *n*, upstairs flat
bovenlicht *n*, skylight

bovenloop, upper reaches
boven'mate, exceedingly
boven'menselijk, superhuman
bovenna'tuurlijk, supernatural
bovenop, on (the) top of
bovenste, topmost
boventoon, overtone
  de boventoon voeren, to (pre-)dominate
box, play-pen
braaf, good, decent, upright
braak, fallow
braam(bes), blackberry
brabbelen, to jabber
braden, to roast
brak, brackish
braken, to vomit
brallen, to brag
bran'card, stretcher
brand, fire
  in brand vliegen, to catch fire
brandbaar, inflammable
branden, to burn
brander, blow-lamp
brandewijn, French brandy
brandkast, safe
brandmerken, to brand
brandnetel, stinging nettle
brandpunt *n*, focus
brandschatten, to hold to ransom
brandspuit, fire-engine
brandstapel, stake; funeral pile
brandstichter, incendiary
brandstof, fuel
brandweer, fire-brigade
branie, daring; swank(-pot)
brasem, bream
braspartij, orgy
bra'voure, bravado
breed, broad, wide
breed'sprakig, prolix
breedte, breadth, width; latitude
breed'voerig, detailed
breekbaar, breakable, fragile
breekijzer *n*, crowbar
breidel, bridle
breidelen, to curb
breien, to knit
brein *n*, brain
breiwerk *n*, knitting

bre'kage, breakage(s)
breken, to break
brem(struik), broom
brengen, to bring, to take
  er toe brengen, to induce
bres, breach
bre'tels, braces
breuk, fracture, fraction, rupture
bre'vet n, certificate
bre'vier n, breviary
brief, letter
briefkaart, postcard
briefwisseling, correspondence
bries, breeze
briesen, to snort
brievenbesteller, postman
brievenbus, letter-box
brik, brig; break, wagonette
bril, glasses
Brits, British
Brit'tanje n, Brit'tannië n, Drittain
broche, brooch
broed n, brood
broeden, to brood
broeder, brother
broeds, broody
broeibak, cold frame
broeien, to brood; to brew; to heat
broeierig, sultry
broeikas, greenhouse
broeinest n, hotbed
broek, (pair of) trousers, knickers
  jong broekje n, whippersnapper
broekspijp, trouser-leg
broer, brother
brok, fragment; lump
bro'kaat, bro'caat n, brocade
brokkelen, to crumble
brommen, to growl, to grumble
bromvlieg, bluebottle
bron, spring, source
bronader, fountain-head
brood n, bread, loaf
  zijn brood verdienen, to earn one's living
brood'dronken(heid), wanton(ness)
broodje n, (bread-)roll
broos, brittle, fragile, frail

bros, brittle; crisp
brouwen, to brew
brouwe'rij, brewery
  leven in de brouwerij brengen, to liven things up
brouwsel n, brew; concoction
brug, bridge
  over de brug komen, to pay up
Brugman: praten als —, to have the gift of the gab
brui: er de — aan geven, to chuck it
bruid, bride
brui(de)gom, bridegroom
bruidsjapon, wedding-dress
bruidsjonker, groomsman, best man
bruidsmeisje n, bridesmaid
bruidspaar n, bride and bridegroom
bruidsschat, dowry
bruikbaar, serviceable
bruikleen: in —, on loan
bruiloft, wedding (feast)
bruin (n), brown
bruisen, to effervesce; to seethe
brullen, to roar
bru'taal, impudent
bru'taalweg, calmly
brutali'teit, insolence
bruto, gross (weight)
bruusk, brusque
bruut, brute: brutish
buffel, buffalo
buf'fet n, sideboard; buffet
bui, shower; fit
buidel, pouch, purse
buigbaar, flexible
buigen, to bend, to bow; to submit
buiging, bow, bend; inflexion
buigtang, (pair of) pliers
buigzaam, pliable; yielding
buiig, showery
buik, belly
  twee handen op één buik, hand in glove
buikje n, tummy; corporation
buikpijn, stomach-ache
buikspreker, ventriloquist
buikvliesontsteking, peritonitis
buil, swelling

buis, tube, pipe; jacket

buiten, outside; beyond; without; in the country

het ging buiten mij om, it occurred without my knowledge

van buiten kennen, to know by heart

buiten(huis) *n*, country-seat

buiten'dien, moreover

buitenge'meen, buitenge'woon, uncommon, extraordinary

buite'nissig, odd

buitenkansje *n*, stroke of luck

buitenkant, outside

buitenland: in het —, abroad

buitenlander, foreigner

buitenlands, foreign

buitenlucht, open air

buitens'huis, out of doors

buiten'spel, off-side

buiten'sporig, excessive

buitenstaander, outsider

buitenste, outermost

buitenwaarts, outwards

buitenwijken, outskirts

bukken, to duck, to stoop

gebukt gaan onder, to be weighed down by

bul, bull, diploma

bulderen, to roar

bulken, to bellow

bulken van het geld, to roll in money

bullebak, bully

bullen, belongings

bult, hump, lump

bundel, bundle; collection (of poems, etc.)

bungelen, to dangle

bunkeren, to take on fuel

burcht, castle, citadel

bu'reau *n*, office; desk

burengerucht *n*, breach of the peace

burge'meester, burgomaster

burger, citizen, civilian

dat geeft de burger moed, that puts heart into a chap

burger-, civil(ian), civic

burgerlijk, bourgeois, civil

burgelijke stand, registry of births, marriages and deaths

bus, tin, canister: bus

in de bus blazen, to loosen the purse-strings

buskruit *n*, gunpowder

buste, bust

bustehouder, brassière

buur, buurman, buurvrouw, neighbour

buurt, neighbourhood

b.v., e.g.

C

For words not given under C, see also K

ca'cao, cocoa

ca'chet *n*, seal, *cachet*

ca'chot *n*, punishment cell

ca'deau *n*, present

ca'mee, cameo

camou'fleren, to camouflage

cam'pagne, campaign

cana'pé, settee

candi'daat, candidate; holder of the first university degree

canon, ground-rent; canon

cano'niek, canonical

ca'outchouc, india-rubber

capiton'neren, to pad; to stuff

capitu'leren, to capitulate

capri'ool, caper

capties maken, to make difficulties

car'bid *n*, carbide

car'bol *n*, carbolic (acid)

carbu'rator, carburettor

carga'door, ship-broker

carrosse'rie, coach-work

carrou'sel, round-about

carri'ère, career

cas'sette, cash-box; casket, canteen (of cutlery)

casta'gnetten, castanets

cas'treren, to castrate

catalogi'seren, to catalogue

ca'talogus, catalogue

catechi'satie, confirmation class, religious instruction

cate'chismus, catechism

catego'rie, category

cate'gorisch, categorical

cause'rie, talk, informal lecture

cavale'rie, cavalry

ceder, cedar

cein'tuur, belt, sash
cein'tuurbaan, circular railway
cel, cell: 'cello
celi'baat n, celibacy
celiba'tair, celibate
cel'list, violoncellist
cen'suur, censorship
cent, 1/100 part of a Dutch guilder; " brass farthing "
cen'traal, central
cen'trale, power-station; tele-phone exchange
centrum n, centre
ceremoni'eel (n), ceremonial
cere'moniemeester, master of ceremonies
certifi'ceren, to certify
cha'grijn n, chagrin
cha'grijnig, cantankerous
champi'gnon, mushroom
chan'tage, blackmail
cha'otisch, chaotic
cha'piter n, subject of discussion
char'geren, to exaggerate
char'mant, charming
char'meren, to charm
chas'seur, page-boy
chauf'feren, to drive (a car)
chef, head, manager, chief
chemi'caliën, chemicals
chemicus, (analytical) chemist
che'mie, chemistry
chemisch, chemical
cheru'bijn, cherub
chi'cane, chicanery
chi'rurg, surgeon
chirur'gie, surgery
chi'rurgisch, surgical
chloor, chlorine
choco'laatje n, chocolate(drop)
choco'la(de), chocolate
choco'la(de)melk, cocoa
Christelijk, Christian
Christen, (a) Christian
Christendom n, Christianity
Christenheid, Christendom
Christus, Christ
chronisch, chronic
chroom n, chromium
cicho'rei, chicory
cijfer n, figure, digit, mark
cijns, tribute money, tax
ci'linder, cylinder

ci'lindrisch, cylindrical
cim'baal, cymbal
cineac, news-theatre
ci'pier, gaoler
ci'pres, cypress
circa, approximately
circu'laire, circular (letter)
circu'leren, to circulate
cirkel(en), (to) circle
cirkel'vormig, circular
cise'leren, to chase; to emboss
ci'taat n, quotation
ci'teren, to quote
ci'troen, lemon
ci'troenpers, lemon-squeezer
ci'viel, civil; moderate
clau'sule, clause; proviso
cle'ment, lenient
cle'mentie, clemency
clo'set n, water-closet
clo'setpapier n, toilet-paper
club, club; armchair
coa'litie, coalition
co'con, cocoon
cognosse'ment n, bill of lading
coif'feren, to dress hair
cokes, coke
col'bert n, jacket
col'bertkostuum n, lounge-suit
collec'tant, person collecting money
col'lecte, collection
collec'teren, to collect money
col'lectie, collection
col'lega, colleague
col'lege n, board; college; uni-versity lecture
    col'lege geven, to lecture
collegi'aal, friendly, harmonious
col'lier, necklace
collo n, (pl. colli), package
co'lonne, column (of soldiers)
colpor'teren, to hawk (printed matter)
colpor'teur, pedlar
comman'dant, commandant, commander, ship's captain
comman'deren, to command, to order about
com'mando n, command
com'mandobrug, navigating bridge
com'mandotoren, conning tower

commen'saal, lodger
commen'taar *n*, commentary
commerci'eel, commercial
com'mies, clerk
commissari'aat *n*, directorate; police-station
commis'saris, company director; chief inspector of police
com'missie, committee, commission
commissio'nair, commission-agent
compa'gnie, company
compa'gnon, (business) partner
comparti'ment *n*, compartment
compen'seren, to compensate
compi'lator, compiler
compi'leren, to compile
com'pleet, complete
comple'teren, to complete
complimen'teren met, to compliment on
complimen'teus, complimentary
compo'neren, to compose (music)
compo'nist, composer
compri'meren, to compress
compromit'tant, compromising
compromit'teren, to compromise
comptabili'teit, accountability
concen'tratievermogen *n*, power of concentration
concen'treren, to concentrate
con'cept *n*, draft (document)
con'cert *n*, concert, recital; concerto
con'cessie, concession
con'ciërge, caretaker, hall-porter
con'cilie *n*, ecclesiastical council
con'cours *n*, competition
  concours hippique, horse-show
concur'rent, competitor
concur'rentie, competition
concur'reren, to compete
concur'rerend, competitive
conden'sator, condenser
conden'seren, to condense
con'ditie, condition
  in conditie, fit
condo'leren, to condole with

conduc'teur, guard, tram *or* bus conductor
con'fectie, ready-made (clothes)
conferen'cier, compère
confi'seur, confectioner
confi'turen, candied fruit
con'frater, colleague
con'fuus, confused, abashed
con'gé *n*: iemand zijn — geven, to send a person packing
conse'quent, consistent
conse'quentie, consequence, consistency
conser'vator, curator
con'serven, preserves
con'siderans, preamble
con'signe *n*, password; instruction
consi'storiekamer, vestry
con'sorten, confederates
consta'teren, to establish
constru'eren, to construct
consu'lent, expert adviser
consul'tatiebureau *n*, welfare clinic
consu'ment, consumer
con'sumptie, consumption, food and/or drink(s)
con'tant, (in) cash
contrac'teren, to contract
contramine: in de —, in a contrary mood
con'trole, check, supervision
contro'leren, to check, to inspect
contro'leur, inspector
conveni'ëren, to be convenient
cor'rector, proof-reader
correspon'deren, to correspond
correspon'dentie, correspondence
corri'geren, to correct
cor'vee, fatigue-duty; tough job
cou'lant, obliging
cou'lissen, wings
cou'pé, compartment; brougham
cou'peren, to cut
cou'rant, newspaper
cour'ante maat, stock size
cou'vert *n*, envelope; cover (at table)
cou'veuse, incubator
cra'paud, easy chair
crea'tuur *n*, creature

cre'peren, to kick the bucket
cri'ant vervelend, inexpressibly
  boring
cri'terium n, criterion
cro'quet, croquette
cru, crude
cul'tures, plantations
cul'tuur, culture
cura'tele, guardianship
cu'rator, curator, official receiver
curiosi'teit, curio
cur'sief, italicized
cursus, school-year, course of
  studies
cynicus, cynic
cynisch, cynical

D

daad, deed, act(ion)
daad'werkelijk, actual
daags, see dag
daal·lor, one and a half guilders
daar, there: as because
daar'achter, behind it
daarbij, near it; moreover
daardoor, through it, as a result
daaren'boven, moreover
daaren'tegen, on the other hand
daar'ginds, over there
daar'heen, thither, there
daargelaten, (quite) apart from
daar'net, just now
daarom, therefore
daarom'trent, thereabouts
daarop, on there; thereupon
daarop'volgend,   subsequent,
  next
daarover, over it, about it
daarvandaan, from there
dadel, date
dadelijk, immediate
dader, perpetrator
dag, day(light)
  dag! hello!, goodbye
  om de drie dagen, every third
  day
  daagse kleren, everyday clothes
dagblad n, daily paper
dagboek n, diary
dagelijks, daily
dagen, to summon: to dawn
dageraad, dawn

dagjesmensen, trippers
dagloner, day labourer
dagtekenen, to date
dagvaarden, to summon
dak n, roof
dakgoot, gutter
daklicht n, skylight
dakloos, homeless
dakkamer, attic
dakpan, tile
dal n, valley
dalen, to go or come down
daling, descent; drop
dam, dam, causeway: king (in
  draughts)
da'mast n, damask
dambord n, draught-board
dame, lady
damhert n, fallow deer
dammen, to play draughts
damp, vapour
dampkring, atmosphere
dan, then: than
  dan ook, in fact
  (hoe, wat, wie) dan ook (how-,
  what-, who-)ever
danig, exceeding, greatly
dank, thanks
  dank zij, thanks to
dankbaar, grateful, gratifying
dankbaarheid, gratitude
danken, to thank, to say grace
dans(en), (to) dance
dapper, brave
dar, drone
darm, intestine
darmontsteking, enteritis
dartel, frisky
dartelen, to frolic, to gambol
das, (neck)tie, scarf: badger
dashond, dachshund
dat, that, which
da'teren, to date
datgene, that (one)
datum, date
dauw, dew
dauwworm, ringworm
daveren, to thunder, to resound
dazen, to talk rot
de, the
debar'keren, to disembark
de'bat n, debate
debat'teren, to debate

debet (n), debit: overdrawn
de'biet n, sale(s)
debi'teren, to debit
   een aardigheid debiteren, to
   crack a joke
debi'teur, debtor
de'buut n, début
december, December
de'ceptie, disappointment
deci'meren, to decimate
decla'meren, to recite
decli'natie, declination; declension
decli'neren, to decline
de'creet n, decree
decre'teren, to decree
deeg n, dough, mixture
deel n, part, share; volume
deel'achtig, participating in
deelbaar, divisible
deelgenoot, participant; partner
deelgenootschap n, partnership
deelnemen aan, to participate in
deelnemer, participant
deelneming, participation; sympathy
deels, partly
deeltal n, dividend
deelteken n, diæresis
deeltje n, particle
deelwoord n, participle
deemoed, meekness
dee'moedig, meek
Deen; Deens (n), Dane; Danish
deerlijk, grievous
deern(e), wench
deernis, compassion
deernis'wekkend, pitiable
de'fect, faulty, out of order: n,
   defect, fault
de'fensie, (national) defence
defi'lé n, march-past; defile
defi'leren, to march past
defini'ëren, to define
defini'tief, definite, definitive
deftig, dignified; distinguished;
   la-di-da
degelijk, sound; substantial; of
   sterling character
   hij weet het wel degelijk, he
   knows (it) perfectly well
degen, sword; foil
de'gene die, the one who

degra'deren, to degrade
deinen, to heave
deining, swell; commotion
dek n, cover; bedclothes; deck
dekbed n, eiderdown
deken, blanket: dean
dekhengst, stallion
dekken, to cover; to lay (the
   table); to serve (a mare)
   zich dekken, to take cover
dekking, cover
deklast, deck cargo
dekmantel, cloak
deksel n, lid, cover
   deksels! by Jove!
dekzeil n, tarpaulin
delen, to divide, to share, to
   split
deler, divisor
deling, division
delfstof, mineral
delgen, to pay off
delgingsfonds, sinking fund
delica'tesse, delicacy
de'licit n, offence
delven, to dig
de'mi(-sai'son), light overcoat
demo'craat, democrat
democra'tie, democracy
demon'teren, to dismantle
dempen, to fill in (with earth);
   to subdue
den(neboom), fir-tree
denderend, smashing
Denemarken n, Denmark
denkbaar, conceivable
denkbeeld n, idea
denk'beeldig, imaginary
denkelijk, probably
denken (aan), to think (of)
   doen denken aan, to remind of
   denk eens aan! just fancy!
denkvermogen n, intellectual
   capacity
denneappel, fir-cone
dennehout n, pine-wood
depo'neren, to deposit, to file, to
   register
de'pot n, depot; branch establishment
depri'meren, to depress
derail'leren, to run off the
   rails

deran'geren, to inconvenience
derde, third
  ten derde, thirdly
derdemachtswortel, cube root
derde'rangs, third rate
deren, to harm
dergelijk, such(like)
  iets dergelijks, something of the sort
der'halve, hence
dermate, to such a degree
dertien(de), thirteen(th)
dertig, thirty
derven, to lack
derwaarts, thither
des, of the
  des te (meer), all the (more)
desalniette'min, nevertheless
desavou'eren, to disavow
desbe'treffend, relating to this
desem n, leaven
desge'lijks, likewise
desge'wenst, if desired
desillusie, disillusionment
des'kundig(e), expert
des'noods, if need be
deson'danks, nevertheless
des'poot, despot
des'sin n, design
des'tijds, at the time
deta'cheren, to detail
de'tail n, detail; retail
deti'neren, to detain
deto'neren, to detonate; to be out of tune, to be out of keeping
deugd, virtue
  lieve deugd! good gracious!
deugdelijk, reliable
deugdzaam, virtuous
deugen: niet —, to be no good
deugniet, rascal, good-for-nothing
deuk(en), (to) dent
deuntje n, tune
deur, door
  met de deur in huis vallen, to come straight to the point
deurwaarder, bailiff
de'vies n, motto, device
de'viezen, foreign currency
de'voot, devout
de'wijl, because

deze, this, these
  deze of gene, (some)one or other
de'zelfde, the same
diaco'nes, protestant nursing sister
diaco'nie, poor relief board
di'aken, church worker; deacon
dia'loog, dialogue
dia'mant, diamond
dia'mantslijper, diamond cutter
diar'ree, diarrhœa
dicht, closed; dense
  dicht bij, near (to)
dichten, to write poetry; to stop a leak
dichter('es), poet(ess)
dichterlijk, poetic(al)
dichtkunst, (art of) poetry
dichtmaat, metre
dic'taat n, dictation; lecture-notes; note-book
dic'tee n, dictation
die, that, those; who, which; he, she, it, they
di'eet n, diet
dief, thief
diefstal, theft
diennan'gaande, as to that
dienaar, servant
diender, cop(per)
  dooie diender, dull dog
dienen, to serve
  waar dient dit voor? what is the use of this?
  daar ben ik niet van gediend, I take exception to that
dienovereen'komstig, accordingly
dienst, service, duty
dienstbode, (house)maid
dienstplicht, compulsory (military) service
dienstregeling, time-table
dienst'vaardig, obliging
dienstweigeraar, conscientious objector
dientafel, (tea-)trolley
dientenge'volge, in consequence
diep, deep; profound
diepgaand, searching
diepgang, draught
diepte, depth

diep'zinnig, profound; abstruse
dier *n*, animal
dierbaar, dearly loved
dierenriem, zodiac
diergaarde, zoo(logical gardens)
dierkunde, zoology
dierlijk, animal; bestial
die'vegge, female thief
differenti'aal-rekening, (differ-
ential) calculus
dij, thigh
dijk, dike, embankment; dam
 aan de dijk zetten, to shelve
dik, thick; fat; dense
 zich dik maken, to get het up
dikkerd, fatty
dikte, thickness
dikwijls, often
dikzak, fatty
dili'gence, stage-coach
dimmen, to dim, to dip
di'neren, to dine
ding *n*, thing
dingen, to bargain
 dingen naar, to compete for, to
 sue for
dinsdag, Tuesday
diplo'maat, diplomat(ist)
diploma'tie, diplomacy
direc'teur, director, manager,
 head(-master)
di'rectie, management
diri'gent, conductor
diri'geren, to conduct
dis, D sharp: table
discon'teren, to discount
dis'conto *n*, (rate of) discount
discu'teren, to discuss, to argue
dispo'neren over, to have at
 one's disposal
dispo'nibel, available
dis'puut *n*, dispute; debating
 society
dissel(boom), pole (of a carriage)
disser'tatie, thesis for a doctorate
distel, thistle
distilla'teur, distiller
distilleerde'rij, distillery
distri'butie, distribution, (food)
 allocation; radio-diffusion
dit, this, these
ditmaal, this time
dobbelaar, gambler

dobbelen, to play dice
dobbelstenen, dice
dobber, float
 een harde dobber hebben, to
 be hard put to it
dobberen, to bob up and down
do'cent, teacher
do'ceren, to teach
doch, but; however
dochter, daughter
docto'raal(e'xamen) *n*, examination for master's degree
docto'randus, person who has
 passed the *doctoraalexamen*
dode, dead (wo)man, deceased
dodelijk, mortal, deadly
doden, to kill, to mortify
doedelzak, bagpipe
doek, cloth; (*n*), canvas; screen
doel *n*, target, goal; aim
doelbe'wust, purposeful
doeleinde *n*, purpose
doelen op, to allude to
doelloos, aimless, pointless
doel'matig, appropriate; efficient
doel'treffend, effective
doemen, to doom
doen, to do, to make; to ask;
 to put
 ik kan er niets aan doen, I
 can't help it
 ik heb met je te doen, I am
 sorry for you
 het doet er niet(s) toe, it makes
 no difference
 doen in, to deal in
 doen en laten, behaviour, doings
does, poodle
doetje *n*, softy
doezelen, to drowse
dof, dull, dim
doffer, cock-pigeon
dog, mastiff
dogger, cod-fisher; dogger
dok *n*, dock
dokken, to dock
 je zult moeten dokken, you'll
 have to fork out
dokter, doctor
dol, mad, frantic; stripped (of a
 screw): rowlock
dolblij, overjoyed

dol'driftig, beside oneself (with rage)

dolen, to wander

dol'fijn, dolphin

dolgraag, only too gladly

dolheid, frenzy

dolk, dagger

dolleman, madman

dollen, to romp

dol'zinnig, frantic

dom, stupid: cathedral, dome

do'mein *n*, domain

domheid, stupidity

dominee, minister, clergyman

domi'neren, to dominate; to play dominoes

domkop, blockhead

dommelen, to doze

domoor, blockhead

dompelaar, diver (bird); plunger

dompelen, to plunge

dona'teur, donor, supporter

donder, thunder

  iemand op zijn donder geven, to give a person a damn' good hiding

  het kan me geen donder schelen, I don't care a damn

donderbui, thunderstorm

donderbus, blunderbuss

donderdag, Thursday

donderen, to thunder

donderslag, thunderclap

donders, deuced

donker, dark

dons *n*, down

donzig, downy

dood, dead: death

doodaf, dead beat

doodbloeden, to bleed to death

doodgaan, to die

doodgraver, grave-digger

doodkist, coffin

doodlopende straat, *cul de sac*

doodop, dead beat

doods, deathly, mortally

doodslag, homicide

doodsnood: in —, worried to death

doodstraf, capital punishment

doodsstrijd, death struggle, throes of death

doodzwijgen, to ignore

doof(heid), deaf(ness)

doofpot, copper peat-extinguisher

  in de doofpot stoppen, to hush up

doof'stom, deaf-mute

dooi(en), (to) thaw

dooier, yolk

doolhof *n*, labyrinth

doop, baptism

doopceel, certificate of baptism

  iemands doopceel lichten, to show a person up

doopsel *n*, baptism

doopsge'zind(e), Mennonite

doopvont, font

door, through; by

  door de week, on week-days

doorbladeren, to glance through

door'boren, to transfix

doorbrengen, to spend

door'dacht, carefully considered

doordat, owing to

doordraaien, to keep going; to remain unsold

  geld er doordraaien, to blue money

doordrijven, to get one's own way

doordringen, to penetrate

door'drongen van, fully alive to

door'een, pell-mell

door'eenmengen, to mix together

dooreten, to go on eating

doorgaan, to go on

  doorgaan voor, to pass for

  er van doorgaan, to bolt

  doorgaande trein, through train

doorgaans, usually

doorgang, passage, way through

doorgangshuis *n*, asylum

doorgeven, to pass (on)

door'gronden, to fathom

doorhalen, to strike out (words); to pull through

door'heen, through

door'kneed in, well-versed in

doorkomen, to get through

door'kruisen, to traverse

doorlichten, to X-ray

doorlopen, to walk *or* run on; to get a move on; to run (of colours); to walk through

door'lopend, continuous, continual
door'luchtig, illustrious
doormaken, to go through
doorn, thorn
doornat, wet through
door'regen spek, streaky bacon
door'schijnend, translucent
doorslaand bewijs, convincing proof
doorslag, carbon copy
de doorslag geven, to turn the scale
doorsnede, section
de doorsneemens, the average person
door'spekken, to interlard
door'staan, to stand, to endure
door'tastend, thorough-going, go-ahead
door'trapt, unmitigated, out and out
door'trokken, soaked; imbued
door'voed, well fed
door'waadbare plaats, ford
door'wrocht, elaborate, thorough
doorzetten, to persevere
doorzicht n, discernment
door'zichtig, transparent
doos, box, case; quod
uit de oude doos, antiquated
dop, shell, husk, pod; top
dopen, to baptize, to dip
doperwten, (green) peas
doppen, to shell
dor, dry, arid
dorp n, village
dorpel, threshold
dorpeling, villager
dorsen, to thresh
dorst, thirst
dorsvlegel, flail
dosis, dose
dot, tuft; pet
dotterbloem, king-cup
douairi'ère, dowager
dou'ane, Customs
dou'blé, plate(d work)
dou'bleren, to double
dou'ceur(tje n), gratuity
dove, deaf person
doven, to extinguish, to dim
dove'netel, dead nettle

do'zijn n, dozen
dra, erelong
draad, thread, wire
draadloos, wireless
draagbaar, stretcher: portable
draagkracht, carrying capacity, range
draaglijk, tolerable
draagstoel, sedan-chair
draai, turn, twist
een draai om de oren, a box on the ears
zijn draai vinden, to find one's niche
draaibaar, revolving
draaibank, lathe
draaiboek n, scenario
draaien, to turn, to revolve; to prevaricate
draaierig, dizzy
draaikolk, whirlpool
draaimolen, roundabout
draaiorgel n, barrel-organ
draaischijf, turn-table
draaispil, capstan
draak, dragon
de draak steken met, to make fun of
drab, dregs
dracht, dress, wear; gestation
drachtig, with young
draderig, stringy
draf, trot: pig-swill
dragen, to bear; to wear; to carry
dra'gonder, dragoon
dralen, to tarry
drama'tiek, drama(tic art)
drang, pressure; urge
drank, drink; medicine
aan de drank zijn, to be addicted to drink
dra'peren, to drape
drassig, marshy
drastisch, drastic
draven, to trot
dreef, avenue, lane; mead(ow)
op dreef, in form
dreg(gen), (to) drag
dreige'ment n, threat
dreigen, to threaten
dreinen, to whine
drek, muck, ordure

drempel, threshold
drenkeling, drowning person
drenken, to water (cattle); to drench
drentelen, to saunter
drenzen, to whine
dres'seren, to train (animals)
dres'soir *n*, sideboard
dres'suur, training (of animals)
dreumes, toddler
dreun, drone, rumbling
dreunen, to drone, to rumble
dribbelen, to toddle
drie, three
drie'delig, tripartite; three-piece
drie'dubbel, triple
Drie'ëenheid, Trinity
driehoek, triangle
driehoeksmeting, trigonometry
drie'jaarlijks, triennial
Drie'koningen, Epiphany, Twelfth-Night
driekroon, tiara
drie'ledig, tripartite
drieling, triplet(s)
drieluik *n*, triptych
drie'maandelijks, quarterly
driepoot, tripod; trivet
driesprong, cross-roads
driest, audacious
drietand, trident
drievoud, treble: *n*, triplicate
driewieler, tricycle
drift, passion; drift
driftig, hot-tempered; in a temper
driftkop, hothead
drijfhout *n*, drift-wood
drijfkracht, drive
drijfnat, sopping wet
drijfveer, mainspring; incentive
drijfwerk *n*, chased work
drijfzand *n*, quicksand(s)
drijven, to float, to drift; to drive; to carry on (a business); to chase (metal work)
dril(len), (to) drill
dringen, to crowd, to jostle
de tijd dringt, time presses
dringend, urgent
drinkebroer, tippler
drinken, to drink
droef, sad

droefenis, sorrow
droef'geestig, mournful
droefheid, sadness
droesem, dregs
droevig, sad
drogbeeld *n*, illusion
droge *n*, dry land
drogen, to dry
dro'gist, druggist
drogiste'rij, chemist's (shop)
drogrede, sophism
drom, throng
dromen, to dream
dromerig, dreamy
drome'rij, reverie
drommel, devil
dronk, drink, draught, toast
dronkaard, drunkard
dronken, drunk(en)
dronkelap, soak(er)
droog, dry
droogleggen, to drain, to reclaim
drooglijn, clothes-line
droogrek *n*, clothes-horse
droogstoppel, old stick
droom, dream
drop, liquorice: drop
druif, grape
druilerig: het is — weer, there is rain in the air
druipen, to drip
druipsteen, stalactite, stalagmite
druisen, to roar, to churn
druk, busy; fussy; gaudy: pressure; print
maak je niet druk, don't fuss
druk bezochte vergadering, well-attended meeting
drukfout, misprint
drukken, to (de)press; to oppress; to print; to shake (hands)
drukkend, oppressive
drukker('ij), printer('s works)
drukletters, type
drukte, bustle; pressure of business; fuss
drukwerk *n*, printed matter
druppel, drop, drip
druppelen, to drip
dubbel, double
dubbelganger, double

dubbelpunt *n*, colon
dubbeltje *n*, ten-cent-piece
dubbel'zinnig, ambiguous
dubbel'zinnigheid, ambiguity, *double entendre*
dubi'eus, doubtful
dubio: in —, in doubt
duchten, to dread
duchtig, thorough, manful
duf, musty
duidelijk, clear, obvious
duidelijkheidshalve, for clarity's sake
duiden op, to point to
duif, dove, pigeon
duig, stave (of a barrel)
  het plan viel in duigen, the plan fell through
duikboot, submarine
duikelen, to tumble
duiken, to dive
duim, thumb; inch
duimstok, foot-rule
duin, dune
duister(nis), dark(ness)
duit, farthing
Duits(er) (*n*), German
Duitsland *n*, Germany
duivel(s), devil(ish)
duivels'toejager, factotum
duiventil, dovecot(e)
duizelen, to get dizzy *or* giddy
duizelig, dizzy, giddy
duizeling, (fit of) dizziness, giddiness
duizend, a thousand
duizendpoot, centipede
duizendschoon, sweet-william
duk'dalf, mooring-buoy
dulden, to bear, to endure
dun, thin
dunk, opinion
dunkt mij, I think
dunnen, to thin
duorijder, pillion-rider
du'peren, to hit; to let down
du'pliek, rejoinder
duplo: in —, in duplicate
dur, major
duren, to last
durf, daring
durven, to dare
dus, so

dus'danig, (in) such (a way)
dusver: tot —, thus far
dutje *n*: een — doen, to have a nap
dutten, to doze
duur, expensive: duration
  op de duur, in time
duurte, high cost(s)
duurzaam, durable
duw(en), (to) push, (to) shove
dwaalbegrip *n*, misconception, fallacy
dwaalspoor *n*, wrong track
dwaas, fool: foolish
dwaasheid, foolishness
dwalen, to wander; to err
dwaling, error
dwang, compulsion
dwangarbeid, penal servitude
dwangarbeider, convict
dwangbuis *n*, straight jacket
dwarrelen, to whirl
dwars, transverse; cross-grained
  het zit me dwars, it worries me, it annoys me
dwarsbomen, to thwart
dwars door, straight through
dwarsdoorsne(d)e, cross-section
dwarsdrijver, obstructionist
dwarskijker, furtive observer
dwarsligger, sleeper
dwarsschip *n*, transept
dwarsschot *n*, bulkhead
dweepziek, fanatic
dweil, floor-cloth; slut
dwepen met, to think the world of; to rave about
dweper, zealot; fan(atic)
dwerg, dwarf, midget
dwingeland, tyrant
dwingen, to force

E

eb, ebb(-tide)
ebbehout *n*, ebony
é'chec *n*, set-back
echt, real, genuine, thorough: matrimony
echtbreuk, adultery
echtelijk, matrimonial
echter, however
echtgenoot, husband
echtgenote, wife

echtpaar *n*, married couple
echtscheiding, divorce
econo'mie, economy; economics
eco'noom, economist
ec'zeem *n*, eczema
edel, noble
Edel'achtbare, Your Worship
edelgesteente *n*, precious stone(s)
edel'moedig, generous
edelsteen, gem
e'ditie, edition
e'doch, however
eed, oath
eega, spouse
eekhoorn, squirrel
eelt *n*, hard skin
een, a(n); one
 een en al, all; nothing but
eend, duck
eender, the same
eendracht, concord
een'drachtig, united
eenheid, unit(y)
eenhoorn, unicorn
een'jarig, yearling
een'kennig, unfriendly, shy
eenletter'grepig, monosyllabic
eenmaal, once
 het is nu eenmaal zo, but there it is
een'parig, unanimous
een'parigheid, unanimity
eens, once, one day; just
 het eens zijn, to agree
eensdeels, partly
eens'denkend, of one mind
eensge'zind, at one, unanimous
eensge'zindheid, harmony, unanimity
eensklaps, suddenly
eensluidend, similar, true
een'stemmig, in unison; with one accord
eens'stemmigheid, unanimity
een'tonig, monotonous
een'voudig, simple
eenvoud, simplicity
eenzaam, lonely, solitary
eenzaamheid, solitude
een'zelvig, self-contained
een'zijdig(heid), one-sided(ness), bias(ed)

eer, honour : before
 eer aandoen, to do credit to
eerbaar, virtuous
eerbetoon *n*, eerbewijs *n*, mark of honour, homage
eerbied, respect
eer'biedig, respectful
eer'biedigen, to respect
eerbied'wekkend, imposing
eerder, before, sooner; rather
eer'gisteren, the day before yesterday
eerherstel *n*, restitution
eer'lang, before long
eerlijk, honest, fair
eerloos, infamous
eerst, first, former
 de eerste de beste, the first (man, opportunity) that comes along
 ten eerste, in the first place
 voor het eerst, for the first time
eerstdaags, one of these days
eersteling, eerstge'boren, first-born
eertijds, formerly
eervol, honourable
Eer'waarde; de — Heer, the Reverend
eerzaam, respectable
eerzucht, ambition
eer'zuchtig, ambitious
eest, oast-house
eetbaar, edible
eetgelegenheid, eating-place
eetgerei *n*, dinner things
eetkamer, dining-room
eetlepel, table-spoon
eetlust, appetite
eetservies *n*, dinner service
eetwaren, provisions
eetzaal, dining hall
eeuw, century, age
eeuwfeest *n*, centenary
eeuwig, eternal, everlasting
 ten eeuwigen dage, for ever
eeuwigheid, eternity
ef'fecten, stocks (and shares)
effec'tief, effective
effen, level, smooth; self-coloured
effenen, to level, to smooth (down)

eg, harrow
e'gaal, smooth, uniform
E'geïsche Zee, Ægean Sea
egel, hedge-hog
eggen, to harrow
ei *n*, egg
eierdooier, egg-yolk
eierdop, egg-shell
eierdopje *n*, egg-cup
eierstok, ovary
eigen, (of one's) own; private
eigenaar, owner
eigen'aardig, peculiar, strange
eigen'aardigheid, peculiarity
eigenbaat, egoism
eigenbelang *n*, self-interest
eigendom *n*, property
eigendomsbewijs *n*, title-deeds
eigendunk, self-conceit
eigenge'maakt, home-made
eigenge'rechtig(heid), self-righteous(ness)
eigenge'reid, opionated
eigenlijk, actual, proper, real
eigen'machtig(heid), high-handed(ness)
eigennaam, proper name
eigenschap, quality, property
eigenwaan, self-conceit
eigenwaarde, self-respect
eigen'wijs, self-opinionated, pig-headed
eigen'zinnig, self-willed
eik, oak
eikel, acorn
eiland *n*, island
eind *n*, end(ing); length, distance
  ten einde te, in order to
  ten einde raad, at one's wits' end
einddiploma *n*, school-leaving certificate
eindelijk, at last
eindeloos, endless
eindexamen *n*, school-leaving examination
eindig, finite
eindigen, to finish (off)
eindproduct *n*, finished article
eindpunt *n*, eindstation *n*, terminus
eis, demand, claim
  aan de eisen voldoen, to satisfy the requirements

eisen, to demand, to claim
eiser, plaintiff, prosecutor
eivol, chock-full
eiwit *n*, white of egg; protein
ekster, magpie
eksteroog, *n*, corn
el, ell (nearly 1 yard)
eland, elk
elas'tiek (*n*), elastic
elas'tiekje *n*, rubber band
elders, elsewhere
electrici'teit, electricity
e'lectrisch, electric
electri'seren, to electrify
elemen'tair, elementary
elf, eleven: elf
  op zijn elf-en-dertigst, at a snail's pace
elfde, eleventh
elftal *n*, eleven, team
elk, each, any
el'kaar, el'kander, each other, one another
  alles bij elkaar genomen, all things considered
  ik kan ze niet uit elkaar houden, I can't tell one from the other
  alles is voor elkaar, everything is settled
elleboog, elbow
el'lende, misery
el'lendeling, rotter
el'lendig, wretched, miserable; rotten
els, alder: awl
e'mail *n*, enamel
embal'lage, packing
em'bleem *n*, emblem
emi'greren, to emigrate
emmer, pail
e'motie, emotion
em'pirisch, empirical
emplace'ment *n*, railway yard
em'plooi *n*, employ(ment)
employ'eren, to employ
en, and
  en . . . en, both . . . and
encanail'leren: zich —, to mix with the lower classes
encyclope'die, (en)cyclopædia
end *n*, distance
endeldarm, rectum

endos'seren, to endorse
enenmale: ten —, absolutely
ener'gie, energy
ener'giek, energetic
enerlei, of the same kind
enerzijds, on the one hand
en'fin, in short
 maar enfin, but there (it is)
eng, narrow; horrible, creepy
engel, angel
engelachtig, angelic
engelenbak, (upper) gallery
Engels(man) (n), English(man)
 Engelse ziekte, rickets
en gros, wholesale
engte, strait(s), isthmus; nar-
 rowness
enig, only, unique; marvellous:
 some, any, a few
eniger'mate, to some extent
enigs'zins, somewhat, in a way
enkel, single, only; ankle
enkeling, individual
enkelvoud n, singular
enkel'voudig, singular, simple
e'norm, enormous
en pas'sant, in passing
en'quête, official inquiry
ensce'neren, to stage(-manage)
ensce'nering, staging
ent(en), (to) graft
enteren, to board
enthousi'ast, enthusiast(ic)
en'tree, entrance; entrée; début
entre'pot n, bonded warehouse
enz(ovoort), etc(etera), and so on
epi'loog, epilogue
e'pitheton n, epithet
epos n, epic
er, there : of it, of them
 er zijn er, die . . ., there are
 those who . . .
 wat is er? what's the matter?
er'barmelijk, pitiable
er'barmen: zich — over, to
 have mercy on
ere-, honorary, of honour
eredienst, divine worship
eren, to honour
erf n, (farm)yard
erfdeel n, portion
erfelijk, hereditary
erfelijkheid, heredity

erfenis, heritage, legacy
erfgenaam, heir
erfgename, heiress
erfgoed n, inheritance
erflater, testator
erflating, bequest
erfpacht, long lease
erfrecht n, law or right of
 succession, hereditary right
erfstuk n, heirloom
erfzonde, original sin
erg, bad; very (much)
 zonder erg, unintentionally
 ik had er geen erg in, I was not
 aware of it
ergens, somewhere, anywhere
ergeren, to annoy; to scandalize
 zich ergeren, to be vexed, to
 take offence
 het is om je dood te ergeren,
 it's infuriating
ergerlijk, annoying, offensive
ergernis, annoyance, offence
er'kennen, to acknowledge, to
 admit
er'kentelijk, grateful
erker, bay window
ernst, seriousness
ernstig, serious
erts n, ore
er'varen, to experience: experienced
er'varing, experience
erven, to inherit : heirs
erwt, pea
es, E♭: ash-tree
esdoorn, maple-tree
es'kader n, eska'dron n, squadron
esp(en), asp(en)
essenti'eel, essential
esta'fette, dispatch-rider; relay
 race
Estland n, Esthonia
e'tage, floor, storey
e'tagewoning, flat
eta'lage, shop-window
e'tappe, stage, lap
eten, to eat, to have a meal: n,
 food; meal
e'thiek, ethics
ethisch, ethical
eti'ket n, label

etmaal *n,* (space of) 24 hours
ets, etching
etsen, to etch
ettelijke, several
etter, pus
etteren, to fester
é'tui *n,* case
euvel *n,* evil
  euvel duiden, to take ill
evacu'eren, to evacuate
evan'gelie *n,* gospel
evan'gelisch, evangelical
even, even, equally; just
  het is mij om het even, it's all
  the same to me
  even . . . als, as . . . as
evenaar, equator
evenals, just as
eve'naren, to equal
evenbeeld *n,* (split) image
even'eens, likewise
evene'ment *n,* event
evengoed, (just) as well
evenknie, equal
evenmin . . . als, no more . . .
  than
even'redig, proportional
even'redigheid, proportion
eventjes, just, (for) a moment
eventu'eel, possible; by any
  chance
evenveel, as much, as many
even'wel, however
evenwicht *n,* balance
even'wichtig, (well-)balanced,
  level-headed
evenwichtsleer, statics
evenwichtstoestand, equilibrium
even'wijdig, parallel
even'zeer, as much
even'zo, likewise
everzwijn *n,* wild boar
e'xamen *n,* examination
  een examen afnemen, to examine
ex'amenopgaaf, examination
  paper
excentrici'teit, eccentricity
excer'peren, to make a *précis* of
excu'seren, to excuse
ex'cuus *n,* excuse, apology
exem'plaar *n,* specimen; copy

exer'ceren, to drill
expe'ditie, expedition; forward-
  ing (business)
exploi'tatie, operation; exploita-
  tion
expo'sitie, exhibition
ex'pres, express
ex'tase, ecstasy
ex'tern, non-resident
extra'heren, to extract
ex'traneus, external (candidate)
ezel, ass, donkey; easel
ezelachtig, asinine
ezelsbrug, mnemonic
ezelsoren maken, to dog-ear

F

f., fl., (= *florijn*), guilder(s)
faam, fame, repute
fabel, fable, fabrication
fabelachtig, fabulous
fabri'cage, manufacture
fabri'ceren, to manufacture
fa'briek, factory
fa'brieksgeheim *n,* trade secret
fa'brieksmerk *n,* trade-mark
fabri'kaat *n,* manufacture
fabri'kant, manufacturer
face-à-'main, lorgnette
facie, mug, phiz
fac'tuur, invoice
facul'teit, faculty
fa'got, bassoon
fail'liet, bankrupt
faillisse'ment *n,* bankruptcy
fakkel, torch
falen, to fail
falie'kant, wrong
fal'saris, forger
fal'set, falsetto
fa'meus, famous, wonderful
famili'aar, familiar, informal
fa'milie, family, relation(s)
fa'naticus, fanatic
fana'tisme *n,* fanaticism
fanta'seren, to indulge in fancies
fanta'sie, fantasy, fancy, imagination
fan'toom *n,* phantom
fat, dandy
fa'taal, fatal

fat'soen *n*, decency, good manners; shape

houd je fatsoen, behave yourself

fatsoe'neren, to shape, to remodel

fat'soenlijk, decent, respectable

fatum *n*, fate

fau'teuil, arm-chair

fauteuils de balcon, dress-circle

fa'zant, pheasant

fee, fairy

feeë'riek, fairy-like

feeks, shrew

feest *n*, feast, festival, fête

feestelijk, festive

dank je feestelijk! thank you for nothing!

feestje *n*, party

feestmaal *n*, banquet

feestvarken *n*, hero of the party

feestvieren, to celebrate, to go on the spree

feilbaar, fallible

feil, fault

feilloos, faultless

feit *n*, fact

feitelijk, actual

fel, fierce

felici'tatie, congratulation

felici'teren met, to congratulate on

ferm, firm; brave

fes'tijn *n*, feast

fes'toen *n*, festoon

fê'teren, to fête

feuille'ton *n*, serial story

fiche, counter

fic'tief, fictitious

fi'deel, jovial

fiedel, fiddle

fielt, knave

fier, proud, undaunted

fiets, bicycle

fietsen, to cycle

figu'rant, super (numerary)

figu'reren, to figure

fi'guur *n*, figure, character

een gek figuur slaan, to cut a ridiculous figure

fijn, fine; subtle

fijnge'voelig, sensitive

fijnproever, connoisseur

fijntjes, nicely, subtly

fijt, whitlow

fiks, robust, vigorous; brave

fil d'é'cosse, lisle

fi'leren, to fillet

fileverkeer *n*, single-line traffic

fili'aal *n*, branch (establishment)

filmjournaal *n*, news-reel

filter, filter; percolator

fil'treren, to filter

Fin(s) (*n*), Finn(ish)

fi'naal, final; quite

financi'eel, financial

fi'nanciën, finance(s)

finan'cieren, to finance

fi'neerhout *n*, veneer

fi'neren, to veneer; to refine

fi'nesses, niceties

fin'geren, to simulate

firma, firm

fir'mant, partner

fiscus, treasurer, treasury

fix'eren, to fix; to look intently at

fla'con, (scent-)bottle

fladderen, to flutter; to flit

flakkeren, to flicker

flam'bouw, torch

fla'nel *n*, flannel

fla'neren, to saunter

flan'keren, to flank

flappen: eruit —, to blurt out

flapuit, blabber

flarden, tatters

aan flarden, in rags; to shreds

flater, blunder

flat'teren, to flatter, to be becoming

flat'teus, flattering

flauw, insipid, feeble, faint

flauwi'teit, feeble joke

flauwte, fainting fit

flauwtjes, faintly

flemen, to cajole

flens, flange

flensje *n*, thin pancake

fles, bottle

op de fles gaan, to go to pot

flessentrekker, swindler

flets, lack-lustre, pale

fleurig, gay, colourful

flikflooien, to cajole

flikje *n*, chocolate drop

flikkeren, to flicker

flink, tough, capable; considerable
flits, flash
flodder, slattern
  losse flodder, blank cartridge
flodderig, shapeless, flimsy
floers *n*, veil
flonkeren, to sparkle, to twinkle
flo'reren, to flourish
flo'ret, foil
floris'sant, flourishing
fluisteren, to whisper
fluit, flute
fluiten, to whistle
fluitje *n*, whistle
fluks, promptly
flu'weel *n*, velvet
fnuiken, to break, to ruin
fnuikend, fatal
foe'draal *n*, case
foefje *n*, trick, dodge
foei! shame (on you)! fie!
foei'lelijk, as ugly as sin
foelie, mace
foe'rier, quartermaster-sergeant
foeteren, to grumble, to rage
fok, foresail; specs
fokhengst, stud-horse
fokken, to breed
foli'ant, folio (volume)
folteren, to torture
fonds *n*, fund
fonkelen, to sparkle
fon'tein, fountain
fon'teintje *n*, small hand-basin
  (fitted in W.C. or passage)
fooi, tip
foppen, to hoax
fopspeen, baby's dummy
for'ceren, to force; to strain
fo'rel, trout
fo'rens, season-ticket holder, commuter
for'maat *n*, size; stature
formali'teit, formality
for'meel, formal
for'mule, formula
formu'lier *n*, form
for'nuis *n*, cooker
fors, robust, strong, vigorous
fort *n*, forte; fort(ification)
for'tuin (*n*), fortune
for'tuinlijk, fortunate

fos'siel *n*, fossil
fouil'leren, to search (a person)
foura'geren, to forage
fourni'turen, haberdashery
fout, mistake, fault, error
fou'tief, wrong, erroneous
fraai, nice, handsome
fractie, fraction
fragmen'tarisch, fragmentary
fram'boos, raspberry
franco, postage paid
franje, fringe
fran'keren, to stamp
Frankrijk *n*, France
Frans (*n*), French; Francis
  een vrolijk Frans, a gay dog
frap'pant, striking
fratsen, pranks
fraude, fraud
fraudu'leus, fraudulent
fre'gat *n*, frigate
fret *n*, ferret
friemelen, to fumble
fries *n*, frieze: Frisian
frik, school-ma'am
fris, fresh, refreshing
  het is frisjes vanavond, it's
    chilly this evening
fri'vool, frivolous
fröbelschool, kindergarten
frommelen, to crumple
fronsen, to frown
fruiten, to fry
fuga, fugue
fuif, party
fuifnummer *n*, gay spark
fuik, eel-pot
fuiven, to feast
functie, function
functio'naris, functionary
functio'neren, to function
fun'dering, foundation
fu'nest, fatal
fun'geren, to function
fust *n*, cask
fut, spirit, go
futili'teit, futility
futloos, lifeless

G

gaaf, sound, whole
gaai, jay

gaan, to go
  hoe gaat het? how are you (getting on)?
  het gaat om . . . it is a question
  of . . .
gaande, afoot, going
gaandeweg, gradually
gaar, cooked, done
gaarkeuken, communal kitchen;
  cook-shop
gaarne, gladly
gaas *n,* gauze; wire netting
gade, spouse
gadeslaan, to watch
gading, liking
gaffel, pitchfork; gaff
gage, pay
gal, bile, gall
ga'lant, courteous: best boy-
  friend
galante'rieën, fancy-goods
ga'lei, galley
gale'rij, gallery
galg, gallows
galgemaal *n,* last meal
galmen, to resound, to reverberate
ga'lon *n,* braid
ga'lop, gallop
gammel, ramshackle
gang, passage; gait; way
  aan de gang, going, working
  op gang, in form; (in) working
  (order)
  ga je gang, go ahead; help
  yourself
gangbaar, current, available
gans, entire: goose
gapen, to yawn; to gape
gaping, gap
gappen, to pinch
garan'deren, to guarantee
garde, guard(s)
garde'robe, wardrobe; cloak-
  room
ga'reel *n,* horse-collar, harness
garen, to gather: *n,* cotton,
  thread
gar'naal, shrimp
gar'neren, to trim
garni'zoen *n,* garrison
gasfabriek, gas-works
gashouder, gasometer

gaskomfoor *n,* gas-ring(s)
gaspedaal *n,* accelerator
gaspit, gas-ring, gas-jet
gasstel *n,* gas-ring(s)
gast, guest
gastheer, host
gasthuis *n,* hospital
gastvrij, hospitable
gast'vrijheid, hospitality
gastvrouw, hostess
gasvormig, gaseous
gat *n,* hole
  een gat in de nacht praten, to
  talk deep into the night
  in de gaten krijgen, to spot
  in de gaten houden, to keep an
  eye on
gauw, quick
gauwdief, sneak-thief
gave, gift
ga'zeus, aerated
ga'zon *n,* lawn
ge'aardheid, disposition
geaffec'teerd, affected
gealli'eerd, allied
ge'armd, arm in arm
ge'baar *n,* gesture
ge'baard, bearded
ge'bak *n,* fancy cake(s)
ge'barenspel *n,* mime
ge'bed *n,* prayer
ge'beente *n,* bones
ge'belgd, offended
ge'bergte *n,* mountain range
ge'beten zijn op, to have a
  grudge against
ge'beuren, to happen
ge'beurtenis, event
ge'bied *n,* territory; field, realm
ge'bieden, to order
ge'bit *n,* set of teeth
ge'bladerte *n,* foliage
ge'bod *n,* command(ment)
ge'boefte *n,* riff-raff
ge'boomte *n,* trees
ge'boorte, birth
ge'boortecijfer *n,* birth-rate
ge'boorteland *n,* native country
ge'boortig uit, born at
ge'boren, born
ge'bouw *n,* building
ge'brek *n,* lack; failing; infirmity

ge'brekkig, defective, faulty; deformed
ge'broed *n*, brood
ge'broeders, brothers
gebrouil'leerd, not on speaking terms
ge'bruik *n*, use; custom
ge'bruikelijk, customary
ge'bruiken, to use; to partake of
ge'bruiksaanwijzing, directions for use
gechar'meerd op, captivated by
gecommit'teerde, delegate
gecompli'ceerd, complicated
gecostu'meerd, in fancy dress
ge'daagde, defendant
ge'daante, shape, figure, form
ge'daanteverwisseling, metamorphosis
ge'dachte, thought
ge'dachteloos, thoughtless
ge'dachtengang, train of thought
ge'deelte *n*, part
ge'deeltelijk, partly
gedele'geerde, delegate
ge'denkdag, anniversary
ge'denken, to commemorate
ge'denkteken *n*, monument
gedenk'waardig, memorable
gedepu'teerde, deputy
ge'dicht *n*, poem
ge'dienstig, obliging
ge'dijen, to thrive
ge'ding *n*, lawsuit; issue
gediplo'meerd, qualified
gedispo'neerd, inclined, disposed
gedistil'leerd, distilled : *n*, spirits
gedistin'geerd, distinguished-looking
ge'doe *n*, fuss; business
ge'dogen, to permit
ge'donder *n*, hell of a mess (row, *etc.*)
ge'drag *n*, behaviour
ge'dragen: zich —, to behave
ge'dragslijn, policy
ge'drang *n*, crowd, crush
ge'drocht *n*, monstrosity
ge'drongen, thick-set; impelled
ge'druis *n*, rumbling, roaring
ge'ducht, formidable
ge'duld *n*, patience
ge'duldig, patient

ge'durende, during
ge'durfd, daring; risky
ge'dwee, submissive
geel (*n*), yellow
geelkoper *n*, brass
geelzucht, jaundice
geen, not a, not any, no
geënga'geerd, engaged
geenszins, by no means
geest, spirit; mind; wit
geest'dodend, soul-destroying
geestdrift, enthusiasm
geestelijk, spiritual, mental
geestelijke, priest
geestelijkheid, clergy
geestesgaven, intellectual gifts
geestesgesteldheid, mentality
geestgrond, sandy peat (behind the dunes)
geestig, witty
geestigheid, wit, witticism
geestkracht, fortitude
geestver'heffend, sublime
geestvermogens, mental faculties
geestverschijning, apparition
geestverwant, kindred spirit
geeuw(en), (to) yawn
gefortu'neerd, wealthy
ge'gadigde, prospective buyer; applicant
ge'gevens, data
ge'goed, well-off
ge'grond, well-founded
ge'haaid, canny
ge'hakt *n*, minced meat
ge'halte *n*, content; quality
ge'hard, seasoned; inured; tempered
ge'harrewar *n*, bickering
ge'havend, battered
ge'heel, whole, all, quite
in het geheel niet, not at all
ge'heelonthouder, teetotaller
ge'heim (*n*), secret
ge'heimenis, mystery
ge'heimhouding, secrecy
ge'heimschrift *n*, cipher
geheim'zinnig, mysterious
ge'hemelte *n*, palate
ge'heugen *n*, memory
ge'hoor *n*, hearing, ear; audience, congregation

ge'hoorzaam, obedient
ge'hoorzaamheid, obedience
ge'hoorzamen, to obey
ge'horig, far from sound-proof, noisy
ge'hucht *n*, hamlet
ge'huichel *n*, hypocrisy
gehu'meurd: goed —, good-tempered
ge'ijkt, recognized, accepted
geil, lecherous, randy; rank
gein, high jinks
geiser, geyser
geit, goat
geitebok, billy goat
ge'jaagd, agitated
gek, mad, foolish; queer: idiot
  voor de gek houden, to make a fool of
gekheid, foolishness, joke
  alle gekheid op een stokje, joking apart
gekkenhuis *n*, madhouse
ge'knipt voor, cut out for
gekscheren, to joke
ge'kunsteld, artificial
ge'laat *n*, countenance
ge'laatskleur, complexion
ge'laatstrek, feature
ge'lag *n*: het — betalen, to foot the bill
  dat is een hard gelag, hard lines!
ge'lagkamer, taproom
ge'lang: naar — van, according to
ge'lasten, to order
ge'laten, resigned
geld *n*, money
geldelijk, financial, monetary
gelden, to apply, to count
  zich doen gelden, to assert one-self
  de algemeen geldende mening, the generally accepted view
geldig, valid
geldschieter, money-lender
geldstuk *n*, coin
geldwolf, money-grubber
geldzuivering, currency reform
ge'leden, ago
ge'leerd, learned
ge'leerde, scholar; scientist

ge'legen, situated; convenient
  er is veel aan gelegen, much depends on it
ge'legenheid, occasion, opportunity; place
ge'lei, jelly
ge'leide *n*, escort
ge'leidelijk, gradually
ge'leiden, to conduct
ge'letterd(e), (man) of letters
ge'lid *n*, rank
ge'liefd, beloved, popular
ge'liefkoosd, favourite
ge'lieven, to please
ge'lijk, equal, alike; level
  je hebt gelijk, you are right
  iemand gelijk geven, to agree with a person
ge'lijkelijk, equally; evenly
ge'lijken, to resemble
ge'lijkenis, resemblance; parable
gelijkge'zind, like-minded
gelijk'luidend, identical
gelijk'matig, equable; even
gelijk'moedigheid, equanimity
gelijk'slachtig, homogeneous
gelijk'stroom, direct current
gelijk'tijdig, simultaneous
gelijk'vloers, on the ground floor; on the same floor
ge'lofte, vow
ge'loof *n*, belief, faith
ge'loofsbrieven, credentials
geloof'waardig, credible
ge'loven, to believe, to think
ge'lovig(en), faithful
ge'lui *n*, ringing
ge'luid *n*, sound
ge'luidloos, noiseless
ge'luimd: goed —, in a good humour
ge'luk *n*, luck, good fortune; happiness
ge'lukken, to succeed
ge'lukkig, happy; fortunate, lucky
ge'lukshanger, charm
ge'lukskind *n*, spoilt child of fortune
ge'luksvogel, lucky one
ge'lukwens, congratulation
ge'lukwensen, to congratulate
geluk'zalig, blessed

ge'lukzoeker, adventurer

ge'maakt, affected, feigned; ready-made

ge'maal, spouse: n, pumping engine

ge'mak n, ease, comfort; convenience

ge'makkelijk, easy, comfortable; convenient

ge'makshalve, for the sake of convenience

gemak'zuchtig, easy-going

gema'lin, spouse

ge'matigd, temperate; moderate

gember, ginger

ge'meen, (in) common; foul

ge'meenlijk, commonly

ge'meenplaats, platitude

ge'meenschap, community; intercourse

gemeen'schappelijk, common, joint

ge'meenschapsgevoel n, public spirit

ge'meente, municipality; congregation; parish

ge'meentebelasting, (local) rates

ge'meentelijk, municipal

ge'meenzaam, familiar

gemelijk, peevish

gemene'best n, commonwealth

ge'middeld, average

ge'mis n, lack, want, loss

ge'moed n, heart, mind, feeling(s)

ge'moedelijk, kindly, informal

ge'moedsaandoening, emotion

ge'moedsrust, peace of mind

ge'moeid, involved

gems, chamois

ge'mutst: goed —, in a good mood

ge'naakbaar, accessible

ge'naamd, named

ge'nade, grace; mercy; pardon

ge'nadeloos, merciless

ge'nadeslag, finishing stroke

ge'nadig, merciful; lightly

ge'naken, to approach

gene, that; the other

deze en gene, several people

ge'neesheer, physician

genees'krachtig, curative

ge'neeskunde, medicine

ge'neesmiddel n, remedy; medicine

ge'negen, inclined, disposed

ge'negenheid, affection

ge'neigd, inclined, prone

gene'raal, general

generale repetitie, dress rehearsal

ge'neren, to incommode

zich generen, to feel embarrassed

ge'neugte, pleasure

ge'nezen, to cure, to heal; to recover

ge'nezing, cure; recovery

geni'aal, brilliant

geniali'teit, genius

ge'nie n, military, engineers; (man of) genius

ge'niepig, underhand

ge'nieten (van), to enjoy

genitief, genitive

ge'nodigden, invited guests

ge'noeg, enough

ge'noegdoening, satisfaction, reparation

ge'noegen n, pleasure

ge'noeglijk, pleasant

ge'noegzaam, sufficient

ge'nootschap n, society

ge'not n, joy, delight

geo'graaf, geographer

geo'loog, geologist

ge'oorloofd, permitted

georiën'teerd (op), with leanings towards, minded

ge'paard gaan met, to be accompanied by

ge'parenteerd, related

ge'past, fitting, seemly

gepast geld, the exact amount

ge'peperd, peppered, pungent

ge'peupel n, mob

gepi'keerd, offended

ge'pluimd, plumed

ge'poseerd, sedate; matronly

ge'raakt, nettled

ge'raamte n, skeleton

ge'raden, advisable

geraffi'neerd, refined; unmitigated; artful

ge'raken, to become, to get
ge'recht *n*, dish: court of justice
ge'rechtelijk, judicial, legal
ge'rechtigd, entitled
ge'rechtigheid, justice
ge'rechtshof *n*, court of justice
ge'reed, ready
ge'reedschap *n*, tools
gerefor'meerd, strict(ly) Calvinist
ge'regeld, regular
gerenom'meerd, renowned
ge'reutel *n*, death-rattle; drivel
ge'richt: het jongste —, the Last Judgement
ge'rief *n*, convenience
ge'rief(e)lijk, convenient
ge'rieven, to oblige
ge'ring, small, slight
ge'ringschattend, disparaging
ge'ringschatting, disdain
Ger'maan, Teuton
ge'roezemoes *n*, buzz, bustle
ge'ronnen, clotted
gerouti'neerd, experienced
gerst, barley
ge'rucht *n*, rumour; noise
ge'ruchtmakend, sensational
ge'ruim, ample
ge'ruisloos, noiseless
ge'ruit, checked
ge'rust, easy
neem (het) maar gerust, you're welcome (to it)
ge'ruststellen, to reassure
gesalari'eerd: (te laag) —, (under)paid
ge'schater *n*, peals of laughter
ge'schenk *n*, present
ge'schieden, to happen, to come about
ge'schiedenis, history; story; affair
geschied'kundig, historical
ge'schiedschrijver, historian
ge'schift, dotty
ge'schikt, suitable; decent
ge'schil *n*, dispute
ge'schoeid, shod
ge'schoold, trained, skilled
ge'schrift *n*, writing
ge'schubd, scaly

ge'schut *n*, artillery
gesel, scourge
geselen, to flog, to scourge
ge'stitueerd: goed —, well-off
ge'slaagd, successful
ge'slacht *n*, stock; generation; sex; gender
ge'slachtelijk, sexual
ge'slachtsboom, family tree
ge'slachtsdelen, genitals
ge'slachtsziekte, venereal disease
ge'slepen, cunning; sharpened
geslepen glas, cut glass
ge'sloten, close(d); uncommunicative
ge'sluierd, veiled
gesp, buckle, clasp
ge'span *n*, team of horses
ge'spannen, tense, strained
gespen, to buckle
ge'spierd, muscular
ge'spikkeld, speckled, dotted
ge'spoord, spurred
ge'sprek *n*, conversation
ge'spuis *n*, rabble
ge'stadig, steady
ge'stalte, figure; stature
ge'stand: zijn woord — doen, to keep one's promise
geste, gesture
ge'steente *n*, stone(s); rock
ge'stel *n*, constitution
ge'steldheid, condition; nature, character
ge'stemd, tuned; disposed
ge'sternte *n*, constellation, star
ge'sticht *n*, institution
ge'streept, striped
ge'stroomlijnd, streamlined
getai'lleerd, tailored, close-fitting
ge'tal *n*, number
ge'tand, toothed, cogged
ge'tapt, popular; tapped
ge'tij *n*, tide
ge'tikt, dotty
ge'titeld, (en)titled
ge'touw *n*, gear; loom
ge'tralied, barred, latticed
getroe'bleerd, deranged
ge'troosten: zich veel moeite —, to take great pains
ge'trouw, faithful

ge'tuige, witness
ge'tuigen, to testify
ge'tuigenis *n*, testimony, evidence
ge'tuigschrift *n*, certificate; testimonial
geul, channel; gully
geur, scent
iets in geuren en kleuren vertellen, to go into elaborate details about something
geuren, to smell
geuren met, to flaunt
geurig, fragrant
ge'vaar *n*, danger
ge'vaarlijk, dangerous
ge'vaarte *n*, huge object
ge'val *n*, case
in geen geval, on no account
ge'vangene, prisoner
ge'vangenis, prison
ge'vangenschap, imprisonment
ge'vat, quick-witted
ge'vecht *n*, fight
gevel, façade
geveltoerist, cat burglar
geven, to give
het geeft niets, it does not matter; it is no use
gever, donor
ge'vest *n*, hilt
ge'vlamd, flamed
ge'vleugeld, winged
ge'vlij: bij iemand in het — komen, to worm oneself into a person's favour
ge'vleugeld, winged
ge'voeglijk, decently; just as well
ge'voel *n*, feeling, sense
ge'voelen *n*, opinion, feeling
ge'voelig, sensitive; tender
ge'voelloos, numb; unfeeling
ge'voelsmens, emotional person
ge'vogelte *n*, birds; poultry
ge'volg *n*, consequence; retinue
gevolg geven aan, to comply with
ge'volgtrekking, conclusion
ge'waad *n*, garment
ge'waagd, bold, *risqué*
aan elkaar gewaagd, well-matched

ge'waarworden, to become aware of
ge'waarwording, sensation
ge'wagen van, to make mention of
gewapender'hand, by force of arms
ge'was *n*, vegetation; crops
ge'weer *n*, gun, rifle
ge'wei *n*, antlers
ge'weld *n*, violence, force
geweld aandoen, to violate
geweld'dadig, violent
ge'weldig, terrific
ge'welf *n*, vault
ge'welfd, vaulted, domed
ge'wennen, to accustom
ge'west *n*, region
ge'westelijk, regional
ge'weten *n*, conscience
ge'wetenloos, unprincipled
ge'wetensbezwaar *n*, scruple
ge'wezen, late; ex-
ge'wicht *n*, weight; importance
ge'wichtig, weighty; important
gewichtig doen, to be pompous
ge'wiekst, smart
ge'wild, in demand; would-be
ge'willig, willing
ge'wis, certain
ge'woon, usual, ordinary; accustomed
ge'woonlijk, usually
ge'woonte, custom, habit
ge'woonterecht *n*, common law
ge'woonweg, simply
ge'wricht *n*, joint
ge'wrichtsband, ligament
ge'wrocht *n*, creation, work
ge'wrongen, laboured; twisted
ge'zag *n*, authority, command
ge'zaghebbend, authoritative
ge'zagvoerder, captain; pilot
ge'zamenlijk, joint; complete
ge'zang *n*, singing; hymn
ge'zant, ambassador, minister
ge'zantschap *n*, legation
ge'zegde *n*, (old) saying; predicate
ge'zeglijk, obedient
ge'zel, mate, companion
ge'zellig, cosy; pleasant; sociable

ge'zelschap *n*, company, party
ge'zelschapsdame, lady-companion
ge'zet, corpulent; set
ge'zeten, established; sitting
ge'zicht *n*, sight; face
ge'zichtseinder, horizon
ge'zichtsbedrog *n*, optical illusion
ge'zichtskring, ken, mental outlook
ge'zichtspunt *n*, point of view
ge'zichtsveld *n*, field of vision
ge'zien, seen; highly thought of; in view of
ge'zin *n*, family
ge'zind, disposed, minded
ge'zindte, religious denomination
ge'zocht, sought (after), far-fetched
ge'zond, healthy, sound
ge'zondheid, health
ge'zusters, sisters
ge'zwel *n*, tumor, swelling
ge'zwind, swift
ge'zwollen, swollen; bombastic
gids, guide
giechelen, to giggle
giek, gig
gier, vulture
gieren, to scream
gierig, miserly
gierigaard, miser
gierigheid, avarice
gierpont, rope-ferry
gierst, millet
gierzwaluw, swift
gietbui, downpour
gieten, to pour; to cast
gieter, watering can; founder
giete'rij, foundry
gietijzer *n*, cast iron
gietkroes, crucible
gif(t) *n*, poison
gift, gift
giftig, poisonous; venomous
giftmenger, poisoner
gij, thou, ye, you
gijlieden, you
gijpen, to gybe
gijzelaar, hostage
gijzelen, to take as a hostage

gilde *n*, guild
gil(len), (to) yell
ginder, ginds, over there
ginnegappen, to giggle
gips *n*, gypsum, plaster (of Paris)
gipsafgietsel *n*, plaster cast
gi'reren, to pay by *giro*
giro(dienst), money order (service), (system of payment by) post-office cheque
gis, guess
op de gis, by guess-work
gispen, to censure
gissen, to guess
gissing, guess
gist, yeast
gisten, to ferment
gisteren, yesterday
gister'avond, last night
gisting, ferment(ation)
git *n*, jet
gi'taar, guitar
glaasje *n*, small glass; slide
gla'ceren, to glaze; to ice
glad, smooth, slippery; glib, cunning
glad mis, all wrong
gladheid, slipperiness
gladjanus, slyboots
gladweg, clean
glans, gloss, sheen, lustre
glansrijk, brilliant
glanzen, to shine, to gleam
glanzig, glossy
glas *n*, glass
glashelder, crystal clear
glazen, (made of) glass
glazenmaker, glazier
glazenwasser, window-cleaner
glazenwisser, squeegee
glazig, glassy, waxy
gla'zuren, to glaze, to ice
gla'zuur(sel) *n*, glaze, enamel (of teeth), icing
gletscher, gletsjer, glacier
gleuf, groove, slit, slot
gleufhoed, trilby
glibberen, to slither
glibberig, slippery
glijbaan, slide
glijden, to slide; to glide
glimlach(en), (to) smile

glimmen, to shine, to gleam
glimp, glimpse
glimworm, glow-worm
glinsteren, to glitter, to glisten
glippen, to slip
glo'baal, rough, broad
gloed, glow; blaze; ardour
gloednieuw, brand-new
gloeidraad, filament
gloeien, to glow
  gloeiend heet, burning hot
gloeikousje *n*, gas-mantle
gloeilamp, electric light bulb
glooien, to slope
glooiing, slope
glorie, glory
glorierijk, **glori'eus**, glorious
gluiper(d), sneak
gluiperig, sneaking
glunderen, to beam (with joy)
gluren, to peer
gniffelen, **gnuiven**, to laugh in one's sleeve
God'dank, thank God
goddelijk, divine
goddeloos, godless
god'dorie, by gad
god'ganselijke dag, whole blessed day
godgeklaagd, crying (to heaven)
godgeleerdheid, theology
godheid, godhead
go'din, goddess
godsdienst, religion
gods'dienstig, religious
godsdienstoefening, divine service
godsdienstwaanzin, religious mania
godslasteraar, blasphemer
gods'lasterlijk, blasphemous
god'vruchtig, pious
god'zalig, godly
goed, good; well: *n*, good(s), material
goe'daardig, good-natured; benign
goeddunken, to think fit: *n*, discretion
goederen, goods
goeder'tieren, merciful
goed'geefs, open-handed
goedge'lovig, credulous

goedge'zind, well disposed
goed'hartig, kind-hearted
goedheid, kindness
  grote goedheid! good gracious!
goedig, sweet natured
goedje *n*, stuff
goedkeuren, to approve of
goedkeuring, approval, assent
goed'koop, cheap
goed'lachs, easily amused
goed'leers, teachable
goed'moedig, good-natured
goedpraten, to explain away
goedschiks of kwaadschiks, willing or unwilling
goeds'moeds, cheerful
goedvinden, to approve
goedzak, gentle soul
goeierd, kind soul
gokken, to gamble, to chance
gokker, gambler
golf, wave; bay; gulf: golf
golfbreker, breakwater
golfkarton *n*, corrugated cardboard
golflengte, wave-length
golfslag, dashing of the waves
golven, to wave, to undulate
gom, gum; rubber
gomelas'tiek *n*, india rubber
gommen, to gum
gondel, gondola
gonzen, to buzz
goochelaar, conjurer, juggler
goochela'rij, conjuring, juggling
goochelen, to conjure, to juggle
goochem, smart
gooi(en), (to), fling, (to) throw
goor, dingy; sallow
goot, gutter; drain
gootsteen, (kitchen) sink
gordel, belt; girdle
gordeldier *n*, armadillo
gordelroos, shingles
gorden, to gird
gor'dijn *n*, curtain
gorgeldrank, gargle
gorgelen, to gargle
gort, groats
gortig: het te — maken, to go too far
goud *n*, gold
gouden, gold(en)

gouden'regen, laburnum

goudgalon n, gold lace

goudhoudend, auriferous

goudklomp, nugget

goudsbloem, marigold

Goudse pijp, church-warden

gouver'nante, governess

gouverne'ment n, government

gouver'neur, governor, private tutor

gouw, district

gouwenaar, church-warden

graad, degree, rank, grade

graadboog, protractor

graaf, count, earl

graafschap n, county

graafwerk n, excavation(s)

graag, eager; gladly

(ja) **graag**, yes please

ik zou graag willen weten, I should (dearly) like to know

graagte, eagerness

graaien, to rummage; to grab

graan n, grain, corn

graanschuur, granary

graansoorten, cereals

graanzuiger, (corn) elevator

graat, fish-bone

hij is niet zuiver op de graat, there's something fishy about him

van de graat vallen, to be ravenous(ly hungry)

grabbel: te — gooien, to throw away

grabbelen, to scramble

grabbelton, lucky dip

gracht, (town) canal; moat

gra'deren, to graduate

gradu'eel verschil n, difference in degree

gradu'eren, to graduate; to confer a degree upon

graf n, grave, sepulchre

gra'fiek, graph; graphic art

grafkelder, (family) vault

grafschrift n, epitaph

grafstem, sepulchral voice

grafzerk, tomb-stone

gram n, gramme

gram'matica, grammar

gram(m)o'foonplaat, gramophone record

gramschap, wrath

gra'naat, shell, grenade

gra'naatappel, pomegranate

gra'naatscherf, (piece of) shrapnel

gra'niet n, granite

grap, joke

uit de grap, for fun

grapjas, **grappenmaker**, wag

grappig, funny

gras n, grass

grasduinen, to browse

grashalm, **grasspriet**, blade of grass

graszode, turf, sod

gratie, grace; free pardon; favour

grati'eus, graceful

gratifi'catie, bonus

grauw (n), grey; rabble

grauw(en), (to) snarl, (to) growl

gra'veerder, engraver

graven, to dig

Graven'hage: 's —, the Hague

gra'veren, to engrave

gra'veur, engraver

gra'vin, countess

gra'vure, engraving

gra'zen, te graze

iemand te grazen nemen, to lead a person up the garden path

greep, grip, grasp; hilt; fork

grein n, grain (1/700 lb)

grendel(en), (to) bolt

grenehout n, deal

grens, bound(ary), frontier, limit

grensgeval n, border-line case

grensrechter, linesman

grenzen aan, to border on

grenzeloos, boundless

greppel, field-drain; narrow ditch

gretig, eager

gribus, hovel, slum

grief, grievance

Griekenland n, Greece

Griek(s) (n), Greek

griend, osier bed

grienen, sniffle

griep, influenza

griesmeel n, semolina

griet, brill

grieven, to grieve

griezel, monstrosity

griezelen, to shudder
griezelig, gruesome
grif, readily
griffel, slate-pencil
griffelkoker, pencil-case
griffie, record-office, secretariate
grif'fier, clerk of the court
grijns, grin, sneer
grijnzen, to sneer, to grin
grijpen, to seize
grijs, grey
grijsaard, old man
grijzen, to (go) grey
gril, caprice; freak
grillig, capricious
gri'mas, grimace
grime, (stage) make-up
grimmig, grim
grinniken, to chuckle, to snigger
grint n, gravel
grissen, to snatch
groef, groove; furrow
groeien, to grow
groeistuipen, growing pains
groen, green
groente(n), vegetables
groenteboer, greengrocer
groentijd, freshmen's initiation period
groep, group; clump
groepsgewijze, in groups
groet, salute, greeting
 de groeten doen, to give one's kind regards
groeten, to greet, to nod good-day
groeve, grave, pit, quarry
groezelig, grubby
grof, coarse; rude; gross
 grof spelen, to play for high stakes
 grof geld verdienen, to earn big money
grollen, antics
grommen, to growl, to grumble
grommig, grumpy
grond, ground, earth, soil
 in de grond van de zaak, basically
 te gronde gaan, to go to pieces
grondbeginsel n, basic principle
grondbelasting, land-tax
grondbezitter, landowner

grondeloos, unfathomable, absymal
gronden, to base
grondgebied n, territory
grondig, thorough
grondkleur, primer; primary colour
grondlegging, foundation
grondoorzaak, root cause
grondpacht, ground rent
grondslag, foundation
grondstelling, axiom
grondstof, raw material
grondverf, undercoat
grondvesten, to found: foundations
grondwerker, navvy
grondwet, constitution
grond'wettelijk, constitutional
groot, large, big, great, tall
 in het groot, on a large scale
grootboek n, ledger
grootbrengen, to bring up
grootdoen, to swagger
groothandel, wholesale trade
grootheid, magnitude
grootheidswaanzin, megalomania
groothertog, grand duke
groothouden: zich —, to put a brave face on it
grootje n, grannie
grootmoeder, grandmother
groot'moedig, magnanimous
grootouders, grandparents
groots, grand(iose)
groot'scheeps, in grand style
grootsheid, grandeur
grootspraak, boasting
grootspreken, to boast
groot'steeds, city
grootte, size
grootvader, grandfather
groot'waardigheidsbekleder, high dignitary
gros n, gross; mass
gros'sier, wholesaler
grot, grotto, cave
grotendeels, for the greater part
gruis n, grit, slack
gruizele'menten, gruzele'menten, smithereens
grut n: klein —, little ones

grutte'rij, corn-chandler's (shop)
gruwel, atrocity, horror
gruweldaad, atrocity
gruwelijk, horrible
gruwen, to shudder; to abhor
guit, little rogue
guitig, roguish
gul, open-handed
gulden, guilder (approx. 2/-): golden
gulheid, generosity
gulp, fly
gulzig, greedy
gulzigaard, glutton
gummi n, (india) rubber
gunnen, to grant
  het is je gegund, you're welcome to it
gunst, favour
  gunst! gracious (me)!
gunstbewijs n, mark of favour
gunsteling, favourite
gunstig, favourable
gut! Lor'!
gutsen, to gush
guur, bleak, raw
gym'nasium n, grammar school
gymnas'tiek, gymnastics
gymnas'tiekzaal, gymnasium

H

haag, hedge
  Den Haag, The Hague
haai, shark
haaibaai, shrew
haak, hook
  niet in de haak, not all that it should be
  tussen haakjes, in brackets; by the way
haakgaren n, **haakkatoen** n, crochet-cotton
haaknaald, **haakpen**, crochet-hook
haaks op, at right angles to
haal, (pen-)stroke; pull
  aan de haal gaan, to take to one's heels
haan, cock
  er zal geen haan naar kraaien, nobody will be any the wiser
  haantje de voorste, cock of the walk

haar, her: n, hair
  het scheelde geen haar, it was touch and go
haard, stove; centre; hotbed
  open haard, fireplace
haardkleedje n, hearth-rug
haardos, head of hair
haarfijn, minute
haarklove'rij, hair-splitting
haarmiddel n, hair restorer
haas, hare
haast, almost: haste
haasten: zich —, to hurry
haastig, hasty
haat, hatred
haat'dragend, vindictive
ha'chee, hash
hachelijk, precarious
hachje n: **bang voor zijn —**, afraid to risk one's life
hage'dis, lizard
hagedoorn, hawthorn
hagel, hail; shot
hagelen, to hail
hagelkorrel, hail-stone; pellet
hagelwit, white as snow
hak, (shoe-)heel
  van de hak op de tak springen, to jump from one subject to another
  iemand een hak zetten, to play a person a dirty trick
hakbijl, chopper
hakblok n, chopping block
haken, to crochet; to hook
  haken naar, to hanker after
hakenkruis n, swastika
hakhout n, copse
hakkelaar, stammerer
hakkelen, to stammer
hakken, to chop, to hack
hakmes n, cleaver
hal, hall
halen, to fetch, to get; to catch
  hij haalt het nooit, he will never manage it
  dat haalt er niet bij, there's no comparison
half, half, semi-
  half zes, half past five
halfbloed, half-breed
half'gaar, underdone; half-witted

halfgod, demigod
halfrond *n,* hemisphere
half'slachtig, half-hearted
half'stok, at half mast
halm, stalk, blade
hals, neck
  om hals brengen, to kill
halsband, (dog-)collar
halssnoer *n,* necklace
hals'starrig, stubborn
halster(en), (to) halter
halte, stop(ping-place)
halter, dumb-bell, bar-bell
hal'veren, to halve
halver'hoogte, half-way up
halverwege, half-way
hamer, hammer, mallet
hameren, to hammer
hamsteren, to hoard
hand, hand
  handen thuis! hands off!
  **de handen uit de mouw
  steken,** to give a helping hand
  er is niets aan de hand, there
  is nothing wrong
  bij de hand, up and doing;
  handy
  met de handen in het haar, at
  one's wits' ends
  op handen dragen, to worship
  van de hand doen, to dispose of
  voor de hand liggen, to go
  without saying
handboeien, handcuffs
handdoek, towel
handdruk, handshake
handel, trade
  in de handel, in business; on
  the market
handelaar, dealer
handelbaar, tractable
handelen, to act; to trade
handeling, act(ion)
handelsrecht, commercial law
handelsvloot, mercantile marine
handelswaren, merchandise
handelwijze, method(s) (of dealing), behaviour
handenarbeid, manual labour,
arts and crafts
handgemeen worden, to come
to blows
handgreep, grip; knack

handhaven, to maintain
handig, handy, deft
handkoffer, suitcase
handlanger, accomplice
handleiding, guide
handschoen, glove
  met de handschoen trouwen
  to marry by proxy
handschrift *n,* manuscript; handwriting
hand'tastelijk, aggressive
hand'tastelijkheden, blows,
fighting; pawing
handtekenen *n,* free-hand drawing
handtekening, signature
handvat *n,* handle
handvest *n,* charter
handwerk *n,* (handi)craft;
needlework
handwerken, to do needlework
handwerksman, artisan
hangbrug, suspension bridge
hangen, to hang
hangend(e), drooping; pending
hanger, (coat-)hanger; pendant
hangerig, listless
hangmat, hammock
hangop, curds
hangslot *n,* padlock
han'sop, child's sleeping suit
hans'worst, clown
han'teren, to handle, to operate
hap, mouthful, bite
haperen, to falter
  er hapert iets, there is a hitch
  somewhere
happen, to take a mouthful
happig, keen, eager
hard, hard
  hard nodig, very necessary
  ik heb er een hard hoofd in, I
  have my doubts (about the
  result)
harden, to harden, to temper
  ik kon het niet langer harden,
  I couldn't stand it any longer
hard'horig, hard of hearing
hard'leers, dunderheaded
hard'lijvig, constipated
hardlopen, to run
hard'nekkig, stubborn
hardop, aloud

hard'vochtig, callous
harig, hairy
haring, herring; tent-peg
hark, rake; gawk
harken, to rake
harlekijn, harlequin
har'monika, concertina
harmo'nie, harmony
harmoni'ëren, to harmonize
harnas n, armour
  iemand in het harnas jagen, to put a person's back up
har'poen, harpoon
harrewarren, to squabble
hars, resin, rosin
hart n, heart
  heb het hart niet! don't you dare!
  van harte bedankt, thank you very much
hartedief, darling
hartelijk, cordial, hearty
harteloos, heartless
hartelust: naar —, to one's heart's content
hartewens, heart's desire
hart'grondig, whole-hearted
hartig, savoury; forthright
hart'roerend, touching
hartstikke, not half
hartstocht, passion
harts'tochtelijk, passionate
hartsvriend(in), bosom friend
hartver'heffend, ennobling, sublime
hartverlamming, heart-failure
hartversterking, pick-me-up
hartzeer n, heart-break
hatelijk, spiteful
hatelijkheid, spite(ful remark)
haten, to hate
have en goed, goods and chattels
  levende have, live-stock
haveloos, ragged
haven, harbour
havenarbeider, dock-worker
havenbestuur n, port authority
havengeld n, harbour dues
havenhoofd n, jetty
havenstad, port
haver, oats
  van haver tot gort kennen, to know inside out

haverklap: om de —, at the slightest provocation; every other minute
havermout, porridge (oats)
havik, hawk
haviksneus, aquiline nose
hazelaar, hazel (nut tree)
hazelip, hare-lip
hazepeper, jugged hare
hazeslaap, snooze
haze'wind, greyhound
hebbelijkheid, peculiar habit
hebben, to have
  hoe laat heb je het? what do you make the time?
  wat heb ik eraan? what's the good of it to me?
  het hebben over, to talk about
hebberig, acquisitive
hebzucht, greed
heb'zuchtig, grasping
hecht, firm, solid: n, handle, haft, hilt
hechten, to attach; to stitch (up)
  ge'hecht aan, fond of, attached to
hechtenis, custody
hechtheid, solidity
hechting, stitch
hechtpleister, adhesive plaster
heden, to-day
  heden ten dage, nowadays
heden'avond, this evening
hedendaags, present-day
heel, whole, entire; quite, very
heelhuids, unscathed
heelkunde, surgery
heen en weer, to and fro
  waar wil je heen? where do you want to go? what are you driving at?
heengaan, to go away
heenweg: op de —, on the way there
heer, gentleman; master; lord
heerbaan, (modern) trunk-road
heerlijk, delicious; delightful
heerschaar, host
heerschap n, gent, cove
heerschap'pij, dominion, rule
heersen, to rule; to prevail
heerser, ruler

heers'zuchtig, ambitious
hees, hoarse
heester, shrub
heet, hot
heetge'bakerd, quick-tempered
hefboom, lever
hefbrug, lift-bridge
heffen, to raise
heffing, levy; stress
  heffing-in-eens, capital levy
heft *n*, handle, haft
heftig, violent; vehement
heg, hedge
heibel, din, racket
heide, moor, heath(er)
heiden, heathen, pagan
heidendom *n*, paganism, pagan
  world
heidens, pagan, heathen(ish)
heien *n*, pile-driving
heiig, hazy
heil *n*, salvation; welfare; good
Heiland, Saviour
heilbot, halibut
heildronk, toast
heilgymnastiek, physiotherapy
heilig, holy, sacred
heiligdom *n*, sanctuary, sanc-
  tum
heilige, saint
heiligen, to hallow, to keep holy
heiligheid, holiness
heiligmakend, sanctifying
heiligschennis, sacrilege
heiligverklaring, canonization
heilloos, evil; disastrous, fatal
heilzaam, salutary
heimelijk, secret, furtive
heimwee *n*, homesickness, nostal-
  gia
heinde en ver, near and far
heining, fence
heipaal, (concrete) pile
hek *n*, railings; gate
hekel, hackle
  ik heb er een hekel aan, I dislike it intensely
  over de hekel halen, to criticize
  sharply
hekeldicht *n*, satire
hekelen, to heckle, to satirize
hekkensluiter, last comer
heks, witch; hag

heksenketel, cacophony
heksentoer, insuperable task
hel, hell: bright
he'laas, alas
held, hero
heldendicht *n*, epic
heldenmoed, heroism
helder, clear, lucid; bright;
  clean
helder'ziend, clairvoyant
held'haftig, heroic
hel'din, heroine
helemaal, altogether
  hele'maal niet, not at all
helen, to receive stolen goods: to
  heal
heler, fence
helft, half
hellebaard, halberd
hellen, to slope, to slant
helling, slope, incline, slipway
helm, helmet: beach-grass
helmhoed, sun-helmet
helmstok, tiller
helpen, to help, to be effective
hels, infernal, hellish
  hèls zijn, to be wild (with rage)
hem, him
hemd *n*, vest, shirt
  het hemd is nader dan de rok,
  blood is thicker than water
hemel, heaven, sky; canopy
hemelgewelf *n*, firmament
hemellichaam *n*, celestial body
hemels, heavenly
hemelsbreed verschil *n*, all the
  difference in the world
hemel'tergend, flagrant, crying
  (to heaven)
Hemelvaart, Ascension
hen, them: hen
hengel, fishing-rod
hengelaar, angler
hengelen, to angle, to fish
hengsel *n*, handle; hinge
hengst, stallion
hennep, hemp
her: van eeuwen —, from times
  immemorial
  van ouds her, of old
her-, re-, again
her'ademen, to breathe again
heral'diek, heraldry: heraldic

he'raut, herald
herberg, inn
herbergen, to accommodate; to harbour
herber'gier, inn-keeper
her'denken, to commemorate; to recall
her'denking, commemoration
herder, shepherd; herdsman
herderlijk, pastoral
herdershond, sheep-dog
herdersstaf, shepherd's crook, crosier
her'drukken, to reprint
hereboer, gentleman farmer
here'miet, hermit
her'enigen, to reunite
herfst(achtig), autumn(al)
herfstdraden, gossamer
her'haald(clijk), repeated(ly)
her'halen, to repeat; to revise
her'haling, repetition; revision
her'inneren aan, to remind of
  zich herinneren, to remember
her'Linering, recollection, memory
her'kauwen, to chew the cud; to ruminate
her'kenbaar, recognizable
her'kennen, to recognize
her'kiezen, to re-elect
herkomst, origin
her'krijgen, to recover
her'leiden, to convert, to reduce
her'leven, to revive; to live again
herme'lijn (n), ermine
her'nemen, to resume; to take again
her'nieuwen, to renew
her'overen, to recapture
herrie, row, hullabaloo
her'rijzenis, resurrection
her'roepen, to revoke
her'scheppen, to re-create; to transform
hersenen, brain(s)
hersenpan, cranium
hersenschim, chimera
hersenschudding, concussion
her'stel n, recovery, convalescence
her'stelbetaling, reparation

her'stellen, to mend; to restore; to recover
her'stellingsoord n, convalescent home
hert n, deer, stag
hertebout, (haunch of) venison
hertenkamp, deer-park
hertog, duke
hertogdom n, duchy
herto'gin, duchess
her'trouwen, to remarry
her'vatten, to resume
her'vormd, reformed; orthodox protestant
her'vorming, reform(ation)
herwaarts en derwaarts, hither and thither
her'winnen, to regain
her'zien, to revise; to review
het, it: the
heten, to be called
het'geen, (that) which
het'zelfde, the same
het'zij ... of (or dan wel), either or whether ... or
heugen: dat zal je —, you won't forget that in a hurry
heuglijk, joyful
heulen met, to be in league with
heup, hip
heus, real; courteous
heuvel, hill
hevel, siphon
hevig, violent
hi'aat n, hiatus
hiel, heel
hier, here
  hier te lande, in this country
hierheen, this way
hier'naast, next to this; next door
hier'namaals n, (life) hereafter
hieruit, out (of) here; from this
hij, he
hijgen, to pant
hijsblok n, pulley-block
hijsen, to hoist
hik, hiccups
hinde, hind
hinderen, to hinder; to annoy
hinderlaag, ambush
hinderlijk, annoying; inconvenient

hindernis, hinderpaal, obstacle
hinken, to limp; to hop
hinniken, to neigh
his'torisch, historic(al)
hit, pony; skivvy
hitte, heat
hobbel(ig), bump(y)
hobbelen, to jolt
hobbelpaard *n*, rocking-horse
hobo, oboe
hoe, how
  hoe eerder hoe beter, the sooner the better
  hoe dan ook, however
hoed, hat
hoe'danigheid, quality
hoede, guard, care
hoeden, to guard
hoef, hoof
hoefijzer *n*, horseshoe
hoegenaamd niets, nothing whatever
hoek, angle; corner, nook
hoekig, angular
hoen *n*, (barndoor) fowl
hoenderhok *n*, hen-coop
hoenderpark *n*, poultry-farm
hoepel, hoop
hoer, whore
hoes, loose cover; dust-sheet
hoest(en), (to) cough
hoeve, farm(stead)
hoeveel, how much, how many
hoe'veelheid, quantity
hoeveelste: de — is het van-daag? what is the date to-day?
hoeven, to need
hoe'ver, how far
  in hoeverre, to what extent
hoe'zeer, how(ever) much
hof, garden: *n*, court
  het hof maken, to court
hofdame, lady-in-waiting
hoffelijk, courteous
hofhouding, royal household
hofmeester('es), steward(ess)
hoge'school, university
hok *n*, kennel, pen, sty, hutch
hokken, to huddle; to hang fire
hokvast, stay-at-home
hol, hollow, concave: *n*, den, cave
  op hol raken, to run wild

Hollands (*n*), Dutch
hollen, to dash (along)
hol'ogig, hollow-eyed
holte, cavity
hom, soft roe
hommel, bumble-bee, drone
homp, lump, chunk
hond, dog, hound
  rode hond, German measles
hondeweer *n*, foul weather
honderd, a hundred
  honderd uit praten, to talk nineteen to the dozen
honderderlei, a hundred and one
honds, churlish
honds'dolheid, rabies
honen, to scoff at
Honga'rije *n*, Hungary
honger(en), (to) hunger
hongerig, hungry
hongerloon *n*, starvation wage
hongersnood, famine
honi(n)g, honey
honi(n)graat, honeycomb
honk *n*, base, home
hono'rair, honorary
hono'rarium *n*, fee
hono'reren, to honour; to pay
hoofd *n*, head; principal, chief
hoofdartikel *n*, leading article
hoofdbreken *n*, brain-racking
hoofdgetal *n*, cardinal number
hoofdkussen *n*, pillow
hoofdkwartier *n*, headquarters
hoofdletter, capital letter
hoofdpijn, headache
hoofdstad, capital, principal town
hoofdstraat, main street
hoofdstuk *n*, chapter
hoofdzaak, main thing
hoofd'zakelijk, mainly
hoofs, courtly
hoog, high, tall
  drie hoog, on the third floor
hoogachten, to esteem
  hoogachtend Uw (dw.), yours faithfully
hoog'dravend, bombastic
hoog'hartig, haughty
Hoogheid, Highness
hooghouden, to uphold
hoog'leraar, professor

hoogmoed, pride
hoog'moedig, proud
hoogmoedswaanzin, megalo-
mania
hoog'nodig, very necessary
hoogoven, blast-furnace
hoogst, highest; extremely
ten hoogste, at most
hoogstaand, of high moral character
hoogstens, at most
hoogte, height, altitude
op de hoogte, well-informed
uit de hoogte, supercilious
hoogtepunt n, acme, zenith
hoogtezon, ultra-violet light
hoogtij vieren, to be rampant
hoogtijdag, heyday; high day
hoogvlakte, plateau
hoogvlieger: hij is geen —,
he's no genius
hoog'waardigheidsbekleder,
(high) dignitary
hoog'water n, high tide
hooi n, hay
teveel hooi op zijn vork
nemen, to bite off more than
one can chew
te hooi en te gras, haphazardly
hooiberg, hay-stack
hooien, to make hay
hooimijt, hay-stack
hooivork, pitchfork
hoon, scorn
hoop, hope: heap, stack
hoopvol, hopeful
hoorbaar, audible
hoorn, horn, bugle; telephone
receiver
hoornblazer, bugler
hoorngeschal n, flourish of trumpets
hoornvlies n, cornea
hoorspel n, radio play
hop(pe), hop
hopeloos, hopeless
hopen, to hope
hopje n, burnt caramel
hopmeester, scoutmaster
hor, gauze screen
horde, horde: hurdle
horen, to hear: to belong (to);
to be right (and proper), ought

horizon'taal, horizontal
horlepijp, hornpipe
hor'loge n, watch
horrelvoet, club-foot
hort: met horten en stoten,
jerkily
horzel, horse-fly
hospes, hospita, landlord, landlady
hossen, to sing and dance arm in
arm
hotsen, to jolt
houdbaar, tenable
houden, to hold; to keep
houden van, to like, to love
houden voor, to take for
zich goed houden, to control
oneself
houding, attitude; bearing
hout n, wood
houterig, starchy
houtje n, bit of wood
op zijn eigen houtje, all off his
own bat
houtskool, charcoal
houtsne(d)e, woodcut
houtsnijwerk n, wood-carving
houtsnip, woodcock
houtvester, forester
houvast n, hold
hou'weel, pick-axe
houwen, to hew
ho'vaardig, haughty
hoveling, courtier
hove'nier, gardener
hozen, to bale
huichelaar, hypocrite
huichela'rij, hypocrisy
huichelen, to dissemble
huid, skin, hide
huidig, present-day
huifkar, covered wagon
huig, uvula
huilebalk, cry-baby
huilen, to cry, to howl
huis n, house, home
huisarts, family doctor
huisbaas, landlord
huisbewaarder, caretaker
huisdier n, domestic animal
huiselijk, domestic(ated); homely
huisgenoot, member of the
household

huis'houdelijk, domestic, household

huishouden *n*, household; housekeeping

huishouden, to keep house

vreselijk huishouden, to play havoc

huishoudkunde, domestic science

huishoudster, housekeeper

huiskamer, living-room

huisraad *n*, household goods

huis-tuin-of-keuken, common or garden

huisvesten, to house

huiswerk *n*, homework

huiveren, to shudder

huiverig voor, wary of

huivering, shudder

huivering'wekkend, horrible

huizenmakelaar, house-agent

hulde(betoon *n*), homage

huldigen, to pay tribute to

hullen, to envelop

hulp, help

hulpe'hoevend, invalid; needy

helpeloos, helpless

hulpmiddel *n*, expedient

hulptroepen, auxiliaries

hulp'vaardig(heid), helpful-(ness)

hulpverlening, assistance

hulpwerkwoord *n*, auxiliary verb

huls, pod; (cartridge-)case

hulst, holly

humeur *n*, mood; temper

hu'meurig, moody

hummel, tiny tot

humor, humour

hun, their; (to) them

hunkeren naar, to hanker after

huppelen, to hop

hups, affable

huren, to hire, to rent

hurken, to squat

hut, cabin, hut

hutkoffer, trunk

hutspot, hotchpotch

huur, rent

huurder, tenant

huurling, hireling, mercenary

huurwaarde, rateable value

huwbaar, marriageable

huwelijk *n*, marriage

huwelijksaanzoek *n*, proposal (of marriage)

huwelijksinzegening, blessing of the Church (after civil marriage)

huwelijksreis, honeymoon

huwelijksvoltrekking, marriage ceremony

huwelijksvoorwaarden, marriage settlement(s)

huwen, to marry

hu'zaar, hussar

hypo'theek, mortgage

hyste'rie, hysteria

hys'terisch, hysterical

I

ide'aal (*n*), ideal

ideali'seren, to idealize

i'dee *n*, idea

ide'ëel, imaginary

idem, ditto

iden'tiek, identical

identifi'ceren, to identify

identi'teit, identity

idi'oom *n*, idiom

idi'oot, idiot: idiotic

ido'laat van, infatuated with

ieder, every, each, any

ieder'een, everyone, anyone

iemand, someone, anyone

iep(eboom), elm (tree)

Ier, Irishman

Iers (*n*), Irish

Ierland *n*, Ireland

iets, something, anything

ietsje, ietwat, somewhat

ijdel, vain

ijdelheid, vanity

ijdeltuit, vain person

ijl: in aller —, hastily

ijl, thin; rarefied

ijlbode, express messenger

ijlen, to be delirious; to hasten

ijlings, in hot haste

ijs *n*, ice

ijsbaan, skating rink

ijsbeer, polar bear

ijsberen, to pace up and down

ijsberg, iceberg

ijselijk, horrible

ijsgang, ice-drift

ijskast, refrigerator
ijskegel, icicle
ijskoud, icy (cold), iced
ijsshots, ice-floe
ijstijd, ice-age
ijsvogel, kingfisher
IJszee, Polar Sea
ijver, diligence
ijveren voor, to champion
ijverig, diligent, keen
ijverzucht, jealousy
ijzel, ice on the roads
ijzen, to shudder
ijzer *n,* iron
ijzerdraad *n,* wire
ijzerhoudend, ferreous
ijzeroer *n,* bog-ore
ijzerwaren, hardware
ijzig, icy-cold; frightful
ijzing'wekkend, ghastly
ik, I
  het ik, the ego
ille'gaal, illegal
il'lusie, illusion
illus'treren, to illustrate
imker, bee-keeper
immer, ever
immers, surely; after all
immo'reel, immoral
impo'neren, to impress
impo'sant, impressive
in'achtneming, observance
inademen, to breathe in
inbakeren, to wrap up warm
inbeelden: zich —, to imagine
inbeelding, imagination; conceit
inbegrepen, including
inbegrip: met — van, inclusive
  of
inbe'slagneming, seizure (of
  goods)
inbinden, to bind
  je moet je wat inbinden, you
  must climb down
inblazen, to suggest
inboedel, household effects
inboeten, to forfeit
  **hij heeft er het leven bij inge-
  boet,** the attempt cost him his
  life
inboezemen, to inspire
inboorling, native

inborst, disposition
inbraak, burglary
inbreken, to burgle, to break in
inbreker, burglar
inbrengen, to bring in; to put
  forward
  hij heeft niets in te brengen,
  he has no say in the matter
inbreuk, infringement
inburgeren, to become current;
  to settle down
incas'seren, to cash; to collect
in'cluis, included
inconse'quent, inconsistent
incou'rante maat, odd size
indampen, to moisten; to reduce by evaporation
indelen, to class(ify), to allocate
indeling, classification, grouping
indenken: zich —, to imagine,
  to visualize, to conceive
inder'daad, indeed
inder'haast, in haste
inder'tijd, at one time, at the
  time
indeuken, to dent
in'dien, if
indienen, to introduce, to submit
indijken, to surround with dikes
indivi'du *n,* individual
individu'eel, individual
indommelen, to doze off
indringen: zich —, to intrude
indroevig, very sad
indrogen, to dry up
indruisen tegen, to run counter
  to
indruk, impression
indruk'wekkend, impressive
indus'trie, industry
industri'eel, industrial(ist)
indutten, to doze off
in'een, together
in'eengedoken, hunched up
in'eenkrimpen, to cower, to
  double up
in'eens, at once
in'eenstorten, to collapse, to
  come crashing down
**in'eenzakken, in el'kaar zak-
  ken,** to collapse, to cave in
inenten, to inoculate, to vaccinate

in'faam, infamous
infante'rie, infantry
infante'rist, infantryman
inferi'eur, inferior
influisteren, to whisper in a person's ear
infor'matie, information
informaties inwinnen, to make inquiries
infor'meren (naar), to inquire (about)
ingaan, to enter; to take effect
niet ingaan op, to ignore
ingang, entrance
met ingang van heden, as from today
ingang vinden, to be well received
ingebeeld, imaginary; conceited
ingeboren, innate
ingehouden, restrained
ingekankerd, inveterate
inge'meen, vile
ingenaaid, in paper covers
ingeni'eur, (qualified) engineer
ingeni'eus, ingenious
ingenomen met, pleased with
ingespannen, strenuous; intent
ingetogen, modest, subdued
inge'val, in case
ingevallen wangen, hollow cheeks
ingeven, to prompt; to administer
ingeving, inspiration
inge'volge, in accordance with
ingewanden, intestines
ingewijde, adept; insider
inge'wikkeld, complicated
ingeworteld, deep-seated
ingezetene, inhabitant
ingezonden stuk n, letter to the editor
ingooien, to throw in(to); to smash
ingrijpen, to intervene
in'grijpend, far-reaching
inhalen, to catch up, to overtake; to take in
inha'leren, to inhale
in'halig, grasping
inham, creek
in'hechtenisneming, arrest

in'heems, indigenous
inhoud, content(s); capacity
inhouden, to contain; to restrain; to dock
inhoudsmaat, cubic measure
inhoudsopgave, table of contents
inhuldigen, to inaugurate
inkalven, to cave in
inkeer: tot — komen, to repent
inkeping, notch
inklaren, to clear (at the customs)
inkleden, to put into words
inkomen, to come in: n, income
daar komt niets van in, nothing doing
inkomsten, income, revenue
inkoop, purchase
inkorten, to shorten, to curtail
inkrimpen, to shrink, to cut down
inkt, ink
inktpotlood n, indelible pencil
inktvis, squid
inkwartieren, to billet
inlaat, inlet
inlander, native
inlassen, to fit in, to insert
inlaten, to let in
zich inlaten met, to have dealings with
inleggeld n, deposit, membership fee
inleiden, to introduce
inleiding, introduction
inleven: zich — in, to imagine oneself as
inleveren, to hand in
inlichten, to inform
inlichting, information
inlijsten, to frame
inlijven, to incorporate
inlossen, to redeem
inluiden, to ring in
inmaak, preserving; preserves
inmaken, to preserve
inmenging, interference
in'middels, meanwhile
innemen, to take (in, up); to capture; to please
innen, to collect
innerlijk, inner; intrinsic: n inner being

innig, heartfelt, intimate
inpakken, to pack (up), to wrap up
inpalmen, to grab; to inveigle
inpeperen, to pay (a person) out
inpikken, to grab; to tackle
inpolderen, to reclaim (land)
inpompen, to pump in; to cram
inpreten, to inculcate
inrichten, to arrange, to rig up, to furnish
inrichting, institute; institution; arrangement, furnishing
inrijden, to ride or drive into; to break or run in
inrit, entrance
inroepen, to call in, to invoke
inruilen, to trade in, to exchange
inruimen, to clear, to vacate; to put back
inrukken, to dismiss
 ruk in! clear out!
inschakelen, to switch on; to put into gear
inschenken, to pour out
inschepen: zich -, to embark
inschieten: erbij - , in go by the board
in'schikkelijk, accommodating
inschikken, to move in closer
inschrijven, to register; to tender; to subscribe
insge'lijks, likewise
in'signe n, badge
inslaan, to beat or smash in; to lay in; to turn into; to catch on
inslag, woof, weft
inslapen, to fall asleep
insluiten, to enclose, to surround; to include, to comprise
inspannen, to put (horses) to; to exert, to strain
in'spannend, strenuous
inspanning, exertion
inspec'teur, inspector
inspraak, dictate(s)
inspreken: iemand moed —, to put heart into a person
inspringen, to leap into the breach
 inspringende regel, indented line

inspuiten, to inject
instaan voor, to vouch for
instal'leren, to install; to induct
in'standhouden, to maintain
in'stantie, authority
 in laatste instantie, in the last resort
instellen, to institute; to focus
 er op ingesteld zijn, to be used to it
instelling, institution
instemmen, to agree
instemming, approval
instinc'tief, instinct'matig, instinctive
instoppen, to tuck in
instorten, to collapse
instru'eren, to instruct
instuderen, to practise; to study
instuif, informal party
in'tegendeel, on the contrary
inte'grerend, integral
intekenen op, to subscribe to
inten'dance, Army Service Corps
interen, to live on one's capital
interes'sant, interesting
interes'seren: zich — voor, to be interested in
interlo'caal gesprek n, trunk call
in'tern, internal; resident
inter'naat n, boarding school, (student) hostel
inter'neren, to intern
interrum'peren, to interrupt
in'tiem, intimate
intimi'teit, intimacy
intocht, (ceremonial) entry
intomen, to curb; to rein in
intrappen, to kick open; to tread down
intre(d)e, entry, commencement
intreden, to enter (upon), to set in
intrek: zijn — nemen in, to take up residence at
intrekken, to draw in; to move in; to withdraw, to retract
intri'gant, intriguer
in'trige, intrigue
introdu'cé, guest
in'tussen, meanwhile

inval, invasion; raid; brain-wave

inva'lide, disabled person, invalid

invaliditeit, disablement

invallen, to fall in; to deputize; to occur to

inven'taris, inventory

inventari'satie, stock-taking

invetten, to grease

invliegen: er —, to fall for a trick

invloed, influence

invloedrijk, influential

invoegen, to insert

invoer, import(s)

invorderen, to collect (debts)

in'vrijheidstelling, release

in'wendig, internal, inward

inwerken op, to act upon

inwijden, to consecrate; to initiate

inwilligen, to comply with

inwinnen, to obtain

inwisselen, to (ex)change, to cash

inzage: ter —, for inspection, on approval

in'zake, with reference to

inzakken, to collapse

inzamelen, to collect

inzegenen, to consecrate

inzender, contributor; exhibitor

inzending, contribution; exhibit(s)

inzepen, to soap

inzet, stake(s)

inzetten, to put in; to start; to stake

inzicht n, insight, understanding

inzien, to glance through; to realize

  iets ernstig inzien, to take a grave view of something

  bij nader inzien, on second thoughts

  mijns inziens, in my opinion

inzinken, to subside; to decline

inzinking, subsidence; relapse

inzitten: erover —, to be worried about something

  hij zit er warmpjes in, he's living in clover

  de inzittenden, the occupants

in'zonderheid, in particular

iro'nie, irony

i'ronisch, ironical

irri'teren, to irritate

ischias, sciatica

iso'latie, insulation

isole'ment n, isolation

iso'leren, to isolate, to insulate

i'voor n, ivory

i'voren, (made of) ivory

J

ja, yes

jaaglijn, tow-rope

jaagpad n, tow-path

jaap, gash

jaar n, year

jaarbeurs, industries fair

jaargang, a year's issue (of a periodical), volume

jaargeld n, annuity

jaargenoot, contemporary

jaargetij(de) n, season

jaarlijks, annual

jaartal n, date

jaartelling, era

jaarwisseling, turn of the year

jacht, hunt(ing); shoot(ing); pursuit: n, yacht

jachten, to hustle

jachtgeweer n, sporting gun

jachthond, gun-dog, hound

jachtschotel, hot-pot

jachtsneeuw, driving snow

jachtvliegtuig n, fighter

jac'quet n, morning-coat

jagen, to hunt; to shoot; to race

jager, hunter, sportsman

jak n, smock

jakhals, jackal

jakkeren, to hustle

jakkes! bah!

ja'loers(heid), jealous(y)

jaloe'zie, jealousy; Venetian blind

jambe, iamb

jammer, distress

  jammer genoeg, unfortunately

  wat jammer! what a pity!

jammeren, to lament

jammerklacht, lamentation

jammerlijk, miserable

Jan en alle'man, every Tom, Dick and Harry
Jan Klaassen en Katrijn, Punch and Judy
Jan Salie, stick-in-the-mud
janboel, muddle
janken, to yelp
janmaat, jack-tar
ja'pon, dress
jarenlang, for years
jarig, one year old
  ik ben jarig, it is my birthday
jarre'tel(le), suspender
jas, coat
jas'mijn, jasmine
jaspanden, coat-tails
jassen, to peel (spuds)
jasses! bah!
ja'wel, certainly
jawoord *n*, consent
je, you; your
jegens, towards
jekker, monkey-jacket
je'never, Dutch gin
je'neverbes, juniper berry *or* tree
jengelen, to whimper
jeugd, youth
jeugdherberg, youth hostel
jeugdig, youthful, young
jeuk, itch
jeuken, to itch; to scratch
jicht, gout
jij, you
j.l., ult., last
jochie *n*, kid, lad (die)
Jodendom *n*, Judaism; Jewry
Jo'din, Jewess
jodium *n*, iodine
joelen, to cheer; to howl
jokken, to fib
jokkebrok, fibber
jol, yawl, dinghy
jolig, jolly
jo'lijt *n*, merry-making
jonassen, to swing a child by its arms and legs
jong, young
jongeling, youth
jonge'lui, young people
jongen, boy: to bring forth young
jongensachtig, boyish
jongensjaren, boyhood

jongenskop, Eton crop
jongge'huwden, newly-weds
jong'leur, juggler
jong'mens *n*, young man
jongs: van — af aan, right from childhood
jongst'leden, last
jonker, nobleman
Jood(s), Jew(ish)
jool, rag, fun
Joost: dat mag — weten, goodness only knows
jota, iota
jou, you
jour'naal *n*, log-book; journal; news-reel
journalis'tiek, journalism
jouw, your
jouwen, to hoot
jubel, rejoicing
jubelen, to shout for joy
jubi'laris, man celebrating some personal anniversary
jubi'leren, to celebrate some anniversary in one's life
jubi'leum *n*, jubilee, anniversary
juffrouw, (unmarried) woman; Miss, (Mrs), Madam
juichen, to shout for joy
juist, exact; right, just (now)
  daarom juist, for that very reason
juistheid, correctness; justness
juk *n*, yoke
jukbeen *n*, cheek-bone
juli, July
jullie, you (people)
juni, June
ju'ridisch, juridical, legal
ju'rist, lawyer
jurk, dress
jus, gravy
jus'titie, judicature; justice, law
ju'weel *n*, jewel; gem
juwe'lier, jeweller

K

ka, kaai, quay
kaak, jaw; gill; pillory
  aan de kaak stellen, to expose
kaakje *n*, biscuit
kaakkramp, lock-jaw

kaal, bald; bare; threadbare; penniless
kaap, cape
kaapstander, capstan
kaapvaarder, privateer
kaapvaart, privateering
kaars, candle
kaarsrecht, bolt upright
kaarsvet n, candle-grease
kaart, card; map, chart; hand (at cards)
kaarten, to play cards
kaartje n, (visiting) card; ticket
kaartlegster, fortune-teller
kaartsysteem n, card index
kaas, cheese
  ik heb er geen kaas van gegeten, I don't know the first thing about it
kaasmijt, cheese-mite
kaasschaaf, cheese slicer
kaasstolp cheese-cover
kaaswei, whey
kaatsbaan, fives-court
kaatsen, to play ball
ka'baal n, shindy
kabbelen, to lap, to ripple
kabel, cable, hawser
kabel'jauw, cod
kabi'net n, cabinet
ka'bouter, goblin, gnome
kachel, stove: tipsy
kachelhout n, firewood
ka'daster n, land-registry
kade, quay
kader n, cadre, framework, scope
kaf n, chaff
kaft, (book-)cover, book-jacket
ka'juit, cabin, ward-room
kakelbont, gaudy, motley
kakelen, to cackle, to chatter
kaken, to gut (herrings)
kake'toe, cockatoo
kakkerlak, cockroach
kale'bas, gourd
ka'lender, calendar
kalf n, calf
kal(e)'fat(er)en, to caulk; to patch up
kalfsvlees n, veal
kalium n, potassium
ka'liber n, calibre
kalk, lime; mortar

kal'koen, turkey
kalkoven, lime-kiln
kalm, calm
kal'meren, to calm
  kalmerend middel, sedative
kalmpjes, calmly
kalmte, calm(ness), composure
ka'lotje n, skull-cap
kalven, to calve
kalverliefde, calf-love
kam, comb; crest; bridge (of a violin)
  over één kam scheren, to treat alike
ka'meel, camel
kame'nier, lady's maid
kamer, room, chamber
kame'raad, comrade
kameraad'schappelijk, friendly
kamerdienaar, valet
kamerheer, chamberlain
kamerjas, dressing-gown
kamermeisje n, parlour-maid
kamerscherm n, screen
kamfer, camphor
kamgaren (n), worsted
ka'mille, camomile
kammen, to comp
kamp n, camp; contest
kampen, to fight; to contend
kam'peren, to camp
kamper'foelie, honeysuckle
kampi'oen(schap n), champion(ship)
kamrad n, cog-wheel
kan, jug, can
ka'naal n, canal; channel
ka'narie, canary
kandelaar, candle-stick
kande'laber, candelabrum
kandi'daat, candidate; holder of the first university degree
kan'dijsuiker, sugar-candy
ka'neel, cinnamon
kanjer, whopper
kanker, cancer; canker
kankeraar, grumbler
kankeren, to cancerate; to grouse
kanni'baal, cannibal
kano, canoe
ka'non n, gun
kano'neerboot, gunboat

ka'nonnenvlees *n*, cannon-fodder
kans, chance
kansel, pulpit
kansela'rij, chancery
kanse'lier, chancellor
kansspel *n*, game of chance
kant, side, edge; lace
  dat raakt kant nog wal, that is quite irrelevant
  iets over zijn kant laten gaan, to put up with something
  kant en klaar, all set and ready
  zich van kant maken, to do oneself in
  op 't kantje af, only just
kan'teel *n*, battlement
kantelen, to topple over; to tilt
kanten, (made of) lace
  zich kanten tegen, to oppose
kan'tine, canteen
kantklossen *n*, lace-making
kan'tongerecht *n*, district court
kan'toor *n*, office
kan'toorbediende, clerk
kan'toorbehoeften, stationery
ka'nunnik, cannon
kap, cap; hood; bonnet; lamp-shade
ka'pel, chapel; band : butterfly
kape'laan, curate
ka'pelmeester, band-master
kaper, privateer
kaphout *n*, copse
kapi'taal *n*, capital
kapitaal'krachtig, financially strong
kapitali'seren, to capitalize
kapi'teel *n*, capital
kapi'tein, captain
ka'pittel *n*, chapter
kaplaars, top-boot, wellington
kapmantel, (hooded) cloak; toilet cape
ka'pot, broken
ka'pothoed, bonnet
kappen, to cut *or* chop down; to dress hair
kapper, hairdresser
kapseizen, to capsize
kapsel *n*, coiffure
kapstok, hall-stand, hat-rack
kaptafel, dressing table
kar, cart

ka'raat *n*, carat
kara'bijn, carbine
ka'raf, carafe, decanter
ka'rakter *n*, character
karakteri'seren, to characterize
karakteris'tiek, characteristic
kara'vaan, caravan
kar'bies, shopping-basket
karbo'nade, chop
kar'bouw, buffalo
kardi'naal, cardinal
karig, parsimonious; sparing, scanty
kar'mijn (*n*), carmine
karmo'zijn (*n*), crimson
karn(ton), churn
karnemelk, buttermilk
karnen, to churn
ka'ronje *n*, shrew
ka'ros, state-coach
karper, carp
kar'pet *n*, carpet
karrepaard *n*, cart-horse
karrespoor *n*, (wheel-)rut
kartelen, to notch, to mill
kar'tets, round of grape-shot
kar'ton *n*, cardboard; carton
kar'wats, riding-whip
kar'wei *n*, job (of work)
kar'wijzaad *n*, caraway-seed
kas, socket; greenhouse; cash (-desk); (watch-)case
  goed bij kas, in funds
kassa, pay-desk, box-office; till
kas'sier, cashier
kast, cupboard; case; quod
kas'tanje, chestnut
kaste, caste
kas'teel *n*, castle
kaste'lein, publican
kas'tijden, chastise
kastje *n*, locker
  van het kastje naar de muur, from pillar to post
kastpapier *n*, lining paper
kat, cat
  de kat uit de boom kijken, to play a waiting game
  als een kat in een vreemd pakhuis, like a fish out of water
  een kat in de zak kopen, to buy a pig in a poke
kater, tom-cat; hang-over

kathe'draal, cathedral
katje n, kitten; catkin
ka'toen, cotton; n, wick
ka'toenspinnerij, cotton-mill
ka'trol, pulley
kattebak, cat's box; dickey seat
kattebelletje n, scribbled note
kattekwaad n, mischief
katterig, chippy
katzwijm, feigned swoon
kauw, jackdaw
kauwen, to chew
kauwgom n, chewing gum
kavalje n, shack; jade
kavelen, to parcel out
kaze'mat, casemate
ka'zerne, barracks
ka'zernewoning, tenement dwelling
ka'zuifel, chasuble
keel, throat
 het hangt me de keel uit, I'm sick and tired of it
keelklep, epiglottis
keelpijn, a sore throat
keer, turn; time(s)
 een doodenkele keer, once in a blue moon
 te keer gaan, to storm
keerdam, weir
keerkringen, tropics
keerpunt n, turning point
keerzijde, reverse side
keet, shed, hut; shindy
keffen, to yap
kegel, cone; skittle
kegelen, to play skittles
kei, boulder, cobble-stone, set; "wizard"
keilen, to fling; to play ducks and drakes
keizer, emperor
keize'rin, empress
keizerlijk, imperial
keizerrijk n, empire
keizersnede, cæsarian
kelder, cellar, vault
kelderen, to go to the bottom; to slump
kelen, to cut the throat of
kelk, chalice; calyx
kelner, waiter
kemelsgaren n, mohair

kemphaan, fighting-cock
kenau, amazon
kenbaar, distinguishable
 kenbaar maken, to make known
kenmerk n, characteristic
kenmerken, to characterize
kennelijk, apparent, clear
kennen, to know
 te kennen geven, to intimate
 men heeft mij er niet in gekend, I was not consulted
kenner, connoisseur
kennis, knowledge; acquaintance
 kennis geven van, to announce
 buiten kennis, unconscious
kennisgeving, notification
kenschetsen, to characterize
kenteken n, distinguishing mark
kenteren, to turn
keper, twill
 op de keper beschouwd, on close inspection; when all is said and done
kerel, fellow
keren, to turn, to stem
kerf, notch
kerfstok, tally-stick
 hij heeft veel op zijn kerfstok, he has a lot to answer for
kerk, church
kerkbank, pew
kerkdienst, (divine) service
kerkelijk, ecclesiastical; church (-going)
kerker, dungeon
kerkgang, church attendance
kerkhof n, churchyard
kerks(ge'zind), churchy
kermen, to moan
kermis, fair
kermiswagen, caravan
kern, kernel, core; crux, gist
kernachtig, pithy
kerngezond, fit as a fiddle
kerrie, curry
kers, cherry
Kerstavond, Christmas Eve
Kerstdag, Christmas Day
 tweede Kerstdag, Boxing Day
Kerstenen, to Christianize
Kerstfeest, Kerstmis, Christmas
kersvers, quite fresh

kervel: dolle —, hemlock
  wilde kervel, sheep's parsley
kerven, to carve, to notch, to cut
ketel, kettle, boiler
ketellapper, tinker
ketelsteen, scale, fur
keten(en), (to) chain
ketsen, to misfire
ketter, heretic
ketteren, to swear, to rage
kette'rij, heresy
ketting, chain; necklace
keu, (billiard) cue
keuken, kitchen; cuisine
keukenfornuis *n*, kitchen-range
keukengerei *n*, kitchen utensils
keur, choice; pick; hall-mark
keuren, to examine; to inspect;
  to sample
keurig, trim, very nice
keuring, medical examination;
  inspection
keurkorps *n*, picked body of men
keurs(lijf *n*), bodice
keurvorst(endom *n*), elector(ate)
keus, choice
keutels, droppings
keuterboer, crofter
keuvelen, to chat(ter)
kever, beetle
kibbelen, to squabble
kiek(je *n*), snapshot
kieken, to take a snap of
kiektoestel *n*, camera
kiel, blouse, smock; keel
kielzog *n*, wake
kiem, germ; seed
kiemen, to germinate
kienen, to play lotto
kier, chink
  op een kier, ajar
kies, molar: delicate
kiesbaar, eligible
kiesdistrict *n*, constituency
kieskauwen, to munch
kies'keurig, fastidious
kieskring, poling district
kiespijn, toothache
kiesrecht *n*, franchise
kietelen, to tickle
kieuw, gill
kievit, lapwing
kievitsei *n*, plover's egg

kiezel *n*, gravel, shingle; silicon
kiezelsteen, pebble
kiezen, to choose; to elect
kiezerslijst, electoral roll
kijf: buiten —, beyond dispute
kijk, view, outlook, idea; prospect
kijken, to (have a) look
kijker, telescope, binoculars;
  viewer
kijkgat *n*, peep-hole
kijven, to quarrel
kik: hij gaf geen —, he did not
  utter a sound
kikken: je hebt maar te —,
  you've only to say the word
kikker, frog; cleat
kikvors, frog
kil, chilly
kilo *n*, kilogram (2·205 lb)
kim, horizon
kin, chin
kina, quinine
kind *n*, child
kinderachtig, childish
kinderbed *n*, cot
kinderbewaarplaats, crèche
kinderjuffrouw,   nurse-maid,
  nannie
kinderkamer, nursery
kinderlijk, childlike
kinderloos, childless
kindersterfte, infant mortality
kinderverlamming,   infantile
  paralysis
kinderwagen, pram
kinds, infantine
kindsbeen: van — af, ever since
  childhood
ki'nine, quinine
kink, kink
  een kink in de kabel, a hitch
kinkel, lout
kinkhoest, whooping-cough
kinnebak, jaw-bone
kip, chicken, hen
kipkar, tip-cart
kiplekker, as right as rain
kippeborst, pidgeon-chest
kippegaas *n*, wire-netting
kippenfokkerij,   poultry   farm
  (-ing)
kippenhok *n*, hen-house

kippekuur, whim
kippevel *n,* goose-flesh
kippig, short-sighted
kirren, to coo
kist, (packing-)case, chest; coffin
kit, coal-hod
kitte'lorig, touchy
kittig, spruce; spry
klaaglied *n,* lamentation, dirge
klaaglijk, plaintive
klaar, clear; ready, finished
  klare wijn schenken, to make one's meaning clear
  klaar wakker, wide awake
klaar'blijkelijk, evident
klaarheid, clarity
klaarkomen, to get ready, to (get) finish(ed)
klaarlichte dag, broad daylight
klaarspelen: het —, to manage it
klacht, complaint
klad, blot; *n* rough draft
  iemand bij de kladden pakken, to grab hold of a person
kladden, to daub, to scrawl
kladpapier *n,* scribbling paper
kladschilderen, to daub
kladwerk *n,* badly written work; daub
klagen, to lament
  het is God geklaagd, it cries out to heaven
klakkeloos, groundless, off-hand, rash
klam, clammy
klamboe, mosquito-net
klamp(en), (to) clamp
klan'dizie, custom(ers)
klank, sound
klankleer, phonetics
klankloos, toneless
klanknabootsend, onomatopœic
klankrijk, klankvol, sonorous
klant, customer, client
klap, blow, smack, crack
klapbes, gooseberry
klapbus, pop-gun
klaplopen, to cadge
klaploper, sponger
klappen: in de handen —, to clap
  met een zweep klappen, to crack a whip

klapper, index: coco-nut
klappertanden: hij klappertandde, his teeth were chattering
klaproos, poppy
klapstoel, tip-up seat, folding chair
klapwieken, to flap the wings
klapzoen, loud kiss
klas, klasse, class(-room), form
klassenstrijd, class-war
klas'siek, classic(al)
klateren, to splatter, to cascade
klatergoud *n,* tinsel
klauteren, to clamber
klauw, claw, talon
klauwzeer *n,* foot-rot
klave'cimbel, harpsichord
klaver, clover
klaver'aas *n,* ace of clubs
kla'vier *n,* keyboard
kleden, to dress; to clothe
klederdracht, local costume
kle'dij, kleding, clothes, attire
kledingstuk *n,* garment
kleed *n,* carpet; cloth; gown
kleedgeld *n,* dress allowance
kleedje *n,* rug, (table-)cloth
kleedkamer, dressing-room, changing-room
kleefpleister *n,* adhesive plaster
kleerborstel, clothes-brush
kleermaker, tailor
klef, sticky, soggy
klei, clay
kleimasker *n,* mud-pack
klein, little, small
  klein geld, small change
  de kleine vaart, inland *or* coastal navigation
klein'burgelijk, bourgeois
kleindochter, granddaughter
klei'neren, to belittle
klei'nering, disparagement
klein'geestig, narrow-minded
kleinge'lovig, of little faith
kleinhandel, retail trade
kleinigheid, trifle
kleinkind *n,* grandchild
kleinkrijgen, to break (a person)
klei'nood *n,* trinket
klein'steeds, provincial

kleintje *n*, baby, little one
  op de kleintjes passen, to take care of the pence
klein'zerig, easily hurt, soft
klein'zielig, petty(-minded)
kleinzoon, grandson
klem, trap; clip; emphasis
klemmen, to pinch, to clench
  een klemmend betoog *n*, a convincing argument
klemtoon, stress
klep, valve; flap; peak
klepel, clapper
kleppen, to clang, to clatter
klepperen, to rattle, to bang to and fro
kleren, clothes
klerenkast, wardrobe
klerk, clerk
klets, smack; twaddle
kletsen, to chatter; to talk rubbish
kletskop, brandy-snap; scald-head
kletskous, gossip, chatter-box
kletteren, to clatter, to patter
kleur, colour; suit (cards)
  kleur bekennen, to follow suit; to show one's colours
kleurecht, fast (dyed)
kleuren, to colour; to blush
kleurenpracht, blaze of colour
kleurling, coloured person
kleurloos, colourless
kleurstof, colouring matter
kleuter, toddler
kleven, to cleave, to stick
kleverig, sticky
kliederen, to make a mess
kliek, clique
kliekjes *n*, scraps, left-overs
klier, gland; dirty rotter
klieven, to cleave
klif *n*, cliff
klikspaan, tell-tale
kli'maat *n*, climate
klimato'logisch, climatic
klimmen, to climb
  bij het klimmen der jaren, with advancing years
klimop, ivy
kling, blade (of a sword)
klingelen, to tinkle

kli'niek, clinic
klink, latch
klinkbout, rivet
klinken, to sound, to ring (out); to clink glasses: to rivet
klinker, vowel: riveter: clinker
klinkklaar, utter, pure
klinknagel, rivet
klip, rock, reef
  blinde klip, sunken rock
klis, klit, burr, burdock; tangle
klodder(en), (to) clot; (to) daub
kloek, brave; stout; substantial: mother hen
klok, clock; bell
  alles wat de klok slaat, all one hears about
klokhuis *n*, core
klokkenspel *n*, carillon, chimes
klokluider, bell-ringer
klokrok, flared skirt
klokslag, stroke (of the clock)
klomp, clog; lump; nugget
klompvoet, club-foot
klont(er), lump, clod, clot
klonteren, to clot
klonterig, lumpy
kloof, cleft, crevice; rift
klooster *n*, monastery, convent
klop, knock, throb
klopjacht, beat(-up)
kloppen, to knock, to tap, to beat; to tally
  dat klopt als een bus, that tallies all along the line
klos, bobbin, reel; coil
klossen, to clump
klotsen, to dash
kloven, to cleave, to split
klucht, farce
kluchtig, funny
kluif, knuckle of pork; (meaty) bone
  een hele kluif, quite a job
kluis, hermitage; strong-room
kluisters, shackles
kluisteren, to fetter
kluit, clod, lump
  flink uit de kluiten gewassen, strapping
kluiven, to gnaw a bone
kluiver, jib
kluizenaar, hermit

klungel, (piece of) trash; bungler

klungelen, to tinker; to bungle

kluts : de — kwijtraken, to lose one's head

klutsen, to whisk

kluwen n, ball (of wool etc.)

knaagdier n, rodent

knaap, boy; coat-hanger

knabbelen, to nibble

knagen, to gnaw

knakken, to snap, to break

knakworst, Frankfurt sausage

knal, report, bang

knallen, to bang, to ring out

knalpatroon, detonator

knalpot, silencer

knap, handsome, pretty; clever; neat

knappen, to snap; to crackle
 een uiltje knappen, to take forty winks

knarsen, to grate; to crunch

knarsetanden, to gnash one's teeth

knauwen, to gnaw, to munch; to damage or hurt seriously

knecht, (man-)servant

knechten, to enslave

kneden, to knead; to mould

kneedbaar, malleable

kneep, pinch; dodge

knel : in de — zitten, to be in a fix

knellen, to pinch

knetteren, to crackle

kneukel, knuckle

kneuzen, to bruise

kneuzing, bruise

knevel, big moustache

knevela'rij, extortion

knevelen, to gag, to pinion

knibbelen, to haggle

knie, knee
 onder de knie krijgen, to master

kniebroek, knickerbockers

kniebuiging, genuflexion; curtsey

knielbank, kneeler

knielen, to kneel

knieschijf, knee-cap

kniesoor, mope

kniezen, to mope

knijpen, to pinch
 ik knijp 'm, I've got the wind up

knikkebollen, to nod (with sleep)

knikken, to nod

knikker, marble

knip, snip; trap; catch, clasp

knipogen, to wink; to blink

knippen, to cut, to clip
 geknipt voor, cut out for

knipperen, to flicker

knipsel n, cutting

knobbel, bump

knobbelig, gnarled

knoedel, dumpling; bun (of hair); knot

knoei : in de — zitten, to be in difficulties

knoeiboel, mess; swindle

knoeien, to make a mess; to bungle

knoeie'rij, corruption; bungling

knoeiwerk n, shoddy work

knoest, knot (in wood)

knoet(je n**),** bun (of hair)

knoflook n, garlic

knok(kel), knuckle

knokken, to scrap

knol, tuber; turnip; jade
 in zijn knollentuin, as pleased as Punch

knolraap, swede

knoop, knot; button; node

knooppunt n, junction

knoopsgat n, button-hole

knop, bud; knob

knopje n, (push-)button, switch

knopen, to tie, to knot
 iets in zijn oor knopen, to make a mental note of something

knorren, to grunt; to grumble

knorrig, peevish

knot, skein

knots, club

knotten, to pollard

knuffelen, to cuddle

knuist, fist

knul, duffer; fellow

knuppel, cudgel

knus(jes), snug

knutselen, to make things (for a hobby)

koddig, droll
koe, cow
  oude koeien uit de sloot halen, to rake up old stories
koeio'neren, to badger
koek, gingerbread
koeke'loeren, to stare inquisitively
koekepan, frying-pan
koekje *n*, sweet biscuit
koekoek, cuckoo; dormer window, skylight
koel, cool
koel'bloedig, cool-headed
koelen, to cool (down)
  zijn woede koelen, to vent one's anger
koelhuis *n*, cold storage
koelinrichting, refrigerating plant
koelte, cool(ness)
koeltje *n*, cool breeze
koen, bold
koepaard *n*, piebald horse
koepel, dome; summer-house
koepeldak *n*, domed roof
koe'rier, courier
koers, course; price (of stocks); rate of exchange
koesteren, to cherish
  zich koesteren, to bask
koeter'waals *n*, double Dutch
koetjes en kalfjes, trifling matters
koets, coach
koet'sier, coachman
koevoet, crow-bar
koffer, suit-case
koffergrammofoon, portable gramophone
koffie, coffee
koffiedik *n*, coffee-grounds
koffiedrinken, to have lunch (i.e. coffee and a bread meal)
kogel, bullet; ball
kogelbaan, trajectory
kogellager *n*, ball-bearing
kok, cook
ko'karde, cockade
koken, to cook; to boil
koker, (long) case
kokette'rie, flirtation
kokhalzen, to retch

kokosmat, coconut mat(ting)
kokosnoot, coconut
kolbak, busby
kolder, staggers; tomfoolery
kolen, coal(s)
  op hete kolen, on tenterhooks
kolenbak, coal-scuttle
kolendamp, carbon monoxide
kolenhok *n*, coal-shed
kolf, (rifle-)butt; retort
koli'brie, humming-bird
ko'liek *n*, colic
kolk, whirlpool; (lock-)chamber
kologen, goggle-eyes
ko'lom, column
koloni'aal, colonial (soldier)
koloni'ale waren, groceries
ko'lonie, colony
kolos'saal, colossal
kom, basin, bowl; the populous part, centre
kom'aan! come along!
kom'af, descent, birth
kom'buis, galley
komedi'ant, play-actor, comedian
ko'medie, play; theatre; comedy
ko'meet, comet
komen, to come
  hoe komt dat? how did that happen?
kom'foor *n*, chafing dish; gas-ring, heater
ko'miek, comical: low comedian
komisch, comic(al)
kom'kommer, cucumber
komma, comma, (decimal) point
komma'punt, semi-colon
kommer, sorrow, distress
kommerlijk, **kommervol**, wretched
kom'pas *n*, compass
kom'pashuisje *n*, binnacle
kom'plot *n*, plot
komst, coming
  op komst, on the way
kond doen, to notify
ko'nijn *n*, rabbit
koning, king
konin'gin, queen
koningschap *n*, kingship
koningsgezind, royalist

koningsmoord, regicide
koninklijk, royal, regal
koninkrijk n, kingdom
konkelen, to scheme
kon'vooi n, convoy
kooi, cage, pen ; bunk
kook, boil
kookboek n, cookery book
kool, cabbage: coal(s) ; carbon
 iemand een kool stoven, to
 play a trick on someone
koolhydraat n, carbohydrate
koolmees, titmouse
koolzaad n, rape-seed
koolzuur n, carbonic acid
koon, cheek
koop, purchase
 te koop, for sale
 te koop lopen met, to show
 off
 op de koop toe, into the bargain
koopacte, title-deed
koophandel, commerce
koopje n, bargain
koopkracht, purchasing power
koopman, merchant
koopvaar'dij, merchant service
koopvaar'dijschip n, merchant-
 ship
koopwaar, merchandise
koor n, choir, chorus ; chancel
koorbank, choir-stall
koord n, cord ; flex
koorddansen n, tight-rope walking
koorhemd n, surplice
koorts, fever
 koorts hebben, to have a temperature
koorts(acht)ig, feverish
kootje n, phalanx
kop, head ; large cup ; bowl (of a
 pipe)
 de kop indrukken, to nip in the
 bud
 op de kop tikken, to pick up, to
 find (a bargain)
 op de kop af, precisely
kopen, to buy
koper, purchaser: n, copper,
 brass
kopergroen n, verdigris
koperslager, coppersmith

kopervijlsel n, brass-filings
ko'pie, copy
kopi'ëren, to copy
ko'pijrecht n, copyright
kopje n, (tea-)cup
 kopje duikelen, to turn somer-
 saults
koplamp, head-light
koppel, belt ; leash: n, couple,
 brace
koppelaar, match-maker
koppela'rij, procuration
koppelen, to couple, to join
koppeling, coupling ; clutch
koppelteken n, hyphen
koppelwerkwoord n, copula
koppensnellen n, head-hunting
koppig, obstinate
koppigheid, obstinacy
kopstuk n, leading light
kopzorg, worry
ko'raal n, choral(e): coral
kor'daat, resolute
koren n, corn
korenschuur, granary
korf, basket ; hive
korfbal, basket-ball
korhoen n, black grouse
kor'nuit, crony
korrel, grain ; pellet ; foresight
korrelig, granular
korst, crust, rind ; scab
korstdeeg n, short pastry
korstmos n, lichen
kort, short, brief
 kort en bondig, terse
 kort maar krachtig, short and
 snappy
kor'tademig, short of breath
kor'taf, curt
kortelings, recently
korten, to deduct ; to while
 away
kortheids'halve, for the sake of
 brevity
korting, discount, deduction
kor'tom, in short
kortsluiting, short circuit
kort'stondig, short-lived
kortweg, without wasting words
kortwieken, to clip the wings of
kort'zichtig, short-sighted
korzelig, grumpy

kost, food; living; board
  kost en inwoning, board and lodging
kostbaar, expensive; precious
kostbaarheden, valuables
kostbaas, landlord
kostelijk, superb; priceless
kosteloos, (cost-)free
kosten, expense(s), cost, charges: to cost
koster, verger
kostganger, boarder
kostgeld *n,* board
kostschool, boarding-school
kostwinner, bread-winner
kot *n,* sty
kotsen, to puke
kotter, cutter
kou(de), cold
  kou vatten, to catch cold
koud, cold
koud'vuur *n,* gangrene
koukleum, chilly person
kous, stocking
  met de kous op de kop, with a flea in one's ear
kouseband, garter
kousje *n,* (incandescent) mantle
kout, chat
kouwelijk, sensitive to cold
ko'zijn *n,* window-sill, window-frame
kraag, collar, ruff
kraai(en), (to) crow
kraakbeen *n,* cartilage
kraakstem, grating voice
kraakzindelijk, spotlessly clean
kraal, bead
kraam, booth, stall
kraambed *n,* childbed
kraamheer, father of the (new-born) child
kraaminrichting, maternity home
kraamvrouw, woman in child-bed
kraan, tap; crane, derrick: dab(-hand)
kraanwagen, break-down truck
krab, crab
krabbel(en), (to) scratch, (to) scrawl
krabben, to scratch

kracht, force, strength, power
  volle kracht vooruit, full speed ahead
  op krachten komen, to regain strength
kracht'dadig, vigorous
krachteloos, powerless
krachtens, by virtue of
krachtig, powerful
krachtprestatie, feat (of strength); (power) output
krachtsinspanning, exertion
kra'kelen, to quarrel
kraken, to crack; to creak; to crunch
kram, staple
kramer, pedlar
krammen, to cramp, to rivet
kramp, cramp; spasm
kram'pachtig, desperate; taut
kranig, smart; brave; brilliant
krank, sick, ill
krank'zinnig, insane
krank'zinnigengesticht *n,* lunatic asylum
krans, wreath
krant, newspaper
krap, tight; short of money
kras, scratch, strong (for one's age)
  dat is kras! that's a bit thick!
krassen, to scratch; to screech
krat, crate
krater, crater
krauwen, to scratch
kreeft, lobster
kreek, creek
kreet, cry, scream
kregel, peevish
kreng *n,* carrion; rotter, bitch
krenken, to offend
krent, currant; skinflint
krenterig, niggardly
kreuk(el)(en), (to) crease
kreunen, to groan
kreupel, lame
kreupelhout *n,* thicket
krib(be), manger, crib
kribbebijter, cross-patch
kribbig, testy
kriebelen, to itch, to tickle; to write a niggling hand
kriebelig, nettled

kriek, black cherry
krieken: bij het — van de dag, at the crack of dawn
krielkip, bantam
krijg, war
krijgen, to get
te pakken krijgen, to get hold of
krijger, warrior
krijgertje n, tig
krijgsgevangene, prisoner of war
krijgs'haftig, warlike
krijgs'haftigheid, valour
krijgslist, stratagem
krijgsman, warrior
krijgsraad, council of war; court-martial
krijgstocht, campaign
krijgsvolk n, soldiers
krijgs'zuchtig, bellicose
krijsen, to screech
krijt n, chalk: lists
krijten, to cry
krijtrots, chalk cliff
krimp geven, to yield
krimpen, to shrink; to back
krimpvrij, unshrinkable
kring, circle
kringloop, cycle
kri'oelen, to swarm
krip n, crape
kris'tal n, crystal
kri'tiek, criticism; review: critical
kritisch, critical
kriti'seren, to criticize
kroeg, pub
kroegbaas, publican
kroep, croup
kroes, mug, crucible: frizzy
krols, on heat
krom, crooked, bent, curved
je lacht je krom, it's a perfect scream
kromliggen, to pinch and scrape
kromming, bend, curve
kromtrekken, to warp
kronen, to crown
kro'niek, chronicle
kroning, coronation, crowning
kronkel, twist, kink
kronkelen, to twist, to wind

kronkelig, winding
kronkeling, convolution
kroon, crown; corolla, chandelier
dat spant de kroon, that crowns everything
kroonlijst, cornice
kroos n, duckweed
kroost n, progeny
kroot, beetroot
krop, gizzard
kropgezwel n, goitre
kropsla, cabbage lettuce
krot n, hovel
kruid n, herb
kruiden, to season
kruide'nier, grocer
kruide'rijen, spices
kruidnagel, clove
kruien, to wheel (in a barrow); to break up, to drift (of ice)
kruier, (luggage-)porter
kruik, stone bottle; hot-water bottle
kruim(el) n, crumb
kruimelig, crumbly
kruin, crown, top
kruipen, to creep; to crawl; to cringe
kruiperig, cringing
kruis n, cross; sharp (in music); croup, crupper, crutch; seat
kruis of munt, heads or tails
kruisbeeld n, crucifix
kruisbes, gooseberry
kruiselings, crosswise
kruisen, to cross; to cruise
kruiser, cruiser
kruisgang, cloister
kruisigen, to crucify
kruiskoppeling, universal joint
kruispunt n, point of intersection, cross-roads
kruistocht, kruisvaart, crusade
kruit n, (gun-)powder
kruiwagen, (wheel)barrow; influential friend
kruk, crutch; door-handle; crank; stool
krul, curl; scroll
krullebol, curly-head
krullenjongen, carpenter's apprentice
kubiek, cubic

kubus, cube
kuch, dry cough
kuchen, to give a slight cough
kudde, herd, flock
kuieren, to stroll
kuif, quif, crest
kuiken *n,* chicken
kuil, pit, (pot-)hole
kuiltje *n,* dimple
kuip, tub
kuipen, to cooper; to intrigue
kuipe'rij, machinations
kuis, chaste
kuisheid, chastity
kuit, calf (of the leg); spawn; roe
kuitschieten, to spawn
kuitbroek, knee-breeches
kul: flauwe —, poppycock
kundig, able; knowledgeable
ter zake kundig, expert
kundigheden, accomplishments
kunne, sex
kunnen, to be able to, may
dat kan (wel), that is (quite) possible, maybe
kunst, art; trick
daar is geen kunst aan, there's nothing to it
kunst-, artificial; art
kunsteloos, artless
kunstenaar, artist
kunstig, ingenious
kunstkenner, connoisseur
kunst'matig, artificial
kunst'nijverheid, applied art
kunstrijden *n,* figure-skating
kunststuk *n,* masterpiece
kunst'vaardig, skilful
kunst'zinnig, artistic
ku'ras *n,* cuirass
kurk(en), (to) cork
kurketrekker, corkscrew
kus, kiss
kushandjes geven, to blow kisses
kussen, to kiss: *n,* pillow, cushion
kussensloop *n,* pillow-case
kust, coast, shore
te kust en te keur, in plenty
kustvaart, coastwise trade
kuur, whim; cure

kwaad, bad; angry
kwaad geweten, guilty conscience
het te kwaad krijgen, to break down
kwaad *n,* evil; harm
kwaa'daardig, malicious
kwaad'denkend, suspicious
kwaadschiks, with an ill grace
kwaadspreke'rij, scandal
kwaad'willig, malevolent
kwaal, complaint, ailment
kwabbig, flabby
kwa'draat *n,* square
kwa'jongen, (young) rascal
kwa'jongensachtig, mischievous
kwak, thud; blob
kwaken, to quack; to croak
kwakkelen, to have poor health
kwakkelwinter, mild winter
kwakzalver, quack
kwal, jelly-fish; rotter
kwalifi'ceren, to describe
kwalijk nemen, to take ill
neem me niet kwalijk, I am sorry
kwanselen, to swop
kwan'suis, for form's sake
kwant, young fellow
kwanti'teit, quantity
kwart, fourth: *n* quarter
kwar'taal *n,* quarter, term
kwar'taalsgewijze, quarterly
kwartel, quail
kwar'tier *n,* quarter of an hour; quarter(s)
kwar'tiermuts, forage-cap
kwartje *n,* 25 cent-piece
kwartjesvinder, confidence trickster
kwartnoot, crotchet
kwarts *n,* quartz
kwast, brush, tassel: knot (in wood): coxcomb: lemon-squash
kwasterig, foppish
kwebbel, chatterbox
kwebbelen, to chatter
kweek(school), training-college
kwee(peer), quince
kwekeling, student teacher
kweken, to grow; to foster
kweker, nurseryman

kweke'rij, nursery
kwekken, to yap; to chatter
kwelen, to warble
kwellen, to torment
kwelling, torment
kwestie, question
kwets, purple plum
kwetsbaar, vulnerable
kwetsen, to wound, to injure
kwet'suur, wound
kwetteren, to twitter
kwezel, pietist
kwibus: een rare —, a queer cove
kwiek, spry
kwijlen, to dribble
kwijnen, to languish
kwijt zijn, to have lost
kwijtraken, to lose
kwijten: zich — van, to discharge
kwijtschelden, to remit, to forgive
kwik n, mercury
kwinke'leren, to warble
kwinkslag, witticism
kwispedoor, spittoon
kwispel(staart)en, to wag the tail
kwistig, lavish
kwi'tantie, receipt
kwi'teren, to receipt

L

la(de), drawer, till
laadboom, derrick
laadvermogen n, loading capacity
laag, layer, stratum: low (-pitched)
 hij gaf me de volle laag, he let me have it
 lager onderwijs, primary education
laag-bij-de-'gronds, crude
laag'hartig, base
laagte, low level, dip
laag'veen n, peat-bog
laagvlakte, plain
laag'water n, low tide
laaie: in lichte —, ablaze
laaien, to blaze
laakbaar, blameworthy

laan, avenue
laantje n, path, lane
laars, boot
 dat lap ik aan mijn laars, I couldn't care less
laat, late
laat'dunkend, arrogant
laatst, last, latest; recently
laatstgenoemde, latter
la'biel, unstable
labora'torium n, laboratory
lach(en), (to) laugh
lachlust: de — opwekken, to raise a laugh
lachspiegel, distorting mirror
lach'wekkend, laughable
la'cune, gap
ladder, ladder
laden, to load, to charge
ladenkast, chest of drawers
lading, load, cargo; charge
laf, cowardly
lafaard, lafbek, coward
lafenis, refreshment
laf'hartig, cowardly
lafheid, cowardice
lager, bearing(s)
Lagerhuis, Lower House, House of Commons
la'gune, lagoon
lak n, sealing-wax; lacquer
 ik heb er lak aan, a fat lot I care
la'kei, footman
laken, to blame: n, cloth, sheet
 de lakens uitdelen, to rule the roost
 hij kreeg van hetzelfde laken een pak, he was treated in just the same way
lakken, to lacquer; to seal
lakmoes n, litmus
laks(heid), lax(ity)
lakschoen, patent leather shoe
lam, paralysed; nasty: n, lamb
lambri'zering, wainscot(ting)
lam'lendig, wretched; indolent
lammeling, wretch
lamp, lamp, bulb, valve
 tegen de lamp lopen, to get into trouble
lam'petkan, ewer
lampi'on, Chinese lantern

lamstraal, wretch
lan'ceren, to launch
land *n*, land, country, field
 ik heb er het land aan, I hate it
 aan land gaan, to go ashore
landarbeider, agricultural labourer
landbouw(kunde), agriculture
landbouw'kundige, agriculturalist
landelijk, rural; nation-wide
landen, to land
landengte, isthmus
landerig, in the dumps
lande'rijen, landed property
landgenoot, compatriot
landgoed *n*, estate
landheer, landowner
landingsgestel *n*, undercarriage
landkaart, map
landleger *n*, land forces
landloper, tramp
landmeter, surveyor
landschap *n*, landscape
landsman: wat is hij voor een
 — ? What nationality is he?
landstaal, vernacular
landstreek, region
landsvrouwe, sovereign lady
landverhuizer, emigrant
landverraad *n*, high treason
landvoogd, governor
lang, long, tall
 lang van stof, long-winded
 lang niet, not nearly
lang'dradig, long-winded
lang'durig, lengthy
langge'rekt, protracted
langs, along, past
 langs elkaar heen praten, to
 talk at cross purposes
lang'uit, at full length
lang'werpig, oblong, elongated
langzaam, slow
langzamerhand, gradually
lank'moedig(heid), long-suffering
lans, lance
lan'taarn, lan'taren, lantern;
 skylight; lamp
lan'taarnpaal, lamp-post
lan'taarnplaatje *n*, lantern-slide
lanterfanten, to loaf

lap, piece (of cloth), rag; patch;
 steak
lapmiddel *n*, makeshift
lappen, to patch; to wipe; to
 manage
lappendeken, patchwork quilt
lappenmand, work basket
 in de lappenmand, under the
 weather
lapwerk *n*, patchwork
larie, stuff and nonsense
larve, larva
las, joint, weld
lassen, to weld
last, load, burden; instruction(s);
 trouble
lastbrief, mandate
laster(en), (to) slander
lasterlijk, slanderous
lastgever, principal
lastig, difficult, tiresome
 lastig vallen, to trouble
lastpost, nuisance
lat, lath, slat
laten, to let; to leave (off)
 ik kan het niet laten, I can't
 help it
 iets laten doen, to have something done
later, afterwards, later
La'tijn(s) (*n*), Latin
latwerk *n*, trellis
lau'rier, laurel
lauw, tepid
lauweren, laurels
lave'ment *n*, enema
laven, to refresh
la'vendel, lavender
la'veren, to tack
la'waai *n*, din
la'wine, avalanche
la'xeermiddel *n*, laxative
la'xeren, to purge
lebberen, to lap, to sip
lector, university lecturer
lec'tuur, reading (matter)
ledematen, limbs
leden, limbs; members
ledepop, dummy
leder *n*, leather
ledig, empty
ledi'kant *n*, bed(stead)
leed *n*, sorrow

leedvermaak *n*, pleasure at other people's misfortune
leedwezen *n*, regret
leefregel, regimen
leeftijd, age
 op leeftijd, elderly
leeftijdsgrens, age-limit
leeftocht, provisions
leefwijze, manner of living
leeg(gieten), (to) empty
leegloper, idler
leegte, emptiness
leek, layman
leem *n*, loam
leemte, gap, hiatus
leen *n*, fief, loan
leenheer, liege lord
leenman, vassal
leenstelsel *n*, feudal system
leep, cunning
leer, doctrine: ladder: *n*, leather
 in de leer bij, apprenticed to
leerboek *n*, text book
leergang, course of study
leergeld *n*: **ik heb — betaald**, I have learnt my lesson
leer'gierig, studious
leerjaar *n*, year's school-work
leerjongen, apprentice
leerkracht, teacher
leerling, pupil
leerlooien, to tan
leerlooie'rij, tannery
leermeester, teacher
leerplan *n*, curriculum
leerrijk, instructive
leerstelling, tenet
leerstoel, chair
leerzaam, instructive; teachable
leesbaar, readable, legible
leeskabinet *n*, reading-room
leest, last
leesteken *n*, punctuation mark
leeuw('in), lion(ess)
leeuwerik, (sky)lark
lef *n*, pluck; swank
le'gaat *n*, legacy
le'gatie, legation
le'gende, legend
leger *n*, army
 Leger des Heils, Salvation Army

legeren, to encamp
le'gering, alloy
legerstede, couch
leges, legal dues
leggen, to lay, to put
legio, legion
legi'oen *n*, legion, army
legiti'matiebewijs *n*, identification paper
legkaart, jig-saw puzzle
lei, slate
leiband, apron strings
leiboom, espalier
leiden, to lead
leider, leader
leiding, guidance, direction, lead; pipe(-line)
leidsel(s) *n*, reins
leidsman, mentor, guide
leien: **alles ging van een — dakje**, everything went smoothly
lek *(n)*, leak(y)
 een lekke band, a puncture
lekken, to leak
lekker, nice
 ik ben niet lekker, I am not very well
 iemand lekker maken, to rouse a person's expectations
 dank je lekker! thanks for nothing!
lekkerbek, gourmet
lekker'nij, delicacy
lel, lobe: slut
lelie, lily
lelijk, ugly; badly
 dat treft lelijk, that's awkward
lemmer *n*, **lemmet** *n*, blade
lende, small of the back, loin
lendenen, loins
lenen, to lend; to borrow
lengte, length, height; longitude
lenig, supple, lithe
lenigen, to alleviate
lening, loan
lenspomp, bilge pump
lente, spring
lepel, spoon, ladle
leperd, shrewd fellow
leraar, school-master
lera'res, school-mistress

LER 117 LIC

leren, (made of) leather: to teach; to learn
 de tijd zal het leren, time will tell
lering, instruction
les, lesson
lesgeld *n,* tuition fee
lesrooster *n,* time-table
lessen, to quench, to slake
lessenaar, desk
leste: ten lange —, at long last
lesvliegtuig *n,* trainer
letsel *n,* injury
letten op, to pay attention to; to look after
 let wel! mark you!
letter, letter, type
letteren, literature
lettergreep, syllable
letterkunde, literature
letterlijk, literal
letterteken *n,* character
letterzetter, compositor
leugen, lie
leugenaar, liar
leugenachtig, mendacious
leuk, nice, cute, amusing
leukerd, fine one
leukweg, coolly
leunen, to lean
leuning, (hand-)rail; parapet; back, arm(-rest)
leunstoel, armchair
leuren met, to hawk
leus, leuze, slogan, device
 voor de leus, for appearance's sake
leut, fun
leuteren, to talk drivel; to loiter
leven, to live, to be alive
levend, (a)live, living
leven *n,* life; noise
levendig, lively
levenloos, lifeless
levensbehoeften, necessities of life
levensbericht *n,* obituary (notice)
levensbeschouwing, philosophy of life
levensbeschrijving, biography
levensge'vaarlijk, deadly dangerous

levensgroot, life-size(d)
levens'krachtig, vigorous
levenskwestie, matter of life and death
levenslang, lifelong
levenslust, *joie de vivre*
levensmiddelen *n,* provisions
levensmoe(de), weary of life
levensonderhoud *n,* subsistence
levensopvatting, outlook (on life)
levens'vatbaar, viable
levensverzekering, life-insurance
levenswandel, conduct
lever, liver
leveran'cier, purveyor, retailer
leve'rantie, delivery, supply
leveren, to supply, to deliver
levertraan, cod-liver oil
leverworst, liver-sausage
lezen, to read; to gather
lezer('es), reader
lezenaar, lectern
lezing, lecture; version
li'as, file
li'bel, dragon-fly
libe'raal, liberal
lichaam *n,* body
lichaamsbeweging, exercise
lichaamsbouw, physique
li'chamelijk, bodily, physical
licht, light, mild, slight; easily: *n,* light
 zijn licht bij iemand opsteken, to ask someone for information
lichtbundel, beam of light
lichtekooi, prostitute
lichtelijk, slightly
lichten, to weigh, to lift
 de bus lichten, to collect the mail
lichter, lighter
lichtge'lovig, credulous
lichtge'raakt, touchy
lichtgevend, luminous
lichtgranaat, star-shell
lichting, draft, class, levy; collection (of mail)
lichtkogel, Very light
lichtma'troos, ordinary seaman
lichtmis, libertine: Candlemas

lichtpunt *n*, point of light; lighting point; ray of hope
licht'vaardig, rash, lightly
licht'zinnig, frivolous, flighty
lid *n*, limb, finger-joint; member; sub-section; term
  uit het lid, dislocated
lidmaat, member of the Protestant Church
lidmaatschap *n*, membership
lidwoord *n*, article
lied(eren) *n*, song(s)
lieden, people
liederlijk, debauched
  zich liederlijk vervelen, to be bored to tears
liedertafel, glee-club; sing-song
liedje *n*, ditty
  het is het oude liedje, it's the same old story
lief, dear, sweet, nice
  meer dan me lief is, more than I care for
  voor lief nemen, to put up with
  lief *n* **en leed** *n*, joys and sorrows
lief'dadig, charitable
lief'dadigheid, charity
liefde, love
liefdeloos, loveless
liefderijk, loving
liefdesgechiedenis, romance
liefdesverklaring, proposal
liefdezuster, sister of mercy
liefelijk, charming, sweet
liefhebben, to love
liefhebber, lover, votary
liefhebbe'rij, hobby
liefje, sweetheart
liefkozen, to fondle
liefst, dearest; preferably
lief'tallig, sweet, winsome
liegen, to tell lies
lier, lyre; winch
lies, groin
lieve'heersbeestje, lady-bird
lieveling, darling
liever, rather, sooner
lieverd, darling
lieverlede: van —, gradually
liften, to hitch-hike
lift(koker), lift(-shaft)
liga, league

liggeld *n*, harbour dues
liggen, to lie
  waar ligt het aan ? what is the cause of it?
ligging, situation
ligplaats, berth
li'guster, privet
lij(boord), lee(-side)
lijdelijk, passive
lijden, to suffer: *n*, suffering, passion
  ik mag hem wel lijden, I rather like him
  lijdend voorwerp, direct object
Lijdensweek, Holy Week
lijdzaam, submissive
lijf *n*, body; bodice
  het heeft weinig om het lijf, it is of little importance
lijfarts, personal physician
lijfblad *n*, favourite newspaper
lijfeigene, serf
lijfrente, annuity
lijfsbehoud *n*, self-preservation
lijfspreuk, motto
lijk *n*, corpse
lijken (op), to resemble; to seem
lijkenhuis(je) *n*, mortuary
lijkkist, coffin
lijkkleed *n*, pall
lijkkoets, hearse
lijkschouwer, coroner
lijkschouwing, post-mortem
lijkverbranding, cremation
lijm, glue; bird-lime
lijmen, to glue
  zich ervoor laten lijmen, to let oneself be talked into it
lijn, line; route
lijnolie, linseed oil
lijnrecht, straight; diametrically
lijntekenen, geometrical drawing
lijntrekken, to slack
lijnwaad *n*, linen
lijnzaad *n*, linseed
lijs, slowcoach
lijst, list; frame
lijster, thrush
lijsterbes, mountain ash
lijvig, corpulent, bulky
lijzig, drawling
lik, lick; swipe
likdoorn, corn

li'keur, liqueur
likkebaarden, to lick one's lips
likken, to lick; to curry favour
lila, lilac(-coloured)
li'miet, limit
limo'nade, (fruit) cordial
linde, lime-tree
lini'aal, ruler
linie, line
  over de hele linie, all round
lini'ëren, to rule
linker-, left
links, (to the) left; left-handed; gauche
  links laten liggen, to cold-shoulder
linksaf, linksom, to the left
linnen *n*, linen
lint *n*, ribbon
lintworm, tapeworm
linzen, lentils
lip, lip
lippenstift, lipstick
liqui'deren, to wind up (a business)
lis, flag, iris; loop
lispelen, to lisp
list, ruse
listig, cunning
lite'rair, literary
lite'rator, man of letters
lits ju'meaux, twin beds
litteken *n*, scar
li'vrei, livery
lob, lobe
lobbes, big good-natured person *or* animal
locomo'tief, (railway-)engine
lodderig, drowsy
loden, lead(en): to plumb
loeder, swine, bitch
loef, luff
  de loef afsteken, to gain the weather-gage (of); to get the better of
loeien, to low; to roar
loens, cross-eyed
loensen, to squint
loep, magnifying glass
loer: op de — liggen, to lie in wait
  iemand een loer draaien, to play a dirty trick on a person

loeren, to peer; to spy
loeven, to luff
lof, praise: *n*, Benediction
lofdicht *n*, panegyric
loffelijk, laudable
lofrede, eulogy
log, unwieldy: log
loge, lodge; (theatre) box
lo'gé(e), guest
lo'geerkamer, spare-room
loge'ment *n*, inn
logenstraffen, to give the lie to
lo'geren, to stay
logger, drifter, lugger
logica, logic
lo'gies *n*, accommodation
  logies met ontbijt, bed and breakfast
logisch, logical
lok, lock (of hair)
lo'kaal *n*, room
lo'kaaltrein, local train
lokaas *n*, bait
lokduif, stool-pigeon
lo'ket *n*, counter, booking-office
lokken, to (al)lure
lokmiddel *n*, lure, bait
lokvogel, decoy
lol, lark, fun
lollig, funny
lommer *n*, shade; foliage
lommerd, pawn-broker's shop
lommerrijk, shady
lomp, boorish, clumsy
lompen, rags
lomperd, lout
lonen, to (re)pay
long, lung
longontsteking, pneumonia
lonk(en), (to) ogle
lont, fuse
  lont ruiken, to smell a rat
loochenen, to deny
lood *n*, lead
  lood om oud ijzer, six of one and half a dozen of the other
  uit het lood geslagen, bewildered
  het loodje leggen, to get the worst of it
loodgieter, plumber
loodlijn, perpendicular (line)

lood'recht, perpendicular, vertical
loods, shed: pilot
loodsen, to pilot
loodswezen *n*, pilotage
loodwit *n*, white-lead
loof *n*, foliage
loog, lye
looien, to tan
looistof, tannin
loom, languid
loon *n*, wages
loop, gait; course; (gun-)barrel
  op de loop gaan, to take to one's heels
loopbaan, career
loopgraaf, trench
loopjongen, errand-boy
looppas: in de —, at the double
loopplank, gangway
loops, on heat
loopvlak *n*, (tire-)tread
loor: te — gaan, to be lost
loos, cunning; false
loot, shoot, cutting
lopen, to walk, to go, to run
lopend, running; current
loper, runner; roundsman; skeleton-key
lor, rag; straw; dud
lor'gnet *n*, pince-nez
lorrenboel, trash
los, loose, detachable: lynx
  er op los, recklessly
  losse arbeider, casual labourer
los'bandig, dissolute
losbarsten, to burst out
losbinden, to untie
los'bladig, loose-leaf
losbol, rake
losgeld *n*, ransom
losjes, loosely
loskopen, to ransom
loslaten, to let go
los'lippig, indiscreet
loslopen, to run free
  het zal wel loslopen, it won't be all that bad
losplaats, discharging-berth
losprijs, ransom
lossen, to discharge, to unload
losstormen op, to rush upon
loszinnig, frivolous

lot *n*, fate; lottery-ticket
loten, to draw lots
lote'rij, lottery
lotgenoot, partner in adversity
lotgevallen, adventures
loupe, magnifying-glass
louter, pure, sheer
louteren, to purify
loven, to praise
  loven en bieden, to haggle
lover *n*, foliage
lozen, to get rid of; to drain
lucht, air; sky; smell
  lucht geven aan, to vent
luchtaanval, air-raid
luchtafweer, anti-aircraft defence
luchtalarm *n*, air-raid alarm
luchtband, pneumatic tire
luchtdruk, atmospheric pressure
luchten, to air, to vent(ilate)
  ik kan hem niet luchten, I can't abide him
luchter, candelabrum, chandelier
lucht'hartig, light-hearted
luchthaven, air-port
luchtig, airy
luchtkasteel *n*, castle in the air
luchtkoker, ventilating-shaft
lucht'ledig *n*, vacuum
luchtmacht, air-force
luchtpijp, windpipe
luchtpost, airmail
luchtstreek, zone, climate
luchtvaart, aviation
luchtverversing, ventilation
lucifer, match
lu'guber, lugubrious
lui, people: lazy
luiaard, sloth
luid, loud
luiden, to ring
  de brief luidt als volgt, the letter reads as follows
luidkeels, at the top of one's voice
luid'ruchtig, noisy
luidspreker, loud-speaker
luier, nappie
luieren, to laze
luiermand, layette; baby basket
luifel, penthouse, canopy
luiheid, laziness

luik *n*, hatch; trap-door; shutter
luilak, lazy-bones
luilakken, to (be) idle
luim, mood, whim, humour
luipaard, leopard
luis, louse
luister, splendour
luisteraar(ster), listener
luisteren, to listen
luisterrijk, splendid, glorious
luistervink, eavesdropper·
luit, lute
luitenant, lieutenant
luiwagen, scrubbing broom
luiwammes, lazy-bones
lukken, to succeed
  het lukt me nooit, I shall never manage it
lukraak, haphazard
lumi'neus, luminous
  een lumineus idee, a brain-wave
lummel, lout
lummelen, to loiter
lunapark *n*, amusement park
lurven: bij de — pakken, to take by the scruff of the neck
lus, loop, noose
lust, inclination, liking
  een lust voor het oog, a sight for sore eyes
lusteloos, listless
lusten, to like, to fancy
lusthof, pleasure garden
lustig, lusty
lustprieel *n*, bower
luttel, little
luwen, to abate, to flag
luxe, luxury
luxu'eus, luxurious
ly'riek, lyric poetry
lyrisch, lyrical

M

maag, stomach: kinsman
maagd, virgin, maid(en)
maagdelijk(heid), virgin(ity)
maagpijn, stomach-ache
maagsap *n*, gastric juice
maagzuur *n*, gastric acid; heart-burn
maagzweer, gastric ulcer

maaien, to mow
maaksel *n*, make, manufacture
maakwerk *n*, hackwork
maal *n*, time: meal
  tienmaal, ten times
maalstroom, whirlpool
maaltijd, meal
maan, moon
  loop naar de maan, go to blazes
maand, month
maandag, Monday
maandblad *n*, monthly periodical
maandelijks, monthly
maandenlang, for months- on end
maandgeld *n*, monthly allowance
maandverband *n*, sanitary towel
maangestalte, phase of the moon
maanjaar *n*, lunar year
maansverduistering, eclipse of the moon
maanziek, moonstruck
maar, but: only; just
maarschalk, marshal
maarschalksstaf, marshal's baton
maart, March
maas, mesh; loop-hole
maasbal, darning ball
maat, measure, size; time, bar: mate, partner
  blinde maat, dummy (at bridge)
maatgevoel *n*, sense of rhythm
maatje *n*, decilitre: pal
maatregel, measure
maat'schappelijk, social
maatschap'pij, society; company
maatstaf, criterion
maatwerk *n*, clothing made to measure
machi'naal, mechanical
ma'chine, engine, machine
ma'chinefabriek, engineering works
ma'chinegeweer *n*, machine-gun
machine'rieën, machinery
ma'chineschrijven *n*, type-writing
machi'nist, ship's engineer; engine-driver

macht, power, might
macht der ge'woonte, force of habit
niet bij machte, unable
machteloos, powerless
machtig, mighty, terrific; rich (food)
een taal machtig zijn, to have command of a language
machtigen, to authorize
machtiging, authorization
machtspositie, position of authority
machtsverheffing, involution
made, maggot, cheese-mite
made'liefje *n*, daisy
maffen, to snooze
maga'zijn *n*, store(s); magazine
maga'zijnmeester, store-keeper
mager, thin, lean, meagre
ma'gie, magic
magiër, magician
magisch, magic(al)
magi'straal, imposing
magi'straat, magistrate
mag'naat, magnate
mag'neet, magnet; magneto
mag'netisch, magnetic
— **magneti'seren,** to magnetize; to mesmerize
magni'fiek, magnificent
ma'honiehout(en) (*n*), mahogany
mailboot, mail-boat
mailzak, mail-bag
maïs, maize
maïskolf, cob of corn
maï'zena, cornflour
majesteit, majesty
majesteitsschennis, *lèse-majesté*
majestu'eus, majestic
majeur, major (key)
ma'joor, major
mak, tame, gentle
makelaar, broker
maken, to make; to mend
dat heeft er niets mee te maken, that has nothing to do with it
hoe maakt U het? how do you do?
makkelijk, easy
makker, comrade

ma'kreel, mackerel
mal, mould, template; stencil: foolish
ma'laise, trade depression
Ma'leier, Malay
melen, to grind
maliënkolder, coat of mail
maling hebben aan, to care not a rap for
in de maling nemen, to make a fool of
malle'jan, lumber wagon
malle'molen, roundabout
mallepraat, silly nonsense
mal'loot, silly creature
mals, tender; lush; gentle (rain)
man, man; husband
aan de man brengen, to sell
op de man af, point blank
manche, game (at cards)
man'chet(knopen), cuff (-links)
mand, basket
door de mand vallen, to make a clean breast of it
man'daat *n*, mandate
manda'rijn, mandarin; tangerine
ma'nege, riding-school
manen, mane: to dun; to exhort
maneschijn, moonlight
man'gaan *n*, manganese
mangat *n*, man-hole
mangel, wringer: *n*, lack
mangelen, to mangle
man'haftig, manly
ma'nie, mania
ma'nier, manner, way
mani'fest *n*, manifesto, manifest
manifes'tatie, manifestation, demonstration
manipu'leren, to manipulate
mank, lame, crippled
manke'ment *n*, defect
man'keren, to be lacking or absent; to fail
wat mankeert je? what's come over you?
man'moedig, manful
man(ne)lijk, male, masculine, manly
mannengek, man-mad woman
mannetje *n*, little man; male (animal)

mannetjesputter, he-man
manoeu'vreren, to manœuvre
mans: niet veel —, not very
  strong
manschappen, ratings, men
manslag, manslaughter
manspersoon, male (person)
mantel, coat, cloak
  iemand de mantel uitvegen,
  to haul someone over the
  coals
mantelpak n, costume
manu'aal n, gesture; manual
manufac'turen, piece-goods
manufactu'rier, draper
manusje n van alles, odd job
  man
manwijf n, virago
manziek, man-mad
map, folder, file
ma'quette, model
marchan'deren, to bargain
mar'cheren, to march
marco'nist, wireless operator
mare, tidings
marechaus'see, military con-
  stabulary
maretak, mistletoe
marge, margin
ma'rine, navy
ma'rineluchtmacht, fleet air
  arm
mari'neren, to pickle, to souse
mari'nier, marine
mar'kant, striking
mar'keren, to mark
mar'kies, marquis: sun-blind
marke'zin, marchioness
markt(plein n), market(-place)
marktkraam, stall
marmer n, marble
mar'mot, marmot; guinea-pig
mars, march: pedlar's pack;
  (fighting) top
  hij heeft heel wat in zijn mars,
  he knows a great deal
marse'pein n, marzipan
marskramer, pedlar
marsoefening, route-march
marssteng, topmast
mars'vaardig, ready to march
marszeil n, topsail
martelaar, martela'res, martyr

martelaarschap n, martyrdom
martelen, to torture, to torment
marteling, torture
marter, marten
masker n, mask
mas'keren, to camouflage
massa, mass, crowd
mas'saal, massive
mas'seren, to massage
mas'sief, solid
mast, mast
mastbos n, fir-wood; forest of
  masts
mat, weary; matt; dim: checkmate: mat
mateloos, boundless
materi'aal n, material(s)
ma'terie, matter
materi'eel, material; plant
  rollend materieel n, rolling
  stock
matglas n, frosted glass
mathe'maticus, mathematician
matig, moderate; abstemious
matigen, to moderate
matigheid, moderation; frugal-
  ity; temperance
mati'neus, up early
matje n, (table-)mat
  op het matje roepen, to carpet
ma'tras, mattress
ma'trijs, matrix
ma'troos, sailor
mattenklopper, carpet-beater
mazelen, measles
mazen, to darn
mecani'cien, mechanic
me'chanica, mechanics
mecha'niek n, mechanism
me'chanisch, mechanical
me'daille, medal
medaill'on n, medallion; locket
mede, with, also: fellow-
mede'deelzaam, communicative
mededelen, to inform
mededeling, communication; information
mededingen, to compete
mededinger, rival
mededogen n, compassion
mede'klinker, consonant
me(d)eleven, to sympathize
me(d)elij(den) n, pity

mede'plichtig, accessary
me(d)evoelen met, to feel for
me(d)ewerken, to co-operate
medewerker, contributor, collaborator
medewerking, active support
medeweten *n*, knowledge
medezeggenschap *n*, say (in the matter)
medi'cijn(en), medicine
medicus, doctor; medical student
medisch, medical
mee, with
meebrengen: met zich —, to bring with one; to entail
meedoen, to take part
mee'dogenloos, merciless
meegaan, to go, to come (along)
mee'gaand, accommodating
meekomen, to come (along); to keep pace
meekrap, madder
meel *n*, meal, flour
meeloper, fellow-traveller
meemaken, to experience
meenemen, to take (along)
meent, common
meepraten, to join in the conversation
meer, more: *n*, lake
meerdere, superior; several
meerderheid, majority
meerder'jarig, of age
meerekenen, to include
meerijden, to drive with, to be given a lift
meermalen, more than once
meermin, mermaid
meervoud *n*, plural
mees, titmouse
meeslepen, to drag along; to carry away
meesmuilen, to smirk
meest(al), most(ly)
meester, master
meeste'res, mistress
meester'knecht, foreman
meesterschap *n*, mastery, command
meesterstuk *n*, masterpiece
meet: van — af aan, from the start
meetkunde, geometry

meet'kundige reeks, geometrical progression
meetronen, to inveigle
meeuw, gull
meevallen, to be better than one expected
dat valt niet mee, that is not easy
meevaller, bit of luck
mee'warig, compassionate
mei, May
meiboom, may-pole
meid, maid(-servant), girl
meidoorn, hawthorn
meineed, perjury
meisje *n*, girl, girl-friend
meisjesachtig, girlish
meisjesgek, philanderer
meisjesnaam, maiden name; girl's name
me'juffrouw, Madam, Miss
mekk(er)en, to bleat
me'laats, leprous
me'laatse, leper
me'laatsheid, leprosy
me'lange, blend
me'lasse, molasses
melden, to report; to announce
meldens'waard(ig), worth mentioning
melding maken van, to mention
mê'leren, to blend
melig, mealy; floury
melk, milk
melkboer, milkman
melken, to milk
melke'rij, dairy-farm
melkinrichting, dairy (shop)
melkkan, milk-jug
melkweg, Milky Way
me'loen, melon
me'morie, memory; memorandum
men, one, people, they, you
me'neer, Sir; (gentle)man
menen, to think, to mean; to fancy
't wordt menens, it's getting serious
mengelmoes *n*, jumble
mengelwerk *n*, miscellany
mengen, to mix, to mingle, to blend
zich mengen in, to meddle with

mengsel *n*, mixture, blend
menie, red-lead
menig, many a
menigeen, many a person
menigmaal, many a time
menigte, crowd
menig'vuldig, manifold
mening, opinion
mennen, to drive (a carriage)
mens, man; human being
  het is een goed mens *n*, she is
  a good soul
mensdom *n*, mankind
menselijk, human
menselijkerwijs gesproken,
  humanly speaking
menselijkheid, humanity
menseneter, cannibal
mensenhater, misanthrope
mensenkenner, judge of character
mensenleeftijd, lifetime
mensheid, mankind
mens'lievend, humane
mens'waardig, worthy of a
  human being
menswording, incarnation
mep(pen), (to) smack
meren, to moor
merendeel *n*, greater part
merendeels, mostly
merg *n*, marrow; pith
mergpijp, marrow-bone
merk *n*, mark, brand
merkbaar, noticeable
merrie, mare
mes *n*, knife
messenlegger, knife-rest
Mes'sias, Messiah
messing *n*, brass
mest, dung, manure
mesten, to fatten; to manure
mesthoop, mestvaalt, dunghill
met, with
  met dat al, for all that
  met Pasen, at Easter
me'taal *n*, metal
me'taalzaag, hacksaw
meta'foor, metaphor
met'een, straight away; presently
meten, to measure
meter, metre; meter

metgezel('lin), companion
me'thodisch, methodical
me'triek, metric: prosody
metrum *n*, metre
metselaar, bricklayer
metselen, to build (using mortar)
metselkalk, mortar
metselwerk *n*, masonry
metten: korte — maken met,
  to make short work of
metter'daad, in fact
metter'tijd, in due course
meubel *n*, piece of furniture
  een raar meubel, a queer
  body
meubelen, to furnish: furniture
meubelmaker, cabinet-maker
meubi'lair *n*, furniture
meubi'leren, to furnish
me'vrouw, Mrs; Madam; lady
middag, midday; afternoon
middageten *n*, middagmaal *n*,
  midday meal
middel(s) *n*, waist(s)
middel(en) *n*, means, remedy
  (-ies)
middelaar, mediator
middelbaar, average, medium
  middelbaar onderwijs *n*, secondary education
middeleeuwen, Middle Ages
middeleeuws, mediæval
Middellandse Zee, Mediterranean
middellijn, diameter
middel'matig, mediocre, average
middelmoot, middle cut
middelpunt *n*, centre, pivot
middelpunt'vliedend, centrifu-
  gal
middelste, middlemost, centre
midden *n*, middle, midst
midden'door delen, to bisect
midden'in, in the middle (of)
middenrif *n*, diaphragm
middenstand, middle-classes
middenweg, (happy) mean
midder'nacht, midnight
mid'scheeps, amidships
mier, ant
mierenhoop, ant-hill
miezerig, drizzly; puny
mijden, to shun

mijl, mile; kilometre
mijlpaal, milestone.
mijmeren, to muse
mijn, my; mine: pit
mijnbouw(kunde), mining
mijnenveger, mine-sweeper
mijnentwille: om —, for my sake
mijnerzijds, on my part
mijngas n, fire-damp
mijn'heer, Sir; Mr; (gentle-) man
mijnwerker, miner
mijnwezen n, mining
mijt, mite
mijter, mitre
mikken (op), to aim (at)
mikpunt n, aim, target, butt
mild, liberal; mild
mild'dadig, generous
mili'cien, conscript
mili'tair, soldier; military
mi'litie, militia
mil'joen n, million
mille, (one) thousand (guilders)
millimeteren, to crop (hair) close
milt, spleen
miltvuur n, anthrax
mi'mitafeltjes, nest of tables
min, wet nurse: love: less; mean, bad
minachten, to regard with disdain
minachting, contempt
minder, less(er), fewer
minderen, inferiors: to decrease
minderheid, minority
minder'jarig, under age
minder'waardig, inferior
minder'waardigheidscomplex n, inferiority complex
mineur, minor (key)
mi'niem, minute
mini'maal, minimum
mi'nister, minister, secretary (of State)
Minister President, Prime Minister
mini'sterie n, ministry, Office
minnaar, lover
minna'res, mistress

minne, love
in der minne schikken, to settle amicably
minnekozen, to bill and coo
minnelijke schikking, amicable arrangement
minnen, to love
minnetjes, poorly
minst, least
minstens, at least
minuti'eus, meticulous
mi'nuut, minute
minver'mogend, poor
minzaam, affable
mirre, myrrh
mirt(eboom), myrtle(-tree)
mis, wrong: Mass
het is mis, it is no good
niet mis, pretty good
mis'baar n, clamour
misbaksel n, monstrosity
misbruik n, abuse
misbruik maken van, to abuse
mis'bruiken, to abuse, to misuse
misdaad, crime
mis'dadig, criminal
misdadiger, criminal
mis'deeld, poor; handicapped
misdienaar, server
mis'doen, to do wrong
mis'dragen: zich —, to misbehave
misdrijf n, offence
misgreep, blunder
mis'gunnen, to begrudge
mis'handelen, to maltreat
miskelk, chalice
mis'kennen, to fail to appreciate
miskraam, miscarriage
mis'leiden, to mislead
mislopen, to go wrong
mis'lukken, to miscarry
mis'lukking, failure
mis'maakt, deformed
mis'moedig, disheartened
mis'noegen n, displeasure
mispel, medlar
mis'plaatst, misplaced, out of place
mis'prijzen, to disapprove of
mispunt n, beast, bounder
mis'rekening, miscalculation
mis'schien, perhaps

misselijk, sick; disgusting
missen, to miss; to lack
missie, mission
missio'naris, (R.C.) missionary
mis'staan, to be unbecoming
misstand, abuse
misstap, false step, slip
mist, fog
misten, to be foggy
mis'troostig, disconsolate
misvatting, misunderstanding
misverstaan, to misunderstand
misverstand *n*, misunderstanding
mis'vormd, misshapen
mi'taine, mitt(en)
mitrail'leur, machine-gun
mits, provided (that)
mits'dien, consequently
modder(ig), mud(dy)
modderpoel, quagmire
mode, fashion
mo'del *n*, model, pattern
modemagazijn *n*, fashion-house, gentlemen's outfitters
modeshow, fashion-parade
modi'eus, fashionable
mo'diste, milliner
moe(de), tired
moed, courage
moedeloos, dejected
moeder, mother; dam; matron
moederliefde, motherly love
moederlijk, motherly
moederloos, motherless
moedermoord, matricide
moedernaakt, stark naked
moeder-'overste, mother superior
moederschap *n*, motherhood
moederschapsuitkering, maternity benefit
moederschip *n*, depot ship
moedertaal, mother tongue
moedervlek, birth-mark, mole
moederziel alleen, quite alone
moedig, courageous
moedwil, wantonness
moed'willig, wilful
moeheid, fatigue
moeien: de politie in een zaak —, to call in the police
er is een week mee ge'moeid, it will take a week

moeilijk, difficult, with difficulty
moeilijkheid, difficulty
moeite, trouble; difficulty
de moeite waard, worth while
moeizaam, laborious
moer, nut: dam
moe'ras *n*, marsh
moe'rassig, marshy
moerbei, mulberry
moeren, to pinch, to steal; to tamper with
moes *n*, mash, pulp
moesgroente, greens
moesson, monsoon
moestuin, kitchen-garden
moet, stain; mark
moeten, must, to have to
wat moet dat ? what's going on (there) ?
je moest je schamen, you ought to be ashamed of yourself
moezen, to mash, to pulp
mof, muff: Hun
moffelen, to enamel: to smuggle away
mogelijk, possible
mogelijker'wijs, possibly
mogelijkheid, possibility
mogen, to be allowed, may; to like
mogendheid, power
moker, sledge-hammer
mokka, mocha
mokkelen, to cuddle
mokken, to sulk
mol, mole: flat, minor (key)
molen, mill
molenaar, miller
molenbeek, mill-race
molenwiek, sail of a windmill
mo'lestverzekering, war-damage insurance
mollen, to do (a person) in
mollevel *n*, moleskin
mollig, chubby
molm, mould
molshoop, mole-hill
molton *n*, swan-skin
mom *n*, mask, cloak
mombakkes *n*, carnival mask
momen'teel, momentary; at present
mo'mentopname, instantaneous photograph

mompelen, to mutter
mond, mouth; muzzle
  met de mond vol tanden, tongue-tied
  iemand naar de mond praten, to play up to a person
mon'dain, fashionable
mondeling, oral
mond-en-'klauwzeer *n,* foot-and-mouth disease
mondig, of age
mondje dicht! mum's the word!
  zij is niet op haar mondje ge'vallen, she has a ready tongue
mondjes'maat, bare minimum
mondkost, provisions
mondspoeling, mouth-wash
mondvoorraad, provisions
monnik, monk
monnikenwerk *n,* labour to no purpose
monnikenwezen *n,* monasticism
monnikskap, cowl
monnikspij, monk's habit
mono'toon, monotonous
monster *n,* monster: (free) sample
monsterachtig, monstrous
monsteren, to muster; to sign on
monstru'eus, monstrous
monstrum *n,* **monstruosi'teit,** monstrosity
mon'tage, assembly, mounting
monter, lively
mon'teren, to assemble, to set (up)
mon'teur, fitter, mechanic
mon'tuur *n,* (spectacle-)frame, mount, setting
mooi, beautiful, fine
mooidoene'rij, airs and graces
moord, murder
moordaanslag, murderous attempt
moord'dadig, murderous
moordenaar, murderer
moordpartij, massacre
Moors, Moorish
moot, fillet (of fish)
mop, joke
  moppen tappen, to crack jokes
mopje *n,* popular tune

mop(s)neus, snub-nose
mopperen, to grumble
mopshond, pug-dog
mo'raal, moral(s)
morali'seren, to moralize
mo'reel, moral: *n,* morale
mores, manners, customs
morgen, morning; tomorrow
  's morgens, in the morning, every morning
morgenland *n,* Orient
morgen'ochtend, tomorrow morning
morgenstond, early morning
mormel *n,* freak
mor'fine, morphia
morrelen, to fumble
morren, to grumble
morsdood, stone-dead
morsen, to spill, to make a mess
mor'tier, mortar
mos *n,* moss
mos'kee, mosque
Moskou, Moscow
mos'kovisch gebak *n,* sponge-cake
mossel, mussel
most, must, new wine
mosterd, mustard
  (als) mosterd na de maaltijd, a bit late in the day
mot, moth: bust-up
motie, motion, vote
mo'tief *n,* motive; motif
moti'veren, to justify, to defend
motor, motor, engine
motorordonnance, despatch rider
motorpech, engine trouble
motregen(en), (to) drizzle
mousse'line, muslin
mous'seren, to effervesce
mout, malt
mouw, sleeve
  ergens een mouw aanpassen, to manage somehow
  ze achter de mouw hebben, to be a sly-boots
  iemand iets op de mouw spelden, to fool a person
mouwschort *n,* overall
moza'iek *n,* mosaic
mud, hectolitre

muf, musty
mug, gnat
muggenzifte'rij, hair-splitting
muil, muzzle: slipper
muilband(en), (to) muzzle
muildier, muilezel, mule
muilkorf, muzzle
muis, mouse; ball of the thumb
muisjes, sugared caraway seeds
  dit muisje zal een staartje
  hebben, we've not heard the
  last of this
muiteling, mutineer
muiten, to mutiny
muite'rij, mutiny
muitziek, mutinous
muizenissen, nagging thoughts
muizeval, mouse-trap
mul, loose, sandy
multiplex n, plywood
mummelen, to mumble
mummie, mummy
mu'nitie, ammunition, munitions
munt, coin(age); currency; mint
  kruis of munt, heads or tails
munteenheid, monetary unit
munten, to mint
  dat was op mij gemunt, that
  (remark) was aimed at me
muntkunde, numismatics
muntmeter, slot-meter
muntstuk n, coin
muntwezen n, coinage
murmelen, to babble
murmu'reren, to grumble
murw, soft, tender; at a low ebb
mus, sparrow
muscus, muskus, musk
musi'ceren, to make music
musicus, musician
mus'kaat(noot), nutmeg
mus'kaatwijn, muscatel
muska'del, muscadine
mus'kiet, mosquito
muskusrat, musquash
muts, cap, bonnet
muur, wall
muuranker, wall-tie
muurschildering, mural
muurvast, firm as a rock
muze, muse
mu'ziek, music
mu'ziekkorps n, band

mu'ziektent, band-stand
muzi'kaal, musical
muzi'kant,   street-musician;
  bandsman
mys'terie n, mystery
mysteri'eus, mysterious
mys'tiek, mystic(ism)
mythe, myth

N

na, after; close
  op één na, all but one
naad, seam, suture
  het naadje van de kous willen
  weten, to want to know every
  detail
naaf, hub
naaidoos, work-box
naaien, to sew
naaister, needle-woman
naaiwerk n, sewing, needlework
naakt, naked, nude
naaktloper, nudist
naald, needle
naaldbos n, pine-wood
naaldenkoker, needle-case
naam, name
naambord n, name-plate
naamgenoot, namesake
naamloze   vennootschap,
  limited company
naamval(suitgang),   case(-end-
  ing)
naäpen, to ape
naäpe'rij,   (slavish)   imitation,
  parody
naar, to;   according   to: unpleasant, nasty
  naar men zegt, according to
  reports
  hij is er naar aan toe, he is in a
  bad way
naar'geestig, gloomy
naarling, nasty specimen
naar'mate, (according) as
naarstig, diligent
naast, next to; nearest
  ten naaste bij, approximately
naast'bijzijnd, nearest
naaste, fellow-man
naasten, to expropriate
naastenliefde,   love   of   one's
  fellow-man

nabestaanden, relatives
nabestellen, to put in a further order
na'bij, near at hand
na'bijgelegen, neighbouring
na'bijheid, neighbourhood; nearness
nablijven, to stay behind
nabootsen, to imitate
nabootsing, imitation
na'burig, neighbouring
nacht, night
  bij nacht en ontij, at all hours of the day and night
nachtbraken, to revel all night
nachtegaal, nightingale
nachtelijk, nocturnal
nachtevening, equinox
nachtgoed *n,* nightwear
nachtkaars, night-light
nachtkastje *n,* bedside cupboard
nachtlogies *n,* a bed for the night
nachtmerrie, nightmare
nachtploeg, night-shift
nachtpon, nightdress
nachtspiegel, chamber(-pot)
nachtuil, screech-owl
nachtverblijf *n,* lodging for the night
nadat, after
nadeel *n,* disadvantage, detriment
na'delig, disadvantageous, detrimental
nadenken, to reflect
na'denkend, thoughtful
nader, nearer; further
  bij nader inzien, on second thoughts
nader'bij, nearer
  van naderbij, more closely
naderen, to approach
nader'hand, afterwards
na'dien, since (then)
nadoen, to imitate
nadruk, emphasis; reprint
na'drukkelijk, emphatic
nagaan, to examine, to trace
nagalmen, to reverberate
nagedachtenis, memory
nagel(en), (to) nail: clove(s)
nagellak, nail-varnish
nagelriem, cuticle

nagemaakt, imitation, spurious
nagenoeg, almost
nagerecht *n,* dessert
nageslacht *n,* posterity
nageven: dat moet ik hem —, I'll say that for him
nahouden: er op —, to maintain
na'ïef, naïve
naijver, jealousy
najaar *n,* autumn
najagen, to pursue
naken, to approach
nakijken, to gaze after; to check
na'komeling, descendant
na'komelingschap, offspring
nakomen, to carry out
nalaten, to leave (behind); to omit
  ik kon niet nalaten u te vertellen, I could not help telling you
na'latenschap, inheritance
na'latig, negligent, remiss
na'latigheid, negligence
naleven, to observe, to live up to
nalezen, to read over *or* again
nalopen, to run after; to be slow
namaak, imitation
namaken, to imitate, to forge
namelijk, namely, i.e.; because
nameloos, unutterable
namens, on behalf of
namiddag, afternoon
nanacht, the early hours
na-oorlogs, post-war
nap, bowl
napluizen, to examine in detail
napraten, to parrot; to stay behind talking
napret, fun after the event
nar, jester
nar'cis, daffodil
nar'cose, narcosis
nar'coticum *n,* narcotic
narcoti'seur, anæsthetist
narekenen, to check
narigheid, unpleasantness
narijden, to ride *or* drive after; to drive
narrig, peevish
na'saal, nasal
naschrift *n,* postscript
naslaan, to look up

nasleep, aftermath
nasmaak, after-taste
naspel *n*, (organ) voluntary; sequel
nasporing, investigation
nastaren, to (turn round and) stare
nastreven, to strive after
nat, wet
natafelen, to linger at the dinner table
natellen, to check
natie, nation
nationali'seren, to nationalize
nattigheid, moisture
 nattigheid voelen, to smell a rat
na'tura: in —, in kind
natu'rel, natural
na'tuur, nature; scenery
 van nature, by nature
na'tuurgetrouw, true to nature
na'tuurkunde, physics
natuur'kundige, physicist
na'tuurlijk, natural, of course
na'tuurschoon *n*, beautiful scenery
na'tuurverschijnsel *n*, natural phenomenon
na'tuurvolk *n*, primitive race
nauw, narrow, tight, close: *n*, straights
 hij neemt het niet te nauw, he is not very particular
nauwelijks, scarcely
nauwge'zet, conscientious
nauw'keurig, accurate
nauw'sluitend, close-fitting
nauwte, defile; straights
navel, navel
navelstreng, umbilical cord
navertellen, to repeat
naver'want, closely related
navolgen, to follow, to imitate
navorsen, to investigate
navraag, enquiries
naweeën, after affects
nawerken, to make its effect felt
nawerking, after-effect
nazaat, descendant
nazien, to check
nazitten, to pursue
nazomer, late summer

neder, down
Nederduits *n*, Low German
nederig, humble
nederlaag, defeat
Nederlander, Dutchman
Nederlands(e) (*n*), Dutch (woman)
nederzetting, settlement
neef, cousin, nephew
nee(n), no
neer, down
neer'buigend, condescending
neerhalen, to haul down; to run down
neerkomen, to come down
 het komt hierop neer, it boils down to this
neerleggen, to put down; to resign
neerslaan, to strike down; to precipitate
 de ogen neerslaan, to cast down one's eyes
neer'slachtig, dejected
neerslag, precipitation, sediment
neet, nit
negen, nine
negende, ninth
negenoog, carbuncle
negentien(de), nineteen(th)
negentig, ninety
neger, negro
negeren, to bully
ne'geren, to ignore
nege'rin, negress
nego'rij, hole, back of beyond
neigen, to incline
neiging, inclination, tendency
nek, (nape of the) neck
 met de nek aankijken, to cold-shoulder
nekken, to break, to ruin
nekvel *n*, scruff of the neck
nemen, to take
 we zullen het er eens van nemen, let's enjoy ourselves
nerf, grain, vein
nergens, nowhere
 ik weet nergens van, I know nothing about it
nering, trade, custom
ner'veus, nervous
nest *n*, nest; minx

nestelen, to nest
　zich nestelen, to ensconce one-
　　self; to nestle
net (*n*), net (work); system: tidy
　neat, decent; just
　achter het net vissen, to miss
　　the boat
　in het net schrijven, to make a
　　fair copy
netel, nettle
neteldoek *n,* muslin
netelroos, nettle-rash
netjes, tidily, neat, nice, decent
nettenboet(st)er, net-mender
netto, nett
netvlies *n,* retina
neuriën, to hum
neu'rose, neurosis
neus, nose, nozzle
　het is maar een wassen neus,
　　there is nothing to it
　met de neus in de boter
　　vallen, to come at the right
　　moment
neusgat *n,* nostril
neusholte, nasal cavity
neushoorn, rhinoceros
neusje van de zalm *n,* acme of
　perfection
neusvleugel, nostril
neuswijs, cocky
neu'traal, neutral
neuzen in, to pry into
nevel, mist, haze
nevelachtig, misty, hazy
nevelvlek, nebula
nicht, cousin, niece
niemand, nobody
nieman'dal, nothing at all
nier, kidney
niet, not
niet(en), (to) staple
nietig, null and void;- diminu-
　tive; trivial
nietigheid, futility
nietigverklaring, nullification
niets, nothing
nietsbe'duidend, **nietsbe'te-**
　kenend, insignificant
nietsnut, good-for-nothing
niets'zeggend, meaningless
niettegen'staande, notwith-
　standing

niette'min, nevertheless
nieuw, new
nieuw'bakken, new-fangled
nieuweling, novice
nieuwer'wets, new-fangled
nieuwigheid, novelty
nieuw'lichter, modernist
nieuws *n,* news
nieuwsblad *n,* newspaper
nieuws'gierig(heid), inquisitive-
　(ness)
nieuwtje *n,* piece of news
niezen, to sneeze
nihil, nil
nijd, envy
nijdas, cross-patch
nijdig, angry
nijgen, to curtsey, to bow
nijlpaard *n,* hippopotamus
nijpen, to nip
　het begint te nijpen, (we)
　　are beginning to feel the
　　pinch
nijptang, (pair of) pincers
nijver, industrious
nijverheid, industry
nikkel *n,* nickel
nikker, nigger
niks, nothing
nimf, nymph
nimmer, never
nippertje: op het —, in the nick
　of time
nis, niche, alcove
ni'veau *n,* level
nivel'leren, to level
n.l., i.e.; you see
nobel, noble-minded
noch . . . noch, neither . . . nor
nochtans, nevertheless
node, reluctantly
nodeloos, needless
nodig, necessary
　nodig hebben, to need
nodigen, to invite
noemen, to name, to call; to
　mention
noemens'waard(ig), worth men-
　tioning
noemer, denominator
noenmaal *n,* luncheon
noest, diligent
nog, still, yet

vandaag nog, this very day
nog vele jaren! many happy
  returns!
noga, nougat
nogal, rather, fairly
nogmaals, once again
nok, ridge of the roof
no'made, nomad
non, nun
nonac'tief, half-pay
nonnenklooster *n*, convent
nonsens, nonsense
nood, need, emergency; distress
noodanker *n*, sheet-anchor
noodbrug, temporary bridge
nooddruft, destitution
noodgedwongen, perforce
noodgeval *n*, emergency
noodlanding, forced landing
nood'lijdend, destitute
noodlot *n*, fate
nood'lottig, fatal
noodmast, jury-mast
noodrem, safety-brake; communication cord
noodtoestand, state of emergency; untenable situation
noodweer *n*, deluge
noodgebouw *n*, temporary building
noodzaak, necessity
nood'zakelijk, necessary
noodzaken, to oblige
nooit, never
Noor, Norwegian
noord, north
noordelijk, northern, northerly
noorden *n*, North
noorder'breedte, North latitude
noorderlicht *n*, northern lights
**noorderzon: met de — ver-
  trekken,** to cut and run
noordpool, north pole
noordpool'cirkel, arctic circle
noordwaarts, northward(s)
Noors (*n*), Norwegian
Noorwegen *n*, Norway
noot, note: nut
  hele, halve noot, kwartnoot
  etc., breve, minim, crotchet *etc.*
  **hij heeft veel noten op zijn
  zang,** he is hard to please
nootmus'kaat, nutmeg

nop(pen), (to) nap
  in zijn nopjes, greatly pleased
nopen, to induce
nopens, concerning
nor, clink, quod
nor'maal, normal
nor'maalschool, teacher training
  college
nor'maliter, normally
nors, gruff
nota, note; bill, account
no'tabelen, leading citizens
no'taris, notary
noteboom, (wal)nut-tree
notedop, nut-shell
notehout *n*, walnut
notekraker, nut-crackers
notenbalken, staves
no'teren, to note (down)
notie, notion
no'titie, note; notice
notulen, minutes
nou, now: you bet!
nouveau'tés, novelties, fancy
  goods
no'velle, short story
no'viet, freshman
novum *n*, novelty
nu, now (that)
  van nu af aan, from now on
nuchter, sober, level-headed
  op de nuchtere maag, on an
  empty stomach
nuf, stand-offish little miss
nukkig, wayward
nul, nought, nil, zero; nonentity
  nul op het re'kwest krijgen, to
  meet with a refusal
nulpunt *n*, zero
nummer *n*, number; issue
  **iemand op zijn nummer zet-
  ten,** to put a person in his place
nummeren, to number
nurks, grumpy
nut *n*, use, benefit
nutteloos, useless
nuttig, useful
nuttigen, to partake of
N.V., Ltd. (Company)

O

o.a., *inter alia*; including
o'ase, oasis

o-benen, bandy legs
ober(kelner), (head-)waiter
ob'ject n, object(ive)
obli'gaat n, obligato
obli'gatie, bond
obliga'toir, obligatory
ob'sceen, obscene
obser'vator, observer
oce'aan, ocean
och, ah!, oh
ochtend, morning
's ochtends, in the morning(s)
ochtendgloren n, day-break
oc'taaf, octave
oc'trooi n, patent; charter
oc'trooiraad, patent-office
o'deur, perfume
oefenen, to train, to practise
oefening, exercise, practice
oer n, bog-ore
Oeral, Urals
oerdier n, protozoon
oergermaans n, primitive ger-
    manic
oermens, prehistoric man
oerwoud n, virgin forest, jungle
oester, oyster
oever, bank, shore
of, or; whether, if
    of . . . of,   either . . . or;
    whether . . . or
offer n, sacrifice, victim
offerande, oblation
offeren, to sacrifice; to offer up
offergave, offering
of'ferte, offer
offer'vaardig, willing to make
    sacrifices
offici'eel, official
offi'cier, officer
    officier van Justicie, public
    prosecutor
offi'ciersaanstelling,   com-
    mission
offici'eus, semi-official
of'freren, to offer
of'schoon, although
ogen, to eye; to be attractive
ogenblik n, moment
ogen'blikkelijk, immediate
ogen'schijnlijk, seemingly
ogenschouw: in — nemen, to
    look over

o.i., in our opinion
oker n, ochre
okkernoot, walnut
oksel, armpit
okshoofd n, hogshead
olie, oil
oliebol, doughnut
olie'dom, fat-headed
oliejas, oilskin (coat)
oliën, to oil
olienoot, monkey-nut
oliesel n, extreme unction
olieslage'rij, oil-mill
olifant, elephant
o'lijf, olive
olijk, roguish
olijkerd, rogue
olm, elm
om, round, about; at
    om de andere dag, every other
    day
    om te, in order to
    de tijd is om, time is up
oma, grandma
om'armen, to embrace
ombrengen, to kill
omdat, because
omdoen, to put on, to wrap
    round
omdraaien, to turn (round), to
    twist
omduwen, to knock over
om'floersen,   to   muffle;   to
    shroud
omgaan, to go round
    het hoekje omgaan, to peg out
omgaande: per —, by return (of
    post)
omgang, social intercourse, deal-
    ings; procession; gallery
omgangstaal, everyday speech
omgangsvormen, manners
omgekeerd, upside-down; re-
    verse(d)
om'geven, to surround
om'geving, surroundings
omgooien, to overturn
omhaal, fuss; verbiage
omhakken, to cut down
om'heen, round (about)
om'heinen, to fence in
om'heining, fence, enclosure
om'helzen, to embrace

om'hoog, up(wards)
om'hullen, to envelope
om'hulsel *n*, cover, wrapping, casing
omkantelen, to topple over
omkeren, to turn (round)
omkijken, to look round
om'kleden, to clothe
omkomen, to perish
om'koopbaar, venal
omkopen, to bribe
omkope'rij, bribery
om'laag, down (below)
om'lijnen, to outline
om'lijsten, to frame
omloop, circulation, course; gallery
omlopen, to walk round
't hooft loopt me om, my head reels
ommekeer, change; turn
ommezien: in een —, in a trice
ommezijde, other side, back
omploegen, to plough up
ompraten, to talk round
om'rasteren, to enclose in wire-netting *or* railings
omrekenen, to convert, to work out
om'ringen, to surround
omroep, broadcasting service
omroepen, to broadcast
omroeper, announcer
omroeren, to stir
omruilen, to exchange
omschakelen, to switch over
om'schrijven, to define; to circumscribe
om'schrijving, definition; paraphrase
om'singelen, to encircle
omslaan, to turn (over); to apportion
om'slachtig, cumbrous; prolix
omslag, wrapper; ado; compress
omslagdoek, wrap
om'sluiten, to enclose
omsmelten, to melt down
om'spannen, to span
omspitten, to dig (over)
omspoelen, to rinse
omspringen met, to handle, to manage

omstander, bystander
om'standig, circumstantial
om'standigheid, circumstance, condition
om'streden, contested
omstreken, environs
omstreeks, about
omtoveren, to transform · as if by magic
omtrek, outline, contour; neighbourhood; circumference
om'trent, about
omvallen, to fall over
omvang, extent; girth
om'vangrijk, extensive
om'vatten, to comprise; to encompass
om'ver, down; over
om'verwerpen, to overthrow
omvouwen, to fold down
omwaaien, to (be) blow(n) down
omwassen, to wash up
omweg, detour, roundabout way
omwenteling, revolution, rotation
omwerken, to remodel, to re-write
omwisselen, to (ex)change
omwoners, neighbours
om'zeilen, to get round
omzet, turnover
omzetbelasting, purchase-tax
omzetten, to transpose; to convert; to sell
om'zichtig(heid), circumspect-(ion)
omzien, to look round
onaan'doenlijk, impassive
on'aangenaam(heid), unpleasant(ness)
onaan'nemelijk, unacceptable, improbable
onaan'tastbaar, unassailable
onaan'zienlijk, insignificant
on'aardig: niet —, not at all bad
on'achtzaam(heid), inattentive(ness)
on'afgebroken, continuous
onaf'hankelijk, independent, irrespective
onaf'scheidelijk, inseparable
onbaat'zuchtig, disinterested

onbe'daarlijk, uncontrollable
onbe'dorven, unspoilt
onbe'duidend, trivial
onbegonnen werk, hopeless task
onbeheerd, ownerless, un-attended
onbeholpen, awkward
onbe'hoorlijk, unseemly
onbehouwen, unwieldy; un-gainly; uncouth
onbe'kend, unfamiliar
onbekommerd, carefree
onbe'kookt, rash, wild
onbe'kwaam, (drunk and) in-capable
onbe'lemmerd, unrestricted
onbe'middeld, without means
onbe'nullig, inane
onbe'paalbaar, indeterminable
onbepaald, indefinite
onbeperkt, unrestricted
  onbeperkt vertrouwen, im-plicit faith
onbe'raden, thoughtless
onbe'rekenbaar, incalculable
onbe'rispelijk, irreproachable
onbeschaafd, ill-mannered; un-civilized
onbeschaamd, shameless; brazen
onbe'scheiden, indiscreet
onbe'schoft, impertinent
onbe'schrijfelijk, indescribable
onbe'schroomd, fearless
onbeslecht, onbeslist, unde-cided
onbesproken, not discussed; un-reserved; beyond reproach
onbe'staanbaar, impossible; in-compatible
onbestelbare brief, dead letter
onbestemd, indeterminate
onbe'stendig, unstable
onbestorven weduwe, grass widow
onbestreden, uncontested
onbesuisd, reckless
onbe'taalbaar, priceless
onbetekenend, insignificant
onbeteugeld, unbridled
onbe'tuigd: ik liet me niet —, I did justice (to the meal)
onbetwist, undisputed
onbe'twistbaar, indisputable

onbevangen, unbiased
onbe'vattelijk, dull-witted; in-comprehensible
onbevlekt, immaculate
onbe'voegd, not qualified; un-authorized
onbe'vredigend, unsatisfactory
onbewaakt, unguarded
onbeweeglijk, motionless, im-movable
onbewerkt, untreated
onbewogen, unmoved
onbe'woonbaar, uninhabitable
onbewoond, uninhabited
onbe'wust, unconscious
onbe'zield, inanimate, lifeless; uninspired
onbezoldigd, unpaid; honorary
onbe'zorgd, carefree
on'billijk, unfair
on'breekbaar, unbreakable
onbruik n, disuse
on'bruikbaar, useless
ondank, ingratitude
on'dankbaar, ungrateful, thank-less
ondanks, despite
on'denkbaar, unthinkable
onder, under(neath); among; during
onder'aan, at the foot of
onder'in, at the bottom (of)
onder'aards, subterranean
onderafdeling, subdivision
onderbewust, subconscious
onderbe'wustzijn n, subcon-scious
onder'breken, to interrupt
onderbrengen, to accommodate, to place
onderbroek, pants
onderbuik, abdomen
onderdaan, subject
onderdak n, shelter, accommoda-tion
onder'danig, submissive
onderdeel n, part
onderdoen: niet — voor, to be in no way inferior to
onderdompelen, to immerse
onder'door, under, through
onder'drukken, to oppress, to suppress

onderduiken, to dive; to go into hiding

ondergaan, to go down; to perish

onder'gaan, to undergo

ondergang, downfall, ruin

onderge'schikt, subordinate; secondary

onderge'tekende, (the) under-signed

ondergoed n, underwear

onder'graven, to undermine

ondergrond, sub-soil; foundation

onder'handelen, to negotiate

onder'handelingen, negotiations

onder'hands, private; under-hand

onder'havige geval, (the) case in question

onder'hevig aan, subject to

onder'horig, subordinate

onderhoud n, maintenance; in-terview

onder'houden, to maintain, to support

 zich onderhouden met, to converse with

onder'houdend, entertaining

onderhuids, subcutaneous, hyperdermic

onderjurk, slip

onderkant, underside

onder'kennen, to discern

onderkin, double chin

onderkomen n, shelter

onderkoning, viceroy

onderkruiper, blackleg

onder'legd: goed —, well-grounded

onderlegger, blotting pad; under-blanket

onderlijf n, abdomen

onderling, mutual

onderlopen, to get flooded

onder'maanse: het —, here below

onder'mijnen, to undermine

onder'nemen, to undertake

onder'nemend, enterprising

onder'nemer, employer, contrac-tor

onder'neming, enterprise; plantation

onderofficier, N.C.O., petty-officer

onder'onsje n, friendly get-together

onderpand n, pledge, security

onderricht n, instruction

onder'schatten, to underesti-mate

onderscheid n, difference, dis-tinction

 jaren des onderscheids, years of discretion

onder'scheiden, to distinguish

onder'scheiding, distinction, honour

onder'scheidingsvermogen n, discrimination

onder'scheidingsteken n, badge, distinguishing mark

onder'scheppen, to intercept

onderschrift n, caption

onder'schrijven, to subscribe to

onders'hands, privately

onderspit: het — delven, to get the worst of it

onderstaand, (mentioned) below

onderstand, support, relief

onderste, bottom (most)

onderste'boven, upside-down

onder steek, bed-pan

onderstel n, under-carriage

onder'steld, hypothetical; supposing

onder'stellen, to (pre)suppose

onder'stelling, hypothesis

onder'steunen, to support

onder'steuning, support, relief

onderstoppen, to tuck in

onder'strepen, to underline

onderstuurman, second mate

onder'tekenaar, signatory

onder'tekenen, to sign

onder'tekening, signature

ondertrouw, registration of in-tended marriage

onder'tussen, meanwhile

onder'vangen, to obviate

onderverhuren, to sub-let

onder'vinden, to experience

onder'vinding, experience

onder'voed, under-nourished

onder'vragen, to interrogate

onder'weg, on the way

onderwerp *n,* subject
onder'werpen, to subject; to subdue; to submit
onder'wijl, meanwhile
onderwijs *n,* education
onder'wijzen, to teach
onder'wijzer, school-teacher
onder'worpen, submissive
onder'zeeboot, submarine
onderzoek *n,* enquiry, investigation, examination, research
onder'zoeken, to investigate, to examine
onder'zoekend, searching
onder'zoekingstocht, exploratory expedition
ondeugd, vice; scamp
on'deugend, naughty
ondienst, disservice
ondienst'vaardig, disobliging
on'diep, shallow
ondiepte, shallow (patch)
ondier *n,* monster
onding *n,* useless *or* ugly thing; absurdity
ondoel'matig, inadequate
on'doenlijk, not feasible
ondoor'dacht, thoughtless
ondoor'dringbaar, impenetrable
ondoor'grondelijk, inscrutable
ondoor'schijnend, opaque
ondoor'zichtig, not transparent
on'draaglijk, unbearable
ondubbel'zinnig, unequivocal
on'duidelijk, indistinct
on'duldbaar, insufferable
ondu'leren, to wave (hair)
onecht, spurious; illegitimate
onedel, ignoble, base
on'eens : het — zijn, to disagree
on'eerbaar, indecent
oneer'biedig, disrespectful
on'effen(heid), uneven(ness)
on'eindig, infinite
on'eindigheid, infinity
on'enigheid, discord
oner'varen, inexperienced
oneven, odd
oneven'redig, disproportionate
onfat'soenlijk, improper
on'feilbaar, infallible
on'fris, stale; sallow
on'gaarne, reluctantly

ongeacht, irrespective of
ongebaand, trackless
onge'bonden, unbound; dissolute
ongebreideld, unbridled
ongebuild meel, wholemeal
ongecompli'ceerd, unsophisticated
onge'daan maken, to undo
onge'dacht, unexpected
onge'deerd, unhurt
ongedierte *n,* vermin
ongeduld *n,* impatience
onge'duldig, impatient
onge'durig, restless
onge'dwongen, unconstrained
ongeëvenaard, unequalled
ongefrankeerd, unstamped, carriage forward
ongegeneerd, unceremonious
onge'grond, groundless
onge'hinderd, unimpeded
ongehoord, unheard-of
onge'huwd, unmarried
ongekend, unprecedented
onge'kleed, not (properly) dressed
ongekunsteld, artless
on'geldig, invalid
on'geldigverklaring, nullification
onge'legen, inopportune
onge'legenheid : in — brengen, to inconvenience
onge'lijk, uneven, unequal
ongelijk *n* (hebben), (to be) wrong
ongelijk'slachtig, heterogeneous
ongelikte beer, rough customer
ongelimiteerd, unlimited
ongelinieerd, ongelijnd, unruled
onge'lofelijk, incredible
ongelogen, really and truly
ongeloof'waardig, improbable
onge'lovig, incredulous
onge'lovige, unbeliever
ongeluk *n,* accident, misfortune
onge'lukkig, unhappy, unfortunate, unlucky
onge'lukkige, poor wretch; cripple
onge'lukkigerwijs, unfortunately

ongemak *n,* inconvenience, discomfort

onge'makkelijk, uncomfortable; hard to please; awkward

ongemanierd, ill-mannered

ongemeen, rare, uncommon

ongemeubileerd, unfurnished

onge'moeid laten, to leave in peace

ongemotiveerd, uncalled-for

onge'naakbaar, unapproachable

ongenade, disgrace, disfavour

onge'nadig, merciless

onge'neeslijk, incurable

onge'nietbaar, unpalatable; unbearable

ongenoegen *n,* displeasure, variance

ongeoorloofd, impermissible

onge'past, improper

ongeraden, ill-advised

ongeregeld, irregular

onge'regeldheden, disturbances

ongerekend, exclusive of

ongerept, inviolate, untouched

ongerief *n,* inconvenience

onge'riefelijk, incommodious

onge'rijmd(heid), absurd(ity)

onge'rust, anxious, uneasy

onge'schikt, unfit, unsuitable

ongeschonden, undamaged; unimpaired

ongeschoold, untrained

onge'steld, unwell

ongestoord, undisturbed

onge'straft, unpunished; with impunity

ongetrouwd, single, unmarried

ongetwijfeld, undoubtedly

ongeval *n,* accident

ongeveer, approximately

ongeveinsd, sincere

onge'voelig, unfeeling

ongewapend, unarmed

ongewenst, undesirable

ongewijzigd, unaltered

ongewild, unintentional

ongewillig, refractory

ongewis, uncertain

onge'woon, unusual

onge'zeglijk, disobedient

onge'zellig, unsociable; cheerless

ongezouten, unsalted; plain

on'gunstig, unfavourable

onguur, sinister, unsavoury

on'handelbaar, intractable

on'handig, clumsy; awkward

on'hebbelijk, rude, objectionable

onheil *n,* calamity

onheil'spellend, ominous

onher'bergzaam, inhospitable

onher'roepelijk, irrevocable

onher'stelbaar, irreparable

on'heuglijk, immemorial

onheus, onhoffelijk, discourteous

on'houdbaar, untenable

onjuist, inaccurate

onkies, indelicate

onklaar, out of order; fouled

onkosten, expenses

on'kreukbaar, unimpeachable

onkruid *n,* weed(s)

onkunde, ignorance

on'kundig van, unaware of

onlangs, recently

on'ledig, occupied

onleesbaar, illegible

on'lekker, out of sorts

on'loochenbaar, undeniable

onlusten, disturbances

onmacht, impotence; swoon

on'machtig, powerless

onmens, brute

on'menselijk, inhuman

on'merkbaar, imperceptible

on'metclijk, vast

on'middellijk, immediate

onmin, discord

on'misbaar, indispensable

onmis'kenbaar, unmistakable

on'mogelijk, impossible, not possible

on'mondig, under age, incapable

onna'denkend, thoughtless

onna'volgbaar, inimitable

on'neembaar, impregnable

onnodig, unnecessary

on'noembaar, on'noemelijk, immeasurable

on'nozel, silly; innocent

onom'stotelijk, incontestable

onomwonden, frank

ononderbroken, uninterrupted

onont'beerlijk, indispensable

onont'koombaar, inescapable
on'ooglijk, unsightly
onoordeelkundig, injudicious
onopgevoed, ill-bred
onop'houdelijk, incessant
onoplettend, inattentive
on'ordelijk, disorderly
onovergankelijk, intransitive
onover'komelijk, insuperable
onover'troffen, unsurpassed
onover'winnelijk, invincible
onpartijdig, impartial
on'passelijk, sick
on'peilbaar, unfathomable
onper'soonlijk, impersonal
onraad n, danger
onrecht n, injustice
  ten onrechte, wrongly
onrecht'matig, unlawful
on'redelijk, unreasonable
onroerende goederen, immov-
  ables
onrust, unrest
onrust'barend, alarming
on'rustig, restless
onruststoker,   onrustzaaier,
  trouble-maker
ons, us: n, 100 grammes
onsamen'hangend, incoherent
on'schadelijk, harmless
on'schatbaar, priceless; invaluable
on'schendbaar, inviolable
onschuld, innocence
on'schuldig, innocent
on'smakelijk, unsavoury
onsolide, flimsy; unsound
on'sterfelijk, immortal
on'stuimig, impetuous; tempestuous
onsympathiek, uncongenial
ont'aard(en), (to) degenerate
ont'aarding, degeneration
on'tactisch, tactless
on'tastbaar, intangible
ont'beren, to lack
ont'bering, hardship
ont'bieden, to summon
ont'bijt(en) (n), (to have) breakfast
ont'binden, to undo; to decompose, to disintegrate, to dissolve; to disband; to factorize

ont'binding, decomposition, dis-
  integration, dissolution
ont'bloot, bare; devoid
ont'bloten, to bare, to uncover, to
  strip
ont'boezeming, effusion
ont'brandbaar, inflammable
ont'branden, to catch fire; to
  flare up
ont'breken, to be missing
  het ontbrak me aan moed, I
  lacked the courage
ont'cijferen, to decipher
ont'daan, cut up, shaken
ont'dekken, to discover
ont'dekking, discovery
ont'dekkingsreiziger, explorer
ont'doen, to divest
ont'dooien, to thaw (out)
ont'duiken, to elude, to evade
ontegen'zeglijk, undeniable
ont'eigenen, to expropriate
on'telbaar, innumerable
on'tembaar, indomitable
ont'eren, to dishonour
ont'erend, degrading
ont'erven, to disinherit
onte'vreden, discontented, dissatisfied
ont'fermen: zich — over, to
  take pity on
ont'futselen, to filch
ont'gaan, to elude
ont'gelden, to suffer for
ont'ginnen, to reclaim
ont'glippen, to slip (out); to
  escape
ont'goocheling, disillusionment
ont'groeien, to outgrow; to become estranged to
ont'groenen, to initiate
ont'haal n, reception
ont'halen, to regale
ont'haren, to depilate
ont'heemde, displaced person
ont'heffen, to relieve; to exempt
ont'heiligen, to desecrate
ont'hoofden, to behead
ont'houden, to remember; to
  withhold
  zich onthouden van, to abstain
  from
ont'hullen, to unveil; to reveal

ont'hutst, disconcerted
on'tijdig, untimely
ont'kennen, to deny
ont'kenning, denial, negation
ont'ketenen, to unchain; to unleash
ont'kiemen, to germinate
ont'kleden, to undress
ont'knoping, denouement
ont'komen, to escape
ont'kurken, to uncork
ont'laden, to unload, to discharge
ont'lasten, to unburden, to relieve, to discharge
ont'leden, to analyse; to dissect
ont'lenen, to borrow, to derive
ont'loken, full-blown
ont'lokken, to elicit
ont'lopen, to evade
ont'luiken, to open, to blossom (out)
ont'luizen, to delouse
ont'mantelen, to dismantle
ont'maskeren, to unmask, to expose
ont'moedigen, to discourage
ont'moeten, to meet
ont'moeting, encounter, meeting
ont'nemen, to deprive of
ont'nuchteren, to disillusion
ontoe'gankelijk, inaccessible
ontoe'geeflijk, unaccommodating
ontoe'laatbaar, inadmissible
ontoe'passelijk, inapplicable
ontoe'reikend, inadequate
ontoe'rekenbaar, not responsible for one's actions
ontoe'schietelijk, unresponsive
on'toombaar, uncontrollable
on'toonbaar, not fit to be seen
ont'plofbare stof, explosive
ont'ploffen, to explode
ont'plooien, to unfurl; to deploy; to unfold, to open out
ont'poppen: zich — als, to turn out to be
ont'raden, to advise against
ont'rafelen, to unravel
ont'redderd, battered
ont'reddering, disorder
ont'rieven, to inconvenience
ont'roeren, to move, to touch
ont'roering, emotion

on'troostbaar, inconsolable
ontrouw, disloyal(ty)
ont'roven, to rob of
ont'ruimen, to vacate, to evacuate
ont'rukken, to snatch away from
ont'schepen, to disembark
ont'schieten, to escape (one's memory)
ont'sieren, to disfigure, to mar
ont'slaan, to discharge
ont'slag n, discharge
 ontslag nemen, to resign
ont'slapen, to pass away
ont'sluieren, to unveil
ont'sluiten, to unlock
ont'smetten, to disinfect
ont'smettingsmiddel n, disinfectant
ont'snappen, to escape
ont'spannen, to relax
ont'spanning, relaxation, recreation
ont'sporen, to be derailed
ont'springen, to have its source
 de dans ontspringen, to have a narrow escape
ont'spruiten, to sprout; to arise from
ont'staan, to originate, to come into being: n, origin
 doen ontstaan, to bring about
ont'steken, to kindle, to ignite; to inflame
ont'steking, inflammation; ignition
ont'steld, alarmed
ont'stellend, alarming, appalling
ont'steltenis, consternation
ont'stemd, upset, put out
ont'stemming, annoyance
ont'stentenis: bij — van, in the absence of
ont'stichten, to give offence
ont'takelen, to dismantle
ont'trekken, to withdraw
 zich onttrekken aan, to shirk
ont'tronen, to dethrone
ontucht, immorality
ontuig n, riff-raff
ont'vallen, to slip out
 zijn vrouw ontviel hem, he lost his wife

ont'vangbewijs *n*, receipt
ont'vangdag, at-home
ont'vangen, to receive
ont'vangenis, conception
ont'vanger, recipient
ont'vangst, reception, receipt
ont'vankelijk, susceptible
ont'veinzen : zich —, to deceive
　oneself
ont'vellen, to skin ; to graze
ont'vlambaar, inflammable ;
　excitable
ont'vlammen, to inflame
ont'vlekken, to dry-clean
ont'vlieden, to flee from
ont'vluchten, to escape from
ont'voeren, to abduct
ont'volken, to depopulate
ont'vouwen, to unfold
ont'vreemden, to steal
ont'waken, to wake up
ont'wapenen, to disarm
ont'waren, to perceive
ont'warren, to disentangle
ont'wennen, to lose the habit
　of
ont'werp *n*, project ; design
ont'werpen, to devise, to design,
　to plan
ont'wijden, to desecrate
on'twijfelbaar, unquestionable
ont'wijken, to evade, to avoid
ont'wijkend, evasive
ont'wikkeld, educated, developed
ont'wikkelen, to develop, to
　generate
ont'wikkeling, development,
　education
ont'winden, to unwind
ont'woekeren aan, ont'wors-
　telen aan, to wrest from
ont'wortelen, to uproot
ont'wrichten, to dislocate
ont'zag *n*, awe
ont'zaglijk, tremendous
ontzag'wekkend, awe-inspiring
ont'zeggen, to deny, to refuse
ont'zenuwen, to unnerve ; to dis-
　prove
ont'zet, appalled : *n*, relief
ont'zetten, to relieve ; to deprive ;
　to put out
ont'zettend, terrible, appalling

ont'zetting, horror ; relief ; dis-
　missal
ont'zield, inanimate
ont'zien, to spare, to save
ont'zinken, to fail
on'uitgesproken, unspoken
onuit'puttelijk, inexhaustible
onuit'spreekbaar, unpronounce-
　able
onuit'sprekelijk, unspeakable
onuit'staanbaar, intolerable
onuit'voerbaar, impracticable
onuit'wisbaar, indelible
onvast, unstable, unsteady
onveranderd, unaltered
onveranderlijk, invariable
onverantwoord, unwarranted ;
　unaccounted for
onverant'woordelijk, irrespon-
　sible, inexcusable
onver'beterlijk, incorrigible
onver'biddelijk, inexorable
onverbloemd, plain
onverbrekelijk, indissoluble
onverdeeld, undivided, unquali-
　fied
onverdiend, undeserved
onver'dienstelijk, undeserving
onver'draagzaam, intolerant
onverdroten, indefatigable
onverenigbaar, incompatible
onverflauwd, unabated
onvergankelijk, imperishable
onver'geeflijk, unpardonable
onverge'lijkelijk, incomparable
onver'getelijk, unforgettable
onverhinderd, unimpeded
onverhoeds, unexpected
onverholen, undisguised
onverhoopt, contrary to expecta-
　tions
onverkiesbaar, ineligible
onverkieslijk, undesirable
onver'klaarbaar, inexplicable
onver'kort, unabridged
onver'krijgbaar, unobtainable
onver'kwikkelijk, unsavoury
onverlaat, miscreant
onvermengd, unmixed
onver'mijdelijk, unavoidable
onverminderd, undiminished
onvermoed, unsuspected
onvermoeibaar, indefatigable

onvermoeid, untiring
onvermogen n, inability; in-
digence
onver'mogend, impecunious;
powerless
onvermurwbaar, inexorable
onverpoosd, unceasing
onverrichter zake, with nothing
accomplished
onversaagd, undaunted
onver'schillig, indifferent, unconcerned
onver'schoonbaar, inexcusable
onver'schrokken, intrepid
onverslapt, unflagging
onver'slijtbaar, indestructible,
very hard-wearing
onver'staanbaar, unintelligible
onverstand n, folly
onver'standig, unwise
onver'stoorbaar, imperturbable
onver'taalbaar, untranslatable
onver'teerbaar, indigestible
onver'togen, unseemly
onvervaard, undismayed
onver'valst, unadulterated
onverwacht(s), unexpected
onverwijld, immediate
onver'woestbaar, inextinguish-
able
onver'zadelijk, insatiable
onver'zettelijk, stubborn
onver'zoenlijk, irreconcilable
onverzorgd, unprovided for, un-
cared for
on'voegzaam, indecent
onvoldaan, unsatisfied; unpaid
onvoldoende, insufficient, unsatisfactory
onvol'prezen, beyond praise
onvoltooid, unfinished; imperfect (tense)
onvol'waardig, debile
on'voorbereid, unprepared, extempore, unseen
onvoor'delig, unprofitable, un-
economical
onvoor'waardelijk, unconditional
onvoor'zichtig, incautious
onvoorzien, unforeseen
on'vriendelijk, unkind
onvriend'schappelijk, unfriendly

onvrij, not free, without any
privacy
on'vruchtbaar, infertile, fruitless
onwaarde: van —, null and void
on'waardig, unworthy, undigni-
fied
onwaar'schijnlijk, improbable
on'wankelbaar, unwavering
onweer n, thunder-storm
onweer'legbaar, irrefutable
onweersbui, thunder-shower
onweer'staanbaar, irresistible
on'wel, unwell
onwel'levend, discourteous
onwel'luidend, inharmonious
onwelge'voeglijk, indecorous
onwel'riekend, malodorous
on'wennig, ill at ease
onweren, to thunder
on'wetend, ignorant
on'wettig, unlawful, illegal,
illegitimate
on'wezenlijk, unreal
onwijs, foolish
onwil, unwillingness
onwille'keurig, involuntary
on'willig, unwilling, obstinate
onwrikbaar, unshakable
onzacht, rough, none too gentle
on'nalig uur, unholy hour
onze, our(s)
on'zedelijk, immoral
on'zeker, uncertain
on'zekerheid, insecurity, un-
certainty
onzelf'standig, dependent on
others
onze-lieve-'heersbeestje n,
lady-bird
onzentwille: om —, for our sake
onzerzijds, for our part
on'zichtbaar, invisible
on'zijdig, neutral, neuter
onzin, nonsense
on'zinnig, senseless
on'zuiver, impure, inaccurate,
out of tune
ooft n, fruit
oog n, eye
oogappel, eyeball
oogarts, occulist, ophthalmic
surgeon
ooggetuige, eye-witness

oogharen, eye-lashes
oogholte, **oogkas**, eye-socket
oogkleppen, blinkers
ooglid *n*, eyelid
oogluikend toelaten, to connive
oogmerk *n*, object, aim
oogopslag, glance, look
oogpunt *n*, point of view
oogst, harvest, crop
oogvlies *n*, cornea
oogwenk, twinkling of an eye
ooi, ewe
ooievaar, stork
ooit, ever
ook, also, too; either
  wat (dan) ook, whatever
  waar (dan) ook, wherever
oom, uncle
oomzegger, nephew
oor *n*, ear; handle
oorbaar, seemly
oorbel, ear-ring
oord *n*, place, region, resort
oordeel *n*, opinion, judgement
oordeel'kundig, judicious
oordelen, to judge
oorijzer *n*, (gold *or* silver) head-
  brooch
oorkonde, charter, (ancient)
  document
oorkussen *n*, pillow
oorlel, ear-lobe
oorlog, war(fare)
oorlogsbodem, warship
oorlogshaven, naval port
oorlogsvloot, navy, fleet
oorlogs'zuchtig, bellicose
oorlogvoerend, belligerent
oorpijn, ear-ache
oorschelp, auricle
oorsprong, origin, source
oor'spronkelijk, original
oorveeg, **oorvijg**, box on the
  ear
oorver'dovend, deafening
oorworm, earwig
oorzaak, cause
oost, east, Orient
oostelijk, easterly, east (of)
oosten *n*, East
Oostenrijk *n*, Austria
oosterling, Oriental
oosters, eastern, oriental

oostindische'kers, nasturtium
oostwaarts, eastward(s)
Oost'zee, Baltic
ootmoed, meekness
oot'moedig, meek
op, on; at; in; up
  het bier is op, the beer is
  finished
  ik heb veel met hem op, I like
  him a lot
  op en top, every inch
opa, grandad
o'paal, opal
opbaren, to place on a bier
opbellen, to ring up
opbergen, to put away
opbeuren, to lift up; to cheer up
opbiechten, to own up
opblazen, to inflate
opbloei, revival
opbod, auction
opbouwen, to build up
opbreken, to break up
opbrengen, to yield; to run in
opbrengst, yield, proceeds
opcenten, surtax
opdagen, to turn up
op'dat, in order that
opdienen, to dish up, to serve
opdiepen, to dig up
opdirken, to titivate
opdissen, to dish up
opdoeken, to close down, to clear
  out
opdoemen, to loom (up)
opdoen, to obtain; to lay in; to
  contract; to dish up
opdonder, biff
opdonderen: donder op! get
  the hell out of here!
opdraaien, to turn up; to take
  the can back
opdracht, instruction(s), commission; dedication
opdragen, to instruct, to order;
  to dedicate
opdrijven, to force up; to drive
opdringen, to thrust upon (a
  person)
op'dringerig, obtrusive
opdruk, surcharge
opduikelen, to rake up
opduiken, to bob up, to crop up

op'een, together, on top of one another

op'eenhoping, accumulation, congestion

op'eens, all at once

opeen'volgend, successive

opeisen, to claim, to demand

open, open

open'baar, public

open'baarheid, publicity

open'baren, to reveal

open'baring, revelation

opendoen, to open; to answer the door

openen, opengaan, to open

open'hartig, frank

open('hartig)heid, frankness

opening, opening

openlijk, public, open

openmaken, to open, to undo

openrijten, to rip open

openslaan, to open

openslaande deur, folding door(s), French window

openslaand raam, casement window

opensperren, to distend

openstaande rekening, un-settled account

openstellen, to (throw) open (to the public)

openvouwen, to open out

ope'ratie, operation

ope'ratiekamer, operating theatre

ope'reren, to operate (on)

ope'rette, operetta

opeten, to eat (up), to finish (up)

opflikkeren, to flare up

opfrissen, to refresh

opgaaf, opgave, statement, re-turn; task, problem, (examina-tion-)paper

opgaan, to rise, to go up; to be absorbed; to come off

dat gaat niet altijd op, that does not always hold good

opgeblazen, puffed-up, bump-tious

opgeld doen, to be at a premium

opgelucht, relieved

opgeruimd, cheerful

opgeschoten jongen, stripling

opgeschroefd, affected, forced

opgesloten, locked up; implied

opgetogen, enraptured

opgeven, to give (up); to cough up; to state

hoog opgeven van, to speak highly of

opgevreten, eaten away, con-sumed

opgewassen tegen, a match for

opgewekt, cheerful

opgewonden, excited

opgezet, swollen; stuffed

groot(s) opgezet, ambitious

opgooien, to toss (up)

opgraven, to dig up

opgravingen, excavations

ophaalbrug, draw-bridge

ophaaldienst, carrier service

ophalen, to draw up; to pick up; to shrug; to sniff (up)

op'handen, at hand

ophef, fuss

opheffen, to lift up; to abolish, to close (down)

ophelderen, to elucidate; to clear

ophemelen, to extol

ophitsen, to incite, to set on

ophoopolon, to buzz off

ophopen, to pile up; to accumu-late

ophouden, to hold up; to up-hold; to cease; to delay

zich ophouden met, to have dealings with

o'pinie, opinion

opiumkit, opium-den

opkikkeren, to perk up

op'klapbaar, folding

opklapbed n, tip-up bed

opklaren, to clear up

opknappen, to smarten up; to cope with; to get well

opkomen, to come up, to (a)rise; to come on; to stick up (for)

het kwam bij me op, it occurred to me

daar kom ik tegen op, I object to that

opkomst, rise; attendance

opkrassen, to clear out

opkroppen, to bottle up

oplaag, oplage, number of copies printed
oplaaien, to flare up
oplappen, to patch up
oplaten, to fly
oplawaai, wallop
opleggen, to impose; to lay on; to store
opleiden, to train
opleiding, training, education
opletten, to pay attention
op'lettend, attentive
opleven, to revive
opleveren, to produce, to present
oplichten, to lift (up); to swindle
oplichter, swindler
oploop, tumult
oplopen, to run up; to rise; to mount up; to incur
op'lopend, short-tempered
op'losbaar, soluble
oplossen, to (dis)solve
oplossing, solution
opluchting, relief
opluisteren, to add lustre to
opmaak, lay-out
opmaken, to make (up); to gather
op'merkelijk, remarkable
opmerken, to observe
opmerking, remark
op'merkzaam maken op, to call attention to
opmonteren, to cheer up
opname, recording, photograph; admission
opnemen, to take (up); to take in; to record
op'nieuw, anew
opnoemen, to enumerate
opoe, granny
opofferen, to sacrifice
oponthoud n, delay
oppas, sitter-in
oppassen, to take care (of); to beware; to try on
oppasser, caretaker, attendant, batman
opperbest, excellent
opperbevel n, supreme command
opperbevelhebber, commander-in-chief
opperen, to propose

opperhoofd n, chief(tain)
oppersen, to press
oppervlak n, (outer) surface
opper'vlakkig, superficial
oppervlakte, surface, area
Opperwezen n, Supreme Being
oppeuzelen, to relish at one's leisure
oppikken, to pick up, to peck up
oppo'neren, to raise objections
opportuni'teit, expediency
oppotten, to hoard
opprikken, to pin up
opraken, to give out
oprakelen, to poke (up); to rake up
oprapen, to pick up
op'recht, sincere
opredderen, to tidy up
oprichten, to erect; to establish
zich oprichten, to raise oneself up
oprichter, founder
oprichting, foundation, establishment
oprijlaan, drive
oprijzen bij, to occur to
oprispen, to belch
oprit, drive
oproep, summons, call
oproepen, to call (up)
oproer n, revolt
op'roerig, rebellious
oproerkraaier, agitator
oproerling, rebel
opruien, to incite to rebellion
opruimen, to clear (away)
opruiming, clearance sale; tidy-up
oprukken, to press onward
opscharrelen, to dig up
opschepen met, to saddle with
opscheppen, to serve; to brag
opschepper, braggart
opschieten, to get (a move) on
met elkaar opschieten, to get on (well) together
opschik, finery
opschikken, to move up
opschommelen, to dig up
opschorten, to suspend
opschrift n, inscription, caption
opschrijfboekje n, note-book

opschrijven, to note down
opschrikken, to start, to be startled
opschrokken, to gobble up
opschudding, commotion
opschuiven, to push up, to move up
opslaan, to raise; to turn up; to lay in; to rise (in price)
opslag, rise; storage
opslobberen, to lap up
opslokken, to gulp down
opslorpen, opslurpen, to drink noisily; to absorb
opsluiten, to lock (up)
opsmuk, finery
opsnijden, to cut up; to brag
opsnij(d)er, braggart
opsnorren, opsnuffelen, to dig up
opsommen, to enumerate
opsou'peren, to blue
opspelen, to kick up a row
opsporen, to track (down)
opspraak, disrepute
opstaan, to rise
opstand, rising; elevation
in opstand komen, to rebel
opstandeling, rebel
op'standig, rebellious
opstanding, resurrection
opstap, step
opstapelen: zich —, to accumulate
opstappen, to get on, to get along
opsteken, to put up; to light; to get up
opsteken van, to profit by
opstel n, essay
opstellen, to draft; to place
opstijgen, to rise; to climb up, to mount
opstoken, to stir up (animosity)
opstootje n, disturbance
opstopper, punch
opstrijken, to run an iron over; to rake in
opstropen, to roll up
opstuiven, to fly up
optekenen, to note down
optellen, to add up
optocht, procession

optornen tegen, to make headway against
optreden, to appear; to act
optrekken, to pull up; to raise
optrekken tegen, to march against
optrekken met, to go about with
optrommelen, to round up
optuigen, to rig; to harness
opvallen, to be conspicuous, to strike
op'vallend, conspicuous
opvangen, to catch; to overhear
opvarenden: de —, those on board
opvatten, to take (up), to interpret, to conceive
weer opvatten, to resume
opvatting, conception
opvliegen, to fly up, to flare up
op'vliegend, irascible
opvoeden, to educate
opvoeding, upbringing
lichamelijke opvoeding, physical training
opvoedingsgesticht n, reformatory school
opvoeren, to raise; to perform
opvoering, performance
opvolgen, to succeed; to carry out
opvolger, successor
opvouwbaar, collapsible
opvreten, to devour
opvrolijken, to cheer up
opwaarts, upward(s)
opwachten, to wait for
opwachting maken, to pay (one's) respects
opwegen tegen, to offset
opwekken, to arouse, to stimulate, to generate
op'wekkend, encouraging
opwellen, to well up
opwelling, surge, impulse
opwerken: zich —, to work one's way up
opwerpen, to throw up; to raise
opwinden, to wind (up), to excite
opwinding, excitement

opzeggen, to recite; to terminate, to cancel
 zijn betrekking opzeggen, to give notice
opzet, plan, intent(ion)
op'zettelijk, met opzet, deliberate
opzetten, to set up; to put on; to turn (against); to swell
 een grote mond opzetten, to harangue
opzicht n, respect
opzichter, superintendent
op'zichtig, flashy
opzien tegen, to look up to; to dread
opzien'barend, sensational
opzoeken, to look up
o'ranje (n), orange
ora'torium n, oratorio; oratory
orchi'dee, orchid
orde, order
 aan de orde, up for discussion
orde'lievend, ordelijk, orderly
ordeloos, disorderly
ordenen, to (put in) order
or'dentelijk, decent
order, order, command
ordi'nair, vulgar
ordner, file
ordon'nans, orderly
o'reren, to hold forth
or'gaan n, organ
organi'seren, to organize
orgel n, organ
orgeldraaier, organ-grinder
oriën'teren zich —, to find one's bearings
origi'neel, original
or'kaan, hurricane
or'kest n, orchestra
or'naat n, robes of office
os, ox, bullock
oscil'leren, to oscillate
ossenhaas, fillet of beef
ostenta'tief, ostentatious
oud, old, ancient
 bij het oude laten, to leave (things) as they were
oud'bakken, stale
oude van dagen, aged
oudejaars'avond, New Year's Eve

ouder, older, elder; parent
ouderdom, (old) age
ouderlijk, parental
ouderling, elder
ouder'wets, old-fashioned
oudge'diende, veteran
oudheid, antiquity
oudheidkunde, archaeology
oudje n, old (wo)man
oudoom, great uncle
oud'roest n, old iron
oudsher: van —, (from) of old
oudst, oldest, elder; senior
oud'strijder, veteran
oudtante, great-aunt
outil'leren, to equip
ouv'reuse, usherette
ouwel, wafer
ouwelijk, elderly
o'vaal, oval
oven, oven, furnace, kiln
over, over, across; via; past; about; left (over)
 over en weer, mutually
 tijd te over, time to spare
 ik heb veel voor hem over, I would do anything for him
 over een paar dagen, in a few days' time
overal, everywhere
overbekend, widely known
overbelasten, to overburden; to overload
overbelicht, over-exposed
overblijfsel n, remains, relic
overblijven, to be left; to stay (at school for lunch)
over'bluffen, to abash
over'bodig, superfluous
over'boord, overboard
overbrengen, to convey
overbrieven, to let on about
over'bruggen, to bridge
overbuur, neighbour across the road
overdaad, excess
over'dadig, excessive
over'dag, during the day
over'dekt, covered in
over'denken, to consider
overdoen, to do again; to pass on
over'donderen, to knock all of a heap

overdracht, transfer

over'drachtelijk, metaphorical

overdragen, to transfer, to convey

over'dreven, exaggerated

overdrijven, to blow over

over'drijven, to exaggerate

overdruk, reprint; overprint

overdrukplaatje *n,* transfer

over'duidelijk, obvious

over'dwars, across, athwart

over'eenbrengen, to reconcile

over'eenkomen, to agree

over'eenkomst, agreement, similarity

overeen'komstig, corresponding (to)

over'eenstemmen, to agree

over'eind, upright, on end

over'erfelijk, hereditary

overgaan, to cross over; to pass (on); to go up (to a higher form)

overgang, transition, change; crossing

overgangsmaatregel, temporary measure

over'gankelijk, transitive

overgave, surrender

overgelukkig, over-joyed

overgeven, to hand over, to surrender; to vomit

overge'voelig, hypersensitive

overgieten, to transfer, to decant

overgooier, tunic

overgordijn *n,* (running) curtain

overgoten met, bathed in

overgrootmoeder, great-grandmother

overgrootvader, great-grandfather

over'haast, precipitate

overhalen, to pull over; to persuade

overhand, upper hand

over'handigen, to hand (over)

over'heen, across, over

  er gaan jaren overheen, it takes years

overheerlijk, exquisite

over'heersen, to (pre)dominate

over'heersing, domination

overheid, authorities

overhellen, to incline, to lean over

overhemd *n,* shirt

overhevelen, to siphon

over'hoop, in confusion; at loggerheads

over'horen : iemand —, to hear a person's lesson

overhouden, to have left

overig, remaining

overigens, for the rest

over'ijld, precipitate

overjas, overcoat

overkalken, to crib

overkant, opposite side

over'kapping, roof(ing)

over'koepelend, co-ordinating

over'komen, to happen to

over'kropt gemoed, pent-up feelings

overladen, to transfer

over'laden, to overload

over'langs, lengthwise

overlast, inconvenience

overlaten, to leave

over'leden, deceased

over'leg *n,* deliberation

overleggen, to produce; to put by

over'leggen, to deliberate

over'leven, to survive

over'levende, survivor

overleveren, to hand down : to deliver up

overlevering, tradition

overlezen, to read through, to read again

over'lijden, to die

overloop, landing

overlopen, to run over; to go over

overloper, deserter, traitor

overmaat, excess

  tot overmaat van ramp, to crown it all

overmacht, superior force; force majeure

overmaken, to do again; to transfer

over'mannen, to overpower; to overcome

over'matig, excessive
over'meesteren, to overpower
overmoed, presumption
over'moedig, presumptuous
over'morgen, the day after tomorrow
overnaads, clinker-built; overcast (seam)
over'nachten, to stay the night
overnemen, to take over; to adopt
over'peinzen, to muse on
over'peinzing, reflection
overplaatsen, to transfer
overplanten, to transplant
over'reden, to persuade
overreiken, to hand
overrijden, to run over
over'rompelen, to take by surprise
overschenken, to decant
overschepen, to tranship
overschieten, to be left
overschoenen, galoshes
overschot n, remainder, surplus
over'schreeuwen, to shout down
over'schrijden, to exceed; to step across
overschrijven, to copy (out); to transfer
overslaan, to skip; to estimate; to crack
overslag, overlap; estimate
over'spannen, to span: overwrought
overspel n, adultery
overstaan: ten — van, in the presence of
over'stag gaan, to go about
overstapje n, transfer ticket
overstappen, to change
overste, lieutenant-colonel; prior
oversteekplaats, (pedestrian) crossing
oversteken, to cross
over'stelpen, to overwhelm
over'stemmen, to drown, to shout down
over'stromen, to flood, to inundate
over'stuur, upset

over'tallig, surplus
over'tekenen, to over-subscribe
overtocht, crossing, passage
over'tollig, superfluous
over'treden, to transgress; to infringe
over'treffen, to surpass
overtreffende trap, superlative
overtrek, (loose) cover
over'trekken, to (re)cover
overtrekken, to cross; to trace to blow over
over'troeven, to over-trump; to score one
over'tuigen, to convince
over'tuiging, conviction
overuren, overtime
overval, surprise attack
over'vallen, to surprise
oververtellen, to repeat
over'vleugelen, to surpass; to outflank
overvloed, abundance
over'vloedig, abundant
over'voeren, to glut
over'vragen, to over-charge
overwaarde, additional value
overweg, level crossing
over'weg kunnen, to get on
over'wegen, to consider
over'wegend, preponderant
over'weging, consideration
over'weldigen, to overpower
over'weldigend, overwhelming
over'weldiger, despotist
overwerken, to work overtime
over'werken, to overwork
overwicht n, preponderance authority
over'winnaar, victor
over'winnen, to conquer
over'winning, victory
overwinstbelasting, excess profits tax
over'winteren, to winter
overzetveer n, ferry
overzicht n, summary
over'zichtelijk, conveniently arranged
over'zien, to survey
overzijde, opposite side
oxi'deren, to oxidize

P

paadje *n*, (foot-)path
paaien, to pacify
paal, pole, pile, post
　als een paal boven water, as clear as daylight
paaps, popish
paar *n*, pair, couple; few
paard *n*, horse
paardebloem, dandelion
paardeknecht, groom
paardekracht, horse-power
paardemiddel *n*, drastic remedy
paardenstoeterij, stud(-farm)
paardenvilder, knacker
paardenvolk *n*, cavalry
paardetoom, bridle
paardevijgen, horse-droppings
paarle'moer *n*, mother of pearl
paars (*n*), violet, purple
paarsgewijs, in pairs
paartijd, mating season
Paasvest, Sunday best
Paasdag: de eerste —, Easter Day
　de tweede Paasdag, Easter Monday
Paasfeest *n*, Easter
pacht, lease, rent
pachten, to rent (a farm)
pachter, tenant farmer
pad, toad: *n*, path
paddestoel, toad-stool, mushroom
padvinder, boy-scout
padvindster, girl-guide
paf staan, to be dumbfounded
pafferig, puffy
pa'gaai(en), (to) paddle
pagina, page
pais en vree, peace and quiet
pak *n*, pack(age); suit
　pak slaag, thrashing
pakhuis *n*, warehouse
pakje *n*, parcel, packet
pakijs, ice-pack
pakken, to pack; to seize; to hug
　iemand te pakken krijgen, to get hold of a person
　ik heb het erg te pakken, I've got it badly
pakkend, fascinating; catchy

pakkerd, hug
pak'ketpost, parcel post
pakpapier *n*, brown paper
pal, pawl, ratchet
　pal staan, to stand firm
　pal oost, due east
pa'leis *n*, palace
pa'let *n*, palette
palfre'nier, footman
paling, eel
palis'sanderhout(en) (*n*), rose-wood
pal'jas, clown; palliasse
palm, palm
Palmpasen, Palm Sunday
pam'flet *n*, pamphlet, lampoon
pan, pan; tile; shindy
　in de pan hakken, to kill to a man
pand *n*, forfeit; premises; (coat-)tail
pandjeshuis *n*, pawn-shop
pandjesjas, tail-coat
pa'neel *n*, panel
pa'neermeel *n*, bread-crumbs
pa'niek, panic
panne, break-down
pannekoek, pancake
pannelap, kettle-holder
pannenbakke'rij, tile-works
panta'lon, trousers; knickers
panter, panther
pan'toffel, slipper
pan'toffelheld, henpecked husband
pantser *n*, armour
pantserdier *n*, armadillo
pantseren, to armour; to brace
pap, milk pudding
pa'paver, poppy
pape'gaai, parrot
pape'rassen, papers, litter
pa'pier *n*, paper
　pa'pieren, papers; stocks and shares; credentials
pa'piermand, waste-paper basket
papil'lotten, curl-papers
papje *n*, paste
papkind *n*, molly-coddle
Pappenheimers: ik ken mijn —, I know the people I'm dealing with
pappie, daddy

pa'raaf, initials
pa'raat, ready
pa'rade, review
para'dijs n, paradise
para'feren, to initial
para'nymf, usher
paranoot, Brazil nut
para'plu, umbrella
para'siet, parasite
par'cours n, course
par'does, slap(-bang)
par'don, pardon; mercy
parel, pearl
parel'moer n, mother of pearl
paren, to mate
  zich paren aan, to be coupled
  with
pa'reren, to parry
par'fum n, scent
parfu'meren, to scent
pari: à —, at par
pari'teit, parity
park n, park
par'keerterein n, car-park
par'keren, to park
par'ket (n), front stalls; public
  prosecutor's office: parquet
  in een lastig parket, in a predicament
par'kiet, parakeet
parle'ment n, parliament
parlemen'tair, parliamentary:
  bearer of flag of truce
parle'vinken, to jabber
parle'vinker, bum-boat
par'mantig, perky
parochi'aan, parishioner
pa'rochie, parish
paro'die, parody
parodi'ëren, to parody
pa'rool n, parole; password
part n, portion
  parten spelen, to play false
par'terre, pit; ground-floor
particu'lier, private: (private)
  individual
par'tij, part(y); game; consignment
  een goede partij doen, to make
  a good match
  partij kiezen, to take sides
  partij trekken van, to take
  advantage of

par'tijdig, biased
par'tijdigheid, partiality
par'tijganger, partisan
par'tijschap n, faction
pas, only (just): pace, step:
  pass
  te pas en te onpas, at random
  te pas, van pas, (be)fitting
Pascha n, Passover
Pasen, Easter
pasgeboren, new-born
pasgeld n, small change
pasge'trouwden, newly-weds
paskamer, fitting-room
pasklaar, ready for fitting
pas'kwil n, absurdity
paslood n, plumb-line
paspoort n, passport
pas'saat, trade-wind
pas'sage, passage; arcade
pas'sagebiljet n, travel-voucher
passa'gier, passenger
passa'gieren, to be on shore-
  leave
passa'giersgoed n, accompanied
  luggage
pas'sant, traveller breaking his
  journey; passer-by
passen, to fit; to try on; to
  match; to be fitting; to pass
  ik pas ervoor, I won't do it
  passen op, to take care (of)
passend, fitting, appropriate
passer, pair of compasses
pas'seren, to pass (over); to
  happen
passie, passion
pas'sief, passive
passiva, liabilities
pasta, paste
pas'tei, patty; paste
pas'toor, parish priest
pasto'rie, parsonage
pa'tates frites, potato chips
pa'tent (n), licence; patent:
  capital
pater, father
pa'triciër, patrician
pa'trijs, partridge
pa'trijshond, spaniel
pa'trijspoort, port-hole
pa'troon, employer: cartridge:
  n, pattern

pa'trouille, patrol
pats, smack; bang!
pauk, kettledrum
paus, pope
pauselijk, papal
pauw, peacock
pauze, interval, pause
pavil'joen *n*, pavilion; marquee
pavoi'seren, to dress overall
pech, bad luck
pe'daal *n*, pedal
pe'dant, pedant(ic)
peddelen, to pedal; to paddle
pe'del, beadle
pedi'cure, chiropodist
pee: ik heb er de — in, I'm fed
to the teeth
 ik heb de pee aan hem, he gets
 my goat
peel, marshy land
peen, carrot
peer, pear; light bulb
 met de gebakken peren zitten,
 to be left holding the baby
pees, tendon; gristle
peet, godparent
peetoom, godfather
peil *n*, gauge, level
 er is op hem geen peil te trekken, he is quite unpredictable
peilen, to gauge, to sound
peilloos, unfathomable
peinzen, to muse
peinzend, thoughtful
pek *n*, pitch
pekel, brine; pickle
pekelvlees *n*, salted meat
pelgrim, pilgrim
pelgrimstocht, pilgrimage
peli'kaan, pelican
pellen, to peel, to shell
pelo'ton *n*, platoon
pels, pelt; fur-coat
pelte'rij, peltry
peluw, bolster
pen, pen, nib, quill; peg, pin
pe'nant *n*, pier
pe'narie: in de —, in a fix
pen'dule, pendulum clock
pe'nibel, grim
peni'tentie, penitence; ordeal
pennen, to pen
pennelikker, pen-pusher

penning, medal; official badge
 op de penning, cheese-paring
penningmeester, treasurer
pens, paunch; tripe
pen'seel *n*, (artist's) brush
pen'sioen *n*, pension
 met pensioen gaan, to retire
 (on a pension)
pen'sion *n*, guest-house; board
pensio'naat *n*, boarding-school
pension'neren, to pension (off)
pentekening, pen-and-ink drawing
peper, pepper
peperduur, ruinous(ly expensive)
peperkoek, gingerbread
peper'munt, peppermint
pepernoot, ginger-nut
per'ceel *n*, plot; premises
per'centsgewijze, proportional
pereboom, pear-tree
perfection'neren, to perfect
per'fide, perfidious
pe'rikel *n*, peril
peri'ode, period
perio'diek, periodical
perk *n*, flower-bed; limit
perka'ment *n*, parchment
permit'teren, to permit
per omgaand, by return (of post)
per'plex, perplexed
per'ron *n*, platform
pers, press: Persian (rug)
persbureau *n*, press-agency
per se, emphatically
persen, to press, to squeeze
perso'neel *n*, staff, personnel
 personele belasting, household
 tax
per'soon(lijk), person(al)
per'soonlijkheid, personality
per'soonsbewijs *n*, identity
card
perspec'tief *n*, perspective
perstribune, press gallery
perti'nent, emphatic, positive
per'vers, perverse
Perzië *n*, Persia
perzik, peach
Perzisch, Persian
pest, plague, pest(ilence)
pesten, to bait, to tease the life
out of

pestkop, bully
pet, cap
't gaat boven mijn pet, it beats me
petekind n, godchild
peter'selie, parsley
pe'tieterig, puny, minute
pe'troleum, paraffin
pe'troleumbron, oil-well
pe'troleumleiding, pipe-line
peukje n, cigar(ette)-butt
peultjes, young pea-pods
peulvruchten, legumes
peuter, tiny tot
peuteren, to fiddle, to tinker
peuterwerk(je) n, finicky job
peuzelen, to eat daintily with relish
ph-: see under f-
pianokruk, music stool
pi'as, clown
piccolo, piccolo: page-boy
picknick(en), (to) picnic
piek, pike; peak
piekeren, to puzzle, to brood
piekfijn, posh
pienter, bright, smart
piepen, to squeak, to cheep
piepjong, very young
piepkuiken n, (young) pullet
piepzak: in de —, in a blue funk
pier, pier, jetty: (earth)worm
ik ben altijd de kwaaie pier, I get the blame for everything
piere'ment n, hurdy-gurdy
pierewaaien, to be on the spree
Pict(er), Peter
Piet de Smeerpoe(t)s, Str{-}welpeter
een hele Piet, quite a lad
piëteit, piety
pieter'selie, parsley
piet'luttig, pettifogging
pietsje n, wee bit
pij, (monk's) habit
pijjekker, pea-jacket
pijl, arrow
pijler, pillar
pijlkoker, quiver
pijn, pain, ache
pijn doen, to hurt
pijnappel, fir-cone
pijnbank, rack

pijnigen, to torture, to rack
pijnlijk, painful
pijn'stillend, sedative, soothing
pijp, pipe; tube; funnel; trouser-leg
pijpkaneel, whole cinnamon
pik, pitch: pickaxe: peck
de pik hebben op, to have a down on
pi'kant, piquant, spicy
pi'keur, riding-master
pikhouweel n, pickaxe
pikken, to peck; to pick: to pitch
pil, pill; chunk
pi'laar, pillar
pilo n, corduroy
pi'loot, pilot
pimpelaar, tippler
pimpelpaars, purple
pin, peg, pin
pin'cet n, tweezers
pinda(kaas), peanut (butter)
pingelen, to haggle
pinguin, penguin
pink, little finger: fishing boat
bij de pinken, all there
Pinksteren, Whitsun(tide)
pi'oenroos, peony
pi'on, pawn
pio'nieren, to pioneer
pi'pet, pipette
pips, off colour
pi'raat, pirate
pi'raatje n, gasper
pisang, banana
pis'ton, cornet
pis'tool n, pistol
pit, kernel, stone, pip; burner; pith
pittig, pithy, racy; spry
plaag, nuisance, plague
plaaggeest, tease
plaat, plate; slab; (gramo{-}phone-)record; picture
plaatijzer n, sheet-iron
plaats, place; room; yard; seat
in plaats van, instead of
ter plaatse, on the spot
plaatsbewijs n, ticket
plaatselijk, local
plaatsen, to place

plaatsruimte, space
plaatsvervanger, deputy
pla'fond n, ceiling
plagen, to tease, to worry
plage'rij, teasing
plag(ge), sod of turf
plagi'aat n, plagiarism
plak, slice; slab
  onder de plak zitten, to be under a person's thumb
plakband, adhesive tape
pla'ket, plaque
plak'kaat n, placard
plakken, to stick
plakzegel, adhesive stamp
pla'muren, to fill (the grain), to stop
plan n, plan, project
  van plan zijn, to intend
pla'neet, planet
pla'neren, to hover
plank, plank, board; shelf
plankenkoorts, stage-fright
plan'kier n, platform
plant, plant
plant'aardig, vegetable
plan'tage, plantation
planten, to plant
plantengroei, vegetation
plantkunde, botany
plant'soen n, gardens, flower-bed
plas, pool, puddle; lake
plasregen, downpour
plassen, to splash; to piddle
plas'tiek n, **plastisch,** plastic
plat, flat; vulgar
pla'taan, plane-tree
platboomd, flat-bottomed
pla'teel n, pottery
platheid, flatness; vulgarity
platina n, platinum
platte'grond, (ground-)plan
platte'land n, country(side)
platte'lands, country, rural
plattrappen, to trample down
platweg, flatly
platzak, penniless, empty-handed
pla'veien, to pave
pla'veisel n, paving
pla'vuis, flag-stone
ple'bejer, plebeian
plebs n, *hoi polloi*
plecht('stat)ig, solemn

plechtigheid, ceremony, solemnity
pleeg-, foster-
pleegzuster, sick-nurse; foster-sister
plegen, to commit
  hij placht te zeggen, he used to say
  overleg plegen, to consult together
plei'dooi n, plea, (address for the) defence
plein n, square, open space
pleister(en) n, (to) plaster
pleisterplaats, road-house
pleit, n, dispute
pleiten, to plead
  dat pleit voor hem, that's a point in his favour
plek, spot
ple'nair, plenary
plengen, to shed
pletten, to roll out, to crush
pletter: te — slaan, to smash to smithereens
pleur('it)is, pleurisy
ple'zier n, pleasure
ple'zierig, pleasant
plicht, duty
plicht(s)getrouw, plicht'-matig, dutiful
plichtpleging, ceremony
plint, plinth; skirting-board
plis'sé, pleat(ing)
ploeg, plough: gang, shift, team
ploegen, to plough
ploegschaar, ploughshare
ploert, cad
ploertendoder, cosh
ploerte'rij, owners of digs
ploeteren, to splash; to plod; to drudge
plof(fen), (to) thud, (to) plop
plom'beren, to fill
plombière, sundae
plomp, unwieldy: thud: water-lily
plons, (s)plash
plonzen, to (s)plash
plooi, fold, pleat, crease
  uit de plooi komen, to unbend
plooibaar, pliable

plooien, to fold, to pleat
plotseling, sudden
pluche, plush
pluim, plume, feather; tuft
pluimpje n, compliment
plui'mage, plumage
pluimstrijker, toady
pluimvee n, poultry
pluis: niet —, fishy
pluisje n, piece of fluff
pluizen, to (give off) fluff
pluk, pick
  een hele pluk, quite a job
plukken, to pick, to pluck
plu'meau, feather duster
plunderen, to plunder
plunje, togs
plunjezak, kit-bag
plus'minus, approximately
p.o., by return (of post)
pochen, to boast
po'cheren, to poach
po'chette, breast-pocket handkerchief
podium n, dais
poedel, poodle
poedelnaakt, stark naked
poeder, powder
poederdons, powder-puff
poedersuiker, icing sugar
poe'ha, fuss, la-di-da
poeieren, to powder
poel, pool, puddle
poe'lier, poulterer
poen, spiv
poes, puss
  niet voor de poes, no chicken-
  feed
poeslief, honey-lipped
poespas, fuss about nothing
poets: een — bakken, to play
  a trick on
poetsen, to polish, to brush
poetskatoen n, cotton waste
poezelig, chubby
poë'zie, poetry
pof: op de —, on tick
pofbroek, plus-fours
poffen, to puff: to pop
poffertjes, small fritters
pofmouw, leg-of-mutton sleeve
pogen, to endeavour
poging, attempt

pok('dalig), pock(-marked)
pokken, smallpox
pol, tussock
po'lair, polar
Polen n, Poland
po'lijsten, to polish
polikli'niek, out-patients' department
polis, insurance policy
po'liticus, politician
po'litie, police
po'litieagent, policeman
po'litiebureau n, police-station
poli'tiek, policy; politics: political
poli'toer(en), (to) French polish
pollepel, wooden spoon
pols, pulse, wrist
polsen, to sound
polsslag, pulse, pulsation
polsspringen n, pole-vaulting
pom'made, pomade
pomp(en), (to) pump
pom'peus, pompous
pom'poen, pumpkin
pond n, pound, 500 grammes
ponsma'chine, punching-
  machine
pont, ferry-boat
pontifex, pontiff
pon'ton, pontoon
pony, pony; fringe
pooier, ponce
pook, poker
pool, pole
poolcirkel, polar circle
poolreiziger, arctic explorer
Pools, Polish
  Poolse landdag, bear-garden
poolshoogte nemen, to see how
  the land lies
poolster, pole-star
poolzee, (ant)arctic sea
poort, gate(way)
poorter, burgher
poos(je n), (little) while
poot, paw, leg
  poot aan spelen, to buckle to
pootaardappel, seed-potato
pootjebaden, to paddle
pop, doll; puppet; dummy;
  court-card; pupa
  nu heb je de poppen aan het
  dansen! that's torn it!

popelen, to quiver, to itch
pope'line, poplin
poppenkast, puppet-show, Punch and Judy show
popperig, diminutive
popu'lair, popular
popu'lier, poplar
por, prod
po'reus, porous
porie, pore
porren, to poke, to prod
porse'lein *n*, china(-ware)
port, postage: port(-wine)
por'taal *n*, porch; hall, landing
porte-bri'sée, sliding doors
por'tée, purport
porte'feuille, portfolio; wallet
porte-man'teau, hall-stand
portemon'naie, purse
portie, share, helping
por'tiek *n*, portico, porch
por'tier, (hall-)porter; door
porto, postage
por'tret *n*, portrait
po'seren, to pose, to sit
po'sitie, position, situation
  in positie, expecting
posi'tief, positive
po'sitiejapon, maternity-gown
pooi'tiovon, wite
post, post; mail; item; picket
  op post, on duty
postbode, postman
postbus, post-office box
postdirecteur, postmaster
postduif, carrier-pigeon
poste'lein, purslane
posten, to post; to picket
pos'teren, to post, to station
poste'rijen, postal service
pos't(h)uum, posthumous
postpapier *n*, note-paper
poststempel *n*, postmark
pos'tuur *n*, figure; posture
postwissel, money order
postzegel, postage stamp
pot, pot, jar; kitty
potas, potash
potdicht, shut tight
potdoof, stone-deaf
poteling, seedling; hefty fellow
poten, to plant, to dibble
poten'tieel, potential

potig, hefty
potlood *n*, pencil; black-lead
pot'nat: één —, six of one and half a dozen of the other
pot'sierlijk, grotesque
potten, to pot; to hoard
pottenbakker, potter
potver'dikkie! Great Scott!
potvis, sperm-whale
pover, poor, meagre
pozen, to pause
praal, pomp, splendour
praalziek, ostentatious
praat(je *n*), talk, chat, gossip
  veel praats hebben, to talk big
praatgraag, praatziek, garrulous
pracht, splendour
prachtband, *de luxe* binding
prachtig, splendid, magnificent
practicum *n*, practical (work)
practisch, practical
pr(a)eses, chairman
prak, hash
prakken, to mash (up)
prakke'zeren, to have a think
prak'tijk, practice
prakti'zeren, to practice
pralen, to shine; to flaunt
prangen, to pinch
prat gaan op, to pride oneself on
praten, to talk
pre'cair, precarious
pre'cies, precise, exact
predi'kant, minister
predi'katie, sermon
prediken, to preach
preek, sermon
preekstoel, pulpit
prefe'reren, to prefer
prei, leek
preken, to preach
pre'laat, prelate
premie, premium
prent, print, picture
prenten, to imprint
prepa'raat *n*, preparation
presen'teerblad *n*, salver, tray
presen'teren, to offer; to present
pre'sent-exemplaar *n*, complimentary copy

pre'sentielijst, attendance list
presi'dentschap *n,* presidency
presi'deren, to preside (at)
pre'sidium *n,* chairmanship
pressen, to press
presse-pa'pier, paper-weight
pressie uitoefenen, to bring pressure to bear
pres'tatie, achievement
pres'teren, to achieve
pret, fun
preten'dent, pretender
pre'tentie, pretension
 zonder pretenties, unassuming
pre'tentieloos, unpretentious
preten'tieus, presumptuous
prettig, pleasant, nice
 prettig vinden, to like
preuts, prudish, squeamish
preva'leren, to prevail
prevelen, to mutter
pri'ëel *n,* arbour
priem, awl
priester, priest
priesterschap *n,* priesthood
prijken, to (be) display(ed)
prijs, price; prize
 op prijs stellen, to appreciate
prijscourant, price-list
prijsgeven, to abandon
prijsnotering, quotation (of prices)
prijsuitdeling, prize-giving
prijsvraag, competition
prijzen, to praise; to price, to mark
prijzens'waardig, praiseworthy
prijzig, expensive
prik, prick, stab
prikkebeen, spindle-shanks
prikkel, sting, goad; spur
prikkelbaar, irritable
prikkeldraad *n,* barbed wire
prikkelen, to prickle; to irritate, to provoke; to stimulate
prikken, to prick; to tingle
pril, tender, vernal
prima, first-rate
pri'mair, primary
pri'meur, scoop
primi'tief, primitive, crude
prin'cipe *n,* principle

principi'eel, fundamental, of *or* on principle
prins, prince
 van de prins geen kwaad weten, to be as innocent as an unborn babe
prinselijk, princely
prin'ses, princess
prin'sesseboon, dwarf bean
priori'teit, priority
prisma *n,* prism
pri'vaat, private: *n,* rears
pri'vaatdocent, external (university) lecturer
pri'vaatles, private tuition
privé, private
pro'baat, proven
pro'beren, to try (out)
pro'bleem *n,* problem
procé'dé *n,* process
proce'deren, to take it to court
pro'cent *n,* percent
pro'ces *n,* lawsuit; process
 iemand een proces aandoen, to bring an action against a person
pro'ces-ver'baal *n,* official report
procla'meren, to proclaim
procu'ratie, power of attorney
procu'reur, attorney
pro Deo, voluntary, for love
produ'cent, producer
produ'ceren, to produce
pro'duct *n,* product(ion)
proef, test; proof
proefkonijn *n,* laboratory rabbit; guinea-pig
proefneming, experiment
proefonder'vindelijk, experimental
proefschrift *n,* thesis
proefstation *n,* research station
proeftijd, noviciate; apprenticeship; probation
proefwerk *n,* test (paper)
proesten, to splutter
proeven, to taste
pro'faan, profane
profa'neren, to profane
pro'feet, prophet
professo'raal, professorial
professo'raat *n,* professorship

profe'teren, to prophesy
profe'tie, prophecy
pro'fiel *n*, profile; cross-section
pro'fijt *n*, profit, advantage
profi'teren van, to profit by, to take advantage of
pro'gramma *n*, programme
progres'sief, progressive
projec'teren, to project, to plan
pro'jectie, projection
pro'leet, pariah
prole'tariër, proletarian
prolon'geren, to continue
pro'loog, prologue
pro'motie, promotion, graduation (ceremony)
pro'motor, company-promoter; director of research (studies)
promo'veren, to obtain a doctor's degree
pronk: te — staan, to be on show
pronken, to show off
pronkjuweel *n*, gem
pronkstuk *n*, show-piece
pronon'ceren, to pronounce
prooi, prey
proost! cheers!
prop, plug, wad
  met een voorstel op de proppen komen, to come out with a suggestion
propae'deutisch, preliminary
propa'geren, to propagate
propje *n*, pellet; tubby little person
proper, clean and tidy
propvol, chock-full
prostitu'ée, prostitute
prote'geren, to patronize, to befriend
protes'teren, to protest
pro'these, artificial teeth (*or* limb *etc.*)
protserig, ostentatious
provi'and, provisions
provian'deren, to provision
provinci'aal, provincial
pro'vincie, province
pro'visie, provision; commission
pro'visiekast, store-cupboard
provi'sorisch, provisional

provo'ceren, to provoke
pro'voost, punishment-cell
proza *n*, prose
pruik, wig
pruikentijd, the time of 18th century dandyism
pruilen, to pout
pruim, plum; quid
pruime'dant, prune
pruimemondje *n*: **een — trekken,** to purse the lips
pruimen, to chew tobacco
Pruisen *n*, Prussia
prul *n*, trash; wastrel
prullenmand, waste-paper basket
prut, curds, mire, grounds
prutsen, to mess about, to botch
pruttelen, to simmer; to grumble
psychi'ater, psychiatrist
psycho'loog, psychologist
puber'teit, adolescence
publi'ceren, to publish
pu'bliek (*n*), public, audience
puffen, to puff
puik, choice
puimsteen, pumice-stone
puin *n*, rubble
puinhoop, ruins, debris
puistje *n,* **nukkel,** pimple
pul, ewer, large vase, tankard
pulken, to pick
pulver *n*, powder
pummel, yokel
pu'naise, drawing-pin
punctu'eel, punctual
punt (*n*), point, tip; full-stop
  dubbel(e) punt, colon
  punt komma, semi-colon
  als puntje bij paaltje komt, when it comes to the point
puntdicht *n*, epigram
punter, punt
puntig, pointed, jagged
pu'pil, ward; pupil
pur'geermiddel *n*, purgative
Puri'tein(s), Puritan(ical)
purper(en) (*n*), purple
put, pit, well
  in de put zitten, to be depressed
putten, to draw, to derive
puur, sheer, neat

Q

quaran'taine, quarantine
quartre-'mains, duet
quitte, quits

R

ra, yard(-arm)
raad, advice; council, board
raadgevend, advisory
raadgeving, (piece of) advice
raadhuis *n*, council offices
raadplegen, to consult
raadsel *n*, riddle, puzzle; enigma
raadselachtig, mystifying
raadsheer, justice
raadslid *n*, councillor
raadsman, adviser
raadzaam, advisable
raaf, raven
raak, well-aimed, to the point
 maar raak, at random
raaklijn, tangent
raam *n*, window; frame
raamkozijn *n*, window-frame, window-sill
raapstelen, turnip-tops
raar, queer; silly
raaskallen, to blather
ra'barber, rhubarb
rab'bijn, rabbi
rad, voluble: *n* wheel
 een rad voor de ogen draaien, to throw dust in (a person's) eyes
radbraken, to wreck, to mangle
radeloos, at a loss, distraught
raden, to guess; to advise
raderboot, paddle-steamer
ra'deren, to erase
radi'caal, radical, fundamental
ra'dijs, radish
radiolamp, (wireless) valve
radio-omroep, broadcasting-service
rafelen, to fray
raffinade'rij, refinery
rage, craze
ragebol, mop (of hair)
ragfijn, gossamer(y)
rakelings langs gaan, to skim past

raken, to hit, to touch; to concern; to get
ra'ket, racquet; rocket
rakker, rascal
ram, ram
ramen (op), to estimate (at)
ramen'as, black radish
ram'meien, to batter, to ram
rammelaar, rattle
rammelen, to rattle, to clank
 door elkaar rammelen, to give a thorough shaking to
rammelkast, tin-can
rammen, to ram
ramp, disaster
rampo'neren, to wreck
rampspoed, adversity
ramp'zalig, disastrous, wretched
ran'cune, rancour
rand, edge, (b)rim
rang, rank, grade
ran'geren, to shunt
rangschikken, to arrange
rangtelwoord *n*, ordinal number
rank, slender, sleek-lined; tendril
ransel, knapsack, satchel; hiding
ranselen, to thrash
rans(ig), rancid
rant'soen *n*, ration
rantsoe'nering, rationing
rap, nimble
ra'paille, ra'palje *n*, rabble
rapen, to gather
rappe'leren, to recall
rap'port *n*, report
rappor'teren, to report
rari'teit, curio(sity)
ras, quick, soon: thoroughbred: *n*, race; breed
rasecht, true-born
rasp, grater, rasp
raspen, to grate, to rasp
raster, lath
rat, rat
rata'plan, caboodle
ratel, rattle; tongue
ratelen, to rattle, to roll
rationali'seren, to rationalize
ratio'neel, rational
ratje'toe, hotchpotch
rats, blue funk
ratsen, to whip, to pinch

rattekruid *n,* arsenic
rauw, raw; raucous
  dat valt me rauw op het lijf, that's an unexpected blow
rauwkost, uncooked vegetables *or* fruit
ravezwart, jet-black
ra'vijn *n,* ravine
ravitai'lleren, to victual
ra'votten, to romp
razen, to roar, to rage
  het water raast, the kettle sings
razend, furious, wild, frantic
razer'nij, frenzy
re'actie, reaction
rea'geerbuis, test-tube
rea'geren, to react, to respond
reali'seren : zich —, to realize
reali'teit, reality
re'bel('leren), (to) rebel
recen'sent, reviewer
re'censie, review
re'cept *n,* recipe; prescription
re'ceptie, reception
re'cherche, criminal investigation department
recher'cheur, detective
recht, straight; right: *n,* right; law
rechtbank, (law-)court(s)
rechtens, by right(s)
rechter, judge
rechter-, right
rechterhand, right hand (side)
rechterlijk, judicial
rechtge'aard, right-minded; honest
rechthoek, rectangle
recht'hoekig, rectangular, right-angled
recht'matig, lawful, legitimate
recht'op, upright, erect
rechts, (on) the right; right-handed; Right(-winged)
rechts'af, to the right
recht'schapen, honest
rechtsgeding *n,* lawsuit
rechts'geldig, legal
rechtsgeleerde, lawyer
rechtsgeleerdheid, · jurisprudence
rechtsom'keert! about turn!

rechtspositie, legal status
rechtspraak, administration of justice
rechtspreken, to administer justice
recht'standig, perpendicular
rechtstreeks, direct
rechtsvervolging, prosecution
rechtzaak, lawsuit
rechtzaal, court-room
rechtzekerheid, legal security
recht'uit, straight (on)
recht'vaardig, just
recht'vaardigen, to justify
recht'zinnig, orthodox
recipi'ëren, to receive
reci'teren, to recite
re'clame, advertisement; claim
  re'clame maken voor, to advertise
recla'meren, to (put in a) claim
reclas'sering, (prisoner) rehabilitation
recomman'deren, to recommend
reconstru'eren, to reconstruct
recru'teren, to recruit
rector principal, master
  rector mag'nificus, Vice-Chancellor
re'çu *n,* receipt ticket
redac'teur, editor
re'dactie, editorial staff
reddeloos, irretrievable
redden, to save, to rescue
  ik kan me wel redden, I can manage (all right)
reddingsboot, life-boat
reddingsgordel, life-belt
rede, reason; speech: roads(tead)
  in de rede vallen, to interrupt
redekavelen, to bandy arguments, to dispute
redekunde, redekunst, (art of) rhetoric
redelijk, reasonable; rational
redeloos, senseless, irrational
reden, reason
redenaar, orator
rede'natie, rede'nering, reasoning
rede'neren, to reason; to hold forth
reder('ij), ship-owner(s)

rederijker, rhetorician
redetwisten, to dispute
redevoering, speech, oration
redeziften, to split hairs
redi'geren, to edit
redmiddel *n,* expedient
re'ductie, reduction
ree(bok), roe(-buck)
reebout, haunch of venison
reebruin (*n*), fawn
reeds, already
re'ëel, real(istic)
reeks, series, row, string
reep, strip, bar; rope
reet, chink
refe'raat *n,* paper, lecture
refe'renties, references
refe'reren, to refer
re'ferte: onder — aan, with
   reference to
reflec'tant, interested party
reflec'teren op, to answer; to
   entertain
refor'matie, reformation
re'frein *n,* refrain
regel, rule; line
regelen, to arrange; to regulate
zich regelen naar, to conform to
regeling, arrangement
regelmaat, regularity
regel'matig, regular
regelrecht, straight
regen, rain
van de regen in de drop, from
   the frying-pan into the fire
regenachtig, rainy
regenen, to rain
regenjas, rain-coat
re'gent, regent, governor
re'gentenregering, oligarchy
regenton, water-butt
re'gentschap *n,* regency, govern-
   orship
re'geren, to govern, to rule
re'gering, government, reign
re'gie, production
regis'seur, producer
re'gister *n,* register; index;
   organ-stop
regis'treren, to register
regle'ment *n,* regulation(s)
reglemen'tair, regular
regu'leren, to regulate

rei, chorus (of dancers)
reiger, heron
reiken, to reach, to stretch
reikhalzend, longingly
reilen: zoals het reilt en zeilt,
   lock, stock and barrel
rein, clean; chaste
je reinste, utter
in het reine brengen, to
   straighten out
reine-claude, greengage
reinigen, to clean(se)
reinigingsmiddel *n,* detergent
reis, journey, voyage
reisbureau *n,* travel-agency
reisgelegenheden, travelling
   facilities
reisgoed *n,* luggage
reis-necessaire, dressing-case,
   toilet-case
reis'vaardig, ready to leave
reisvereniging, travel association
reizen, to travel
reiziger, traveller, passenger
rek, elasticity: *n,* rack
dat is een hele rek, it's a tidy
   stretch
rekbaar(heid), elastic(ity)
rekel, rascal
rekenen, to reckon, to count; to
   charge
reken maar! you bet!
rekenfout, (mathmatical) error
rekening, bill, account
rekening houden met, to take
   into consideration
rekening-cou'rant, current account
rekenkunde, arithmetic
rekenliniaal, slide-rule
rekenmachine, calculating-
   machine
rekenschap, account
zich rekenschap geven van,
   to realize (to the full)
rekken, to stretch; to protract
rekstok, horizontal bar
re'k(w)est *n,* petition
rekwi'reren, to requisition
rel, riot
re'laas *n,* account
re'latie, (business) relation, connection

rela'tief, relative

reli'ëfdruk, die-stamping

re'ligie, religion

reli'kwi, reli'qui, relic

reling, (ship's) rail(s)

relletje n, disturbance

rem, brake

rem'bours n, cash on delivery

re'mise, remittance; tram depot; draw(n game)

remmen, to brake; to restrain, to retard

rempla'cant, substitute

rempla'ceren, to replace

renbaan, race-course; speedway

ren'dabel, profitable, paying

ren'deren, to pay (its way)

rendier n, reindeer

rennen, to run

renom'mee, fame

renpaard n, race-horse

rente, interest

rentekaart, insurance card

renteloos, free of interest

rente'nieren, to live on private means

rentestandaard, rate of interest

rentmeester, agent

rep en roer, an uproar

repa'ratie, repair(o)

repa'reren, to repair, to mend

repatri'ëren, to return home, to repatriate

repe'teren, to repeat; to re-hearse; to coach (for an ex-amination)

repe'titie, (revision-)test; re-hearsal

repe'titor, coach, tutor

re'pliek, rejoinder

repor'tage, commentary

reppen van, to make any men-tion of

zich reppen, to hurry (up)

repre'saillemaatregel, reprisal

re'prise, repeat(-performance)

rep'tiel n, reptile

repub'liek, republic

republi'kein(s), republican

repu'tatie, reputation

requi'reren, to requisition

reser'vaat n, reserve

re'serve, reserve(s)

re'servewiel n, spare wheel

resi'dentie, royal residence; resi-dency

reso'luut, resolute

reso'neren, to resound

respec'tievelijk, respectively

res'pijt n, respite

res'sort n, jurisdiction

ressor'teren onder, to come under the jurisdiction of

rest, rest, remainder

res'tant n, remnant

restau'ratie, restoration, renova-tion; refreshment-room, din-ing-car

resten, to remain

res'terend, remaining

restitu'eren, to pay back

resul'taat n, result

resu'meren, to summarize

reti'rade, toilet

retou'cheren, to touch up

re'tour, return

re'traite, retreat

reu, male dog

reuk, smell, scent, odour

reukwater n, scent

reü'nie, reunion

reü'nisten, past members

reus, giant

reus'achtig, tremendous

reutel(en), (to) rattle

reuze, enormous, wizard

reuzel, lard

reuzenarbeid, gigantic task

re'vanche, revenge

reven, to reef (down)

revé'rence, curtsey

re'vers, lapel

re'visie, revision

revolution'nair, revolutionary

re'vue, review; revue

r(h)e'torisch, rhetorical

r(h)euma'tiek, rheumatism

riant, delightful

rib, rib

ribbel(ig), rib(bed)

ribbenkast, body

richel, ledge, ridge

richten, to direct, to aim; to address

zich richten naar, to conform to

richting, direction, trend

iets in die richting, something of the sort

richtlijn, guiding principal

richtsnoer, guidance

ridder, knight

ridderlijk, chivalrous

ridderorde, order of knighthood

ridderroman, romance of chivalry

ridderslag, accolade

ridderstand, knighthood, knightage

rieken, to smell

riem, strap, belt: oar: ream

riet n, reed; cane

rieten dak n, thatched roof

rietje n, (drinking-)straw

rietsuiker, cane-sugar

rif n, reef

rij, row

op de rij af, consecutively

rijbaan, riding track; carriage-way

rijbewijs n, driving-licence

rijbroek, riding breeches

rijden, to ride, to drive, to run

rijdier n, mount

rijgen, to tack; to thread

rijgnaald, rijgpen, bodkin

rijk, rich, wealthy, sumptuous: n, state, realm

het Britse Rijk, the British Empire

het rijk alleen hebben, to have it all to oneself

rijkdom, riches, wealth

rijkelijk, richly, amply

rijknecht, groom

rijksambtenaar, civil servant

rijksbureau n, government department

rijks'daalder, 2½ guilders

rijkskosten: op —, at the public expense

rijksweg, trunk road

rijkswege: van —, on government authority

rijm n, rhyme

rijmelaar, versifier

rijmela'rij, doggerel

rijmen, to rhyme; to tally, to reconcile

Rijn, Rhine

Rijnvaart, Rhine trade

rijp, ripe, mature: hoar-frost

rijpelijk, seriously

rijpen, to ripen, to mature

het heeft gerijpt, there has been a hoar-frost

rijs(hout) n, osier(s)

rijschool, riding-school

rijst, rice

rijste'brij, rijstepap, rice-pudding

rijsttafel, meal of savoury dishes with rice

rijtuig n, carriage

rijweg, carriage-way

rijwiel n, (bi)cycle

rijwielstalling, cycle store-(house)

rijzen, to (a)rise

rijzig, tall

riksja, rickshaw

rillen, to shiver, to shudder

rimboe, jungle

rimpel(en) (to) wrinkle (up); (to) ripple; (to) gather

ring, ring

ringbaard, dundreary whiskers

ringeloren, to browbeat

ringsteken, to tilt at the ring

ringwerpen n, quoits

rinkelen, to jingle, to tinkle

rins, acidulous

rio'lering, sewerage

ri'ool n, sewer, drain

ris, bunch

ri'see, laughing stock

risico n, risk

ris'kant, risky

ris'keren, to risk

rist, string

risten, to strip, to string

rit, (tram-, bus-)ride, drive, rally

ritme n, rhythm

ritmisch, rhythmic(al)

ritselen, to rustle

ritssluiting, zip-fastener

ritu'eel n, ritual

ritus, rite

rivali'teit, rivalry

ri'vier, river

rob, seal

robbedoes, tomboy

robber, rubber
ro'bijn, ruby
ro'buust, robust
rochelen, to rattle, to ruckle
roddelen, to gossip
rode'hond, German measles
roebel, rouble
roe(de), rod, birch; rood
roef, deck-house: whiz!
roeiboot, rowing-boat
roeien, to row
roeipen, rowlock
roeispaan, oar
roek, rook
roekeloos, reckless
roem, glory, renown
roemen, to praise; to boast
Roe'menië n, Roumania
roemer, goblet
roemrijk, roemvol, glorious
roep, call, cry; fame
roepen, to call (out)
roeping, calling, vocation
roepstem, call (of duty)
roer n, rudder, helm
roerdomp, bittern
roerei n, scrambled egg
roeren, to stir; to move
roerend, moving, pathetic
 roerende goederen, movables
roerganger, helmsman
roerig, restless
roerloos, motionless: rudderless
roerpen, tiller
roersteven, sternpost
roes, intoxication, fever of excitement
roest, perch, roost: n, rust,
 blight
 oud roest, scrap iron
roesten, to rust
roestig, rusty
roestvrij, rustproof, stainless
roet n, soot
 roet in het eten gooien, to
 throw a spanner in the works
roezemoezig, rowdy
roffel, (drum-)roll
rogge, rye
rok, skirt; tails
rokbeschermer, dress-guard
rokkostuum n, dress-suit
roken, to smoke

rol, roll; part, role
 aan de rol zijn, to be on the
 spree
rolgordijn n, blind
rol'lade, collared beef
rollen, to roll
rolletje n, roll, packet; castor
rolluik n, roller shutter
rolmops, Bismarck herring
rolpens, spiced mince pudding
 done up in tripe
rolschaats(:n), (to) roller-skate
rolstoel, wheel-chair
roltrap, escalator
rolvast, word-perfect
rolveger, carpet-sweeper
rolverdeling, cast
roman, novel
roman'tiek, romantic(ism)
romantisch, romantic
Ro'mein(s), Roman
rommel, mess, rubbish, junk
rommelen, to rummage; to
 rumble
rommelig, untidy
rommelkamer, lumber-room
romp, trunk; hull; fuselage
rompslomp, fuss and bother
rond, round; forthright
 in het rond, round (about)
rondas, buckler
rondbazuinen, to blaze abroad
rond'borstig, forthright
ronde, round(s), lap, heat
ron'deel n, rondeau
rondhout n, spa
ronding, rounding, curve, camber
rondje n, round (of drinks or
 cards)
rondkomen, to make ends meet
rondom, all round
rondreis, tour
rondreizend, itinerant, touring
rondrit, (coach-)tour
rondschrijven n, circular letter
rondtasten, to grope about
rondte: in de —, in a circle,
 round about
ronduit, outright
rondvaart, boat-trip
rondvertellen, to spread
rondvlucht, (joy-)flight

rondvraag, question time
rondwaren, to haunt
ronken, to snore; to roar
ronselen, to recruit
röntgenen, to (give) X-ray (treatment)
rood (*n*), red
  rood koper, copper
roodborstje *n*, robin
roodgloeiend, red-hot
roodvonk, scarlet fever
roof, plunder, robbery, prey
roofdier *n*, beast of prey
roofoverval, hold-up
rooftocht, foray
roof'zuchtig, rapacious
rooien, to dig (up); to manage
rook, smoke
  onder de rook van, within a stone's throw of
rookgordijn *n*, smoke-screen
rooktabak, pipe-tobacco
rookvlees *n*, smoked beef
room, cream
roomboter, butter
roomijs *n*, ice-cream
Rooms(-Katholiek), Roman (Catholic)
roomsoes, cream-puff
roos, rose; dandruff; bull's eye
roos'kleurig, rosy
rooster, grating, grate, grill, ventilator; rota, time-table
roost(er)en, to roast, to grill, to toast
ros *n*, steed
ro'sarium *n*, rose-garden
rosbief *n*, roast beef
rose (*n*), pink
roskammen, to curry; to slate
rossen, to tear (along)
rot, rotten
  zich rot lachen, to laugh oneself stupid
ro'teren, to rotate
rots, rock, cliff
rotsachtig, rocky
rotsblok *n*, boulder
rotspartij, rockery
rotsvast, firm as a rock
rotten, to rot, to decay
rotting, cane
rotzooi, ruddy mess(-up)

rou'leren, to be in circulation
rouw, mourning
rouwbeklag *n*, condolence
rouwdienst, memorial service
rouwen, to rue
rouwig, sorry
rouwkoets, funeral coach
rouwrandjes *n*, dirty nails
roven, to pillage, to steal, to kidnap
rover, robber
ro'yaal, generous, sporting, lavish, ample
royal'istisch, royalist
royali'teit, open-handedness
ro'yeren, to strike off the register
rozebottel, rose-hip
rozelaar, rose-bush
rozenkrans, rosary; garland of roses
ro'zet, rosette
ro'zijn, raisin
rubber, rubber
ru'briek, heading, rubric, column
ruchtbaar maken, to make known
ruchtbaarheid, publicity
rug, back, ridge
  achter de rug, over and done with
ruggegraat, backbone
ruggelings, backward(s), back to back
ruggespraak, consultation
rugleuning, back of the chair
rugzak, rucksack
rui(en), (to) moult
ruif, manger
ruig, shaggy, hairy; rough
ruiken, to smell, to scent
ruiker, posy
ruil, exchange
ruilen, to (ex)change, to swop
ruim, ample, spacious, wide: *n*, hold
ruimen, to clear (away)
  het veld ruimen, to give way to
ruimschoots, amply
ruimte, room, space
ruin, gelding
ru'ïne, ruin(s), wreck
ruï'neren, to ruin
ruisen, to rustle, to rush, to swish

ruit, (glass) pane(l); check; diamond
ruiten'boer, knave of diamonds
ruiter, horseman, trooper
ruiteraanval, cavalry charge
ruite'rij, calvalry
ruiterlijk, frank
ruiterpad *n*, bridle-path
ruitewisser, squeegee, wind-screen wiper
ruitijd, moulting season
ruk(ken), (to) tug, (to) jerk
rukwind, squall
rul, loose, running
ru'moer *n*, clamour
ru'moerig, noisy
run, tanning
rund *n*, ox
runderen, cattle
runderhaas, fillet of beef
runderlap, beefsteak
rundvee *n*, (horned) cattle
rundvet *n*, suet
rundvlees *n*, beef
runenschrift *n*, runic script
rups, caterpillar
Rus(sisch), Russian
rust, rest, quiet, peace; half-time
  op de plaats rust! stand easy!
rustbank, rustbed *n*, couch
rusteloos, restless, untiring
rusten, to rest
  wel to rusten! good night!
rustend, retired
rus'tiek, rustic, rural
rustig, quiet, tranquil
rustoord *n*, retreat
rustpoos, breathing-space
rutschbaan, switch-back, chute
ruw, rough, coarse, raw
ruzie, quarrel, row

S

saai, dull, drab
saam'horigheid, solidarity
saam'horigheidsgevoel *n*, team-spirit
sabbat, sabbath
sabbelen, to suck
sabel, sabre
sabelbont *n*, sable

sabo'teren, to sabotage
sacramen'teel, sacramental
sa'disme *n*, sadism
saf'fiaan *n*, morocco
saf'fier, sapphire
saf'fraan, saffron
sage, saga, legend
sa'jet(ten), wool(len)
sakker'loot! by Jove!
Saksisch (*n*), Saxon
  Saksisch porcelein, Dresden china
sa'lade, salad
sa'laris *n*, salary
saldo *n*, balance
  per saldo, after all
salie, sage
salmi'ak, sal-ammoniac
sa'lon, drawing-room; saloon
sa'lonmuziek, light music
sal'peterzuur *n*, nitric acid
salto mor'tale, somersault
salu'eren, to salute
sa'luut *n*, salute; cheerio!
salvo *n*, salvo, volley; round
samen, together
samendoen, to put together; to go shares
samenflansen, to concoct, to slap together
samengesteld, compound(ed), complex, composite
samenhangen, to be connected
samenhokken, to herd together
samenkomen, to (for)gather
samenloop van omstandig-heden, coincidence
samenscholing, gathering
samensmelten, to fuse, to amal-gamate
samenspannen, to conspire (to-gether)
samenspanning, plot, conspir-acy
samenspel *n*, *ensemble*, team-work
samenspraak, dialogue, con-fabulation
samenstellen, to compose
samenstelling, composition, compound
samenstroming, concourse; confluence

samentrekken, to contract, to concentrate

samenvallen, to coincide

samenvatten, to summarize

samenvloeien, to unite; to merge, to blend

samenvoegen, to join

samenweefsel *n,* texture, web

samenzweerder, conspirator

samenzwering, conspiracy

sanctie, sanction

san'daal, sandal

sani'tair, sanitary

sans-a'tout, no trumps

santenkraam, (the whole) bang shoot

sap *n,* sap, juice

sapperde'kriek, sapper'loot! by Jove!

sappig, juicy, luscious

sar'castisch, sarcastic

sarren, to bait

sas: in zijn —, pleased as Punch

sa'tanisch, fiendish

sater, satyr

sa'tijn, *n,* satin

sa'tiricus, satirist

sau'cijzebroodje *n,* sausage-roll

saus, sauce

sausen, to flavour; to pelt (with rain)

sauskom, sauce-boat

sau'teren, to quick-fry

savou'reren, to relish

sawa(h), paddy-field

scal'peren, to scalp

scan'deren, to scan

schaaf, plane, slicer

schaafwond, graze, abrasion

schaakmat, checkmate; stalemate

schaakspel *n,* game of chess; chess-set

schaal, scale; shell; dish

schaldier *n,* crustacean

schaalverdeling, graduation

schaambeen *n,* pubis

schaamdelen, private parts

schaamrood *n,* blush of shame

schaamte(loos), shame(less)

schaap *n,* sheep; ninny
  zwaart schaap, scapegoat

schaar, (pair of) scissors, shears; host

schaars, scarce, sparse

schaarste, scarcity, shortage

schaats(en) (rijden), (to) skate

schab'loon, stencil-plate, template

schacht, shaft

schade, damage, harm, detriment
  de schade inhalen, to make up arrears

schadelijk, harmful, noxious

schadeloos stellen, to indemnify

schaden, to harm, to do damage to

schadepost, financial set-back

schadevergoeding, compensation

schaduw(en), (to) shadow, (to) shade

schaduwrijk, shady

schaduwzijde, shaded side; drawback

schaffen, to provide

schaften, to knock off for lunch

schakel, link

schakelaar, switch

schaken, to play chess: to abduct

scha'kering, shade

schalk, rogue

schalks, roguish

schallen, to (re)sound, to ring out

schal'mei, shawm

schamel, meagre, wretched

schamen: zich —, to be ashamed

schampen, to graze; to mock

schamper, scornful

schan'daal *n,* scandal, shame

schan'dalig, disgraceful, shameful

schanddaad, outrage

schande, disgrace, shame

schandelijk, disgraceful

schandpaal, pillory

schandvlek, stain, disgrace

schapebout, leg of mutton

schapewolkjes, fleecy clouds

schappelijk, fair, decent

schar, dab

scharen, to range, to rally

scharensliep, scharenslijper, knife-grinder
schar'laken *n*, scarlet
schar'minkel, spindle-shanks
schar'nier *n*, hinge
scharrelen, to rummage; to get along somehow
schat, treasure, wealth; darling
schatbewaarder, treasurer
schateren, to scream (with laughter)
schatkist, treasury
schatrijk, fabulously rich
schattebout, poppet
schatten, to value; to estimate
schattig, sweet
schatting, estimate, valuation; tribute
schaven, to plane; to graze; to polish
scha'vot *n*, scaffold
scha'vuit, rascal
schede, sheath; vagina
schedel, skull
scheef, crooked, lop-sided, raked
scheve voorstelling, misrepresentation
scheve verhouding, wry relationship
scheel, cross-eyed
scheelkijken, scheelzien, to squint
scheenbeen *n*, shin(-bone)
scheepgaan, to embark
scheepsbeschuit, ship's biscuit
scheepsbouw, ship-building
scheepsjournaal *n*, log(-book)
scheepsrecht *n*, maritime law
scheepsroeper, loud hailer
scheepsruimte, tonnage; cargo space
scheepsterm, nautical term
scheepsvolk *n*, (ship's) crew
scheepvaart, shipping
scheepvaartkunde, navigation
scheerapparaat *n*, (safety) razor
scheerlijn, guy(-rope)
scheermes *n*, cut-throat razor
scheermesje *n*, razor-blade
scheerriem, strop
scheerzeep, shaving-soap
schegbeeld *n*, figure-head
scheidbaar, separable

scheiden, to separate, to part; to divorce
scheiding, separation; parting; divorce
scheiding van tafel en bed, legal separation
schei(ds)lijn, dividing-line
scheidsmuur, partition-wall; barrier
scheidsrechter, umpire, referee; arbitrator
scheikunde, chemistry
schei'kundig, chemical
schei'kundige, (analytical) chemist
schel, shrill, glaring; bell
schelden (op), to swear (at)
scheldnaam, (rude) name
scheldpartij, slanging-match
scheldwoord *n*, term of abuse
schelen, to matter; to make a difference
het kan me niet schelen, I don't mind
we schelen maar twee jaar, there is only two years between us
schellak, shellac
schellen, to ring (the bell)
schellinkje *n*, gallery
schelm, rascal
schelmenroman, picaresque novel
schelms, roguish
schelp, shell, scallop
schelpdier *n*, shell-fish
schelvis, haddock
schema *n*, sketch diagram, rough draft
sche'matisch, schematic
schemer(ing), twilight, dusk
schemer(acht)ig, dim, vague
schemerdonker (*n*), twili(gh)t, half-dark(ness)
schemeren, to dawn, to grow dusk; to be dimly visible
zitten schemeren, to sit in the twilight
schemerlamp, shaded lamp
schenden, to violate; to damage, to disfigure; to desecrate
schenkel, shank; femur
schenken, to pour (out); to present with, to grant

schenking, gift
schep, shovel, scoop
  een schep geld, heaps of money
schepel, bushel
schepeling, member of the crew
schepen, to ship: sheriff
schepje *n,* spoonful
  er een schepje opdoen, to go one better
scheppen, to scoop, to shovel, to ladle: to create
  een luchtje scheppen, to take a breather
  vreugde scheppen, to derive great pleasure
scheppend, creative
schepper, creator
schepping, creation
scheprad *n,* paddle wheel, water-wheel
schepsel *n,* creature
scheren, to shave, to shear, to skin
  scheer je weg! be off with you!
scherf, fragment, splinter
schering en inslag, warp and woof; everyday occurrence
scherm *n,* screen, curtain
  achter de schermen, behind the scenes
schermdegen, foil
schermen, to fence
scher'mutseling, skirmish
scherp, sharp, keen; trenchant
  scherpe hoek, acute angle; sharp corner
scherp *n,* edge; live cartridge
scherpen, to sharpen; to whet
scherp'hoekig, acute-angled
scherprechter, executioner
scherpschutter, marksman
scherpte, sharpness, definition
scherpziend, keen-sighted; penetrating
scherp'zinnig, acute, astute
scherp'zinnigheid, acumen
scherts, joking, jest, joke
schertsen, to jest
schets(en), (to) sketch
schetteren, to blare; to rant, to gas
scheur, tear, crack
scheurbuik, scurvy

scheuren, to tear; to plough up; to crack
scheuring, split, cleavage
scheut, dash; shooting pain
scheutig, open-handed
schichtig, shy, skittish
schielijk, quick, swift
schier, nearly
schiereiland *n,* peninsula
schietbaan, rifle-range
schieten, to shoot, to fire
  een plan laten schieten, to drop a plan
  te binnen schieten, to dawn on
schietgat *n,* loop-hole
schietkatoen *n,* gun-cotton
schietlood *n,* plummet
schietschijf, target
schiften, to sift, to screen; to curdle
schijf, disk; slice; target, dial
schijn, light; appearance, semblance
schijnaanval, sham-attack
schijnbaar, seemingly
schijnbeeld *n,* phantom
schijnbeweging, apparent movement; feint
schijnen, to shine; to seem
schijngestalte, phase
schijn'heilig, hypocritical
schijnsel *n,* light, glimmer
schijntje *n,* scrap
schijnwerper, spot-light, search-light, flood-light
schijt(en), (to) shit
schik: in zijn — zijn, to be pleased (with life)
schikgodinnen, Fates
schikken, to arrange, to settle to be convenient (to)
  zich schikken, in, to resign oneself to
schikking, arrangement, agreement
schil, peel, skin
schild *n,* shield
  iets in het schild voeren, to be up to something
schilder, painter; decorator
schilderachtig, picturesque
schilderen, to paint; to depict; to hang about

schilde'rij, painting, picture
schilderkunst, painting, art
schilderstuk *n,* painting, picture
schildklier, thyroid gland
schildknaap, shield-bearer, varlet
schildpad, tortoise(-shell), turtle
schildwacht, sentry
schilferen, to peel, to flake off
schillen, to peel
schillenboer, kitchen-waste collector
schim, shadow, ghost
schimmel, mildew; grey (horse)
schimmelen, to go mouldy
schimmel(plant), fungus
schimpen (op), to scoff (at)
schinkel, shank, femur
schip *n,* ship; nave
  schoon schip maken, to clear out (*or* up)
schipbreuk lijden, to be shipwrecked; to miscarry
schipbrug, pontoon-bridge
schipper, skipper, bargee
schipperen, to manage somehow
schisma *n,* schism
schitteren, to glitter, to be brilliant; to be conspicuous
schitterend, brilliant, splendid
schlager, (song-)hit
schmink(en), (to) make up
schobbejak, blackguard
schoeisel *n,* foot-wear
schoelje *n,* bad lot
schoen, shoe
  de stoute schoenen aantrekken, to pluck up courage
  iemand iets in de schoenen schuiven, to lay something at a person's door
schoener, schooner
schoenlapper, cobbler
schoenmaker, shoe-repairer
schoensmeer, shoe-polish
schoep, paddle, blade
schoffel(en) (to) hoe; (to) shuffle
schoft, cad : withers
schoftje *n,* gutter-snipe
schok, shock, jolt
schokbreker, shock-absorber
schokken, to shake; to jerk, to jolt

schol, plaice: (ice-)floe
scholen, to shoal, to flock together; to school
scho'lier, pupil
schommel, swing; lumbersome woman
schommelen, to swing, to rock, to roll; to fluctuate
schone, beauty
schonk(ig), big bone(d)
schoof, sheaf
schooier, beggar, tramp; wretch
school, school; shoal
schoolblijven: moeten —, to be kept in
schoolbord *n,* black-board
schoolgeld(en) *n,* school-fees
schoolgeleerdheid, book-learning
schooljuffrouw, school-mistress
schoolmeester, school-master; pedant
schoolplicht, compulsory school-attendance
schoolreisje *n,* school outing
schools, scholastic
schoolslag, breast stroke
schoolverzuim *n,* absence(s)
schoolwet, education act
schoolziek, shamming (illness)
schoon, clean; beautiful, fine
schoonheid, beauty
schoonheidsmiddel *n,* beauty preparation
schoonhouden, to keep clean
schoonmaak, (spring-)cleaning; clear-out
schoonmaken, to clean
schoonouders, schoonvader en schoonmoeder, father- and mother-in-law
schoonrijden *n,* figure-skating
schoonschrift *n,* calligraphy; copy-book
schoonzoon, son-in-law
schoonzuster, sister-in-law
schoor, shore, prop
schoorsteen, chimney(-pot); funnel
schoorsteenmantel, mantelpiece
schoorsteenplaat, hearth-plate
schoorsteenveger, sweep

SCH 172 SCH

schoorvoetend, reluctantly
schoot, lap; womb, bosom; sheet
schootkindje *n,* pampered child, baby
schootsvel *n,* leather apron
schop, spade; shovel: kick
schopje *n,* trowel, child's spade
schoppen to kick (up)
schoppen'heer *etc,* king *etc* of spades
schopstoel: hij zit op de —, he may be turned out at any moment
schor, hoarse: mud-flat
schoren, to shore up
schorpi'oen, scorpion
schorr(i)emorrie *n,* riff-raff
schors, bark
schorsen, to suspend; to adjourn
schorse'neer, salsify
schort, apron, pinafore
schort: wat — eraan? what is the matter?
schot *n,* shot; partition, bulkhead
Schot, Scot(sman)
shotel, dish, saucer
schots, (ice-)floe
schots en scheef door elkaar, here, there and everywhere
Schotse ruit, tartan
shouder, shoulder
schouderblad *n,* shoulder-blade
schout, sheriff
schout-bij-'nacht, rear-admiral
schouw, fireplace; scow
schouwburg, theatre
schouwing, autopsy
schouwspel *n,* spectacle
schraag, trestle
schraal, meagre, lean, bleak
schraalhans is daar keukenmeester, you'll get nothing but short commons there
schraapijzer *n,* scraper
schraapzucht, rapacity
schragen, to shore up; to sustain
schram(men), (to) scratch
schrander, shrewd, intelligent
schransen, to gorge

schrap, scratch
zich schrap zetten, to take a firm stand, to brace oneself
schrapen, to scrape; to clear
schrappen, to scrap(e), to cross out
schrede, stride, step
schreeuw(en), (to) yell, (to) cry (out)
schreeuwend, crying; garish; blatant
schreeuwlelijk, bawler
schreien, to cry (out), to weep
schriel, frail; meagre; mingy
schrift *n,* (hand)writing; exercise-book
de Heilige Schrift, (the) Holy Scripture(s)
schriftelijk, written, in writing
schriftgeleerde, scribe
schriftvervalsing, forgery
schrijden, to stride
schrijfbehoeften, stationary
schrijfbureau *n,* desk
schrijffout, slip of the pen
schrijfletters, script
schrijfmachine, typewriter
schrijfmap, writing-case
schrijftaal, formal language
schrijftrant, style (of writing)
schrijlings, astride
schrijnen, to smart; to gall
schrijnwerker, cabinet-maker
schrijven, to write; *n,* communication
schrik, fright, terror
schrikaanjagend, terrifying
schrikachtig, nervy
schrik'barend, appalling
schrikbeeld *n,* nightmarish vision
schrikbewind *n,* reign of terror
schrikkeljaar *n,* leap-year
schrikken, to have a (nasty) fright, to be taken aback
wakker schrikken, to wake with a start
schrik'wekkend, terrifying
schril, shrill, glaring
schrobben, to scrub
schrob'bering, wigging
schroef, screw, propeller
op losse schroeven staan, to be uncertain

schroeien, to scorch, to singe
schroevedraaier, screw-driver
schroeven, to screw
schrokken, to gorge
schromelijk, gross
schromen, to have qualms
schroom, diffidence
schroom'vallig, diffident
schroot n, canister-shot
schub(ben), (to) scale
schuchter, bashful
schuddebollen, to nod (with sleep)
schudden, to shake; to shuffle
schuieren, to brush
schuif, slide, damper
schuifdak n, sunshine roof
schuifdeur, sliding door
schuifelen, to shuffle, to slither
schuifladder, extending ladder
schuifraam n, sash-window
schuiftrompet, trombone
schuilen, to (take) shelter, to lurk
schuilgaan, to go in, to hide
schuilhouden, to lie low
schuilkelder, air-raid shelter
schuilkerk, clandestine church
schuilnaam, pen-name
schuilplaats, hiding-place
schuim n, foam, froth, lather, scum; meringue
schuimbekken, to foam at the mouth
schuimen, to foam, to froth, to lather; to skim
schuimkoppen, white horses
schuin, slanting, oblique; smutty
schuit, boat, barge
schuiven, to push
  laat hem maar schuiven, he can fend for himself
  met de eer gaan schuiven, to take the credit
schuld, debt; fault, blame, guilt
schuldbekentenis, IOU; confession of guilt
schuldbe'wust, guilty
schuldeiser, creditor
schuldenaar, debtor
schuldig, guilty
  schuldig zijn, to be guilty; to owe

schuldige, culprit, guilty party
schulp, shell
schulpen, to scallop
schunnig, shabby; bawdy
schuren, to scour, to sandpaper; to graze
schurft, scabies, mange
schurk, scoundrel
schurken, to writhe, to rub
schurkenstreek, caddish trick
schutblad n, fly-leaf, bract
schutkleur, camouflage
schutsengel, guardian angel
schutlsuis, lock
schutspatroon, patron saint
schutten, to pass through a lock; to dam up
schutter, marksman
schutterig, clumsy, awkward
schutte'rij, civic guard
schutting, fence
schuur, barn
schuurkatoen n, schuurlinnen n, emery cloth
schuurmiddel n, abrasive
schuurpapier n, sand-paper
schuw, timid, shy
schuwen, to shun, to fight shy of
schuwlelijk, dreadfully ugly
scorbutt, scurvy
sculptie, essay
scru'pule, scruple
sec, neat, dry, bare
secon'dair, secondary
secon'dant, second
se'conde(wijzer), second (s-hand)
secreta'resse, (female) secretary
secretari'aat n, secretaryship; secretariate
secreta'rie, town clerk's office
secre'taris, secretary
secre'taris-gene'raal, permanent under-secretary
sectie, section; incision, autopsy
secu'lair, secular
se'cuur, safe; accurate; certain
sedert, since, for
sein n, signal
seinen, to signal, to wire
seinhuisje n, signal-box
seinpaal, semaphore

seinsleutel, transmitting key
seinwachter, signalman
sei'zoen *n,* season
sei'zoenopruiming, (clearance) sale(s)
sekse, sex
sekte, sect
selderij, celery
sema'foor, semaphore
semi-arts, first part of the qualifying examination in medicine; student who has passed this examination
se'naat, senate
se'niel, senile
sen'satie, sensation
sensu'eel, sensual
sentimen'teel, sentimental
sepa'reren, to separate
sep'time, seventh
septisch, septic
sera'fijn(en), seraph(im)
serge, serge
serie, series
seri'eus, serious
sérieux: au — nemen, to take seriously
se'ring, lilac
ser'pent *n,* serpent; shrew
serpen'tine, streamer
serre, conservatory, sun-parlour
ser'veerboy, dumb waiter
ser'veren, to serve
ser'vet *n,* napkin
ser'viel, servile
ser'vies *n,* dinner-service, tea-set
sext, sixth
sexu'eel, sexual
sfeer, (atmo)sphere
sferisch, spherical
shag, cigarette tobacco
sibbekunde, geneaology
sidderen (voor), to quake (at the thought of)
siddering, shudder
sieraad *n,* ornament, (piece of) jewellery
sieren, to adorn, to enhance
sierlijk, elegant
sierplant, ornamental plant
si'gaar, cigar
si'garenwinkel, tobacconist's (shop)

siga'ret, cigarette
si'gnaal *n,* signal
signale'ment *n,* (police) description
signa'leren, to see, to signalize
  overal signaleren, to circulate a description
sijpelen, to seep
sijs: een rare —, a queer bird
sik, goatee
sikkel, sickle, crescent: shekel
sikke'neurig, querulous
sikkepit: geen —, not a thing
simpel, simple, silly
simu'lant, humbug
simu'leren, to simulate
sinaasappel, orange
sinds('dien), (ever) since (then)
singel, girdle; (street on either side of a) town canal
sint, saint
sintel, cinder
Sinter'klaas, Santa Claus
Sinterklaas'avond, St Nicholas' Eve (Dec. 5)
Sint Juttemis: met —, on the Greek calends
sip kijken, to look glum
Sire, your Majesty
si'rene, siren
si'roop, syrup
sissen, to hiss, to sizzle
sisser: met een — aflopen, to fizzle out
sjaal, shawl
sjab'loon, stencil-plate, template
sjacheren, to run a shady business; to haggle
sjees, gig
sjerp, sash
sjezen, to be ploughed
sjoelbak, shovelboard
sjofel, shabby
sjokken, to trudge
sjorren, to lash (up); to haul
sjouwen, to lug; to drudge
sjouwer, dock-hand; porter
ske'let *n,* skeleton
skiën, to ski
sla, salad; lettuce
slaaf, slave
slaafs, slavish, servile
slaags raken, to come to blows

slaan, to hit, to strike, to beat, to smack;
 dat slaat op mij, that applies to me
slaap, sleep: temple
 slaap hebben, to feel sleepy
 slaap vatten, to get to sleep
slaapdrank, sleeping draught
slaapdronken, not fully awake
slaapje *n*, nap; bed-mate
slaapkop, sleepy-head
slaapliedje *n*, lullaby
slaapmiddel *n*, opiate
slaapmuts, night-cap
slaapplaats, (sleeping-)berth
slaapwagen, sleeping-car
slaap'wekkend, soporific
slaapzaal, dormitory
slaapziekte, sleeping sickness
slaatje *n*, salad
slab(be), bib
sla'bakken, to slack(en), to dawdle
slaboon, French bean
slachten, to slaughter
slachting, slaughter
slachtoffer *n*, victim
sla'dood: lange —, lofty (fellow)
slag, blow, stroke, beat, crash; battle; knack; turn; kind
 men moet een slag maken om aan de slag te komen, one has to make a trick in order to get the lead
 een slag om de arm houden, not to commit oneself
 zijn slag slaan, to strike while the iron is hot
slagader, artery
slagbal *n*, rounders
slagboom, boom, barrier
slagen, to succeed, to pass
slager('ij), butcher('s shop)
slaghamer, mallet
slaghout *n*, bat
slaglinie, slagorde, line of battle
slagregen, down-pour
slagroom, (whipped) cream
slagtand, fang, tusk
slag'vaardig, ready for battle
slagwerk *n*, striking mechanism; percussion (section)

slagwoord *n*, **slagzin,** slogan
slagzij(de) (maken), (to) list, (to) bank
slagzwaard *n*, broadsword
slak, snail, slug: slag
slaken, to utter, to heave
slakkegang, snail's pace
slakkehuis *n*, snail-shell; cochlea
slam'pamper, gadabout, lout
slang, snake, serpent; hose (-pipe)
slangemens, contortionist
slangenbezweerder, snake-charmer
slank, slim, slender
slaolie, salad oil
slap, slack, soft, flabby, weak; spineless
slape'loosheid, insomnia
slapen, to (be a)sleep
slaperig, sleepy
slapjes, slack, weak
slappe'koord *n*, slack-rope
slappeling, weakling, jelly-fish
slavenarbeid, slavery
slavendrijver, slave-driver
slaver'nij, slavery, servitude
Slavisch, Slav(onic)
slecht, bad, poor
slechten, to level (out), to demolish; to settle
slechts, only
sle(d)e, sled(ge); (ship's) cradle
 een slee van een wagen, a sleek limousine
sleef, ladle
sleep, train, trail, tow
sleepboot, tug
sleepnet *n*, drag-net
sleeptouw *n*, tow-rope
sleets zijn, to be hard on one's clothes
slenteren, to saunter
slepen, to drag; to tow
sleper, haulier
sleperspaard *n*, dray-horse
slet, slut
sleuf, groove; slot
sleur, rut, humdrum routine
sleuren, to drag (on)
sleutel, key; clef
sleutelbeen *n*, collar bone

sleutelbloem, primrose, primula
Sleutelstad, Leyden
slib *n,* silt, mire
slier(t), stream(er); winding trail
slijk *n,* mire, slime
  aardse slijk, filthy lucre
slijm *n,* slime; phelgm, mucus
slijmvlies *n,* mucous membrane
slijpen, to sharpen, to grind; to cut and polish
slij'tage, wear (and tear)
slijten, to wear out, to wear off; to spend, to retail
slijte'rij, off-license shop
slikken, to swallow
sliknat, sopping wet
slim, clever, crafty; bad
slinger, festoon; pendulum; sling; (crank-)handle
slingeren, to swing; to lurch; to wind; to lie about; to fling
slingerplant, creeper
slinken, to shrink (to nothing), to subside
slinks, sly, underhand
slip, tail(-end)
  slip vangen, to draw (a) blank
slipgevaar ! beware of skidding!
slipover, pull-over
slippedrager, pall-bearer
slippen, to slip, to skid
slippertje maken, to take French leave
slobberen, to suck in, to guzzle noisily
slobkous, gaiter, spat
slodderig, slovenly
sloddervos, slattern
sloep, (ship's) boat, (naval) barge
sloerie, slut
slof, slipper; briquette; carton
  het op zijn sloffen doen, to take things easy,
sloffen, to shuffle
slok, gulp, draught
slokdarm, gullet
slokje *n,* sip, drop
slokken, to guzzle
slons, slattern, frump
sloof, apron: drudge
sloom, languid
  slome duikelaar, slowcoach
sloop, pillow-case; dismantling

sloot, ditch
slop *n,* back street
slopen, to demolish, to break up
slordig, untidy, slipshod
  een slordig sommetje, a tidy sum
slorpen, to sip noisily, to gulp
slot *n,* lock; castle; conclusion
  ten slotte, finally
  per slot van rekening, when all is said and done
slotakkoord *n,* final chord
slotrede, peroration
slotsom, conclusion; upshot
slotzin, closing sentence
sloven, to drudge (and toil)
sluier(en), (to) veil
sluif, slit; sheath
sluik, lank
sluikhandel, trafficking, smuggling
sluimer(en), (to) slumber
sluipen, to steal, to creep
sluipmoordenaar, assassin
sluis, lock; floodgate
sluisdeur, lock-gate
sluiskolk, lock-chamber
sluitboom, (drop-)boom
sluiten, to shut (up), to close (down), to lock (up); to conclude; to fit
sluiting, closing(-down); fastening
sluitring, washer
sluitsteen, key-stone
slungel, stripling
slurf, trunk, proboscis
slurpen, to sip noisily, to gulp
sluw, sly, wily
smaad, libel, contumely
smaak, taste, flavour; relish; palate
  in de smaak vallen, to be popular, to be to (a person's) liking
smaakvol, in good taste
smachten, to pine (away)
smachtend, love-lorn
smadelijk, ignominious
smak, thud
smakelijk, toothsome
  smakelijk eten ! I hope you'll enjoy your meal

smakeloos, tasteless; in bad taste

smaken (naar), to taste (of)

smakken, to fall with a thud; to fling; to smack (one's lips)

smal, narrow

smaldeel *n,* squadron

smalen op, to jeer at

smalfilm, 16 mm. film

smaragd(en), emerald

smart, grief, anguish

smartelijk, grievous

smeden, to forge; to plan

smede'rij, smithy, forge

smeedijzer *n,* wrought iron

smeekbede, supplication

smeer, grease

smeerkaas, cheese spread

smeerkees, smeerlap, muckrake(r); blackguard

smeermiddel, *n,* lubricant

smeerolie, lubricating oil

smeerpoets, dirty tyke

smekeling, suppliant

smeken, to implore, to beseech

smelten, to (s)melt, to fuse

  smeltende tonen, mellow tone(s)

smeltkroes, crucible

smeren, to spread; to grease, to lubricate

  'm smeren, to beat it

smerig, filthy, shabby

smeris, cop(per)

smet, stain, blemish

smetteloos, spotless, blameless

smeuig, smooth; colourful

smeulen, to smoulder

smid, blacksmith

smidse, forge, smithy

smiezen: ik heb het in de —, I've got it taped

smijten (met), to chuck; to throw (about)

smoel, mug, phiz

smoesje *n,* bit of eye-wash, excuse

smoezelig, soiled

smoezen, to whisper together

smoking, dinner-jacket

smokkela'rij, smuggling

smokkelen, to smuggle; to cheat

smokkelwaar, contraband

smokken, to smock

smoor: de — hebben, to be utterly fed up

smoordronken, dead drunk

smoorheet, sweltering

smoorverliefd, madly in love

smoren, to strangle, to stifle

smullen, to tuck in

smulpaap, gourmand(izer)

snaak(s), wag(gish)

snaar, string, chord

snakken naar, to yearn for, to gasp for

snappen, to get, to twig; to nab

snars, the slightest bit

snater: hou je —! hold your tongue!

snateren, to quack, to cackle

snauw(en), (to) snarl

snavel, beak, bill

sne(d)e, cut; slice

  goud *or* **verguld op snee,** with gilt edges

snedig, witty

sneeuw(en), (to) snow

sneeuwjacht, blizzard, driving snow

sneeuwklokje *n,* snowdrop

sneeuwpop, snow-man

snel, quick, fast

snelbuffet *n,* snack-bar

snelduik(en), (to) crash-dive

snelheid, speed

snellen, to hurry

snelschrijven *n,* shorthand

snerpend, biting, bitter

snert, pea-soup; trash(y)

snertvent, rotter

sneu, rotten (luck)

sneuvelen, to be killed (in action)

snibbig, snappily, snappish

snijbiet, beet spinach

snijbloemen, cut flowers

snijboon, runner bean

  rare snijboon, queer cove

snijden, to cut (in), to carve; to intersect; to finesse

snijtand, incisor

snijzaal, dissecting-room

snik, sob, gasp

  niet goed snik, not all there

snikheet, sweltering

snikken, to sob

snip(penjacht), snipe(-shooting)

snipper, snippet, scrap; candied peel

snipperuur *n,* spare hour

snit, cut

snoeien, to prune, to lop, to clip

snoek, pike

 een snoek vangen, to fall in the water; to catch a crab

snoep(e'rij), sweets

snoepen, to eat sweets, to tuck in

snoepreisje *n,* joy-ride

snoer *n,* flex; string; line

snoeren: iemand de mond —, to shut a person up

snoes, duck(y)

snoeshaan, chap, specimen

snoet, snout; face

snoeven, to boast

snoezig, sweet, dinky

snood, vile

snor, moustache

snorken, to snore

snorren, to roar, to drone, to hum

snotaap, snotjongen, urchin

snotneus, snotty nose; urchin

snuffelen, to sniff; to ferret (about)

snufje *n,* knick-knack

snugger, bright, brainy

snuif(je) *n,* (pinch of) snuff

snuiste'rij, trinket

snuit, snout, trunk; (little) face

snuiten, to blow (one's nose); to snuff

snuiter, chap, fellow

snuiven, to (give a) sniff, to snort

snurken, to snore

soci'ale ver'zorging, welfare work

socië'teit, club(-house)

soebatten, to beg

soep, soup; balderdash

soepballetje *n,* (force-)meat ball

soepel, supple

soepkip, boiling fowl

soes, puff

soezen, to doze

sok, sock

sokophouder, suspender

sol'daat, soldier

 sol'daat maken, to finish up

sol'deerbout, soldering-iron

sol'deren, to solder

sol'dij, army pay

soli'dair, loyal

so'lide, sound, substantial

so'list, soloist

sollen, to romp; to push around

sollici'tant, applicant

sollici'teren, to apply

solospel *n,* solo (performance)

som, sum

somber, gloomy, sombre

somma, (total) amount

som'meren, to summon

sommige(n), some

som(tijd)s, sometimes; perhaps

sonate, sonata

so'noor, sonorous

soort, brand, species; *n,* kind

soortelijk ge'wicht *n,* specific gravity

soortgelijk, similar

soos, club

sop *n,* broth; (soap-)suds

 het ruime sop, the sea

soppen, to sop, to steep

so'praan, soprano, treble

sor'teren, to (as)sort, to grade

sor'tering, assortment

souff'leren, to prompt

souff'leur(shokje *n*), prompter('s box)

sou'peren, to sup

sou'tane, cassock

souterrain *n,* basement

souvereini'teit, sovereignty

spaak, spoke, rung

 spaak lopen, to come to grief

spaander, sliver, chip

Spaans (*n*), Spanish

spaarbank, savings bank

spaarkas, thrift club

spaarpot, money-box

spaarzaam, sparing, thrifty

spade, spade

spalk(en), (to) splint

span *n,* span; team, yoke

spanbroek, (pair of) tights

span'deren, to spend

spandoek, banner

Spanje *n,* Spain

spankracht, tensile strength
spannen, to stretch, to strain
  de haan spannen, to cock (a rifle)
  het zal er om spannen, it will be touch and go
spannend, tense, thrilling
spanning, tension; span
spanwijdte, span
spar, rafter; spruce(-tree)
sparappel, fir-cone
sparen, to save (up); to spare
spartelen, to sport, to splash, to kick
spatader, varicose vein
spatbord *n,* mud-guard
spatie, space
spatten, to splash, to spatter
spece'rij, spice
specht, woodpecker
speci'aal, special
specie, mortar
specifi'ceren, to specify
speci'fiek, specific
specu'laas, spice cake *or* biscuit
specu'lant, speculator
specu'leren, to speculate
speeksel *n,* saliva
speelbal, cue ball; plaything
speelbank, gaming-room
speelgoed *m,* toy(s)
speelkwartier *n,* break, recreation
speelplaats, playground
speelpop, puppet
speels(heid), playful(ness)
speeltuin, playground
speen, teat, dummy
speenvarken *n,* sucking-pig
speer, spear, javelin
spek *n,* bacon, fat pork; blubber
spekken: zijn beurs —, to line one's purse
spektakel *n,* racket; spectacle
spekzool, crepe sole
spel *n,* game; pack, hand (of cards), play(ing), acting
  op het spel staan, to be at stake
spelbreker, spoil-sport
**spel(den), (to) pin
  ik kon er geen speld tussen krijgen, I couldn't get a word in edgewise; he had a water-tight argument

spelen, to play, to act; to chime
spelenderwijs, frivolously
speler, player, musician, actor
spelevaren *n,* boating
spelfout, spelling mistake
speling, (free) play; scope; freak
spelleider, games master
spellen, to spell
spelletje *n,* game
spe'lonk, cave, grotto
spelregel, rule (of the game): spelling-rule
spenen, to wean
sperballon, barrage balloon
speruur *n,* curfew
spervuur *n,* barrage
sperzieboon, French bean
spett(er)en, to spatter
speuren, to search
speurhond, sleuth-hound, gun-dog
speurzin, keen nose
spichtig, spiky, spidery
spie, cent, bean, dough
spiegel, mirror
spiegelbeeld *n,* reflection; phantom
spiegelei *n,* fried egg
spiegelen: zich — aan, to learn from
spiegelgevecht *n,* mock battle
spiegelglas *n,* plate glass
spiegeling, reflection
spiegelkast, (mirror-fronted) wardrobe
spiegelruit, plate glass window
spieken, to crib
spier, muscle
spiernaakt, stark naked
spierwit, white as a sheet
spies, spear
spijbelen, to play truant
spijker, nail
  spijkers met koppen slaan, to get down to business
  spijkers op laag water zoeken, to make a song and dance about nothing; to quibble
spijl, bar, spike
spijs, fare
spijskaart, menu
spijsvertering, digestion
spijt, regret; spite

spijten, to upset
  het spijt me, I am sorry
spijtig: het is —, it is a pity
spijzen, food
spikkel, speck
spiksplinternieuw, gleaming new
spil, pivot, axis; capstan
spillebeen, spindle-shank(s)
spilziek, spendthrift
spin(nekop), spider
spi'nazie, spinach
spinnen, to spin; to purr
spinne'rij, spinning-mill
spinneweb, n, cobweb
spinnewiel n, spinning-wheel
spinnijdig, as cross as two sticks
spinrag n, cobweb
spi'on, spy; window mirror
spio'neren, to spy
spi'raal, spiral; woven bed-spring
spiri'tisme n, spiritualism
spiritus, methylated spirit(s)
spit, n, spit: lumbago
spits, point(ed), sharp: peak
  spitse toren, steeple, pinnacle
  op de spits drijven, to bring to a head
spitsboef, scoundrel
spitsboog, pointed arch
spitsen, to sharpen; to prick up
spitsuur n, rush hour, peak hour
spits'vondig(heid), (over)-subtle(ty)
spitten, to dig
spleet, slit, split
splijten, to split, to cleave
splinter(en), (to) splinter
splinternieuw, brand-new
split, slit, placket
splitsen, to split (up), to fork
splitsing, split(ting up), fork, fission
spoed(en), (to) haste(n)
spoedgeval n, emergency case
spoedig, soon, speedy
spoel, spool, coil, reel
spoelen, to rinse, to wash
spoelkom, slop-basin
spoken, to haunt; to be astir
sponde, bed(side)
spons, sponge

spon'taan, spontaneous
spook n, ghost; freak, bogey
spookhuis n, haunted house
spookverschijning, apparition
spoor n, spur: foot-mark, track, scent, trace; rail(way)
spoorbaan, railway
spoorboekje n, (railway) time-table
spoordijk, railway embankment
spoorlijn, railway(-line)
spoorloos, without a trace
spoorslags, hell for leather
spoorstudent, student travelling from a distance
spoorverbinding, railway communication; connection
spoorweg, railway
spoorwegovergang, level crossing
spo'radisch, sporadic
sporen, (to go) by rail
sport, sport; rung
sportbroek, slacks, flannels
sportbroekje n, shorts
spor'tief, sporting; informal
sportjasje n, sports-coat
sportkousen, knee-length stockings
spot, mockery
spotgoedkoop, dirt-cheap
spotprent, caricature, cartoon
spotten (met), to mock; to defy
spraak(gebrek n), (impediment of) speech
spraakgebruik n, usage
spraakkunst, grammar
spraakleraar, teacher of elocution
spraakzaam, talkative
sprake, talk, question
  ter sprake, up for discussion
sprakeloos, speechless
sprank(elen), (to) spark(le)
spreekbeurt, lecturing engagement
spreekbuis, voice-tube; mouthpiece
spreekgestoelte n, rostrum, pulpit
spreekkamer, consulting-room
spreektaal, conversation(al language)

preekuur *n*, consulting-hour

preekwoord *n*, proverb

preek'woordelijk, proverbial

preeuw, starling

prei, bed-spread

spreken, to speak (to), to mention

  het spreekt vanzelf, it stands to reason

sprekend, striking, telling

spreker, speaker

sprenkelen, to sprinkle

spreuk, motto, maxim

spriet, blade (of grass); antenna

sprietig, spindly

springen, to jump; to snap, to burst; to become insolvent

  ik zit erom te springen, I just can't wait for it

spring-in-'t-veld, tomboy

springlevend, very much alive

springpaard *n*, vaulting-horse

springstof, explosive

springtij, *n*, **springvloed**, spring tide

springtouw *n*, skipping-rope

sprinkhaan, locust, grass-hopper

sprint(en), (to) sprint

sprits, butter-biscuit

sproeien, to sprinkle, to spray

sproet, freckle

sprokkelen, to gather (wood)

sprong, jump, leap, bound

sprookje *n*, fairy-tale

sprookjesachtig, make-believe, dream-like

sprot, sprat

spruit, sprout; offspring

spruiten, to sprout; to spring

spruitjes, Brussel sprouts

spugen, to spit

spuien, to sluice; to vent(ilate)

spuigaten: dat loopt de — uit, that crowns everything

spuit, syringe; gamp; shooting-iron

spuiten, to gush(out), to spray

spuitfles, (soda-water) siphon

spuitgast, fireman

spuitwater *n*, soda-water

spul *n*, stuff; trouble

  spullen, bits and pieces; togs

spullebaas, showman, booth attendant

sputteren, to sputter

spuug *n*, spit

spuwen, to spit, to vomit

staaf, bar, rod

staak, stake, bean-stick

staal *n*, steel: sample, piece

staal(draad)kabel, steel-wire rope

staan, to stand, to be; to suit

  laat staan, leave alone; let alone

  erop staan, to insist on it

  hoe staat hij ervoor? how is he doing?

  staande houden, to stop; to maintain

  zich staande houden, to keep on one's feet; to hold one's own

  op staande voet, then and there

staanplaats(en), standing-room

staar, cataract

staart, tail; pigtail

staat, state; rank; list

  in staat zijn, to be able

  staat maken op, to depend on

staat'huishoudkunde, economics

staatkunde, politics

staatsambtenaar, civil servant

staatsexamen *n*, matriculation

staatsgreep, *coup d'état*

statie, state; procession

staatsman, statesman

staatsrecht *n*, constitutional law

staatsschuld, national debt

sta'biel, stable

stad, town, city

stad'huis *n*, town hall, city hall

stadion *n*, stadium

stadium *n*, stage, phase

stadslichten, side-lights

stadsschouwburg, municipal theatre

stads'timmerhuis *n*, corporation department of works

staf, staff; mace, crosier

stafkaart, ordnance-map

stafrijm *n*, alliteration

stag'neren, to stagnate

sta-in-de-weg, obstacle

staken, to stop, to strike

staking, stoppage, suspension, strike; tie

stakker(d), poor devil, poor thing
stal, stable, cow-shed, stall
stalen, (to) steel, iron
stalknecht, groom
stallen, to stable, to put away
stalles, stalls
stalmeester, equery
stalvoe(de)r n, fodder
stam, stem, trunk; tribe, race
stamboek n, herd-book, stud-book
stamboekvee n, pedigree cattle
stamboom, family tree
stamelen, to stammer
stamgast, habitué
stamhouder, son and heir
stamhuis n, dynasty
stamkaart, national registration card
stammen, to hail, to date
stamouders, ancestors
stampen, to pound, to mash; to stamp, to drum; to pitch
stamper, pestle, (potato-)masher, rammer; pistil
stamppot, mashed vegetables
stampvoeten, to stamp (one's foot)
stampvol, packed out
stamroos, standard rose
stamvader, ancestor
stand, position, attitude; score class, order, state
  tot stand komen, to come into being
standaard, standard; stand
standbeeld n, statue
stander, (hall-)stand
standhouden, to hold (one's own)
standje n, ticking-off; cross-patch; shindy
standplaats, stand, pitch, (taxi-)rank; post, living
standpunt n, point of view
stand'vastig, steadfast
stang, bar, rod, stancheon
  op stang jagen, to bait
stank, stench
stap, step, pace; move
  op stap, on (our) way
stapel, pile, heap
  van stapel lopen, to glide off the stocks; to go (off) smoothly

stapelen, to stack, to heap
stapel(gek), quite daft
stappen, to step, to get
stapvoets, at a walking-pace
star, fixed, rigid
staren, to stare, to gaze
startbaan, runway
starten, to start
Statenbijbel, Authorized Version (of the Dutch Bible)
Staten-Gene'raal, States General, the Upper and Lower Chambers
statie, Station of the Cross
sta'tief n, tripod, stand
statiegeld n, deposit
statig, stately, majestic
sta'tion n, station
sta'tionschef, station-master
statis'tiek, statistics
sta'tuut n, statute, regulation
sta'vast, (high) resolve
staven, to substantiate
stedeljik, urban, municipal
stedeling, townsman
steeds, ever, still: town(ish)
steeg, alley, lane
steek, stitch, sting, stab, dig; cocked hat
  in de steek laten, to leave in the lurch
  geen steek, not a thing
steek'houdend, sound, valid
steekproef, sample taken at random
steekvlam, torch flame
steel, stem, stalk; handle
steelpan, saucepan
steels, stealthy
steen, stone
steenbakke'rij, brick-works
steenbok, ibex; Capricorn
steendruk, lithograph(y)
steengroeve, quarry
steenhouwer, stone-mason
steenkool, (bituminous) coal
steenoven, brick-kiln
steenpuist, boil
steentijdperk n, stone-age
steentje n, stone, pebble
  een steentje bijdragen, to do one's (little) bit
steevast, regularly

steiger, landing-stage; scaffolding
steigeren, to rear
steil, steep, sheer
stek, cutting
stekeblind, blind as a bat
stekel, prickle, spine
stekelbaars, stickleback
stekelig, prickly; caustic
stekelvarken *n,* porcupine
steken, to sting, to stab, to smart; to stick
 blijven steken, to get stuck
 van wal steken, to push off
stekker, plug(-top)
stel *n,* set, couple; stove
stelen, to steal
stelkunde, algebra
stel'lage, scaffolding
stellen, to put; to adjust; to suppose; to manage
stellig, definite
stelling, proposition, thesis, theorem; position, line of fortifications; scaffolding
stelpen, to sta(u)nch
stelregel, maxim
stelsel *n,* system
stelsel'matig, systematic
stelten, stilts
 op stelten staan, to be at sixes and sevens
stem, voice, part; vote
stembanden, vocal chords
stembiljet *n,* voting-paper
stembuiging, modulation
stembureau *n,* polling-station
stembus, ballet-box
stemgeluid *n,* voice
stemge'rechtigd, entitled to vote
stemhamer, tuning-key
stemhebbend, voiced; entitled to vote
stemloos, voiceless
stemmen, to vote; to tune (up)
 iemand gunstig stemmen, to put a person in a good mood
stemmer, tuner; voter
stemmig, demure
stemming, mood, atmosphere: vote
stempel *n,* stamp, (post)mark; stigma

stempelen, to stamp, to (post-, hall-)mark
stempelkussen *n,* ink-pad
stemplicht, compulsory voting
stemrecht *n,* franchise
stemspleet, glottis
stemvork, tuning-fork
stengel, stalk, stem
stenigen, to stone (to death)
steno(gra'fie), shorthand
step, step; scooter
steppehond, prairie-dog
ster, star
stereo'tiep, stereotype(d)
sterfbed *n,* death-bed
sterfelijk(heid), mortal(ity)
sterfgeval *n,* death
sterftecijfer, mortality-rate
ste'riel, sterile
sterk, strong; extraordinary; greatly
 sterk verhaal, tall story
sterken, to strengthen; to comfort
sterkgekleurd, highly coloured
sterkte, strength; all the best!
sterk'water *n,* spirits
sterrekijker, telescope
sterrenbeeld *n,* constellation
sterrenkunde, astronomy
sterrenwacht, observatory
sterrenwichelarij, astrology
sterretje *n,* star, asterisk
sterveling, mortal
sterven (aan), to die (from)
steun, support
steunbeer, buttress
steunen, to support, to lean: to groan
steunfonds *n,* relief-fund
steunpilaar, pillar, mainstay
steuntrekkend, on the dole
steunzool, arch support
steven, prow
stevig, firm, substantial, sturdy
stichtelijk, edifying
 dank je stichtelijk! thank you for nothing!
stichten, to found, to establish; to edify
stichting, foundation, institution; edification
stief(moeder), step(mother)

stiekem, on the quiet
stier, bull
stierlijk: zich — vervelen, to be bored stiff
stift, stylo, pin, pencil(-lead)
stifttand, crowned tooth
stijf, stiff, starchy
stijfkop, pig-headed person
stijfsel, starch, paste
stijgbeugel, stirrup
stijgen, to rise; to (dis)mount
stijl, style: stanchion
stijlfiguur, figure of speech
stijven, to starch; to encourage
stikdonker n, pitch-dark(ness)
stikken, to stifle, to suffocate: to stitch
stikstof, nitrogen
stikvol, chock-full
stil, silent, quiet; still
  de stille week, Holy Week
stilhouden, to stop; to keep quiet
stilleggen, to stop
stillen, to quiet(en), to alleviate
stilletje n, commode
stilletjes, quietly, stealthily
stilliggen, to lie still, to lie idle
stilstaan, to stand still; to pull up
  stilstaan bij, to give (some) thought to
stilstaand, stationary, stagnant
stilstand, standstill
stilte, silence
  in stilte, quietly, privately
stilzwijgen n, silence
stil'zwijgend, tacit
stimu'lans, stimulant, stimulus
stimu'leren, to stimulate
stinkdier n, skunk
stinken, to stink
stip(pel), dot, speck
stipt, punctual, prompt; strict
stoeien, to romp
stoel, chair
stoelendans, musical chairs
stoelgang, motion(s)
stoep, front-door step(s); pavement, kerb
stoer, stalwart
stoet, procession
stoete'rij, stud(-farm)

stoethaspel, duffer
stof, material, (subject-)matter: n, dust
  lang van stof, long-winded
stofbril, goggles
stofdoek, duster
stof'feerder, upholsterer
stoffelijk, material, mortal
stoffen, to dust
stoffer, brush
stof'feren, to upholster
stoffig, dusty
stofgoud n, gold-dust
stofje n, speck of dust: bit of material
stoflaken n, dust-sheet
stofnest n, dust-trap
stofregen, drizzle
stofwisseling, metabolism
stofzuiger, vacuum-cleaner
stoï'cijn(s), stoic(al)
stok, stick; perch, roost; truncheon; stock(s)
  het aan de stok krijgen, to fall out
stokboon, runner-bean
stokdoof, stone deaf
stoken, to burn, to keep a fire going; to distil; to stir up
stoker, fireman, stoker; distiller; firebrand
stokje n, stick, baton
  er een stokje voor steken, to scotch
stokken, to falter, to break down: to stake
stokoud, ancient
stokpaard n, hobby(-horse)
stokroos, hollyhock
stokstijf, rigid
stokvis, stockfish
stola, stole
stollen, to congeal
stolp, glass cover
stolpplooi, box-pleat
stom, dumb, mute, speechless; stupid
stomen, to steam, to smoke; to dry-clean; to cram
stome'rij, dry-cleaners
stommelen, to clump (about)
stommeling, stommerik, fathead

stommi'teit, stupidity, blunder

stomp, blunt, obtuse: stump: punch, dig

stompen, to punch, to jab

stomp'zinnig, obtuse

stomverbaasd, stupefied

stomvervelend, deadly dull

stoof, foot-warmer

stoofpeer, stewing pear

stookgat n, stoke-hole

stookolie, fuel-oil

stoom, steam

stoomgemaal n, steam pump

stoomketel, boiler

stoomwals, steam-roller

stoornis, disturbance

stoot, bump, jab, dig

stootblok n, buffer

stoottroepen, shock troops

stop, plug, stopper; darn

stopcontact n, (wall-)socket

stoplap, stop-gap

stopnaald, darning-needle

stoppel, stubble

stoppen, to stop (up); to put; to fill; to darn; to constipate

stoptrein, slow train

stopverf, putty

stopwoord n, expletive

stopzetten, to stop, to shut down

storen, to disturb, to interrupt

 zich storen aan, to bother about

storing, interference, failure, dislocation

storm, gale, storm

stormen, to storm, to blow a gale

stormenderhand, by storm

stormklok, gale tocsin

stormladder, rope-ladder

stormlamp, hurricane-lamp

stormloop, rush, stampede

stormram, battering-ram

stormsein n, storm-cone

stormtroep, assault party

stormvloed, gale-swept high water

stortbui, heavy shower

storten, to plunge, to dump, to shed; to pay in

stortregenen, to pour with rain

stortvloed, torrent

stortzee, (green) sea

stoten, to bump, to knock, to butt

 zich stoten aan, to take offence at

stotend, offensive

stotteren, to stammer

stout, naughty; bold

stout'moedig, undaunted

stoven, to stew

straal, ray; radius; jet

straalaandrijving, jet propulsion

straalbreking, refraction

straalvliegtuig n, jet-plane

straat, street, road; straits

straatarm, poor as Job

straatdeun, street-song

straatjongen, street-arab

straatlantaarn, street-lamp

straatmaker, road-mender

straatschende'rij, hooliganism

straatstenen, paving-stones

straatweg, high-road

straf, punishment, penalty: severe, strong

strafbaar, punishable

straffeloos, with impunity

straffen, to punish

strafkolonie, convict settlement

strafport, postage due

strafrecht n, criminal law

strafschop, penalty kick

straftijd, term of imprisonment

strafwerk n, imposition

strafwet, criminal law

strafwetboek n, penal code

strak, tight, hard

strak(je)s, in a moment, soon

stralen, to shine, to beam

stralend, radiant

stralenkrans, halo

stram, stiff, rigid

stra'mien n, canvas

strand n, beach

stranden, to (be) strand(ed)

strandjutter, beach-comber

stra'teeg, strategist

streek, district, region: trick; stroke

 van streek, upset

streekroman, regional novel

streep, stripe, stroke, line
 er een streep onder zetten, to call it a day
streepje *n*, dash, hyphen
strekken, to stretch
 iemand tot eer strekken, to do a person credit
strekking, purport
strelen, to stroke; to tickle
stremen, to curdle; to hold up
streng, severe, strict, strand, skein
strengelen, to twine
streven naar, to strive for
striem, weal
striemen, to lash
strijd, fight, struggle, conflict
strijdbaar, fit for service
strijden met, to fight (against), to go against
strijdig, contrary
strijdkrachten, military forces
strijd'lustig, bellicose, pugnacious
strijdperk *n*, lists
strijd'vaardig, fighting-fit
strijkbout, flat-iron
strijken, to iron : to haul down; to stroke, to brush
strijkgoed *n*, ironing
strijkijzer *n*, iron
strijkinstrument *n*, stringed instrument
strijkkwartet *n*, string quartet
strijkplank, ironing-board
strijkstok, bow
strik, bow(-tie); snare
strikken, to tie; to (en)snare
strikt, strict
strikvraag, catch question
stro *n*, straw
stroef, stiff, harsh
stroken met, to tally with
stromen, to flow
stroming, current; trend
strompelen, to hobble
stronk, stump, stalk
strontje *n*, sty
strooibiljet *n*, handbill
strooien, to strew, to sprinkle: straw
strooisel *n*, litter

strook, strip; frill; counterfoil
stroom, stream, flood, current
stroom'af(waarts), downstream
stroomgebied *n*, (river-)basin
stroom'op(waarts), upstream
stroomsterkte, amperage
stroomversnelling, rapid(s)
stroop, syrup, treacle
strooplikken, to curry favour
strooptocht, marauding expedition
strootje *n*, gasper
strop, noose; tough luck
stropdas, stock, tie
stropen, to skin, to strip; to poach, to pillage
stroper, poacher
strot, throat
strottehoofd *n*, larynx
strozak, palliasse
strubbelingen, friction, snags
struc'tuur, structure
struif, omelet
struik, bush, shrub
struikelblok *n*, stumbling-block
struikelen, to stumble, to trip (up)
struikgewas *n*, brushwood
struikrover, highwayman
struis, robust
struisveer, ostrich-feather
struisvogel, ostrich
struisvogelpolitiek, escapism
stu'deerkamer, study
stu'dentencorps *n*, students' union
stu'dentenhaver, almonds and raisins
studenti'koos, undergraduate, varsity
stu'deren, to study, to read; to practice; to be at the university
studie, study
studiebeurs, scholarship
studieboek *n*, text-book
stuf *n*, (india-)rubber
stug, dour, gruff; tough
stuifmeel, *n*, pollen
stuip, convulsion; daft notion
stuiptrekking, convulsion
stuit(been *n***),** tail-bone
stuiten, to check; to bounce

tuiten op, to encounter
tegen de borst stuiten, to go against the grain
tuitend, offensive
tuiven, to blow dust about; to dash
stuiver, 5-cent piece
stuivertje wisselen, general post
stuk (n), piece; play; document; lot: broken, to pieces
een stuk of vier, three or four
aan één stuk door, without a break
op geen stukken na, not by a long chalk
klein van stuk, small
iemand van zijn stuk brengen, to upset a person
stuka'door, plasterer
stukgoed (eren) n, general cargo; piece-goods
stukhakken, to chop up
stukloon n, piece-rates
stukslaan, to smash (to pieces)
stumper(d), duffer; wretch
stuntelig, clumsy
sturen, to send; to steer
stutten, to prop (up)
stuur n, handle-bar(s), (steering-) wheel, helm
stuurboord n, starboard
stuurknuppel, control-column
stuurman, mate; cox(swain)
stuurs, surly
stuurstang, control-column
stuw, weir
stuwa'door, stevedore
stuwen, to drive; to stow; to dam up
stuwkracht, driving force
su'biet, sudden, at once
su'bliem, sublime
sub'sidie, subsidy
sub'stantie, substance
substitu'eren, to substitute
sub'tiel, subtle
suc'ces n, success
suc'cessie, succession
suc'cessierechten, death-duties
succes'sievelijk, successively
suc'cesvol, successful
suf, muzzy; nitwitted
suffen, to day-dream

suffer(d), noodle
sugge'reren, to suggest, to prompt
suiker, sugar
suikergoed n, candy
suikeroom, rich uncle
suikerpot, sugar-bowl
suikerriet n, sugar-cane
suikerstrooier, sugar-caster
suikerziekte, diabetes
suizebollen, to have a reeling head
suizen, to whisper, to murmur
su'kade, candied peel
sukkel, muggins
aan de sukkel zijn, to be an invalid
sukkelaar, weakling; booby
sukkeldraf, jog-trot
sukkelen, to be in poor health; to plod
sul, nincompoop
summum n, acme
supple'toir, supplementary
sup'poost, custodian
surro'gaat n, substitute
surveil'leren, to supervise, to invigilate
sussen, to soothe; to salve
symboliek, symbolism
sym'bool n, symbol
sympa'thiek, congenial, engaging
symp'toom n, symptom
syno'niem (n), synonym(ous)
syn'thetisch, synthetic
sys'teem n, system

T

taai, tough, dogged, tedious
taai-'taai n, tough kind of gingerbread
taak, task
taal, language
taalboek n, grammar
taaleigen n, idiom
taalfout, solecism
taalgeleerde, taal'kundige, linguist
taart, tart, gâteau
ta'bak, tobacco
ergens tabak van hebben, to be fed up with something

TAB 188 TEG

ta'bakszak, tobacco-pouch

tabbard, tabberd, tabard

ta'bel, table, index

tabel'larisch, tabulated

ta'blet, tablet

tachtig, eighty

tachtiger, octogenarian; writer of the movement of 1880

tac'tiek, tactic(s)

tactloos, tactless

tafel, table

tafelblad *n*, table-top, table-leaf

tafeldame, partner (at table)

tafeldekken, to lay the table

tafelen: lang —, to linger over a meal

tafelgebed *n*, grace

tafelgoed *n*, table-linen

tafelheer, partner ·(at table)

tafelkleed *n*, table-cover

tafellaken *n*, table-cloth

tafelschuier, crumb-brush

tafelstoel, high chair

tafe'reel *n*, scene

tafzij(de), taffeta

taille, waist(-line), bodice

tak, branch

takel, tackle, rigging

takelen, to rig (out); to hoist

takelwagen, break-down lorry

takkenbos, faggot

tal *n*, number

een viertal, twaalftal, twintigtal *etc*, (about) four, a dozen, a score *etc*.

talen, to be interested in

talg, talk, tallow, talc(um powder)

talloos, countless

talmen, to linger

talrijk, numerous

talstelsel *n*, (numerical) system

tam, tame(d), domestic(ated)

tamboe'rijn, tambourine

tamelijk, fair(ly), rather

tand, tooth, prong

iemand aan de tand voelen, to put a person through his paces

tandarts, dentist

tandestoker, tooth-pick

tandheelkunde, dental surgery

tandrad *n*, cog-wheel

tandradbaan, rack-railway

tandvlees *n*, gum(s)

tanen, to tan; to wane

tang, (pair of) tongs, forceps: witch

dat slaat als een tang op een varken, that is neither here nor there

tanig, tawny

tanken, to (re)fuel

tankschip *n*, tanker

tantali'seren, to tantalize

tante, aunt; woman

tantième *n*, bonus

ta'pijt *n*, carpet

tapisse'rie, tapestry

tapkast, bar

tappen, to tap; to crack

taps, tapering

taptemelk, skimmed milk

taptoe, tattoo

tapverbod *n*, prohibition

tapzaag, tenon saw

tarbot, turbot

ta'rief *n*, tariff, terms, fare

tarten, to defy

tarwe, wheat

tas, (hand)bag, brief-case

tast: op de —, by feeling

tastbaar, tangible

tasten, to feel, to grope

tateren, to jabber

tatoe'ëren, to tattoo

taxa'teur, valuer

tax'eren, to value, to assess

te, at, in; too; to

tech'niek, technique; technics

technisch, technical

te(d)er, tender, delicate

teef, bitch, vixen

teelaarde, humus

teelbal, testicle

teelt, cultivation, culture, breeding

teen, toe: osier

teenhout *n*, osier(s)

teer, tar: (*see* **teder**)

teerling, die

tegel, tile

tege'lijk(ertijd), at the same time

tege'moet-, to ... to meet

tege'moetgaan, to go to meet; to head for

tege'moetkomen, to (come to) meet (halfway)

tege'moetkomend, accommodating

tege'moetzien, to await

tegen, against; towards; at
  ik kan er niet tegen, I cannot stand it

tegen-, counter-

tagen'aan, against, into

tegenbeeld n, counterpart

tegenbericht n, word to the contrary

tegenbenzoek n, return visit

tegenbezwaar n, (counter-)objection

tegencandidaat, opposing candidate

tegendeel n, contrary

tegengaan, to counter(act)

tegengesteld, opposite

tegengif n, antidote

tegenhanger, counterpart

tegenhouden, to check, to hold

tegenkanting, opposition

tegenkomen, to come across

tegenligger, oncoming vehicle or vessel

tegenlopen: het liep me tegen, I had bad luck

tegen'over, opposite (to), (as) against, towards

tegen'overgesteld(e n), contrary

tegenpartij, opponent

tegenpool, antipole

tegenprestatie: als —, in return

tegenslag, set-back

tegenspartelen, to struggle; to protest

tegenspeler, opponent; opposite number

tegenspoed, adversity

tegenspraak, contradiction

tegenspreken, to contradict

tegenstaan, to be repugnant to

tegenstand, resistance

tegenstander, adversary

tegenstelling, contrast

tegenstemmen, to vote against

tegenstribbelen, to struggle; to protest

tegen'strijdig, conflicting

tegenvallen, to be disappointing
  het viel tegen, it was worse than (or not what) I'd expected

tegenvaller, blow

tegenvoeter, antipode

tegenwaarde, equivalent

tegenweer, resistance

tegenwerken, to oppose

tegenwerking, obstruction (ism)

tegenwerping, objection

tegenwicht n, counterpoise

tegen'woordig, present(-day), nowadays

tegen'woordigheid, presence

tegenzin, aversion
  met tegenzin, reluctantly

tegenzitten: alles zit me tegen, I'm up against it

te'goed n, credit: owing

te'huis n, home

teil, (zinc, enamel) bowl or bath

teisteren, to ravage

teken n, sign, token
  in het teken staan van, to be overshadowed by

tekenen, to draw; to sign

tekenfilm, cartoon

tekenhaak, T-square

tekening, drawing, plan; marking(s)

te'kort (n), shortage, deficit, short

te'kort doen, to stint; to wrong

te'kortkoming, shortcoming

tekst, text, script, words

tekstuitlegger, exegete

tekstwoord n, text

tel, count; second
  in tel zijn, to be highly thought of

tele'foon(tje n), telephone(-call)

tele'fooncel, call-box

tele'fooncentrale, telephone-exchange

tele'foongids, telephone-directory

telegra'feren, to wire, to cable

te'leurstellen, to disappoint

te'leurstelling, disappointment

telex, teleprinter

telg, offspring

telkenmale, telkens (weer), again and again, every time

tellen, to count, to total

te'loorgaan, to get lost
telwoord *n*, numeral
temen, to drawl, to moan
temmen, to tame
tempel, temple
tempera'mentvol, temperamental
tempera'tuur, temperature
temperen, to temper, to moderate
tempo *n*, tempo, pace
ten'dens, tendency
tenger, slight, delicate
tenge'volge van, as a result of
te'nietdoen, to nullify, to vitiate
ten'lastelegging, charge
ten'minste, at least
tennissen, to play tennis
tent, tent, booth, "dive"
ten'tamen *n*, preliminary examination
tentdoek *n*, canvas
ten'toonspreiden, to display
ten'toonstelling, exhibition, show
te'nue *n*: (groot) —, (full) dress
ten'zij, unless
tepel, nipple, teat
ter'aardebestelling, interment
ter'dege, thoroughly
te'recht, rightly
te'rechtbrengen, to make a job of
te'rechtkomen, to turn out all right; to turn up; to end up
te'rechtstaan, to stand one's trial
te'rechtstelling, execution
te'rechtwijzing, reprimand
teren op, to live on
tergen, to provoke
ter'handstelling, presentation
tering, consumption
ter'loops, incidental
term, term
ter'mijn, term; instalment
op korte termijn, at short notice; short-term
ter'nauwernood, scarcely
ter'neerdrukken, to depress
ter'neergeslagen, disheartened
terpen'tijn, turpentine
ter'ras *n*, terrace

ter'rein *n*, terrain, ground, field
ter'reinknecht, groundsman
ter'reur, reign of terror
ter'rine, tureen
ter'sluiks, stealthily
ter'stond, at once
terts: (grote) —, (major) third
te'rug, back
te'rugblik, retrospect(ion)
te'rugdeinzen, to shrink (back)
te'rugdenken aan, to recall (to mind)
te'ruggetrokken, retiring
te'ruggeven, to give back, to return
terug'houdend, reserved
te'rugkaatsen, to strike back, to rebound, to (be) reflect(ed), to (re-)echo
te'rugkeer, return
te'rugkeren, to return, to turn back
te'rugkomen, to come back, to return
te'rugkrabbelen, to back out
te'ruglopen, to walk back; to decline
te'rugnemen, to take back, to withdraw
te'rugreis, return-journey, way back
te'rugroepen, to call back, to recall
te'rugschrikken, to recoil
te'rugslaan, to hit back, to repulse; to back-fire
te-rugslag, reaction
te'rugtraprem, back-pedal brake
te'rugtrekken, to draw back, to retract; to retreat
zich terugtrekken, to retire
te'rugwerkende kracht hebben, to be retrospective
ter'wijl, while; whereas
ter'wille van, for the sake of
ter'zijde, aside
testa'ment *n*, will, Testament
testen, to test
teug, gulp
teugel, rein
teugelloos, unbridled
teugje *n*, sip

teuten, to dawdle
te'veel *n*, surplus
tevens, as well
tever'geefs, to no purpose
te'vreden, content(ed), satisfied
te'vredenheid, satisfaction, contentment
te'waterlating, launching
te'weegbrengen, to bring about
tex'tiel, textile
te'zamen, together
thans, at present
thea'traal, theatrical
thé com'plet, afternoon tea
thee, tea
theelichtje *n*, (heated) tea-pot stand
theeleut, inveterate tea-drinker
Theems, Thames
theemuts, tea-cosy
theeservies *n*, tea-set
theestoof, tea brazier
theezeefje *n*, tea-strainer
thema *n*, theme; exercise
theo'loog, theologian, theological student
theo'reticus, theorist
theo'retisch, theoretical
theo'rie, theory
thera'pie, therapy, therapeutics
thermosfles, thermos (flask)
thesau'rier, treasurer
thuis, (at) home
thuisbrengen, to take home; to place
thuishoren, to belong
thuiskrijgen: zijn trekken —, to find one's pranks coming home to roost
tien, ten
tiend(e), tithe
tien'delig, ten-piece, in ten parts; decimal
tien'tallig, decimal
tientje *n*, ten-guilder note; tenth share (in a lottery ticket)
tier(e)lan'tijntje *n*, frill, furbelow
tieren, to thrive: to rage
tij *n*, tide
tijd, time; tense
tijdelijk, temporary; temporal
tijdens, during
tijdgenoot, contemporary

tijdig, timely, in good time
tijding(en), tidings, news
tijdlang: een —, for some time
tijdopname, time-exposure; timing
tijdpassering, pastime
tijdperk *n*, period
tijd'rovend, protractive
tijdsbestek *n*, space of time
tijdschrift *n*, periodical
tijdstip *n*, epoch, moment
tijdstroom, trend of the times
tijdsverloop *n*, lapse
tijdvak *n*, period
tijdverdrijf *n*, pastime
tijdverspilling, waste of time
tijgen, to set (out)
tijger, tiger
tijk, tick(ing)
tik, tap, rap
tikje *n*, gentle tap; touch, shade
tikken, to tap; to tick; to type
tik-tak-tol, noughts and crosses
til, dove-cot
  iets op til, something brewing
tillen, to raise, to lift
timmeren, to carpenter, to hammer
timmerman, carpenter
tingelen, to tinkle
tinne, pinnacle, battlement
tinnen, pewter
tint, tint, shade
tintelen, to sparkle, to twinkle; to tingle
tip, tip, corner
tippel(en), (to) tramp
tippen, to tap, to dab: to tiptoe
ti'ran, tyrant
tiranni'seren, to bully
titel, title, heading
titelplaat, frontispiece
titula'tuur, style, titles
tjilpen, to chirp
tjokvol, chock-full
tobbe, tub
tobben, to brood; to slave; to have a tough time
toch, still, for all that; surely, after all
  zeg het toch! do tell me!
  waarom toch? whatever for?
tocht, draught; trip, drive

tochtdeur, hall-door
tochten, to be draughty
tochtig, draughty
toe, to
  toe maar !, toe nou ! go on!
  er slecht aan toe zijn, to be in a bad way
  het is tot dear aan toe, it is bad enough
toebedelen, ['tubədelə], to allot
toebehoren, to belong to: *n,* accessories
toebereidselen, preparations
toebrengen, to inflict on
toedekken, to cover up; to mulch
toedienen, to administer to
toedoen, to close; to matter: *n,* influence
toedracht, (case-)history
toedragen, to think of (a person) with
  zich toedragen, to come about
toeëigenen: zich —, to appropriate
toegaan: het gaat er raar toe, there are strange goings-on there
toegang, admission, entry
toegangsbewijs *n,* ticket of admission
toe'gankelijk, accessible, open
toegedaan, (kindly) disposed to(wards)
toe'geeflijk, lenient
toegenegen, affectionate
toegeven, to admit; to give way (to)
toegewijd, devoted
toegift, encore
toehoorders, audience, observers
toejuichen, to applaud; to welcome
toekennen, to confer upon, to attach to
toekeren, to turn to(wards)
toekijken, to look on
toekomen, to come to(wards); to make ends meet; to be due to
  doen toekomen, to send
toe'komend, future; due
toekomst(ig), future

toekrijgen: ik kreeg ... toe, that was thrown in (for nothing); I had ... for pudding
toelage, allowance
toelaten, to admit, to permit
toelatingsexamen *n,* entrance examination
toeleggen op, to contribute towards
  zich toeleggen op, to apply oneself to
toelichten, to elucidate
toeloop, concourse, rush
toelopen, to run (up) to; to taper
toen, then; when
toenaam: met naam en —, in detail
toenadering, rapprochement
toename, increase
toenemen, to increase
toenmaals, at that time
toen'malig, then, of the day
toenter'tijd, at the time
toe'passelijk, applicable, appropriate
toepassen, to apply
toepassing: van —, applicable
  in toepassing brengen, to put into practice
toer, tour; feat; rev(olution); row (of knitting)
  een hele toer, quite a job
toereiken, to hand (to)
toe'reikend, sufficient
toe'rekenbaar, responsible
toeren: gaan —, to go for a drive
toe'rist(enverkeer *n*), tourist (traffic)
toer'nooi *n,* tournament
toe'schietelijk, responsive, obliging
toeschijnen, to seem to
toeschouwer, spectator, onlooker
toeschrijven, to attribute
toeslaan, to slam
toeslag, excess (fare); bonus
toespeling, allusion
toespijs, dessert
toespraak, address
toespreken, to speak to, to address

toestaan, to allow, to grant

toestand, state of affairs, situation, position, condition

toestel *n,* apparatus, machine

toestemmen (in), to consent (to)

toestemming, permission

toestoppen, to stop up; to slip into (a person's) hand; to tuck in

toestromen, to pour (in)

toet, face: bun

toetakelen, to doll up; to knock about

toetasten, to help oneself

toeten: hij weet van — noch blazen, he doesn't know a thing (about it)

toeter(en), (to sound the) horn

toetje *n,* pudding, second course

toetreden tot, to join

toets, key; test

toetsen, to test

toetssteen, touchstone

toeval *n,* accident; epileptic fit

toe'vallig, (by) chance
  wat toevallig! what a coincidence!

toeverlaat, refuge

toevertrouwen, to (en)trust with
  dat is hem wel toevertrouwd, you can leave that to him

toevloed, influx

toevlucht, recourse

toevluchtsoord *n,* asylum

toevoegen, to add

toevoer, supply

toewenden, to turn to(wards)

toewensen, to wish

toewijding, devotion

toewijzen, to allocate

toezeggen, to promise

toezicht *n,* supervision

toezien, to look on; to take care (of)

tof, ripping

toga, gown, cassock

toi'lettafel, dressing-table

toilet'teren: zich —, to dress

tokkelen, to pluck, to strum

tol, toll: top

tolboom, turnpike

tole'reren, to tolerate

tolk, interpreter; spokesman

tollen, to play with a top, to spin round

tollenaar, publican

to'maat, tomato

tomeloos, unbridled

tom'poes, cream slice: chubby umbrella

ton, barrel; buoy; ton; 100,000 guilders

tondeldoos, tinder-box

ton'deuse, hair-clippers

to'neel *n,* stage; scene, theatre

to'neelgezelschap *n,* repertory company

to'neelkijker, (pair of) opera glasses

to'neelknecht, stage-hand

to'neelrecensent, dramatic critic

to'neelschool, school of dramatic art

to'neelschrijver, playwright

to'neelspel *n,* play; acting

to'neelspeler, actor

to'neelstuk *n,* play

to'neelvereniging, dramatic club

to'neelvoorstelling, theatrical performance

to'neelzolder, fly

tonen, to show

tong, tongue: sole

tongval, accent

tonicum *n,* tonic

toog, arch: cassock

tooi, attire; finery

tooien, to adorn

toom, bridle
  in toom houden, to keep in check

toon, tone; pitch

toonaangevend, leading

toonaard, key

toonbaar, presentable

toonbank, counter

toonbeeld *n,* model

toonder, bearer

toonhoogte, pitch

toonkamer, show-room

toonkunst, music

toonladder, scale; gamut

toonloos, toneless; unaccented

toonsoort, key

toontje lager zingen, to come down (a) peg or two

toonval, cadence
toonvast, in tune, note-perfect
toonzaal, show-room
toonzetting, (musical) setting
toorn, rage
toorts, torch
toost, toast
top, top, tip: agreed!
topo'grafisch, topographical, ordnance
topprestatie, record
toppunt *n,* summit, height; limit
tor, beetle
toren, tower
torenhoog, towering
torenspits, spire
torentje *n,* turret
torentrans, gallery
tornen, to unpick; to meddle
torpe'deren, to torpedo; to scotch
tor'pedojager, destroyer
torsen, to labour under (the weight of)
tossen, to toss
tot, till, (up) to; as
  tot aan, as far as
  tot op, to within; up till
to'taal, total, utter
totdat, until
tou'cheren, to touch (up)
tour'nee, tour
touw *n,* rope, string
  op touw zetten, to set on foot
  ik kon er geen touw aan vast-knopen, I couldn't make head or tail of it
touwtje *n,* piece of string
  touwtje springen, to skip
touwtrekken *n,* tug-of-war
tovenaar, magician
tovena'res, enchantress
toverachtig, magic, enchanting
toverdrank, magic potion
toveren, to work charms, to conjure (up)
toverkol, witch
toverlantaarn, magic lantern
tovermiddel *n,* charm
toverstaf, magic wand
traag, slow, sluggish
traan, tear: oil
trachten, to attempt, to try

tra'ditie, tradition
tra'gedie, tra'giek, tragedy
tragisch, tragic
trainen, to train, to coach
trai'neren, to hold up
tra'ject *n,* stretch, stage, line
trak'taat *n,* treatise, tract; treaty
trak'tatie, treat
trakte'ment *n,* salary
trak'teren (op), to treat (to)
tralies, bars, grating
traliewerk *n,* trellis
tram(halte), tram(-stop)
tranen, to water
trans, gallery, battlement
transfor'mator, transformer
tran'sito(haven), transit(-port)
transpi'reren, to perspire
transpor'teren, to transport; to bring forward
trant, style, manner
trap, kick; stairs; degree
  een hele trap, quite a way (by bike)
trapgevel, step-gable
trapje *n,* step, stair
trapleer, step-ladder
trapleuning, banisters
traploper, stair-carpet
trapnaaimachine, treadle sewing-machine
trappelen, to stamp
trappen, to kick; to tread; to pedal
trappenhuis *n,* staircase well
trappers, pedals: brogues
trapsgewijs, step by step
tra'want, satellite
trechter, funnel, hopper
trechtermonding, estuary
tred, step, pace; gait
trede, step, stair
treden, to tread; to go, to come
treeft(je *n),* trivet
treeplank, footboard
tref, bit of luck
treffen, to hit, to strike; to meet
  het (goed) treffen, to be lucky
treffend, striking, touching
treffer, good shot, hit
trein, train
treiteren, to bait, to nag

trek, pull, draught; stroke; feature, trait; inclination, appetite; migration
 in trek, in demand
trekharmonica, accordian
trekken, to draw, to drag; to migrate, to trek
trekker, trigger; hiker
trekking, (lottery) draw
trekpaard *n,* draught-horse
trekpen, drawing-pen
trekpleister, vesicant plaster; (fatal) attraction
trektocht, hiking-tour
tres, braid
treurdicht *n,* elegy
treuren, to grieve
treurig, sad
treurmars, funeral march
treurspel *n,* tragedy
treurwilg, weeping-willow
treurzang, dirge
treuzelen, to dawdle
tri'bune, platform, gallery, stand
tricot *n,* stockinette; tights
tries(ig), gloomy
trijp *n,* velveteen
trillen, to vibrate, to quiver
tri'omf, triumph
triom'fanteliik, triumphant
triom'feren, to triumph
triplex, three-ply
trippelen, to trip
trip'tiek, triptych; triptyque
troebel, turbid
troef, trump(s)
troel, slut
troep, crowd, troop, pack, company; rowdy lot, mess
troepenmacht, military forces
troetelkind *n,* spoiled child
troeven, to trump
trog, trough
trom, drum
trommel, tin, (bread-)bin; drum
trommelen, to drum; to strum
trommelvlies *n,* ear-drum
trom'pet, trumpet
trom'petgeschal *n,* blare of trumpets
tronen, to sit enthroned; to lure
tronie, mug, dial
troon, throne

troonsbestijging, accession
troost, consolation
troosteloos, disconsolate
troosten, to comfort
tropen, tropics
tros, cluster, bunch; hawser
trots, proud: pride: despite
trot'seren, to brave, to face
trot'toir *n,* pavement
trot'toirband, kerb
trouw, faith(ful), loyal(ty)
trouw-, marriage-, wedding-
trouwakte, marriage-certificate
trouweloos, disloyal
trouwen (met), to marry, to be married (to)
 zo zijn we niet getrouwd, that's not playing fair
trouwens, for that matter
trouw'hartig, candid
truc, trick, stunt
trui, jersey, sweater
Tsjech(isch *n***),** Czech
tsjirpen, to chirp
tucht, discipline
tuchtigen, to chastise
tuchtschool, Borstal (institution)
tuig *n,* rigging, harness; scum
tui'gage, rigging
tuiltje *n,* posy
tuimelen, to tumble, to topple over
tuimel, spill, fall
tuin, garden
tuinboon, broad bean
tuinbouw, horticulture
tuinder, market-gardener
tuinhuisje *n,* summer-house
tui'nieren, to garden
tuinman, gardener
tuit, spout
tuiten, to tingle
tuk op, keen on
tukje *n,* snooze
tulband, turban; ring(-cake)
tule(n), tulle
tulp, tulip
tunnel, tunnel, subway
ture'luurs, dotty
turen, to peer, to pore over
turf, peat
turfmolm, turfstrooisel *n,* moss-litter

turnen, to do gymnastics
tussen, between, among
  iemand er tussen nemen, to pull a person's leg
tussen'beide komen, to intervene
tussen'door, through
tussenhandel, middleman's trade
tussen'in : er —, in between
tussenkamer, middle room
tussenkomst, intervention
tussenmuur, partition-wall
tussenpersoon, middleman; go-between
tussenpoos, interval
tussenschot *n,* partition
tussentijd, interim
  tussentijdse verkiezing, by-election
tussenuur *n,* free period
tussenvoegen, to insert
tussenvoegsel *n,* interpolation
tussenwerpsel *n,* interjection
tussenzetsel *n,* insertion
tutoy'eren, to drop the formalities
twaalf, twelve
twaalftallig, duodecimal
twaalfuurtje *n,* midday meal
twaalfvingerige darm, duodenum
twee, two
tweede, second
tweede'hands, second-hand
tweedekker, double-decker; biplane
tweede'rangs, second-rate
tweedraads, two-ply
tweedracht, discord
tweegevecht *n,* dual
twee'hoevig, cloven-hoofed
tweeklank, diphthong
twee'ledig, twofold, dual
tweeling, (pair of) twin(s)
tweeloopsgeweer *n,* double-barrelled gun
tweemaal, twice
tweepersoons, double
twee'slachtig, bisexual; amphibious; ambiguous
tweespalt, discord
tweespan *n,* pair (of horses)

tweespraak, duologue
tweesprong, fork; cross-roads
twee'stemmig, two-part
tweestrijd, inner conflict
twee'talig, bilingual
twee'zijdig, bilateral
twijfel(achtig), doubt(ful)
twijfelen (aan), to doubt
twijg, twig
twintig, twenty
twist(en), (to) quarrel
twistappel, bone of contention
twistgesprek *n,* dispute
twistpunt *n,* vexed question
twistziek, quarrelsome
ty'peren, to typify
ty'perend voor, typical of
tyfus, typhus, typhoid
typisch, typical; quaint

U

u, you
überhaupt, at all; anyway
ui, onion; joke
uier, udder
uil, owl
uilskuiken *n,* numbskull
uit, out (of), from; finished
  ergens op uit, out for (bent on) something
uitbeelden, to depict, to render
uitbesteden, to put out to contract; to board out
uitblijven, to stay away; to fail to materialize
uitblinken, to excel
uitbotten, to bud
uitbouw, extension
uitbraak, escape (from prison)
uitbraken, to vomit; to belch out
uitbrander, dressing-down
uitbreiden, to extend
uitbuiten, to exploit
uit'bundig, exuberant
uitdagen, to challenge
uitdelen, to distribute
uitdenken, to think up
uitdeinen, to serve; to have its day
uitdiepen, to deepen
uitdijen, to expand

uitdoen, to take off; to put out

uitdoven, to extinguish

uitdraaien, to turn out

 zich er uitdraaien, to wriggle out of it

 op (ruzie) uitdraaien, to end in (a quarrel)

uitdrage'rij, junk-shop

uitdrinken, to drink up, to finish

uit'drukkelijk, express

uitdrukken, to express; to stub out

uitdrukking, expression

uitduiden, to point out

uit'eengaan, to separate

uit'eenlopend, divergent

uit'eenzetten, to state, to explain

uiteinde n, extremity

uit'eindelijk, ultimate

uiten, to utter, to express

uiten'treuren, on and on (and on)

uiter'aard, naturally

uiterlijk, outward; at the latest: n, appearance

uitermate, exceedingly

uiterst, ut(ter)most, extreme

uiterste n, extreme

uiterwaarden, water meadows

uitflappen, to blurt out

uitfluiten, to cat-call

uitfoeteren, to blow up

uitgaan, to go out

 uitgaan op, to end in; to go out (to look) for

uitgang, exit; ending

uitgangspunt n, point of departure

uitgave, expense; publication, edition

uitgebreid, extensive

 uitgebreid lager onderwijs n, "secondary modern" education

uitgehongerd, famished

uitgelaten, elated

uitgeleide doen, to see off

uitgelezen, select

uitgemergeld, emaciated, exhausted

uitgestreken: met een — gezicht, without batting an eyelid

uitgeteerd, emaciated

uitgeven, to spend; to issue; to publish

 zich uitgeven voor, to pose as

uitgever, publisher

uitgewekene, refugee

uitgezonderd, except (for)

uitgieren: het — van het lachen, to scream with laughter

uitgifte, issue

uitglijden, to slip

uitgommen, to rub out

uitgroeien, to (out)grow

uithaal, whoop; swerve

uithalen, to turn out; to unpick; to be up to (tricks)

 de kosten er uithalen, to cover the costs

uithangbord n, sign(board)

uithangen, to hang out; to act

uit'heems, foreign; outlandish

uithoek, out-of-the-way place

uithollen, to hollow out

uithoren, to wheedle information from

uithouden: het —, to stand (it)

uithoudingsvermogen n, stamina

uit'huizig, gadabout

uithuw(elijk)en, to give in marriage

uiting, expression

uitje n, jaunt: small onion

uitjouwen, to barrack (at)

uitkeren, to pay

uitkering, pay(ment), benefit

uitkienen, to figure (out)

uitkiezen, to select

uitkijk, view; look-out

uitkijken, to look out, to look forward

 je raakt er nooit uitgekeken, there's no end to be seen there

uitklaring(skosten), clearance (dues)

uitkleden, to undress, to strip

uitknijpen, to squeeze out; to do a bunk; to peg out

uitknipsel n, cutting

uitkno(b)belen, to figure out

uitkoken, to boil (out), to scald, to render

uitkomen, to come out, to work out

  ervoor uitkomen, to state openly

uitkomst, result; remedy

uitkramen, to spout, to parade

uitlaat, exhaust

uitlachen, to laugh at, to have a good laugh

uitlaten, to let out; to leave off (wearing)

  zich uitlaten, to express an opinion

uitleenbibliotheek, lending-library

uitleg, explanation, construction

uitleggen, to lay out; to explain; to let out

uitlenen, to lend

uitleven: zich —, to live one's (own) life (to the full)

  uitgeleefd, decrepit

uitleveren, to deliver up

uitlezen, to finish (reading)

uitlokken, to invite

uitlopen, to run out; to sprout

  uitlopen op, to lead to

uitloper, runner; spur

uitloven, to offer

uitmaken, to break off; to constitute; to decide; to matter; to put out

  iemand uitmaken voor al wat lelijk is, to call a person all the names under the sun

uitmesten, to clear out

uitmonden in, to discharge into

uitmoorden, to massacre

uitmunten, to excel

uit'muntend, excellent

uit'nemendheid: bij —, *par excellence*

uitnodigen, to invite

uitnodiging, invitation

uitoefenen, to exercise; to carry on, to hold

uitpakken, to unpack

uitpluizen, to go through with a fine tooth-comb

uitpraten, to finish talking; to talk over

  zich ergens uitpraten, to talk one's way out of something

uitpuilen, to bulge

uitputten, to exhaust

uitreiken, to distribute, to issue

uitrekenen, to calculate

uitroeien, to root out, to exterminate: to row out

uitroepen, to call (out), to exclaim; to proclaim

uitroep(steken *n***),** exclamation(-mark)

uitrusten, to rest; to equip

uitrusting, outfit, equipment

uitschakelen, to cut out (of the circuit); to count out

uitscheiden (met), to stop

uitschelden, to slang

uitschot *n,* trash, rejects

uitschuiftafel, extending table

uitslaan, to knock (shake, fling) out; to break out; to sweat

uitslag, result; rash; condensation

uitslapen, to sleep long enough, to lie in; to sleep off

uitsloven, to slave

uitsluiten, to exclude

  uitgesloten! out of the question!

uit'sluitend, exclusively

uitsluitsel *n,* decisive answer

uitsmijter, fried-egg on bread and ham

uitspanning, tea-garden(s)

uitspansel *n,* firmament

uitsparen, to save

uitspatting, extravagance, excess

uitspelen, to finish (a game); to play (off)

uitspoken, to be up to (mischief)

uitspraak, pronunciation; verdict

uitspreiden, to spread (out)

uitspreken, to pronounce, to express; to finish speaking

uitspringen, to jut out; to jump out

uitstaan, to stick (out); to bear interest

uitstallen, to display

uitstapje *n,* outing

uitstappen, to alight, to get out

uit'stedig, out of town

uitsteeksel *n*, protuberance
uitstek: bij —, pre-eminently
uitsteken, to put out, to stick out
uitstekend, protruding
uit'stekend, excellent
uitstel *n*, postponement
uitstellen, to postpone
uitstippelen, to work out (in detail
uitstorten, to pour out
uitstralen, to radiate
uitstrekken, to stretch (out)
uitstulping, bulge
uittocht, exodus
uittreden, to resign
uittrekken, to pull out; to take off; to march out
uittreksel *n*, extract, *précis*
uitvaagsel *n*, scum
uitvaardigen, to issue·
uitval, sally, break-through; outburst
uitvallen, to fall out; to turn out; to flare up; to make a sortie
uitvaren, to sail (out); to storm
uitverkiezing, predestination
uitverkocht, sold out
uitverkoop, (clearance-)sale
uitverkoren, chosen
uitvinden, to invent
uitvissen, to fish out; to ferret out
uitvlucht, pretext
uitvoer, export(s)
  ten uitvoer brengen, to put into effect
uit'voerbaar, practicable
uitvoeren, to export; to carry out, to perform
uit'voerig, detailed, fully
uitvorsen, to unearth
uitvragen, to ask out; to pump
uitwasemen, to exhale; to emanate
uitwedstrijd, away match
uitweg, way out, escape, outlet
uitweiden, to digress
uit'wendig, external
uitwerken, to work out, to elaborate; to mature, to wear off
uitwerking, effect; elaboration

uitwerpselen, excrements
uitwijken, to move to one side; to flee the country
uitwijzen, to show; to decide; to expel
uitwippen, to nip out(side)
uitwisselen, to exchange
uitwonen, to dilapidate
uitwonend, non-resident
uitzenden, to send out; to broadcast
uitzet, outfit, trousseau
uitzetten, to expand; to turn out; to set (out); to lower (boats)
uitzicht *n*, view, prospect
uitzieken, to get over an illness
uitzien, to look out
uitzingen: het —, to hold out
uitzitten: zijn straf —, to serve one's sentence
uitzoeken, to pick out
uitzondering, exception
uitzuigen, to suck out; to bleed white
uk(je *n*), nipper
una'niem, unanimous
unicum *n*, unique specimen
unie, union
u'niek, unique
univer'seel, universal; sole
universi'tair, universi'teit, university
urenlang, for hours
urmen, to worry, to fumble
uur *n*, hour; o'clock
uurwerk *n*, timepiece
uw, your
uwentwil(le): om —, for your sake
uwerzijds, for your part

V

vaag, vague
vaak, often
vaal, faded, sallow
vaandel *n*, colour(s)
vaandeldrager, standard-bearer
vaandrig, ensign; standard-bearer
vaarboom, punting-pole
vaardig, skilful; ready

vaargeul, fairway, channel
vaars, heifer
vaart, speed; waterway
(grote) vaart, (ocean-going) trade
vaartuig *n*, vessel
vaarwater *n*, fairway
iemand in het vaarwater zitten, to thwart a person
vaar'wel, farewell
vaas, vase
vaatdoek, dish-cloth
va'cantie, holiday(s), vacation
vaca'ture, vacancy
vacci'neren, to vaccinate
vacht, pelt, coat
vadem, fathom
vader, father
vaderlander, patriot
vaderlands'lievend, patriotic
vaderlands, native, national
vaderliefde, paternal love
vaderlijk, paternal
vadermoorder, parricide : stick-up collar
vaderschap *n*, paternity, father-hood
vadsig, slothful, flaccid
vagevuur *n*, purgatory
vak *n*, compartment, panel; subject, trade
vakje *n*, pigeon-hole
vakman, expert
vakterm, technical term
vakvereniging, trade-union
val, (down)fall; trap; valance
valbijl, guillotine
valbrug, draw-bridge
valdeur, trapdoor
va'lies *n*, portmanteau
valk(e'nier), falcon(er)
valkuil, pitfall
val'lei, valley
vallen, to fall
er valt niets aan te doen, nothing can be done about it
valluik *n*, trapdoor
valpoort, portcullis
valreep: één op de —, one for the road
vals, false, vicious
vals spelen, to cheat; to play out of tune

valscherm *n*, parachute
valsheid in geschrifte, forgery
valstrik, trap
va'luta, currency
valwind, squall
van, of; from
van de week, this week
van'af, (as) from
van'avond, this evening
van'daag, today
van'daan, from
van'daar, hence
vandaar dat, that is why
van'door: er — (gaan), to be off
vangarm, tentacle
vangen, to catch
vangnet *n*, safety net
vangst, haul, catch
va'nille, vanilla
van-, this (afternoon, morning)
van'nacht, last night, tonight
van'ouds (her), of old
van'waar, whence
van'wege, on account of
vanzelf'sprekend, self-evident, quite obvious
varen, to sail, to fare : fern
laten varen, to give up, to drop
varensgezel, sailor
varia, miscellaneous (items)
vari'ëren, to vary
varken *n*, pig
varkensdraf, hogwash
varkenshoeder, swineherd
varkenskot *n*, pigsty
varkensvlees *n*, pork
vast, fixed, permanent, firm, regular, stock; solid; certainly
maar vast, in the meantime
vastbe'raden, resolute
vastbinden, to tie up (tight)
vastdoen, to fix
vaste'land *n*, continent, main-land
vastenavond, Shrove Tuesday
vastentijd, Lent
vastgrijpen, to catch hold of
vastheid, firmness, consistency, stability
vasthouden, to hold (on to), to clutch; to detain
vast'houdend, tenacious; conservative

vastklampen : zich — aan, to cling to

vastleggen, to fix, to tie up ; to record

vastlopen, to run aground ; to jam ; to bog down

vastmaken, to fasten

vastpakken, to seize

vastraken, to run aground ; to get jammed

vastroesten, to rust (solid) ; to root (deeply)

vaststaan, to stand firm ; to be definite (ly established)

vaststellen, to fix, to establish

vastzetten, to fix (in position) ; to corner

vastzitten, to be stuck
er aan vastzitten, to be entailed

vat *n,* cask, vat, vessel ; hold

vatbaar, susceptible, capable

vatenkwast, washing-up mop

vatten, to catch ; to understand ; to set

vechten, to fight

vecht'lustig, pugnacious

vechtpartij, scrap

vee *n,* cattle

veearts, veterinary surgeon

veeg, streak : ominous
een veeg uit de pan, a piece of one's mind

veel, much, a good deal, many

veelal, often

veelbe'lovend, promising

veelbe'tekend, significant, suggestive

veelbe'wogen, eventful

veeleer, rather

veel'eisend, exacting

veelhoek, polygon

veelom'vattend, comprehensive

veel'soortig, manifold

veelvoud *n,* multiple

veelvraat, glutton

veel'vuldig, frequent ; manifold

veel'zeggend, significant

veel'zijdig, many-sided, catholic, versatile

veem *n,* warehouse (-company)

veen *n,* peat (-moor)

veenkolonie, fen-colony

veer, feather ; spring : *n,* ferry (-boat)

veerkracht, resilience

veer'krachtig, buoyant, resilient

veertien, fourteen

veertig, forty

veestapel, live-stock

veeteelt, stock-breeding

vegen, to sweep, to brush, to wipe

vege'tariër, vegetarian

vege'teren, to vegetate

veil : zijn leven — hebben, to hold one's life cheap

veilen, to auction

veilig (heid), safe (ty)

veiligheidshalve, for safety's sake

veiligheidsraad, Security Council

veiligheidsstop, fuse

veiligheidsverdrag *n,* security pact

veiling, auction

veine, (run of) luck

veinzen, to feign, to sham

vel *n,* skin, hide ; sheet
om uit je vel te springen, enough to make you wild

veld *n,* field
het veld ruimen, to retire from the field ; to make way
uit het veld geslagen, taken aback

veldbed *n,* camp-bed

veldfles, water-bottle, flask

veldheer, general

veldloop, cross-country run

veldpost, army post-office

veldprediker, army-chaplain

veldslag, battle

veldtocht, campaign

veldwachter, village policeman

velen, to stand : many (people)

velerlei, all kinds of

velg, rim

vellen, to fell : to pass

ven *n,* fen

ven'duhuis *n,* auction room (s)

ve'nijn *n,* venom

ve'nijnig, venomous

ven'noot, partner

ven'nootschap, partnership, company

venster *n*, window

vensterbank, window-sill

vensterglas *n*, window-pane

vent, chap, cove

venten, to peddle, to hawk

venter, hawker, costermonger

ven'tiel *n*, valve

venti'leren, to ventilate

ver, far, distant

ver'aangenamen, to make pleasant

ver'achtelijk, contemptible, contemptuous

ver'achten, to despise

ver'ademen, to breathe again

veraf, far (away)

ver'afgoden, to idolize

ver'afschuwen, to detest

ver'anderen, to change, to alter

ver'andering, change, transformation

ver'anderlijk, changeable, variable, inconstant

verant'woordelijk, responsible

verant'woordelijkheid(sgevoel *n*), (sense of) responsibility

ver'antwoorden, to answer for; to justify

ver'antwoording, account; justification

var'armen, to impoverish; to become poor

ver'assen, to cremate

ver'band *n*, connection; context; bandage, dressing; bond

ver'bandkist, first-aid box

ver'bannen, to exile

ver'basteren, to degenerate, to corrupt

ver'bazen, to astonish, to amaze

ver'beelden, to represent

  zich verbeelden, to imagine, to fancy

ver'beelding, imagination, (self-)conceit

ver'beiden, to await; to (a)bide

ver'bergen, to hide

ver'beten, obdurate, pent-up, grim

ver'beteren, to improve; to correct

ver'beteringsgesticht *n*, approved school

ver'beurdverklaren, to confiscate

ver'beuren, to forfeit

ver'beuzelen, to fritter away

ver'bidden, to mollify

ver'bieden, to forbid, to prohibit

ver'bijsteren, to bewilder

ver'bijten: zich —, to clench one's teeth

ver'binden, to join, to connect

  zich verbinden tot, to commit oneself to

ver'binding, connection, communication

ver'bindingsofficer, liaison officer

ver'bintenis, contract

ver'bitterd, embittered

ver'bleken, to grow pale; to fade

ver'blijden, to cheer (up)

ver'blijf *n*, stay; residence

ver'blijfkosten, hotel expenses

ver'blijven, to stay, to remain

ver'blinden, to blind, to dazzle

ver'bloemen, to disguise

ver'bluffend, staggering

ver'bod *n*, prohibition, ban

ver'boemelen, to squander

ver'bolgen, incensed

ver'bond *n*, alliance; covenant

ver'bouwen, to rebuild; to grow

verbouwe'reerd, flabbergasted

ver'branden, to burn (down); to be burnt (down, out, up), to tan

ver'brandingsproces *n*, process of combustion; cremation

ver'brassen, to dissipate

ver'breden, to widen

ver'breiden, to spread

verbreken, to break (off), to cut (off)

ver'brijzelen, to shatter

ver'broedering, fraternization

ver'brokkelen, to crumble

ver'bruien: het bij iemand —, to get into a person's bad books

ver'bruik *n*, consumption

ver'bruiken, to consume, to use up

ver'buigen, to bend, to buckle; to decline
ver'buiging, declension
ver'chroomd, chromium-plated
ver'dacht, suspect(ed); suspicious; prepared
ver'dagen, to adjourn
ver'dampen, to evaporate
ver'dedigen, to defend
ver'dediger, defender, council for the defence
ver'dediging, defence
ver'deeldheid, disagreement
ver'dekt, under cover
ver'delen, to divide (up)
ver'delgen, to destroy
ver'denken, to suspect
verder, further(more)
ver'derf n, ruin
ver'derfelijk, pernicious
ver'dichten, to invent
ver'dienen, to earn; to deserve
ver'dienste, wages, profit; merit
ver'dienstelijk, useful
ver'diepen: zich — in, to become engrossed in
ver'dieping, floor, storey
ver'dikke(me), ver'dikkie! drat it! by Jove!
ver'dobbelen, to gamble away
ver'doemen, to damn
ver'doemenis, damnation
ver'doen, to waste
ver'domd, damn(ed)
ver'dommen: ik verdom het! I'm damned if I do!
ver'donkeremanen, to spirit away
ver'doolde, pervert
ver'dorie! darn (it)!
ver'dorren, to wither, to parch
ver'dorven, depraved
ver'doven, to deaden, to benumb, to stun, to give an anæsthetic; to deafen
ver'dovingsmiddel n, anæsthetic, narcotic
ver'draagzaam, tolerant
ver'draaid, distorted: deuced: dash it all!
ver'draaien, to distort, to twist
ver'drag n, treaty
ver'dragen, to bear

ver'driet n, grief; regrets
ver'drieten, to grieve
ver'drietig, pained, sad, sullen
ver'drijven, to drive off; to dispel; to while away
ver'dringen, to oust
 zich verdringen om, to crowd round
ver'drinken, to be drowned; to drown; to squander on drink; to inundate
ver'drogen, to dry up
ver'dromen, to waste (time) in dreaming
ver'drukking: in de — komen, to suffer
ver'drukte, underdog, oppressed
ver'dubbelen, to (re)double
ver'duidelijken, to elucidate
ver'duisteren, to eclipse, to black out; to embezzle
ver'duiveld, devilish; darned
ver'dunnen, to thin, to dilute
ver'duren, to put up with
ver'dwaasd, vacant
ver'dwijnen, to disappear
ver'edelen, to enhance the quality of
vereen'voudigen, to simplify
vereen'zelvigen, to identify
ver'eeuwigen, to immortalize
ver'effenen, to settle
ver'eisen, to require
ver'eiste n, requirement
veren, to (be) spring(y)
veren(bed n), feather(-bed)
ver'en(ig)en, to unite, to join; to reconcile
ver'eniging, association, union
ver'eren, to honour
ver'ergeren, to deteriorate, to aggravate
verf, paint; dye
ver'fijnen, to refine
ver'filmen, to film
ver'flauwen, to flag, to fade
ver'foeien, to detest
ver'fomfaaien, to dishevel
ver'fraaien, to beautify
ver'frissen, to refresh
ver'frommelen, to crumple up
verg., cf.

ver'gaan, to perish, to decay, to go down

hoe zal het ons vergaan ? what is in store for us ?

een lawaai, dat horen en zien me verging, a noise fit to wake the dead

ver'gaarbak, reservoir

ver'gaderen, to assemble

ver'gadering, meeting

ver'gallen, to embitter, to spoil

vergalop'peren zich —, to let oneself in for something

ver'gankelijk, transitory

vergapen: zich —, to become infatuated

ver'garen, to collect

ver'gassen, to vaporize; to gas

ver'gasten, to treat, to feast

ver'geeflijk, pardonable

ver'geefs, (in) vain

ver'geetachtig, forgetful

ver'geetboek n: in het — raken, to be forgotten

ver'gelden, to repay, to pay for

ver'geldingsmaatregel, retaliatory measure

ver'gelen, to turn yellow

verge'lijk n, agreement; comparison

verge'lijken, to compare

verge'lijkend, comparative; competitive

verge'lijking, comparison, simile; equation

verge'makkelijken, to facilitate

vergen, to make demands on, to require

verge'noegd, contented

ver'getelheid, oblivion

ver'geten, to forget

ver'geven, to forgive

ver'gevensgezind, forgiving

ver'geving, pardon, forgiveness

vergevorderd, (far-)advanced

verge'wissen: zich —, to make sure

verge'zellen, to accompany

vergezicht n, prospect

verge'zocht, far-fetched

ver'giet, colander

ver'gieten, to shed; to refound

ver'gif(t) n, poison

ver'giffenis, forgiveness

ver'giftig, poisonous

ver'giftigen, to poison

ver'gissen: zich —, to be mistaken, to make a mistake

ver'gissing, mistake, slip

ver'goddelijking, deification

ver'goeden, to compensate (for), to reimburse

ver'goelijken, to palliate

ver'gooien, to throw away

zich vergooien, to throw oneself away; to play the wrong card

ver'grijp n, offence, breach

ver'grijpen: zich — aan, to lay hold on

ver'grooien, to disappear in time; to grow out of shape

ver'grootglas n, magnifying-glass

ver'groten, to enlarge, to increase, to magnify

ver'gruizen, to crush

ver'guizen, to vilify

ver'guld, gilt; delighted

ver'gulden, to gild

ver'gunnen, to permit

ver'gunning, permission, licence

ver'haal n, story: redress

op zijn verhaal komen, to take it easy (for a bit)

ver'haasten, to quicken, to expedite, to precipitate

ver'halen, to relate; to vent

het verhalen op, to take it out of

ver'handelen, to deal in; to discuss

ver'handeling, treatise

ver'harden, to harden

verharde weg, metalled road

ver'haren, to moult

ver'haspelen, to make a hash of

ver'heerlijken, to glorify, to elate

ver'heffen, to lift (up), to raise, to exalt

ver'heimelijken, to secrete

ver'helderen, to clarify

ver'helen, to conceal

ver'helpen, to remedy

ver'hemelte n, palate; canopy

ver'heugen, to delight
  zich verheugen, to rejoice
  zich verheugen op, to look forward to
ver'heven, exalted, lofty
ver'hinderen, to prevent, to hinder
ver'hip! dash!
ver'hitten, to heat
ver'hoeden, to forefend
ver'hogen, to raise, to heighten
ver'hoging, increase; platform; temperature
ver'holen, secret
ver'hongeren, to starve (to death)
ver'hoor n, interrogation, hearing
ver'horen, to hear, to grant; to interrogate
ver'houden: zich — als, to be in the ratio of
ver'houding, relation(ship), proportion
ver'huiswagen, removal-van
ver'huizen, to move (house)
ver'huizing, move
ver'hullen, to conceal
ver'huren, to let (out on hire)
ver'huur, hire, hiring out
ver'huurder, landlord, lessor
verifi'ëren, to verify
ver'ijdelen, to frustrate
vering, springiness, springs
ver'jaard, fallen by default, out of date
ver'jaardag, birthday
ver'jagen, to drive away
ver'jaren, to have one's birthday
ver'kalken, to harden, to calcerate
ver'kapt, disguised, veiled
ver'kavelen, to parcel out
ver'keer n, traffic; intercourse
ver'keerd, wrong, mis-(understood etc)
ver'keersheuvel, traffic-island
ver'keerstoren, control-tower
ver'keersweg, thoroughfare
ver'kennen, to reconnoitre
ver'kenner, scout
ver'kenning(svlucht), reconnaissance (flight)
ver'keren, to be, to move

ver'kering hebben, to be courting
ver'kerven: het bij iemand —, to incur a person's displeasure
ver'kiesbaar, eligible
ver'kies(e)lijk, preferable; desirable
ver'kiezen, to prefer; to elect, to chose
ver'kiezing, election; preference
ver'kiezingsdag, polling-day
ver'kijken: zich —, to make a mistake
  je kans is verkeken, you've missed your chance
ver'kikkerd, dead keen
ver'killen, to chill
ver'klappen, to let on (about)
ver'klaren, to explain; to declare, to certify
ver'klaring, explanation; declaration; certificate
ver'kleden: (zich) —, to change
ver'kleinen, to reduce, to cut down; to belittle
ver'kleinwoord n, diminutive
ver'kleumen, to get numb with cold
ver'kleuren, to fade
ver'klikken, to split (on)
ver'klikker, tell-tale
ver'klungelen, to fritter away
ver'kneukelen, ver'kneuteren: zich —, to gloat
ver'knippen, to cut up; to spoil by cutting wrongly
ver'knocht, devoted
ver'knoeien, to bungle; to waste
ver'koelen, to cool (off)
ver'koken, to boil away; to overcook
ver'kolen, to char, to carbonize
ver'kondigen, to proclaim
verkoop, sale
ver'kooplokaal n, auction-room
ver'koopster, shop-assistant
ver'kopen, to sell: to crack (jokes)
ver'koping, (auction-)sale
ver'korten, to shorten; to beguile
ver'kouden worden, to catch cold
  je bent verkouden, you've got a cold; you've walked right into it

ver'koudheid, cold
ver'krachten, to violate, to rape
ver'kreuk(el)en, to crumple (up)
ver'krijgbaar, obtainable
ver'krijgen, to obtain
ver'kroppen, to swallow
ver'kropt, pent-up
ver'kruimelen, to crumble (away)
ver'kwanselen, to barter away, to squander
ver'kwikken, to refresh
ver'kwisten, to waste, to dissipate
ver'laden, to ship
ver'lagen, to lower
ver'lakken, to diddle
ver'lammen, to paralyse
ver'lamming, paralysis
ver'langen, to desire, to long; to require
ver'laten, to leave, to desert: lonely, deserted
zich verlaten op, to rely on
ver'leden, last: n, past
ver'legen, shy, embarrassed: — perished
ver'legenheid, shyness, embarrassment, quandary
ver'leggen, to shift
ver'leidelijk, tempting
ver'leiden, to tempt, to seduce
ver'lenen, to grant, to give
ver'lengen, to lengthen, to extend
ver'lengstuk n, extension piece
ver'leppen, to wilt; to jade
ver'leren, to lose the art
ver'licht, lit (up); enlightened; relieved
ver'lichten, to light (up), to illuminate; to lighten; to alleviate
ver'liefd, in love, amorous
ver'lies n, loss
ver'liezen, to lose
ver'lof n, leave, permission; licence
ver'lokken, to entice
ver'loochenen, to deny, to belie
ver'loofde, fiancé(e)

ver'loop n, course, (re)lapse
ver'lopen, to elapse; to go down(hill); to go (off): expired: down-and-out
ver'loren gaan, to get lost; to be wasted
ver'loskunde, obstetrics
ver'lossen, to deliver
ver'lossing, redemption; deliverance
ver'loten, to raffle
ver'loven, to get engaged
ver'loving, engagement
ver'luchten, to illuminate
ver'luiden, to murmur
ver'lummelen, to laze away
ver'lustigen: zich — in, to revel in
ver'maak n, pleasure, amusement
ver'maard, celebrated
ver'mageren, to reduce or lose weight
ver'mageringskuur, slimming course
ver'makelijk, amusing
ver'maken, to amuse; to alter; to bequeath
vermale'dijd, accursed
ver'manen, to admonish
ver'mannen: zich —, to brace oneself
ver'meend, supposed
ver'meerderen, to increase
ver'meien: zich —, to enjoy oneself
ver'melden, to mention, to record
vermeldens'waard, worth mentioning
ver'menen, to opine
ver'mengen, to mix, to mingle
vermenig'vuldigen, to multiply
ver'metel, audacious
ver'mijden, to avoid, to evade
vermil'joen (n), vermilion
ver'minderen, to reduce, to diminish
ver'minken, to maim, to mutilate
ver'mist, missing
ver'moedelijk, presumably probable

ver'moeden, to presume; to suspect: *n*, conjecture; suspicion
ver'moeid(heid), tired(ness), fatigue(d)
ver'moeiend, tiring
ver'mogen *n*, fortune; ability, capacity
 niets vermogen, to be powerless
ver'mogend, wealthy
ver'mogensbelasting, property-tax
ver'molmd, mouldered
ver'mommen, to disguise
ver'moorden, to murder
ver'morzelen, to crush
ver'murwen, to mollify
ver'nachelen, to fox
ver'nauwen, to take in, to narrow
ver'nederen, to humble, to humiliate
ver'nemen, to learn, to hear
ver'nielen, to destroy, to wreck
ver'nielziek, verniel'zuchtig, destructive
ver'nietigen, to destroy; to annul, to reverse
ver'nieuwen, to renew
ver'nikkelen, to nickle(-plate); to diddle
ver'nis *n*, varnish; veneer
ver'noemen naar, to name after
vernuft *n*, ingenuity, wit
veron'aangenamen, to make unpleasant
veron'achtzamen, to neglect
veronder'stellen, to suppose, to assume
ver'ongelijkt, hurt, injured
ver'ongelukken, to be wrecked, to crash, to be killed
veront'heiligen, to desecrate
veront'reinigen, to pollute
veront'rusten, to alarm
veront'schuldigen, to excuse
 zich verontschuldigen, to apologize, to excuse oneself
veront'waardigd, indignant
veront'waardiging, indignation
ver'oordelen, to condemn, to convict

ver'oorloofd, allowed, permissible
ver'oorloven: zich —, to permit oneself, to take the liberty of; to afford
ver'oorzaken, to cause
ver'orberen, to consume
ver'ordening, regulation(s), by-law
ver'ouderd, obsolete, aged
ver'overen, to conquer, to capture
ver'pachten, to let (out) on lease
ver'pakken, to pack
ver'panden, to pawn; to pledge
ver'patsen, to trade
verper'soonlijken, to personify
ver'pesten, to contaminate; to wreck
ver'pieterd, scrubby (little)
ver'plaatsen, to move, to transfer
 zich verplaatsen, to imagine oneself
ver'planten, to transplant
ver'pleegster, nurse
ver'plegen, to nurse
ver'pletteren, to shatter
ver'plicht, obliged, indebted; compulsory
ver'plichten, to oblige; to compel
ver'plichting, obligation, commitment
ver'pozen: zich —, to relax
ver'praten: tijd —, to spend time talking
 zich verpraten, to let on
ver'prutsen, to muck up
ver'raad *n*, treason
ver'raden, to betray
ver'rader, traitor
ver'raderlijk, treacherous, insidious
ver'rassen, to surprise
ver'rassing, surprise
verre'gaand, gross, outrageous
ver'regend, washed out (by the rain)
verreikend, far-reaching
ver'reisd, travel-weary

ver'rekenen, to settle
  zich verrekenen, to miscalculate
verrekijker, telescope
ver'rekken, to sprain, to strain: to go to hell
verre'weg, by far
ver'richten, to carry out, to do
ver'rijken, to enrich
ver'rijzen, to (a)rise, to spring up
ver'roeren, to stir
ver'roest, rusty: darn(ed)
ver'rotten, to rot
ver'ruilen, to exchange
ver'ruimen, to broaden
ver'rukkelijk, delicious; gorgeous
ver'rukking, rapture
ver'rukt, delighted
vers, fresh, new(-laid): n, verse, poetry, poem
ver'sagen, to quaver
ver'schaffen, to provide
ver'schalken, to beguile
ver'schansen, to entrench, to ensconce
ver'scheiden, various, several: n, decease
ver'scheidenheid, diversity
ver'schepen, to (tran)ship
ver'scherpen, to intensify
ver'scheuren, to tear (to pieces), to rend
ver'schiet n, distance; prospect
ver'schieten, to use up; to turn pale, to fade
ver'schijnen, to appear
ver'schijning, appearance; figure
ver'schijnsel n, phenomenon; symptom
ver'schil n, difference
ver'schillen, to differ
ver'schillend, different
ver'schonen, to put on clean sheets or clothes; to excuse; to spare
ver'schoppeling, outcast
ver'schrikkelijk, terrible
ver'schrikking, fright, horror
ver'schroeien, to scorch
ver'schrompelen, to shrivel (up)

ver'schuilen, to hide, to shelter
ver'schuiven, to shift
ver'schuldigd, indebted, due
versie, version
ver'sieren, to adorn
ver'siering, decoration
ver'siersel n, ornament
ver'sjacheren, to barter away, to squander
ver'sjouwen, to shift
ver'slaafd, addicted
ver'slaan, to beat, to defeat; to cover
ver'slag n, report
ver'slagen, defeated; put out
ver'slaggever, reporter, commentator
ver'slapen: zich —, to oversleep
ver'slappen, to weaken, to flag
ver'slepen, to tow away, to shift
ver'slijten, to wear out; to while away
  waar verslijt je me voor? what do you take me for?
ver'slikken: zich —, to choke
ver'slinden, to devour
ver'slingeren: zich —, to throw oneself away
ver'sloffen, ver'slonzen, to neglect
versmaat, metre
ver'smachten, to pine away
ver'smaden, to despise
ver'smelten, to melt, to blend
ver'snapering, titbit, refreshment
ver'snellen, to accelerate
ver'snelling, acceleration; gear
ver'snipperen, to cut up; to fritter away
ver'snoepen, to spend on sweets
ver'soberen, to live more simply
ver'spelen, to throw away
ver'sperren, to block (up)
ver'spieden, to spy out
ver'spillen, to waste
ver'splinteren, to (break into) splinter(s)
ver'spreiden: (zich) —, to spread, to scatter
ver'spreken: zich —, to make a slip (of the tongue)

verspringen *n,* long-jump
ver'staan, to understand, to hear
ver'staanbaar, audible, intelligible
ver'stand *n,* sense(s), mind; knowledge
  met dien verstande, on the understanding
  daar staat mijn verstand bij stil, it is beyond me
ver'standelijk, intellectual, rational
ver'standhouding, understanding, terms
ver'standig, sensible
ver'standshuwelijk *n,* marriage of convenience
ver'standskies, wisdom tooth
ver'standsmens, man of thought
ver'standsverbijstering, mental derangement
ver'stard, rigid
ver'steend, petrified; fossilized
ver'stek, *n,* default
ver'stekeling, stowaway
ver'stelbaar, adjustable
ver'steld, dumbfounded
ver'stellen, to adjust; to mend
ver'sterken, to fortify, to reinforce, to intensify; to amplify
ver'sterker, amplifier
ver'stevigen, to consolidate
ver'stijven, to stiffen; to grow numb
ver'stikken, to stifle
ver'stoken, to consume, to burn
ver'stoken van, without
ver'stokt, hardened, confirmed
ver'stolen, furtive
ver'stommen, to fall silent, to be struck dumb
ver'stoord, disturbed; vexed
ver'stoppen, to block (up); to hide
ver'stoppertje *n,* hide-and-seek
ver'storen, to disturb, to upset
ver'stoten, to cast off
ver'stouten: zich —, to make bold
ver'stouwen, to stow (away)
ver'strekken, to furnish, to issue
verstrekkend, far-reaching, sweeping

ver'strijken, to expire, to elapse
ver'strikken, to ensnare
ver'strooid, scattered; absent-minded
ver'strooien: zich —, to disperse; to find amusement
ver'stuiken, to sprain
ver'stuiven, to (be) blow(n) about
ver'suft, stupefied; doting
ver'takken: zich —, to branch
ver'talen, to translate
ver'taling, translation
verte, distance
ver'tederen, to mollify; to mellow
ver'teerbaar, digestible
ver'tegenwoordigen, to represent
ver'tellen, to tell, to say
  zich vertellen, to miscount
ver'telling, ver'telsel *n,* story
ver'teren, to consume, to spend; to digest: to perish
ver'tering, food and/or drink(s)
ver'tier *n,* (signs of) life, gaiety
ver'tikken, to jib, to refuse flatly
ver'tillen, to lift
  zich vertillen, to strain oneself (lifting something)
ver'timmeren, to make alterations to
ver'toeven, to sojourn
ver'tolken, to interpret
ver'tonen, to show, to produce
ver'toon *n,* show, presentation
ver'tragen, to retard
ver'traging, delay
ver'trappen, to trample under foot
ver'trek *n,* room: departure
ver'trekken, to leave; to distort
ver'troebelen, to confuse
ver'troetelen, to molly-coddle
ver'trouwd, trusty, safe; conversant
ver'trouwelijk, confidential; intimate
ver'trouweling, confidant(e)
ver'trouwen, to (en)trust; to rely: *n,* trust, confidence
ver'twijfeld, desperate

ver'twijfeling, desperation
veruit, by far
veruitziend, far-sighted
ver'vaard, alarmed
ver'vaardigen, to manufacture
ver'vaarlijk, frightful, terrific
ver'vagen, to fade
ver'val *n*, decline; disrepair; fall
ver'vallen, to lapse, to be cancelled, to expire, to fall (due); to go to ruin
ver'valsen, to fake
ver'vangen, to replace
ver'vat, couched; included
ver'velen: (zich) —, to (be) bore(d)
  tot vervelens toe, *ad nauseam*
ver'velend, boring; annoying
ver'veling, boredom
ver'vellen, to peel; to slough
verveloos, in need of a coat of paint
verven, to paint; to dye
ver'versen, to refresh; to renew
ver'vlakken, to become colourless
ver'vliegen, to evaporate, to vanish
ver'vloeken, to curse
ver'voegen, to conjugate
  zich vervoegen bij, to apply to
ver'voer *n*, transport
ver'voeren, to transport
ver'voering, rapture
ver'voermiddel *n*, (means of) conveyance
ver'volg *n*, continuation; future
ver'volgen, to continue; to pursue; to persecute, to prosecute
ver'volgens, after that
ver'volgverhaal *n*, serial story
ver'vreemden, to alienate, to grow estranged
ver'vroegen, to put forward
ver'vuilen, to get filthy
ver'vullen, to fill, to fulfil
ver'vulling, fulfilment
ver'waaid, dishevelled
ver'waand, conceited
ver'waardigen: (zich) —, to vouchsafe
ver'waarlozen, to neglect

ver'wachten, to expect
ver'wachting, expectation
ver'want, related
  verwanten, relatives
ver'wantschap, relationship affinity
ver'warmen, to heat
ver'warren, to confuse, to (en)tangle
ver'warring, confusion, disorder
ver'waterd, watered (down)
ver'wedden, to bet
ver'weer *n*, resistance; defence
ver'weerd, weather-beaten
ver'weking, softening
ver'wekken, to arouse, to raise; to beget
ver'welken, to wither, to wilt
ver'welkomen, to welcome
ver'wennen, to spoil
ver'wensen, to curse
ver'weren, to weather: to defend
ver'werken, to cope with; to work up
ver'werpen, to reject
ver'werven, to acquire
ver'wezen, dazed
ver'wezenlijken, to realize
  zich ver'wezenlijken, to materialize
ver'wijden, to widen
ver'wijderen, to remove, to turn out
  zich verwijderen, to withdraw
ver'wijdering, removal, expulsion; estrangement
ver'wijfd, effeminate
ver'wijlen, to linger
ver'wijt(en) (*n*), (to) reproach
ver'wijzen, to refer
ver'wikkelen, to implicate, to complicate
ver'wikkeling, complication, plot
ver'wilderen, to run wild, to degenerate
ver'wisselen, to (ex)change
ver'wittigen, to notify
ver'woed, furious
ver'woesten, to devastate
ver'wonden, to injure, to wound

ver'wonderen, to surprise
  zich verwonderen, to be surprised
ver'wonen, to pay in rent
ver'wording, degeneration
ver'wringen, to twist, to distort
ver'zachten, to alleviate
ver'zadigen, to saturate; to satisfy
ver'zaken, to forsake
ver'zakken, to sag, to subside
ver'zamelen, to collect, to muster (up)
ver'zamelnaam, collective
ver'zanden, to silt up
ver'zegelen, to seal (up)
ver'zeilen, to land (up)
ver'zekeren, to assure, to insure; to secure
  zich verzekeren, to make sure
ver'zekering, assurance, insurance
ver'zenden, to send (off)
ver'zet n, resistance
ver'zetje n, break
ver'zetten, to move; to get through; to get over
  zich verzetten, to oppose, to resist
ver'zien : het — hebben op, to be out to get
verziend, long-sighted
ver'zilveren, to silver(-plate); to convert into cash
ver'zinken, to become immersed; to countersink
ver'zinnen, to think (up)
ver'zinsel n, fabrication
ver'zitten, to move to another chair; to shift one's position
ver'zoek n, request
ver'zoeken, to request; to tempt
ver'zoeking, temptation
ver'zoekschrift n, petition
ver'zoenen, to reconcile
ver'zolen, to re-sole
ver'zorgen, to take care of
ver'zot op, mad on
ver'zuchten, to sigh
ver'zuchting, sigh, moan
ver'zuim n, omission; non-attendance
  zonder verzuim, without fail

ver'zuimen, to fail (in); to miss
ver'zuipen, to drown; to blue on drink
ver'zuren, to (turn) sour
ver'zwakken, to weaken
ver'zwaren, to increase (the standard of)
  ver'zwarende omstandigheden, aggravating circumstances
ver'zwelgen, to swallow up
ver'zwijgen voor, to keep from
ver'zwikken, to sprain
vest n, waistcoat
vesti'aire, cloak-room
vesti'bule, hall
vestigen, to establish; to fix
  zich vestigen, to settle
vesting, fortress
vet, fat; greasy; rich: n, fat
  vet gedrukt, in heavy type
vete, feud
veter, (shoe-)lace
vete'raan, veteran
vetgehalte n, fat content
vetmesten, to fatten (up)
vetplant, succulent plant
vettigheid, richness, greasiness
vetvrij, grease-proof
vetzak, fatty
vetzucht, obesity
veulen n, foal
vezel, fibre
vgl., cf.
via'duct n, (railway-)bridge, viaduct
vib'reren, to vibrate
vici'eus, vicious
vief, lively
vier, four
  onder vier ogen, in private
vieren, to celebrate: to ease off
vierendelen, to quarter
vierhoek, quadrilateral
vierkant (n), square
vierkantsvergelijking, quadratic equation
vierkantswortel, square root
vierling, (set of) quadruplets
viersprong, cross-road(s)
viervoeter, quadruped
vies, dirty, filthy; wry
  ik ben er vies van, it turns my stomach

viezerik, muck-pot, filthy specimen
vijand, enemy
vij'andelijk, enemy('s)
vij'andig, hostile
vijandschap, enmity
vijf, five
vijfling, (set of) quintuplets
vijftien, fifteen
vijftig, fifty
vijg, fig
vijl(en), (to) file
vijver, pond
vijzel, mortar
villen, to skin, to fleece
vilt n, felt
vin, fin
vinden, to find; to think; to get on
vindingrijk, inventive
vinger, finger
  door de vingers zien, to overlook
vingerafdruk, finger-print
vingerdoekje, n, small napkin
vingerhoed, thimble
vingervlug, nimble-fingered
vingerwijzing, hint, pointer
vink, finch
vinnig, cutting, sharp
vio'list, violinist
violon'cel, violoncello
vi'ool, violin: violet, pansy
vi'oolsleutel, treble clef
virtu'oos, virtuoso
vis, fish
visboer, fishmonger
viscouvert n, fish-knife and fork
visie, visi'oen n, vision
vi'site, visit(or)(s)
vislijm, isinglass
vissen, to fish
visser, fisherman
visse'rij, fishing(-industry)
vissnoer n, fishing-line
visspaan, fish-slice
visvangst, fishing
vi'taal, vital
vi'trage, (curtain-)net
vi'trine, show-case
vitten op, to find fault with
vi'zier n, visor
  in het vizier krijgen, to catch
  sight of

vla, (dessert) cream
vlaag, gust; fit
Vlaams, Flemish
vlag, flag
vlaggen, to put out the flag(s)
vlak, flat, smooth; right, close:
  n (sur)face
vlakgom n, india-rubber
vlakte, plane; stretch
vlam, flame
vlammen, to blaze, to be ardent
vlas n, flax
vlasblond, flaxen
vlassen op, to be all agog for
vlecht, plait
vlechten, to plait, to weave
vleermuis, bat
vlees n, meat, flesh
vleesboom, fleshy growth
vleeshouwer, butcher
vleesmes n, carving-knife
vleesmolen, mincing-machine
vleeswording, incarnation
vleet : geld bij de —, pots of
  money
vlegel, flail; (insolent) youth
vleien, to flatter, to coax
vlek, blot, spot, stain
vlekkeloos, spotless
vlekkenwater n, dry cleaner
vlerk, wing, arm; lout
vlet(schuit), flat-bottomed boat
vleug, nap; glimmer; whiff
vleugel, wing; grand piano
vlezig, fleshy, plump
vlieg, fly
vliegdekschip n, aircraft-
  carrier
vliegdienst, air-service
vliegen, to fly
  in brand vliegen, to burst into
  flames
vliege'nier, airman
vliegenkast, meat-safe
vliegenklap, fly-swatter
vliegensvlug, as quick as lightning
vlieger, kite; airman
vlieghaven, airport
vliegkunst, aviation
vliegmachine, aeroplane
vliegtuig n, aircraft, plane
vliegveld n, airfield

vliegwerk *n*, stage machinery
vliegwiel *n*, fly-wheel
vlier(bes), elder(berry)
vliering, loft
vlies *n*, fleece; film, membrane
vlijen, to nestle
vlijmscherp, sharp as a razor
vlijt, diligence
vlijtig, industrious
vlinder, butterfly
vlo, flea
vloed, flood (tide), flow
vloedgolf, tidal wave
vloeibaar, liquid
vloeiblok *n*, blotting-pad
vloeien, to flow; to blot
vloeiend, flowing; fluent
vloeipapier *n*, blotting-paper;
  tissue-paper
vloeistof, liquid
vloeitje *n*, cigarette-paper
vloek, curse, oath
vloeken, to swear, to curse; to
  clash
vloer, floor(ing)
vloeren, to floor
vloerkleed *n*, carpet
vlok, flake, tuft
vlonder, plank (thrown across a
  ditch); wooden platform
vloot, fleet
vlootbasis, naval base
vlootvoogd, admiral of the fleet
vlos(sig), floss(y)
vlot, fluent, smooth, slick, sprightly; afloat: *n*, raft
vlotgaand, shallow-draught
vlotten, to float; to proceed
  smoothly
vlucht, flight; wing-span
vluchteling, fugitive
vluchten, to fly, to flee
vluchtheuvel, traffic island;
  mound
vluchtig, cursory, fleeting, volatile
vlug, quick
vlugschrift *n*, pamphlet
vlugzout *n*, sal volatile
vocabu'laire *n*, vocabulary
vocht *n*, fluid, moisture
vochtig, damp, moist
vod *n*, rag, tatter

voddenkoopman, rag-and-bone
  man
voeden, to feed, to nourish
voeder(en) (*n*), (to) fodder
voederzak, nose-bag
voeding, feed; nourishment
voedingsbodem, breeding-
  ground
voedingsleer, dietetics
voedsel *n*, food
voedster, wet-nurse
voedsterkind *n*, foster-child
voedzaam, nourishing
voeg, joint
voegen, to join, to add; to point;
  to behove
  zich voegen, to join; to comply
voegwoord *n*, conjunction
voelbaar, perceptible
voelen, to feel
voelhoren, voelspriet, feeler
voer, *n*, fodder; load
voeren, to take, to carry (on), to
  wield, to conduct: to feed: to
  line
voering, lining
voerloon *n*, carriage
voerman, carter
voertaal, official language
voertuig *n*, vehicle
voet, foot; footing
  voet bij stuk houden, to stick
  to one's guns
voetangel, mantrap
voetbal(schoen), football(boot)
voet(en)bank, foot-stool
voet(en)einde *n*, foot (of the
  bed)
voetganger, pedestrian
voetkussen *n*, hassock
voetreis, walking tour
voetspoor *n*, foot-mark
voetstuk *n*, pedestal
voetvolk *n*, foot(-soldiers)
voetzoeker, (jumping) cracker
vogel, bird
vogelbekdier *n*, platypus
vogelverschrikker, scarecrow
vogelvlucht, bird's-eye view
vogelvrij, outlawed
vol, full
vo'lant, flounce
volbloed, thorough(bred)

vol'brengen, to accomplish

vol'daan, satisfied; paid

vol'doen, to satisfy, to give satisfaction, to pay

voldoen aan, to fulfil

vol'doend, satisfactory; sufficient

vol'doening, satisfaction; settlement

vol'dongen, accomplished

vol'dragen, fully developed

vol'eind(ig)en, to complete

vol'gaarne, right gladly

volgauto, car in procession

volgeboekt, booked up

volgeling, follower

volgen, to follow

volgend, following, next

volgens, according to

volgieten, to fill

volgnummer n, serial number

volgorde, order, sequence

volgzaam, docile

vol'harden, to persevere

volhouden, to keep up, to maintain, to insist

voli'ère, aviary

vol'ijverig, sedulous

volk n, nation, people

Volkenbend, League of Nations

volkenkunde, ethnology

volkenrecht n, international law

vol'komen, complete

vol'korenbrood n, whole-meal bread

volksaard, national character

volksbuurt, working-class quarter

volksconcert n, popular concert

volksdans, folk-dance

volksdracht, national costume

volksgebruik n, national custom

volkshogeschool, village college

volkskunde, folk-lore

volkslied n, national anthem; folk-song

volksmond : in de — heten, to be popularly called

volksstam, tribe

volksstemming, plebiscite

volkstelling, census

volkstuin, allotment

volksuitgave, popular edition

volksuniversiteit, people's college

volksverhaal n, folk-tale

volksverhuizing, mass-migration

vol'ledig, complete, full

vol'leerd, consummate

vollopen, to fill up

vol'maakt, perfect

volmacht, power of attorney, proxy

vol'mondig, whole-hearted

volon'tair, student apprentice

volop, plenty (of)

volproppen, to stuff, to clutter up

vol'slagen, utter, total

vol'staan : laat ik — met te zeggen, suffice it to say

vol'strekt, absolute, at all

vol'tallig, complete, plenary

volte, crowd

vol'tooien, to complete

voltreffer, direct hit

vol'trekken, to solemnize, to execute

vol'uit, in full

volvette kaas, full-cream cheese

vol'voeren, to carry out

vol'waardig, sound (in body and mind)

vol'wassen(e), grown-up, full-grown, adult

volzee, high sea

volzin, sentence

vondeling, foundling

vondst, find

vonk(en), (to) spark

vonnis n, sentence, verdict

voogd('es), guardian

voog'dij, guardianship

voor, for; before; in front of: furrow

voor . . . uit, ahead

voor'aan, in front, at this end

voor'aanstaand, prominent

vooraanzicht n, front view

voor'af, beforehand

voor'afgaand, foregoing, preliminary

voor'al, especially, by all means, on any account

voorals'noĝ, as yet
vooravond, early evening; eve
voorbaat : bij —, in anticipation
voor'bariĝ, premature
voorbedachte : met — rade, with malice aforethought
voorbede, intercession
voorbeeld *n,* example, model
voor'beeldiĝ, exemplary
voorbehoedmiddel *n,* prophylactic
voorbehoud *n,* reservation
voorbehouden, to reserve
voorbereiden, to prepare
voorbereiding, voorbereidsel *n,* preparation
voorbericht *n,* preface
voorbeschikken, voorbestemmen, to predestine
voorbidden, to lead in prayer
voor'bij, past
voor'bijgaan, to pass (by)
voor'bijgaand, passing, temporary
voor'bijganger, passer-by
voor'bijpraten : zijn mond —, to let one's tongue run away with one
voor'bijstreven, to outstrip, to overshoot
voorbode, herald, prelude
voordat, before
voordeel *n,* advantage, profit
voor'deliĝ, economical, advantageous
voordeur, front door
voor'dien, until then
voordoen, to give a demonstration; to put on
  zich voordoen, to arise; to (re)present oneself
voordracht, recitation, lecture; delivery, rendering; nomination
voordragen, to recite; to propose
voor'eerst, in the first place; for the present
voorgaan, to lead (the way); to come first
voorgaand, preceding
voorganger, predecessor; minister

voorgerecht *n,* entrée
voorgeslacht *n,* ancestors
voorgevel, façade
voorgevoel *n,* presentiment
voor'ĝoed, for good
voorgrond, foreground, fore-(front)
voorhamer, sledge-hammer
voor'handen, available
voorhebben, to intend; to have the advantage
voor'heen, formerly
voorhistorisch, prehistoric
voorhoede, advanced guard; forwards
voorhoofd *n,* forehead
voor'in, in (the) front
voor'ingenomen, prejudiced
voorjaar *n,* spring
voorkamer, front room
voorkauwen, to repeat over and over again
voorkennis, (fore)knowledge
voorkeur, preference
voorkomen, to occur; to seem; to drive up; to get ahead; to appear: *n,* appearance; incidence
voor'komen, to prevent; to anticipate
voor'komend, charming, considerate
voorlaatst, penultimate, last but one
voorland *n,* foreland; future
voorleggen, to submit to
voorletter, initial
voorlezen, to read (out) to
voorlichten, to light the way; to enlighten
voorlichting, information
voorliefde, predilection
voorliegen, to tell lies about
voorlijk, forward
voorlopen, to go in front; to gain, to be fast
voorloper, precursor
voor'lopig, interim, provisional, for the time being
voor'maliĝ, one-time
voor'meld, above-mentioned
voormiddag, morning
voornaam, Christian name

voor'naam, distinguished, prominent

het voornaamste is, the main point is

voornaamwoord *n,* pronoun

voor'namelijk, principally

voornemen: zich —, to resolve, to propose

voornemen *n,* intention

voor'noemd, afore-mentioned

voor'onder *n,* forecastle

voor'oordeel *n,* prejudice

voor'oorlogs, pre-war

voor'op, in front

voor'opgezet, preconceived

voor'opstellen, to take for granted; to put first and foremost

voorouders, ancestors

voor'over, forward

voorplecht, forecastle

voorpost, outpost

voorpraten, to prompt

voorproefje *n,* foretaste

voorraad, stock, store

vorraadschuur, granary

voor'radig, in stock

voorrang, precedence; right of way

voorrangsweg, major road

voorrecht *n,* privilege

voorrede, preface

voorrijder, postilion; outrider

voorruit, wind-screen

voorschieten, to advance

voorschijn: te — brengen, to produce

te — halen, to take out

te — komen, to appear

te — roepen, to evoke

voorschoot, apron

voorschot *n,* advance

voorschrift *n,* regulation, order

voorschrijven, to prescribe, to lay down

voorsnijmes *n,* carving knife

voorspel *n,* voluntary, prologue; prelude

voorspelen, to play for

voor'spellen, to predict; to presage

voorspiegelen, to hold out prospects of

voorspoed, prosperity

voor'spoedig, prosperous, successful

voorspraak, intercession; advocate

voorsprong, start, lead

voorstaan, to stand in front; to come to mind

zich laten voorstaan op, to pride oneself on

voorstad, suburb

voorstander, advocate

voorste, foremost, front

voorstel *n,* proposal, suggestion

voorstellen, to (re)present, to introduce; to propose

zich voorstellen, to introduce oneself; to imagine; to intend

voorstelling, performance; representation

zich een voorstelling maken van, to visualize

voorstemmen, to vote in favour (of)

voorsteven, stem

voort-, on, forward

voortaan, in future

voortbestaan *n,* future life

voortbrengen, to produce, to beget

voortbrengsel *n,* product

voort'durend, continual, continuous

voorteken *n,* sign, omen

voortgang, progress; haste

voortkomen uit, to emanate from

voortmaken, to make haste

voortplanten, to propagate

voor'treffelijk, excellent

voortrein, relief train

voortrekken, to favour

voortrekker, pioneer

voorts, further(more)

voortslepen, to drag along

voortspruiten uit, to arise from

voort'varend, go-ahead

voort'varendheid, enterprise, drive

voortvloeien uit, to result from

voort'vluchtig, at large, fugitive

voortwoekeren, to spread

voortzetten, to continue

voor'uit, forward, ahead; before(hand)

voor'uitbetalen, to pay in advance

voor'uitgaan, to go on ahead; to make progress

voor'uitgang, progress, improvement

voor'uitkomen, to get on

voor'uitlopen op, to anticipate

vooruit'strevend, progressive

voor'uitzicht *n*, prospect

voorvader, ancestor

voorval *n*, incident

voorvechter, champion

voorvoegsel *n*, prefix

voor'waar, verily

voorwaarde, condition

voorwaarts, forward(s)

voorwenden, to feign

voorwendsel *n*, pretext, pretence

voor'wereldlijk, prehistoric

voorwerp *n*, object

voorwoord *n*, foreword

voorzeggen, to prompt

voorzet, centre

voorzetsel *n*, preposition

voor'zichtig, careful, cautious

voor'zichtigheid, caution

voor'zien, to foresee; to provide (for)

 het op iemand voorzien hebben, to have one's eye on a person

 het niet op iemand voorzien hebben, to have no time for a person

voor'zienigheid, providence

voorzitter, chairman

voorzorg(smaatregel), precaution(ary measure)

voos, spongy, rotten

vorderen, to (make) progress; to requisition, to demand

vordering, progress: claim

voren: naar —, to the front

 te voren, before(hand)

 van voren, (from) in front

 van voren af aan, from the beginning

vorig, last, previous

vork, fork

vorm, form, shape, mould

vormelijk, formal

vormen, to form, to constitute

vorming, formation; education

vormleer, accidence

vorm(e)loos, shapeless

vormsel *n*, confirmation

vorsen, to search

vorst, frost: prince, monarch

vorstelijk, royal, regal

vorstendom *n*, principality

vorstenhuis *n*, dynasty

vors'tin, queen

vos, fox; bay (horse)

vossen, to swot

vouw, fold, crease

vouwbeen *n*, paper-knife

vouwen, to fold

vraag, question, request, demand

vraagbaak, fund of information

vraaggesprek *n*, interview

vraagstuk *n*, problem

vraagteken *n*, question-mark

vraat'zuchtig, voracious(ly)

vracht, freight, load, cargo

vrachtauto, lorry

vrachtboot, cargo-boat

vrachtbrief, bill of lading

vrachtgoed *n*, goods, cargo

vrachtrijder, carrier (service)

vrachtwagen, lorry

vragen, to ask; to charge; to require

vrede, peace

vredesnaam: in —, for goodness' sake

vredestichter, peacemaker

vredig, peaceful

veedzaam, peaceable

vreemd, strange; foreign, alien

vreemde: in den —, abroad

vreemdeling, stranger; foreigner

vreemdelingeverkeer *n*, tourist traffic

vreemd'soortig, unusual

vrees, fear

vreesaanjagend, terrifying

vreetzak, greedy-guts

vrek(kig), miser(ly)

vreselijk, frightful

vreten, to devour, to eat, to stuff

vreugde, joy

vreugdebetoon *n*, rejoicing(s)

vreugdeschot *n*, salute

vreugdevol, joyful
vreugdevuur *n*, bonfire
vrezen, to fear
vriend, friend
vriendelijk, kind, friendly
vriendendienst, kind turn
vrien'din, (lady, girl) friend
vriendschap, friendship
vriend'schappelijk, friendly, amicably
vriespunt *n*, freezing-point
vriezen, to freeze
vrij, free: rather, quite
  vrije etage, self-contained flat
  vrij beroep, profession
  het vrij veld, the open
  zo vrij zijn om te, to take the liberty of
vrijaf, time off
vrijbiljet *n*, free pass
vrijblijvend, subject to alteration in price; without obligation
vrijbrief, free pass; passport
vrijbuiter, privateer
vrijdag, Friday
vrijen, to make love
vrijer, suitor, sweetheart
vrijgeleide *n*, safe-conduct
vrijgeven, to decontrol; to give (time) off
vrij'gevig, liberal
vrijgevochten, undisciplined
vrijge'zel, bachelor
vrijheid, liberty, freedom
vrijkomen, to get off; to fall vacant; to be decontrolled; to be liberated
vrijkopen, to ransom
vrijlaten, to release. to emancipate; to leave free
vrijloop, free wheel
vrij'metselaar, freemason
vrij'moedig, frank, outspoken
vrijpleiten, to exonerate
vrij'postig, forward, impertinent
vrijspreken, to acquit
vrijstaan, to be detached
  het staat je vrij om te, you are at liberty to
vrijstellen, to exempt, to excuse
vrijster, sweetheart; (old) maid
vrijuit, freely

vrijwaren voor, to safeguard against
vrijwel, practically
vrij'willig, voluntary
vrij'williger, volunteer
vrij'zinnig, liberal
vroedschap, City Fathers
vroedvrouw, midwife
vroeg, early
  vroeg of laat, sooner or later
vroeger, earlier, former, previous
  ik woonde daar vroeger, I used to live there
vroegte, early morning
vroeg'tijdig, early
vrolijk, cheerful
vrome, pious person
vroom, pious
vroomheid, piety
vrouw, woman; wife
vrouwelijk, female, feminine
vrouwenarts, gynæcologist
vrouwen'kiesrecht *n*, women's suffrage
vrucht, fruit, fœtus
vruchtbaar, fertile; fruitful, prolific
vruchtbeginsel *n*, ovary
vruchtdragend, fruit-bearing; fruitful
vruchteloos, fruitless, in vain
vruchtenbowl, fruit-cup
vruchtvlees *n*, pulp
vuig, sordid
vuil, dirty: *n*, dirt, muck
vuilak, filthy blighter
vuilbek, foul-mouthed fellow
vuil(ig)heid, filth; obscenity
vuilmaken, to (make) dirty; to waste
vuilnis, refuse
vuilnisbak, dustbin
vuilnisbelt, rubbish-dump
vuilnisman, dustman
vuist, fist
  voor de vuist (weg), extempore
vul'gair, vulgar
vul'kaan, volcano
vulkachel, slow-combustion stove
vullen, to fill, to stuff
vulpen, fountain-pen
vulpotlood *n*, propelling pencil

vulsel n, filling; stuffing
vuns, vunzig, musty, fusty
vuren, to fire
vurehout(en) (n), deal
vurig, fiery; fervent, ardent
vuur n, fire
  vuur geven, to fire; to give (a person) a light
vuurbaak, beacon(-light)
vuurmond, gun
vuurpeloton n, firing-squad
vuurpijl, rocket
  de klap op de vuurpijl, the crowning sensation
vuurproef, ordeal by fire; crucial test
vuurrood, flaming red
vuurspuwende berg, volcano
vuursteen, flint
vuurtoren, lighthouse
vuurvast, fire-proof
  vuurvaste steen, fire-brick
vuurwapen n, fire-arm
vuurwerk n, firework(s) (display)
vuurzee, blaze

W

waag, weigh-house
waaghals, dare devil
waagschaal: zijn leven in de —stellen, to risk one's life
waagstuk n, risky enterprise
waaien, to blow, to fan
  ik laat de boel maar waaien, I couldn't care less (about it)
waaier, fan
waakhond, watch-dog
waaks, waakzaam, watchful
waakzaamheid, vigilance
Waals(e), Walloon
waan, delusion
waanwijs, (self-)conceited
waanzin, madness
waan'zinnig, mad, crazy
waar, where: true: ware(s), commodity, stuff
  niet waar? isn't that so?
waar-(aan etc), (to etc) what, which, whom
waar'achtig, true, real(ly and truly), actually
waarborg(en), (to) guarantee

waard, landlord: worth
  waarde vriend, dear friend
waarde, value
waardeloos, worthless
waar'deren, to appreciate, to value
waardevol, valuable
waardig, dignified, worthy
waardigheid, dignity
waar'din, landlady
waarheen, waar . . . heen, whither, where
waarheid, truth
waarlijk, truly
waarmaken, to verify
waarmerk(en) (n), (to) stamp, (to) hall-mark
waar'neembaar, perceptible
waarnemen, to observe; to avail oneself of; to deputize; to discharge
waarom, why
waar'schijnlijk, probable
waar'schijnlijkheid, probability
waarschuwen, to warn
waarschuwing, warning; demand-note, reminder
waartoe, for which, for what, where, to which
waarzegster, fortune-teller
waas n, film, haze, bloom; air
wacht, watch(man), guard(-duty)
  in de wacht slepen, to scrounge, to rake in
wachten (op), to wait (for)
  zich wachten voor, to beware of
wachter, watchman
wachtgeld n, reduced salary, retainer
wachtkamer, waiting-room
wachtlijst, waiting-list
wachtmeester, sergeant
wachtrol, watch-bill
wachtwoord n, password
wad n, mud-flat
waden, to wade
wafel, waffle, wafer; trap
wagen, car, cart: to risk, to venture
wagenrennen, chariot races
wagenspoor n, (cart-)rut
wagenziek, train-sick, car-sick

wagenwijd, wide

waggelen, to totter, to waddle, to wobble

wa'gon, (railway-)carriage, van, truck(-load)

wak *n*, hole (in the ice)

waken, to (keep) watch; to wake

wakend, watchful

waker, watchman

wakker, awake

 wakker schrikken, to wake with a start

wal, rampart; bank

 aan wal, ashore

 langs de wal, alongside

 aan lager wal, on one's beam ends

 van wal steken, to push off; to fire away

 van twee wallen eten, to have it both ways

walg(e)lijk, disgusting

walgen, to be nauseated

walging, loathing

walm(en), (to) smoke

walnoot, walnut

wals, waltz; (motor-)roller

walvis(vaarder), whale(r)

wambuis *n*, jacket, doublet

wanbedrijf *n*, crime

wanbegrip *n*, fallacy

wanbeheer *n*, **wanbeleid** *n*, mismanagement

wanbetaling, non-payment

wanbof(fen), (to have) bad luck

wand, wall

wandaad, outrage

wandelaar, walker, stroller

wandelen, to walk, to wander

 gaan wandelen, to go for a walk

wandeling, walk, stroll

wandelkaart, large-scale map

wandelpad *n*, footpath

wandelstok, walking-stick

wandluis, bed-bug

wandschildering, mural

wandtapijt *n*, hanging carpet, tapestry

wanen, to fancy

wang, cheek

wangedrag *n*, misconduct

wangedrocht *n*, monster

wanhoop, despair

wanhopen, to despair

wan'hopig, desperate, despairing, hopeless

wankel, unsteady, rickety

wankelbaar, unstable

wankelen, to stagger, to sway from side to side; to waver

wankel'moedig, irresolute

wanklank, jarring note

wanneer, when(ever)

wanorde, disorder

wan'staltig, deformed

want, for: mitten: *n*, rigging

wantoestand, chaotic situation

wantrouw(en), (to) distrust

wan'trouwend, **wan'trouwig**, suspicious

wanverhouding, disparity

wapen *n*, weapon, arm; coat of arms

wapendrager, armour-bearer

wapenen, to arm, to reinforce

wapenfeit *n*, feat of arms

wapenrusting, (suit of) armour

wapenschild *n*, escutcheon

wapenschouwing, inspection, review

wapenspreuk, heraldic device

wapenstilstand, armistice, truce

wapperen, to flutter

war: in de —, in a muddle, upset

warboel, muddle, clutter

ware, right person (*or* thing) (for the job)

 je ware, the real thing

wa'rempel, truly, actually

waren, to wander

warenhuis *n*, departmental store

warm, warm, hot

warmen, to warm

warmoeze'nier, market-gardener

warmpjes, warmly

warmte, warmth, heat, temperature

warnet *n*, tangle, labyrinth

warrelen, to whirl

wars van, averse to

wartaal, gibberish

warwinkel, muddle, clutter

was, wax: wash(ing)

 goed in de slappe was zitten, to be in velvet

wasbaar, washable
wasbak, wash-basin
wasbenzine, benzine
wasbleek, waxen
wascommode, wash-stand
wasecht, washable, fast
wasem(en), (to) steam
was(-en-strijk)inrichting,
  laundry
wasgoed n, washing
washandje n, washing-glove
wasketel, (wash-)boiler
wasknijper, clothes-peg
waskom, wash-bowl
waslijn, clothes-line
waslijst, laundry list ; catalogue
wasmerk n, laundry-mark
wasmiddel n, detergent
waspit, taper
wassen, to wash ; to shuffle : to
  swell, to wax : wax(en)
wassenbeeld n, waxwork (model)
wasse'rij, laundry
wastafel, wash-basin, wash-stand
wasvrouw, washer-woman
wat, what, which ; how ; some-
  (thing), any(thing) ; somewhat
  wat voor, what (sort of)
  wat (dan) ook, wat maar,
    whatever
  wàt blij, only too pleased
water n, water
waterbouwkunde, hydraulic
  engineering
waterdamp, vapour
waterdicht, waterproof, water-
  tight
wateren, to (make) water
waterglas n, tumbler ; water-
  glass
waterhoen n, moor-hen
waterig, watery
waterkamp n, boating camp
waterkant, water's edge, water-
  front
waterkering, weir
waterklerk, ship-broker's clerk
waterkoud, raw
waterkruik, pitcher
waterlaarzen, waders
waterlanders, tears
waterleiding, waterworks
waterlinie, flooding defence line

waterpas n, spirit-level
waterplaats, urinal ; watering-
  place
waterpokken, chicken-pox
waterrijk, abounding in water
waterschap n, district controlled
  by polder-board
waterscheiding, watershed
watersnood, floods
waterspiegel, water-level
waterstaat, Ministry of Works
waterstand, water(-level)
waterstof, hydrogen
watertanden : doen —, to make
  the mouth water
waterverf, water-colour, distemper
watervlak n, expanse of water
watervliegtuig n, sea-plane
watervrees, hydrophobia
waterzoeker, water-diviner
waterzucht, dropsy
watje n, piece of cotton wool
watjekou, clout
watten, cotton-wool, wadding
wat'teren, to pad, to quilt
wauwelen, to blather
wazig, hazy, filmy
web(be) n, web
wecken, to bottle
wedden, to bet
weddenschap, wager
we(d)er, again, re-
wederantwoord n, rejoinder
wederdienst, service in return
wederhelft, better half
weder'kerend, reflexive
weder'kerig, mutual
weder'om, (once) again
weder'opbouw, rebuilding, reconstruction
weder'opstanding, resurrection
weder'rechtelijk, unlawful
weder'waardigheden, vicissi-
  tudes
wederwoord n, repartee
wederzijds, mutual
wedijveren, to compete
wedijver(ing), rivalry
wedloop, (running-)race
wedren, race(-meeting)
westrijd, match, competition
weduwe, widow

weduwnaar, widower

wee, sickly, faint: *n*, woe, labour pain

weefgetouw *n*, loom

weefsel *n*, tissue, fabric, texture

weegschaal, (pair of) scales, weighing-machine

week, week: soft

 was in de week zetten, to put washing in to soak

weekblad *n*, weekly (paper)

weekdier *n*, mollusc

week'hartig, soft-hearted

weeklacht, lamentation

weeklagen, to (be)wail

weelde, luxury, profusion

weelderig, luxurious, luxuriant

weemoed, melancholy

wee'moedig(heid), melancholy

weer, again, re-: *n*, weather

 in de weer zijn, to be on the move; to be busy

weerbaar, defensible; able-bodied

weer'barstig, unruly

weerbericht *n*, weather-forecast

weerga, equal

weer'galmen, to reverberate

weergeven, to render, to reflect

weerglas *n*, barometer

weerhaak, barb(ed hook)

weerhaan, weathercock

weer'houden, to restrain, to suppress

weer'kaatsen, to reflect, to (re)echo

weerklank, echo

weer'klinken, to resound

weerkunde, meteorology

weer'leggen, to refute

weerlicht *n*, summer lightning

weerloos, defenceless

weermacht, (fighting) services

weer'omstuit: van de —, in sympathy

weerschijn, reflection

weersgesteldheid, weather conditions

weerskanten, both sides

weer'spannig, recalcitrant

weer'spiegelen, to reflect

weer'staan, to resist

weerstand, resistance

weer'streven, to oppose

weersverwachting, weather-forecast

weerwil: in — van, in spite of

weerzien *n*, meeting, reunion

weerzin, aversion

weerzin'wekkend, repugnant

wees(huis *n***),** orphan(age)

weetal, know-all

weet'gierig, studious

weg, way, road: away, gone

 veel van iemand weg hebben, to be very like a person

wegbergen, to put away

wegbrengen, to take away; to see off

wegcijferen, to efface, to set aside

wegdek *n*, road surface

wegen, to weigh

wegennet *n*, road-system

wegens, on account of

weggaan, to leave, to go away

wegkomen, to get away

weglaten, to omit, to leave out

wegleggen, to put aside

 weggelegd zijn voor, to be in store for

wegmaken, to get rid of, to lose; to put under an anæsthetic

wegnemen, to take away, to allay

 dat neemt niet weg dat, that does not alter the fact that

wegomlegging, diversion

wegpinken, to brush away

wegpraten, to explain away

wegraken, to get lost

wegscheren: zich —, to make oneself scarce

wegtrekken, to pull away; to march away; to disappear

wegvagen, to sweep away

wegvallen tegen, to cancel (out)

wegwerken, to get rid of

wegwijs maken, to show the ropes

wegwijzer, sign-post

wei, whey; serum: meadow

weide, meadow, pasture

weiden, to graze; to travel

weids, grandiose

weifelen, to waver

WEI 223 WER

weigeren, to refuse, to misfire, to jib
weiland n, pasture
weinig, little, few
weitas, game-bag
wekelijks, weekly
weken, to soak, to soften
wekken, to wake, to arouse, to create
wekker, alarm-clock
wel, well; very much; certainly, probably, quite
wel neen, oh no
ik geloof het (or van) wel, I think so
ik zie het wél! I do see it!
hij is niet ziek, wel? he isn't ill is he?
welbehagen n, well-being
welbeschouwd: alles —, after all
welbespraakt, fluent, eloquent
welbezocht, (much) frequented
weldaad, good deed
wel'dadig, beneficial, pleasant
wel'dadigheid, charity
weldoen, to do good
weldoener, benefactor
weldoordacht, well thought-out
weldra, soon
Weledelgeboren heer, Esquire
wel'eer, of old
Weleerwaard(e heer), Reverend
welgeaard, good-natured
welgedaan, plump
welgemutst, good-humoured
welgesteld, well-to-do
welgevallen n, pleasure, discretion
zich laten welgevallen, to put up with
welge'vallig, agreeable
welgezind, kindly disposed
welhaast, soon
welig, lush
weliswaar, it is true
welk, which, what
welkom, welcome
welkomstgroet, (word of) welcome
wellen, to weld: to cook without boiling
welletjes, enough
wel'levendheid, good manners

wellicht, perhaps
wel'luidend, melodious
wellust, lust; delight
welnaad, weld
welnemen: met Uw —, by your leave
wel'nu, well (now)
weloverwogen, (well-)considered
welp, cub
wel'riekend, fragrant
welslagen n, success
wel'sprekend, eloquent
welstand, well-being, prosperity
welste: van je —, like nobody's business
welvaart, prosperity
welvaren, to thrive
welven, to vault, to arch
welving, vault(ing), camber
wel'voeglijk, seemly
wel'willend, obliging, sympathetic
welzijn n, welfare, health
wemelen van, to swarm with
wenden: (zich) —, to turn; to apply
wending, turn
wenen, to weep
wenk: een — geven, to beckon; to drop a hint, to give the tip
wenkbrauw, eyebrow
wenken, to beckon
wennen, to get used to
wens, wish
wenselijk, desirable
wensen, to wish, to desire
wentelen, to roll (over)
wenteling, revolution
wentelteefje n, sop in the pan
wenteltrap, winding staircase
wereld, world
uit de wereld helpen, to dispose of
werelddeel n, continent
wereldlijk, wordly, secular
wereldreiziger, globe-trotter
werelds, wordly(-minded)
wereldstad, metropolis
wereldtaal, universal language
wereldtentoonstelling, world fair
weren, to avert; to (de)bar
zich weren, to exert oneself

werf, shipyard, dockyard; wharf
werfdepot n, recruiting-office
werk n, work, job
　er werk van maken, to do something about it
werkborstel, scrubbing brush
werkelijk, real
werkelijkheid, reality
werkeloos, unemployed, idle
werke'loosheid, unemployment
werken, to work, to be active; to warp
　naar binnen werken, to get down (one's throat)
werkezel, (hard) worker
werkgever, employer
werking, action, operation
werkkamer, work-room, study
werkkrachten, energies; labour
werkkring, occupation
werkloon n, wage(s)
werkloos, unemployed, idle
werkman, workman, working-man
werknemer, employee
werkplaats, workshop
werkster, charwoman
werktuig n, tool
werktuigkunde, mechanics
werk'tuiglijk, mechanical
werkvolk n, workers
werkvrouw, charwoman
werkwoord n, verb
werkzaam, active, (hard-)working
werkzaamheden, activities, duties, tasks
werpen, to throw
werpspeer, javelin
wervel, vertebra
wervelkolom, spinal column
werven, to rope in, to enlist
werwaarts, whither
wesp, wasp
westelijk, westerly, western
westen n, west
　buiten westen, unconscious
westerlingen, western world
westers, western
wet, law, act
　de wet voorschrijven, to lay down the law
wetboek n, code

weten, to know; to manage: n, knowledge
　er iets op weten, to know the answer
　te weten, to wit
wetenschap, science; learning, knowledge
wetenschappelijk werk n, research; scientific work
wetgevend, legislative
wethouder, alderman
wetsontwerp n, bill
wettelijk, wettig, legal, lawful
wettigen, to legalize; to justify
weven, to weave
wezel, weasel
wezen, to be: n, being, essence
　— hij mag er wezen, he's got what it takes
wezenlijk, real, essential
wezenloos, vacant
wichelroede, divining-rod
wicht n, creature
wie, who(m), anyone who
　wie ook, whoever
wiebelen, to wobble
wieden, to weed
wieg, cradle
　in de wieg gelegd voor, cut out for
wiegelied n, lullaby
wiegen, to rock
wiek, wing, sail
wiel n, wheel
wielrennen n, cycle-racing
wielrijder, cyclist
wiemelen, to fidget
wier n, sea-weed
wierook, incense
wig, wedge
wij, we
wijd, wide, spacious
wijd en zijd, far and wide
wijdbeens, with legs apart
wijden, to consecrate, to dedicate, to devote, to ordain
wijdte, width
wijduitstaande, distended, bulging, prominent
wijdvertakt, widespread
wijf n, hag, woman
wijfje n, wifey; female (animal)
wijfjesvos, vixen

wijk, district; refuge
wijken, to yield; to pass (off)
wijkgebouw *n*, parish-hall
wijkverpleegster, wijkzuster, district-nurse
wijlen, (the) late
wijn, wine
wijnberg, hill vineyard
wijngaard, vineyard
wijnlezen *n*, vintage
wijnsteen(zuur *n*), tartar(ic acid)
wijs, manner, way; tune; mood: wise
　van de wijs, at sea
　wijs maken, to convince; to dupe
wijsbegeerte, philosophy
wijselijk, wisely
wijsgeer, philosopher
wijsheid, wisdom
wijsje *n*, tune, air
wijsneus, know-all
wijsvinger, forefinger
wijten, to impute
　het is aan het weer te wijten, it is due to the weather
wijwater *n*, holy water
wijze, manner, way
wijzen, to point (out), show
wijzer, pointer, hand
wijzerplaat, (clock-)face
wijzigen, to modify
wikkelen, to wrap (up); to involve
wikken en wegen, to weigh (up)
wil, will, wish
　tegen wil en dank, against one's will
　ter wille van, for the sake of
　ter wille zijn, to oblige
wils, wild
wild *n*, game
　in het wild(e weg), wildly, at random
wildbraad *n*, venison
wilde, savage
wildebras, young tough, tomboy
wildernis, wilderness
wildvreemd, utterly strange
wilg, willow
willekeur: naar — handelen, to do as one pleases
wille'keurig, arbitrary

willen, to want, to like, to be willing
　dat wil zeggen, that is to say
willens, on purpose
willig, willing
willoos, will-less
wilsbeschikking, will
wilskracht, will-power
wimpel, pennant
wimper, eyelash
wind, wind
　ik heb er de wind onder, I've got them under my thumb
windas *n*, windlass
windbuks, air-gun
winden, to wind
winderig, windy
windhond(rennen), greyhound (racing)
windhoos, whirlwind
windpokken, chicken-pox
windsel *n*, bandage
windstil(te), calm
windstoot, gust of wind
windstreek, point of the compass
windvaan, windwijzer, weather vane
wingerd, vine(yard); (Virginia) creeper
wingewest *n*, (conquered) province
winkel(en), (to) shop
winkelhaak, set-square; three-cornered tear
winkelhuis *n*, shop with residence over
winke'lier, shopkeeper, retailer
winkeljuffrouw, shop-assistant
winkelstand, tradespeople
winkelweek, shopping-week
winnaar, winner
winnen, to win, to gain
winst, profit, gain
winst'gevend, profitable
winter, winter; chilblain(s)
wintergezicht *n*, wintry scene
wintergoed *n*, winter clothes
wintergroen *n*, evergreen
winterhanden, chilblained hands
winters, wintry
winterslaap, hibernation
wip, seesaw; jiffy
wipneus, snub nose

wippen, to rock (to and fro), to nip; to kick out
wipplank, seesaw
wipstoel, rocking-chair
wirwar, tangle
wis, certain
wiskunde, mathematics
wispel'turig, fickle
wissel, points; bill of exchange
wisselbeker, challenge-cup
wisselen, to (ex)change; to shed milk-teeth
wisselgeld *n,* (small) change
wisseling, (ex)change
wisselspoor *n,* siding
wisselstroom, alternating current
wissel'vallig, precarious
wisselvalligheid, vicissitude
wisselwerking, interaction
wissen, to wipe
wissewasje *n,* slightest little thing, trifle
wit, white
 Witte Donderdag, Maundy Thursday
witgloeiend, white-hot
witkalk, whitewash
witkiel, porter
witlof *n,* chicory
wittebroodsweken, honeymoon
witten, to whitewash
woede(n), (to) rage
woedend, furious
woekeraar, usurer
woekeren, to be rife
woekeren met, to make the most of
woekerplant, parasite
woelen, to toss and turn
woelig, turbulent, restless
woelwater, fidget
woensdag, Wednesday
woerd, drake
woest, wild, waste, desolate
woesteling, ruffian
woeste'nij, wilderness
woes'tijn, desert
wol, wool
 hij is in de wol geverfd, he has been through the mill; he's a double-dyed rogue
wolf, wolf

wolfram *n,* tungsten
wolk, cloud
wolkenkrabber, sky-scraper
wolkje *n,* little cloud; puff, drop
wollen, woollen
wollig, woolly
wond(en), (to) wound
wonder *n,* wonder, miracle
wonder'baarlijk, miraculous, stupendous
wonderkind *n,* infant prodigy
wonderlijk, strange, surprising
wondermiddel *n,* panacea
wonderolie, castor-oil
wondroos, erysipelas
wonen, to live
woning, house, flat
woningbureau *n,* estate-agent's office
woningnood, housing shortage
woningtoestanden, housing conditions
woon'achtig, resident
woonhuis *n,* private house
woonkamer, living-room
woonplaats, (place of) residence
woonschip *n,* **woonschuit,** house-boat
woonwagen, caravan
woonwijk, residential district
woord *n,* word
 het hoogste woord hebben, to monopolize the conversation
 het woord voeren, to speak, to be spokesman
 onder woorden brengen, to put into words
 iemand te woord staan, to see a person
woordelijk, literal, word for word, verbatim
woordenboek *n,* dictionary
woordenschat, vocabulary
woordentwist, dispute
woordenwisseling, altercation
woordsoort, part of speech
woordspeling, play on words, pun
woordvoerder, spokesman
worden, to be(come), to get, to grow, to go
worgen, to strangle
worm, worm, grub
wormstekig, maggoty

worp, throw; litter
worst, sausage
worstelen, to struggle, to wrestle
wortel, root; carrot
wortelen, to be rooted
woud n, forest
wraak, revenge
wraak'gierig, wraak'zuchtig, vindictive
wrak, rickety, dilapidated : n, wreck
wrakhout n, wreckage
wrang, sour, tart; bitter
wrat, wart
weed, cruel
wreedaard, (cruel) brute
wreef, instep
wreken, to revenge, to avenge
wrevel, resentment
wrevelig, resentful
wriemelen, to crawl, to tickle
wrijfwas, furniture-polish
wrijven, to rub; to polish
wrijving, friction
wrikken, to jerk
wringen, to wring, to wrench
zich wringen, to wriggle
wrochten, to work, to do
wroeging, remorse
wroeten, to root, to rummage
wrok, rancour
wrokken, to fret
wrong, knot (of hair)
wrongel, curds
wuft, frivolous, flighty
wuit, projecting jaw
wuiven, to wave
wulps, lewd
wurgen, to strangle
wurmen, to wriggle

Z

zaad n, seed, semen
op zwart zaad zitten, to be on the rocks
zaag, saw; interminable grumbler
zaagmeel n, zaagsel n, sawdust
zaaien, to sow
zaak, business, affair; case; cause
het is zaak, the great thing is
ter zake, to the point
niet veel zaaks, no great shakes
zaakgelastigde, agent

zaakwaarnemer, solicitor
zaal, hall, ward, auditorium
zacht, soft, mild, gentle
zacht'aardig, gentle
zachtjes, gently, quietly
zachtjes aan, gradually
zacht'moedig, gentle
zacht'zinnig, good-natured
zadel n, saddle
zadeldek n, saddle-cloth
zadelen, to saddle
zagen, to saw; to harp (on a subject)
zak, pocket; sack, bag
zakboekje n, note-book, diary
zakdoek, handkerchief
zakelijk, business-like, to the point
zakenbrief, business letter
zakformaat n, pocket-size
zakken, to sink, to fall; to fail
zakkenroller, pickpocket
zaklantaarn, torch
zaklopen n, sack-race
zalf, ointment
zalig, blessed; heavenly
zaliger, late
zaligheid, bliss
Zaligmaker, Saviour
zaligsprekingen, beatitudes
zaligverklaring, beatification
zalm, salmon
zalven, to anoint
zalvend, unctuous
zamen: te —, together
zand n, sand
zandbak, sand-pit
zanderig, sandy
zandgebak n, shortbread
zandgroeve, sand-pit
zandloper, hour-glass
zandplaat, sand-bank
zandruiter, thrown rider
zandtaart, shortbread
zandverstuiving, drift-sands
zandweg, sandy lane
zang, song, canto
zanger('es), singer
zangerig, melodious, sing-song
zanggezelschap n, choral society
zangles, singing lesson
zangstem, singing voice; voice part
zanguitvoering, choral concert

zangvogel, singing-bird
zaniken, to natter
zanikkous,   cantankerous
  grumbler
zat, more than enough, tight
  zich zat eten, to eat one's fill
Zaterdag, Saturday
zatlap, soak(er)
ze, they, them; she
zede, custom
  zeden, morals; manners
zedelijk, moral
zedeloos, immoral
zedenkunde, ethics
zedenpreek, homily
zedenspreuk, maxim
zedig, modest, demure
zee, sea
  recht door zee, straight
zeeboot, ocean steamer
zeeëngte, straits
zeef, sieve, strainer
zeegat n, entrance to channel
zeegezicht n, seascape
zeehond, seal
zeekasteel n, leviathan
zeem n, wash-leather
zeemacht, naval forces
zeeman, seaman
zeemanskunst, seamanship
zeemeermin, mermaid
zeemeeuw, sea-gull
zeemlap, (wash-)leather
zeemleer n, chamois leather
zeemogendheid, sea-power
zeen, sinew
zecofficier, naval officer
zeep, soap
zeepbel, soap-bubble
zeepsop n, soap-suds
zeer, very (much): sore
  zeer doen, to hurt
zeeramp, shipping disaster
zeerecht n, maritime law
zeerob, seal; seadog
zeerover, private
zeerste: ten —, highly, greatly
zeeschildpad, turtle
zeeslang, sea-serpent
zeesleepboot, deep-sea tug
zeesoldaat, marine
zeespiegel, sea-level
zeester, star-fish

zeestraat, straights
Zeeuw(se), inhabitant of Zealand
zeevaart, navigation
zeevaartschool, nautical college
zeevarend, seafaring
zeeverkenners, sea-scouts
zee'waardig, seaworthy
zeeweg, sea-route
zeewering, sea-wall
zeewier n, seaweed
zeeziek, seasick
zege, victory, triumph
zegel, seal; stamp
zegelen, to seal
zegellak, sealing-wax
zegelrecht n, stamp-duty
zegelring, signet-ring
zegen(ing), blessing
zegenen, to bless
zegenrijk, full of blessings
zegepoort, triumphal arch
zegepraal, victory
zegeteken n, trophy
zegetocht, triumphal march
zegevieren, to triumph
zegevuur n, bonfire
zeggen, to say, to tell
  liever gezegd, rather
  wat zegt U? (I beg your)
    pardon?
  er valt niets op te zeggen,
    there is nothing to be said
    against it
  dat zegt niets, that doesn't
    mean a thing
  je hebt niets te zeggen, your
    opinion is not asked for
zeggenschap, say, part-interest
zegsman, informant
zegswijze, expression
zeil n, sail, tarpaulin, American
  cloth, lino(leum)
zeildoek n, canvas, oil-cloth
zeilen, to sail
zeilwagen, land-yacht
zeilwedstrijd, sailing regatta
zeis, scythe
zeker, certain, (for) sure
  dat weet je zeker wel, I expect
    you know that
zekerheid, certainty; security
  voor alle zekerheid, to be on
    the safe side

zekerheidshalve, for safety('s sake)

zekering, fuse

zelden, seldom, rarely

zeldzaam, rare, scarce; exceptionally

zelf, (one)self

ik (*etc*) **zelf,** I (*etc*) myself

de eenvoud zelf, simplicity itself

zelfbeheersing, self-control

zelfbehoud *n,* self-preservation

zelfbe'wust, self-assured

zelfge'noegzaam, self-sufficient

zelfkant, selvage

zelfmoord, suicide

zelfs, even

zelf'standig, independent

zelfstanding naamwoord *n,* noun

zelfverloochening, self-denial, self-sacrifice

zelfvertrouwen *n,* self-confidence

zelfverzekerd, self-confident

zelfvoldaan, self-satisfied

zelfzucht, egoism

zelf'zuchtig, selfish

zemelaar, cantankerous grumbler

zemelen, bran

zemen, to clean

zendeling, missionary

zenden, to send

zender, sender; transmitter

zending, mission; consignment

zendstation *n,* transmitting station

zenuw, nerve; tendon

zenuwachtig, nervous, nervy; flustered

zenuwarts, nerve-specialist

zenuwgestel *n,* nervous system

zenuwontsteking, neuritis

zenuwpees, bundle of nerves

zenuwpijn, neuralgia

zenuw'slopend, nerve-racking

zenuwtrekking, nervous spasm

zenuwziek, neurotic

zes(de), six(th)

zeshoek, hexagon

zestien(de), sixteen(th)

zestig, sixty

zet, move, coup; push

een hele zet, a tough job

zetbaas, manager

zetel, seat; see

zetmeel *n,* starch

zetsel *n,* forme; brew

zetten, to set, to put; to make; to stake

ik kan het niet zetten, I can't stomach it

zetting, arrangement

zeug, sow

zeulen, to lug

zeuren, to whine, to nag

zeurkous, zeurpiet, grouser

zeven, seven: to sieve, to strain

zeventien(de), seventeen(th)

zeventig, seventy

zich, one (him, her, it, your)self, themselves

zicht *n,* sight; visibility

op zicht, on approval; at sight

zichtbaar, visible

zich'zelf, one (him, her, it)self, themselves

uit zichzelf, of his own accord

zieden, to seethe

ziek, ill, sick; diseased

zieke, patient

ziekelijk, sickly, in bad health

ziekenauto, ambulance

ziekenfonds *n,* national health insurance

ziekte, illness, disease

ziekteuitkering, sickness benefit

ziel, soul; heart, lifeblood

zieleheil *n,* salvation

zielig, pitiful, pathetic

zielkunde, psychology

zielsbedroefd, heart-broken

zielsverwant, congenial

zielverheffend, exalting

zien, to see, to look

er uit zien, to look (like)

iemand niet kunnen zien, to hate the sight of a person

iets zien te doen, to try and do something

laten zien, to show

hij ziet niet op geld, he is not worried about money

zienderogen, visibly

ziener, seer

ziens: tot —, good-bye for now

zienswijze, way of thinking, attitude

zier, scrap

ziezo, there we are

ziften, to sift

zi'geuner, gipsy

zij, she; they

zijbeuk, aisle

zij(de), side : silk
  op zij, ter zijde, aside
  ter zijde staan, to help

zijdelings, sidelong, indirect, oblique

zijden, silk(en)

zijderups, silk-worm

zijgen, to sink down

zijkant, side

zijn, to be : his, its, one's
  zij zijn weg(gegaan), they have gone
  dat mag er zijn, that takes a lot of beating

zijnerzijds, for his part

zijrivier, tributary

zijspan n, side-car

zijspoor n, siding

zijwaarts, sideways, sideward

zilt, salt(y)

zilver(en) n, silver

zin, sense; mind, way; sentence
  er zin in hebben, to feel like it
  naar mijn zin, to my liking

zindelijk, clean

zingen, to sing

zink n, zinc

zinken, to sink : zinc

zinloos, senseless

zinnebeeld n, emblem, symbol

zinne'beeldig, symbolic

zinnelijk, sensual, sensory

zinnen, to brood

zinsbedrog n, illusion

zinsnede, passage, clause

zinsontleding, analysis

zinspelen op, to hint at

zinspreuk, motto

zinsverband n, context

zinswending, turn of speech

zintuig n, sense

zin'tuiglijk, sensory

zinvol, pregnant

zit : een hele —, a long time sitting down

zitbad n, hip-bath

zitbank, settee

zitdag, session

zitje n, (cosy) nook

zitkamer, sitting-room

zitplaats, seat

zitten, to sit; to be; to fit
  gaan zitten, to sit down
  iemand laten zitten, to walk out on a person
  er zit niets anders op, there's no alternative
  daar zit ik met de gebakken peren, I'm left holding the baby

zittend, sitting, sedentary

zitting, session; seat

zitvlak n, bottom

zo, so, like that; in a minute; just now : straight : if
  de zaak zit zo, it's like this
  zó gaat het niet, that won't do
  zo iets, such a thing
  zo maar, just like that; for no reason in particular

zoals, (such) as, like

zo'danig, such, in such a way

zodat, so that

zode, sod

zo'doende, in that way

zo'dra, as soon as

zoek, missing
  op zoek naar, in search of

zoekbrengen : de tijd —, to pass the time

zoeken, to look (for), to seek : n, search

zoeklicht n, searchlight

zoekmaken, to mislay

zoekraken, to get lost

zoel, mild

zoemen, to buzz, to drone

zoen(en), (to) kiss

zoenoffer n, (expiatory) sacrifice

zoet, sweet; good

zoetekauw : een — zijn, to have a sweet tooth

zoetemelkse kaas, cream cheese

zoethoudertje, n, sop

zoethout n, liquorice(-root)

zoetig, slightly sweet

zoetigheid, sweet things

zoetjes aan, gradually

zoetluidend, melodious
zoet'sappig, mealy-mouthed
zoet'vloeiend, mellifluous
zoetwater n, fresh water
zoet'zuur, partially sweet(ened); sweet pickle
zoëven, just now
zog n, (mother's) milk; wake
zogen, to suckle
zoge'naamd, so-called; ostensibly
zolang, as long as; meanwhile
zolder, loft, attic
zoldering, ceiling
zolderkamer, garret
zolderverdieping, attic, top storey
zolen, to re-sole
zomen, to hem
zomer(s), summer(-like)
zomersproeten, freckles
zo'n, such (a), a sort of
zon, sun
zondaar, sinner
zondag, Sunday
zondagsruiter, would-be horseman
zondagsviering, Sunday observance
zonde, sin; shame; waste
zondebok, scape-goat
zonder, without
zonderling, queer; eccentric
zondeval, Fall
zondig, sinful
zondigen, to sin, to offend
zondvloed, Flood
Zon-en-feestdagen, Sundays and bank-holidays; high-days and holidays
zonnebaden n, sun-bathing
zonnebrand, sun-burn
zonnebril, sun-glasses
zonneklaar, clear as daylight
zonnen, to bask (in the sun)
zonnescherm n, sun-shade, sun-blind
zonneschijn, sunshine
zonnestand, sun's altitude, position of the sun
zonnesteek, sun-stroke
zonnestelsel n, solar system
zonnestilstand, solstice

zonnestraal, sunbeam; ray of sunshine
zonnetent, awning
zonnetijd, solar time
zonnewijzer, sun-dial
zonnig, sunny
zons'ondergang, sunset
zons'opgang, sunrise
zonsverduistering, eclipse of the sun
zoogdier n, mammal
zooi, mob, bang shoot
zool, sole
zoölo'gie, zoology
zoom, seam, hem; edge; outskirts
zoon, son
zootje n, mess; lot
zorg, care, concern, worry
het zal mijn zorg zijn! fat lot I care !
zorg baren, to cause anxiety
zorgeloos, care-free
zorgen voor, to look after; to provide (for)
zorg, dat je op tijd bent, mind you're not late
zorg'vuldig, careful
zorg'wekkend, worrying, alarming
zorgzaam, careful, conscientious
zot, fool(ish)
zotteklap, zottepraat, silly nonsense
zout (n), salt(ed)
zouteloos, saltless; insipid, pointless
zouten, to salt (down)
zoutje n, cocktail biscuit
zoutvaatje n, salt-cellar
zoutzak, sack of potatoes
zoutzuur n, hydrochloric acid
zoveel, so much, so many
honderd zoveel, a hundred and something
zover, so far, thus far
in zover(re), to the extent, in so far as
voor zover, as far as
zo'waar, believe it or not
zo'wel, as well
zo'zeer, so much
zucht, sigh; craving

zuchten, to sigh

zuid, south

zuidelijk, southern, south(erly), southward(s)

zuiden *n,* south

zuiderhalfrond *n,* southern hemisphere

zuiderling, southerner

Zuid'poolzee, Antarctic (Ocean)

zuidvruchten, subtropical fruit

zuid'wester, sou(th)wester

Zuidzee: Stille —, Pacific (Ocean)

zuigeling, infant (in arms)

zuigen, to suck

zuiger, piston

zuigfles, feeding-bottle

zuil, pillar, column

zuilengalerij, colonnade

zuinig, economical

zuinigheid, economy, thrift

zuipen, to booze, to swill

zulplap, sot

zuivel, dairy produce

zuiver, pure, sheer; clear

zuiveren, to purify, to clean(se), to refine; to clear

zuivering, purge

zuiveringszout *n,* epsom salts

zulk, such

zullen, shall, will

dat zal wel, I quite believe it

wat zou dat ? so what !

zus en zo, so-and-so, this and that

zus(je *n),* sister

zuster, sister; nurse

zusterovertse, Mother Superior

zuur, sour: *n,* acid; pickles

zuurdeeg *n,* **zuurdesem,** leaven

zuurkool, sauerkraut

zuurpruim, grouch

zuurstof, oxygen

zuurtje *n,* acid-drop

zwaai, swing, sweep

zwaaien, to wave, to wield, to swing

zwaan, swan

zwaar, heavy; hard; severe; full-bodied, stodgy

zwaard *n,* sword; lee-board

zwaardvechter, gladiator

zwaar'lijvig, corpulent

zwaar'moedig(heid), melancholy

zwaarte, weight

zwaartekracht, gravitation

zwaartepunt *n,* centre of gravity; crux

zwaar'tillend, pessimistic

zwaar'wichtig, weighty

zwabber, swab, mop

aan de zwabber, on the razzle

zwabberen, to swab, to mop

zwachtel, bandage

zwachtelen, to swathe

zwager, brother-in-law

zwak, weak, delicate, feeble: *n,* weakness

zwakkeling, weakling

zwakte, weakness

zwak'zinnig, mentally deficient

zwalken, to drift about

zwaluw, swallow

zwaluwstaart, swallow-tail; dovetail

zwam, fungus

zwammen, to gas

zwamneus, gas-bag

zwang, vogue

zwanger, pregnant

zwangerschap, pregnancy

zwarigheid, difficulty, objection

zwart *(n),* black

zwart maken, to blacken; to denigrate

zwarte kunst, black magic

zwaat'gallig, melancholy, pessimistic

zwartje *n,* darky

zwavel, sulphur

zwavelstok, safety-match

zwavelzuur *n,* sulphuric acid

Zweeds, Swedish

zweefvliegen, to glide

zweefvliegtuig *n,* glider

zweem, trace

zweep, whip, hunting-crop

zweepslag, lash (with the whip)

zweer, ulcer

zweet *n,* sweat

zwelgen, to guzzle; to revel

zwellen, to swell

zwembad *n,* **zwembassin** *n,* swimming-bath

zwembroek, bathing-trunks

zwemen naar, to be somewhat like
zwemgordel, life-jacket
zweminrichting, public baths
zwemmen, to swim
zwempak *n,* bathing-costume
zwemvest *n,* life-jacket
zwemvlies *n,* web
zwendel(a'rij), swindle, racket
zwengel, pump-handle, crank
zwenken, to swing round, to swerve
zweren, to swear : to fester
zwerftocht, peregrination, ramble
zwerk *n,* firmament
zwerm(en), (to) swarm
zwerven, to roam, to wander
zwerver, wanderer, vagabond
zweten, to sweat
zwetsen, to gas ; to brag
zweven, to float, to glide, to hover
zwezerik, sweetbread

zwichten voor, to yield to
zwiepen, to swish
zwier, flourish, dash
  aan de zwier zijn, to be on the spree
zwieren, to glide to and fro, to reel
zwierig, stylish, flamboyant
zwijgen, to be silent, to keep quiet
  tot zwijgen brengen, to silence
zwijgend, silent, tacit
zwijgzaam, taciturn
zwijm, swoon
zwijmelen, to feel dizzy
zwijn *n,* hog, swine
zwijnenboel, pigsty
zwijntje *n,* fluke
zwik, caboodle
zwikken, to sprain
Zwitser(s), Swiss
zwoegen, to toil
zwoel, sultry
zwoerd *n,* bacon-rind, pork-rind

AN ENGLISH–DUTCH DICTIONARY

For notes on the use of this Dictionary see the Introduction

A

a(n), een
abandon, opgeven, ver'laten: overgave
abashed, ver'legen
abate, ver'flauwen
abbey, ab'dij
abbot, abt
abbess, ab'dis
abbreviate, afkorten, ver'korten
abbreviation, afkorting
abdicate, afstand doen van
abdomen, onderlijf n
abduct, ont'voeren
aberration, dwaling
abeyance: in —, tijdelijk in on-bruik
abhor, ver'afschuwen
abhorrent, weerzin'wekkend
abide, toeven; uitstaan
to abide by, zich houden aan
ability, ver'mogen n, be'kwaam-heid
abject, ver'slagen; laag'hartig
abjure, afzweren
ablaze, in lichte laaie
able, in staat; be'kwaam
to be able to, kunnen
able seaman, vol matroos
abnegation, ver'loochening
abnormal, abnor'maal
aboard, aan boord
abode, woonstede
abolish, afschaffen
abolition, afschaffing
abominable, af'schuwelijk
abomination, afschuw, gruwel
aborigines, inboorlingen
abortion, ab'ortus

abortive, voor'barig
abound, in overvloed zijn
abounding in, rijk aan
about, om(streeks), onge'veer; over; in de buurt
about to go, op het punt te gaan
above, boven
the above, het bovenstaande
abrasion, schaafwond
abrasive, schuurmiddel n: afschurend
abreast, naast el'kaar; ter (or op de) hoogte (van)
abridge, ver'korten
abroad, in (or naar) het buiten-land; naar alle kanten verspreid
abrogate, afschaffen
abrupt, ab'rupt, kort'af
abscess, ab'ces n
abscond, er van'door gaan
absence, af'wezigheid, ge'brek n
absent, af'wezig
to absent oneself, ver'stek laten gaan
absentee, af'wezige
absenteeism, absente'isme n
absent-minded(ness), ver'strooid(heid)
absolute, vol'slagen, vol'strekt; defini'tief; abso'luut
absolution, abso'lutie
absolve, ver'geven, vrijspreken
absorb, (in zich) opnemen
absorbed, ver'diept
absorbent, absor'berend
absorbing, boeiend
abstain, zich ont'houden
abstemious, matig
abstinence, ont'houding
abstract, ab'stract: uittreksel n

abstruse, duister
absurd, onge'rijmd ; be'lachelijk, gek
abundance, overvloed
abundant, meer dan vol'doende
abundantly, in overvloed, rijkelijk
abuse, misbruik n; scheldwoorden: mis'bruiken; uitschelden
abusive, be'ledigend
abut on, grenzen aan
abysmal, bodemloos, grenzeloos
abyss, afgrond
academic(al), aca'demisch
academy, aca'demie
accede to, be'stijgen, aan'vaarden; toestemmen in
accelerate, ver'snellen, gas geven; in snelheid toenemen
acceleration, ver'snelling
accelerator, gaspedaal n
accent, ac'cent n, klemtoon
accent(uate), accentu'eren
accept, aannemen
acceptable, be'vredigend; welkom
acceptance, gunstige ont'vangst
access, toegang
accessary, mede'plichtige
accessible, (gemakkelijk) be'reikbaar; ge'naakbaar
accession, (troons)bestijging: toetreding; aanwinst
accessories, toebehoren n
accessory, mede'plichtige
accident, ongeluk n; toeval n
accidental, toe'vallig; per ongeluk: kruis n of mol
acclaim, toejuiching; accla'matie: toejuichen
acclimatize, acclimati'seren
accolade, ridderslag; acco'lade
accommodate, onderdak ver'lenen, (her)bergen; aanpassen
accommodating, in'schikkelijk
accommodation, accommo'datie
accompaniment, bege'leiding
accompany, verge'zellen, ge'paard gaan met; bege'leiden
accomplice, mede'plichtige
accomplish, vol'brengen
accomplished, ta'lentvol; vol'dongen (fact)

accomplishment, gave, pres'tatie
accord, over'eenstemming: ver'lenen; over'eenstemmen
of my own accord, uit eigen be'weging
according to, volgens
accordingly, dienovereen'komstig
accordion, accorde'on
accost, aanklampen
account, ver'slag n; rekening; rekenschap; be'lang n
to account for, ver'klaren
to take into account, in aanmerking nemen
on account of, van'wege
on no account, in geen ge'val
accountancy, boekhouding
accountant, (hoofd)boekhouder
accoutrements, uitrusting
accredit, toeschrijven aan
accredited, er'kend
accretion, aanwas
accrue, toenemen
accumulate, (zich) ophopen
accumulator, accu(mu'lator)
accuracy, nauw'keurigheid
accurate, nauw'keurig; pre'cies
accursed, ver'vloekt
accusation, be'schuldiging
accuse, be'schuldigen
accused, ver'dachte
accustom, wennen aan
accustomed, ge'wend; ge'woon
ace, aas; kraan
acerbity, scherpheid
ache, pijn (doen); hunkeren (naar)
achieve, be'reiken
achievement, pres'tatie; bereiken n
acid, zuur (n)
acknowledge, er'kennen; be'antwoorden
acknowledgement, er'kenning; be'antwoording; be'richt van ont'vangst n
acme, toppunt n
acolyte, misdienaar
acorn, eikel
acoustic, ge'luids-
acoustics, a'custica, acus'tiek

acquaint, in kennis stellen
acquaintance, kennis
acquainted, be'kend, op de hoogte
acquiesce in, instemmen met; be'rusten in
acquire, ver'werven, aanschaffen
acquirements, kundigheden
acquisition, aanwinst
acquisitive, heb'zuchtig
acquit, vrijspreken; kwijten
acquittal, vrijspraak
acre, 4047 vierkante meter (m²)
acrid, scherp
acrimonious, bits
acrobat, acro'baat
across, aan (or naar) de overkant (van); (dwars) over or door
act, daad; be'drijf n, nummer n; wet: handelen, werken; (to'neel)spelen
acting, waarnemend: to'neelspel n
action, handeling, werking; actie
activate, aanzetten (tot)
active, ac'tief
activity, be'drijvigheid
actor, to'neelspeler
actress, to'neelspeelster
actual, werkelijk
actually, eigenlijk, feitelijk
actuate, (aan)drijven
acumen, scherp'zinnigheid
acute, scherp; a'cuut
adamant(ine), onver'murwbaar
adapt, aanpassen, be'werken
adaptability, aanpassingsvermogen n
adaptable, aan te passen; plooibaar
adaptation, be'werking; aanpassing
add (to), toevogen aan, voegen bij
add to, ver'meerderen
add up, optellen; oplopen
addict, ver'slaafde
addicted, ver'slaafd
addition, optelling; toevoeging
in addition, boven'dien
additional, extra
addled, be'dorven; ver'dwaasd
address, a'dres n; toespraak: adres'seren; aanspreken, toespreken

adenoids, neusamandelen
adept, be'dreven(e) (in)
adequate, vol'doende, ge'schikt
adhere, (aan)kleven; aanhangen, blijven bij
adherent, aanhanger
adhesion, ad'hesie
adhesive, plak-: plakmiddel n
adjacent, aan'grenzend
adjective, bij'voeglijk naamwoord n
adjoin, grenzen aan
adjourn, ver'dagen; (uit'een)-gaan
adjudicate, uitspraak doen
adjunct, aanhangsel n; be'paling
adjure, be'zweren
adjust, regu'leren, (ver')stellen
adjustable, ver'stelbaar
administer, be'heren; toedienen
administration, be'heer n, re'gering
administrative, administra'tief
admirable, loffelijk; uit'stekend
admiral, admi'raal
admiralty, admirali'teit
admiration, be'wondering
admire, be'wonderen
admissible, ver'oorloofd; aan'nemelijk
admission, toegang (sprijs), toelating; er'kenning
admit, toelaten tot, opnemen in; toegeven
admittance, toegang
admittedly, weliswaar
admonish, ver'manen
ad nauseam, tot ver'velens toe
ado, drukte
adolescence, puber'teit
adolescent, opgroeiend: jonge man, jong meisje n
adopt, aannemen
adorable, allerliefst
adoration, aan'bidding
adore, aan'bidden; dol zijn op
adorn, (ver')sieren
adornment, ver'siering, sieraad n
adrift, drijvend, los
adroit(ness), handig(heid)
adulation, kruipe'rij
adult, vol'wassen(e)
adulterate, ver'valsen

adultery, overspel *n*
advance, voor'uitgang; opmars; voorschot *n*: naar voren komen oprukken; voorschieten
 in advance, van te voren
advanced, (ver)ge'vorderd
advancement, voor'uitgang, be'-vordering
advantage, voordeel *n*
 to take advantage of, ge'bruik maken van
advantageous, gunstig
advent, (aan)komst; Ad'vent
adventure, avon'tuur *n*, (ge'waag-de) onder'neming
adventurer, avontu'rier; specu'-lant
adventurous, avon'tuurlijk; ge'waagd
adverb, bijwoord *n*
adversary, tegenstander
adverse, on'gunstig; na'delig
adversity, tegenspoed
advertise, adver'teren, re'clame maken (voor); be'kend maken
advertisement, adver'tentie, re'-clame
advice, raad
advisable, raadzaam
advise, aanraden
advisedly, met over'leg
adviser, raadsman
advisory, raadgevend
advocate, voorspraak; voor-stander: be'pleiten
aerial, an'tenne
aerodrome, vliegveld *n*
aeronautics, luchtvaartkunde
aeroplane, vliegtuig *n*
aesthetic, aes'thetisch
afar, verre
affable, minzaam
affair, zaak; ver'houding
affect, (be')treffen; voorwenden
affectation, ge'maaktheid; voor-wendsel *n*
affected, ge'maakt
affection, ge'negenheid
affectionate, aan'hankelijk, harte-lijk; toegenegen
affidavit, be'ëdigde ver'klaring
affiliated to, aangesloten bij
affinity, ver'wantschap

affirm, plechtig ver'klaren
affirmation, be'vestiging
affirmative, be'vestigend
afflict, kwellen, teisteren
affliction, kwelling, ramp
affluent, (schat)rijk
afford, zich ver'oorloven; ver'-schaffen
afforestation, aanplant(ing)
affront, be'lediging
afield: far —, ver weg
afloat, drijvend
afoot, aan de gang
aforementioned, aforesaid, voor'noemd
afraid, bang
afresh, op'nieuw
aft, (naar) achter
after, (daar')na: na'dat
after-effect(s), nawerking
aftermath, nasleep
afternoon, (na)middag
afterthought, latere over'weging
afterwards, later, nader'hand
again, weer (eens); te'rug
 again and again, telkens weer
against, tegen
agate, a'gaat
age, leeftijd, ouderdom; eeuw: ouder worden
 of age, meerder'jaarig
aged, be'jaard; oud
agency, a'gentschap *n*
agenda, a'genda
agent, tussenpersoon, a'gent
agglomeration, op'eenhoping
aggrandize, ver'heffen
aggravate, (ver')ergeren
aggravating, ver'velend; ver'-zwarend
aggregate, (ge'zamenlijk) to'taal *n*
aggression, ag'gressie
aggressive, aggres'sief
aggressor, aanvaller
aghast at, ont'zet over
agile, be'hendig
agitate, a'geren; schudden
agitation, actie; be'roering; ge'-jaagdheid
agitator, opruier
aglow, gloeiend
agnostic, ag'nosticus

ago, ge'leden
agog: to be —, zitten te springen
agonizing, (vreselijk) pijnlijk
agony, folterende pijn
agrarian, a'grarisch
agree, het eens zijn; over'eenkomen; toestemmen
  fish doesn't agree with me, ik
kan niet tegen vis
agreeable, aangenaam; be'reid
agreement, over'eenkomst
agricultural, landbouw('kundig)
agriculture, landbouw
aground, aan de grond
ahead, voor'op, voor'uit; in het
voor'uitzicht
aid, hulp
ail, man'keren; sukkelen
ailment, kwaal
aim, doel(einde) *n*: mikken op;
munten op; streven naar
aimless, doelloos
air, lucht; schijn; wijs: luchten
  airs (and graces), airs
aircraft, vliegtuig(en) *n*
aircraft-carrier, vliegdekschip *n*
airfield, vliegveld *n*
airforce, luchtmacht
airgun, windbuks
airily, lucht'hartig
air-lift, luchtbrug
air-line, luchtvaartlijn
air-liner, lijnvliegtuig *n*
airman, vlieger
airport, vlieghaven
air-raid, luchtaanval
airtight, luchtdicht
airways, luchtvaartmaatschappij
airy, luchtig
aisle, zijbeuk, gangpad *n*
ajar, op een kier; ge'prikkeld
akimbo: arms —, met de handen in de zij
akin, ver'want
alacrity, levendigheid
  with alacrity, vol'gaarne
alarm, a'larm *n*; ont'steltenis:
ont'stellen
alarm-clock, wekker
alarmist, alar'mist(isch)
alas, he'laas
alb, albe
albeit, (al)hoe'wel

albumen, eiwit *n*
alcohol, alcohol
alcoholic, alco'holisch: alco-
ho'list
alcove, nis; al'koof
alderman, wethouder
ale, bier *n*
alert, waakzaam
algebra, algebra
alien, vreemd(eling)
alienate, ver'vreemden
alight, aan(gestoken): af (*or*
uit)stappen; neerstrijken
align, op één lijn plaatsen
alike, evenzeer
  to be alike, op el'kaar lijken
alive, levend, in leven; zich
be'wust van
alkali(ne), al'kali(sch) (*n*)
all, al(le); alles, allen; ge'heel,
alle'maal
  all along, steeds
  all but, bijna
  all in, bek'laf: alles inbegrepen
  all right, in orde
  all the more, des te meer
  after all, ten'slotte
  all in all, al met al
  at all, über'haupt
  not at all, hele'maal niet
  for all that, desondanks
  for all I know, voor zo'ver ik
weet
allay, stillen
allegation, be'wering
allege, be'weren
alleged(ly), zoge'naamd
allegiance, trouw
allegory, allego'rie
allergic, al'lergisch
alleviate, ver'lichten
alley(way), steeg
alliance, ver'bond *n*
allied, ver'bonden; ver'want
alliteration, allite'ratie
allocate, toewijzen
allot, toebedelen
allotment, volkstuintje *n*
allow, toestaan; rekenen
allowance, toelage
  to (make) allow(ance) for,
rekening houden met
alloy, le'gering

all-round, veel'zijdig
allude to, zinspelen op
alluring, aan'lokkelijk
allusion, toespeling
ally, bondgenoot: ver'binden
almighty, al'machtig
almond, a'mandel
almoner, administra'teur
almost, bijna
alms, aalmoes
aloft, in 't want, in de hoogte
alone, al'leen
  let alone, laat staan
along, langs; mee; voort
  along with, met . . . mee,
    samen met
alongside, langs'zij
aloof, op een afstand
aloud, hardop
alphabet, alfabet *n*
alphabetical, alfa'betisch
already, al, reeds
also, ook; boven'dien
altar, altaar *n*
alter, ver'anderen, (zich) wijzigen
alteration, ver'andering
altercation, twistgesprek *n*
alternate, afwisselen
  on alternate days, om de andere
    dag
alternately, om de beurt
alternating current, wissel-
    stroom
alternative, alterna'tief (*n*)
alternatively, aan de andere
    kant
although, hoe'wel
altitude, hoogte
alto, alt
altogether, hele'maal; alles bij
    el'kaar
altruism, altru'ïsme *n*
aluminium, alu'minium *n*
always, al'tijd
amalgamate, samensmelten
amass, op'eenhopen
amateur, ama'teur
amaze, ver'bazen
amazement, ver'bazing
ambassador, (af)gezant
amber, barnsteen *n*
ambiguity, dubbel'zinnigheid
ambiguous, dubbel'zinnig

ambition, eerzucht; aspi'ratie,
    ide'aal *n*
ambitious, eer'zuchtig; groots
    opgezet
amble, kuieren
ambulance, ziekenauto
ambush, hinderlaag
amenable, ont'vankelijk (voor)
amend, ver'beteren, wijzigen
amendment, amende'ment *n*
amends: to make —, het weer
    goedmaken
amenity, ge'mak *n*
amiable, be'minnelijk
amicable, vriend'schappelijk
amidships, mid'scheeps
amid(st), te midden van
amiss, ver'keerd
amity, pais en vree
ammonia, ammoni'ak
ammunition, (am)mu'nitie
amnesty, amnes'tie
among(st), onder, tussen
amorous, ver'liefd; liefdes-
amount, be'drag, hoe'veelheid
  to amount to, be'dragen; be'-
    tekenen
amphibian, amfi'bie; twee'slach-
    tig
ample, ruim (vol'doende)
amplify, aanvullen; ver'sterken
amply, ruimschoots
amputate, ampu'teren
amuse, ver'maken; pret hebben
amused: to be —, grappig vin-
    den
amusement, ver'maak *n*, tijd-
    verdrijf *n*
amusing, amu'sant, onder'houd-
    end
anaemia, bloedarmoede
anaesthetic, ver'dovend: ver'-
    dovingsmiddel *n*
analogous, ana'loog
analogy, analo'gie
analyse, anali'seren
analysis, ana'lyse
anarchy, anar'chie
anathema, banvloek; pesti'len-
    tie
anatomy, anato'mie
ancestor, voorvader
ancestral, voorvaderlijk

ancestry, voorgeslacht *n*; af-stamming
anchor, anker *n*: (ver)'ankeren
anchorage, ankergrond; steun
anchovy, an'sjovis
ancient, (zeer) oud
and, en
anecdote, anek'dote
anew, op'nieuw
angel, engel
angelic(al), engelachtig, engelen-
anger, boosheid: ver'toornen
angle, hoek; ge'zichtspunt *n*: hengelen
Anglican, Angli'caan(s)
angry, boos
anguish, zielssmart; folterende pijn
angular, hoekig
animal, dier *n*: dierlijk, dieren-
animate, levend: be'zielen
animated, geani'meerd
animation, enthousi'asme
animosity, vij'andigheid
ankle, enkel
annals, an'nalen
annex, anne'xeren; toevoegen
annexe, uitbouw, depen'dance; bijlage
annihilate, ver'nietigen
anniversary, jaarfeest *n*, ge'denk-dag
announce, aankondigen
announcement, aankondiging
announcer, omroeper
annoy, ergeren
annoyance, ergenis
annoying, ver'velend
annual, jaarlijks: éénjarige plant; jaarboek *n*
annuity, jaargeld *n*, lijfrente
annul, te niet doen
anoint, zalven
anomaly, afwijking
anon, straks
anonymous, ano'niem
another, een ander(e), nog een
answer, antwoord *n*, oplossing: (be')antwoorden
answerable, aan'sprakelijk; te be'antwoorden
ant, mier
antagonism, vijandschap

antagonist, tegenstander
antagonize, ophitsen
antarctic, Zuidpool(gebied *n*)
antecedent, voor'afgaand: ante-ce'dent *n*
anteroom, voorvertrek *n*
anthem, mo'tet *n*
ant-hill, mierenhoop
anthology, bloemlezing
anthracite, antra'ciet
anti-aircraft, luchtafweer-
antics, dolle streken
anticipate, ver'wachten;voor'uit-lopen op, vóór zijn
anticipation, ver'wachting
anticlimax, anti'climax
antidote, tegengif *n*
antipathy, antipa'thie
antiquarian, oudheid'kundig(e), anti'quair
antiquated, ouder'wets
antique, an'tiek; antiqui'teit
antiquity, oudheid; ouderdom
antiseptic, anti'septisch (middel *n*)
antithesis, tegenstelling, tegen-ge'stelde *n*
antlers, ge'wei *n*
anvil, aanbeeld *n*
anxiety, be'aangdheid; vurig ver'-langen *n*
anxious, be'zorgd
  to be anxious to, heel graag willen
any, ieder, iemand; wat (ook), enig
  not any, geen; niets
  have you any bread (*etc*) ? hebt U (ook) brood (*etc*)?
anybody, anyone, iemand, ieder-een; wie ook
anyhow, hoe dan ook; zo maar
anything, iets; alles
anyway, in ieder ge'val
anywhere, ergens; over'al
apace, vlug
apart, uit el'kaar; afgezien; afgezonderd
apartment, ver'trek *n*
apathetic, a'patisch
apathy, onver'schilligheid
ape, aap (zonder staart): naäpen

aperture, opening

apex, top(punt *n*)

apiary, bijenstal

apiece, per stuk, elk

apologetic, veront'schuldigend

apologize, zich veront'schuldigen

apology, veront'schuldiging

apoplectic fit, be'roerte

apostate, af'vallig(e)

apostle, a'postel

apostrophe, apos'trof

appal, ont'zetten

appalling, schrik'barend

apparatus, appa'raten, appa'raat *n*, toestel(len) *n*

apparel, kle'dij

apparent, duidelijk; ogen'schijnlijk

apparently, blijkbaar

apparition, ('geest)ver'schijning

appeal, be'roep *n*, smeekbede; aantrekkingskracht: een be'roep doen (op), smeken; in be'roep gaan (bij); aantrekken

appear, (ver')schijnen, blijken

appearance, ver'schijning, optreden *n*; voorkomen *n*

appease, sussen, stillen

appeasement, ver'zoening

append, (bij) voegen

appendage, aanhangsel *n*

appendicitis, blinde'darmontsteking

appendix, ap'pendix; aanhangsel *n*

appertain to, be'trekking hebben op; be'horen aan

appetite, (eet)lust

appetizing, smakelijk

applaud, toejuichen, applaudis'seren

applause, ap'plaus *n*, toejuiching-(en)

apple, appel

appliance, appa'raat *n*; toepassing

applicable, toe'passelijk

applicant, sollici'tant

application, aanbrengen *n*; (ma'nier van) toepassing, ge'bruik *n*; sollici'tatie; ijver

applied, toegepast

apply, aanbrengen; toepassen, van toepassing zijn; zich wenden; sollici'teren; toeleggen (op)

appoint, be'noemen, aanwijzen

appointed time, vastgesteld uur

appointment, afspraak; be'noeming, ambt *n*

apportion, ver'delen

apposite, toe'passelijk

appraisal, schatting

appreciable, aan'merkelijk

appreciate, waar'deren, ge'voelig zijn voor; stijgen

appreciation, waar'dering, ge'voel *n*; stijging

appreciative, dankbaar

apprehend, ge'vangen nemen; vatten; vrezen

apprehension, in'hechtenisneming; be'grip *n*; angst

apprehensive, angstig

apprentice, leerling: in de leer doen

approach, nader'bij komen (*n*); toegang(sweg); aanpak: naderen; zich wenden tot

approachable, toe'gankelijk

approbation, goedkeuring

appropriate, ge'schikt: zich toeëigenen, be'stemmen

approval, goedkeuring, bijval

on approval, op zicht

approve, goedkeuren, er'kennen

approximate, be'naderen

the (approximate) **length is** (approximately), de lengte is onge'veer

approximation, schatting

apricot, abri'koos

April, a'pril

apron, schort, voorschoot

apse, apsis

apt, ge'neigd; passend; vlug

aptitude, aanleg

aquarium, a'quarium *n*

aquatic, water-

aqueduct, waterleiding

aquiline, arends-

Arab, Ara'bier

Arabian, Arabic, A'rabisch

arable, bouw-

arbitrary, wille'keurig

arbitration, arbi'trage

arc, boog

arcade, gale'rij

arch, boog, ge'welf *n*; aarts-, schalks

archaeology, oudheidkunde

archaic, ver'ouderd

arched, ge'bogen

archer, boogschutter

archery, boogschieten *n*

architect, archi'tect

architectural, bouw'kundig

architecture, bouwkunde, bouwstijl

archives, ar'chief *n*, ar'chieven

archway, poort

arctic, Noordpool(gebied *n*)

ardent, vurig

arduous, zwaar

area, oppervlak *n*, ge'bied *n*

arena, a'rena

argue, debat'teren; tegenspreken; be'togen

argument, argu'ment *n*, de'bat *n*; ge'dachtengang

argumentative, twistziek

arid, dor

aright, juist

arise, ont'staan, zich voordoen; ver'rijzen

aristocracy, aristocra'tie

aristocrat, aristo'craat

arithmetic, rekenkunde

ark, ark

arm, arm, leuning: wapen *n*: be'wapenen

 arm in arm, ge'armd

armament, be'wapening

armchair, fau'teuil

armful, vracht

armistice, wapenstilstand

armour, harnas *n*; wapenrusting

armoured, pantser-

armoury, wapenzaal

armpit, oksel

army, leger *n*

aroma, a'roma *n*

aromatic, geurig

around, rond('om); over'al; in de buurt (van)

arouse, opwekken; wakker maken

arraign, aanklagen; be'schuldigen

arrange, (rang)schikken; regelen, afspreken; arran'geren

arrangement, schikking; afspraak; arrange'ment *n*

arrant, door'trapt

array, (slag)orde; uitstalling; dos: opstellen; uitdossen

arrears, achterstand

arrest, ar'rest *n*, arres'tatie: arres'teren; tegenhouden

arrival, (aan)komst; aangekomene

arrive, (aan)komen

arrogance, aanmatiging

arrogant, arro'gant

arrow, pijl

arsenal, arse'naal *n*

arsenic, ar'senicum *n*

arson, brandstichting

art, kunst(greep)

arterial road, hoofdverkeersweg

artery, (slag)ader

artful, ge'slepen

arthritis, ge'wrichtsontsteking

artichoke, arti'sjok

article, ar'tikel *n*; voorwerp *n*; lidwoord *n*

 article of clothing, kledingstuk *n*

articulate, duidelijk: articu'leren; koppelen

artifice, kunst(greep)

artificer, handwerksman

artificial, kunst'matig, ge'kunsteld, kunst-

artillery, artille'rie

artisan, handwerksman

artist, kunstenaar, schilder

artistic, kunst'zinnig, artis'tiek

artistry, kunstenaarstalent *n*

artless, argeloos; ruw

as, (zo)als: ter'wijl; daar

 (just) as . . . (as), even . . . (als)

 as to, wat betreft

asbestos, as'best *n*

ascend, (be')stijgen

ascendancy, overwicht *n*

Ascension, Hemelvaart

ascent, stijgen *n*, be'stijging; helling

ascertain, te weten komen
ascetic, as'ceet: as'cetisch
ascribe, toeschrijven
ash, as: es(seboom)
Ash Wednesday, As'woensdag
ashamed, be'schaamd
 to be ashamed, zich schamen
ashen, lijkbleek
ashore, aan wal, aan land
ash-tray, asbak
aside, op'zij, ter'zijde
asinine, ezelachtig
ask, vragen
 to ask a question, een vraag
 doen
askance, wan'trouwend
askew, scheef
aslant, schuin
asleep, in slaap
 to be asleep, slapen
asparagus, as'perge
aspect, as'pect n, kant; aanblik;
 ligging
aspersion, laster
asphalt, asfalt n
asphyxiate, (ver')stikken
aspirant, aspi'rant; postu'lant
aspiration, aspi'ratie
aspire, streven (naar)
ass, ezel
assail, be'stormen, aanvallen
assailant, aanvaller
assassin, sluipmoordenaar
assassinate, ver'moorden
assault, be'storming, aanval(len),
 be'stormen
assay, proef(neming): toetsen
assemble, (zich) ver'zamelen;
 mon'teren
assembly, bij'eenkomst; mon'-
 tering
assent, instemming: instemmen
assert, be'weren; doen gelden,
 opkomen voor
assertion, be'wering
assess, ta'xeren; aanslaan
asset, creditpost; voordeel n
assiduous, naarstig
assign, toewijzen; vaststellen
assignment, opdracht
assimilate, ver'werken, opnemen
assimilation, assimi'latie

assist, helpen
assistance, hulp
assistant, assis'tent, be'diende
 hulp-
assizes, rechtzitting(en)
associate, partner; ver'want
 ver'binden, associ'eren, omgaar
association, associ'atie; ge'noot
 schap n
assorted, ge'mengd
assortment, sor'tering; ver'-
 zameling
assuage, stillen, lessen
assume, aannemen; voorwenden;
 op zich nemen
assumption, veronder'stelling;
 aanvaarding
assurance, ver'zekering
assure, ver'zekeren
assuredly, stellig; zelfbe'wust
astern, achter('uit)
astir, op de been
astonish, ver'bazen
astonishment, ver'bazing
astound, (ten hoogste) ver'bazen
astray, op een dwaalspoor
astride, schrijlings (op)
astrology, sterrenwichelarij
astronomical, astro'nomisch
astronomy, sterrenkunde
astute, slim
asunder, uit el'kaar
asylum, ge'sticht n; a'siel n
asymmetric(al), asym'metrisch
at, aan (position); in, op, te
 (place); om (time); naar (direction); voor (price)
 at (my) leisure, op mijn ge'mak
 at that moment, op dat ogenblik
 at the time, toen
atheism, athe'ïsme n
athlete, at'leet
athletic, at'letisch
athletics, atle'tiek
Atlantic, At'lantische Oce'aan
atlas, atlas
atmosphere, dampkring;
 (atmo')sfeer
atmospheric, atmos'ferisch
atom, a'toom n; greintje n
atomic, a'tomisch, a'toom-
atone, boeten

atonement, boete(doening), ver'zoening
atrocious, af'schuwelijk
atrocity, gruwel(daad)
atrophy, atro'fie; (doen) uitteren
attach, vastmaken, ver'binden; hechten
attachment, onderdeel n, ver'binding; ge'hechtheid
attack, aanval(len)
attain, be'reiken, be'halen
attainable, be'reikbaar
attainment, be'reiken n; ta'lent n
attempt, poging, aanslag : trachten
attend, bijwonen; verge'zellen
  attend to, opletten; ver'zorgen
attendance, opkomst; aan'wezigheid
  in attendance, aan'wezig; in het ge'volg
attendant, be'diende; be'zoeker: bege'leidend; dienstdoend
attention, aandacht; at'tentie; houding
attentive, op'lettend; at'tent
attenuate, ver'dunnen; ver'zachten
attest, ge'tuigen van, attes'teren
attic, zolder (kamer)
attire, tooi(en)
attitude, houding
attorney, gevol'machtigde, pro cu'reur
attract, (aan)trekken
attraction, aantrekking(skracht)
attractive, aan'trekkelijk
attribute, eigenschap, kenmerk n; attri'buut n : toeschrijven
attune, (over'een)stemmen met
auburn, kas'tanjebruin
auction, veiling : veilen
auctioneer, afslager
audacious, ver'metel
audacity, ver'metelheid, bru-tali'teit
audible, hoorbaar
audience, ge'hoor n, toehoorders; audi'ëntie
audit, ac'countantsverslag n: verifi'ëren
audition, to'neel-(or mu'ziek-) proef

auditor, ac'countant; toehoorder
auditorium, zaal
augment, ver'meerderen, uit-breiden
augur, voor'spellen
august, ver'heven : au'gustus
aunt, tante
aura, geur; lichtkrans
auspices, au'spiciën
auspicious, gunstig
austere, streng, sober
austerity, ver'sobering
Austria, Oostenrijk n
authentic, authen'tiek
authenticate, verifi'ëren
authenticity, echtheid
author, schrijver; schepper, oor-sprong
authoritarian, autori'tair (per'-soon)
authoritative, autori'tair, ge'-zaghebbend
authority, autori'teit; bron; machtiging
authorize, machtigen; be'krach-tigen
autobiography, autobiogra'fie
autocracy, onbeperkte heer-schap'pij
autocrat, auto'kraat
autograph, handtekening. (eigen'handig) tekenen
automatic, auto'matisch (pis'tool n)
automaton, auto'maat
automobile, automo'biel
autonomous, auto'noom
autopsy, lijkschouwing
auto-suggestion, autosug'gestie
autumn(al), herfst(-)
auxiliary, hulp (troep)
avail, baten
  of no avail, vruchteloos
  to avail oneself of, be'nutten
available, be'schikbaar
avalanche, la'wine
avarice, gierigheid
avaricious, gierig; be'gerig
avenge, wreken
avenue, laan; weg
aver, (plechtig) ver'klaren
average, ge'middeld (doen) : ge'-middelde n

averse to, af'kerig van
aversion, afkeer, tegenzin
avert, afwenden
aviary, voli'ère
aviation, luchtvaart, vliegwezen *n*
aviator, vlieger
avid, gretig, be'gerig
avoid, (ver')mijden
avoidance, ver'mijding
avow, be'lijden, be'kennen
avowal, be'kentenis, be'lijdenis
await, afwachten; wachten op
awake, wakker; zich be'wust (worden) van; ont'waken; wekken
awaken, wekken
awakening: rude —, ont'nuchtering
award, be'kroning, prijs: toekennen, toewijzen
aware, zich be'wust
awareness, be'sef *n*
awash, over'spoeld
away, weg; er op los
  do away with, opruimen
awe, ont'zag *n*
awe-inspiring, ontzag'wekkend
awful, ver'schrikkelijk, vreselijk
awfully, (heel) erg
awhile, een tijdje *n*
awkward, on'handig; lastig
awning, dekzeil *n*, zonnescherm *n*
awry, scheef
axe, bijl: drastisch be'perken
axiom, axi'oma *n*
axis, as(lijn); spil
axle, as
aye, ja, stem vóór; immer
azure, hemelsblauw

B

babble, babbelen, kabbelen
babel, spraakverwarring
baboon, bavi'aan
baby, kindje *n*, baby; benjamin: jong, klein
babyish, kinderachtig
bacchanal, baccha'naal *n*: bac'chantisch
bachelor, vrijge'zel
bacillus, ba'cil

back, rug, achterkant, rugleuning: te'rug, achter-: achter'uitgaan; wedden op; bijvallen
back to front, achterste voren
at the back, achter'aan (*or* 'in)
on the back, achter'op
to back down, zich te'rugtrekken
to back out, te'rugkrabbelen
to back up, steunen
back-biting, kwaadspreke'rij
backbone, ruggegraat
backfire, te'rugslaan
background, achtergrond
backing, steun; achterkant (bekleding)
back-stage, achter de schermen
backward(s), achter'uit, te'rug-; achterlijk, traag
backwards and forwards, heen en weer
backwater, kreek, uithoek; boegwater *n*
bacon, (ge'rookt) spek *n*
bacteria, bac'teriën
bad, slecht, naar; vals; be'dorven
to go bad, be'derven
bad luck, pech
badge, in'signe *n*
badger, das: lastig vallen
badly, erg; dolgraag
bad-tempered, slecht-gehu'meurd
baffle, smoorplaat: ver'bijsteren
bag, zak, tas; vangst: gappen
baggage, ba'gage
baggy, uitgezakt, hang-
bagpipe, doedelzak
bail, borg(tocht): borgstaan: hozen
bailiff, rentmeester; deurwaarder
bait, lokaas *n*: van aas voor'zien; aanhitsen
baize, baai
bake, bakken
baker, bakker
bakery, bakke'rij
balance, evenwicht *n*; saldo *n*, rest ('ant *n*); weegschaal: in evenwicht brengen, opwegen tegen; sluitend maken (*or* zijn)

balanced, even'wichtig
balance-sheet, ba'lans
balcony, bal'kon n
bald, kaal; naakt
bale, baal: in balen ver'pakken
baleful, onheil'spellend, ge'pij-
nigd
balk, balk: ver'ijdelen, tegenstribbelen
ball, bal(len); bal n (dance)
ballad, bal'lade,
ballast, ballast
ball-bearing, kogellager n
ballet, bal'let n
balloon, bal'lon: bol staan
ballot, (ge'heime) stemming; lot
n
balm, balsem, geur
balmy, zacht, geurig; ge'tikt
balsam, balsem
Baltic, Oost'zee
balustrade, balu'strade
bamboo, bamboe
bamboozle, beetnemen; in de
war brengen
ban, ver'bod n, ban(vloek):
ver'bieden; ver'bannen
banal, ba'naal
banana, ba'naan
band, band, rand; troep; ka'pel:
ver'enigen
bandage, ver'band n
bandit, ban'diet
bandstand, mu'ziektent
bandy, telkens (or over en) weer
lan'ceren
bandy-legged, met o-benen
bane, vloek
bang, klap, knal: (dicht)slaan
banish, ver'bannen
banishment, ver'banning
banisters, trapleuning
banjo, banjo
bank, oever, berm; bank: ophopen; depo'neren; overhellen;
afdekken
 to bank on, specu'leren op
banker, ban'kier
bank-holiday, offici'ele va'cantie-
dag
bank-note, bankbiljet n
bankrupt, fai'lliet
bankruptcy, faillisse'ment n

banner, ba'nier, vaandel n
banns, (kerkelijke) huwelijks-
afkondiging
banquet, gastmaal n: banket'-
teren
banter, gekscheren (n)
baptism, doop
Baptist, doopsge'zinde
baptize, dopen
bar, stang, reep, staaf; barri'ère;
bar; balie; maat: uitgezonderd: afsluiten, ver'sperren;
uitsluiten
barb, weerhaak
barbarian, bar'baar(s)
barbarity, bar'baarsheid
barbarous, bar'baars
barbed, met weerhaken; heke-
lend
 barbed wire, prikkeldraad n
barber, kapper
bard, zanger-dichter
bare, (ont')bloot, kaal; mini'-
maal: ont'bloten
barefaced, onbe'schaamd
bare-foot(ed), bloots'voets
bare-headed, bloots'hoofds
barely, nauwelijks
bargain, over'eenkomst; koopje
 into the bargain, op de koop
toe
 to bargain for, rekenen op
barge, schuit, sloep: botsen, zich
werken
baritone, bariton
bark, schors: ge'blaf n: bark:
schaven: blaffen
barley, gerst
barmaid, buf'fetjuffrouw
barn, schuur
barometer, barometer
baron, ba'ron; mag'naat
baroque, ba'rok(stijl)
barracks, ka'zerne(woning)
barrage, gor'dijnvuur n
barrel, vat n, ton; loop
barren, on'vruchtbaar, dor
barricade, barri'cade: barri-
ca'deren
barrier, barri'ère, con'trole
barrister, advo'kaat
barrow, handkar: grafheuvel

barter, ruilhandel drijven; ver'kwanselen
base, basis, voetstuk *n* : ge'meen, on'edel : ba'seren
baseball, honkbal *n*
basement, souter'rain *n*
bash, opstopper : (in) slaan
bashful, schuchter
basic, fundamen'teel, grond-
basin, kom, bak ; dok *n* ; stroom-gebied *n*
basis, basis
bask, zich koesteren
basket, mand
basket-ball, korfbal *n*
bass, bas: baars
bassoon, fa'got
bastard, bastaard : on'echt
baste, met vet over'gieten : rijgen : ranselen
bastion, basti'on *n*
bat, slaghout *n* : vleermuis : bat-ten
 off one's own bat, op eigen houtje
batch, par'tij, baksel *n* ; groep
bath, bad *n* : in bad doen (*or* gaan) **(public) baths,** badinrichting
bathe, (zich) baden : betten
 bathed (in light), badend (in licht)
bathing-costume, badpak *n*
bathing-trunks, zwembroek
bath-robe, badjas
bathroom, badkamer
batman, oppasser
baton, stok (je *n*)
battalion, batal'jon *n*
batten, (schalm)lat
batter, be'slag *n* : beuken
battery, batte'rij, accu ; aan-randing
battle, (veld)slag ; strijd (en)
battle-axe, strijdbijl
battle-dress, veldte'nue *n*
battle-field, slagveld *n*
battlement, kan'teel
battleship, slagschip *n*
bawdy, vuil
bawl, schreeuwen, brullen
bay, baai ; erker, hoek : vos: blaffen
 at bay, in het nauw

bayonet, bajo'net
bazaar, ba'zaar
be, zijn ; zitten, worden
 to be hungry, sleepy, thirsty, cold, honger, slaap, dorst, het koud hebben
 how are you ? hoe maakt U het ?
 how is it that, hoe komt het dat
beach, strand *n*
beacon, baken *n*
bead, kraal ; parel (tje *n*)
beak, snavel
beaker, beker (glas *n*)
beam, balk ; stralenbundel : stralen (van)
 on the beam, op zij
bean, boon
bear, beer : (ver)dragen ; baren
 to bear down, neerdrukken ; afkomen op
 to bear out, staven
 to bear witness, ge'tuigen
beard, baard : trot'seren
bearer, drager, brenger ; toonder
bearing, houding ; be'trekking ; richting ; kogellager *n*
beast, beest *n*
beastly, beestachtig ; akelig
beat, (maat)slag ; ronde : (ver)-slaan, kloppen ; la'veren
beating, afranseling ; klappen *n*
beautiful, mooi
beautify, ver'fraaien
beauty, schoonheid ; pracht-exemplaar *n*
beaver, bever
becalmed : to be —, door wind-stilte over'vallen worden
because, omdat
 because of, van'wege
beckon, wenken
become, worden
 to become of, ge'beuren met
becoming, be'tamelijk, flat'teus
bed, bed (ding) (*n*)
bedaub, be'kladden ; opdirken
bed-clothes, dek *n*, beddegoed *n*
bedding, beddegoed *n* ; onderlaag
bedlam, gekkenhuis *n*
bed-pan, ondersteek
bedraggled, nat en ver'wilderd
bedridden, bed'legerig
bedroom, slaapkamer

bedspread, sprei
bedstead, ledi'kant n
bee, bij
beech, beuk(e'hout n)
beef, rundvlees n
beefsteak, runderlap
beehive, bijenkorf
beer, bier n
beet, biet
beetle, kever
beetroot, rode biet
befall, over'komen
befit, be'tamen
befog, be'nevelen
before, voor('af, 'op or 'uit), te
voren; voordat
before long, weldra
beforehand, voor'af, van te voren
befriend, vriendschap be'wijzen
befuddle, be'nevelen
beg, bedelen; smeken, ver'zoe-
~ken; zo vrij zijn
beget, voortbrengen
beggar, bedelaar; stakker: tarten
beggarly, ar'moedig
begin, be'ginnen
beginning, be'gin n
begrudge, mis'gunnen
beguile, be'driegen; ver'drijven
behalf: on — of, ten be'hoeve
van, uit naam van
behave (oneself), zich (netjes)
ge'dragen
behaviour, ge'drag n
behead, ont'hoofden
behind, achter(ste n)
behold, aan'schouwen
beige, beige
being, wezen n
to come into being, ont'staan
for the time being, voor'lopig
belated, (ver')laat
belch, boeren; uitbraken
belfry, klokketoren
Belgium, België
belie, logenstraffen
belief, ge'loof n
believe, ge'loven
believer, ge'lovige; voorstander
(van)
belittle, klei'neren
bell, bel, klok

bellicose, oorlogs'zuchtig
belligerent, oorlogvoerend;
strijd'lustig
bellow, ge'brul n: brullen
bellows, blaasbalg
belly, buik: uitbollen
belong, (be')horen
to belong to, (toebe)horen aan
belongings, spullen
beloved, ge'liefd(e)
below, onder, be'neden
belt, gordel, riem; zone: afranselen
bemoan, be'jammeren
bench, (recht)bank
bend, bocht: (zich) buigen,
ver'buigen
beneath, be'neden, onder
benediction, zegen; Lof n
benefactor, weldoener
benefice, bene'ficie
beneficial, heilzaam
benefit, voordeel n; uitkering:
goed doen, voordeel trekken
benevolent, wel'willend
benign, goed('aard)ig, wel'dadig
bent, ge'bogen: be'sloten, uit op:
aanleg
benumb, ver'kleumen
bequeath, ver'maken
bequest, le'gaat n
bereave, be'roven
bereaved, diep be'droefd
bereavement, zwaar ver'lies n
beret, ba'ret
berry, bes
berth, ligplaats; kooi: meren
beseech, smeken
beset, vol: om'ringen
beside, naast
beside oneself with, buiten
zichzelf van
besides, boven'dien: be'halve
besiege, be'legeren; be'stormen
besmirch, be'vuilen; be'zoedelen
best, (het) best
best man, bruidsjonker
best part of, bijna
at best, in het gunstigste ge'val
to make the best of, zich schikken in
bestial, beestachtig

bestow, ver'lenen, schenken
bet, wedden(schap)
betoken, be'duiden
betray, ver'raden
betrayal, ver'raad *n*
betroth, ver'loven
better, beter : ver'beteren
better off, er beter aan toe
had better, moet(en) maar
between, tussen
bevel, afschuinen
beverage, drank
bewail, be'jammeren
beware of, oppassen voor
bewilder, ver'bijsteren
bewitch, be'heksen
beyond, voor'bij ; boven ; meer
dan
it is beyond me, het gaat mij te
hoog
bias, neiging : bevoor'oordelen
bib, slabbetje *n*
Bible, Bijbel
bibliography, bibliogra'fie
bicker, kibbelen
bicycle, fiets
bid, bod *n* : bieden ; ge'lasten
bide, beiden
bier, (lijk)baar
biff, mep
big, groot
bigamy, biga'mie
bigot(ed), kwezel(achtig)
bilge, vulling, ruimwater *n*;
kletskoek
bilious attack, maagstoring
bill, rekening ; wetsontwerp *n*;
aanplakbiljet *n* : snavel
billet, kwar'tier *n* : inkwartieren
billiards, bil'jart *n*
billion, bil'joen *n*
billow, baar : bollen ; in wolken
opstijgen
bin, bak
bind, (in-, vast- *or* ver')binden ;
ver'plichten
binder, (boek)binder ; omslag
binding, band *n* : bindend
binoculars, kijker
biography, levensbeschrijving
biology, biolo'gie
birch, berk(ehout *n*)
bird, vogel

birth, ge'boorte
to give birth to, het leven
schenken aan
birthday, ver'jaardag
birth-rate, ge'boortecijfer *n*
biscuit, koekje *n*, biskwietje *n*
bishop, bisschop
bishopric, bisdom *n*
bit, beetje *n*, stukje : bit *n*
wait a bit, even wachten
bitch, teef
bite, beet, hap : bijten
bitter, bitter
blab, ver'klikken
black, zwart, blauw (*eye*)
blackberry, braam
blackbird, merel
blackboard, schoolbord *n*
blackguard, schobbejak
blackmail, chan'tage : geld afpersen
blackout, ver'duistering ; tijde-
lijke bewuste'loosheid
blacksmith, smid
bladder, blaas
blade, kling, lemmet *n*, mesje *n*;
spriet
blame, (de) schuld (geven)
blameless, onbe'rispelijk
blanch, (ver')bleken, pellen
bland, (poes)lief
blank, blanco ; wezenloos ; rijm-
loos ; los (*cartridge*)
to draw blank, botvangen
blanket, deken
blare, schallen
blasphemy, godslastering
blast, rukwind, luchtdruk :
ver'rek ! : laten springen
blast-furnace, hoogoven
blatant, over'duidelijk
blaze, laaiend vuur *n*, (vlammen)-
zee : opvlammen, in lichte laaie
staan
bleach, (doen ver')bleken
bleak, troosteloos
bleat, blaten
bleed, bloeden ; uitzuigen
blemish, smet, ont'siering : be'-
kladden
blend, mengsel *n* : (zich) ver'mengen, harmoni'ëren
bless, zegenen

...essing, zegen(ing)

...light, plantenziekte; be'derf *n*

...lind, blind; doodlopend: rol-gordijn *n*; foefje *n*: ver'blinden

...lindfold, ge'blinddoekt: blind-doeken

...lindness, blindheid

...link, knipperen

...liss, geluk'zaligheid

...lister, blaar

...lizzard, sneeuwjacht

...lock, blok *n*: (ver')stoppen

...lockade, blok'kade: blok'keren

...lockhead, domkop

...lond(e), blond('ine)

...lood, bloed *n*

...loodshed, bloedvergieten *n*

...loodshot, met bloed be'lopen

...loody, bloed(er)ig; ver'domd

...loom, bloem; waas *n*; bloei(en)

...lossom, bloesem: bloeien

...lot, vlek, smet: afvloeien; be'-kladden

to blot out, ver'nietigen

...lotting-paper, vloeipapier *n*

...louse, blouse

...low, slag: waaien, blazen; snuiten

to blow up, opblazen; op-vliegen, uitschelden: opsteken

blow-lamp, brander

blue, blauw (*n*)

blueprint, blauwdruk; plan *n*

bluff, bluf(fen); steil(e oever): rond'borstig

bluish, blauwachtig

blunder, blunder; struikelen

blunt, stomp, bot (maken); ab'rupt

blur, ver'vagen

blurt out, er'uit flappen

blush, blos: blozen, zich schamen

bluster, bulderen

boar, zwijn *n*

board, plank, bord *n*; kost(geld *n*); be'stuur *n*

to (go on) board, aan boord gaan

above board, bona fide

boarding-house, pen'sion *n*

boarding-school, kostschool

boast, pochen; bogen (op)

boat, boot

boatswain, bootsman

bob, korte buiging: dobberen: kort knippen

bobbin, spoel

bode ill (well), wat slechts (goeds) be'loven

bodice, (onder)lijfje *n*

bodily, li'chamelijk; in zijn ge'heel

body, lichaam *n*, lijf *n*; sub'stan-tie; carrosse'rie; groep

bodyguard, lijfwacht

bog, moe'ras *n*

to be bogged (down), vast-zitten

bogey, boeman, schrikbeeld *n*

bogus, vals

boil, kook: steenpuist: koken

to boil down, inkoken; neer-komen (op)

boiler, ketel, boiler

boisterous, on'stuimig

bold, stout('moedig); scherp

bolster, peluw: sterken

bolt, bout; grendel(en); ervan doorgaan

bolt upright, kaarsrecht

bomb(ard), bom(bar'deren)

bombastic, bom'bastisch

bomber, bommenwerper

bond, band; obli'gatie; entre'pot *n*: ver'binden

bondage, slaver'nij

bone, been *n*, graat; ba'lein

bone-dry, kurkdroog

bonfire, (vreugde)vuur *n*

bonnet, kap

bonny, leuk, fris, knap

bonus, premie, tan'tième *n*

bony, knokig, vol benen (*or* graten)

boob(y), uilskuiken *n*

book, boek(je) *n*: be'spreken, boeken

bookcase, boekenkast

booking-office, lo'ket *n*, plaats-kaartenbureau *n*

book-keeping, boekhouden *n*

book-seller, boekhandelaar

boom, (haven)boom: hausse: ge'dreun *n*: dreunen

boon, weldaad

boost, aanjagen, opdrijven; een zetje geven

boot, laars; bak: trappen
 to boot, op de koop toe
booth, kraam
booty, buit
booze, zuippartij: zuipen
border, grens; rand; bloembed *n*:
 om'zomen
 to border on, grenzen aan
bore, boren; ver'velen
 to be bored, zich ver'velen
boredom, ver'veling
born, ge'boren
borough, (stads)ge'meente
borrow, lenen (van), ont'lenen
 (aan)
bosom, boezem; schoot
boss, baas: bult: comman'deren
botany, plantkunde
both, beide, allebei
 both . . . and, zo'wel . . . als
bother, last, drukte: bah! lastig
 vallen
bottle, fles: inmaken, bottelen
 to bottle up, opkroppen
bottom, bodem; zitvlak *n*:
 onder'aan, onderste
 he is at the bottom of it, hij zit
 er achter
bough, (grote) tak
boulder, grote kei
bounce, stuiten; springen
bound, ver'bonden; ver'plicht:
 sprong: springen; be'grenzen
 to be bound, moeten; op weg zijn
boundary, grens(lijn)
boundless, onbe'grensd
bounteous, bountiful, mild, over-
 vloedig
bout, par'tij; peri'ode, vlaag
bow, buiging: boeg: boog;
 strik; strijkstok: buigen
bowels, ingewanden; schoot
bower, pri'eel *n*
bowl, schaal, bak: bowlen
 to bowl over, om'vergooien;
 van (zijn) stuk brengen
box, doos(je *n*), kist(je *n*); loge:
 buks(boom): oorvijg: boksen
Boxing Day, tweede Kerstdag
box-office, plaatsbu'reau *n*
boy, jongen
boycott, boycot(ten)
boyhood, jongens(jaren)

boyish, jongens(achtig)
brace, klamp; boor: paar *n*:
 (zich) scherp zetten
bracelet, armband
braces, bre'tels
bracing, op'wekkend
bracken, varens
bracket, kar'beel, arm; haakje
 n: samenkoppelen
brag, pochen
braid, vlecht(en); ga'lon
braille, brailleschrift *n*
brain, hersenen
brains, hersens, ver'stand *n*
brain-wave, lumi'neus idee *n*
brainy, knap
braise, smoren
brake, rem(men)
bramble, braam(struik)
bran, zemelen
branch, tak; bijkantoor *n*; fili'-
 aal *n*; afdeling: zich ver'-
 takken
brand, merk *n*; brandmerk(en)
 (*n*)
brandish, (dreigend) zwaaien
brand-new, splinternieuw
brandy, cog'nac
brass, (geel)koper(en) (*n*)
 brass band, fan'farekorps *n*
brassiere, bustehouder
brat, aap, wicht *n*
bravado, bra'voure
brave, moedig: trot'seren
bravery, moed
brawl, vechtpartij
brawn, spieren; hoofdkaas
bray, balken
brazen, bru'taal
breach, (in)breuk, schending;
 bres: door'breken
bread, brood *n*
 slice of bread and butter,
 boterham
breadth, breedte; ruimte
break, breuk, onder'breking,
 pauze: (ver)breken
 to break down, afbreken;
 weigeren; vastlopen; over'stuur
 raken
 to break up, stukbreken; zich
 (*or* doen) ver'spreiden; eindigen

break-down, de'fect *n* ; mis'lukking; instorting
breakers, branding
breakfast, ont'bijt(en) (*n*)
breakwater, golfbreker
breast, borst
breath, adem ; zuchtje *n*
  out of breath, buiten adem
breathe, ademen, ademhalen
breathless, ademloos, buiten adem
breeches, (knie)broek
breed, ras *n* : voortbrengen, fokken
breeding, fokken *n* ; (innerlijke) be'schaving
breeze, bries
breezy, winderig ; vrolijk
brevity, kortheid
brew, brouwsel *n* : brouwen ; broeien
brewery, brouwe'rij
bribe, omkoopgeld *n* : omkopen
bribery, omkope'rij
brick, baksteen, blok
  you're a brick, het is ge'weldig van je
  to drop a brick, een flater be'gaan
bricklayer, metselaar
brickwork, metselwerk *n*
bridal, bruids-
bride(groom), bruid(egom)
bridesmaid, bruidsmeisje *n*
bridge, brug : bridge *n* : over'bruggen
bridle, teugel, toom : tomen
brief, kort : instru'eren
brief-case, aktentas
brig, brik
brigade, bri'gade
brigand, ban'diet
bright, hel(der) ; pienter ; hoopvol
brighten, oplichten ; opvrolijken
brilliance, schittering ; geniali'teit
brilliant, schitterend ; bril'jant
brim, rand
brimful, boordevol
brine, pekel ; zilte nat *n*
bring, (mee)brengen
  to bring about, te'weegbrengen

to bring back, te'rugbrengen ; oproepen
to bring on, ver'oorzaken
to bring out, doen uitkomen
to bring round, bijbrengen ; overhalen
to bring up, bovenbrengen ; grootbrengen ; te berde brengen
brink, rand
brisk, kwiek
bristle, borstel(haar *n*) : gaan over'eind staan ; wemelen van
Britain, Brit'tanje *n*
British, Brits
Briton, Brit
brittle, broos, bros
broach, aansteken ; ter sprake brengen
broad, breed ; ruim
broadcast, uitzending : uitzenden ; ver'spreiden
broaden, (zich) ver'breden ; ver'ruimen
broad-minded, ruim van opvatting
broadside, breedzij(vuur *n*)
brocade, bro'kaat *n*
brogue, (Iers) ac'cent *n* ; stevige schoen
broil, roosteren
broke, blut
broken-hearted, diep onge'lukkig
broker, makelaar
bronchitis, bron'chitis
bronze, brons *n* : bronzen
brooch, broche
brood, broedsel *n* : broeden
brook, beek : dulden
broom, bezem ; brem
broth, boui'llon
brothel, bor'deel *n*
brother, broer, broeder
brotherhood, broederschap
brother-in-law, zwager
brow, voorhoofd *n* ; rand
browbeat, intimi'deren
brown, bruin (*n*)
  brown paper, pakpapier *n*
browse, grasduinen
bruise, (blauwe) plek : kneuzen
brunette, bru'nette
brunt, volle kracht

brush, borstel, kwast, pen'seel *n*; staart; scher'mutseling: (af)-borstelen, (af)vegen
 to brush past, rakelings gaan langs
brush(wood), kreupelhout *n*
brusque, bruusk
Brussels sprouts, spruitjes
brutal, beestachtig
brutality, wreedheid
brute, bruut
bubble, (lucht)bel: borrelen
buccaneer, boeka'nier
buck, mannetjes(damhert *n*): bokken
 to buck up, opfleuren; opschieten; aanpakken
bucket, emmer
buckle, gesp: vastgespen; krommen
bud, knop: uitbotten
budding, in de dop
budge, (zich) ver'roeren
budget, be'groting
buff, okergeel (*n*): po'lijsten
buffalo, buffel
buffer(-state), buffer(staat)
buffet, buf'fet *n*: stomp(en)
buffoon, pi'as
bug, beestje *n*
bugle, si'gnaalhoorn
build, bouw(en)
 to build up, opbouwen; be'bouwen
builder, aannemer
building, ge'bouw *n*
bulb, (bloem)bol; gloeilamp
bulge, uitpuiling: uitpuilen
bulk, massa; grootste deel *n*
bulkhead, schot *n*
bulky, lijvig, groot
bull, stier: bul
bullet, kogel
bulletin, bulle'tin *n*
bullion, (goud)staven
bullock, os
bully, bullebak: donderen
bulwark, bolwerk *n*
bumble-bee, hommel
bump, knobbel: stoot(en); hotsen
 to bump into, aanbotsen tegen
bumptious, aan'matigend

bumpy, hobbelig
bun, luxe broodje *n*; knoet
bunch, bos(je. *n*), tros: op'eenhopen
bundle, pak *n*, bos: samenbinden
bung, spon
 to bung up, (ver')stoppen
bungalow, bungalow
bungle, (ver')knoeien
bunk, kooi: kletspraat: er vandoor gaan
bunting, vlaggen
buoy, boei
buoyant: to be —, drijven; veerkracht hebben
burden, last: laden; drukken
bureau, bu'reau *n*
burglar, inbreker
burglary, inbraak
burial, be'grafenis
burlesque, (parodi'erende) klucht: koddig
burly, stoer
burn, brandwond: (ver')branden; aanbranden
burnish, po'lijsten
burrow, hol *n*: wroeten
burst, barst(en); vlaag: springen
bury, be'graven; ver'bergen
bus, bus
bush, struik; rimboe
business, zaak, zaken
businesslike, zakelijk
bust, borstbeeld *n*, buste
bustle, drukte: queue: druk in de weer zijn
busy, (druk)bezig
 to be busy, het druk hebben
busybody, be'moeial
but, maar: be'halve
butcher, slager; beul: afslachten
butler, hoofdbediende
butt, ton: kolf; peukje *n*: schietbaan: stoten
butter, boter: smeren
buttercup, boterbloem
butterfly, vlinder
buttocks, billen
button, knoop: knopen
buttonhole, knoopsgat *n*: aanklampen
buttress, beer: steunen
buxom, mollig

buy, koop : kopen
buyer, (in)koper
buzz, ge'gons *n* ; gonzen
by, door ; bij ; langs ; per ; volgens
  by train, met de trein
  by night and by day, 's nachts en over'dag
  by and large, over het alge'meen
bye-election, tussentijdse ver'- kiezing
bye-law, plaatselijke ver'orde- ning
by-product, nevenprodukt *n*
bystander, toeschouwer

C

cab, taxi ; ca'bine
cabbage, kool
cabin, hut ; ca'bine
cabinet, kabi'net *n*, kastje *n* ; mi'nisterraad
cable, kabel : telegra'feren
caboodle, rata'plan
cackle, kakelen
cacophony, tegen'strijdig ge'- schetter *n*
cactus, cactus
cad, ploert
caddie, golfjongen
caddy, (thee)busje *n*
cadence, ca'dans
cadet, ca'det
cadge, schooieren
café, ca'fé(-restau'rant) *n*
cage, kooi ; opsluiten
cajole, aftroggelen
cake, cake, ge'bak(je) *n* ; taart ; koek(en)
calamity, ramp
calculate, (be')rekenen
calendar, ka'lender
calf, kalf *n* : kuit
calibre, ka'liber *n*
call, tele'foontje *n* : roepen (*n*) ; noemen
  to give a call, roepen
  to pay a call, een be'zoek afleggen
  to be called, heten
  to call off, aflasten

to call on, bc'zoeken ; een be'roep doen op
calling, roeping
callous, onge'voelig
calm, kalm(te) : be'daren
calumny, laster
camel, ka'meel
camera, fototoestel *n*
camouflage, camou'flage : camou'fleren
camp, kamp('eren) (*n*)
campaign, veldtocht ; cam'pagne
can, kan, blik *n* ; kunnen
canal, ka'naal *n*, gracht
canary, ka'narie
cancel, schrappen, afzeggen
cancer, kanker
candid, open('hartig)
candidate, kandi'daat
candle, kaars
candlestick, kandelaar
candour, op'rechtheid
candy, kan'dij ; kon'fijten
  candied peel, su'kade
cane, rotting : riet(en) : afran- selen
cannibal, kanni'baal
cannon, ka'non *n* ; ge'schut *n*
canny, slim
canoe, kano
canon, canon ; ka'nunnik
canopy, balda'kijn
cant, ge'kwezel *n* : kantelen
cantankerous, cha'grijnig
canteen, kan'tine
canter, (in) korte ga'lop (draven)
canvas, (zeil)doek *n*
canvass, stemmen werven ; col- por'teren
canyon, diep ra'vijn *n*
cap, pet ; dop : over'treffen
  capped, ge'huld (in)
capable, be'kwaam, flink
  capable of, in staat tot ; vat- baar voor
capacious, ruim
capacity, inhoud ; ver'mogen *n* ; hoe'danigheid
cape, kaap : cape
caper, capri'olen maken
capital, hoofdstad ; kapi'taal *n* ; hoofdletter : kapi'teel *n* : prima
capitalist, kapita'list

capitulate, capitu'leren
caprice, gril
capsize, omslaan
capstan, kaapstander
captain, kapi'tein, ge'zagvoerder, aanvoerder
caption, onderschrift *n*
captivate, be'toveren
captive, ge'vangen(e)
captivity, ge'vangenschap
capture, ver'overing: ver'overen, ge'vangennemen
car, auto
caravan, woonwagen, kam'peerwagen; kara'vaan
carbolic, car'bol(zuur *n*)
carbon, koolstof; doorslag-(papier *n*)
card, kaart(je *n*)
cardboard, kar'ton *n*
cardigan, vest *n*
cardinal, kardi'naal: hoofd-
cards, kaartspel *n*
  to play cards, kaarten
care, zorg; lust hebben
  to take care of, zorgen voor; passen op
  I don't care, het kan me niets schelen
  to care about, geven om
  to care for, (iets) voelen voor
career, loopbaan, carri'ère
carefree, onbe'zorgd
careful, voor'zichtig; zorg'vuldig
careless, slordig
caress, liefkozing: liefkozen
caretaker, conci'ërge
cargo, lading, vracht
cargo-boat, vrachtschip *n*
caricature, karika'tuur
carillon, klokkenspel *n*
carnage, slachting
carnal, vleselijk
carnation, anjer
carnival, carna'val *n*
carol, (Kerst)lied *n*: kwelen
carouse, zwelgen
carp, karper: vitten
carpenter, timmerman: timmeren
carpet, ta'pijt *n*
carriage, rijtuig *n*, wa'gon; ver'voer *n*; houding

carrier, voerman; ba'gagedrager
carrion, aas
carrot, wortel
carry, dragen, houden
  to carry away, meeslepen
  to carry off, in de wacht slepen; klaarspelen
  to carry on, doorgaan; uitoefenen; zich (slecht) ge'dragen
  to carry out, uitvoeren
cart, kar: ver'voeren
cartilage, kraakbeen *n*
carton, kar'ton *n*
cartoon, (spot)prent; tekenfilm
cartridge, pa'troon
carve, snijden; beeldhouwen
carving, snijwerk *n*: voorsnij-
cascade, kleine waterval; stortvloed: neerstorten
case, koker, koffer, kist: ge'val *n*, zaak
  in case, voor het ge'val dat
casement window, openslaand raam *n*
cash, (ge'reed) geld *n*, con'tant(en): wisselen
cashier, kas'sier: cas'seren
cask, vat *n*
cassock, sou'tane
cast, worp; afgietsel *n*; rolverdeling: werpen; gieten
cast iron, ge'goten ijzer *n*
castle, kas'teel *n*
castor, rolletje *n*
casual, noncha'lant; toe'vallig; vluchtig
casualty, ongeval *n*
  casualties, doden en ge'wonden
cat, kat
catalogue, ca'talogus
catapult, katapult
cataract, waterval: staar
catastrophe, cata'strofe, ramp
catch, vangst; valstrik; haak: (op)vangen; halen; be'trappen; vatten; (blijven) haken; treffen
  to catch on, ingang vinden
  to catch up, inhalen
categorical, cate'gorisch
category, catego'rie
cater, maaltijden ver'zorgen; rekening houden (met)

caterpillar, rups
cathedral, kathe'draal
catholic, katho'liek; veel'zijdig
cattle, vee n
cauliflower, bloemkool
cause, oorzaak, (be'weeg)reden; zaak: ver'oorzaken
causeway, dam
caustic, brandend; bijtend
caution, voor'zichtigheid: waarschuwen
cautious, voor'zichtig
cavalry, cavale'rie
cave(rn), grot
  to cave in, inzakken
cavity, holte
caw, krassen
cease, ophouden (met)
ceaseless, voort'durend
cedar, ceder(hout n)
cede, afstaan
ceiling, pla'fond n; maximum n
celebrate, vieren
celebrated, ver'maard
celebration, viering, feest n
celebrity, be'roemdheid
celery, selderij
celestial, hemels, hemel-
celibacy, celi'baat n
cell, cel
cellar, kelder
cello, cel
cellophane, cello'faan n
cellulose, cellu'lose
cement, ce'ment
cemetry, be'graafplaats
censor, censor: censu'reren
censure, be'risping: bekriti'seren
census, volkstelling
centenary, eeuwfeest n
centigrade, Celsius
central, cen'traal, midden-, hoofd-
centralize, centrali'seren
centre, middelpunt n, centrum n
  in the centre of, midden in
century, eeuw
cereal, graan(pro'duct) n
ceremonial, ceremoni'eel (n)
ceremony, cere'monie, formali'teit(en)
certain(ty), zeker(heid)

certificate, di'ploma n, akte, at'test n
certify, (plechtig) ver'klaren
cessation, staken n
chafe, schuren
chaff, kaf n: voor de gek houden
chagrin, ergernis
chain, ketting; keten(en); reeks
chair, stoel
chairman(ship), voorzitter-(schap n)
chalice, kelk
chalk, krijt n
challenge, uitdaging: uitdagen, aanroepen, be'twisten
chamber, kamer
chamois, gems; zeemleer n
champ, kauwen
champion, kampi'oen; voorstander: voorstaan
chance, kans; toeval n: toe'vallig: wagen
chancel, koor n
chancellor, kanse'lier
chandelier, kroon(luchter)
change, ver'andering, overgang; kleingeld n: ver'anderen; (ver)wisselen, (ver')ruilen; (zich) ver'kleden; overstappen
  to change one's mind, zich be'denken
changeable, ver'anderlijk
change-over, overgang
channel, Ka'naal n; vaargeul, goot; weg
chant, (be')zingen; dreunen
chaos, chaos
chap, kerel: barsten
chapel, ka'pel
chaperon, chape'ron('neren)
chaplain (to the forces), (leger)-predi'kant
chapter, hoofdstuk n; ka'pittel n
char, schroeien, ver'kolen
character, ka'rakter n; type n
characteristic, kenmerk(end (voor)) (n)
characterize, kenmerken
charcoal, houtskool
charge, aanval(len); (be')last-(en); lading; be'schuldiging: laden; be'schuldigen

to be in charge of, de leiding hebben van; be'last zijn met
to (make a) charge, rekenen
charitable, mens'lievend
charity, lief'dadigheid(s-), naastenliefde
charm, charme; tovermiddel *n*; ge'lukshanger: be'koren; be'toveren
charming, char'mant; aller'aardigst
chart, kaart; grafische voorstelling: in kaart brengen
charter, charter(en) (*n*)
charwoman, werkster
chary, huiverig
chase, jacht(stoet): (na)jagen; drijven
chasm, kloof
chassis, chassis *n*
chaste, kuis
chasten, chastise, kas'tijden
chat, babbeltje *n*: babbelen
chatter, kletsen, ratelen
chatterbox, kletskous
cheap, goed'koop, waardeloos
cheat, valse speler: be'driegen, vals spelen
check, rem; ruit: stuiten; contro'leren
check(mate), schaak(mat) (zetten)
in check, in toom
to check up, nagaan
cheek, wang; brutali'teit
cheek-bone, jukbeen
cheer, juichkreet: (toe)juichen; opmonteren
three cheers, een hoe'raatje *n*; lang leve . . .
cheerful, vrolijk
cheerless, troosteloos
cheese, kaas
chemical, chemisch(e stof), schei'kundig
chemist, schei'kundige; dro'gist
chemistry, scheikunde
cheque, cheque
chequered, af'wisselend
cherish, koesteren
cherry, kers(eboom)
cherub, cheru'bijn
chess: **to play —,** schaken

chess(-set), schaakspel *n*
chest, borst(kas); kist
chestnut, kas'tanje(boom)
chew, kauwen
chick, kuiken *n*
chicken, kip
chicken-pox, waterpokken
chicory, cicho'rei; witlof
chide, be'rispen
chief, hoofd(-) (*n*); voor'naamste
chiefly, voor'namelijk
chieftain, opperhoofd
chilblain(ed feet), winter(voeten)
child(ren), kind(eren) *n*
childbirth, be'valling
childhood, kinderjaren
childish, kinderachtig, kinderlijk
childlike, kinderlijk
chill, kou: afkoelen
chill(y), kil; koel
chime, klokkenspel *n*, klokslag: luiden
chimney, schoorsteen
chin, kin
china, porse'lein(en) (*n*)
chink, spleet: rinkelen
chip, scherf; fiche: stoten, bikken
chiropodist, pedi'cure
chirp, tjilpen
chisel, beitel(en)
chit, jong ding *n*: briefje *n*
chivalrous, ridderlijk
chivalry, ridderlijkheid
chlorine, chloor *n*
chock, klos
chock-full, propvol
chocolate, choco'la(de), choco'laatje *n*
choice, keus: prima
choir, koor *n*
choke, (doen) stikken, zich ver'slikken; ver'stoppen
choose, (uit)kiezen, ver'kiezen
chop, karbo'nade; kaak: (fijn)hakken
chopper, hakbijl
choppy, woelig
choral, koor-
chord, ak'koord *n*; snaar
chortle, hardop grinniken van pret

chorus, koor *n* ; re'frein *n*
christen, dopen
Christendom, Christenheid
christening, doop(dienst)
Christian, Christen : Christelijk
  Christian name, voornaam
Christianity, Christendom *n* ;
  Christelijkheid
Christmas, Kerstmis : Kerst-
  Christmas Day, Eerste Kerstdag
chromium(-plated), (ver')-
  chroom(d) (*n*)
chronic, chronisch
chronicle, kro'niek : boekstaven
chronological, chrono'logisch
chubby, mollig
chuck, aai : smijten
chuckle, ge'grinnik *n* : grinniken
  (om)
chug, puffen
chum, maat
chunk, klomp, homp.
church, kerk
  Church of England, Angli'-
  kaanse Kerk
churchyard, kerkhof *n*
churlish, lomp
churn, karn, melkbus : karnen ;
  woelen
chute, glijbaan, glijkoker
cider, cider
cigar, si'gaar
cigarette, siga'ret
cinder, sintel
cinema, bios'coop
cinnamon, ka'neel
cipher, cijferschrift *n* ; nul
circle, cirkel(en) ; kring
circuit, kring(loop) ; (stroom)-
  baan
circuitous, om'slachtig
circular, cirkel'vormig, rond-
  (gaand) : circu'laire
circulate, (laten) circu'leren
circulation, circu'latie ; bloedsomloop ; oplaag
circumference, omtrek
circumscribe, om'schrijven
circumspect, om'zichtig
circumstance, om'standigheid,
  bij'zonderheid
circus, circus *n*

cistern, waterreservoir *n*
cite, ci'teren ; noemen
citizen, (staats)burger
city, stad(s-)
civic, burger-, stads-
civil, burgerlijk, burger- ; be'leefd
  civil servant, ambtenaar
civilian, burger
civilization, be'schaving
civilize, be'schaven
clad, ge'kleed
claim, aanspraak (maken op) ;
  vordering : (op)eisen ; be'weren
clamber, klauteren
clammy, klam
clamorous, luid('ruchtig)
clamour, ge'tier *n* : schreeuwen
clamp, klamp(en)
clan, stam
clang, galm : kletteren
clap, slag ; klap(pen (met)),
  applaudis'seren ; slaan
clarify, klaren ; ophelderen
clarity, duidelijkheid
clash, botsing : botsen ; vloeken
clasp, gesp(en) ; (vast)grijpen
class, klas(se) ; stand ; lesuur *n* :
  plaatsen
classic, klas'siek (werk *n*)
classical, klas'siek
classify, klassifi'ceren
classroom, klaslokaal *n*
clatter, ge'kletter *n* : kletteren
clause, clau'sule, bijzin
claw, klauw(en), poot
clay, klei
clean, schoon(maken), rein(igen) ;
  zindelijk
cleanliness, zindelijkheid
cleanse, zuiveren
clear, helder, duidelijk ; vrij-
  (maken) : ophelderen ; vrijspreken ; ont'ruimen
  to clear off, maken dat men
  wegkomt
  to clear up, ver'duidelijken ;
  opruimen ; ophelderen
clear-cut, scherp om'lijnd
clearing, open plek
cleavage, scheuring
cleave, kloven ; kleven
cleft, kloof : ge'spleten
clemency, mildheid

clench, ballen; vastklemmen
  clenched teeth, tanden op el'kaar
clergy, geestelijken
X**clergyman**, dominee
clerical, administra'tief; geest- elijk
clerk, klerk, grif'fier
clever, knap
click, klik(ken)
client, klant
cliff, klif
climate, kli'maat *n*
climax, climax
climb, (be')klim(men)
  to climb down, afklimmen; inbinden
clinch, vastklinken; be'klinken, be'slechten
cling, zich vastklemmen, plakken
clinic, kli'niek
clink, klink(en)
clip, klem(metje *n*); mep: klem- men; knippen
clippers, schaar, ton'deuse; klip- pers
clipping, (uit)knipsel *n*
cloak, (dek)mantel: hullen
cloak-room, garde'robe
clock, klok
clockwise, met de klok mee
clockwork, (met) mecha'niek *n*
clod, (aard)kluit
clog, klomp: ver'stoppen
cloister, klooster(gang)
close, dicht'bij; scherp; nauw; in'tiem: ingesloten ruimte; einde *n*: (af)sluiten
  to close down (*or* **up**), sluiten
close-fisted, gierig
closet, kabi'net *n*; opsluiten
clot, kluit: klonteren, stollen
cloth, stof; kleed *n*, doek
clothe, kleden
clothes, kleren
clothes-line, drooglijn
clothes-peg, knijper
clothing, kleding
cloud, wolk: ver'troebelen
X **to cloud over**, be'trekken
cloudy, be'wolkt; troebel
clout, mep (geven)
clove, kruidnagel

clover, klaver
clown, clown
club, knots; club, socië'tiet klaver: knuppelen
cluck, klokken
clue, aanwijzing, sleutel
clump, groep, brok: klossen
clumsy, on'handig
cluster, tros, bos, groep: zich scharen
clutch, klauw; koppeling: (vast)- pakken
clutter, warboel: volproppen
coach, koets, dili'gence, touring- car, spoorrijtuig *n*; trainer, repe'titor: trainen, repe'teren
coagulate, stremmen
coal, kolen(-); steenkool
coalesce, samensmelten
coalition, coa'litie
coarse, grof
coast, kust: glijden, freewheelen
coat, jas, mantel; vel *n*; (verf)- laag: be'dekken
  coat of arms, wapen *n*
coat-hanger, kleerhanger
coax, vleiend be'praten
cobble(-stone), keisteen
cobbler, schoenlapper
cobweb, spinneweb *n*
cock, haan: de haan spannen van; scheefhouden
cock-eyed, scheef
cockpit, cockpit
cocktail, cocktail
cocky, bru'taal
cocoa, ca'cao
coconut, kokosnoot
cod, kabel'jauw
code, code(stelsel *n*); wet
coercion, dwang
coffee, koffie
coffin, doodkist
cog, tandrad *n*
cogent, effec'tief
cogitate, nadenken
coherent, samenhangend, logisch
coil, tros, spi'raal: oprollen
coin, munt(stuk *n*): smeden
coincide, samenvallen
coincidence, samenloop van om- standigheden
coke, cokes

colander, ver'giet

cold, koud; koel: ver'koudheid

  to have a cold, ver'kouden zijn

collaborate, samenwerken

collapse, instorting: in el'kaar zakken

collapsible, op'vouwbaar

collar, kraag, boord, halsband

colleague, col'lega

collect, (zich) ver'zamelen

collection, ver'zameling, col'-lecte; buslichting

collector, ver'zamelaar

college, college n, (hoge')school

collide, botsen

colliery, kolenmijn

collision, botsing, aanvaring

colon, dubbel punt

colonel, kolo'nel

colonial, koloni'aal

colonize, koloni'seren

colonnade, zuilengang

colony, ko'lonie

colossal, reus'achtig

colour, kleur(en), verf

colourful, kleurrijk

colt, (hengst)veulen

column, zuil; ko'lom

coma, coma n

comb, kam(men); afzoeken

combat, strijd: be'strijden

combination, combi'natie

combine, syndi'caat n; com'bine: combi'neren

combustion, ver'branding

come, komen, meegaan

  to come about, ge'beuren

  to come across, overkomen; tegenkomen

  to come round, aanlopen; (bij)draaien; bijkomen

  to come in, binnenkomen; mode worden

  to come off, afkomen; doorgaan, lukken

comedian, ko'miek, komedi'ant

comedy, blijspel n

comely, be'vallig

comet, ko'meet

comfort, troost(en); ge'mak n, welstand

comfortable, be'hagelijk

  to be comfortable, ge'makkelijk zitten (or liggen)

comfortably off, in goede doen

comic, komisch; (kinder)krantje n

coming, (op)komend; komst

comma, komma

command, be'vel(en) (n); com'-mando n (voeren); be'schikking: be'schikken over; be'strijken

 commanding officer, com-man'dant

commandeer, (op)vorderen

commander, be'velhebber; kapi'tein-luitenant

commandment, ge'bod n

commemorate, her'denken

commence, be'ginnen

commend, prijzen; aanbevelen

commendable, prijzens'waardig

comment, opmerking(en maken)

commentary, commen'taar n

commentator, ver'slaggever

commerce, handel(sverkeer n)

commercial, handels-

commiserate, sympathi'seren

commission, opdracht (geven); (offi'ciers) aanstelling; pro'visie: machtigen: aanstellen; in dienst stellen

commissioner, ge'volmachtigde, (hoofd)commis'saris

commit, plegen, be'gaan; toevertrouwen

 to commit oneself, zich ver'binden

commitment, ver'plichting

committee, comi'té n, be'stuur n, com'missie

commodious, ruim

commodity, ge'bruiksartikel n

common, ge'meen('schappelijk), ge'woon, algemeen: meent

 common sense, ge'zond ver'-stand n

 in common, ge'meen

commonplace, alle'daags: ge'-meenplaats

commonwealth, gemene'best n

commotion, opschudding

communal, gemeen'schappelijk

communicate, ver'binding heb-

ben, zich in ver'binding stellen ;
mededelen

communication, mededeling,
schrijven *n* ; ver'binding (sweg)

communicative, mede'deelzaam

communion, ge'meenschap ;
Com'munie

communism, commu'nisme *n*

community, ge'meenschap ;
broederschap

compact, com'pact : over'eenkomst

companion, metgezel ; ge'zelschapsdame

companionable, ge'zellig

companionship, ge'zelschap *n*,
vriendschap

company, ge'zelschap *n* ; ven'-
nootschap ; compag'nie ; be'-
zoek *n*

comparable, te verge'lijken

comparative, be'trekkelijk,
verge'lijkend

compare, (te) verge'lijken (zijn)

comparison, verge'lijking

compartment, afdeling ; cou'pé

compass, kom'pas *n* ; passer ;
omtrek, be'stek *n* ; vatten

compassion, er'barmen *n*

compassionate, mee'warig

compatriot, landgenoot

compel, (af)dwingen

compensate for, schadeloos stellen voor, ver'goeden ; opwegen
tegen

compensation, ver'goeding,
compen'satie

compete, wedijveren, mededingen (naar)

competence, be'voegdheid, be'-
kwaamheid

competent, be'kwaam, be'voegd

competition, wedstrijd ; concur'rentie

competitive, verge'lijkend

competitor, deelnemer, concur'rent

compile, samenstellen

complacent, gauw te'vreden

complain, klagen

complaint, (aan)klacht ; kwaal

complement, aanvuling ; be'-
manning

complete, vol'ledig, vol'tallig,
vol'slagen ; vol'tooien ; be'-
sluiten, aanvullen

complex, com'plex (*n*)

complexion, ge'laatskleur

compliance, inwilliging

complicate, compli'ceren

complicated, inge'wikkeld

complication, compli'catie

complicity, mede'plichtigheid

compliment, compli'ment ('eren)
(*n*)

complimentary, complimen'-
teus ; pre'sent-, vrij-

comply with, vol'doen aan

component, be'standdeel *n* :
samenstellend

compose, samenstellen, compo'neren

to be composed of, be'staan uit

to compose oneself, be'daren

composer, compo'nist

composite, samengesteld

composition, samenstelling; compo'sitie ; opstel *n*

composure, zelfbeheersing

compound, samengesteld :
samenstelling, ver'binding : erf
n : (ver')mengen

comprehend, (om')vatten

comprehension, be'grip *n*

comprehensive, veelom'vattend

compress, kom'pres *n* : samen-
persen, compri'meren

comprise, be'vatten

compromise, compro'mis *n* : tot
een schikking komen ; compromit'teren

compulsion, dwang

compulsory, ver'plicht

compunction, scru'pules

compute, be'rekenen

comrade, kame'raad

concave, hol

conceal, ver'bergen

concede, toegeven, toestaan

conceit, ver'waandheid ; spits'-
vondigheid

conceited, ver'waand

conceivable, denkbaar

conceive, zich een voorstelling
maken van ; be'vrucht worden

concentrate, (zich) concen'treren

concentric, con'centrisch
concept, be'grip n
conception, voorstelling, opvatting; be'vruchting
concern, zaak, be'lang n; be'-
zorgdheid; onder'neming:
aangaan
to be concerned, be'lang hebben bij; be'trokken zijn bij;
zich bezighouden met; be'zorgd
zijn over
as far as I'm concerned, wat
mij be'treft
concerning, be'treffende
concert(o), con'cert n
concerted, ge'zamenlijk
concession, con'cessie
conciliate, gunstig stemmen
concise, be'knopt
conclude, (be')sluiten; opmaken
conclusion, be'sluit n, slot n;
ge'volgtrekking
conclusive, afdoend
concoct, brouwen; ver'zinnen
concord, eendracht
concrete, be'ton(nen) (n);
con'creet
concubine, bijzit
concur, het eens zijn; bijdragen
concurrence, instemming;
samenwerking
concurrent, gelijk'tijdig
concussion, (hersen)schudding
condemn, ver'oordelen, afkeuren
condensation, conden'satie
condense, conden'seren; samenvatten
condescend, zich ver'waardigen
condescending, neer'buigend
condition, voorwaarde; con'-
ditie, staat, toestand
(weather) conditions, (weers)-
om'standigheden
condolence, deelneming
condone, ver'goelijken
conducive, be'vorderlijk
conduct, ge'drag(en) (n); be'-
handeling: (ge')leiden; diri'-
geren
conductor, (ge')leider; diri'gent;
conduc'teur
cone, kegel; (denne)appel
confectionery, suikergoed n

confederate, mede'plichtige:
ver'bonden
confederation, ver'bond n
confer, ver'lenen(aan); be'raadslagen
conference, confe'rentie
confess, be'kennen; be'lijden;
biechten
confession, be'kentenis; biecht
confidant(e), ver'trouweling(e)
confide in, in ver'trouwen nemen
confide to, toevertrouwen
confidence, ver'trouwen n
confident, vol ('zelf)ver'trouwen;
over'tuigd
confidential, ver'trouwelijk
confine, grens: be'perken
to be confined to one's bed or
barracks, het bed moeten
houden; kwar'tier-arrest
hebben
confinement, be'valling; ge'-
vangenschap
confirm, be'vestigen; be'krachtigen; vormen
confirmed, vaststaand; chronisch, ver'stokt
confiscate, ver'beurd ver'klaren
conflagration, vlammenzee
conflict, con'flict n: in strijd zijn
conflicting, (tegen')strijdig
conform, zich schikken (naar);
over'eenkomen
confound, in de war brengen;
ver'vloeken
confront, contron'teren
to be confronted by, komen te
staan tegen'over; zich ge'plaatst
zien in
confuse, ver'warren
confusion, ver'warring
confute, weer'leggen
congeal, stollen
congenial, prettig, sympa'thiek
congenital, (aan)ge'boren
congest, (zich) ophopen
conglomeration, conglome'raat
n
congratulate, ge'lukwensen
congratulation, ge'lukwens
congregate, (zich) ver'zamelen
congregation, ge'meente; ver'-
zameling

congress, con'gres *n*
conical, kegelvormig
coniferous, kegeldragend
conjecture, gissing
conjugate, ver'voegen
conjunction, voegwoord *n*
 in conjunction with, samen met
conjure, goochelen : be'zweren
 to conjure up, oproepen
conjurer, goochelaar
connect, (aan el'kaar) ver'binden; in ver'band brengen;
 aansluiten (op)
connexion, ver'binding; ver'band
 n; re'latie
connive at, door de vingers
 zien; — (**with**), in ge'heime
 ver'standhouding staan (met)
connoisseur, fijnproever, kenner
connote, (tege'lijk) be'tekenen
conquer, ver'overen, over'winnen; meester worden
conscience, ge'weten *n*
conscience-smitten ge'kweld
conscientious, plichtsgetrouw
conscious, (zich) be'wust; bij
 kennis
consciousness, be'wustzijn *n*
conscript, dienst'plichtig(e) :
 oproepen, vorderen
conscription, con'scriptie
consecrate, (in)wijden
consecutive, op'eenvolgend,
 samenhangend
consent, toestemming, instemming; toe(*or* in)stemmen
consequence, ge'volg *n*
 in consequence, dientenge'-
 volge
 of consequence, be'langrijk
consequent, daaruit voortvloei-
 end
consequently, dientenge'volge
conservation, in'standhouding,
 be'houd *n*
conservative, conserva'tief
conservatory, serre
conserve, op peil houden; conser'veren
consider, over'wegen; be'-
 schouwen als, in aanmerking
 nemen, rekening houden met;
 menen

all things considered, alles
 welbe'schouwd
considerable, aan'zienlijk
considerate, at'tent
consideration, over'weging; factor; conside'ratie; ver'goeding
considered, welover'wogen;
 ge'acht
considering, ge'zien; (alles)
 welbe'schouwd
consign, depo'neren; overleveren, toevertrouwen
consignment, zending
consist of, be'staan uit
consistency, consis'tentie
consistent, conse'quent; op één
 lijn met
consolation, troost
consolidate, ver'sterken; con-
 soli'deren
consonant, medeklinker
consort, ge'maal : omgaan
conspicuous, in het oog lopend;
 treffend
conspiracy, samenzwering
conspirator, samenzweerder
conspire, samenzweren; samenwerken
constable, po'litieagent; slot-
 voogd
constancy, stand'vastigheid;
 trouw
constant, vast; voort'durend;
 trouw : con'stante
constellation, sterrenbeeld *n*
consternation, ont'steltenis
constipation, consti'patie
constituency, kiesdistrict *n*
constituent, be'standdeel *n*;
 kiezer
constitute, vormen; aanstellen
constitution, ge'stel *n*;
 samenstelling; grondwet
constitutional, aangeboren, voor
 het ge'stel; constitutio'neel
constrain, be'dwingen
constraint, (be')dwang; ge'-
 dwongenheid
constrict, be'klemmen; binden;
 samentrekken
construct, (op)bouwen
construction, (aan)bouw, con'-
 structie; uitleg

constructive, opbouwend
construe, ver'klaren; con-stru'eren
consul(ate), consul('aat *n*)
consult, raadplegen
consultation, raadpleging, con'sult *n*; be'raadslaging
consume, ver'bruiken, ver'orber-en; ver'teren, ver'nietigen
consummate, vol'maakt: in-ver'vulling doen gaan
consumption, ver'bruik *n*, con'sumptie; tering
contact, con'tact *n*; zich in ver'binding stellen met
contagious, be'smettelijk; aan'stekelijk
contain, be'vatten; inhouden
container, blik *n*, doos
contaminate, veront'reinigen
contemplate, (over')peinzen; be'schouwen; van plan zijn
contemplation, ge'peins *n*, over'weging; be'spiegeling
contemporary, van de'zelfde tijd, hedendaags: tijdgenoot
contempt, ver'achting
contemptible, ver'achtelijk
contemptuous, minachtend
contend, be'togen
  to contend with, kampen met, aankunnen
content(s), inhoud; ge'halte *n*
content(ed), te'vreden
contention, twist; be'wering
contentment, te'vredenheid
contest, (wed)strijd: be'twisten
contestant, mededinger, deel-nemer
context, ver'band *n*
continent, vaste'land *n*, wereld-deel *n*
continental, continen'taal
contingency, eventuali'teit
contingent, af'hankelijk, even-tu'eel: contin'gent *n*; situ'atie
continual(ly), voort'durend, her'haald(elijk)
continuance, voortzetting
continuation, voortzetting, ver'volg *n*
continue, voortgaan (met); voortzetten

continuity, samenhang; con-tinuï'teit
continuous, on'afgebroken, door'lopend
contort, (ver')draaien
contour, con'tour
contraband, contrabande
contract, con'tract *n* (aangaan); (zich) samentrekken; aannemen, oplopen
contraction, inkrimping, samen-trekking
contractor, aannemer
contradict, tegenspreken, ont'kennen
contradiction, tegenspraak, tegen'strijdigheid
contradictory, (tegen')strijdig, weer'spannig
contralto, alt
contraption, uitvindsel *n*, meka'niek(je *n*)
contrary, tegengesteld(e *n*), tegen-; ba'lorig
  contrary to, tegen . . . in
  on the contrary, in'tegendeel
contrast, tegenstelling: tegen-over al'kaar stellen, een con'trast *n* vormen
contravene, in strijd zijn met
contribute, bijdragen
contribution, bijdrage
contributory, secun'dair, zij-
contrition, diep be'rouw *n*
contrivance, uitvinding
contrive, be'ramen; ervoor zor-gen
control, be'heer(sing) (*n*); con'trole; stuurinrichting: in be'dwang houden, be'heersen, be'heren, regelen
controversial, be'twistbaar, strijd-
controversy, ge'schil *n*
convalescence, her'stel *n*
convene, bij'eenroepen, bij'een-komen
convenience, ge'rief(elijkheid) (*n*), ge'mak *n*
convenient, ge'schikt, ge'rie-felijk
convent, nonnenklooster *n*; zusterschool

convention, con'ventie; samenkomst; over'eenkomst

conventional, conventio'neel

converge, conver'geren; zich
concen'treren

conversant, ver'trouwd

conversation, ge'sprek n

converse, omgekeerd(e n):
conver'seren

conversion, omzetting; be'-
kering

convert, be'keerling: omzetten,
ver'anderen; be'keren

convex, bol

convey, ver'voeren, overdragen;
betekenen, overbrengen

conveyance, ver'voer(middel) n;
overdracht; overbrengen n

convict, dwangarbeider:
schuldig ver'klaren

conviction, over'tuiging:
schuldigverklaring

convince, over'tuigen

convivial, feestelijk

convoy, kon'vooi('eren) (n)

convulse, (doen) schudden;
samentrekken; stuiptrekken

coo, kirren (n)

cook, kok('kin): koken; knoeien
met

cooker, for'nuis n

cookery, koken n; kook-

cooking, koken n, keuken:
moes(appel), stoof(peer)

cool, koel(te); kalm; bru'taal:
ver'koelen, afkoelen

coop, hok: opsluiten

co-operate, samenwerken

co-operative, be'hulpzaam;
coöpera'tief

co-ordinate, coördi'neren

cope, koorkap: klaarspelen
   to cope (with it), het aankunnen

copious, ruim

copper, (rood)koper(en) (n);
kopergeld n; wasketel:
smeris

copse, kreupelbosje n

copy, ko'pie; exem'plaar n:
namaken, nadoen
   to copy out, overschrijven

copyright, ko'pijrecht n

coquetry, kokette'rie

coral, ko'raal: ko'ralen

cord, koord n

cordial, hartelijk: sap n, drank

corduroy, ribfluweel n

core, klokhuis n; kern

cork, kurk(en)

corkscrew, kurketrekker

corn, koren n: likdoorn

corner, hoek: in het nauw
drijven

cornflour, mai'zena

coronation, kroning

coroner, magi'straat bij een
lijkschouwing

coronet, kroontje n

corporal, korpo'raal: lijf-

corporate, met rechtspersoon-
lijkheid; ge'zamenlijk

corporation, rechtspersoon, cor-
po'ratie; buikje n

corps, korps n

corpse, lijk n

corpulent, zwaar'lijvig

correct, juist, goed, cor'rect:
corri'geren

correction, cor'rectie

corrective, ver'beterend; cor-
rec'tief n

correspond, over'eenkomen;
correspon'deren

correspondence, correspon'dentie; over'eenkomst

correspondent, correspon'dent

corresponding, overeen'komstig

corridor, gang

corroborate, be'vestigen

corrode, aantasten, ver'roesten

corrosion, cor'rosie

corrugated, golf-

corrupt, cor'rupt, ver'dorven:
be'derven

corruption, cor'ruptie, ver'derf n

corset(s), kor'set n

cosh, ploertendoder

cosmetic, kos'metisch: schoonheidsmiddel n

cosmopolitan, kosmopo'litisch

cost, prijs, kosten

costermonger, venter

costly, duur, kostbaar

costume, kos'tuum n, klederdracht

cosy, knus: muts

cot, kinderbedje n
cottage, huisje n
cotton, ka'toen(en) (n), garen n: snappen
cotton-wool, watten
couch, rustbank: stellen
cough, hoest(en)
council, raad
counsel, raad(geven), be'raadslaging; advo'caat
count, tel(ling): graaf: (mee)tellen; rekenen
  to count out, uittellen; uitschakelen
countenance, ge'laat(suitdrukking) (n): sanctio'neren
counter, toonbank, balie, lo'ket n; fiche, teller: tegen ... in: be'antwoorden
counter-, tegen-
counteract, neutrali'seren, tegenwerken
counterbalance, tegenwicht; opwegen tegen
counterfeit, nagemaakt: namaken
counterfoil, strook
countermand, annu'leren
counterpart, tegenhanger
countersign, medcondertekenen
countess, gra'vin
countless, talloos
country, (platte')land n, streek: landelijk
  in the country, buiten
countryman, landgenoot; buitenman
countryside, landschap n
county, graafschap n
couple, paar n, stel n: koppelen; combi'neren
coupon, bon, cou'pon
courage(ous), moed(ig)
courier, koe'rier
course, (be')loop (n), koers, richting; gang; renbaan; cursus; ge'dragslijn
  in due course, te zijner tijd
  in the course of, in de loop van
  of course, na'tuurlijk
court, hof(houding) (n), (binnen)plaats; rechtbank, rechtszaal; baan: het hof maken; zoeken

courteous, hoffelijk
courtesy, hoffelijkheid; gunst
courtier, hoveling
court-martial, (voor de) krijgsraad (brengen)
courtyard, binnenplaats
cousin, neef, nicht
cove, inham: vent
covenant, ver'bond n; con'tract n
cover, deksel n; (buiten)band; dekking: (be')dekken; ver'bergen; afleggen; onder vuur hebben; ver'slaan
covert, heimelijk: schuilplaats
covet, be'geren
cow, koe: intimi'deren
coward, lafaard
cowardice, lafheid
cower, in'eenkrimpen
cowhide, rundleer n
cowl, monnikskap; schoorsteenkap
cowslip, sleutelbloem
coxswain, stuurman
coy, schuchter
crab, krab
crack, barst(en), kier; klap(pen); krieken n: prima: kraken; tappen (jokes); overslaan
  to crack up, be'zwijken, ophemelen
cracker, knalbonbon, voetzoeker; cracker
crackle, knappen, kraken
cradle, wieg; bakermat
craft, ambacht n, kunst'vaardigheid; sluwheid; vaartuig(en) n
craftsman(ship), vakman(schap n)
crafty, listig, sluw
crag, steile rots(punt n)
cram, (vol)proppen, schrokken; (in)pompen
cramp, kram(p): opsluiten, be'krimpen; be'lemmeren
crane, kraan(vogel): uitrekken
crank, slinger; zonderling: aanslingeren
crash, klap, slag; botsing, neerstorting: in('een)storten, neerstorten; over de kop gaan
crass, grof

crate, krat
crater, krater
cravat, cra'vate
crave, hunkeren; smeken
craving, be'geerte
crawl, slakkengang: kruipen; wemelen
crayon, kleurpotlood *n*; kleuren
craze, rage
crazy, gek; fanta'sie-
creak, kraken
cream, (slag)room, crème; puik *n*: afromen
creamy, roomachtig
crease, vouw(en); kreuken
create, scheppen; te'weegbrengen
creation, schepping; cre'atie
creative, scheppend
creature, schepsel *n*
credentials, ge'loofs(*or* intro'ductie)brieven
credible, geloof'waardig
credit, kre'diet *n*, te'goed *n*, batig saldo *n*; ge'loof *n*, eer: credi'teren; ge'loven; toeschrijven
creditor, schuldeiser
credulous, lichtge'lovig
creed, ge'loofsbelijdenis
creek, kreek
creep, kruipen, sluipen
creeper, klimplant
cremate, ver'assen
creosote, creo'soot
crepe, crêpe
crescent, wassende maan; ge'bogen straat
cress, sterre'kers
crest, kuif, pluim; helmteken *n*; top
crestfallen, ter'neergeslagen
crevasse, gletscherspleet
crevice, scheur
crew, be'manning, ploeg; troep
crib, kribbe; spiekbriefje *n*: spieken
crick, kramp
cricket, cricket *n*: krekel
crime, misdaad, misdrijf *n*
criminal, mis'dadig, straf-: misdadiger
crimson, karmo'zijn(rood) (*n*)
cringe, in'eenkrimpen, kruipen

crinkle, kronkel(en)
crinoline, crino'line
cripple, ge'brekkige: ver'minken; ont'wrichten, ver'lammen
crisis, crisis
crisp, bros; scherp
criss-cross, kriskr̄as
criterion, maatstaf
critic, criticus
critical, kritisch; kri'tiek
criticism, kri'tiek
criticize, (be)kriti'seren
croak, ge'kwaak *n*: kwaken, krassen
crochet, haken
crock, aarden pot; wrak *n*
crockery, ser'viesgoed *n*
crocodile, kroko'dil
crocus, krokus
crony, boezemvriend(in)
crook, staf; oplichter: krommen
crooked, scheef, krom; vals
croon, neuriën; croonen
crop, oogst, ge'was *n*; krop; zweep: afvreten; kortknippen
croquet, croquet *n*
croquette, cro'quet
cross, kruis(ing) (*n*): dwars-; boos: (el'kaar) kruisen; tegenwerken
to cross oneself, een kruis slaan
to cross out, doorhalen
to cross (over), oversteken
it crossed my mind, het schoot me door het hoofd
cross-country, dwars door het land
cross-examination, kruisverhoor *n*
cross-eyed, scheel
crossing, kruispunt *n*; overtocht; oversteekplaats
cross-purposes: at —, langs el'kaar heen
cross-roads, kruispunt *n*; tweesprong
cross-section, (dwars)doorsnee
crosswise, kruiselings
crochet, kwartnoot
crouch, in el'kaar duiken
croup, kroep
crow, kraai(en)
crowbar, koevoet

rowd, menigte, stel *n* : (zich) (ver')dringen

rowded, vol, druk

rown, kroon, krans ; kruin, bol : kronen (tot) ; be'kronen

rucial, kri'tiek

rucible, smeltkroes

rucifix, kruisbeeld *n*

rucifixion, kruisiging

rucify, kruisigen

rude, ruw ; grof

ruel(ty), wreed(heid)

ruet, peper-en-'zoutstel *n*

ruise, (zee)reis: kruisen

ruiser, kruiser

rumb, kruimel(en)

rumble, (ver')kruimelen ; af- brokkelen

rumple, ver'frommelen

runch, (fijn)kauwen, knarsen

rusade, kruistocht ; cam'pagne

rush, ge'drang *n* : (samen)- persen, ver'brijzelen ; ver'plet- teren

rust, (met een) korst (be'dek- ken)

rutch, kruk ; kruis *n* ; vork

crux, kern

cry, kreet, leus: huilen ; schreeuwen, roepen

crying, ge'huil *n* : schreeuwend

crypt, crypt

cryptic, ge'heim('zinnig)

crystal, kris'tal(len) (*n*)

crystallize, kristalli'seren

cub, welp, jong *n* ; vlegel

cube, kubus, blokje *n* ; der- de'macht

cubic, kubusvormig ; ku'biek, inhouds- ; derde'machts-

cuckoo, koekoek ; sul : stapel

cucumber, kom'kommer

cud : to chew the —, her'kauwen

cuddle, pakkerd ; knuffelen

cudgel, knuppel(en)

cue, vingerwijzing, wachtwoord *n* : keu

cuff, man'chet: oorveeg (geven)

cuff-link, man'chetknoop

cul-de-sac, doodlopende weg

culinary, keuken-, kook-

cull, plukken ; uitzoeken

culminate, culmi'neren

culpable, be'rispelijk

culprit, schuldige

cult, cultus

cultivate, be (*or* ver)'bouwen ; aankweken, ont'wikkelen

cultural, cultu'reel

culture, cul'tuur, be'schaving ; aankweking ; teelt

cultured, be'schaafd ; ge'kweekt

cumbersome, on'handelbaar

cumulative, cumula'tief

cunning, listig(heid)

cup, kopje *n* ; kelk : hol maken

cupboard, kast

cupid, cupido(otje *n*)

cur, (straat)hond

curate, hulppredikant

curb, trot'toirband, rand : be'- teugelen

curds, wrongel

curdle, schiften

cure, ge'nezing, ge'neesmiddel *n*, kuur : ge'nezen ; zouten en roken

curfew, avondklok ; spertijd

curio, curiosi'teit

curiosity, nieuws'gierigheid ; curiosi'teit

curious, nieuws'gierig ; vreemd, curi'eus

curl, krul(len)

currant, krent, bes

currency, be'taalmiddel *n* ; ruchtbaarheid

current, stroom ; stroming : cou'rant, actu'eel ; in omloop, heersend

curriculum, leerplan *n*

curry, kerrie(schotel) : met kerrie kruiden

curse, ver'vloeking, vloek(en), ver'vloeken

cursory, vluchtig

curt, bruusk, kort'af

curtail, ver'korten ; be'knotten

curtain, gor'dijn *n*, doek *n*

curtsy, révé'rence (maken)

curve, bocht, kromming, rond- ing : (zich) buigen

cushion, kussen ; bil'jartband

custard, custard

custody, zorg, be'waring ; hech- tenis

custom, ge'woonte, (oud) ge'bruik *n*; klan'dizie
customs, dou'ane(rechten)
customary, ge'bruikelijk
customer, klant
cut, snee, knip; ver'mindering; snit: (door)snijden, (af)-knippen; slijpen; graven; banen; (door')klieven; ver'minderen; cou'peren; ne'geren; ver'zuimen; maaien
to take a short cut, afsnijden
to cut across, oversteken
to cut down, vellen; ver'minderen
to cut in, snijden; in de rede vallen
to cut off, afsnijden; afsluiten, iso'leren; ver'breken
to cut out, (uit)knippen, ver'wijderen; afslaan; schrappen, uitscheiden met
to cut up, kleinsnijden, ver'snipperen; erg aangrijpen; opspelen
cuticle, nagelriem
cutlery, be'stek *n*, zilver *n*
cutlet, kote'let
cutting, scherp; holle weg; uitknipsel *n*; stek
cycle, kringloop, cyclus: fietsen
cyclist, fietser
cyclone, cy'cloon
cygnet, jonge zwaan
cylinder, ci'linder
cymbal, cim'baal
cynic, cynicus
cynical, cynisch
cypress, ci'pres
cyst, cyste
Czech, Tsjech(isch (*n*))

D

dab, tik, likje *n*; schar: kei: betten, aantippen
dabble, ploeteren; liefhebberen
dachshund, taks
dad(dy), pappie, vader
daffodil, gele nar'cis
daft, dwaas
dagger, dolk

daily, dagelijks, dag-
dainty, sierlijk, fijn, tenger kies'keurig: lekker'nij
dairy, melkinrichting, melke'rij: melk-, zuivel-
daisy, made'liefje *n*, mar'griet
dale, dal *n*
dally, talmen; spelen
dam, dam; moer: afdammen
damage, schade(n); be'schadigen
damages, schadevergoeding
damask, da'mast(en) *n*
dame, vrouwe, moedertje *n*
damn, donder: ver'domme (ver')doemen
damnable, ver'vloekt
damp, vochtig(heid); gas *n*: be'vochtigen; doen dempen be'koelen
damsel, jonge dame
damson, da'mastpruim
dance, dans(partij), bal *n*: dansen
dandelion, paardebloem
dandle, spelen met
dandruff, roos
dandy, fat: reuze
danger(ous), ge'vaar(lijk) (*n*)
dangle, bengelen
Danish, Deens (*n*)
dank, muf en vochtig
dapper, kwiek
dappled, ge'vlekt
dare, (aan)durven; tarten
daring, durf: ge'durfd
dark, donker (*n*); duister (*n*)
darken, donker maken (or worden)
darkness, donker *n*
darling, lieveling; liefste
darn, stop(pen): ver'dikkeme!
dart, pijl(tje *n*): schieten
dash, streepje *n*; scheutje *n*, snuifje *n*; run; zwier: jakkes! slaan; hollen; ver'nietigen
dastardly, laf'hartig
data, ge'gevens
date, datum, jaartal *n*; afspraak: dadel(palm): da'teren, ver'ouderen
out of date, uit de tijd: ver'lopen
to date, tot op heden

up to date, tot dusver; op de hoogte: mo'dern

daub, (be')smeren; kladschilderen

daughter, dochter

daughter-in-law, schoondochter

daunt, afschrikken

dauntless, onver'vaard

davit, davit

dawdle, treuzelen

dawn, dageraad: aanbreken; doordringen tot

day, dag; tijd
 all day, de hele dag

daybreak, het aanbreken van de dag

daydream, mijmeren, dromen

daylight, daglicht *n*

daytime: in the —, over'dag

daze, ver'bijstering: ver'doven, ver'bijsteren

dazzle, ver'blinden

deacon, kape'laan, hulppredikant

deaconess, diaco'nes

dead, dood(s), levenloos, ge'voelloos; abso'luut; pal: dode(n); holst *n*
 dead beat, doodop

deaden, dempen, ver'doven

dead-lock, im'passe

deadly, dodelijk; dood(s)-, ver'schrikkelijk

deaf (and dumb), doof('stom)

deafen, ver'doven

deafening, oorver'dovend

deal, trans'actie, be'handeling: vurehout *n*: handelen; geven; toebrengen
 a good (*or* great) deal, nogal (*or* heel) veel
 to deal out, uitdelen
 to deal with, te doen hebben met, be'handelen, helpen; afrekenen met

dealer, handelaar; gever

dealings, zaken, omgang

dean, deken

dear, lief, dierbaar; duur; ach!
 Dear Sir, Mijne Heren, Zeer geachte Heer
 Dear Mr X, Geachte Heer X
 Dear John, Beste Jan

dearly, dolgraag, innig; duur

dearth, schaarste, ge'brek *n*

death, dood; sterfgeval *n*
 to (bleed) to death, dood(bloeden)

death-duties, suc'cessierechten

debar, uitsluiten, be'letten

debase, ver'lagen; ver'nederen

debatable, be'twistbaar

debate, de'bat('teren (over)) (*n*); be'twisten

debauched, liederlijk

debauchery, los'bandigheid

debility, ge'brek *n*

debit, debet(saldo) *n*: debi'teren

débris, puin *n*, rommel

debt(or), schuld(enaar)
 to be in debt, schuld(en) hebben

début, de'buut *n*

decade, de'cennium *n*

decadence, deca'dentie

decamp, opbreken; zijn biezen pakken

decant, overgieten

decanter, ka'raf

decapitate, ont'hoofden

decay, ver'rotting: (in) ver'val (raken) (*n*); (doen) ver'rotten

decease, over'lijden (*n*)

deceased, over'leden (e)

deceit, be'drog *n*

deceitful, vals

deceive, be'driegen

decency, fat'soen *n*

decennial, tienjaarlijks

decent, net(jes), aardig; be'hoorlijk

deception, be'drog *n*

deceptive, be'drieglijk

decide, (doen) be'sluiten; be'slissen

decided, be'slist; vastbesloten

deciduous tree, loofboom

decimal, tien'tallig, tien'delig

decipher, ont'cijferen

decision, be'slissing, be'sluit *n*; be'slistheid

decisive, be'slissend; be'slist

deck, dek *n*: tooien

deck-chair, ligstoel

declaim, decla'meren

declaration, ver'klaring; aangifte

declare, ver'klaren, be'kendma- ken; aangeven

decline, daling, achter'uitgang: be'danken (voor); afdalen, achter'uitgaan; ver'buigen

decompose, ont'binden

decorate, ver'sieren; schilderen (en be'hangen); deco'reren

decoration, ver'siering; deco'- ratie

decorative, decora'tief

decorous, wel'voeglijk

decorum, de'corum *n*

decoy, lok(aas *n*): in de val lokken

decrease, afname: ver'minderen

decree, de'creet *n*: decre'teren

decrepit, af'tands

decry, afkeuren, in diskrediet brengen

dedicate, wijden; opdragen

dedication, (toe)wijding; op- dracht

deduce, afleiden

deduct, aftrekken

deduction, aftrek, korting; ge'volgtrekking

deed, daad, akte

deem, achten

deep, diep

deepen, dieper worden (*or* maken)

deer, hert(en) *n*

deface, ont'sieren

defamatory, lasterlijk

defame, be'lasteren

default, ver'zuim *n*; in ge'breke blijven

defeat, nederlaag: ver'slaan; ver'ijdelen

defeatist, defai'tist

defect, ge'brek *n*

defection, af'valligheid

defective, ge'brekkig, de'fect

defence, ver'dediging

defenceless, weerloos

defend, ver'dedigen

defendant, ge'daagde

defensive, ver'dedigend

defer, uitstellen; zich onder- werpen aan

deference, eerbied

defiance, tarting

in defiance of . . ., . . . ten spijt

defiant, uit'dagend

deficiency, te'kort *n*

deficient, ontoe'reikend

deficit, te'kort *n*

defile, bergengte: defi'leren; be'vuilen, be'zoedelen

define, defini'eren

definite, be'paald, defini'tief, vast

definition, om'schrijving; scherpte

deflate, laten leeglopen; de'flatie tot stand brengen van

deflect, ombuigen

deform, mis'vormen

deformed, mis'maakt

defraud, valselijk be'roven

defray, be'strijden

deft, vaardig

defunct, over'leden; ver'ouderd

defy, trot'seren

degenerate, ont'aard(en)

degradation, degra'datie

degrade, degra'deren; ver'- nederen

degree, graad, mate, rang

dehydrate, drogen

deify, ver'goddelijken

deign, zich ver'waardigen

deity, godheid

dejected, neer'slachtig

delay, ver'traging, uitstel(len) (*n*); ver'tragen

delectable, ge'notvol

delegate, afgevaardigde: afvaardigen, overdragen

delegation, dele'gatie

delete, doorhalen

deliberate, op'zettelijk, wel- overwogen, be'dachtzaam: over'wegen, be'raadslagen

delicacy, fijnheid; hachelijkheid; zwak ge'stel *n*; delica'tesse

delicate, fijn(ge'voelig); teer

delicious, heerlijk

delight, ge'not *n*, ver'rukking: ver'rukken, ge'noegen be'zorgen

delightful, ver'rukkelijk, enig

delineation, tekening, omtrek

delinquent, schuldig(e)

delirious, aan het ijlen; waan'zinnig

deliver, be'zorgen, overleveren; geven; ver'lossen

delivery, be'zorging, over'handig-
ing; voordracht; ver'lossing
dell, (nauw) dichtbegroeid dal *n*
delude, mis'leiden, be'goochelen
deluge, wolkbreuk, (stort)vloed:
over'stromen, over'stelpen
delusion, be'drog *n*, waan
de luxe, luxe
delve, delven; vorsen
demagogue, dema'goog
demand, vraag, aanspraak: eisen,
vragen
demarcation, afbakening
demeanour, optreden *n*
demented, waan'zinnig
demigod, halfgod
demise, over'lijden *n*; overdracht
demobilize, demobili'seren
democracy, democra'tie
democratic, demo'cratisch
demolish, afbreken
demolition, afbraak
demon, boze geest, duivel
demonic, de'monisch
demonstrate, demon'streren,
aantonen
demonstration, demon'stratie,
be'wijs *n*, ver'toon *n*
demonstrative, demonstra'tief;
aan'wijzend
demoralize, demorali'seren
demur, pro'test('eren) (*n*)
demure, zedig; preuts
den, hol *n*; hok *n*
denial, ont'kenning, ver'loochening
Denmark, Denemarken *n*
denomination, be'naming;
ge'loofsrichting
denote, duiden op, aanduiden
denouement, ont'knoping
denounce, openlijk ver'oordelen,
aanbrengen
dense, dicht; dom
density, dichtheid; domheid
dent, (in)deuk(en)
dental, tand . . .
dentist, tandarts
dentures, kunstgebit *n*
denude, ont'doen van
deny, ont'kennen; ver'loochenen;
ont'houden

depart, ver'trekken
departed, over'ledene (*n*)
department, afdeling
departure, ver'trek *n*; afwijking
depend on, af'hankelijk zijn van,
ver'trouwen op, afhangen van
dependable, be'trouwbaar
dependant, af'hankelijk persoon
dependent, af'hankelijk
depict, afbeelden
deplete, ver'minderen, uitputten
deplorable, betreurens'waardig
deplore, be'treuren
deploy, ont'plooien
depopulate, ont'volken
deport, depor'teren; ge'dragen
deportment, optreden *n*
depose, afzetten
deposit, be'zinksel *n*, laag; stort-
ing, waarborgsom: achterlaten;
depo'neren
depot, de'pot *n*
depraved, ont'aard
depravity, ver'dorvenheid
deprecate, (ernstig) afkeuren
depreciate, in waarde (doen)
dalen; onder'schatten
depreciation, waardeverminder-
ing; ge'ringschatting
depredation, plundering
depress, neerdrukken; depri'meren
depression, daling, uitholling;
ma'laise; neer'slachtigheid
deprive of, ont'nemen
depth, diepte, hoogte
deputation, afvaardiging
deputize, waarnemen
deputy, afgevaardigde; plaatsvervanger: plaatsvervangend
derail, (doen) derai'lleren
derange, in de war brengen
derelict, ver'laten (schip *n*);
ver'vallen
deride, honend uitlachen
derision, be'spotting
derisive, spottend
derive, afleiden; ont'lenen,
ver'krijgen
derogatory, ge'ringschattend
derrick, laadboom; boortoren

descant, dis'cant

descend, afdalen; overgaan (op)

descendant, afstammeling

descent, (af)daling; afstamming

describe, be'schrijven

description, be'schrijving, signale'ment *n*; soort

descriptive, be'schrijvend

descry, be'speuren

desecrate, ont'wijden

desert, woes'tijn: ver'diende loon *n*: ver'laten; deser'teren

deserter, deser'teur, af'vallige

deserve, ver'dienen

deservedly,. te'recht

deserving, waardevol, ver'dienstelijk

design, ont'werp(en) (*n*), des'-sin *n*; oogmerk *n*, opzet

designate, be'noemd: aan-duiden; (be')noemen

designer, ont'werper

desirable, wenselijk

desire, ver'langen (*n*), be'geerte: be'geren

desist, ophouden (met)

desk, bu'reau *n*, lessenaar; kas

desolate, ver'laten, triest: ver'woesten

desolation, woeste'nij; trooste-loosheid; ver'woesting

despair, wanhoop: wanhopen

desperado, woesteling

desperate, tot het uiterste ge'dre-ven, wanhopig, schreeuwend

desperation, de moed der wan-hoop, ver'twijfeling

despicable, ver'achtelijk

despise, ver'achten, ver'smaden

despite, on'danks

despoil, plunderen

despondent, moedeloos

despot, des'poot

despotism, despo'tisme *n*

dessert, des'sert *n*

destination, (plaats van) be'-stemming

destine, be'stemmen

he was destined never to re-turn, het lot wilde, dat hij nooit te'rug zou komen

destiny, (nood)lot *n*; be'stem-ming

destitute, be'hoeftig, be'rooid

destroy, ver'nietigen, ver'nielen

destroyer, tor'pedojager

destruction, ver'nietiging, ver'-woesting; ver'derf *n*

destructive, ver'nielziek, schade-lijk; afbrekend

desultory, te hooi en te gras

detach, scheiden, losmaken; de-ta'cheren

detached, los(geraakt), vrij-staand; onbe'vangen

detachment, detache'ment *n*: losmaken *n*; onbe'vangenheid

detail, de'tail *n*; deta'chering: deta'cheren

detailed, uit'voerig

detain, ophouden, vasthouden

detect, be'speuren, be'trappen

detective, detec'tive, recher'cheur

detention, oponthoud *n*; ge'vang-enhouden *n*, schoolblijven *n*

deter, afschrikken

detergent, wasmiddel *n*

deteriorate, achter'uitgaan

deterioration, achter'uitgang

determination, vastbe'raden-heid; vaststellen *n*; be'slissing

determine, be'sluiten; vaststel-len, be'palen

determined, vastbe'sloten, vast-be'raden

deterrent, afschrikkend middel *n*

detest, ver'afschuwen

detestable, ver'foeilijk

dethrone, ont'tronen

detonate, (doen) ont'ploffen

detour, omweg

detract from, afbreuk doen aan'

detriment(al), schade(lijk)

deuce, twee, veertig ge'lijk: drommel

devastate, ver'woesten

develop, (zich) ont'wikkelen, uit-werken

development, ont'wikkeling

deviate, afwijken

device, toestel *n*; list; sym'bool *n*, de'vies *n*

devil, duivel

devilish, duivels; ver'duiveld

devious, om'slachtig

devise, ver'zinnen

evoid of, zonder

evolve, overdragen (aan), overgaan (op)

evote, (toe)wijden

evoted, (toe)gewijd, ver'knocht

evotee, enthousi'ast

evotion, toewijding, ver'knochtheid; de'votie; ge'bed n

evour, ver'slinden

evout, vroom

ew(drop), dauw(droppel)

exterous, be'hendig

iabetes, suikerziekte

iabolic(al), duivels

iadem, dia'deem

iaeresis, deelteken n

iagnose, diag'nose opmaken

iagnosis, diag'nose

iagonal, diago'naal

iagram, dia'gram n

ial, wijzer(plaat), schijf; facie: draaien

ialect, dia'lect n

ialogue, dia'loog

iameter, middellijn

iametrically, diame'traal; lijnrecht

iamond, dia'mant(en); ruit (-'vormig)

iaphragm, middenrif n; dia'fragma n

iarrhoea, dia'rree

iary, dagboek n, a'genda

iatribe, schimprede

ice, dobbelstenen: dobbelen

ickens, drommel

ictate, voorschrift n; stem: dic'teren; voorschrijven

ictation, dic'teren n; dic'tee n; voorschrift n

ictator, dic'tator

ictatorial, dictatori'aal

ictatorship, dicta'tuur

iction, dictie

ictionary, woordenboek n

ictum, uitspraak; ge'zegde n

idactic, di'dactisch

iddle, be'dotten

ie, sterven, doodgaan; snakken naar

to die out, uitsterven

ie-hard, onver'zettelijk

iesel, diesel

diet, di'eet (houden) (n)

differ, ver'schillen; het niet eens zijn

difference, ver'schil n

different, ver'schillend, anders

differentiate, onder'scheiden; onderscheid maken

difficult, moeilijk

difficulty, moeilijkheid, be'zwaar n

diffident, be'schroomd

diffuse, dif'fuus: (zich) ver'spreiden

dig, por; steek: graven, omspitten, rooien (potatoes); porren; vorsen

digest, overzicht n: ver'teren; ver'werken

digestion, (spijs)ver'tering

dig(ging)s, kamers

digit, vinger; cijfer n

dignified, waardig

dignify, opluisteren

dignitary, waardigheidsbekleder

dignity, waardigheid

digress, afdwalen, uitweiden

dilapidated, bouw'vallig

dilate, (zich) uitzetten

dilatory, traag

dilemma, di'lemma n

dilettante, dilet'tant

diligence, vlijt; dili'gence

diligent, vlijtig

dilute, ver'dund: ver'dunnen

dim, flauw, vaag, schemerig; dom: dof worden, ver'flauwen, ver'zwakken

dimension, afmeting, di'mensie

diminish, ver'minderen

diminutive, klein: ver'kleinwoord n

dimple, kuiltje n

din, la'waai n

dine, di'neren

diner, eter

dinghy, jol

dingy, vuil, goor

dining-car, restau'ratiewagen

dining-room, eetkamer, eetzaal

dinky, snoezig

dinner, warme maaltijd, di'ner n

dinner-service, eetservies n

dint: by — of, door middel van

diocese, bisdom *n*
dip, duik(en); inzinking: dompelen; dalen; salu'eren (met)
diphtheria, difte'ritis
diphthong, tweeklank
diploma, di'ploma *n*
diplomacy, diploma'tie
diplomat, diplo'maat
diplomatic, diploma'tiek
dire, ver'schrikkelijk
direct, rechtstreeks, di'rect; on'middellijk; open'hartig: leiden; ge'lasten; de weg wijzen; richten; adres'seren
direction, richting; aanwijzing; leiding
directly, on'middellijk; pre'cies
director, direc'teur; raadsman
directory, ad'resboek *n*, gids
dirge, klaagzang
dirt, vuil *n*; aarde
dirt-cheap, spotgoedkoop
dirty, vuil(maken); ge'meen
disability, onvermogen *n*
disabled, inva'lide
disablement, invalidi'teit
disadvantage, nadeel *n*
  at a disadvantage, in een na'delige po'sitie
disadvantageous, na'delig
disagree with, het on'eens zijn met; slecht be'komen
disagreeable, on'aangenaam
disagreement, (menings)verschil *n*
disallow, van de hand wijzen
disappear(ance), ver'dwijnen (*n*)
disappoint, te'leurstellen
  to be disappointing, tegenvallen
disappointment, te'leurstelling, tegenvaller
disapproval, afkeuring; misnoegen *n*
disapprove, afkeuren; erop tegen zijn
disarm, ont'wapenen
disarmament, ont'wapening
disaster, ramp
disastrous, ramp'spoedig
disavow, loochenen
disband, ont'binden

disbelief, ongeloof *n*
disbelieve, onge'lovig zijn, i▐ twijfel trekken
disburse, uitbetalen
disc, schijf
discard, op'zij ge'legde kaart ver'werpen, afdanken; uittrek ken; wegleggen
discern, onder'scheiden
discernible, waar'neembaar
discernment, onder'scheidings vermogen *n*, inzicht *n*
discharge, ont'lading; ont'plof fing; ont'slag *n*; afvoer; etteren (*n*); zich kwijten van (*n*) lossen; afschieten; ont'laden; ont'slaan; uitmonden; afdoe▐
disciple, dis'cipel
disciplinary, discipli'nair, tucht-
discipline, disci'pline: discipli'neren
disclaim, van de hand wijzen, ont'kennen
disclose, ont'hullen, blootleggen; loslaten
discolour, (doen) ver'kleuren
discomfort, onbe'haaglijkheid
disconcert, van de wijs brengen
disconcerting, storend
disconnect, uitschakelen, afkoppelen
disconnected, on'samenhangend
disconsolate, troosteloos
discontent(ment), onte'vredenheid
discontented, onte'vreden
discontinue, opheffen, ophouden met, staken; opzeggen
discord, tweedracht; disso'nant
discordance, wangeluid *n*
discordant, dishar'monisch; tegen'strijdig
discount, korting: discon'teren; buiten be'schouwing laten
discourage, ont'moedigen; afraden; weer'houden
discouragement, ont'moediging; tegenwerping; afschrikking
discourse, ver'handeling (houden)
discourteous, on'hoffelijk
discover, ont'dekken
discovery, ont'dekking

discredit, schande, oneer: in diskrediet brengen (n); geen ge'loof hechten aan (n)

discreet, dis'creet

discrepancy, onregel'matigheid, ver'schil n

discretion, goedvinden n; tact; onderscheid n

discriminate, onder'scheiden, onderscheid maken (n)

discrimination, onderscheid-(ingsvermogen) n

discursive, on'samenhangend

discuss, be'spreken

discussion, be'spreking, dis'cussie

disdain, ver'achting: ver'smaden

disdainful, ver'achtelijk

disease, ziekte; kwaal

diseased, ziek, be'smet

disembark, (zich) ont'schepen

disengage, losmaken

disengaged, onbe'zet

disentangle, ont'warren

disfavour, tegenzin; ongenade

disfigure, ont'sieren, mis'vormen

disgorge, uitbraken; uitstorten

disgrace, schande; ongenade: te schande maken; laken

disgraceful, schandelijk

disgruntled, ver'zuurd

disguise, (ver')mom(ming): ver'mommen, ver'bloemen

disgust, afkeer, walging: doen walgen

 to be disgusted at, walgen van

 to be disgusted with, meer dan ge'noeg hebben van

disgusting, walgelijk, af'schuwelijk

dish, schaal; ge'recht n

 to dish up, opdoen

disharmony, disharmo'nie

dish-cloth, vaatdoek

dishearten, ont'moedigen

dishevelled, ver'fomfaaid

dishonest(y), on'eerlijk(heid)

dishonour, oneer, schande: ont'eren

dishonourable, ont'erend; on'-eervol

disillusion, ont'goochelen

disillusionment, ont'goocheling

disinclination, tegenzin

disinclined, onge'negen

disinfect, ont'smetten

disinfectant, ont'smettingsmiddel n

disinherit, ont'erven

disintegrate, uitel'kaar vallen, (zich) ont'binden

disinterested, be'langeloos

disjointed, on'samenhangend

dislike, afkeer: on'prettig vinden

dislocate, ont'wrichten

dislodge, losmaken; ver'drijven

disloyal(ty), ontrouw

dismal, triest

dismantle, ont'mantelen

dismay, ont'zetting: ont'stellen

dismiss, ont'slaan, wegsturen; afwijzen

dismissal, ont'slag n

dismount, afstijgen; demon'-teren

disobedience, onge'hoorzaamheid

disobedient, onge'hoorzaam

disobey, geen ge'hoor geven (aan), onge'hoorzaam zijn

disorder, wanorde; onge'regeldheid; onge'steldheid

disorderly, wan'orderlijk; op'-roerig

disorganize, in de war sturen

disown, ver'loochenen

disparage, klei'neren

disparity, onge'lijkheid

dispassionate, onpar'tijdig, ob-jec'tief

dispatch, ver'zending; (offici'eel) be'richt n; spoed: ver'zenden; afmaken; ver'orberen

dispel, ver'drijven

dispensary, apo'theek

dispensation, uitdeling; dis-pen'satie; be'schikking

dispense, uitdelen; klaarmaken

 to dispense with, het stellen zonder

dispersal, ver'spreiding

disperse, ver'strooien

dispirit, ont'moedigen

displace, ver'plaatsen, ver'vangen

displacement, (water)ver'plaatsing

display, ver'toon *n*, demon'stratie: (ver')tonen, ten'toonspreiden; ont'plooien

displease, mis'hagen

displeased, ont'stemd

displeasing, on'aangenaam

displeasure, mis'noegen *n*

disport, ver'maken

disposal, opruimen *n*; (be')schikking

dispose, (rang)schikken: be'wegen

  to dispose of, van de hand doen, ver'maken

disposed, ge'neigd, ge'stemd

disposition, rangschikking; aard, neiging

dispossess, uit het be'zit stoten

disproportionate, oneven'redig

disprove, weer'leggen

dispute, woord'entwist, dis'puut *n*: (be')twisten, dispu'teren; be'strijden

disqualification, diskwalifi'catie; be'lemmering

disqualify, diskwalifi'ceren; onge'schikt maken

disquiet, onrust: veront'rusten

disregard, veron'achtzaming: veron'achtzamen

disrepair, ver'val *n*

disreputable, be'rucht; haveloos

disrespect, oneer'biedigheid

disrupt, uit'eenrukken

disruption, scheuring

dissatisfaction, onte'vredenheid

dissatisfied, onte'vreden

dissect, ont'leden

dissemble, (zich) ont'veinzen, veinzen

disseminate, ver'spreiden

dissension, tweedracht

dissent, van mening ver'schillen

dissenter, afgescheidene

dissertation, ver'handeling

disservice, ondienst

dissimilar(ity), onge'lijk(heid)

dissipate, ver'strooien; ver'doen

dissipated, ver'lopen, los'bandig

dissociate, (af)scheiden, niet stellen achter

dissolute, liederlijk

dissolution, opheffing

dissolve, (zich) oplossen ont'binden; wegsmelten

dissonant, wan'luidend

dissuade, afraden, afbrengen (van)

distance, afstand; verte

distant, ver; weg; koel

distaste, afkeer

distasteful, on'smakelijk

distemper, (honde)ziekte; tempera; vloebaren

distend, opzwellen, opensperren

distil, distil'leren; puren

distillery, distilleerde'rij

distinct, duidelijk; ver'schillend; be'slist

distinction, onderscheid *n*, onder'scheiding; aanzien *n*

distinctive, kenmerkend

distinguish, onder'scheiden, onderscheid maken

distinguished, aan'zienlijk

distort, ver'wringen; ver'draaien

distract, afleiden; krank'zinnig maken

distraction, afleiding; rade'loosheid

distraught, radeloos

distress, ellende, smart: be'droeven

distribute, uitdelen, ver'spreiden

distribution, uitreiking, ver'deling

district, streek, wijk

distrust, wantrouwen (*n*)

disturb, storen; komen aan; veront'rusten

disturbance, storing; ver'warring; stoornis

disuse, onbruik *n*

disused, oud, in onbruik ge'raakt

ditch, sloot: lozen

ditty, deuntje *n*

divan, divan(bed *n*)

dive, duik(en); tent: tasten

diver, duiker; duikvogel

diverge, uit'eenlopen

divergence, ver'schil *n*

divers(e), ver'scheiden

diversion, ver'legging, wegomlegging; ont'spanning

diversity, ver'scheidenheid

divert, ver'leggen; afleiden

divest, ont'doen

divide, (zich) ver'delen; stemmen

dividend, divi'dend *n*; deeltal *n*

dividers, (steek)passer

divine, goddelijk, gods-; aan'biddelijk: godgeleerde: peilen, gissen

divinity, god(delijk)heid; godgeleerdheid

divisible, deelbaar

division, (ver')deling, afdeling; di'visie; ver'deeldheid; stemming

divorce, (echt)scheiding: (zich laten) scheiden (van)

divulge, be'kend maken

dizzy, duizelig, duizeling'wekkend

do, doen
 how do you do? hoe maakt u het?
 that will do, dat is ge'noeg
 did you say that you did want it or that you didn't? zei je, dat je het wel wilde of dat je het niet wilde?
 to do away with, afschaffen
 to do out of, afzetten; pro'n'teren van
 to do up, vastmaken, inpakken; opknappen
 to do well, het goed maken; er goed aan doen
 to do with, ge'bruiken; maken met
 to do without, het stellen zonder

docile, volgzaam

dock, dok(ken) (*n*); be'klaagdenbank: korten

dockyard, ma'rinewerf

doctor, dokter; doctor: be'handelen

doctrine, leer(stuk *n*)

document, docu'ment('eren) (*n*)

documentary, documen'tair(e film)

dodder, wankelen

dodge, foefje *n*: op'zijspringen; ont'wijken

doe, hinde; wijfje *n*

doff, afzetten, uittrekken

dog, hond: (achter)volgen

dog-ear, ezelsoren maken

dogged, hard'nekkig

doggerel, rijmela'rij

doggo: to lie —, zich koest houden

dogma, dogma *n*

dogmatic, dog'matisch

dog-tired, hondsmoe

doily, kleedje *n*

doings, ge'doe *n*; spul(len) *n*

doldrums, streek der windstilten; put

dole, steun
 to dole out, ronddelen

doleful, somber

doll, pop
 to doll up, opdirken

dollar, dollar

dolphin, dol'fijn

dolt, domkop

domain, do'mein *n*, landgoed *n*; ge'bied *n*

dome, koepel

domestic, huis('houd)elijk, huis-(houd)-; binnenlands

domesticated, huiselijk; ge'temd

domicile, domi'cilie *n*

dominant, (over')heersend; domi'nerend; domi'nant

dominate, (over')heersen, be'heersen; be'strijken

domination, over'heersing

domineer, de baas spelen over

domineering, bazig

dominion, heerschap'pij; ge'bied (met zelf bestuur) *n*

dominoes, dominospel *n*

don, ge'leerde: aandoen

donate, schenken

donation, do'natie

done, klaar, af; gaar
 done for, op; er ge'weest

donkey, ezel

donor, schenker, donor

doom, noodlot *n*, ondergang; laatste oordeel *n*: doemen

door, deur, ingang
 out of doors, buiten

doorstep, stoep; pil

door-way, deuropening

dope, spanlak; be'dwelmend middel *n*; inlichtingen; stomkop: be'dwelmen

dormant, slapend
dormer window, koekoek
dormitory, slaapzaal
dorsal, rug(ge)-
dose, dosis : do'seren
dot, stip(pelen), punt
dotage, kindsheid
dote, kinds zijn ; ver'zot zijn op
dotty, niet goed snik
double, dubbel, tweepersoons-:
  dubbele   *n,*   dubbelganger:
  (zich)ver'dubbelen, dubbelvou-
  wen; zich omwenden; dou'bleren
 to double up, in'eenkrimpen;
  opschieten
double-barrelled, dubbel(loops)
double-cross, dubbel spel spelen (*n*)
doublet, wambuis *n*
doubt, twijfel(en), be'twijfelen
doubtful, twijfelachtig
doubtless, onge'twijfeld
douche, douche
dough, deeg *n* ; duiten
doughnut, oliebol
doughty, koen
dour, stug
douse, drijfnat maken
dove, duif(je *n*)
dovecot, duiventil
dowager, douai'rière
dowdy, lijzig ge'kleed, sjofel
down, naar be'neden, neder; af:
 down: dons *n*
 down and out, door en door;
  aan lager wal
 a down on, iets tegen
 down payment, bedrag *n* in'eens
 down with, weg met
downcast, (ter')neergeslagen
downfall, val; zware bui
down-hearted, neer'slachtig
downhill, de heuvel af; berg'afwaarts
downpour, plasregen
downright, uitgesproken
downstairs, (naar) be'neden
downstream, stroom'afwaarts
down-trodden,   platgetrapt;
  ver'trapt
downward(s), naar be'neden
downy, donzig

dowry, bruidschat
doze, dutje *n* ; dutten
dozen, do'zijn *n*
drab, saai ; vaal(bruin)
draft,   schets,   klad   *n* ;   de
  tache'ment *n* ; wissel : inlijven
  deta'cheren
draftsman, ont'werper
drag, rem : slepen ; dreggen
  kruipen
 to drag on, zich voortslepen
dragon, draak
dragon-fly, waterjuffer
dragoon, dra'gonder: ringeloren
drain, afvoer(buis), ri'ool *n* ; afvoeren;   lopen ;   droogleggen ;
  ont'trekken
 to be a drain on, veel vergen
  van
drainage, afwatering ; afvoer
draining-board, aanrecht *n*
drainpipe, afvoerbuis
drake, woerd
dram, drachme; boompje *n*
drama, drama('tiek) (*n*)
dramatic, dra'matisch
dramatics, to'neelkunst
dramatist, drama'turg
dramatize, (zich laten) dramati'-
  seren
drape, drape'rie : dra'peren
drapery, drape'rie ;   manufac'-
  turen
drastic, drastisch
drat, drommels
draught, tocht, trek ; vangst;
  diepgang ; teug : trek- ; ge'tapt
draughts, damspel *n*
draughty, tochtig
draw,   ge'lijk   spel(en)   (*n*) ;
  at'tractie; ver'loting : trekken :
  tekenen
 to draw near, naderen
 to draw up, stilhouden; opstellen; bijschuiven
drawback, be'zwaar *n*, nadeel *n*
drawbridge, ophaalbrug
drawer, la(de) : tekenaar
drawers, panta'lon
drawing, tekening, tekenen *n*
drawing-pin, pu'naise
drawing-room, sa'lon
drawl, ge'teem *n* : temen

drawn, afgetobd; onbe'slist

dread, (met) angst (en beven tege'moetzien)

dreadful, vreselijk

dream, droom: dromen

dreamy, dromerig; vaag

dreary, somber

dredge, baggermolen; (uit)baggeren

dregs, be'zinksel *n*; grondsop *n*

drench, door'weken

dress, ja'pon; kleding, te'nue *n*: gala-: (zich) (aan)kleden; tooien; ver'binden

  to dress up, (zich) opdirken

dresser, (keuken)buf'fet *n*

dressing, ver'band *n*; saus

dressing-gown, kamerjapon

dressmaker, naaister

dressmaking, naaien *n*

dress-rehearsal, gene'rale repe'titie

dress-suit, rokkos'tuum *n*

dressy, pronkziek; ge'kleed

dribble, druppelen, kwijlen; dribbelen

drier, droogtoestel *n*

drift, drijven (*n*); jachtsneeuw; neiging, strekking: zich laten meeslepen, dwalen

driftwood, drijfhout *n*

drill, dril(boor); oefening, exer'citie; kleine voor: (door)boren; drillen

drink, (iets te) drinken, borreltje *n*

  to drink to, drinken op

drip, druppel(en), druipen

dripping, braadvet *n*

drive, rit; oprijlaan; drijfkracht; cam'pagne; slag: (voort)drijven; rijden; slaan

  to drive at, doelen op

drivel, ge'wauwel *n*: wauwelen

driver, be'stuurder

driving licence, rijbewijs *n*

drizzle, motregen(en)

droll, grappig, zot

drone, dar, luilak; ge'gons: gonzen, dreunen

droop, hangen; omvallen

drop, druppel; glaasje *n*; daling; hoogte: (laten) vallen;

(laten) dalen; weglaten; afzetten

  to drop in, (even) langskomen

  to drop off, in slaap vallen

dropsy, waterzucht

dross, afval

drought, droogte

drown, ver'drinken; over'stemmen

  to be drowned, ver'drinken

drowse, dommelen

drowsy, slaperig; slaap'wekkend

drudge, werkezel: sloven

drudgery, ge'zwoeg *n*

drug, be'dwelmend middel *n*: be'dwelmen

drum, trom(mel), ton: trommelen

drummer, trommelslager

drunk, dronken: dronkeman

drunkard, dronkaard

dry, droog: (af)drogen

dry-clean(ing), chemisch reinigen (*n*)

dual, twee'ledig, dubbel

dub, tot ridder slaan

dubious, twijfelachtig, dubi'eus

ducal, her'togelijk

duchess, herto'gin

duchy, hertogdom *n*

duck, eend; snoes; nul: duiking: (onder)duiken

duct, ka'naal *n*, buis

dud, sukkel, blindganger: snert

due, ver'schuldigd, ver'diend, ge'past; ver'wacht; zuiver: wat iemand toekomt

  due to, dank zij, ten ge'volge van

duel, du'el *n*; duel'leren

duet, du'et *n*, quatre'mains

duffer, sufferd

dug-out, uitgegraven schuilplaats

duke, hertog

dull, dof; saai; traag; somber: afstompen

duly, dan ook; dus, naar be'horen

dumb, stom, sprakeloos

dumb-bell, halter

dumbfound, ver'stomd doen staan

dummy, pop; blinde: namaak-

dump, belt, stortplaats; opslagplaats: storten, neerzetten

dumpling, knoedel
dumpy person, propje *n*
dunce, domkop
dune, duin *n*
dung, (be)mest(en)
dungarees, over'all
dungeon, kerker
dupe, dupe: be'driegen
duplicate,   dupli'caat   (*n*):
  ver'dubbelen
 in duplicate, in duplo
duplicity, dubbel'hartigheid
durable, duurzaam
duration, duur
duress, dwang
during, tijdens
dusk, schemering
dusky, donker, schemerig
dust, stof *n*: afstoffen; be'stuiven
dustbin, vuilnisbak
dustman, vuilnisman
dustpan (and brush), (veger
  en) blik *n*
dusty, stoffig; poeierig
Dutch, Nederlands (*n*): Neder-
  landers
dutiful, plichtgetrouw
duty, plicht; functie; (invoer)-
  rechten
dwarf,   dwerg;   minia'tuur:
  over'schaduwen
dwell, wonen
 to dwell (up)on, lang stilstaan
  bij
dweller, be'woner
dwelling, woning
dwelling-place, woonplaats
dwindle (away), wegteren; uitsterven, ver'dwijnen
dye, verf (stof); verven, kleuren
dynamic, dy'namisch
dynamite, dyna'miet *n*
dynamo, dy'namo
dynasty, dynas'tie
dysentery, dysente'rie

E

each, elk, ieder; per stuk
 each other, el'kaar
eager,   enthousi'ast,   gretig,
  ver'langend

to be eager, dolgraag (zouden)
  willen
eagerness,   enthousi'asme   *n,*
  ver'langen *n*
eagle, arend
ear, oor *n*; ge'hoor *n*: aar
ear-drum, trommelvlies *n*
earl, graaf
early, (te) vroeg, vroeger, vroeg'-
  tijdig
ear-mark, be'stemmen
earn,   ver'dienen;   ver'werven,
  be'zorgen
earnest, ernstig, vurig
 in earnest, in (alle) ernst
earnings, verdiensten
ear-ring, oorbel
ear-splitting, oorver'dovend
earth,   aarde,   grond;   hol   *n*;
  aardverbinding
 what (*or* how) on earth . . . wat
  (*or* hoe) in vredesnaam . . .
earthenware, aardewerk *n*
earthly, aards, stoffelijk
earthquake, aardbeving
earthworm, aardworm
earthy,   grond-;   laag   bij   de
  gronds
ease,   ge'mak   *n*:   ver'lichten;
  losser   maken;   voor'zichtig
  schuiven; ver'minderen
easel, ezel
easily,   (ge')makkelijk;   verreweg
east, Oosten (*n*); oost(waarts)
Easter, Pasen
 Easter Day, eerste Paasdag
easterly, oostelijk, ooster-
eastern, oosters, oostelijk
easy, (ge')makkelijk; kalm
easy-going, gemak'zuchtig; flegma'tiek
eat, (op)eten; vreten
eaves, overhangende dakrand
eavesdrop, afluisteren
ebb, eb(ben); ver'val *n*: afnemen
ebony, ebbenhout(en) (*n*)
eccentric,   ex'centrisch;   ex-
  cen'triek: zonderling
ecclesiastical, geestelijk, kerkelijk
echo, echo; weerklank: weer'-
  klinken; weergeven, her'halen

eclipse, ver'duistering: ver'duisteren; in de schaduw stellen
economic, eco'nomisch
economical, zuinig, voor'delig; eco'nomisch
economics, econo'mie
economist, eco'noom
economize, be'zuinigen
economy, zuinigheid; be'heer *n*
ecstasy, ex'tase
ecstatic, geest'driftig
eddy, draaikolk: dwarrelen
edge, rand; scherpe kant
on edge, zenuwachtig
edible, eetbaar
edict, e'dict *n*
edifice, ge'bouw *n*
edify, stichten
edit, uitgeven; redi'geren
edition, uitgave, e'ditie
editor, redac'teur, be'werker
editorial, hoofdartikel *n*
  editorial board (staff), re'dactie
educate, onder'wijzen, opvoeden
education, onderwijs *n*, ont'wikkeling
educational, opvoedings-, onderwijs
eel, paling
eerie, griezelig
efface, uitwissen; wegcijferen
effect, ge'volg *n*, uitwerking, resul'taat *n*; ef'fect *n*: be'werkstelligen
  in effect, in feite: van kracht
effective, ge'slaagd, treffend; af'doend; van kracht
effeminate, ver'wijfd
effervesce, mous'seren; bruisen
efficacy, doel'treffendheid
efficiency, vaardigheid; nuttig ef'fect *n*
effigy, beeltenis, beeldenaar
effort, krachtsinspanning, poging; pres'tatie
effrontery, brutali'teit
effusive, uit'bundig
egg, ei *n*
  to egg on, aanzetten
egoist, ego'ist
egotism, eigenwaan
eiderdown, donzen deken

eight(h), acht(ste)
eighteen(th), achttien(de)
eighty, tachtig
Eire, Ierland *n*
either, één (van beide); beide; elk: ook
either . . . or, of . . . of
ejaculate, uitroepen
eject, uitwerpen, uitzetten
eke out, rekken
elaborate, inge'wikkeld, door'wrocht, uitgebreid: be'werken, bijwerken; uitweiden
elapse, ver'strijken, ver'lopen
elastic, e'lastisch; rekbaar: elas'tiek *n*
elasticity, elastici'teit; rekbaarheid
elated, opgetogen
elbow, elleboog: door'heenwerken
elder, ouder(e), oudst(e); ouderling
elderly, op leeftijd
elect, ge'kozen(e), uitverkoren(e): (ver')kiezen (als), uitkiezen
election, (uit)ver'kiezing
elector(ate), kiezer(s)
electric(al), e'lektrisch
electrician, elektri'cien
electricity, elektrici'teit
electrify, elektrifi'ceren; elektri'seren
elegant, ele'gant
elegy, ele'gie
element, ele'ment *n*; be'standdeel *n*
elemental, na'tuur-, essen'tieel
elementary, elemen'tair; een'voudig
  elementary school, lagere school
elephant, olifant
elevate, ver'heffen
elevation, ver'hoging, hoogte; ver'heffing; opstand
eleven, elf (tal *n*)
elf, ka'bouter, elf
elicit, ont'lokken
eligible, ver'kiesbaar; be'voegd; ge'schikt
eliminate, uitschakelen

ellipse, el'lips

elm, iep(enhout *n*)

elocution, voordracht

elongate, (zich) ver'lengen, uitrekken

elope, weglopen

eloquence, wel'sprekendheid

else, anders; verder

elsewhere, ergens anders

elucidate, toelichten

elude, ont'wijken, ont'duiken, ont'gaan

elusive, moeilijk te vinden (*or* vatten)

emaciate, uitmergelen

emanate from, voortkomen uit, uitstralen van

emancipation, emanci'patie

embalm, balsemen

embankment, kade

embargo, be'slag *n*, ver'bod *n*

embark, (zich) inschepen

to embark on, aanvangen

embarrass, ver'legen maken, in ver'legenheid brengen; be'moeilijken

embarrassing, pijnlijk

embarrassment, ver'legenheid

embassy, ambas'sade, ge'zantschap *n*

embedded, ge'nesteld, vastge'raakt

embellish, ver'fraaien

ember, gloeiend kooltje (*or* stuk hout) *n*

embezzle, ver'duisteren

embitter, ver'bitteren, ver'gallen

emblem, zinnebeeld *n*

embody, be'lichamen; be'vatten

embossed, gebosse'leerd, in re'liëf

embrace, om'helzing: (el'kaar) om'helzen; om'sluiten; zich eigen maken

embroider, bor'duren

embroidery, bor'duurwerk *n*

embroil, ver'wikkelen

embryo(nic), embryo('naal) (*n*)

in embryo, in wording

emendation, ver'betering

emerald, sma'ragd(en)

emerge, te voorschijn komen

emergency, nood(geval *n*), noodtoestand

emigrant, emi'grant: emi'grerend

emigrate, emi'greren

eminence, emi'nentie, ver'maardheid

eminent, uit'zonderlijk (ver'maard)

emissary, ge'zant

emit, uitstralen, afgeven; uiten

emolument, ver'dienste

emotion, (ge'moeds)aandoening, e'motie

emotional, emotio'neel, ge'voels-

emperor, keizer

emphasis, nadruk

emphasize, de nadruk leggen op, duidelijk doen uitkomen

emphatic, na'drukkelijk

empire, (keizer)rijk *n*

emplacement, stelling

employ, (in)dienst(hebben); ge'bruiken, bezighouden

employee, werknemer

employer, werkgever

employment, werk *n*; ge'bruik *n*

employment exchange, arbeidsbeurs

empower, machtigen

empress, keizer'in

empty, leeg (maken *or* worden); niets'zeggend: lozen

emulate, nastreven

emulsion, e'mulsie

enable, in staat stellen

enact, tot wet ver'heffen; opvoeren

enamel, e'mail('leren) (*n*), brandverf, gla'zuur *n*: lakken

enamour, be'koren; ver'zotten

encamp, een kamp opslaan; legeren

encase, om'sluiten, opsluiten

enchant, be'toveren; ver'rukken

enchanting, sprookjesachtig, char'mant; be'toverend

encircle, om'ringen, om'singelen

enclose, insluiten

enclosure, om'sloten ruimte: bijlage

encompass, om'sluiten; be'vatten

encore, bis('seren): toegift
encounter, ont'moeting; treffen
n: tegenkomen; onder'vinden
encourage, aanmoedigen
encouragement, aanmoediging
encroach on, doordringen tot;
inbreuk maken op
encrust, be'slaan; be'zetten
encumber, be'lasten
encumbrance, be'letsel *n*
encyclopaedia, encyclope'die
end, eind(igen) (*n*); doel *n*
no end of, vreselijk veel
in the end, ten'slotte
make both ends meet, rondkomen
endanger, in ge'vaar brengen
endear, ge'liefd maken, innemen
endeavour, poging: trachten
ending, eind *n*; uitgang
endless, eindeloos, zonder einde
endorse, endos'seren; onder'-
schrijven
endow, be'giftigen
endowment, schenking
endue, be'giftigen
endurance, uithoudingsvermogen *n*; ver'dragen *n*
endure, ver'dragen; ver'duren
enemy, vijand(elijk)
energetic, encr'giek; krachtig
energy, ener'gie
enfold, om'wikkelen; om'helzen,
om'strengelen
enforce, (krachtig) uitvoeren;
dwingen tot
enforcement, handhaving
enfranchise, vrijmaken; kiesrecht ver'lenen
engage, in dienst nemen; in
be'slag nemen; slaags raken
met; in el'kaar grijpen
engaged, ver'loofd; in ge'sprek,
be'zet, bezig
to get engaged, zich ver'loven
met
engagement, afspraak; ver'loving; in'dienstneming; ge'vecht
n
engaging, in'nemend
engender, ver'wekken; ver'oorzaken

engine, ma'chine, motor, locomo'tief
engineer, inge'nieur, technicus,
machi'nist, lid van de ge'nie-
troepen: klaarspelen
engineering, tech'niek
England, Engeland *n*
English(man), Engels(man) (*n*)
engrave, gra'veren; inprenten
engraving, gra'vure, gra'veren *n*
engross, ver'diepen; fasci'neren
engulf, ver'zwelgen
enhance, ver'hogen
enigma(tic)(al), raadsel(achtig)
(*n*)
enjoin, be'velen
enjoy, ge'nieten (van)
enjoyable, prettig
enjoyment, ple'zier *n*, ge'nieten *n*
enlarge, (zich) ver'groten
to enlarge on, uitweiden over
enlighten, opheldering geven
aan; ver'lichten
enlist, (in) dienst nemen; een
be'roep doen op
enliven, opvrolijken
enmity, vijandschap
ennoble, adelen
enormous, kolos'saal
enormously, e'norm
enough, ge'noeg; heel
kind enough, zo vriendelijk
enrage, woedend maken
enrapture, in ver'voering
brengen
enrich, ver'rijken
enrol, (zich laten) inschrijven;
lid worden
ensconce, ver'schansen; nestelen
ensign, vlag; vaandrig
enslave, knechten
ensue, het ge'volg zijn, volgen
ensure, ver'zekeren
entail, met zich meebrengen
entangle, vastraken; ver'strikken
enter, binnengaan, binnenkomen;
gaan in; opgeven; boeken
enterprise, onder'neming(sgeest)
enterprising, onder'nemend
entertain, ver'maken, onder'houden; ont'halen, ont'vangen;
over'wegen; koesteren

entertaining, amu'sant: so'ciale plichten

entertainment, amuse'ment *n*

enthrall, boeien

enthrone, op de troon plaatsen, wijden

enthusiasm, enthousi'asme *n*

enthusiast(ic), enthousi'ast

entice, (ver')lokken

entire, (ge')heel

entirely, helemaal

entirety, ge'heel *n*

entitle, (be')titelen; het recht geven

entity, eenheid, ge'heel *n*, (aan)-zijn *n*

entomb, be'graven

entrails, ingewanden

entrance, ingang; opkomen *n*: in ver'voering brengen

entreat, smeken

entreaty, smeekbede

entrust, toevertrouwen

entry, intocht, ingang; boeking; inschrijving

enumerate, opnoemen

envelop, hullen

envelope, enve'loppe

enviable, benijdens'waardig

envious, af'gunstig

environment, om'geving

environs, omstreken

envisage, voor'zien

envoy, ('af)ge'zant

envy, afgunst: be'nijden

epaulet, epau'let

ephemeral, kort'stondig

epic, epos *n*, heldendaden: episch

epicure, gastro'noom

epidemic, epide'mie; rage

epigram, epi'gram *n*

epilepsy, epilep'sie

epilogue, epi'loog

Epiphany, Drie'koningen

episcopal, episco'paal

episode, epi'sode

epistle, (zend)brief

epitaph, grafschrift *n*

epithet, e'pitheton *n*

epitome, kwintessens

epoch, tijdperk *n*

equal, ge'lijk (zijn aan); eve'naren

  equal to, opgewassen tegen

equality, ge'lijkheid

equalize, ge'lijk maken

equally, even('zeer)

equanimity, gelijk'moedigheid

equation, verge'lijking

equator, evenaar

equatorial, equatori'aal

equilateral, gelijk'zijdig

equilibrium, evenwicht *n*

equinox, dag-en-'nachtevening

equip, uitrusten, toerusten

equitable, billijk

equity, billijkheid

equivalent, ekwiva'lent (*n*)

equivocal, dubbel'zinnig, twijfel-achtig

era, tijdperk *n*, jaartelling

eradicate, uitroeien

erase, schrappen; uitwissen

erect, over'eind (zetten); oprich-ten

ermine, herme'lijn (*n*)

erode, uitschuren

erosion, e'rosie

erotic, e'rotisch

err, dwalen

errand, boodschap

erratic, inconse'quent, onregel'-matig

erroneous, on'juist

error, fout, a'buis *n*

erudite, ge'leerd

erupt, uitbarsten, uitspuwen

escalator, roltrap

escapade, esca'pade

escape, ont'vluchting: ont'snap-pen, ont'komen aan; ont'gaan

escarpment, steile wand

escort, ge'leide *n*, es'corte *n*: bege'leiden, escor'teren

especial, bij'zonder

especially, bijzonder, voor'al

espionage, spion'nage

espouse, huwen; om'helzen

espy, be'speuren

Esq(uire): A. Man —, de Wel-edelgeboren Heer A. Man

essay, opstel *n*: pogen

essence, wezen *n*, es'sentie; es'sence

essential, essen'tieel: hoofd-zaak

essentially, in wezen

establish, oprichten; (vast)-
stellen; vestigen; instellen
establishment, (handels)huis *n*,
instelling; oprichten *n*
estate, landgoed *n*, vast goed *n*
  estate agent, makelaar
esteem, achting: achten
estimable, achtens'waardig; te
be'rekenen
estimate, schatting: schatten
estimation, mening; schatting,
achting
estrange, ver'vreemden
estuary, ri'viermond
etc(etera), enz(ovoorts)
etch, etsen
etching, ets
eternal, eeuwig
eternity, eeuwigheid
ether, ether
ethereal, e'therisch
ethical, ethisch
ethics, ethica
ethnology, volkenkunde
etiquette, eti'quette
etymology, etymolo'gie
eulogy, lofrede
Europe, Eu'ropa *n*
European, Euro'pees: Europe'aan
evacuate, evacu'eren
evade, ont'wijken
evaluate, ta'xeren, schatten
evangelic(al), evan'gelisch
evangelist, evange'list
evaporate, ver'dampen; ver'-
dwijnen
evasion, ont'wijking, ont'duiking
evasive, ont'wijkend
eve, (voor)avond, dag voor
even, ge'lijk ('matig); effen; even;
quitte; gelijk'moedig: zelfs;
pre'cies; nog: ge'lijkmaken
  even so, maar toch
evening, avond
evening-dress, avondtoilet *n*
event, ge'beurtenis, ge'val *n*;
nummer *n*
  at all events, in ieder ge'val
eventful, veelbe'wogen
eventual, uit'eindelijk; even-
tu'eel
eventually, ten'slotte

ever, ooit, ten allen tijde
evergreen, altijd groen(e plant)
everlasting, eeuwig('durend)
evermore, altijd
every, ieder; alle
  every other week, om de twee
  weken
  every now and then, telkens
everybody, everyone, ieder'een
everyday, alle'daags, dagelijks
everything, alles
everywhere, overal (waar)
evict, uitzetten
evidence, be'wijs(materi'aal *or*
stuk) *n*, ge'tuigenis; blijk *n*
  to give evidence, ge'tuigenis
  afleggen
evident, duidelijk, klaar'blijkelijk
evil, kwaad (*n*); onheil *n*, euvel *n*
evildoer, boosdoener
evince, (aan)tonen
evoke, oproepen
evolution, evo'lutie
evolve, (zich) ont'plooien
ewe, ooi
ewer, lam'petkan
exact, pre'cies: eisen
exacting, veel'eisend
exactitude, nauw'keurigheid
exaggerate, over'drijven
exalt, ver'heffen; ver'heerlijken
exaltation, ver'heerlijking;
(geest)ver'voering
examination, e'xamen *n*; onderzoek *n*; ver'hoor *n*
examine, exami'neren; onder'-
zoeken, onder'vragen; goed
be'kijken
example, voorbeeld *n*, mo'del *n*
  to set an example, een voorbeeld geven
exasperate, gruwelijk ergeren
excavate, uitgraven, opgraven
excavation, opgraving
exceed, te boven gaan,
over'schrijden
exceedingly, bij'zonder
excel, uitmunten; over'treffen
excellence, voor'treffelijkheid
excellency, excel'lentie
excellent, uit'stekend
except, be'halve: uitzonderen

exception, uitzondering
to take exception to, min denken over
exceptional, onge'woon, exceptio'neel
excerpt, (aangehaalde) passage
excess, overmaat; surplus *n*; uitspatting: extra
excessive, over'dadig, buiten'sporig
exchange, ruil(en); beurs; cen'trale; (uit)wisseling: (in)-wisselen
exchequer, schatkist
excise, ac'cijns: uitsnijden
excitable, gauw opgewonden
excite, opwinden, prikkelen; opwekken
excitement, opwinding
exclaim, uitroepen
exclamation, uitroep
exclude, uitsluiten, buitensluiten
exclusive, uit'sluitend; exclu'sief
excommunicate, in de ban doen
excrements, uitwerpselen
excrescence, uitwas; over'tolligheid
excretion, afscheiding
excruciating, folterend, pijnlijk
excursion, ex'cursie, uitstapje *n*; uitweiding
excusable, be'grijpelijk
excuse, ex'cuus *n*: excu'seren, niet kwalijk nemen; veront'schuldigen; vrijstellen
excuse me, par'don; neem me niet kwalijk
execute, uitvoeren; ter dood brengen
execution, uitvoering; te'rechtstelling
executioner, beul
executive, uitvoerend(e macht); be'drijfsleider
executor, execu'teur
exemplary, voor'beeldig
exemplify, als voorbeeld dienen van, be'lichamen
exempt, vrij(gesteld): vrijstellen
exercise, oefening: (uit)oefenen; in acht nemen
exert, aanwenden, inspannen
exertion, inspanning; ge'bruik *n*

exhale, uitademen
exhaust, uitlaat: uitputten
exhaustion, uitputting
exhibit, inzending, be'wijsstuk *n*: ten'toonstellen; (ver')tonen
exhibition, ten'toonstelling; ver'toon *n*, ver'toning
exhibitor, expo'sant
exhilarate, stimu'leren, opvrolijken
exhort, aansporen, ver'manen
exhume, opgraven
exigency, dringende aange'legenheid; noodgeval *n*
exile, balling(schap)
exist, be'staan
existence, be'staan *n*
exit, uitgang; aftreden *n*
exonerate, zuiveren
exorbitant, buiten'sporig
exorcize, be'vrijden; uitdrijven
exotic, uit'heems
expand, (doen) uitzetten, (zich) uitbreiden, (zich) uitspreiden; uitwerken
expanse, uitge'strektheid
expansion, uitzetting, uitbreiding
expatiate, uitweiden
expatriate, ver'bannen
expect, ver'wachten; denken
expectant, vol verwachting
expectant mother, aanstaande moeder
expectation, ver'wachting
expediency, opportuni'teit; eigenbelang *n*
expedient, be'vorderlijk, raadzaam, redmiddel *n*
expedite, be'spoedigen
expedition, expe'ditie
expel, uitdrijven; wegsturen, roy'eren
expend, uitgeven; be'steden
expenditure, uitgeven *n*, be'steden *n*; uitgaven
expense, (on)kosten, uitgave
expensive, duur
experience, er'varing: onder'vinden
experienced, er'varen
experiment, proef: experimen'teren

experimental, proef (onder'vindelijk)

expert, des'kundig(e), be'dreven

expiate, boeten voor

expire, aflopen; de laatste adem uitblazen; uitademen

expiry, afloop

explain, uitleggen

explanation, ver'klaring

explanatory, ver'klarend

explicit, uit'drukkelijk

explode, (doen) ont'ploffen; losbarsten; ont'zenuwen

exploit, (helden)daad; exploi'teren

exploration, onder'zoeking-(stocht)

explore, ver'kennen, onder'zoeken

explorer, ont'dekkingsreiziger

explosion, ont'ploffing; uitbarsting

explosive, springstof: ont'plofbaar; op'vliegend

exponent, expo'nent

export, uitvoer(artikel *n*): uitvoeren

expose, blootstellen; uitstallen; ont'hullen, aan de dag brengen; be'lichten

exposed, onbe'schut

exposition, uit'eenzetting; ten'toonstelling

exposure, ont'maskering; blootstellen *n*; be'lichting

expound, uit'eenzetten

express, uit'drukkelijk, speci'aal, op'zettelijk; ex'presse: ex'pres-(trein): uitdrukken; uitpersen

expression, uitdrukking

expressive, expres'sief; veel'zeggend

expropriate, ont'eigenen

expulsion, uitdrijving; wegsturen *n*, roye'ment *n*

expunge, uitwissen

exquisite, buitengewoon fijn; zeer ver'fijnd

extant, nog be'staand

extemporaneous, extempore, geimprovi'seerd, on'voorbereid

extemporize, improvi'seren

extend, (zich) uitstrekken,
ver'lengen; uitbreiden; ver'lenen

extension, bijgebouw *n*; ver'lenging; lijn

extensive, uitgebreid, uitgestrekt

extent, uitge'strektheid; omvang
to what (*or* **this**) **extent,** in hoe(*or* zo)'verre

extenuate, ver'zachten, ver'goelijken

exterior, buiten(kant), uit'wendig

exterminate, uitroeien

external, uit'wendig, buiten-(lands); uiterlijk(heid)

extinct, uitgestorven

extinguish, blussen, doven; een eind maken aan

extort, afpersen

extortionate, buiten'sporig

extra, extra

extract, passage; ex'tract *n*; (uit)trekken, uithalen; afpersen

extraction, ex'tractie; afkomst

extraneous, vreemd, niet ter zake dienend

extraordinary, buitenge'woon zeldzaam

extravagance, buiten'sporigheid, ver'kwisting; uitspatting

extravagant, ver'kwistend; buiten'sporig, over'dreven

extreme, uiterst(e *n*)

extremist, extre'mist(isch)

extremity, uiterste (nood) (*n*), uiteinde *n*

extricate, loswerken, losmaken, ont'warren

exuberant, uit'bundig

exude, afscheiden; ver'spreiden

exult, jubelen

exultant, triom'fantelijk, opgetogen

exultation, tri'omf, opge'togenheid

eye, oog *n*: aankijken
to catch a person's eye, de aandacht van iemand trekken
to see eye to eye, het ge'heel eens zijn
to set eyes on, onder ogen krijgen

eyebrow, wenkbrauw
eyelash, wimper
eyelid, ooglid *n*
eye-opener, open'baring
eyesight, ge'zicht *n*
eyesore, gruwel (voor het oog)
eyrie, arendsnest *n*

F

fable, fabel
fabric, stof, weefsel *n*; struc'tuur
fabricate, fabri'ceren; ver'zinnen
fabulous, legen'darisch; fabelachtig
façade, gevel; voorwendsel *n*
face, ge'zicht *n*; wijzerplaat; oppervlakte; pres'tige *n*: no-minaal: liggen op; het ge'zicht keren naar; onder de ogen zien; be'dekken
  face to face, van aangezicht tot aangezicht
  in the face of, ondanks; in aanmerking ge'nomen
  on the face of it, ogen'schijnlijk
  faced with, ge'plaatst voor (*or* in)
  at its face value, zonder meer
facet, fa'cet *n*
facetious, gek(scherend), schertsend
facial, ge'zichts-
facile, (licht')vaardig, opper'vlakkig
facilitate, verge'makkelijken
facility, ge'mak(kelijkheid) (*n*)
facing, tegen'over, met het ge'zicht naar (*or* op): be'leg *n*
fact, feit *n*
  in (point of) fact, in feite, eigenlijk, zelfs, immers
faction, par'tij (strijd)
factor, factor
factory, fa'briek
factual, feitelijk
faculty, ver'mogen *n*, aanleg; facul'teit; ver'gunning
fad, be'vlieging
fade, (doen)ver'schieten; ver'weken; wegsterven

fag, cor'vee(ër); strootje: (zich) afsloven
faggot, bos hout
fail, mis'lukken, (laten) zakken; nalaten; in de steek laten; opraken
  without fail, zonder man'keren
failing, ge'brek *n*: bij ge'brek aan
failure, mis'lukk(el)ing
fain, gaarne
faint, flauw(te), vaag, zwak: flauwvallen
faint-hearted, blo'hartig
fair, billijk, eerlijk; be'hoorlijk; blond; mooi, net: kermis, markt
fairly, tamelijk; eerlijk
fairway, vaarwater *n*; baan
fairy, fee
fairyland, sprookjesland *n*
fairy-tale, sprookje *n*
faith, ge'loof *n*; ver'trouwen *n*; trouw
faithful, trouw; ge'lovig(en)
  yours faithfully, Uw dw. (*i.e.* dienstwillige)
faithless, onge'lovig; trouweloos
fake, be'drog *n*; namaak: knoeien met; namaken; fin'geren
falcon, valk
fall, val(len), daling; overgave, ondergang; ver'val *n*: be'zwijken; dalen
  to fall back on, zijn toevlucht nemen tot; te'rugtrekken op
  to fall out, ruzie krijgen; uit het ge'lid treden
  to fall short, te'kortschieten
  to fall through, in duigen vallen
  to fall to, aanpakken, toetasten; dichtvallen; ten deel vallen
fallacy, dwaalbegrip *n*, drogrede
fallow, braak: geelbruin
false, on'juist; vals; on'trouw; scheef; loos
  false teeth, kunstgebit *n*
falsehood, on'waarheid
falsify, ver'valsen
falter, wankelen, weifelen; stamelen
fame, roem, ver'maardheid
famed, be'roemd

familiar, be'kend, ver'trouwd; famili'aar

familiarity, familiari'teit

family, ge'zin *n*, fa'milie; ge'slacht *n*; kinderen

famine, hongersnood; schaarste

famish, uithongeren, ver'hongeren

famous, be'roemd; prachtig

fan, waaier, venti'lator: enthousi'ast: waaieren; aanwakkeren

fanatic, dweper; fana'tiek(eling)

fanaticism, fana'tisme *n*

fancier, lief hebber

fanciful, fan'tastisch; grillig

fancy, ver'beelding(skracht); be'vlieging: fanta'sie-, luxe: zich in(*or* ver')beelden; een i'dee hebben; zin hebben in

fancy-dress, gecostu'meerd

fanfare, fan'fare

fang, giftand, slagtand

fanlight, raam boven een deur

fantastic, fan'tastisch, grillig

fantasy, fanta'sie

far, ver; veel

far off, ver weg

the far side, de overkant

as far as, voor zover tot aan

by far, far and away, verreweg

far and wide, heinde en ver

farce, klucht, pas'kwil *n*

farcical, kluchtig, be'spottelijk

fare, ta'rief *n*, vracht(je *n*); ver'voerskosten; kost: gaan

farewell, afscheid(s-) (*n*): a'dieu!

far-fetched, verge'zocht

farm, boerde'rij, fokke'rij, kweke'rij: een boerde'rij hebben (van)

farmer, boer

farmhand, boeren'arbeider

farmhouse, boeren'huis *n*, boerde'rij

farming, boerenbe'drijf *n*

farmstead, boerde'rij

farmyard, (boeren')erf *n*

far-off, ver

far-reaching, verstrekkend

farrier, hoefsmid

farrow, worp: biggen

far-sighted, verziend; voor'uitziend

farther, verder

farthest, verst

farthing, kwart penny; duit

fascinate, boeien, fasci'neren

fascination, iets boeiends, be'koring; ge'boeide be'langstelling

fashion, mode; ma'nier: scheppen, vormen

fashionable, modi'eus, deftig, (in de) mode

fast, snel, hard; vóór; ge'raffi'neerd: vast; wasecht; trouw: vasten

to be fast asleep, als een roos slapen

fasten, vastmaken; gooien

fastening, sluiting, knip

fastidious, kies'keurig

fat, dik, vet (*n*)

fatal, dodelijk; nood'lottig; be'slissend

fatalist(ic), fata'list(isch)

fate, lot *n*; dood

fated: he seems —, het schijnt zijn voorbestemming te zijn; hij schijnt ten ondergang ge'doemd

fateful, ge'wichtig

father, vader; pater

fathom, vadem: peilen

fathomless, peilloos

fatigue, ver'moeidheid, ver'moeienis; cor'vee: afmatten

fatten, aanzetten; vetmesten

fatty, vet(tig): dikkerd

fatuous, stom, dwars

fault, fout, de'fect *n*; schuld

to find fault with, vitten op; aanmerkingen maken op

faultless, onbe'rispelijk, feilloos

faulty, ge'brekkig, de'fect

favour, (be')gunst(igen); ingang; voorliefde; in'signe *n*: de voorkeur geven aan

in favour of, vóór; ten gunste van

to do someone a favour, iemand een ge'noegen doen

favourable, gunstig

favourite, gunsteling, favo'riet: lievelings-

favouritism, be'voorrechting

fawn, beige: jong hert *n*: flikflooien

fealty, (leenmans)trouw

fear, angst, vrees: vrezen, bang zijn

fearful, vreselijk

fearless, onbe'vreesd

feasible, uit'voerbaar; aan'nemelijk

feast, feest(maal) n: zich ver'gasten aan, ont'halen

feat, pres'tatie

feather, veer, pluim: veren

feature, (ge'laats)trek; onderdeel n, (op'vallende) eigenschap: gaan over

February, februˈari

fecund(ity), vruchtbaar(heid)

federal, fedeˈraal

federation, fedeˈratie

fee, honoˈrarium n, be'drag n, (school)geld n

feeble, zwak, flauw

feed, voer(en) (n); voeding: eten

 fed up: to be —, er ta'bak van hebben

feeder, slab

feel, ge'voel n: (zich) voelen; (be')tasten; aanvoelen; ge'loven; (meelij) hebben

 to feel like, aanvoelen als; zich voelen (als); zin hebben in

feeling, ge'voel(en) n

feign, veinzen

felicitous, ge'lukkig

felicity, ge'luk('zaligheid) (n)

feline, katachtig

fell, hevig: (neer)vellen

fellow, kerel: mede-

fellowship, ge'meenschap

felonious, mis'dadig; snood

felony, zware misdaad

felt, vilt(en) (n)

female, vrouwelijk (per'soon), vrouwspersoon; wijfje n

feminine, vrouwelijk

fen, moe'rasland n, polder

fence, om'heining, schutting; heler: om'heinen; schermen

fend for oneself, voor zich'zelf zorgen

 to fend off, afweren

fender, haardrand;. stootmat

ferment, gist(ing); be'roering: (doen) gisten

fern, varen

ferocious, woest

ferret, fret: opsporen; snuffelen

ferro-concrete, ge'wapend be'ton n

ferry, veer(pont) (n): overzetten

fertile, vruchtbaar; rijk

fertilize, vruchtbaar maken; be'vruchten

fertilizer, (kunst)mest

fervent, vurig, innig

fervid, heftig

fervour, vuur n

festal, feestelijk, feest-

fester, zweren; woekeren

festival, feest n

festive, feestelijk, feest-

festivity, festivi'teit

festoon, slinger: met slingers tooien

fetch, (af)halen; opbrengen

fête, lief'dadigheidsfeest (in de open lucht) n

fetish, fetisj

fetter, keten(en)

feud, vete

feudal, feoˈdaal

fever, koorts(achtige opwinding)

feverish, koorts(acht)ig

few, weinig(en)

 a few, een paar, enkele

fiancé(e), ver'loofde

fiasco, fiˈasco n

fib, leugentje n; jokken

fibre, vezel; stoerheid, aard

fickle, wispel'turig

fiction, ro'mans en korte ver'halen; fictie, ver'dichtsel n

fictitious, fic'tief, gefin'geerd

fiddle, vi'ool (spelen); peuteren; scharrelen

fiddlesticks! nonsens!

fidelity, trouw, ge'trouwheid

fidget, draaitol: wiebelen

fie on you! schaam je!

field, veld n, akker; ge'bied n: fielden

field-marshal, veldmaarschalk

fiend, duivel; mani'ak

fiendish, duivels

fierce, woest, fel

fiery, vuur(rood); vurig

fife, fluit: pijpen

fifteen(th), vijftien(de)
fifth, vijfde: kwint
fifty, vijftig
fig, vijg; zier
fight, ge'vecht *n*, strijd; vecht-
lust: (be')vechten
figment, ver'zinsel *n*
figurative, fi'guurlijk
figure, cijfer *n*; prijs; ge'daante,
fi'guur *n*: voorkomen
figure of speech, zegswijze
to figure out, uitkienen
figurehead, boegbeeld *n*; leider
in naam
filament, (gloei)draad
filch, kapen
file, dos'sier *n*, map; file; vijl-
(en); opbergen; (een voor een)
trekken
filigree, fili'graan *n*
filings, vijlsel *n*
fill, (op)vullen; stoppen
fillet, fi'let: fi'leren
filling, vulling
fillip, prikkel
filly, jonge merrie
film, film, vlies(je) *n*, waas *n*;
(ver')filmen
filmy, vliezig, wazig
filter, filter: fil'treren; sijpelen
filter through, uitlekken
filth, vuiligheid; vuile taal
filthy, vuil, vies
fin, vin
final, laatste, eind-, slot-; defini'tief: eindwedstrijd
finally, ten'slotte
finance, fi'nanciën: finan'cieren
financial, finan'cieel
financier, finan'cier
find, vondst: (be')vinden; ont'-
dekken; merken; (op)zoeken
finding, be'vinding
fine, mooi; (haar)fijn; best:
geldboete
finery, opschik
finesse, fi'nesse, listigheid: snijden
finger, vinger: be'tasten
finger-nail, nagel
finger-print, vingerafdruk
finicky, kies'keurig, piete'peute-
rig

finish, eind(igen) (*n*); afwerking: af(*or* op)maken; afwerken
finite, eindig
Finn(ish), Fin(s) (*n*)
fiord, fjord
fir, den(ne boom)
fire, vuur *n*, brand; haard: (af)-
vuren, (af)schieten, lossen;
bakken; aanwakkeren; op
straat zetten
to catch fire, vlam vatten
on fire, in brand; brandend (van
ver'langen)
to set fire to, to set on fire, in
brand steken
fire-arm, vuurwapen *n*
fire-brand, brandende spaander;
stokebrand
fire-engine, brandspuit
fire-escape, brandtrap
fire-extinguisher, blusappa-
raat *n*
fire-fly, glimworm
fire-guard, haardhekje *n*
fire-light, vuurgloed
fireman, brandweerman; stoker
fire-place, open haard
fire-proof, brandvrij, vuurvast
fireside, (open) haard
firewood, brandhout *n*
fireworks, vuurwerk *n*
firm, vast(be'raden), stevig,
hecht; stand'vastig: firma
firmament, uitspansel *n*
first, (voor het) eerst; ten eerste
at first, in het be'gin
first of all, eerst, om te be'ginnen
first aid, eerste hulp
first-hand, uit de eerste hand
first-rate, eersteklas, prima
fiscal, fis'caal, be'lasting-
fish, vis(sen); opdiepen
fisher(man), visser, hengelaar
fishery, visse'rij
fishing, vissen *n*; visge'legenheid
fishing-rod, hengel
fishmonger, visboer, viswinkel
fishy, visachtig, vis-; ver'dacht
fissure, kloof, spleet
fist, vuist
fit, ge'zond; ge'schikt; klaar:
aanval; bui, toeval *n*: passen;

kloppen met; voor'zien, uitrusten

to fit in, plaats (*or* tijd) vinden voor; zich aanpassen, passen bij

fitful, on'rustig, grillig, hokkend

fitting, ge'past; pas: fitting

fittings, toebehoren *n*, be'nodigdheden

five, vijf

fix, knel: vastmaken; vaststellen; vestigen; opknappen; fi'xeren

fixed, vast

fixture, vaste fitting; (datum ven een) wedstrijd

fizz, sissen

fizzle, sissen, sputteren

to fizzle out, met een sisser aflopen

flabbergast, stomverbaasd doen staan

flabby, pafferig

flag, vlag; pla'vuis; lis: ver'slappen

flagon, (1½ liter)fles; schenkkan

flagpole, flagstaff, vlaggestok

flagrant, schandelijk

flagship, vlaggeschip *n*

flake, vlok: (af)schilferen

flamboyant, zwierig, op'zichtig

flame, vlam(men); vuurrood zijn

flange, flens

flank, flank('eren)

flannel, fla'nel(len) (*n*); waslapje *n*

flannels, sportbroek

flap, klep, (tafel)blad *n*, pand: klapperen; (op en neer) slaan met

flare, opflikkering; fakkel, si'gnaalvlam

to flare up, opvlammen; opstuiven

flash, flits(en); flikkeren; schieten

flashlight, zaklantaren

flashy, op'zichtig

flask, fla'con

flat, plat, vlak; vierkant (*refusal*); standaard (*rate*); ver'schaald; mat; te laag: flat, é'tage; mol

flat-bottomed, platboomd

flatten, plat maken

flatter, vleien, flat'teren

flattery, vleie'rij

flatulence, opgeblazen ge'voel *n*

flaunt, geuren met

flavour, smaak; tintje *n*: kruiden, toebereiden

flavouring, a'roma *n*

flaw, fout; leemte

flawless, gaaf; onbe'rispelijk

flax, vlas *n*

flaxen, vlassig

flay, villen

flea, vlo

fleck, (be')spikkel(en)

flee, vlieden

fleece, vacht: villen

fleecy, wollig; schapen-

fleet, vloot; leger *n*: snel

fleeting, bliksemsnel, voor'bijflitsend

Flemish, Vlaams

flesh, vlees *n*

fleshy, vlezig

flex, snoer *n*: buigen

flexible, buigzaam; soepel

flick, tik(ken), knip(pen)

flicker, flikkeren

flight, vlucht; groep, zwerm; trap

flighty, wuft

flimsy, dun, teer, flodderig

flinch, te'rugdeinzen; (in'een)-krimpen

fling, smijten (met); stormen

flint, vuursteen(tje *n*)

flip, (weg)slaan

flippant, onge'past spottend

flirt, flirt(en); spelen

flit, fladderen, dartelen

float, dobber, drijver: (laten) drijven, vlot maken

floating, vlottend

flock, kudde, schare: (samen)-stromen

flog, (af)ranselen

flood, over'stroming; (zond)-vloed, zee: (doen) over'stromen; stromen

floodlight, floodlight *n*: ver'lichten

floor, vloer, ver'dieping: over'donderen

flop, fi'asco *n*; (in el'kaar) ploffen

floral, bloemen-

florid, bloemrijk

florin, tweeshillingstuk *n*, gulden

florist, bloe'mist

flotilla, flot'tielje

flounce, stuiven

flounder, ploeteren, spartelen; worstelen

flour, bloem, meel *n*

flourish, zwierig ge'baar *n*, krul, ge'schal *n*: ge'dijen; zwaaien; geuren met

flout, in de wind slaan

flow, stroom; vloed: stromen

flower, bloem, bloei(en)

fluctuate, schommelen, op en neer gaan

flue, rookkanaal *n*

fluent, vloeiend

fluff, pluisjes: pluizen

fluffy, donzig

fluid, vloeibaar; on'vast: vloei-stof

fluke, ankerhand: bof

fluorescent, fluore'scerend

flurry, vlaag; trilling: zenuw-achtig maken

flush, blos; opwelling, rood: ge'lijk: blozen: (schoon)spoe-len

fluster, ner'veus maken

flute, fluit; groef: groeven

flutter, ge'klapwiek *n*: fladderen, klapwieken; flikkeren

flux, voort'durende ver'andering

fly, vlieg(en); gulp: vluchten (uit): oplaten; voeren

flying-boat, vliegboot

foal, veulen *n*

foam, schuim(en) (*n*)

foamy, schuimend

focus, brandpunt *n*; haard: stellen, zijn blik fi'xeren

fodder, (vee)voer *n*

foe, vijand

fog, mist: be'nevelen

foggy, mistig; vaag

foible, zwak(ke punt) *n*

foil, schermdegen: ver'ijdelen, over'treffen

foist off on, aansmeren

fold, vouw(en), plooi; kooi, kudde: slaan

folder, map; folder

folding, op'vouwbaar, vouw-

foliage, ge'baderte *n*

folio, folio *n*

folk, mensen: volks-

follow, volgen (op), opvolgen; be'grijpen

follower, volgeling

following, aanhang

folly, dwaasheid

foment, (aan)kweken

fomentation, (warme) omslag

fond, innig

to be fond of, houden van

fondle, liefkozen

font, doopvont

food, voedsel *n*, eten *n*; stof

foodstuffs, voedingsmiddelen

fool, dwaas; nar: dwaars doen; voor de gek houden

foolhardy, roekeloos

foolish, dwaas

foot, voet, poot; voeteneinde *n*; voetvolk *n*: lopen; be'talen

on foot, te voet; aan de gang

to put one's foot in it, zich vergalop'peren

football(er), voetbal(ler)

footfall, voetstap

foothold, vaste voet

footing, houvast; (vaste) voet

footlights, voetlicht *n*

footman, li'vreiknecht, la'kei

footmark, voetafdruk

footpath, voetpad *n*

footprint, voetindruk

footstep, voetstap

footwear, schoeisel *n*

fop(pery), fat(terigheid)

for, voor; naar; ge'durende; wegens; ondanks: want; (om)dat

O! **for** . . . had ik maar . . .

forage, fou'rage: foura'geren

foray, rooftocht: plunderen

forbear, voorzaat: nalaten

forbid, ver'bieden; ver'hoeden

forbidding, afschrik'wekkend

force, (strijd)kracht, ge'weld *n*; dwingen, for'ceren

in force, van kracht

forceful, krachtig
forceps, tang
forcible, geweld'dadig; krachtig
ford, voord; door'waden
fore, voor('aan): voorgrond
forearm, voorarm
forebode, voor'spellen
foreboding, voorgevoel *n*; voor'-
  spelling
forecast, voor'spelling: voor'-
  spellen
forecastle, bak
forefather, voorvader
forefinger, wijsvinger
foregoing, voor'afgaand(e *n*)
foregone conclusion, uitge-
  maakte zaak
foreground, voorgrond
forehead, voorhoofd *n*
foreign, buitenlands; vreemd
foreigner, vreemdeling, buitenlander
foreman, (ploeg)baas
foremost, voorste, eerste
forenoon, voormiddag
foresee, voor'zien
foreshadow, de voorbode zijn
  van
foreshorten, ver'korten
foresight, voorzorg
forest, woud *n*
forestall, voor'komen, voorzijn
forester, houtvester
forestry, boswezen *n*, bosbouw
foretaste, voorsmaak
foretell, voor'spellen
forethought, be'leid *n*
forever, (voor) altijd
forfeit, boete, pand *n*; ver'spelen
forfeiture, ver'beurdverklaring
forgather, samenkomen
forge, smidsvuur *n*, smidse:
  smeden; ver'valsen
  to forge ahead, ge'stadig voor'-
  uitkomen
forgery, ver'valsing
forget, ver'geten
  I forget your name, ik ben Uw
  naam ver'geten
forgetful, ver'geetachtig
forgive, ver'geven
forgiveness, ver'giffenis
forgiving, vergevensge'zind

forgo, opgeven
fork, vork; tweesprong, ver'tak-
  king: zich splitsen
  to fork out, dokken
forked, ge'vorkt; zigzag
forlorn, troosteloos, zielig
form, vorm, ge'daante, lichaam
  n; klas; bank; formu'lier *n*;
  stijl; formali'teit; con'ditie:
  (zich) vormen, (zich) opstellen
formal, for'meel
formality, formali'teit
formation, vorming, for'matie
former, eerst(genoemd); vroeger
formidable, ge'ducht, ontzag'-
  wekkend
formula, for'mule; vorm
formulate, formu'leren
fornication, ontucht
forsake, ver'laten
fort, fort *n*
forth, voort; uit; te voorschijn
  and so forth, enzovoorts
forthcoming, (tege'moet)komend
forthright, open'hartig
forthwith, ter'stond
fortification, ver'sterking
fortify, ver'sterken
fortitude, geestkracht
fortnight, veertien dagen
fortress, vesting
fortuitous, toe'vallig
fortunate, ge'lukkig
fortune, for'tuin *n*; For'tuna
  good fortune, ge'luk *n*
  to tell fortunes, waarzeggen
forty, veertig
forward, voor'uit, voorwaarts;
  naar voren; voorst; voorlijk;
  vrij'postig: voor(speler): door-
  sturen, ver'zenden; voor'uit-
  helpen
fossil, fos'siel *n*
fossilize, ver'stenen
foster, kweken; koesteren
foster(-mother), pleeg(moeder)
foul, vies; laag; vals, ge'meen:
  be'vuilen; on'klaar raken (*or*
  maken)
found, stichten, oprichten; ba'seren
foundation, funda'ment *n*; oprichting; stichting; grond(slag)

founder, stichter, oprichter; grondlegger: ver'gaan; mis'lukken
foundling, vondeling
foundry, (me'taal)gieter'ij
fount, bron: lettertype *n*
fountain, fon'tein; bron
fountain-pen, vulpen
four, vier(tal *n*)
  on all fours, op handen en voeten
fourteen(th), veertien(de)
fourth, vierde (man); kwart (*n*)
fowl, ge'vogelte *n*; hoender
fox, vos: be'dotten
foxglove, vingerhoedskruid *n*
fraction, breuk; mi'niem ge'deelte *n*, onderdeel *n*
fractious, twistziek
fracture, breuk: breken
fragile, broos, breekbaar
fragment, frag'ment *n*, brokstuk *n*
fragrance, geur
fragrant, geurig
frail, teer
frailty, zwakheid
frame, lijst, mon'tuur *n*, ko'zijn *n*; lichaamsbouw: inlijsten; (op)stellen
  frame of mind, ge'moedstoestand
framework, ge'raamte *n*
franc, frank
franchise, kiesrecht *n*; (burger)recht *n*
frank, open'hartig
frantic, dol, razend, wild, radeloos
fraternal, broederlijk
fraud, be'drog *n*, fraude; oplichter
fraudulent, fraudu'leus
fraught with, zwanger van
fray, strijd: (uit)rafelen, ver'stlijten
freak, gril, ge'drocht *n*
freckle(d), (vol) sproet(en)
free, vrij; gratis; los(lippig); open(lijk); over'vloedig: be'vrijden, vrijlaten
  free from (*or* **of**), zonder, be'vrijd van
  to set free, be'vrijden

freedom, vrijheid
free-hand, met de hand
freehold, vrij (grondbezit *n*)
freeze, (doen) (be')vriezen
freight, vracht(prijs)
freighter, vrachtboot, vrachtschip *n*
French, Frans(en) (*n*)
  French bean, sperzieboon
  French polish, poli'toeren
  French windows, openslaande deuren
Frenchman, Fransman
frenzied, razend
frenzy, razer'nij
frequency, veel-vuldigheid, fre'quentie
frequent, veel'voorkomend, ge'regeld: dikwijls be'zoeken
frequently, her'haaldelijk
fresco, fresco *n*
fresh, vers, fris; nieuw; zoet
freshman, eerste'jaars (stu'dent)
fret, kniezen, pruilen; wegvreten
fret-work, uitgezaagd werk *n*
friar, monnik
friction, wrijving
Friday, vrijdag
friend, vriend('in), kennis
  to make friends with, be'vriend raken met
friendly, vriend('schapp)elijk
friendship, vriendschap
frieze, rand, fries
frigate, fre'gat *n*
fright, schrik; vogelverschrikker
frighten, doen schrikken
frightful, ver'schrikkelijk
frigid, ijzig; kil
frill, ge'rimpelde strook; tierlan'tijntje *n*
fringe, franje; pony; buitenkant: om'zomen; grenzen (aan)
frippery, prullen
frisk, dartelen; vluchtig fouill'eren
frisky, dartel
fritter, bei'gnet: ver'kwisten
frivolous, licht'zinnig; beuzelachtig
frizzle, sissen; fri'seren; bakken

fro: to and —, heen en weer, op en neer

frock, jurk(je *n*)

frog, kikvors

frolic, jo'lijt: dartelen

from, van('daan), van'af; uit; wegens

front, voorkant, voorste deel (*n*); front *n*: voor-, voorste
  at the front (of), voor'aan (in)
  in front of, voor
  in the front (of), voor'in (in)

frontier, grens

frost, vorst; rijp

frostbite, be'vriezing

froth, schuim *n*

frown, frons: het voorhoofd fronsen
  to frown upon, niet graag zien

frugal, sober, karig

fruit, vrucht(en), fruit *n*

fruitful, vruchtbaar

fruition, ver'vulling

fruitless, vruchteloos

frustrate, ver'ijdelen; tegenwerken

frustrated, te'leurgesteld en on-be'vredigd

frustration, wan'hopig ge'voel van onbe'vredigdheid

fry, bakken, braden

fuddle, be'nevelen

fuel, brand(stof): tanken

fugitive, vluchteling: (voort')- vluchtig

fulfil, ver'vullen; waarmaken; be'antwoorden aan

full, vol('ledig)
  full of, vol
  in full, ten volle; vol'uit
  fully, vol'komen, ten volle

fumble, tasten; frommelen

fume, damp(en): koken

fumigate, met dampen ont'smetten

fun, pret
  for (*or* **in**) **fun,** voor de grap
  to make fun of, de gek steken met

function, functie: functio'neren

functional, functio'neel; prak-tisch

fund, fonds *n*: voorraad

funds, geld *n*

fundamental, fundamen'teel, grond(beginsel *n*)

funeral, be'grafenis(-); lijk-, graf-

fungus, zwam

funk, rats: niet aandurven

funnel, trechter; pijp

funny, grappig; raar

fur, bont *n*; be'slag *n*, ketelsteen

furious, woedend

furl, oprollen

furnace, (smelt)oven, kachel

furnish, meubi'leren; voor'zien van, 'ver'schaffen

furnishings, stof'fering (en meu-bi'lering)

furniture, meubelen

furrow, voor; groef

further, verder, nader: be'vorderen

furtive, steels, heimelijk

fury, woede, razer'nij

fuse, (doorgeslagen) stop; lont: samensmelten

fuselage, romp

fusion, samensmelting; fusie

fuss, drukte: zich druk maken; zenuwachtig maken

fussy, lastig; druk

fusty, muf

futile, ver'geefs, zinloos, onbe'nul-lig

future, toekomst: toe'komstig
  in future, voortaan

G

gabble, snateren

gaberdine, gabar'dine

gable, gevelspits

gadget, snufje *n*, ge'val *n*

gag, prop: mop: knevelen

gaiety, vrolijkheid

gain, winst: be'halen; toene-men; ver'werven; be'reiken; voorlopen

gainsay, tegenspreken

gait, gang

gaiter, slobkous

gala, feest *n*: gala-

galaxy, schitterende ver'zameling

gale, storm

gall, gal: gruwelijk ergeren

gallant, fier, hoffelijk

gallantry, dapperheid; hoffelijkheid

galleon, gal'joen n

gallery, gale'rij; mu'seum n

galley, ga'lei; kom'buis

gallon, 4½ liter

gallop, ga'lop('peren)

gallows, galg

galore, in overvloed

galosh, overschoen

galvanize, galvani'seren

gamble, gokje n; gokken

gambler, gokker

gambol, dartelen

game, spel(letje) n; par'tij(tje n); wild n: flink; be'reid: lam: gokken

gamekeeper, jachtopziener

gamut, toonladder; re'gister n

gander, gent

gang, troep, bende

gangrene, gan'green n

gangster, gangster

gangway, pad n; loopplank

gaol, ge'vangenis

gaoler, ci'pier

gap, gat n, opening, hi'aat n

gape, gapen

garage, ga'rage: stallen

garb, kle'dij

garbage, vuilnis

garden, tuin('ieren)

gardener, tuinman, tui'nier

gargle, gorgelen

garish, schel, op'zichtig

garland, guir'lande: om'kransen

garlic, knoflook

garment, kledingstuk n, ge'waad n

garner, graanschuur: binnenhalen

garnish, gar'neren

garret, zolderkamer

garrison, garni'zoen n: legeren

garrulous, praatziek

garter, kouseband

gas, gas n: ver'gassen

gash, snee; snijden, scheuren

gasp, snak(ken)

gastric, maag-

gate, hek n, poort; ingang

gate-crash, binnenvallen

gateway, poort, hek n

gather, (zich) ver'zamelen; binnenhalen; krijgen (speed); samentrekken; opmaken(uit)

gathering, bij'eenkomst

gauche, links

gaudy, op'zichtig

gauge, (standaard)maat; meetinstrument n, manometer: meten, ijken; schatten

gaunt, (brood)mager

gauntlet, (kap)handschoen, pantserhandschoen; spitsroede

gauze, gaas n

gawky, slungelig

gay, vrolijk

gaze, starre blik: staren

gazette, staatscourant

gear, ver'snelling; inrichting; tuig: instellen

to change gear, overschakelen

out of gear, uitgeschakeld; in de war

gelatine, gela'tine

gem, edelsteen; ju'weel n

gender, ge'slacht n

general, algemeen: gene'raal

in general, over het algemeen

generalize, generali'seren

generally, ge'woonlijk; (over het) algemeen

generate, opwekken

generation, gene'ratie; opwekking

generator, gene'rator

generosity, edel'moedigheid

generous, edel'moedig; ro'yaal

genetics, ge'netica

genial, vriendelijk; groeizaam

genitive, genitief

genius, ge'nie n; ta'lent n

genteel, deftig(doend)

gentle, licht, zacht('aardig); matig

gentleman, gentleman, heer

genuine, echt, op'recht

geographic(al), aardrijks'kundig

geography, aardrijkskunde

geology, geolo'gie

geometry, meetkunde

Georgian, achttiende-'eeuws

geranium, ge'ranium

germ, kiem, ba'cil
German, Duits(er) (n)
  German measles, rode hond
Germany, Duitsland n
gesticulate, gesticu'leren
gesture, ge'baar n
get, krijgen; komen; worden
  I have got, ik heb
  I have got to, ik moet
    to get something done, iets
    (laten) doen; iets ge'daan
    krijgen
    to get about, buitenkomen,
    rondlopen
    to get along, (weg)gaan; op-
    schieten; het maken
    to get around, overal komen;
    be'kend worden; om'zeilen
    to get at, be'reiken; achter
    komen; be'doelen
    to get away, wegkomen;
    ont'snappen
    to get back, te'rugkomen;
    te'rugkrijgen
    to get in, binnenkomen, in-
    stappen
    to get off, (er) afkomen (van),
    afstappen van; afkrijgen
    to get on, opstappen; aan-
    krijgen; opschieten; het stel-
    len; het maken
    to get out, (onder')uitkomen,
    uitstappen; voor de dag halen;
    to get over, te boven komen
    to get through, doorkomen;
    antwoord krijgen
    to get to, komen in (or aan)
    to get up, opstaan; opsteken;
    op touw zetten
geyser, geiser
ghastly, af'grijselijk, doodsbleek
ghost, spook n; zweem
giant, reus('achtig)
gibber, brabbelen
gibberish, koeter'waals n
gibbet, galg
giblets, afval van ge'vogelte
giddy, duizelig; duizeling'wekkend; mal
gift, ge'schenk n; gave
gifted, be'gaafd
gig, sjees
gigantic, mas'saal, ge'weldig

giggle, giechelen
gild, ver'gulden
gill, kieuw: 0.14 liter
gilt, ver'guld (sel n)
gin, jonge jenever
ginger, gember
gingerly, be'hoedzaam
gipsy, zi'geuner('in)
giraffe, gi'raffe
gird, om'gorden
girder, (stalen) balk
girdle, gordel
girl, meisje n
girl-friend, vrien'din
girlish, meisjesachtig
girth, omvang; buikriem
gist, kern
give, geven; doorzakken, buigen
  to give away, weggeven; ver'-
  klappen
  to give in, zich ge'wonnen
  geven
  to give out, uitdelen; aankondigen; be'zwijken
  to give up, overgeven; (het)
  opgeven
given, be'paald; ge'neigd (tot)
gizzard, spiermaag; strot
glacier, gletsjer
glad, blij (de)
gladden, ver'blijden
glade, open plek
gladly, graag
glamorous, be'toverend
glamour, be'tovering
glance, (vluchtige) blik: een
  blik werpen; afschampen
gland, klier
glare, ver'blindend licht n;
  woeste blik : woest kijken
glaring, schel; vlammend; in
  het oog springend
glass, glas(werk) n : glazen
  glasses, bril
glaze, gla'zuur n: van glas
  voor'zien; gla'zuren
gleam, schijnsel n, straaltje n,
  glans: glimmen
glean, lezen; ver'garen
glee, vreugde, schelms ge'not n
glen, bergdal n
glib, glad, rad
glide, zweven, glijden

glider, zweefvliegtuig *n*

glimmer, flikkering; glimp: flikkeren

glimpse, glimp

glint, glinstering

glisten, glinsteren

glitter, ge'schitter *n*: schitteren

gloat, zich ver'lustigen, leedvermaak hebben

globe, (aard)bol

globule, pareltje *n*

gloom, duister *n*; droef'geestigheid

gloomy, duister, somber; droef'geestig

glorify, ver'heerlijken

glorious, roemrijk; heerlijk

glory, glorie, heerlijkheid

gloss, glans

　to **gloss over,** ver'doezelen

glossy, glanzend

glove, handschoen

glow, gloed; blos: gloeien; stralen

glower, dreigend kijken

glow-worm, glimworm

glue, (hout)lijm: lijmen

glum, sip

glut, (over)ver'zadiging: over'voeren

glutton, gulzigaard; werkezel

gnarled, knoestig, knokig

gnash one's teeth, knarsetanden

gnat, mug

gnaw, (af)knagen

gnome, aardmannetje *n*

go, (weg)gaan; lopen; worden; horen

　as things go, verge'leken bij anderen

　to **go by,** gaan per (*or* over); voor'bijgaan; zich laten leiden door; be'kend staan onder

　to **go down,** afgaan; naar be'neden gaan, ondergaan, zinken; er'in gaan

　to **go into,** binnengaan; ingaan (op); treden in (details); zich ver'diepen in

　to **go off,** af(*or* weg)gaan; aflopen

　to **go on,** gaan op; voor'uitgaan, voortgaan

　to **go up,** stijgen

　to **go with,** meegaan met; passen bij, horen bij

　to **go without,** het stellen zonder

　to **let go,** loslaten

goad, prikkel(en); aanzetten

go-ahead, vooruit'strevend

goal, doel(punt) *n*

goat, geit

gobble, schrokken; klokken

goblet, bo'kaal

goblin, ka'bouter

god, god

goddess, go'din

godly, god'vruchtig

god(mother), peet(tante)

godsend, zegen

goggle, kijken met grote ogen

going: to get (*or* to keep) —, aan de gang brengen, (*or* houden); lopen

gold, goud(en) (*n*)

golden, gouden; gulden

goldfish, goudvis

gold-leaf, bladgoud (*n*)

golf, golf *n*

golf-course, golf-links, golf-baan

gondola, gondel

gone, weg; op; zoek; dood

gong, gong

good, goed; zoet: bestwil

　a good deal, vrij veel

　for good, voor'goed; ten goede

good-bye, dag

good-looking, knap

good-natured, ge'moedelijk, goed'aardig

goodness, goedheid; voeding: goeie ge'nade!

good-night, wel te rusten

goods, goederen, spullen

goodwill, wel'willendheid; klan'dizie

goose, gans

gooseberry, kruisbes(sen)

gore, ge'ronnen bloed *n*; spietsen

gorge, bergengte: (zich) volstoppen

gorgeous, magni'fiek

gospel, evan'gelie *n*

gossamer, herfstdraad

gossip, ge'roddel *n*; rodde-
laar(ster); roddelen, kletsen
gothic, gotisch
gout, jicht
govern, re'geren; leiden
governess, gouver'nante
government, re'gering; be'leid *n*
governor, gouver'neur; cu'rator
gown, ja'pon; toga
grab, greep: grijpen naar
grace, gratie; ge'nade; tafelgebed *n*; res'pijt *n*: ver'eren
graceful, graci'eus
gracious, minzaam, hoffelijk:
(grote) goedheid!
grade, graad, kwali'teit: sor'teren
gradient, hellingshoek
gradual, ge'leidelijk
graft, (poli'tieke) knoeie'rij:
enten, transplan'teren
grain, graan *n*, korrel; greintje
n; nerf
grammar, gram'matica
grammar-school, gym'nasium
n
gramophone, grammo'foon
granary, graanschuur
grand, groot(s), prachtig
grandchild, kleinkind *n*
grandeur, grootsheid
grandiose, grandi'oos
grandmother, grootmoeder
granite, gra'niet(en) (*n*)
granny, grootje *n*, oma
grant, toelage: (toe)geven;
ver'lenen; inwilligen
grape, druif
grapefruit, grapefruit
graph, gra'fiek
graphic, grafisch; aan'schouwelijk
graphite, gra'fiet *n*
grapple, worstelen
grasp, greep; i'dee *n*; be'reik *n*:
vastpakken
grasping, in'halig
grass, gras *n*
grasshopper, sprinkhaan
grassy, gras(rijk)
grate, rooster: raspen; knarsen;
tegen de borst stuiten
grateful, dankbaar

gratification, vol'doening
gratify, strelen; be'vredigen
gratifying, be'vredigend, dankbaar
grating, traliewerk *n*; knarsen *n*
gratitude, dankbaarheid
gratuitous, gratis; spon'taan;
mis'plaatst
gratuity, fooi
grave, graf *n*: ernstig
gravel, grint(-) (*n*)
graveyard, kerkhof *n*
gravitation,   aantrek-
king(skracht)
gravity, zwaartekracht; ernst
centre of gravity, zwaartepunt *n*
gravy, jus
graze, schaafwond: even aanraken; schaven: grazen, weiden
grazing, weiland *n*
grease, smeer, vet *n*: (in)smeren,
invetten
greasy, vet(tig), vuil
great, groot; voor'naamste;
nobel; enthousi'aste
a great deal (of), heel veel
great-grandchild, achterkleinkind *n*
great-grandmother, overgrootmoeder
greatly, zeer
greed, gulzigheid, hebzucht
greedy, gulzig; hebberig
Greek, Griek(s) (*n*)
green, groen: brink; baan
greens, bladgroenten
greengrocer, groenteboer
greenhouse, broeikas
greet, (be)groeten
greeting, groet
grey, grijs (worden), grauw
greyhound, haze'wind: wind-
honden-
grid, (braad)rooster; hoogspan-
ningsnet *n*
grief, ver'driet *n*
grievance, grief
grieve, treuren; be'droeven
grievous, hevig; schreeuwend
grill, rooster(en)
grim, onver'biddelijk; onaan'-
lokkelijk; akelig

grimace, gri'mas
grime, vuil *n*: be'vuilen
grin, grijns: grijnzen
grind, ge'zwoeg *n*: malen;
slijpen; knarsen (op)
grindstone, slijpsteen
grip, (hand)greep, vat *n*, houvast
n; tas; be'grip *n*: (vast)pak-
ken
gristle, kraakbeen *n*
grit, gruis *n*; durf
grizzle, grienen
grizzly, grijs(achtig)
groan, ge'kreun *n*: kreunen
grocer, kruide'nier
groceries, kruide'nierswaren
groggy, wankel
groin, lies
groom, stalknecht: ver'zorgen
groove, groef; sleur: groeven
grope, (rond)tasten
gross, bruto; grof: gros *n*
grotesque, gro'tesk
grotto, grot
ground, grond(-); ter'rein *n*:
aan de grond lopen; grondig
onder'leggen
  to cover ground, ter'rein
  be'strijken
  to give ground, wijken
  to stand one's ground, standhouden; voet bij stuk houden
grounds, ter'rein *n*, park *n*;
(koffie)dik *n*; reden(en)
ground-floor, (op de) bc'ne-
denver'dieping
groundless, onge'grond
group, groep('eren)
grouse, korhoen(ders) *n*: kankeren
grove, bos(je *n*)
grovel, kruipen
grow, (aan)groeien; ver'bouwen,
kweken; worden
  to grow up, opgroeien, ouder
  worden; ont'staan
growing, toenemend
growl, grom(men)
grown-up, vol'wassen(e)
growth, groei; aanwas; ge'zwel
n
grub, larve; kost: wroeten
grudge, wrok: mis'gunnen

grudgingly, met tegenzin
gruel, gruwel
gruelling, af'mattend
gruesome, griezelig
gruff, bars
grumble, mopperen
grunt, ge'knor *n*; ge'brom *n*;
knorren; brommen
guarantee, (waar)borg, ga'rantie: waarborgen, garan'deren
guard, wacht; scherm *n*,
be'scherming; hoede; con-
duc'teur: (be')waken; be'schermen
guarded, voor'zichtig
guardian, voogd, be'waarder:
be'scherm-
guess, gis(sing): raden
guest, gast, lo'gé(e)
guidance, leiding, ad'vies *n*
guide, gids; padvindster: leiden
guild, gilde *n*
guilder, gulden
guile, list
guileless, argeloos
guillotine, guillo'tine
guilt, schuld
guiltless, on'schuldig
guilty, schuldig, schuldbe'wust
guise, voorkomen *n*, vorm; mom
n
guitar, gi'taar
gulf, golf; kloof
gull, meeuw: beetnemen
gullet, slokdarm, keel
gullible, lichtge'lovig
gully, geul
gulp, slok, teug: opslokken;
inslikken
gum, gom(men); tandvlees *n*
gun, ka'non *n*, ge'weer *n*, pis'tool
n
gunner, artille'rist, kon'stabel
gunpowder, buskruit *n*
gunwale, dolboord *n*
gurgle, kabbelen, klokken, kirren
gush, stroom: gutsen, stromen
gushing, dwepend
gust, vlaag
gusto, animo
gusty, stormachtig
gut, darm: schoonmaken; uit-
branden

gutter, goot
guttersnipe, straatkind *n*
guy, stormlijn: vent: voor de gek houden
guzzle, opschrokken
gymnasium, gymnas¹tiekzaal
gymnastics, gymnas¹tiek

H

haberdashery, garen en band *n*
habit, ge¹woonte; pij; rijkleed *n*
habitable, be¹woonbaar
habitation, woonplaats
habitual, ge¹woon(lijk), ge¹woonte-, regel¹matig
hack, rijpaard *n*: hakken
hackneyed, afgezaagd
haddock, schelvis
haemorrhage, bloeding
hag, heks
haggard, uitgeteerd
haggle, knibbelen
hail, hagel(en): toejuichen, (luidkeels) be¹groeten; aanroepen; af¹komstig zijn
hair, haar *n*: haren
to split hairs, muggeziften
hairdresser, kapper
hairy, harig, be¹haard
half, half: (de) helft
half past one, half twee
half-way, halver¹wege
hall, hal, zaal
hallmark, keur; stempel(en) (*n*)
hallow, heiligen
hallucination, halluci¹natie
halo, aure¹ool, halo
halt, halt (houden); hokken
halter, halster
halve, hal¹veren
ham, ham
hamlet, ge¹hucht *n*
hammer, hamer(en)
hammock, hangmat
hamper, mand: be¹lemmeren
hand, hand; wijzer; arbeider; spel *n*: over¹handigen, aangeven
  at hand, bij de hand; op handen
  in hand, in be¹dwang; onder handen; over

on the other hand, aan de andere kant
to hand down, overleveren
to hand in, inleveren
to hand out, uitdelen
to hand over, overdragen, over¹handigen
to hand round, ronddienen, ronddelen
handbag, handtas
handbill, strooibiljet *n*
handcuff, handboei
handful, hand(je)vol
handicap, handicap(pen)
handicraft, handwerk *n*, handenarbeid
handiwork, (hand)werk *n*
handkerchief, zakdoek
handle, handvat *n*, knop, oor *n*: be¹dienen; han¹teren; aanpakken; be¹handelen; handelen in
handle-bars, stuur *n*
handmade, handwerk
handshake, handdruk
handsome, knap; flink, ro¹yaal
handwriting, (hand)schrift *n*
handy, handig; bij de hand; van pas
hang, slag: (op)hangen; laten hangen; be¹hangen
to hang about, rondlummelen
to hang on, (zich) vasthouden; wachten
hangar, han¹gar
hanging, drape¹rie
hang-over, kater
hank, streng
hanker, hunkeren
haphazard, luk¹raak
happen, (toe¹vallig) ge¹beuren
  I happen to . . . ik . . . . toe¹vallig; ik . . . nu eenmaal
happenings, ge¹beurtenissen
happiness, ge¹luk *n*
happy, ge¹lukkig
harangue, heftige toespraak (houden)
harass, be¹stoken; kwellen
harbour, haven: (ver¹)bergen, koesteren
hard, hard(¹vochtig); moeilijk; vast
to try hard, zijn best doen

harden, harder worden (*or* maken)
hard-hearted, hard'vochtig
hardly, nauwelijks: hard
hardship, ont'bering, last
hardware, ijzerwaren
hardwood, hardhout(en) (*n*)
hardy, ge'hard, sterk
hare, haas
harlequin, harle'kijn
harm, schade, letsel *n*: kwaad
  doen
harmful, na'delig, schadelijk
harmless, on'schadelijk; argeloos
harmonic, har'monisch
harmonica, mondharmonika
harmonious, har'monisch, harmoni'eus
harmonize, (doen) harmoni'-
  eren; harmoni'seren
harmony, harmo'nie
harness, (paarden)tuig *n*; ga'-
  reel *n*: optuigen
harp, harp: hameren
harpoon, har'poen('eren)
harpsichord, klave'cimbel
harrow, eg(gen); aangrijpen
harry, plunderen; kwellen
harsh, ruw, wrang; hard
hart, mannetjeshert *n*
harvest, oogst(tijd): oogsten
hash, ha'chee; knoeieboel
haste, haast
hasten, zich haasten, ver'haasten
hasty, haastig; driftig
hat, hoed
hatch, luik *n*: uitbroeden, uitkomen
hatchet, bijl
hate, haat: haten, een hekel
  hebben aan
hateful, akelig
hatred, haat
haughty, hoog'hartig
haul, vangst: slepen, halen
haunch, lende, hurk
haunt, oord *n*, speelplaats; hol
  n: veel'vuldig be'zoeken;
  achter'volgen
haunted, spook-, door geesten
  be'zocht
have, hebben; laten; moeten;
  nemen; krijgen

haven, (veilige) haven
haversack, broodzak
havoc, ver'woesting
hawk, havik: venten
hawser, tros
hawthorn, hagedoorn
hay, hooi *n*
hayrick, haystack, hooiberg
hazard, risico *n*: wagen
hazardous, ris'kant
haze, waas *n*, nevel
hazel, hazelaar: lichtbruin
hazy, wazig; vaag
he, hij
head, hoofd(-) (*n*), kop; spits:
  tegen-: leiden; sturen
  to keep one's head, zijn
    ver'stand bij el'kaar houden
  to lose one's head, in de war
    raken
headache, hoofdpijn
head-dress, headgear, hoofd-
  tooi
heading, ru'briek, opschrift *n*
headland, voorgebergte *n*
headlight, koplamp
headline, kop
headlong, hals over kop
headmaster, direc'teur,
  (school)hoofd *n*
headquarters, hoofdkwartier *n*
headstrong, koppig
headway, voortgang
heal, ge'nezen
health, ge'zondheid
healthy, ge'zond
heap, hoop, massa: ophopen
hear, horen; luisteren
hearing, ge'hoor *n*; ver'hoor *n*
hearken, luisteren
hearsay, praatjes
hearse, lijkwagen
heart, hart *n*; moed; kern, binnenste *n*
  by heart, uit het hoofd
  to take heart, moed scheppen
heart-breaking, hartver'scheur-
  end
heart-broken, ge'broken
hearten, opbeuren
heart-felt, innig
hearth, haard
heartless, harteloos

hearty, hartelijk; ge'zond; stevig; hart'grondig

heat, hitte; vuur *n*; loop: ver'warmen; opwinden

heater, ver'warmingsapparaat *n*

heath, heide

heathen, heiden(s)

heather, heide

heave, hijsen, lichten; trekken; slaken; deinen

to heave to, bijdraaien

heaven, hemel

heavenly, hemels, hemel-

heavy, zwaar, klef

Hebrew, He'breeuws *n*; He'-breeër

heckle, jouwen, scherp onder'vragen

hectic, koortsachtig

hedge, heg: om'heinen; er omheen draaien

hedgehog, egel

hedgerow, haag

heed, aandacht: letten op

heedless, achteloos

heel, hiel,hak: overhellen

hefty, stoer

heifer, vaars

height, hoogte; top(punt *n*)

heighten, ver'hogen; ver'sterken

heinous, snood

heir, erfgenaam

heiress, erfgename

heirloom, erfstuk *n*

helicopter, helikopter

hell, hel

hello, hal'lo

helm, roer *n*

helmet, helm

helmsman, roerganger

help, hulp; steun, helper(s): helpen; nalaten

I can't help it, ik kan er niets aan doen

help yourself gaat Uw gang!

helpful, hulp'vaardig; be'vorderlijk, ge'makkelijk

helping, portie

helpless, hulpeloos

helter-skelter, hals over kop

hem, zoom: zomen

hemisphere, halfrond *n*

hemp, hennep

hen, kip: wijfjes-

hence, van'daar (dat); hie van'daan, van nu af aan

henceforth, van nu af aan

henchman, handlanger

henpeck, op de kop zitten

her, haar

herald, he'raut, voorbode: aan kondigen

heraldry, heral'diek

herb, kruid *n*

herd, kudde: hokken, (samen-drijven

herdsman, veehoeder

here, hier

hereabout(s), hier in de buurt

hereafter, hier'na(maals *n*)

hereby, hierbij, hierdoor

hereditary, erfelijk, erf-

heredity, erfelijkheid, overerving

heresy, kette'rij

heretic(al), ketter(s)

hereupon, hierop

herewith, hierbij

heritage, erfdeel *n*, erfgoed *n*

hermetic(al), her'metisch

hermit, kluizenaar

hero, held

heroic, held'haftig, helden-

heroics, bombast

heroine, hel'din

heron, reiger

herring, haring

hesitant, aarzelend

hesitate, aarzelen

hesitation, aarzeling

heterogeneous, hetero'geen

hew, houwen

heyday, bloeitijd

hiatus, hi'aat *n*

hibernate, winterslaap doen

hiccup(s), hik(ken)

to have hiccups, de hik hebben

hide, huid: afrossen: (zich) ver'bergen

hide-and-seek, ver'stoppertje *n*

hidebound, be'krompen

hideous, af'zichtelijk, af'schu-welijk

hierarchy, hiërar'chie

high, hoog; adellijk

highland, hoogland(s) (*n*)

highly, hoog-, zeer

high-pitched, hoog, schel

highway, grote weg

highwayman, struikrover

hike, trektocht: trekken

hilarious, uitgelaten

hill, heuvel, berg

hillock, heuveltje *n*

hilly, heuvelachtig

hilt, ge'vest *n*

him, hem

hind, achter(ste): hinde

hinder, (ver)hinderen

hindrance, be'lemmering

hinge, schar'nier *n*; spil: draaien

hint, wenk; zweem: laten door-schemeren

  to hint at, zinspelen op

hip, heup: rozebottel

hippopotamus, nijlpaard *n*

hire, huur: (ver')huren

hire-purchase, huurkoop: op afbetaling kopen

his, zijn, van hem

hiss, sissen; (uit)fluiten

historian, ge'schiedschrijver

historic, his'torisch; ge'wichtig

historical, his'torisch

history, ge'schiedenis

hit, slag; treffer; suc'ces *n*: slaan; raken, treffen

  to hit upon, treffen, vinden

hitch, ruk; kink in de kabel: (op)trekken; vastmaken

hitch-hike, liften

hither, hier(heen)

hitherto, tot nu toe

hive, korf; mierennest *n*

hoard, voorraad: opsparen, ham-steren

hoarding, re'clamebord *n*

hoar-frost, rijp

hoarse, hees, schor

hoax, beetneme'rij: beetnemen

hobble, strompelen

hobby, liefhebbe'rij, stokpaardje *n*

hobnob, keuvelen

hockey, hockey *n*

hod, (kalk)bak

hoe, schoffel(en)

hog, varken *n*; zwijn *n*

hoist, hijstoestel *n*: (op)hijsen

hold, houvast *n*, vat *n*; invloed;

ruim *n*; (vast)houden; be'vat-ten; (in zijn be'zit) hebben; opgaan

to hold out, geven; volhouden; in leven blijven

to hold up, ophouden; aan-houden

to hold with, goedkeuren, het eens zijn met

to get hold of, te pakken krijgen; vastpakken

hole, gat *n*, hol *n*

holiday, va'cantie(dag), feestdag

holiness, heiligheid

Holland, Nederland *n*

hollow, hol(te); leeg

  to hollow out, uithollen

holly, hulst

holster, holster

holy, heilig

homage, hulde(betuiging)

home, (t.)huis *n*, tehuis *n*: bin-nenlands: naar huis; raak

  at home, thuis

homeland, ge'boorteland *n*

homeless, dakloos

homely, huiselijk; ge'moedelijk

home-made, eigengemaakt

homesick: to be —, heimwee hebben

homestead, hofstede

homeward, huiswaarts

homicide, doodslag

homogeneous, homo'geen

honest(y), eerlijk(heid)

honey, honing

honeycomb, honingraat

honeymoon, huwelijksreis

honeysuckle, kamper'foelie

honk, toeteren; snateren

honorary, ere-

honour, eer(gevoel *n*); eerbewijs *n*: (ver')eren

honourable, eervol

hood, kap

hoodwink, zand in de ogen strooien

hoof, hoef

hook, haak: aan de haak slaan

hooligan, straatvlegel

hoop, hoepel

hoot, krassen; toeteren; uitjouw-en

hop, sprong: hop(plant): hink-
en, springen
hope, hoop(volle ver'wachting):
hopen
hopeful, hoopvol
hopeless, hopeloos, wan'hopig
horde, horde
horizon, horizon
horizontal, horizon'taal
horn, horen
hornet, horzel
horoscope, horos'coop
horrible, horrid, af'grijselijk,
af'schuwelijk
horrify, ont'zetten
horror, afgrijzen n; gruwel(daad)
horse, paard n; cavale'rie
horseback: on —, te paard
horseman, ruiter
horse-power, paardekracht
horse-shoe, hoefijzer n
horticulture, tuinbouw
hose, (tuin)slang; kousen
hosiery, trico'tages
hospitable, gastvrij
hospital, ziekenhuis n
hospitality, gast'vrijheid
host, gastheer, waard; (leger-)
schaar; Hostie
hostage, gijzelaar
hostel, te'huis n
hostess, gastvrouw
hostile, vij'andelijk, vij'andig
hostility, vij'andelijkheid, vij'-
andigheid
hot, heet, warm
hotel, ho'tel n
hothouse, broeikas
hound, (jacht)hond
hour, uur n
house, huis n: huisvesten
to keep house, de huishouding
doen
household, huisgezin n:
huis('houd)elijk
householder, ge'zinshoofd n
housekeeper, huishoudster
housekeeping, huishouden n;
huishoud(geld n)
housetop, dak(rand) (n)
housewife, huisvrouw
housework, huishoudelijk
werk n

housing, woning-, woon-: huis
vesting
hovel, krot n
hover, zweven, hangen
how, hoe
however, hoe . . . dan ook, ho
. . . toch: echter
howl, huilen, janken; gillen
joelen
howler, bok
hub, naaf; middelpunt n
hubbub, herrie
huddle, (bij or in el'kaar) kruiper
hue, tint: ge'gil n
hug, pakken; tegen zich aan-
drukken; koesteren
huge, reus'achtig
hulk, romp
hulking, log
hull, romp
hum, ge'gons n: gonzen, snorren;
neuriën
human, menselijk, mens(en-)
human being, menselijk wezen
n
humane, mens'lievend
humanitarian, humani'tair
humanity, het mensdom n
humanly, menselijkerwijs
humble, nederig: ver'nederen
humbug, bedrieger('ij)
humdrum, saai(e sleur)
humid(ity), vochtig(heid)
humiliate, ver'nederen
humility, ootmoed
humorist, humo'rist
humorous, grappig, humo'ristisch
humour, humor; hu'meur n;
luim: toegeven aan
hump, bult
hunch, zo'n idee n: samentrekken, krommen
hunchback, ge'bochelde
hundred(th), honderd(ste)
hunger, honger
hungry, hongerig
to be hungry, trek (or honger)
hebben
hunk, homp
hunt, jacht(stoet): jagen (op);
(af)zoeken
to hunt down, in het nauw
drijven; opsporen

hunter, jager; jachtpaard *n*

hurdle, horde; hindernis

hurl, slingeren

hurrah, hoe'ra

hurricane, or'kaan

hurried, haastig, ge'haast

hurry, (zich) haasten

 to be in a hurry, haast hebben

hurt, pijn doen; deren, kwetsen

hurtle, ratelen, schieten

husband, man, echtgenoot; zuinig be'heren

husbandry, (zuinig) be'heer *n*

hush, stilte: stil! : tot zwijgen
brengen

husk, schede, schil

husky, schor; potig

hussy, meid

hustle, ge'jacht *n*: jachten,
drijven; dringen

hut, hut, ba'rak

hybrid, hy'bride: bastaard-

hydraulic, hy'draulisch

hydrogen, waterstof

hygiene, ge'zondheidsleer

hygienic, hygi'ënisch

hymn, ge'zang *n*

hyphen(ate), (door een) streepje
n (ver'binden)

hypnotize, hypnoti'seren

hypocrisy, huichela'rij

hypocrite, huichelaar

hypocritical, huichelachtig

hypothesis, hypo'these

hysterical, hys'terisch

hysterics, zenuwaanval

I

I, ik

ice, ijs(je) *n* : (doen) be'vriezen;
gla'ceren

iceberg, ijsberg

ice-cream, roomijs *n*

iced, ijskoud; gegla'ceerd

icicle, ijskegel

icing sugar, poedersuiker

icy, ijskoud, glad; ijs-, ijzig

idea, i'dee *n*

ideal, ide'aal (*n*)

idealism, idea'lisme *n*

idealist(ic), idea'list(isch)

idealize, ideali'seren

identical, iden'tiek

identification, identifi'catie

identify, identifi'ceren, vereen'zelvigen

identity, identi'teit

idiom, idi'oom *n*

idiosyncracy, eigen'aardigheid

idiot(ic), idi'oot

idle, nietsdoend; lui; leeg:
niets doen

 to be idle, niets doen; stilliggen

idler, leegloper

idol, a'god (sbeeld *n*)

idolatry, afgodendienst

idolize, ver'afgoden

idyll, i'dylle

if, als, in'dien, of

ignite, in brand steken (*or* raken)

ignoble, laag

ignominious, smadelijk

ignorance, on'wetendheid

ignorant, on'wetend, on'kundig

ignore, ne'geren

ill, ziek; slecht, kwaad (*n*);
kwalijk

 to cause ill feeling, kwaad
bloed zetten

ill-advised, onver'standig

ill-bred, on'opgevoed

illegal, on'wettig, onrecht'matig

illegible, on'leesbaar

illegitimate, on'wettig; ongeoorloofd

ill-fated, ramp'spoedig

illicit, onge'oorloofd

illiterate, onge'letterd: analfa'-
beet

illness, ziekte

illogical, on'logisch

ill-treat, slecht be'handelen

illuminate, ver (*or* be)'lichten,
toelichten; ver'luchten

illumination, ver'lichting; ver'-
luchting

illusion, il'lusie

illustrate, illus'treren; toelichten

illustration, illus'tratie, toe-
lichting

illustrious, door'luchtig

image, (even)beeld *n*, beeltenis

imaginable, denkbaar

imaginary, denk'beeldig

imagination, ver'beelding-(skracht)

imaginative, vindingrijk, rijk aan ver'beelding; fan'tastisch

imagine, zich voorstellen

imbecile, imbe'ciel

imbibe, drinken; (in zich) opnemen

imbue, door'drenken

imitate, nabootsen

imitation, nabootsing: namaak-

immaculate, onbe'rispelijk

immaterial, on'stoffelijk; onver'schillig, onbe'langrijk

immature, on'rijp

immeasurable, on'meetbaar; niet te over'zien, on'noemelijk

immediate, on'middellijk, naast

immense, on'metelijk

immerse, onderdompelen, indompelen

immersed, onder'water; ver'-diept

immigrant, immi'grant: immi'grerend

immigration, immi'gratie

imminent, op handen, dreigend

immobile, onbe'weeglijk

immoderate, on'matig

immodest, onbe'scheiden; on'-zedig

immoral, immo'reel

immortal(ity), on'sterfelijk-(heid)

immovable, on'wrikbaar

immune, im'muun voor; vrijgesteld

immutable, onver'anderlijk

imp, duiveltje *n*

impact, botsing, samentreffen *n*; ef'fect *n*

impair, na'delig be'ïnvloeden, schaden

impart, ver'lenen; mededelen

impartial(ity), onpar'tijdig(heid)

impassable, onbe'gaanbaar

impassioned, harts'tochtelijk

impassive, onver'stoorbaar; ge'voelloos

impatient, onge'duldig

impeach, in twijfel trekken; aanklagen

impeccable, onbe'rispelijk, feilloos

impede, be'lemmeren

impediment, be'letsel *n*, ge'brek *n*

impel, voortdrijven, aanzetten

impend, dreigen

impenetrable, ondoor'dringbaar

impenitent, onboet'vaardig, ver'-stokt

imperative, hoogstnood'zakelijk; ge'biedend

imperceptible, on'merkbaar

imperfect, imper'fect(um *n*); afwijkend, on'gaaf

imperial, keizerlijk, keizer(s)-, rijks-

imperialism, imperia'lisme *n*

imperil, in ge'vaar brengen

imperious, aan'matigend

impermeable, ondoor'dringbaar

impersonal, onper'soonlijk

impersonate, voorstellen

impertinent, onbe'schaamd

imperturbable, onver'stoorbaar

impervious, ondoor'dringbaar; doof (voor)

impetuous, on'stuimig

impetus, drijfkracht; stuwkracht

impinge on, raken

impious, goddeloos

impish, schelms

implacable, onver'zoenlijk

implant, inplanten

implement, werktuig *n*: uitvoeren

implicate, ver'wikkelen, be'trekken (bij)

implication, bijgedachte

implicit, onvoor'waardelijk; stilzwijgend, er in be'grepen

implore, (af)smeken

imply, impli'ceren, inhouden, te ver'staan geven

impolite, onbe'leefd

import, invoer(en)

importance, be'tekenis, be'lang *n*

important, be'langrijk, ge'wichtig(doend)

importunity, op'dringerigheid

impose on, opleggen; misbruik maken van

imposing, indruk'wekkend

mpossible, on'mogelijk

mpostor, be'drieger ·

mpotent, impo'tent, machteloos

mpoverish, ver'armen, uitputten

mpracticable, onuit'voerbaar

mpregnable, on'neembaar; onaan'tastbaar

mpregnate, impreg'neren; be'vruchten

mpress, stempel(en) (n); indruk maken op, op het hart drukken; rekwi'reren

mpression, indruk, i'dee n; afdruk; oplage

impressionable, ont'vankelijk

impressive, indruk'wekkend

imprint, afdruk; stempel(en) (n): inprenten

imprison, ge'vangen zetten (or houden)

imprisonment, ge'vangenschap

improbable, onwaar'schijnlijk

impromptu, voor de vuist

improper, incor'rect, onfat'soenlijk

improve, ver'beteren; voor'uitgaan

improvement, ver'betering; voor'uitgang

improvident, onbe'zonnen

improvise, improvi'seren

imprudent, onvoor'zichtig

impudence, brutali'teit

impudent, bru'taal

impulse, stoot; opwelling, aandrift

impulsive, stuw-; impul'sief

impunity: with —, onge'straft

impure, on'zuiver; on'kuis

impute, toeschrijven

in, in, (naar) binnen

inability, onvermogen n

inaccessible, onbe'reikbaar; onge'naakbaar

inaccurate, onnauw'keurig

inactive, nietsdoend

inactivity, nietsdoen n ·

inadequate, ontoe'reikend

inadvertent, onop'zettelijk

inadvisable, onver'standig

inalienable, onver'vreemdbaar

inane, zinloos

inanimate, levenloos

inappropriate, onge'schikt

inarticulate, ongearticu'leerd; sprakeloos

inasmuch as, voorzo'ver; aange'zien

inattentive, onop'lettend; onat'tent

inaudible, on'hoorbaar

inaugural, inaugu'reel

inaugurate, inhuldigen; inluiden

incalculable, onbe'rekenbaar

incandescent, gloei-

incantation, toverformule

incapable, onbe'kwaam; niet in staat

incapacitate, onge'schikt maken; ver'hinderen

incendiary, brand-; opruiend: brandstichter

incense, wierook: ver'toornen

incentive, prikkel

inception, ont'staan n

incessant, onop'houdelijk

incest, bloedschande

inch, duim

incident, voorval n; epi'sode

incidental, toe'vallig; bij'komstig

incidentally, ter'loops, tussen twee haaktjes

incision, insnijding

incite, aanzetten

inclement, guur; onmee'dogend

inclination, buiging, helling; neiging

incline, helling: overhellen (tot)

to be inclined, ge'neigd zijn, de neiging hebben

include, be(or om)'vatten; meerekenen

to be included, (er'bij) inbegrepen zijn

including, met inbegrip van, waar'onder

inclusive, allesom'vattend, inclu'sief; tot en met

incoherent, onsamen'hangend

income, inkomen n, inkomsten

income-tax, inkomstenbelasting

incomparable, niet te verge'lijken; weergaloos

incompatible, onver'enigbaar

incompetent, onbe'voegd; in-
effici'ent
incomplete, onvol'ledig
incomprehensible, onbe'grijpelijk
inconceivable, on'denkbaar
inconclusive, niet be'slissend,
niet over'tuigend
incongruous, niet passend, onge'rijmd
inconsiderate, onat'tent
inconsistent, inconse'quent,
tegen'strijdig
inconspicuous, onop'vallend
incontestable, onbe'twistbaar
inconvenience, last (aandoen)
inconvenient, lastig, onge'legen;
onge'riefelijk
incorporate, opnemen; ver'enig-
en
incorrect, on'juist
incorrigible, onver'beterlijk
increase, toename, ver'hoging:
toenemen, ver'hogen
increasingly, steeds meer
incredible, onge'lofelijk
incredulous, onge'lovig
incriminate, be'schuldigen; in
een ten'lastelegging be'trekken
incubator, broedmachine
inculcate, inprenten
incur, zich op de hals halen; lopen
incurable, onge'neeslijk(e zieke)
indebted, schuldig, ver'plicht
indecent, on'zedelijk; onwel'-
voeglijk
indecision, be'sluiteloosheid
indecisive, onbe'slist; be'sluiteloos
indeed, inder'daad; werkelijk,
(ja) zelfs
indefatigable, onver'moeibaar,
onver'moeid
indefinite, onbe'paald
indelible, onuit'wisbaar; inkt-
indemnity, schadeloosstelling
independence, onaf'hankelijk-
heid
independent, onaf'hankelijk
indescribable, onbe'schrijfelijk
index, re'gister n; aanwijzing:
wijs-
Indian, Indisch: Indiër

india-rubber, gummi
indicate, aanwijzen; wijzen op
indication, aanwijzing
indicator, wijzer
indictment, aanklacht
indifferent, onver'schillig; (middel')matig
indigenous, in'heems
indigestible, onver'teerbaar
indigestion, indi'gestie
indignant, veront'waardigd
indignation, veront'waardiging
indignity, smaad
indirect, indi'rect
indiscreet, indis'creet
indiscretion, onbe'scheidenheid
indiscriminate, lukraak, zonder
onderscheid; ver'ward
indispensable, on'misbaar
indisposed, onge'steld; onge'negen
indisputable, onbe'twistbaar
indistinct, on'duidelijk
individual, individu'eel: indivi'du n
individuality, individuali'teit
indivisible, on'deelbaar
indolent, vadsig
indomitable, onover'winnelijk,
on'tembaar
indoor(s), binnen(s'huis)
induce, ertoe brengen; te'weegbrengen; afleiden
inducement, stimu'lans, lokmiddel n
induction, in'ductie; aanvoering;
instal'latie
indulge, toegeven aan
to indulge in, zich permit'teren
indulgence, toe'geeflijkheid; uitspatting; aflaat
industrial, industri'eel, be'drijfs-
industrialist, industri'eel
industrious, vlijtig
industry, indus'trie, be'drijf-
(sleven) n ; vlijt
inebriated, dronken
inedible, on'eetbaar
ineffective, ineffectual, ondoel'-
treffend, vruchteloos
inefficient, ondoel'matig, onbe'kwaam
inept, onge'rijmd, dwaas

inequality, onge'lijkheid

inert(ia), in'ert(ie) ; stil(stand)

inestimable, on'schatbaar

inevitable, onver'mijdelijk

inexcusable, onver'geeflijk

inexhaustible, onuit'puttelijk

inexorable, onver'biddelijk

inexpensive, voor'delig

inexperienced, oner'varen

inexplicable, onver'klaarbaar

inexpressible, onuit'sprekelijk

infallible, on'feilbaar

infamous, schandelijk, be'rucht

infancy, kindsheid

infant, zuigeling, kind(er-)

infantry, infante'rie

infatuated, ver'zot (op)

infect, be'smetten ; aansteken

infection, in'fectie

infectious, be'smettelijk ; aan'stekelijk

infer, afleiden ; laten doorschemeren

inference, ge'volgtrekking ; bijgedachte

inferior, inferi'eur ; onderge'schikt(e)

 to be inferior to, lager zijn dan ; onderdoen voor

inferiority, minder'waardig-heid (s)

infernal, hels, duivels

inferno, hel

infest, teisteren

infidel, onge'lovig(e)

infidelity, ontrouw

infinite, on'eindig (veel)

infinitesimal, on'eindig klein

infinity, on'eindigheid

infirmary, ziekenafdeling, ziekenhuis n

infirmity, ge'brek n

inflame, (in geestdrift doen) ont'steken

inflammable, ont'vlambaar

inflammation, ont'steking

inflate, opblazen, oppompen ; opdrijven

inflation, in'flatie

inflexible onver'zettelijk, rots-vast, star

inflict, toebrengen, opleggen, ver'oorzaken ; lastig vallen met

influence, invloed ; be'invloeden

influential, invloedrijk

influenza, griep

influx, toevloed

inform, mededelen, be'richten ; aanbrengen

informal, infor'meel

informant, zegsman ; aanbrenger

information, inlichting(en), be'-richt(en) n

infrequent, zeldzaam

infringe, inbreuk maken ; over'treden

infuriate, woedend maken

infuse, laten trekken ; be'zielen

ingenious, ver'nuftig

ingenuity, ver'nuft n

ingenuous, onge'kunsteld

ingot, baar, staaf

ingrained, inge'worteld

ingratiate, zich in de gunst dringen

ingratitude, on'dankbaarheid

ingredient, be'standdeel n

inhabit, wonen in

inhabitant, in(or be')woner

inhale, inha'leren

inherent, inhe'rent

inherit, erven

inheritance, erfenis

inhibition, remming

inhospitable, ongast'vrij, on-her'bergzaam

inhuman, on'menselijk

inimical, vij'andig

inimitable, onna'volgbaar

iniquitous, hoogst onrecht'vaar-dig

iniquity, onrecht'vaardigheid, ver'derf n

initial, be'gin-, eerst: voorletter : para'feren

initially, in het be'gin

initiate, inwijden

initiative, initia'tief n

inject, inspuiten

injudicious, onoordeel'kundig

injunction, be'vel n

injure, wonden ; schade doen, kwetsen

injurious, schadelijk

injury, ver'wonding ; schade ; be'lediging

injustice, onrecht('vaardigheid) (*n*)

ink, inkt

inkling, flauw i'dee *n*

inlaid, ingelegd

inland, binnen(land)(s); het land in

in-laws, schoonfamilie

father-(mother- *or* sister-)in-law, schoonvader(moeder *or* zuster)

inlet, inham, zeegat *n*

inmate, (tijdelijk) ('mede) be'woner

inn, herberg

innate, aangeboren

inner, binnen-; innerlijk

innermost, binnenste

innkeeper, waard

innocence, onschuld

innocent, on'schuldig

innocuous, on'schadelijk

innovation, nieuwigheid

innuendo, (hatelijke) toespeling

innumerable, on'telbaar

inoculate, inenten

inoffensive, on'schuldig

inopportune, onge'legen

inordinate, buiten'sporig

inquest, ge'rechtelijk onderzoek naar de doodsoorzaak *n*

inquire, infor'meren (naar), vragen (naar)

inquiry, vraag, poging (om inlichtingen te winnen); onderzoek *n*

inquisitive, nieuws'gierig

inroad, inval, ver'overing; gat *n*

insane, krank'zinnig

insatiable, onver'zadelijk

inscribe, schrijven op, gra'veren; inschrijven

inscription, opschrift *n*; opdracht

inscrutable, ondoor'grondelijk

insect, in'sekt *n*

insensible, onge'voelig voor; onbe'wust

inseparable, onaf'scheidelijk

insert, inlas(sen), insteken, plaatsen

inside, binnen(kant); naar binnen; in

insidious, arg'listig; ver'raderlijk

insight, inzicht *n*

insignia, onder'scheidingstekens

insignificant, zonder be'tekenis onbe'tekenend, onbe'duidend

insincere, onop'recht

insinuate, indringen; insinu'eren

insipid, flauw

insist, er op staan; (blijven) volhouden; (er op) aandringen

insistent, vol'hardend; dringend

insolent, onbe'schoft

insoluble, onop'losbaar

insomnia, slape'loosheid

inspect, onder'zoeken; inspec'teren

inspection, in'spectie; onderzoek *n*

inspector, inspec'teur

inspiration, inspi'ratie; be'zielend voorbeeld *n*; ingeving

inspire, inspi'reren; inblazen; inboezemen

install, instal'leren

instalment, ter'mijn; ge'deelte *n*, aflevering

instance, voorbeeld *n*; plaats; ver'zoek *n*: aanhalen

instant, ogenblik *n*: ogen'blikkelijk

instantaneous, on'middellijk

instead of, in plaats van

instep, wreef

instigate, aanstichten

instil, bijbrengen

instinct(ive), in'stinct('ief) (*n*)

institute, insti'tuut *n*: instellen

institution, instelling; tra'ditie

instruct, onder'richten; ge'lasten; mededelen

instruction, onderricht *n*; in'structie

instructive, leerzaam

instrument, instru'ment *n*

instrumental, instrumen'taal; be'vorderlijk (voor)

insubordinate, weer'spannig

insufferable, onuit'staanbaar

insufficient, onvol'doende

insular, eiland-; geïso'leerd, be'krompen

insulate, iso'leren

insult, be'lediging: be'ledigen

insuperable, onover'komelijk

insurance, ver'zekering

insure, ver'zekeren

insurgent, oproerling; op'roerig

insurrection, opstand

intact, in'tact, gaaf

intake, inlaat; aanvoer

intangible, on'tastbaar

integral, inte'grerend; inte'graal

integrate, (tot één ge'heel) ver'-enigen

integrity, on'kreukbaarheid

intellect(ual), intel'lect(u'eel) (*n*)

intelligence, intelli'gentie; in-lichtingen

intelligent, intelli'gent, be'vat-telijk

intelligible, be'grijpelijk

intemperate, on'matig

intend, van plan zijn; be'doelen

intense, in'tens

intensify, ver'hogen, ver'scher-pen

intensity, intensi'teit

intensive, inten'sief

intent, ('in)ge'spannen: be'doe-ling

intention, be'doeling

intentional, op'zettelijk

inter, ter aarde be'stellen

interaction, wisselwerking

intercede on behalf of, voor-spraak zijn van

intercept, onder'scheppen, de pas afsnijden

interchange, ver'wisselen, afwis-selen

interchangeable, ver'wisselbaar

intercourse, omgang, ver'keer *n*

interest, be'lang(stelling) (*n*); aandeel *n*; rente: interes'seren **to be interested in,** be'lang stellen in (*or* hebben bij)

interfere, tussen'beide komen; zich mengen in

interference, be'moeienis; stoor-nis; storing

interim, tussentijd(s)

interior, in'wendig(e *n*), binen-(lands); binnenhuis(*or* land) *n*

interlock, interlock: in el'kaar grijpen

interlude, pauze, tussenperiode; tussenspel *n*

intermarry, onder el'kaar huwen

intermediary, be'middelaar; be'middeling

intermediate, tussen-

interminable, eindeloos

intermingle, (zich) ver'mengen

intermittent, bij vlagen, af en toe onder'broken

intern, inter'neren

internal, in'wendig; binnenlands

international, internatio'naal

interplay, wisselwerking

interpolate, interpo'leren

interpose, in het midden breng-en; tussen beide komen

interpret, ver'tolken, uitleggen

interpreter, tolk

interrogate, onder'vragen

interrupt, onder'breken, in de rede vallen; be'lemmeren

intersect, door'snijden; el'kaar snijden

intersperse, door'spekken; ver'spreiden

interval, pause, tussentijd (*or* ruimte)

intervene, tussen'beide komen; liggen (tussen)

intervention, tussenkomst

interview, inter'view(en) (*n*)

interweave, door'eenweven

intestine, darm

intestines, ingewanden

intimate, in'tiem, ver'trouwd: laten merken

intimation, aanduiding

intimidate, intimi'deren

into, in, tot (in)

intolerable, onver'draaglijk

intolerant, onver'draagzaam

intonation, into'natie

intoxicant, be'dwelmend (mid-del *n*)

intoxicate, dronken maken

intoxication, dronkenschap; roes

intractable, on'handelbaar; hard'nekkig

intransigent, intransi'gent

intrepid, onver'saagd

intricate, inge'wikkeld

intrigue, in'trige, ge'konkel *n*;
amou'rette : intri'geren
intrinsic, intrin'siek
introduce, introdu'ceren; breng-
en in; indienen
introduction, invoeren *n*; inleiding
intrude, (zich) in(*or* op)dringen;
storen
intuition, intu'ïtie; ingeving
intuitive, intuï'tief
inundate, onder water zetten;
over'stromen
inure, harden
invade, binnenvallen
invalid, zieke, inva'lide; on'geldig
invaluable, on'schatbaar
invariable, con'stant
invariably, zonder uitzondering
invasion, inval; inbreuk
invective, scheldwoorden
inveigle, ver'lokken
invent, uitvinden, ver'zinnen
invention, uitvinding, ver'zinsel
n
inventive, vindingrijk
inventor, uitvinder
inventory, inven'taris
inverse, omgekeerd
invert, omkeren, omzetten
invest, be'leggen; ver'lenen
investigate, navorsen, nasporen
investigation, onderzoek *n*
investment, (geld)be'legging
inveterate, ver'stokt
invidious, hatelijk
invigorate, kracht geven
invincible, onover'winnelijk
invisible, on'zichtbaar
invitation, uitnodiging
invite, uitnodigen; vragen om
inviting, aan'lokkelijk
invoice, fac'tuur
invoke, aan(*or* op)roepen; een
be'roep doen op
involuntary, onwille'keurig
involve, met zich meebrengen,
be'trekken
involved, (in)ge'wikkeld
invulnerable, on'kwetsbaar
inward, naar binnen; innerlijk

irate, woedend
Ireland, Ierland *n*
Irish, Iers (*n*)
irksome, ver'velend, lastig
iron, (strijk)ijzer *n* : ijzeren :
strijken
ironic(al), i'ronisch
ironmongery, ijzerwaren
irony, iro'nie
irreconcilable, onver'zoenlijk
irrefutable, onweer'legbaar
irregular, onregel'matig; tegen
de regel
irrelevant, niet ter zake dienend
irreparable, onher'stelbaar
irrepressible, onbe'dwingbaar
irreproachable, onbe'rispelijk
irresistable, onweer'staanbaar
irresolute, be'sluiteloos
irrespective of, afge'zien van,
ongeacht
irresponsible, onverant'woordelijk
irretrievable,   onher'stelbaar;
reddeloos
irreverent, oneer'biedig
irrevocable, onher'roepelijk
irrigate, be'vloeien
irrigation, irri'gatie
irritable, prikkelbaar
irritate, prikkelen; irri'teren
irritation,   ge'prikkeldheid;
branderigheid
island, eiland *n*; vluchtheuvel
isle, eiland *n*
isolate, iso'leren
issue, uitgifte, nummer *n*; uit-
stroming; uitkomst; kwestie:
ver'strekken;   uitgeven;
(voort)komen uit
it, het
Italian, Itali'aan(s) (*n*)
italic, cur'sief
Italy, I'talië *n*
itch, jeuk(en); er om zitten te
springen
item, stuk *n*, punt *n*; be'richt *n*
itinerant, rondtrekkend
itinerary, reisplan *n*
its, zijn
itself, (zich')zelf
ivory, i'voor *n*; i'voren
ivy, klimop

J

ab, steek: steken

abber, kakelen

ack, (op)krik(ken); boer

acket, jasje *n*; omslag

ade, ne'friet: knol: afjakkeren

agged, ruw, ge'tand, puntig

am, jam: opstopping: (samen) duwen, klemmen; storen

January, janu'ari

Japanese, Ja'pans (*n*); Ja'panner

ar, pot: schok: krassen; een schok geven

argon, vaktaal

aundice, geelzucht

aunt, uitstapje *n*

aunty, zwierig

avelin, werpspies

aw, kaak: kletsen

azz, jazz

ealous, ja'loers; angst'vallig be'zorgd

eer, schimpen

jelly, ge'lei, gela'tinepudding

jellyfish, kwal

jeopardize, in ge'vaar brengen

jerk, ruk(ken), schok(ken)

jersey, trui(tje *n*)

jest, echerts(en)

jester, nar

jet, straal(buis), gaspit: git *n*

jettison, over'boord werpen

jetty, havenhoofd *n*, pier

Jew, Jood

jewel, (edel)steen, ju'weel *n*

jeweller, juwe'lier

jewellery, ju'welen

Jewish, Joods

jib, kluiver; arm; weigeren, er niet van ge'diend zijn

jig, horlepijp: dansen

jigsaw puzzle, legpuzzel

jilt, de bons geven

jingle, (laten) rinkelen

job, kar'wei, werk(je) *n*, baan(tje *n*)

jockey, jockey: manoeu'vreren

jocular, schertsend

jocund, vrolijk

jog, stoten; wippen; sukkelen; opfrissen

join, ver'binding, naad: ver'binden, ver'enigen, samenkomen, in el'kaar slaan; zich voegen bij, meedoen, komen bij

joint, ge'wricht *n*; ver'binding, naad: groot stuk vlees *n*: ge'zamenlijk

joke, grap(pen maken)

joker, grappenmaker; joker

jolly, jolig; reuze

jolt, schok: hotsen

jostle, (ver')dringen

jot, jota: vlug no'teren

journal, dagboek *n*; tijdschrift *n*

journalism, journalis'tiek

journalist, journa'list

journey, reis (maken)

joust, steekspel *n*

jovial, jovi'aal

joy(ful), vreug'de(vol)

jubilant, jubelend, in de wolken

jubilee, jubi'leum *n*

judge, rechter, jurylid *n*, kenner: (be')oordelen

judgement, uitspraak, oordeel *n*, vonnis *n*

judicial, ge'rechtelijk

judicious, oordeel'kundig

jug, kan

juggle, goochelen

juice, sap *n*

juicy, sappig

July, juli

jumble, warboel: door el'kaar gooien

jump, sprong: springen; op-schrikkèn

jumper, jumper: springer

junction, knooppunt *n*, kruispunt *n*

juncture, stadium *n*, ogenblik *n*

June, juni

jungle, rimboe

junior, junior, jonger(e)

junk, (oude) rommel: jonk

junket, met leb ge'stremde melk

jurisdiction, juris'dictie

jury, jury

just, recht'vaardig; welverdiend; ge'grond: pre'cies; net: maar; even: een'voudig

justice, recht('vaardigheid) (*n*), ge'rechtigheid; jus'titie; recht-er

   to do justice, billijk be'handelen; eer aandoen, goed doen uitkomen

justifiable, gerecht'vaardigd; ver'dedigbaar

justification, grond, recht'vaardiging

justify, recht'vaardigen

jut out, uitsteken

jute, jute

juvenile, jeugd(ig), jong(eling)

K

kangaroo, kangoeroe

keel, kiel

keen, scherp('zinnig); enthousi'ast

keep, kost; slottoren: (onder')houden, be'waren; weer'houden; (goed)blijven

   to keep away, wegblijven

   to keep on, blijven, door-; aan (*or* op)houden

   to keep up, volhouden; onder'houden

   to keep up with, bijhouden

keeper, oppasser, opzichter

keeping, hoede; over'eenstemming

keg, vaatje *n*

ken, ge'zicht(skring) (*n*)

kennel, hondehok *n*, kennel

kerb, trot'toirband

kernel, kern

kettle, ketel

key, sleutel(-); toets; toon-aard

keyboard, toetsenbord *n*

keynote, grondtoon

khaki, kaki *n*

kick, schop(pen); te'rugstoot: trappen; stoten

kid, geitje *n*; glacé *n*; kind *n*: voor de gek houden

kidnap, ont'voeren

kidney, nier

kill, doden

   to be killed, sneuvelen, omkomen

kiln, oven

kilt, kilt

kin, fa'milie

kind, soort: vriendelijk

kindergarten, fröbelschool

kind-hearted, goed'hartig

kindle, aansteken

kindly, goe'daardig, vriendelijk

   kindly leave off, wees zo goed o te houden

kindness, vriendelijkheid

kindred, ver'want(en)

king, koning

kingdom, koninkrijk *n*

kink, slag, kink; kronkel

kinship, ver'wantschap

kinsman, bloedverwant

kiosk, ki'osk

kipper, bokking

kiss, kus(sen)

kit, uitrusting; ba'gage; ge'reedschap *n*

kitchen, keuken

kite, vlieger; wouw

kitten, katje *n*

knack, slag, kneep

knapsack, ransel, rugzak

knave, schurk; boer

knavish, schurken-

knead, kneden

knee, knie

kneel, knielen, ge'knield liggen

knell, doodsklok

knickers, broek(je *n*)

knife, mes *n*: door'steken

knight, (tot) ridder (slaan)

knighthood, ridderorde, ridderschap

knit, breien; samengroeien

knitting, breiwerk *n*

knob, knop; knobbel

knock, slag, klop(pen), slaan, stoten

   to knock down, om'vergooien, aanrijden; toeslaan

   to knock off, afslaan; ophouden, schaften

   to knock out, uitkloppen; be'wusteloos slaan

   to knock over, om'vergooien

knocker, klopper

knoll, heuveltje *n*

knot, knoop; kwast: knopen

knotty, vol knopen; vol kwasten; lastig

know, (het) weten; (her¹)kennen

knowing, schrander; veelbe¹tekenend

knowledge, (voor)kennis; wetenschap

knuckel, knokkel

L

label, eti¹ket *n*, label: van (een) eti¹ket(ten) voor¹zien

laboratory, labora¹torium *n*

laborious, ar¹beidzaam; zwaar

labour, arbeid(en); werkkrachten; weeën: doorzagen over

labourer, arbeider

labour-exchange, arbeidsbureau *n*

labyrinth, doolhof *n*

lace, kant; veter; ga¹lon *n*: vastrijgen

lacerate, (ver¹)scheuren

lack, ge¹brek (hebben aan) *n*
to be lacking, ont¹breken

laconic, laco¹niek

lacquer, lak(werk *n*)

lad, knaap

ladder, ladder

laden, be¹laden; be¹zwangerd

ladle, scheplepel: opscheppen

lady, dame

lag, achterblijven; be¹kleden

lagoon, la¹gune

lair, hol *n*

laity, leken

lake, meer *n*

lamb, lam (svlees) *n*: lammeren

lame, kreupel, zwak

lament, weeklacht: be¹treuren

lamentable, jammerlijk

lamentation, weeklacht

lamp, lamp, lan¹taren

lamp-post, lan¹tarenpaal

lance, lans; lan¹ceren

land, land(e¹rij) (*n*): neerkomen; (doen) be¹landen; aan land zetten

landed, land-, grond-

landing, landing; overloop
 landing-stage, steiger

landlady, hospita

landlord, huisbaas, landheer; hospes, waard

landmark, baken *n*, be¹kend punt *n*; mijlpaal

land-owner, grondbezitter

landscape, landschap *n*

landslide, (aard)ver¹schuiving

lane, landweg(getje *n*); rijbaan; vaargeul

language, taal

languid, loom, flauw

languish, ver¹slappen; wegkwijnen; smachten (naar)

languor, slapte; matheid

lank, schraal; sluik

lanky, slungelachtig

lantern, lan¹taren

lap, schoot; ronde: (op)leppen; kabbelen

lapel, re¹vers

lapse, a¹buis *n*; ver¹val(len) (*n*); ver¹loop *n*

larceny, diefstal

larch, lariks

lard, reuzel

larder, pro¹visiekamer (*or* -kast)

large, groot

largely, grotendeels

lark, leeuwerik; pretje *n*: lol maken

larva, larve

larynx, strottehoofd *n*

lascivious, wel¹lustig

lash, zweepkoord *n*; zweepslag: geselen; (doen) zwiepen; vastsjorren

lass, meisje *n*

lassitude, matheid

last, (het) laatst; ver¹leden: leest: duren, het uithouden
 last straw, laatste druppel
 at last, ten¹slotte; eindelijk

lasting, blijvend; duurzaam

lastly, ten¹slotte

latch, klink, slot *n*

late, (te) laat; re¹cent; wijlen, ge¹wezen

lately, (in de) laatst(e tijd)

latent, la¹tent

lateral, zij(delings)

lath, lat

lathe, draaibank

lather, schuim(en) (*n*)

Latin, La'tijn(s) (*n*), Ro'maans
latitude, breedte; speling
latter, laatst(genoemd)(e)
latterly, tegen het eind; in de laatste tijd
lattice, traliewerk *n*
laud, loven
laudable, lof'waardig
laugh, lach(en)
  to laugh at, lachen om; uitlachen
laughable, lach'wckkcnd
laughter, ge'lach *n*
launch, (zware) sloep: te water laten; insturen; afschieten; op touw zetten, ont'ketenen
laundry, wasse'rij; was(goed *n*)
laurel, lau'rier; lauwer-
  laurels, lauweren
lava, lava
lavatory, W.C., toi'let *n*
lavender, la'vendel
lavish, kwistig; over'laden
law, recht(en) (*n*); wet
law-abiding, orde'lievend
law-court, rechtbank
lawful, wettig, recht'matig
lawless, los'bandig
lawn, ga'zon *n*; ba'tist *n*
lawsuit, pro'ces *n*
lawyer, advo'caat
lax(ity), laks(heid)
laxative, la'xeermiddel *n*
lay, lied *n*: leke(n)-: leggen; dekken
  to lay down, voorschrijven; geven; neerleggen
  to lay in, inslaan
layer, laag
layette, kinderuitzet
layman, leek
lay-out, plan *n*, aanleg
laze, luieren
lazy, lui
lead, leiding; eerste plaats, voorsprong; riem; voorbeeld *n*: lood *n*: leiden, ertoe brengen; voor('op)gaan; aanvoeren
leaden, loodzwaar
leader, leider; hoofdartikel *n*
leadership, leiding; leiderschap *n*
leading, voor'aanstaand, hoofd-

leaf, blad *n*
leaflet, blaadje *n*, folder
leafy, be'bladerd
league, (ver')bond (*n*): drie mij.
leak, lek(ken) (*n*)
leakage, lek *n*; uitlekking
lean, mager; schraal: overhellen; leunen; zetten
leaning, neiging
lean-to, afdak *n*
leap, sprong: springen
leap-year, schrikkeljaar *n*
learn, leren; ver'nemen
learned, ge'leerd
learner, leerling
learning, ge'leerdheid, wetenschap
lease, huurcon'tract *n*, pacht; huurtijd: (ver')huren
leasehold, pacht(goed *n*)
leash, riem
least, minst
  at least, tenminste, minstens
leather, leer *n*: leren
leave, ver'lof *n*; afscheid *n*: ver'trekken (uit), weggaan; (ver')laten; achter(*or* na)laten; overlaten
  to leave alone, afblijven van; met rust laten
  to leave off, ophouden (met)
  to leave out, weglaten; er buiten laten
leaven, zuurdeeg *n*
lecture, lezing (houden), col'lege (geven) (*n*); de les lezen
lecturer, spreker, lektor
ledge, richel, rand
ledger, grootboek *n*
lee, lij
leech, bloedzuiger
leek, prei
leer, gluren
left, linker(hand); links
left-handed, links
leg, been *n*, poot; (broeks)pijp; e'tappe
legacy, le'gaat *n*; erfenis
legal, rechts'kundig, rechterlijk; wettig; wettelijk; rechts'geldig
legation, ge'zantschap *n*
legend, le'gende; onderschrift *n*
legendary, legen'darisch

legible, leesbaar
legion, legi'oen *n* : legio
legislation, wetgeving
legislative, wetgevend
legitimate, wettig; gerecht'vaardigd; recht'matig
leisure, vrije tijd
leisurely, be'daard
lemon(ade), ci'troen(limo'nade)
lend, (uit)lenen; ver'lenen
length, lengte, duur; eind(je) *n*
at length, eindelijk; uit'voerig
lengthen, ver'lengen; langer
worden
lengthwise, in de lengte
lengthy, lang('durig)
lenient, cle'ment
lens, lens
Lent, Vasten(tijd)
leopard, luipaard *n*
leper, me'laatse
leprosy, me'laatsheid
less, min(der)
lessen, ver'minderen, (doen)
afnemen
lesser, minder
lesson, les; schriftlezing
lest, voor het ge'val dat; opdat
. . . niet; dat
let, laten, toestaan; ver'huren
to let down, neerlaten, uitleggen; du'peren, in de steek laten
to let go, loslaten; laten gaan
to let in, binnen laten
to let off, laten gaan
lethargic, slaperig, loom
letter, brief; letter
lettuce, (krop)sla
level, vlak, ge'lijk (met): hoogte;
ni'veau *n* : ge'lijk maken
level-headed, ver'standig, nuchter
lever, hefboom
levy, heffing, lichting: heffen,
werven
lewd, on'tuchtig, ob'sceen
liability, aan'sprakelijkheid,
ver'antwoording; blok aan het
been *n*
liable, licht ge'neigd; vatbaar;
aan'sprakelijk
to be liable to, (licht) kunnen;
last hebben van

liaison, ver'binding(s-); liai'son
liar, leugenaar
libel, smaadschrift *n* : op schrift
be'lasteren
liberal, vrij('gevig); ruim; libe'-
raal
liberate, be'vrijden
liberty, vrijheid
librarian, bibliothe'caris
library, biblio'theek
licence, ver'gunning; vrijheid
licentious, los'bandig
lichen, korstmos *m*
lick, (af)likken
lid, deksel *n*
lie, leugen : liegen; (gaan) liggen
to lie down, gaan liggen;
liggen te rusten
liege, soeve'rein, leen-
lieutenant, luitenant
life, leven(sbeschrijving) (*n*)
life-belt, reddingsgordel
life-boat, reddingsboot
lifeless, levenloos
lifelike, na'tuurgetrouw
lifelong, levenslang
lifetime, leven(sduur) (*n*)
lift, lift: (op)tillen; optrekken;
gappen
ligament, band, pees
light, licht (*n*); vuurtje *n* : aan
steken; ver'lichten; ver'helderen
lighten, lichter worden; ophelderen; weerlichten; ver'lichten
lighter, aansteker: lichter
light-hearted, luchtig
lighthouse, vuurtoren
lighting, ver'lichting
lightly, zachtjes; licht('vaardig); luchtig
lightning, bliksem(snel)
lightship, lichtschip *n*
lightweight, (van) licht (ge'-
wicht)
like, (zo)als: houden van, aardig
vinden; graag willen
it is just like him, het is echt
iets voor hem; het lijkt sprekend op hem
nothing like, lang niet
something like, onge'veer,
zo(iets) als

likeable, prettig
likelihood, kans
likely, waar'schijnlijk
 he is likely to, het is aan'nemelijk dat hij
likeness, ge'lijkenis
likewise, even'eens; insge'lijks
liking, voorliefde, zin
lilac, se'ring; lila (n)
lilting, zwierig
lily, lelie
limb, lid n; tak
limbs, ledematen
lime, kalk: li'moen: linde
limelight, voorgrond
limit, grens: be'perken
limitation, be'perking; grens, te'kortkoming
limited company, naamloze vennootschap
limp, slap: mank lopen
limpid, helder
line, lijn; linie; rij; regel; spoor n: lini'ëren; voeren, be'kleden
linen, linnen(goed) n
liner, lijnboot, lijnvliegtuig n
linger, dralen
linguistic, taal('kundig)-
lining, voering, be'kleding
link, schakel'(en); inhaken; ver'binden; met elkaar in ver'band brengen
linoleum, li'noleum n
linseed, lijnzaad n
lint, pluksel n
lintel, bovendrempel
lion(ess), leeuw('in)
lip, lip; rand
lipstick, lippenstift
liqueur, li'keur
liquid, vloeibaar: vloeistof
liquidate, liqui'deren
liquor, (sterke) drank
liquorice, drop
lisle, fil d'écosse
lisp, ge'lispel n: lispelen
list, lijst; slagzij: overhellen
listen, luisteren
listless, lusteloos
lists, strijdperk n
literal, letterlijk
literary, lite'rair

literature, litera'tuur
lithe, lenig
litre, liter
litter, afval, rommel; nest n, worp: (met rommel) be'zaaien
little, klein; weinig: beetje n
 a little late, wat laat
liturgy, litur'gie
live, levend(ig); ge'laden, scherp: (blijven) leven; wonen
livelihood, kost, be'staan n
lively, levendig, be'drijvig, druk
liver, lever
livery, li'vrei
livestock, vee n
livid, doodsbleek; wit
living, levend, levens-: kost; leven n: predi'kantsplaats
living-room, huiskamer
lizard, hage'dis
load, vracht, lading: (in)laden, be'laden; over'laden
loaf, brood n: lummelen
loam, leem
loan, lening: (uit)lenen
loath, onge'negen
loathe, walgen van
loathsome, walgelijk
lob, hoog slaan
lobby, hal, fo'yer
lobe, lel
lobster, kreeft
local, plaatselijk; lo'kaal
locality, om'geving
localize, lokali'seren
locate, opsporen, thuisbrengen; vestigen
location, ligging; plaatsbepaling
lock, slot n; sluis: lok: op slot doen (or gaan), (op)sluiten; vastraken
locker, kastje n
locket, medail'lon n
locomotive, locomo'tief: be'wegings-
locust, sprinkhaan
lodge, (por'tiers)woning: lo'geren, in de kost zijn, onderbrengen; blijven steken; indienen
lodger, kostganger
lodgings, (ge'huurde) kamers
loft, zolder; gale'rij

fty, hoog; ver'heven

g, blok hout *n*; log(boek *n*): blok-: no'teren; afleggen

ggerheads: to be at —, over'hoop liggen

gic, logica

gical, logisch

in, lende(stuk *n*)

iter, omhangen

ll, hangen

ondon, Londen(s) (*n*)

ne(ly), eenzaam, ver'laten

ng, lang: door: ver'langen

nging, ver'langen *n*

ngitude, lengte

ngitudinal, in de lengte

ng-sighted, vèrziend

ng-suffering, lank'moedig

ng-winded, lang'dradig

ok, (aan)blik; voorkomen *n*: kijken; er uitzien

oks, uiterlijk

to look after, zorgen voor

to look at, be'kijken, kijken naar

to look back, omzien; te'rugzien

to look for, zoeken (naar); ver'wachten

to look forward to, zich ver'heugen op

to look into, onder'zoeken

to look like, lijken op, er uitzien als

to look on, toekijken

to look out, uitkijken

to look up, opkijken; opzoeken; opknappen

lookout, uitkijk

to keep a lookout for, uitkijken naar

loom, weefgetouw *n*: opdoemen

loop, lus

loophole, (schiet)gat *n*; uitvlucht

loose, los, vrij

loosen, los(ser) maken

loot, buit: plunderen

lop, (af)snoeien

lop-sided, scheef

loquacious, praatziek

lord, heer, lord

lordly, vorstelijk, voor'naam

lore, kunde, kennis

lorgnette, face-à-main

lorry, vrachtauto

lose, (doen) ver'liezen, kwijtraken; missen; voor'bij laten gaan

loss, ver'lies *n*

lost, ver'loren; ver'dwaald; ver'ongelukt

to get lost, ver'dwalen

lot, lot *n*; per'ceel *n*; stel *n*: heel wat

lotion, huid-(wond- *or* haar-)water *n*

lottery, lote'rij

loud, luid('ruchtig)

lounge, sa'lon, conver'satiezaal: leunen, liggen

louse, luis

lout, pummel

lovable, lief

love, liefde; liefje *n*: nul: houden van; dolgraag (willen)

lots of love, veel liefs

(to fall) in love with, ver'liefd (worden) op

to make love, het hof maken

lovely, prachtig, mooi; heerlijk

lover, ge'liefde; liefhebber

loving, aan'hankelijk; liefhebbend

low, laag; bijna op (*or* leeg): loeien

lower, laten zakken; strijken: dreigend kijken

lowland, laagland *n*

lowly, nederig

loyal(ty), trouw

lubricant, smeermiddel *n*

lubricate, smeren

lucid(ity), helder(heid)

luck, ge'luk *n*

bad luck, pech

good luck, ge'luk *n*: suc'ces!

lucky: to be —, boffen; ge'luk brengen

lucrative, winstgevend

ludicrous, be'lachelijk

lug, slepen

luggage, ba'gage

lugubrious, lu'guber

lukewarm, lauw

lull, stilte: sussen

lullaby, wiegeliedje *n*
lumber, ge'kapt hout *n*; rommel: dreunen
luminous, lichtgevend
lump, klomp, brok, klontje *n*, knobbel: rond
lunacy, krank'zinnigheid
lunar, maan-
lunatic, krank'zinnig(e)
lunch, lunch(en)
lung, long
lunge, uitval (doen); dres'seren
lurch, stoot: steek: voor'uit(*or* op'zij)schieten, slingeren
lure, lokstem: (ver')lokken
lurid, gloeiend; gruwelijk
lurk, zich schuil houden, ver'borgen zijn, loeren
luscious, heerlijk sappig
lush, mals
lust, (wel)lust, zucht: be'geren
lustre, glans; luister
lusty, fors
lute, luit
luxuriant, welig; weelderig
luxurious, weelderig
luxury, weelde, luxe
lying, leugenachtig
lynch, lynchen
lyre, lier
lyric, lyrisch (ge'dicht *n*)
lyrical, lyrisch

M

mace, staf: foelie
machination, kuipe'rij
machine, ma'chine; organi'satie
machinery, machine'rieën; mecha'nisme *n*; organi'satie(s)
mackerel, ma'kreel
mad, gek; dol
madam, me'vrouw, juf'frouw
madden, gek maken; gruwelijk ergeren
madman, gek
madness, krank'zinnigheid; gekkigheid
madrigal, madri'gaal *n*
magazine, tijdschrift *n*; maga'zijn *n*
maggot, made

magic, toverkunst, tove'rij tover(achtig)
magician, tovenaar
magistrate, magis'traat
magnanimous, groot'moedig
magnate, mag'naat
magnet, mag'neet
magnetic, mag'netisch
magnificence, luister, pracht
magnificent, luisterrijk, groots
magnify, ver'groten
magnitude, grootte
magpie, ekster
mahogany, ma'honie(hout) *n*
maid, meisje *n*
maiden, maagd(elijk): onge'trouwd, meisjes-; eerste
mail, post(-): maliënkolder
maim, ver'minken
main, hoofd-, voor'naamste
 mains, hoofdleiding, net *n*
mainland, vaste'land *n*
mainly, hoofd'zakelijk
mainsail, grootzeil *n*
mainstay, grote stag; steunpilaar
maintain, handhaven; onder'houden; be'weren
maintenance, onderhoud *n*
maize, maïs
majestic, majestu'eus
majesty, majesteit
major, groot(ste), hoofd-: ma'joor; majeur
majority, meerder('jarig)heid
make, merk *n*: maken; dwingen, laten; ver'dienen; schatten, denken; halen; opmaken (*a bed*); zetten (*tea*); doen (*a promise*)
 to make out, opstellen; be'weren; snappen, ont'cijferen; onder'scheiden
 to make up, maken; ver'zinnen; ver'goeden, aanvullen; het weer goedmaken; (zich) opmaken
 to make up for, goedmaken; inhalen
make-believe, een spelletje *n*: ver'zonnen
maker, schepper, fabri'kant
makeshift, geimprovi'seerd (lapmiddel *n*)

make-up, geestesgesteldheid; schmink, make-up
malady, kwaal
malaria, ma'laria
male, mannelijk (per'soon or dier n), mannen-
malevolent, boos'aardig
malice, boos opzet n, haat
malicious, boos'aardig
malign, be'lasteren
malignant, kwaad'aardig
malleable, smeedbaar; kneedbaar
malnutrition, onder'voeding
malt, mout(en)
mammal, zoogdier n
mammoth, mammoet: reuzen-
man, man; (de) mens: be'mannen, be'zetten
manage, aankunnen; leiden; klaarspelen
management, be'heer n; di'rektie, be'stuur n
manager, direk'teur, chef
mandate, opdracht; man'daat-(gebied) n
mane, manen
manger, voerbak, kribbe
mangle, mangel(en); ver'scheuren
manhandle, ver'sjouwen, toetakelen
manhood, mannelijke leeftijd
mania, waanzin; ma'nie
maniac, waan'zinnige
manicure, mani'cure
manifest, duidelijk; mani'fest n: tonen
manifestation, uiting
manifesto, mani'fest n
manifold, veel'vuldig
manipulate, han'teren; be'werken; knoeien met
manipulation, han'tering; manipu'latie
mankind, mensdom n
manly, man'haftig
mannequin, manne'quin
manner, ma'nier (van doen); soort
mannerism, hebbelijkheid, ge-manië'reerdheid

manoeuvre, ma'noeuvre; manoeu'vreren
manor, ambachtshuis n
mansion, herenhuis n
manslaughter, doodslag
mantelpiece, schoorsteenmantel
mantle, mantel; gloeikousje n
manual, hand(en)-: manu'aal n
manufacture, fabri'kage, fabri'-kaat n: fabri'ceren
manure, mest: be'mesten
manuscript, handschrift n
many, veel; velen
  a good many, heel wat
  a great many, heel veel, heel wat
map, (land)kaart, platte'grond
maple, esdoorn
mar, ont'sieren; be'derven
maraud, plunderen
marble, marmer(en) (n); knikker
march, mars: (doen) mar'cheren; oprukken
March, maart
mare, merrie
margarine, marga'rine
margin, kant(lijn); speling
marginal, kant-
marigold, goudsbloem
marine, zee; scheeps: mari'nier
mariner, zeeman
marital, echtelijk
maritime, zee(vaart)-
mark, plek, streep, vlek, spoor; moet, put; merk n; stempel, (ken)teken n; doel n; peil n: een vlek (etc) achterlaten; aanduiden; (ken)merken; prijzen; corri'geren; letten op
  to mark time, de pas mar'keren
marked, duidelijk; ver'dacht
market, markt: aan de markt brengen
market-place, markt(plein n)
marksman, scherpschutter
marmalade, marme'lade
maroon, paarsrood (n)
  to be marooned, stranden
marquis, mar'kies
marriage, huwelijk n
marrow, merg(pompoen) (n)

marry, trouwen (met); uit-huwelijken

marsh(y), moe'ras(sig) (n)

marshal, maarschalk: ordenen; ge'leiden

martial, krijgs('haftig)

martyr, martelaar: de martel-dood doen sterven

martyrdom, martelaarschap n; marteling

marvel, wonder n : zich ver'won-deren

marvellous, wonder'baarlijk, fan'tastisch; heerlijk

masculine, mannelijk

mash, pap: (fijn)stampen

mask, masker(en) (n); mas'ke-ren

mason, steenhouwer, metselaar

masquerade, maske'rade: zich ver'mommen

mass, massa: mis

massacre, massamoord; slacht-ing

massage, mas'sage: mas'seren

massive, mas'saal

mast, mast

master, (jonge) heer; ge'zag-voerder; leraar; meester(-): hoofd-: meester worden

masterful, bazig

masterly, meesterlijk

masterpiece, meesterstuk n

mastery, overhand; meester-schap n

mat, mat(je n), kleed(je) n; ver'warde massa: plakkerig maken

mat(t), mat

match, lucifer: par'tij, com-bi'natie; wedstrijd; huwelijk n: eve'naren; bij el'kaar pas-sen

matchless, onverge'lijkelijk

mate, maat; levensgezel('in); stuurman: (zich) paren

material, stof(felijk), materi'aal (n), materi'eel (n); essenti'eel

materialist(ic), materia'list(isch)

materialize, ver'wezenlijkt wor-den; ver'wezenlijken; ver'-schijnen

maternal, moederlijk, moeder-

maternity, moederschap n kraam-

mathematical, wis'kundig

mathematician, wis'kundige

mathematics, wiskunde

matins, metten

matrimonial, huwelijks-

matrimony, huwelijk (se staat) n

matron, ma'trone; moeder; direc'trice

matter, stof; kwestie; pus: van be'lang zijn

as a matter of fact, eigenlijk; overigens

as a matter of course, als van-zelf'sprekend

for that matter, wat dat be'treft, trouwens

it does not matter, het geeft niets, het doet er niet toe

what is the matter? wat scheelt er aan?

matter-of-fact, zakelijk

mattress, ma'tras

mature, rijp(en); ver'vallen

maturity, rijpheid; ver'valtijd

maul, toetakelen

mauve, lichtpaars

maxim, stelregel

may, meidoorn: mei: mogen, misschien kunnen

maybe, mis'schien

mayonnaise, mayon'naise

mayor, burge'meester

maze, doolhof n

me, mij, me

mead, mee: dreef

meadow, weide

meagre, schraal

meal, maal(tijd) (n): meel n

mean, ge'meen, krenterig; ge'ring, schriel: middenweg, ge'middelde n: be'doelen, me-nen: be'tekenen

meander, kronkelen; dolen

meaning, be'tekenis; be'doeling: veelbe'tekenend

meaningless, niets'zeggend

means, middel(en) n

by all means, ge'rust

by no means, geenszins

meantime: in the —, in'tussen

meanwhile, onder'tussen

measles, mazelen

measure, maat(regel): (op)meten; zijn

measurement, maat

meat, vlees *n*; kost

meat-safe, vliegenkast

mechanic, mecani'cien

mechanical, machi'naal, werktuig'kundig; werk'tuiglijk

mechanics, werktuigkunde

mechanism, mecha'nisme *n*, mecha'niek *n*

mechanize, mechani'seren

medal, me'daille

meddle with, zich be'moeien met; komen aan

meddlesome, be'moeiziek

mediaeval, middel'eeuws

mediate, als be'middelaar optreden

medical, medisch: keuring

medicinal, genees'krachtig

medicine, ge'neeskunde; ge'neesmiddel *n*, drankje *n*

mediocre, middel'matig

mediocrity middel'matigheid

meditate, be(*or* over)'peinzen

meditation, over'peinzing; medi'tatie

Mediterranean, Middellandse Zee

medium, middel('matig) (*n*); medium *n*

medley, mengelmoes *n*; potpour'ri

meek, zacht'moedig

meet, (el'kaar) ont'moeten; (aan)treffen; samenkomen; afhalen; vol'doen aan

meeting, ver'gadering, samenkomst; ont'moeting

megaphone, mega'foon

melancholy, zwaar'moedig(heid)

mellow, zacht (en sappig); rijp; zoet'vloeiend

melodious, wel'luidend

melodrama, melo'drama *n*

melody, melo'die

melon, me'loen

melt, (doen) smelten

member, lid(maat) (*n*)

membership, lidmaatschap *n*; ledental *n*

membrane, vlies *n*

memento, aandenken *n*

memoirs, me'moires

memorable, gedenk'waardig

memorandum, memo'randum *n*; nota

memorial, ge'denkteken *n*; her'denkings-

memorize, uit het hoofd leren

memory, ge'heugen *n*; her'innering; nagedachtenis

menace, (voort'durende) be'dreiging

menagerie, menage'rie

mend, repa'reren; beteren

mendicant, bedel(end): bedelaar

menial, nederig, onderge'schikt

mental, geestelijk, geest(es)-; hoofd-

  mental arithmetic, hoofdrekenen *n*

mentality, mentali'teit

mention, (ver')melding: ver'melden

mentor, mentor

menu, me'nu *n*

mercantile, handels-

mercenary, geld'zuchtig: huurling

merchandise, koopwaar

merchant, koopman: koopvaar'dij-

merciful, ge'nadig; ge'zegend

merciless, mee'dogenloos

mercury, kwik(zilver) *n*

mercy, ge'nade; zegen

mere, louter

  a mere (nothing), maar een (kleinigheid)

merely, alleen maar

merge, overgaan(in); samensmelten

meridian, meridi'aan

meringue, schuim(gebak) *n*

merit, ver'dienste: ver'dienen

mermaid, zeemeermin

merriment, vrolijkheid

merry, vrolijk

merry-go-round, draaimolen

merry-making, pret(make'rij): pretmakend

mesh, maas

mess, rommel, bende; lelijke toestand; me'nage, (offi'ciers)-tafel : vuil maken

to mess about, friemelen, klungelen

to mess up, ver'knoeien

message, boodschap, be'richt *n*

messenger, (voor)bode

Messiah, Mes'sias

Messrs., de Heren; Firma

messy, slordig, vuil

metal, me'taal *n* : me'talen

metallic, me'talen, me'taalachtig

metamorphosis, ge'daantever-wisseling

metaphor, beeldspraak

metaphorical, fi'guurlijk

mete out, toemeten

meteor, mete'oor

meteorological, meteoro'logisch

meter, meter

method, me'thode; sys'teem *n*

methodical, syste'matisch

Methodist, Metho'dist

meticulous, (al te) zeer nauwge'zet

metre, meter; metrum *n*

metropolis, wereldstad

metropolitan, hoofd'stedelijk, Londense: metropo'liet

mettle, tempera'ment *n*

to put a person on his mettle, een uitdaging voor iemand zijn, uitdagen

mew, stal(woning): mi'auwen

mica, mica *n*

microbe, mi'crobe

microphone, micro'foon

microscope, micros'coop

mid, midden

midday, twaalf uur: middag-

middle, middel(ste) (*n*), midden(-) (*n*)

middle-classes, middenstand

middle-aged, van middelbare leeftijd

middle-ages, middeleeuwen

middleman, tussenpersoon

middling, middel'matig

midge, mug

midget, dwergje *n* : minia'tuur

midnight, midder'nacht(elijk)

midriff, middenrif *n*

midshipman, adelborst

midst, (te) midden (van)

midsummer, mid'zomer

midway, halver'wege

midwife, vroedvrouw

mien, voorkomen *n*

might(y), macht(ig)

migrate, trekken

migration, trek

mild, zacht('aardig); licht

mildew, (be')schimmel(en)

mile, mijl

mileage, afstand in mijlen

milestone, mijlpaal

militant, strijdend; strijd'lust-ig

militarism, milita'risme *n*

military, mili'tair, krijgs-

militate, (tegen)werken

militia, mi'litie

milk, melk(en)

milkman, melkboer

Milky Way, Melkweg

mill, molen; fa'briek: malen; kartelen; kri'oelen

miller, molenaar

millet, gierst

milliner's (shop), hoedenzaak

million, mil'joen *n*

millionaire, miljo'nair

mime, ge'barenspel *n*: met ge'baren uitbeelden

mimic, mimicus: nabootsen

mince, ge'hakt *n*: fijnhakken

mind, geest, ver'stand *n*, ge'dachte; zin: er iets op tegen hebben; letten op; oppassen

to make up one's mind, be'sluiten

mindful, ge'dachtig (aan)

mine, van mij, het (*or* de) mijne: mijn; bron: delven

miner, mijnwerker

mineral, delfstof: mine'raal *n*

mingle, (zich) mengen; omgaan

miniature, minia'tuur (*n*)

minimize, zo klein mogelijk maken; ge'ringschatten

minimum, minimum *n*

mining, mijn(bouw)

minion, gunsteling

minister, predi'kant; mi'nister; ge'zant: ver'zorgen

ministry, predi'kantschap *n*; minis'terie *n*

mink, nerts *n*

minor, klein, minder (be'langrijk); mi'neur: minder'jarige

minority, minder('jarig)heid

minstrel, min'streel

mint, kruize'munt: munt(en)

minus, min; zonder

minute, mi'nuut; ogenblik *n*; notule: mi'niem; minuti'eus

miracle, wonder *n*

miraculous, wonder'baarlijk

mirage, fata mor'gana; zinsbegoocheling

mire, slijk *n*

mirror, spiegel: weer'kaatsen

mirth, vrolijkheid

misadventure, ongeluk *n*; onge'lukkig voorval *n*

misapprehension, mis'vatting

misbehave, zich mis'dragen

misbehaviour, wangedrag *n*

miscalculate, zich ver'rekenen; misrekenen

miscarriage, mis'lukking; miskraam

miscarry, mis'lukken; ver'loren gaan

miscellaneous, veel'soortig

miscellany, ge'mengde ver'zameling

mischief, (katte)kwaad *n*; on'deugendheid

mischievous, on'deugend; kwaa'daardig

misconception, dwaalbegrip *n*, mis'vatting

misconduct, wangedrag *n*; wanbeheer *n*: slecht be'heren

misconstrue, ver'keerd opvatten

miscreant, laag: onverlaat

misdeed, misdaad

misdemeanour, wangedrag *n*

miser, vrek

miserable, diep onge'lukkig; naar'geestig; el'lendig

misery, el'lende

misfire, ketsen; overslaan

misfit: to be a —, niet passen; uit de toon vallen

misfortune, ongeluk *n*

misgiving, bang ver'moeden *n*

misguided, ver'doold; onver'standig

mishap, ongeluk(je) *n*

misinform, ver'keerd inlichten

misinterpret, ver'keerd uitleggen

misjudge, ver'keerd (be')oordelen

mislay, kwijtraken

mislead, mis'leiden

mismanagement, wanbeheer *n*

misnomer, ver'keerde be'naming

misplace, ver'keerd plaatsen

misplaced, mis'plaatst

misprint, drukfout: ver'keerd drukken

misrepresent, een ver'keerde voorstelling geven van

miss, (me')juffrouw: misslaan; mislopen; missen; ver'zuimen

misshapen, mis'vormd

missile, projec'tiel *n*

mission, missie; zending

missionary, zendeling(s-)

missive, schrijven *n*

mist, nevel, lage wolk; waas *n*

mistake, ver'gissing; fout: aanzien, veer'keerd be'grijpen, mis'kennen

to be mistaken, zich ver'gissen; mis'plaatst zijn

mistress, me'vrouw; juffrouw, lera'res; mai'tresse

mistrust, wantrouwen (*n*)

misty, nevelachtig, wazig; be'slagen

misunderstand, ver'keerd be'grijpen

misunderstanding, misverstand *n*

misuse, misbruik *n*: mis'bruiken; mis'handelen

mite, dreumes; mijt

mitigate, ver'zachten, ver'lichten

mitre, mijter; ver'stek *n*

mitt(en), want, vuisthandschoen

mix, (ver')mengen; zich laten mengen; omgaan met

to mix up, ver'warren

mixture, mengsel *n*, mengeling

moan, ge'kerm *n*; ge'jammer *n*: kermen, suizen; jammeren

moat, gracht

mob, (mensen)massa; ge'peupel *n*; bende: zich ver'dringen om, als één man te lijf gaan

mobile, be'weeglijk, rondtrekkend

mobilize, mobili'seren

mock, schijn-, kunst-: (be')spotten; be'spottelijk maken; naäpen

mockery, spotter'nij; aanfluiting

mode, mode; ma'nier

model, mo'del *n*: model'leren, boet'seren

moderate, (ge')matig(d): matigen; be'daren

moderation, matigheid

in moderation, met mate

modern(ize), mo'dern(i'seren)

modest, be'scheiden; zedig

modification, wijziging

modify, wijzigen; matigen

moist(en), vochtig (maken)

moisture, vocht(igheid) (*n*)

molasses, me'lasse

mole, mol: pier: moedervlek

molecule, mole'cule

molest, lastig vallen

mollify, ver'tederen

moment, ogenblik *n*; be'lang *n*

momentarily, voor een ogenblik

momentary, kort'stondig

momentous, ge'wichtig

momentum, arbeidsvermogen van be'weging *n*, vaart

monarch, vorst('in)

monarchy, monar'chie

monastery, klooster *n*

monastic, klooster(achtig)

Monday, maandag

monetary, munt-, geldelijk

money, geld *n*

mongrel, bastaard(hond)

monk, monnik

monkey, aap

monocle, mo'nocle

monogram, mono'gram *n*

monologue, al'leenspraak

monopolize, monopoli'seren

monopoly, mono'polie *n*

monotonous, een'tonig

monotony, een'tonigheid

monsoon, moesson

monster, monster *n*; ge'drocht *n*

monstrosity, monstrum *n*

monstrous, monsterachtig

month(ly), maand(elijks)

monument, monu'ment *n*

monumental, monumen'taal

mood, stemming, hu'meur *n*: wijs

moody, hu'meurig; ont'stemd

moon(light), maan(licht *n*)

moor, heide: Moor: meren

moorings, meertouwen; ligplaats

moot, be'twistbaar

mop, zwabber; (afwas)kwast: dweilen, zwabberen; afvegen

mope, mokken

moral, zedelijk, zeden-, mo'reel: mo'raal

morals, zeden

morale, mo'reel *n*

morality, zedelijke be'ginselen; zedelijkheid; morali'teit

moralize, morali'seren

morbid, ziekelijk; patho'logisch

more, meer, nog (meer)

some more, nog wat

more or less, min of meer

moreover, boven'dien

morgue, morgue

morning, morgen, ochtend

in the morning, 's ochtends; morgenochtend

morose, gemelijk

morsel, bete; stukje *n*

mortal, sterfelijk; dodelijk, doods-: sterveling

mortality, sterfte(cijfer *n*)

mortally, dodelijk

mortar, metselkalk; mor'tier; vijzel

mortgage, hypo'theek (nemen op)

mortify, diep ver'nederen; kas'tijden

mortuary, lijkenhuis *n*

mosaic, moza'ïek (*n*)

mosque, mos'kee

mosquito, mus'kiet

moss, mos *n*

most, meest; bij'zonder: het (*or* de) meeste

at the most, op zijn hoogst (*or* meest)

to make the most of, zoveel mogelijk profi'teren van

mostly, groten'deels; meestal

moth, nachtvlinder, mot

mother, moeder

motherly, moederlijk

mother-or-pearl, paarle'moer-(en) (*n*)

motif, mo'tief *n*

motion, be'weging; motie; stoelgang: wenken

motionless, onbe'weeglijk

motivate, moti'veren

motive, be'weegreden

motley, bont

motor, motor: rijden

motor-cycle, motorfiets

motorist, automobi'list

mottle, vlekken

motto, motto *n*

mould, vorm(en); schimmel; teelaarde: boet'seren

mouldy, be'schimmeld; snert

moult, ruien

mound, wal, terp

mount, berg: rijdier *n*: (be')stijgen

mountain(eer), berg(beklimmer)

mountainous, bergachtig

mourn, (be')treuren

mourner, rouwdrager

mournful, treurig; droevig

mourning, rouw

mouse, muis

mouse-trap, muizeval

moustache, snor

mouth, mond(ing); opening

mouthful, hapje *n*

mouthpiece, mondstuk *n*; woordvoerder

movable, be'weegbaar; ver'anderlijk

move, zet; stap; ver'huizing: (zich) be'wegen; ver'huizen; ont'roeren

movement, be'weging

moving, roerend

mow, maaien

much, veel; zeer; verreweg; vrijwel

muck, drek, vuil *n*

mud, modder

muddle, warboel: in de war

brengen, door el'kaar gooien; scharrelen

muddy, modderig

mudguard, spatbord *n*

muff, mof: be'derven

muffle, instoppen; dempen

muffler, bouf'fante

mug, kroes: sul: smoel

mulberry, moerbei

mule, muildier *n*

multifarious, veel'soortig

multiple, veel'voudig; veelvoud *n*

multiplication, vermenig'vuldiging

multiply, (zich) vermenig'vuldigen

multitude, menigte; groot aantal *n*

mum: to keep —, stilzwijgen

mumble, mompelen

mummy, mummie: mammie

mumps, de bof

munch, (hoorbaar) k(n)auwen (op)

mundane, werelds

municipal, ge'meente-, stedelijk, stads-

municipality, ge'meente

munition, krijgsvoorraad

mural, muurschildering

murder, moord: ver'moorden

murderer, moordenaar

murderous, moord'dadig

murky, zwart, somber

murmur, ge'murmel *n*: murmelen; mopperen

muscle, spier

muscular, ge'spierd; spier-

muse, muze: mijmeren

museum, mu'seum *n*

mush, moes *n*; ge'wauwel *n*

mushroom, champi'gnon

music, mu'ziek

musical, muzi'kaal; mu'ziek-

musician, musicus; muzi'kant

muslin, neteldoek *n*

mussel, mossel

must, moet(en), moest(en)

mustard, mosterd

muster, monstering: monsteren; ver'zamelen

musty, muf, schimmelig

mute, stom; sour'dine: dempen
mutilate, ver'minken
mutineer, muiter
mutiny, muite'rij, opstand
mutter, mompelen, prevelen
mutton, schapevlees *n*
mutual, onderling, weder'zijds;
  weder'kerig
muzzle, muil(band); mond
my, mijn
myriad, on'telbaar; tien'duizend-
  tal *n*
myself, me('zelf), (ik')zelf
mysterious, geheim'zinnig
mystery, ge'heim *n*; raadsel *n*
mystic, mysticus
mystic(al), ver'borgen; mys'tiek
mysticism, mys'tiek
mystify, ver'bijsteren
myth, mythe; ver'dichtsel *n*
mythical, mythisch; ver'dicht
mythology, mytholo'gie

N

nag, hit; vitten
nail, spijker; nagel; vastspijk-
  eren
naïve, na'ïef
naked, naakt; bloot
name, naam; (be')noemen; opnoemen; thuisbrengen
nameless, onbe'kend; ano'niem,
  naamloos
namely, namelijk
namesake, naamgenoot
nap, dutje *n*: nop; dutten
nape, nek
napkin, ser'vet *n*; luier
narcissus, nar'cis
narcotic, slaap'wekkend middel
  n: ver'dovend
narrate, ver'halen
narrative, ver'haal *n*; ver'halend
narrow, smal, nauw; klein
narrow-minded, klein'geestig
nasal, na'saal, neus-
nasty, akelig; smerig; naar,
  lelijk
nation, volk *n*, natie
national, natio'naal; volks-,
  staats-
nationalist(ic), nationa'list(isch)

nationality, nationali'teit
nationalize, nationali'seren
native, inboorling: ge'boorte-
  moeder-; aangeboren; in'heems
nativity, ge'boorte
natural, na'tuurlijk, na'tuur-
  natural history, na'tuurlijke
  his'torie
naturalist, natura'list
naturalize, naturali'seren
naturally, na'tuurlijk; van
  na'ture
nature, na'tuur; aard
naught, nul; niets
naughty, on'deugend
nausea, misselijkheid; walging
nauseate, misselijk maken
nautical, zee(vaart'kundig)
naval, ma'rine-, zee-
nave, schip *n*
navel, navel
navigable, be'vaarbaar
navigate, be'sturen
navigation, stuurmanskunst,
  navi'gatie
navigator, navi'gator
navy, ma'rine, vloot
nay, neen; ja (zelfs)
near, dichtbij, na'bij
nearly, bijna
  not nearly, lang niet
neat, net(jes); handig; puur
necessarily, nood'zakelijk-
  (erwijs)
necessary, nood'zakelijk: be'-
  hoefte
necessitate, nood'zakelijk maken
necessity, nood(zaak); be'hoefte
neck, hals(stuk *n*)
necklace, (hals)ketting, (hals-)
  snoer *n*
necktie, (strop)das
nectar, nectar
need, be'hoefte, nood(zaak): nodig hebben; hoeven, moeten
  there is no need . . . het is niet
  nodig . . .
needful, nodig
needle, naald
needless, on'nodig
needlework, naaiwerk *n*, hand-
  werk(en) *n*
needy, be'hoeftig

negation, ont'kenning, ver'loochening

negative, ont'kennend; negatief
(*n*)

neglect, ver'zuim(en) (*n*), ver'-
waarlozing: ver'waarlozen

negligence, ver'waarlozing, on'-
achtzaamheid

negligent, achteloos

negligible, niet noemens'waard

negotiate, onder'handelen

negotiation, onder'handeling

negro, neger(-)

neigh, hinniken

neighbour, buurman (*or* vrouw);
naaste

neighbourhood, buurt, om'-
geving

neighbouring, na'burig

neighbourly, vriendelijk

neither, geen van beide:
even'min

neither . . . nor, noch . . . noch

nephew, neef

nerve, zenuw; geestkracht;
(bru'tale) moed: ver'mannen

nervous, zenuw(achtig); bang

nest, nest *n*; (zich) nestelen

nestle, zich nestelen

net, net *n*; tule, vi'trage: met
een net vangen

nether, onder-

Netherlands, Nederland(s) (*n*)

netting, gaas *n*

nettle, (brand)netel: pi'keren

network, net(werk) *n*

neurotic, zenuw(patient),
zenuwziek

neuter, on'zijdig

neutral, neu'traal (land *n*)

neutralize, neutrali'seren; neu'-
traal ver'klaren

never, nooit; niet eens

nevertheless, desondanks

new, nieuw, vers

newborn, pasgeboren

newcomer, nieuweling

new-fangled, nieuwer'wets

newly, pas, opnieuw

news, nieuws(berichten) (*n*),
be'richt *n*

newspaper, krant

newsreel, jour'naal *n*

next, volgend, aan'staande:
daar'na

next door, hier'naast

next (door) to, naast

nib, pen

nibble, knabbelen

nice, aardig; lekker; net(jes); fijn

nicety, nauwge'zetheid; fi'nesse

niche, nis, hoekje *n*

nick, keep: inkepen

nickname, bijnaam

nicotine, nico'tine

niece, nicht

niggard(ly), vrek(kig)

night, nacht, avond

at (*or* in the) night, 's nachts

nightdress, nachtjapon

nightfall, het vallen van de avond

nightingale, nachtegaal

nightmare, nachtmerrie

nimble, kwiek

nine(teen), negen(tien)

ninety, negentig

nip, kneep: halfje *n*: knijpen

nipple, tepel

nitrogen, stikstof

nitwit, domoor

no, neen: niet, geen

no one, niemand

nobility, adel(stand)

noble, edel(man), adellijk; groots

nobody, niemand: nul

nocturnal, nachtelijk, nacht-

nod, knik(ken); knikkebollen

noise, la'waai *n*, ge'luid *n*

noiseless, ge'ruisloos

noisy, luid'ruchtig, druk

nomad, no'made; zwerver

nominal, in naam; nomi'naal

nominate, be'noemen; kandi'daat stellen

nomination, be'noeming; kandi'-
daatstelling

nonchalant, onver'schillig

non-committal, (op'zettelijk)
vaag

nonconformist, afgescheiden(e)

nondescript, onbe'paald; onop'vallend

none, geen (één), niemand, niets:
geenszins

nonentity, nul

nonsense, onzin

nook, hoekje *n*, plekje *n*

noon, twaalf uur ('s middags)

noose, strop, strik

nor, noch, en . . . ook niet.

normal, nor'maal

normally, ge'woonlijk

north, (naar het) noorden; noord(en)-

northerly, northern, noordelijk

Norway, Noorwegen *n*

Norwegian, Noor(s) (*n*)

nose, neus

nosegay, ruiker

nostril, neusgat *n*

not, niet

notable, op'merkelijk, aan'zienlijk: no'tabele

notably, met name, voor'al

notation, schrijfwijze

notch, kerf: kerven

note, aantekening, no'titie; briefje *n*; nota; toon, noot; be'tekenis: no'teren; opmerken

notebook, aantekenboekje *n*

noted, be'kend, be'roemd

noteworthy, opmerkens'waardig

nothing, niets

notice, aandacht; aankondiging: (op)merken

  to give notice, de dienst (*or* huur) opzeggen; kennis geven

  to take notice of, aandacht schenken aan

noticeable, merkbaar

notification, kennisgeving

notify, ver'wittigen; be'kend maken

notion, i'dee *n*

notorious, be'rucht

notwithstanding, (des)ondanks

nought, niets; nul

nourish, voeden; koesteren

nourishment, voeding, voedsel *n*

novel, ro'man: nieuw

novelist, ro'manschrijver

novelty, nieuwigheid

November, november

novice, nieuweling

now, nu

nowadays, tegen'woordig

nowhere, nergens

noxious, schadelijk

nozzle, tuit

nucleus, kern

nude, naakt (*n*); naaktstudie

nudge, duwtje *n*: zachtjes aanstoten

nugget, (goud)klomp

nuisance: **to be a —,** lastig zijn

null and void, van nul en gener waarde

nullify, nietig ver'klaren; opheffen

numb, ver'kleumd, ver'doofd: ver'doven

number, ge'tal *n*; aantal *n*; nummer(en) (*n*); tellen, rekenen

numeral, cijfer *n*; telwoord *n*

numerical, nume'riek

numerous, talrijk

nun, non

nunnery, nonnenklooster *n*

nuptial, huwelijks-

nurse, ver'pleegster; kindermeisje *n*: ver'plegen; zogen; ver'zorgen; koesteren

nursery, kinderkamer; kweke'rij

nurture, (op)voeden; koesteren

nut, noot; moer

nutmeg, nootmus'kaat

nutrition, voeding(s'waarde)

nutritive, voedzaam

nymph, nimf

O

oaf, pummel

oak, eik(enhout *n*) (en)

oar, riem

oasis, o'ase

oats, haver

oath, eed; vloek

oatmeal, havermeel *n*, havermout

obdurate,   onver'murwbaar, ver'stokt

obedience, ge'hoorzaamheid

obedient, ge'hoorzaam

obeisance, diepe buiging

obese, zwaar'lijvig

obey, ge'hoorzamen

obituary notice, in Me'moriam

object, voorwerp *n*; doel *n*: be'zwaar hebben (*or* maken) (tegen)

objection, be'zwaar *n*, tegenwerping

objectionable, on'aangenaam,
afkeurens'waardig

objective, objec'tief (*n*)

obligation, ver'plichting

obligatory, ver'plicht

oblige, ver'plichten; ge'noegen
doen

obliging, voor'komend

oblique, schuin; zijdelings

obliterate, uitwissen

oblivion, ver'getelheid

oblivious, onbe'wust

oblong, lang'werpig: rechthoek

obnoxious, aan'stotelijk

oboe, hobo

obscene, on'zedelijk

obscure, ob'scuur; onbe'kend;
ver'borgen;   on'duidelijk:
on'zichtbaar maken; be'lemmeren; ver'doezelen

obscurity,   on'duidelijkheid;
onbe'kendheid

obsequious, kruiperig

observance, in'achtneming

observant, op'merkzaam

observation, waarneming, obser'vatie; opmerking

observatory, sterrenwacht

observe, (op)merken, waarnemen; in acht nemen

obsess, (ge'heel) ver'vullen

obsession, ob'sessie

obsolete, ver'ouderd

obstacle, hindernis; be'letsel *n*

obstetrics, ver'loskunde

obstinate, hard'nekkig

obstreperous, wild, luid'ruchtig

obstruct, ver'sperren, be'lemmeren

obstruction, hindernis, be'letsel
n; be'lemmering

obtain, ver'krijgen, ver'werven,
be'halen; gelden

obtainable, ver'krijgbaar

obtrude, (zich) opdringen

obtuse, stomp('zinnig)

obviate, uit de weg ruimen

obvious, overduidelijk

occasion, ge'legenheid; aanleiding (geven tot)

occasionally, nu en dan

occult, oc'cult

occupant, be'woner, inzittende

occupation, be'roep *n*, bezigheid;
be'zetting

occupy, be'zetten, innemen;
be'wonen

occur, voorkomen; opkomen (bij)

occurrence, voorval *n*, ge'beurtenis

ocean, oce'aan

ocean-going, zee-

o'clock, uur

octagonal, acht'hoekig

octave, oc'taaf

October, oc'tober

octopus, achtarm

oculist, oogarts

odd, on'even; los; over; vreemd

  odd job, kar'weitje *n*

  odd moment, ver'loren ogenblik *n*

oddity, eigen'aardigheid, vreemde
snuiter

oddment, res'tant *n*

odds, kans;   (alle)   nadelen;
ver'schil *n*

ode, ode

odious, ver'foeilijk

odorous, kwalijk (*or* wel')riekend

odour, reuk; lucht(je *n*)

of, van, uit; met; over

off, van (. . . af); weg; at; vrij

offal, afval

offence, over'treding; aanstoot,
be'lediging; aanval

offend, be'ledigen, ergeren

offensive, be'ledigend; on'aangenaam; aanval(s-)

offer, (aan)bod *n*: (aan)bieden;
aanvoeren; zich voordoen

offering, gift

offhand, op het eerste ge'zicht

office, kan'toor *n*, ambt *n*,
functie; zorg

officer, offi'cier; functio'naris

official, offici'eel;   ambtenaar,
be'ambte

officiate, dienst doen; de dienst
leiden

officious, be'moeiziek

offing, ver'schiet *n*

offset, (laten) opwegen tegen

offspring, kroost *n*

often, vaak
ogle, (toe)lonken
ogre, boeman
oil, olie, pe'troleum : smeren
oilcloth, zeildoek *n*
oil-painting, schilde'rij in olie-
    verf
oilskin, oliegoed *n* ; oliejas
oily, olieachtig
ointment, zalf
old, oud
old-fashioned, ouder'wets
oligarchy, oligar'chie
olive, o'lijf(boom)
omelet, ome'let
omen, voorteken *n*
ominous, onheil'spellend
omission, ver'zuim *n*, weglating
omit, weglaten ; nalaten
omnipotent, al'machtig
omniscient, al'wetend
on, op ; aan ; bij, met ; over : verder ;
    aan de gang
once, eens, één keer ; eenmaal
  at once, on'middellijk
  once in a while, zo nu en dan
  once or twice, een paar keer
one, één : men
onerous, zwaar
oneself, (zich')zelf, zich
one-sided, een'zijdig
onion, ui
onlooker, toeschouwer
only, slechts, (al'leen) maar ;
    pas, nog : enig
  only too, maar al te
onset, aanval ; aanvang
onslaught, woeste aanval
onto, op
onus, last
onward(s), voorwaarts
ooze, (door)sijpelen
opal, o'paal
opaque, ondoor'schijnend
open, open('baar) ; open'hartig ;
    blootgesteld : openlucht : open-
    gaan ; opendoen
opening, opening ; be'gin *n* ;
    kans : inleidend
opera, opera
opera-glasses, to'neelkijker
operate, ope'reren ; werken ;
    be'dienen

operation, ope'ratie ; handeling
operator, telefo'nist(e) ; be'dien-
    er
opinion oordeel *n*, mening
opium, opium *n*
opponent, tegenstander
opportune, gunstig
opportunist, opportu'nist
opportunity, ge'legenheid
oppose, tegenwerken ; stellen
    tegen'over
opposite, tegen'over (gesteld)
opposition, tegenstand ; oppo'-
    sitie
oppress, (onder')drukken
oppression, onder(*or* ver)'druk-
    king
oppressive, drukkend
optic, ge'zichts-, oog-
optical, ge'zichts-
optimistic, opti'mistisch
option, keus
optional, faculta'tief
opulence, rijkdom
or, of
oracle, o'rakel *n*
oral, mondeling ; mond-
orange, sinaasappel : o'ranje
oration, rede
orator, redenaar
oratorio, ora'torium *n*
oratory, wel'sprekendheid ; ka'pel
orb, bol
orbit, baan ; kring
orchard, boomgaard
orchestra(l), or'kest(-) (*n*)
orchid, orchi'dee
ordain, voorschrijven ; wijden
ordeal, be'proeving, proef
order, (volg)orde ; stand ;
    be'vel(en) (*n*) ; be'stelling :
    ordenen ; be'stellen
  in order that, opdat
  in order to, om te
  out of order, niet op volgorde ;
    niet in orde
orderly, ordelijk ; ordon'nans ;
    zaalmeisje (*or* knecht) (*n*)
ordinance, ver'ordening
ordinarily, ge'woonlijk
ordinary, ge'woon
ordnance, ge'schut *n* ; staf-
ore, erts *n*

organ, orgel; *n* or'gaan *n*
organic, or'ganisch
organism, orga'nisme *n*
organist, orga'nist
organization, organi'satie
organize, organi'seren
orgy, baccha'naal *n*
Orient, Oosten *n*
Oriental, Oosters: Oosterling
orientate, orien'teren
orifice, opening
origin, oorsprong; afkomst
original, oor'spronkelijk; origi'-
neel (*n*)
originate, ont'staan (uit); in
het leven roepen
ornament, sieraad *n*, ver'siersel *n*
ornamental, sier-
ornate, zwierig; bloemrijk
ornithologist, vogel'kundige
orphan, wees(-), ouderloos
orphanage, weeshuis *n*
orthodox, ortho'dox; ge'bruikelijk
oscillate, slingeren; oscil'leren
osier, rijs *n*
ossify, ver'benen; ver'stenen
ostensible, ogen'schijnlijk
ostentation, uiterlijk ver'toon *n*
ostentatious, praalziek
ostracize, doodverklaren
ostrich, struisvogel
other, ander; nog
the other day, onlangs
otherwise, anders
otter, otter
ought, moest(en)
ounce, (approx.) kwart ons *n*
our(selves), ons(zelf)
ours, de (*or* het) onze, van ons
oust, ver'dringen
out, (er')uit; (naar) buiten; weg
out and out, door en door
out of, uit; buiten; zonder
outbreak, uitbarsting; oproer *n*
outbuilding, bijgebouw *n*
outburst, uitbarsting
outcast, ver'stoteling
outcome, resul'taat *n*
outcry, luid pro'test *n*
outdoor, openlucht-
outer, buiten-
outfit, uitrusting, uitzet

outgoing, uitgaand, aftredend:
uitgave
outgrow, groeien uit; ont'groeien
outhouse, bijgebouw *n*, schuurtje
n
outing, uitstapje *n*
outlandish, vreemd'soortig
outlaw, banneling; vogel'vrij
ver'klaren
outlay, uitgave(n)
outlet, afvoer(kanaal *or* buis) *n*;
uitweg
outline, omtrek; schets(en):
aftekenen
outlive, over'leven
outlook, (voor')uitzicht *n*; opvatting
outlying, afgelegen
outnumber, (in aantal) over'treffen
out-of-date, ver'ouderd
out-of-the-way, afgelegen; buite'nissig
outpost, buiten(*or* voor)post
output, opbrengst
outrage, annranding; schande
outrageous, schan'dalig
outright, in'eens; rond'uit
outset, begin *n*
outside, buiten(kant)
outsider, buitenstaander
outskirts, buitenkant
outspoken, open'hartig
outstanding, voor'treffelijk
outstrip, achter zich laten;
over'treffen
outward, uit-, naar buiten
(to all) outward appearances,
uiterlijk (*n*)
outwardly, uiterlijk
outweigh, zwaarder wegen dan
outwit, ver'schalken
oval, o'vaal (*n*)
ovation, o'vatie
oven, oven
over, boven; over('heen); door;
meer dan: om
over again, nog eens
overall, huishoudschort *n*: to'taal
overalls, ove'rall
overbearing, aan'matigend
overboard, over'boord
overcast, be'trokken

overcharge, te veel vragen
overcoat, overjas
overcome, over'stelpt, be'vang-
en : over'winnen
overcrowded, over'vol
overdo, te veel doen ; over'drijv-
en
overdue, achter'stallig, te laat
overflow, overloop: over'stromen, overlopen
overgrown, over'woekerd
overhang, uitstekende rand :
overhangen
overhaul, nakijken en repa'reren ;
inhalen
overhead, boven (het hoofd) :
boven'gronds, lucht-
overheads, vaste uitgaven
overhear, horen ; afluisteren
overjoyed, dolblij
overlap, ten dele be'dekken,
ge'deeltelijk samenvallen
overlook, over'zien ; over het
hoofd zien
overnight, in één nacht ; de
avond te'voren
overpower, over'weldigen
overrate, over'schatten
overrule, ver'werpen
overrun, over'stromen, over'-
woekeren
overseas, over'zee(s)
overseer, opzichter
overshadow, over'schaduwen
oversight, a'buis n
oversleep, zich ver'slapen
overstep, over'schrijden
overtake, inhalen
overtax, te veel vergen van
overthrow, ten val brengen
overtime, overwerk n
overture, voorstel n ; ouver'ture
overturn, om'verwerpen, omslaan
overwhelm, over'stelpen
overwork, zich over'werken
overwrought, over'spannen
owe, schuldig zijn
owing to, dank zij
owl, uil
own, eigen(dom n) : be'zitten ;
er'kennen
owner, eigenaar

ownership, eigendom (srecht n)
ox, os
oxygen, zuurstof
oyster, oester

P

pace, pas, tempo n : stappen
pacific, vrede'lievend
Pacific, Stille Oce'aan
pacifist, paci'fist
pacify, tot be'daren brengen
pack, pak(ken) (n) ; hoop ; spel
n : ver'(or in)pakken ; proppen
package, pak n
packet, pakje n
packing, ver'pakking
pact, ver'drag n
pad, kussen(tje) n ; blok n :
capiton'neren ; opvullen
paddle, pa'gaai(en) ; pootje
baden
paddock, paddock
padlock, hangslot n
pagan, heiden(s)
page, bladzijde: page
pageant, ver'toning ; optocht
pail, emmer
pain, pijn (doen)
to take pains, moeite doen
painful, pijnlijk
painstaking, nauwge'zet
paint, verf : verven ; schilderen
paint-brush, verfkwast, pen'seel
n
painter, schilder
painting, schilde'rij n ; schilderkunst
pair, paar n
pal, maat
palace, pa'leis n
palatable, smakelijk
palate, ge'hemelte n ; smaak
palatial, vorstelijk
palaver, samenspreking ; ge'klets
n
pale, bleek, licht: paal: ver'bleken
palette, pa'let n
paling, om'heining
palisade, palis'sade
pall, lijkkleed n ; mantel ; gaan
tegenstaan

pallid, bleek
pallor, bleekheid
palm, palm(tak)
 to palm off on, aansmeren
palpable, in het oog springend
palpitate, snel kloppen; trillen
paltry, nietig
pamper, ver'wennen
pamphlet, pam'flet n
pan, pan
panacea, pana'cee
pancake, pannekoek
pandemonium, pande'monium n
pane, ruit
panegyric, lofrede
panel, pa'neel n, vak n
pang, steek; plotseling ge'voel, n
panic, pa'niek: het hoofd ver'liez-en
panic-stricken, ver'lamd van schrik
panorama, pano'rama n
pansy, vi'ooltje n
pant, hijgen; snakken (naar)
pantomime, sprookjesvoorstel-ling; panto'mime
pantry, pro'visiekast
pants: (pair of) —, onder-broek
papal, pauselijk
paper, pa'pier(en) (n); krant; ver'handeling; (e'xamen)op-gave: be'hangen
par, pari
 on a par, ge'lijk
parable, ge'lijkenis
parachute, para'chute
parade, pa'rade; ap'pel n; ver'toon n; para'deren; aan-treden; pronken met
paradise, para'dijs n
paradox, para'dox
paraffin, pe'troleum
paragon, toonbeeld n
paragraph, a'linea
parallel, paral'lel, even'wijdig: eve'naren
paralyse, ver'lammen
paralysis, ver'lamming
paramount, hoogst
parapet, borstwering, leuning
paraphernalia, spullen

parasite, para'siet
parasol, para'sol
parcel, pakje n, pak'ket n
parch, ver'dorren, uitdrogen
parchment, perka'ment n
pardon, ver'giffenis; gratie (ver'lenen): ver'geven: par'don!
pare, schillen; (af)snijden; be'-knotten
parent, ouder
parentage, afkomst
parental, ouder(lijk)
parenthood, ouderschap n
parish, pa'rochie
park, park('eren) (n)
parley, onder'handeling: on-der'handelen
parliament, parle'ment n
parliamentary, parlemen'tair
parlour, sa'lon
parochial, parochi'aal; klein'-burgerlijk
parody, paro'die
parole, erewoord n
paroxysm, hevige aanval
parrot, pape'gaai
parry, afweren
parsimonious, karig
parsley, peter'selie
parsnip, pasti'naak
parson, dominee
part, deel n, ge'deelte n; rol; stem; steek: scheiden
partake, ge'bruiken
partial, ge'deeltelijk; par'tijdig; ge'steld(op)
partially, ten dele
participant, deelnemer
participate, deelnemen (aan)
particle, deeltje n
particular, bij'zonder(heid); kies'keurig, pre'cies
 that particular one, die ene daar; die be'paalde
 in particular, in het bij'zonder
particularly, (in het) bij'zonder, voor'al
parting, afscheid n; scheiding
partisan, aanhanger: par'tijdig
partition, ver'deling; tussen-schot n; vak n: ver'delen
partly, ge'deeltelijk, deels
partner, partner, compa'gnon

partnership, ven'nootschap
partridge, pa'trijs
part-time job, niet-vol'ledige be'trekking
party, ge'zelschap *n*, krans; par'tij (tje *n*)
pass, pas; stand van zaken: pas'seren, voor'bijgaan; aangeven; slagen; vellen (*judgement*); doorbrengen; goedkeuren; ge'beuren; ermee doorkunnen
passable, redelijk; be'gaanbaar
passage, (door)gang; pas'sage; voor'bijgaan *n*
passenger, passa'gier
passer-by, voor'bijganger
passing, voor'bijgaand; over'-lijden *n*
 in passing, ter'loops
passion, hartstocht (elijke liefde); Lijden (sverhaal) *n*
passionate, harts'tochtelijk
passive, pas'sief
passport, paspoort *n*
password, wachtwoord *n*
past, voor'bij; ver'leden (*n*); vorig; over
paste, kleefpasta (*or* pap); pas'tei: plakken
pastel, pas'tel (tekening)
pastime, tijdverdrijf *n*
pastor, (zielen)herder
pastoral, herderlijk, herders-, landelijk; ziel-
pastry, korstdeeg *n*; ge'bakje *n*
pasture, weide; gras *n*
pat, tikje *n*; kluitje *n*: zachtjes kloppen
patch, lap(je *n*); plek(je *n*): oplappen
pate, bol
patent, pa'tent (*n*); duidelijk
paternal, vader(lijk)
path, pad *n*; baan
pathetic, aan'doenlijk; zielig
pathology, patholo'gie
pathos, pathos
pathway, pad *n*
patience, ge'duld *n*; pa'tience *n*
patient, ge'duldig: pa'tient
patriarch, patri'arch
patriot, patri'ot

patriotic, vaderlands'lievend
patrol, pa'trouille: patroui'lleren
patron, vaste klant; be'schermheer (*or* vrouw); be'scherm-
patronage, klan'dizie; be'gunstiging
patronize, be'gunstigen, vaste klant zijn van
patronizing, neer'buigend
patter, ge'kletter *n*, ge'trippel *n*; ge'babbel *n*: kletteren, trippelen
pattern, pa'troon *n*; voorbeeld *n*
patty, pas'teitje *n*
paunch, buik,
pauper, arme
pause, rust, onder'breking: pau'seren, (even) wachten
pave, pla'veien; banen
pavement, trot'toir *n*
pavilion, pavil'joen *n*
paw, poot: krabben; aanraken
pawn, pi'on; werktuig *n*: pand *n*: ver'panden
pay, loon; *n*, sol'dij: (uit-) be'talen; schenken (*attention*); maken (*compliments*); afleggen (*visit*); lonen
 it does not pay, het loont de moeite niet; het heeft geen zin
payment, be'taling; loon *n*
pea, erwt
peace, vrede; rust
peaceable, vrede'lievend, vreedzaam
peaceful, rustig; vreedzaam
peach, perzik
peacock, pauw
peak, piek; klep; hoogtepunt *n*
peal, ge'rommel *n*; ge'lui *n*; ge'schater *n*: luiden
peanut (butter), pinda(kaas)
pear, peer
pearl, parel
peasant, boer
peat, turf
pebble, kiezelsteen
peck, kwart schepel: pikken
peculiar(ity), eigen'aardig (heid)
pecuniary, geldelijk, geld-
pedagogue, peda'goog
pedal, pe'daal *n*: peddelen
pedant(ic), pe'dant

peddle, venten
pedestal, voetstuk *n*
pedestrian, voetganger: alle'-
daags
pedigree, stamboom, ras-
pedlar, marskramer
peek, kijkje *n*: gluren
peel, schil(len)
peep, gluren
peer, edelman; weerga: turen
peerage, adelstand
peerless, weergaloos
peeved, gepi'keerd
peevish, korzelig
peg, pen, haak, knijper, haring
to peg away, ploeteren
pelican, peli'kaan
pellet, propje *n*, klontje *n*, korrel,
balletje *n*
pelt, vel *n*: be'kogelen; kletteren
pen, pen: kooi
penal, straf-, strafbaar
penalize, straffen
penance, boete(doening)
pencil, potlood *n*
pendant, hanger; luchter
pending, hangend; in afwachting
van
pendulum, slinger
penetrate, doordringen, door'-
boren
penetrating, scherp('zinnig)
penguin, pinguïn
peninsula, schiereiland *n*
penitence, be'rouw *n*
penitent, be'rouwvol; boeteling
penknife, zakmes *n*
penniless, straat'arm
penny, 4 cent; stuiver
pension, pen'sioen *n*, uitkering
pensioner, gepensio'neerde
pensive, peinzend
penthouse, afdak *n*
pent-up, opgekropt; opgesloten
penury, armoede
people, mensen; volk *n*; fa'milie
pepper, peper
peppermint, peper'munt
per, per
perambulator, kinderwagen
perceive, waarnemen, be'merken

percent, pro'cent *n*
percentage, percen'tage *n*
perceptible, waar'neembaar,
merkbaar
perception, waarneming(svermogen *n*)
perch, stok(je *n*), zitplaats:
baars: gaan zitten
percolate, fil'treren; doorsijpelen
percussion, slag(-)
peremptory, ge'biedend, be'slissend
perennial, overblijvend; altijd
durend
perfect, vol'maakt, vol'slagen:
perfectio'neren
perfection, vol'maaktheid, per'-
fectie
perfectly, vol'maakt, vol'komen
perfidious, trouweloos
perforate, perfo'reren
perform, doen; opvoeren, ten
beste geven, uitvoeren
performance, opvoering, uitvoering; optreden *n*; pres'tatie
perfume, par'fum; geur
perfunctory, noncha'lant, vluchtig
perhaps, mis'schien
peril(ous), ge'vaar('lijk) (*n*)
perimeter, omtrek
period, peri'ode, uur *n*
periodical, perio'diek: tijdschrift *n*
periodically, van tijd tot tijd
periphery, omtrek
periphrasis, om'schrijving
periscope, peri'scoop
perish, omkomen, ver'gaan
perishable, aan be'derf onder'hevig; ver'gankelijk
perjure oneself, een meineed
doen
perjury, meineed
perk up, opkikkeren
perky, par'mantig
permanent, vast, perma'nent
permeate, (door')dringen,
(door')trekken
permissible, ge'oorloofd
permission, ver'lof *n*
permit, ver'gunning: toestaan

pernicious, ver'derfelijk; kwaa'daardig

perpendicular, loodrecht: loodlijn

perpetrate, be'gaan

perpetual, aan'houdend, eeuwig('durend)

perpetually, con'stant

perpetuate, ver'eeuwigen

perplex, ver'bijsteren

perplexity, ver'bijstering

persecute, ver'volgen

perseverance, vol'harding

persevere, vol'harden

Persian, Per'zisch (n); Pers

persist, hard'nekkig doorgaan, volhouden

persistent, hard'nekkig

person, per'soon, mens

personal, per'soonlijk

personality, per'soonlijkheid

personally, per'soonlijk; wat mij be'treft

personification, verper'soonlijking

personnel, perso'neel n

perspective, perspec'tief n

perspiration, transpi'ratie

perspire, transpi'reren

persuade, over'reden, over'tuigen

persuasion, over'reding(skracht)

persuasive, over'redend

pert, vrij'postig

pertain, be'horen (tot), be'trekking hebben (op)

pertinent, ter zake dienend

perturb, veront'rusten

perusal, studie

peruse, bestu'deren

pervade, ver'vullen, trekken door

perverse, weer'barstig, dwars; ver'draaid; ver'dorven

pervert, be'derven; ver'draaien

pessimism, pessi'misme n

pessimist(ic), pessi'mist(isch)

pest, plaag

pester, plagen; lastig vallen

pestilence, dodelijke epide'mie

pet, lieveling(sdier n); lievelings-: ver'troetelen

petal, bloemblad n

petite, klein en tenger

petition, ver'zoek(schrift) n, smeekbede

petrify, ver'lammen

petrol, ben'zine

petticoat, onderjurk

petty, klein, nietig

petulant, kribbig

pew, kerkbank

pewter, tin(nen) (n)

phantom, schim

phase, fase; stadium n; schijngestalte

pheasant, fa'zant

phenomenal, fenome'naal

phenomenon, ver'schijnsel n; wonder n

philanthropist, filan'troop

philosopher, filo'soof

philosophic(al), filo'sofisch

philosophy, filoso'fie

phlegm, slijm n

phlegmatic, flegma'tiek

phosphorescent, fosfores'cerend

photograph, foto(gra'feren)

photographer, foto'graaf

photography, fotogra'fie

phrase, frase; uitdrukking: uitdrukken

physical, li'chamelijk, lichaams-; na'tuur('kundig)

physician, dokter, inter'nist

physicist, natuur'kundige

physics, na'tuurkunde

physiology, fysiolo'gie

physique, lichaamsbouw

pianist, pia'nist

piano, pi'ano

pick, keus; beste n; hou'weel n: plukken; peuteren; uitzoeken

to pick up, oprapen; op de kop tikken; oppikken; ophalen

pickaxe, hou'weel n

picket, paal; pi'ket, post

pickle, tafelzuur n; lastpost; pekelen; inmaken

pickpocket, zakkenroller

picnic, picknick(en)

pictorial, in beeld: geïllus'treerd tijdschrift n

picture, schilde'rij n; plaat; (toon)beeld n: zich voorstellen

picturesque, schilderachtig
pie, pas'tei, taart
piebald, bont (paard *n*)
piece, stuk(je) *n*
piecemeal, bij stukken en brok-
ken
pier, pier
pierce, door'boren; door'zien
piercing, door'dringend
piety, vroomheid
pig, varken *n*
pigeon, duif
pigeon-hole, vak(je) *n*
pig-headed, eigen'wijs
pigment, pig'ment *n*
pigsty, varkenskot *n*
pigtail, vlecht
pike, piek; snoek
pile, stapel; hoop: aambei:
nop: heipaal: (op)stapelen,
ophopen
pilfer, ont'futselen
pilgrim(age), pelgrim(stocht)
pill, pil
pillage, plunderen
pillar, (steun)pi'laar, zuil
pillory, schandpaal: aan de kaak
stellen
pillow, (hoofd)kussen *n*
pillow-case, kussensloop
pilot, loods(en); pi'loot.
be'sturen
pimple, puistje *n*
pin, speld(en); pen; vastgekneld
houden
pinafore, schortje *n*
pincers, nijptang; schaar
pinch, kneep; snuifje *n*; nood:
knijpen, klemmen; gappen
pine, pijnboom; pijnhout *n*:
smachten (naar), kwijnen
pine-apple, ana'nas
pinion, klein tandrad *n*: binden
pink, roze (*n*); kleine anjer
pinnace, pi'nas
pinnacle, (berg)spits, torentje
n; toppunt *n*
pint, (*approx*) halve liter
pioneer, pio'nier(en)
pious, vroom
pip, pit
pipe, pijp, buis; fluit(en)
piper, doedelzakspeler

piping, ge'fluit *n*: buizen(net *n*):
kokend
piquant, pi'kant
pique, pi'keren; prikkelen
pirate, zeerover(sschip *n*)
pistil, stamper
pistol, pis'tool *n*
piston, zuiger
pit, kuil; mijn, groeve; par'terre
pitted, vol kuiltjes; pok'dalig
pitch, pek *n*: toonhoogte; graad:
pik-: gooien; opslaan; stampen; storten
pitcher, kan
pitchfork, hooivork
piteous, beklagens'waardig
pitfall, val(strik)
pith, pit *n*
pitiable, pitiful, beklagens'waardig; jammerlijk
pitiless, mee'dogenloos
pittance, schijntje *n*
pity, medelijden (hebben met)
(*n*)
what a pity, wat jammer
pivot, spil: draaien
placard, plak'kaat *n*: re'clame
maken voor, be'plakken
place, plaats(en); thuisbrengen
to take place, plaatsvinden
placid, kalm
plague, pest; plaag: plagen;
lastig vallen
plaid, ge'ruite stof
plain, duidelijk; een'voudig;
effen: onaan'trekkelijk: vlakte
plaintiff, aanklager
plaintive, klaaglijk
plait, vlecht(en)
plan, plan *n*, platte'grond:
ont'werpen, uitwerken, op touw
zetten; van plan zijn
plane, vlak *n*; peil *n*; vliegtuig
n: schaaf: pla'taan: schaven
planet, pla'neet
plank, plank
plant, plant(en); instal'latie
plantation, plan'tage
planter, planter
plaque, pla'quette
plasma, plasma *n*
plaster, pleister(en) (*n*); be'-
smeren

plastic, plastic *n* : plastisch

plate, bord *n* ; plaat ; goud en zilver *n*, pleet *n*

plateau, hoogvlakte

platform, per'ron *n*, podium *n*

platinum, platina *n*

platitude, ge'meenplaats

platoon, pelo'ton *n*

platter, schotel

plausible, geloof'waardig

play, spel(en) (*n*) ; to'neelstuk *n* ; speling

player, (to'neel)speler

playful, speels, schertsend

playground, speelplaats

playmate, speelmakker

play-pen, box

plaything, stuk speelgoed *n* ; speelbal

playwright, to'neelschrijver

plea, (dringend) ver'zoek *n* ; veront'schuldiging ; pleit *n*

plead, aanvoeren ; smeken ; (be')pleiten

pleasant, prettig, aardig

pleasantry, geestigheid

please, een ple'zier doen (*n*), be'hagen ; ver'kiezen : alstublieft

be pleased to . . ., met ge'noegen . . .

pleasing, aangenaam ; in'nemend

pleasure, ge'noegen *n*, ple'zier *n*

pleat, plooi(en)

plebeian, ple'bejer ; ple'bejisch

plebiscite, plebis'ciet *n*

pledge, ge'lofte ; pand *n*, teken *n* : be'loven, ver'binden

plenipotentiary, gevol'machtigd(e)

plenteous, plentiful, over'vloedig

plenty (of), ruim vol'doende, veel

pliable, pliant, buigzaam ; plooibaar

pliers, buigtang

plight, toestand

plod, zwoegen

plop, plons : plonzen

plot, kom'plot *n*, in'trige ; stukje grond *n* : be'ramen, samenspannen ; in kaart brengen

plough, ploeg(en)

pluck, moed : plukken ; tokkelen

plucky, flink

plug, stop(contact *n*), prop : (dicht)stoppen

plum, pruim

plumage, ge'vederte *n*

plumb, loodrecht ; pre'cies : peilen

plumber, loodgieter

plumbing, loodgieterswerk *n*

plume, pluim

plump, mollig : (neer)ploffen

plunder, buit : plunderen

plunge, sprong : indompelen ; (zich) storten

plural, meervoud *n*

plus, plus

plush, pluche

plutocrat, pluto'craat

ply, han'teren ; uitoefenen ; over'laden (met) ; ge'regeld rijden, be'varen

pneumatic, lucht-, pneu'matisch

pneumonia, longontsteking

poach, stropen : po'cheren

pocket, zak(-) : in de zak steken ; (in)slikken

pock-marked, pok'dalig

pod, peul

poem, ge'dicht *n*

poet(ic), dichter(lijk)

poetry, poëzie, dichtwerk *n*, ge'dichten

poignant, schrijnend ; scherp ; aan'grijpend

point, punt (*n*) ; zin : wissel : wijzen, richten

point of view, ge'zichtspunt *n*

to point out, aanwijzen ; er op wijzen

point-blank, à bout por'tant, bot'weg, op de man af

pointed, puntig ; scherp ; ad rem

pointer, wijzer ; aanwijzing

pointless, zinloos

poise, houding

poised, in evenwicht

poison, ver'gift(igen) (*n*)

poisonous, ver'giftig

poke, (op)por(ren) ; steken

poker, pook : poker

poky, benepen en slonzig

polar, pool-

pole, paal, stok ; pool

police, po'litie
policeman, (po'litie)a'gent
policy, poli'tiek; polis
polish, was, smeerpoets; glans:
Pools (n): wrijven, poetsen;
be'schaven, opknappen
polite, be'leefd
political, poli'tiek; staats-
politician, po'liticus
politics, poli'tiek, staatkunde
polka, polka
poll, stemming; aantal stemmen
(n): stemmen (ver'krijgen)
pollen, stuifmeel n
pollinate, be'stuiven
pollute, be'zoedelen, veront'reinigen
polo, polo n
polygamy, polyga'mie
pomp, praal
pompous, praalziek, hoog'dravend
pond, vijver
ponder, (be')peinzen
ponderous, zwaar'wichtig;
zwaar op de hand
pontifical, pauselijk; pontifi'-
caal
pontoon, pon'ton: vingt-et-'un
pony, puny
poodle, poedel
pool, plas; pot: bij el'kaar doen
poop, achterdek n, achtersteven
poor, arm('zalig); slecht
poorly, arm('zalig); niet lekker,
minnetjes
pop, knallen; wippen; puilen
pope, paus
poplar, popu'lier
poppy, klaproos
poppycock, larie
populace, ge'peupel n
popular, popu'lair; volks-
populate, be'volken
population, be'volking
populous, dichtbevolkt
porcelain, porse'lein(en) (n)
porch, por'tiek
porcupine, stekelvarken n
pore, porie: zich ver'diepen
(in)
pork, varkensvlees n
porous, po'reus

porridge, havermoutpap
port, haven: bakboord n: port
portable, koffer-, draagbaar
portend, voor'spellen
portent, voorteken n
porter, kruier; por'tier
portfolio, porte'feuille
porthole, pa'trijspoort
portico, zuilenportiek (or gale'rij)
portion, deel n, portie
portly, welgedaan
portmanteau, va'lies n
portrait, por'tret n
portray, (af)schilderen
pose, houding; aanstelle'rij:
po'seren; zich voordoen als;
stellen
position, po'sitie; houding; stelling
positive, posi'tief; stellig
positively, abso'luut
possess, be'zitten
possession(s), be'zit(tingen) (n)
possessive, hebberig; be'zittelijk
possibility, mogelijkheid
possible, mogelijk
possibly, mis'schien
not possibly, on'mogelijk
post, stijl, paal: post; be'trekking. op do post doen; (over)-
plaatsen; aanplakken
postage, port; post-
postal, post-
postcard, briefkaart
poster, aanplakbiljet n
posterior, achter-; later
posterity, nageslacht n
posthumous, pos'tuum
postman, postbode
post-mortem, lijkschouwing
postpone, uitstellen
postscript, post'scriptum n
postulate, postu'leren
posture, houding
post-war, na-oorlogs
posy, tuiltje n
pot, pot(ten); fuik; bom (duit-
en): inmaken
potash, potas
potato, aardappel
potent, krachtig
potentate, poten'taat

potential, potenti'eel (*n*); potenti'aal
potion, drank
potter, pottenbakker: prutsen
pottery, aardewerk *n*; pottenbakkerij
pouch, zak, buidel
poultice, kom'pres *n*, pap
poultry, pluimvee *n*
pounce, zich storten
pound, (*approx*) half kilogram, pond *n*: schutstal: beuken (op); bonzen (op); fijnstampen
pour, gieten, schenken; stromen
pout, pruilen
poverty, armoede
poverty-stricken, arm('oedig)
powder, poeier(en), (be')poeder-(en); buskruit *n*
power, macht, kracht; mogendheid
powerful, machtig, krachtig
powerless, machteloos
power-station, elektrici'teits-centrale
practicable, uit'voerbaar
practical, praktisch
practically, nage'noeg
practice, oefening; prak'tijk; ge'woonte
practise, (be')oefenen; (prak'-tijk) uitoefenen
prairie, prairie
praise, lof: prijzen, loven
praiseworthy, loffelijk, lof'waardig
prance, dansen, steigeren; trots stappen
prank, (dolle) streek
prate, wauwelen
prattle, babbelen
prawn, steurgarnaal
pray, ge'lieve: bidden
prayer, ge'bed *n*
preach, preken, prediken
preacher, prediker
preamble, inleiding
precarious, hachelijk
precaution, voorzorg (smaatregel)
precede, voor('af)gaan
precedence, voorrang
precedent, prece'dent *n*
precept, grondregel, voorschrift *n*

precinct, ter'rein *n*
precious, kostbaar, dierbaar; edel; ge'wild
precipice, hoge rotswand
precipitate, plotseling; over-ijld, onbe'zonnen: neerslag: ver'haasten
precipitous, zeer steil
precise, juist, pre'cies
precision, nauw'keurigheid
preclude, uitsluiten
precocious, voorlijk
preconceived, voor'opgezet
precursor, voorloper
predatory, roof-
predecessor, voorganger
predicament, hachelijke po'sitie
predict, voor'spellen
predominant, over'heersend, over'wegend
predominate, over'heersen
pre-eminence, superiori'teit
pre-eminent, uit'blinkend
pre-eminently, bij uitstek
preen, gladstrijken
preface, voorbericht *n*: inleiden
prefer, de voorkeur geven aan, liever willen
preferable, wenselijker, beter
preferably, bij voorkeur
preference, voorkeur
pregnancy, zwangerschap
pregnant, zwanger; ge'laden
prehistoric, voorhistorisch
prejudice, voor'oordeel *n*: be-voor'oordelen
prejudicial, schadelijk
prelate, pre'laat
preliminary, voor'afgaand (e for-mali'teit)
prelude, voorspel *n*; pre'lude
premature, vroeg'tijdig, voor'-barig
premeditated, voor'opgezet
premier, eerste (mi'nister)
premise, pre'misse: voor'op-stellen
premises, pand *n*, per'ceel *n*
premium, premie
premonition, voorgevoel *n*
preoccupation, af'wezige ge'-dachten
preoccupy, in be'slag nemen

preparation, (voor)bereiding
preparatory, voorbereidend
prepare, (zich) voorbereiden, be'reiden
preponderance, overwicht n
preposterous, ab'surd
prerogative, (voor)recht n
presage, voor'spellen
Presbyterian, Presbyteri'aan(s)
prescribe, voorschrijven
prescription, re'cept n; voorschrift n
presence, aan'wezigheid
present, aan'wezig, tegen'woordig: heden n: ca'deau n: schenken; presen'teren; ver'tonen; opvoeren; voorstellen
at present, op het ogenblik
presentable, presen'tabel
presentation, schenking; uitreiking; opvoering
present-day, heden'daags
presentiment, voorgevoel n
presently, straks
preservation, be'houd n; con'ditie
preserve, wildpark n; ge'bied n: redden; be'waren, goedhouden, conser'veren
preserves, con'serven
preside, presi'deren, de leiding hebben
presidency, presi'dentschap n
president, presi'dent; voorzitter
press, pers(en); drukken; (aan)dringen; pressen
pressing, dringend
pressure, druk(ken n); drang; pressie
prestige, pres'tige n
presumably, ver'moedelijk
presume, veronder'stellen; zo vrij zijn; ge'bruik maken (van)
presumption, veronder'stelling; aanmatiging
presumptuous, aan'matigend
pretence, voorwendsel n; aanstelle'rij
pretend, doen alsof; aanspraak maken (op)
pretension, pre'tentie
pretentious, pretenti'eus

pretext, voorwendsel n
pretty, lief, knap: nogal
prevail, heersen; zegevieren
to prevail upon, overhalen
prevalent, heersend; veel'voorkomend
prevent, voor'komen, ver'hinderen
prevention, voor'komen n
preventive, prevent'ief
previous, voor'afgaand, vorig
previously, vroeger; van te voren, al eerder
pre-war, voor'oorlogs
prey, prooi
price, prijs: prijzen
priceless, on'schatbaar; kostelijk
prick, prik(ken)
prickle, stekel(tje) n; prikkel
prickly, stekelig; kriebelig
pride, trots, hoogmoed
to pride oneself, prat gaan
priest, priester
prig, pe'dante kwezel
prim, stijf, preuts
primarily, in de eerste plaats
primary, pri'mair
prime, eerst: bloei(tijd): voorbereiden
primeval, oor'spronkelijk, oer-
primitive, primi'tief
primrose, sleutelbloem
prince, prins, vorst
princely, vorstelijk
princess, prin'ses
principal, voor'naamst; hoofd(-) (n)
principally, voor'namelijk
principle, prin'cipe n
print, druk(ken); prent; afdruk; afdrukken; be'drukken; prenten
printer, drukker
prior, voor'afgaand, eerste: prior
priority, voorrang
priory, prio'rij
prism, prisma n
prison, ge'vangenis
prisoner, ge'vangene
privacy, vrijheid; ge'heimhouding
private, vrij, pri'vé, per'soonlijk; particu'lier; ge'heim: sol'daat

privateer, kaper(schip *n*)

privation, ont'bering

privilege, voorrecht *n* : be'voorrechten

prize, prijs : be'kroond

probability, waar'schijnlijkheid

probable, waar'schijnlijk, ver'moedelijk

probation, proef(tijd)

probe, peilen; doordringen; son'deren

problem, pro'bleem *n*, vraagstuk *n*

problematic(al), twijfelachtig

procedure, handelwijze

proceed, voortgaan; voortkomen **he proceeded to tell me,** hij ver'telde me ver'volgens

proceedings, handelingen; ma'nier van doen

proceeds, opbrengst

process, pro'ces *n*, procédé *n* : be'handelen

procession, stoet, optocht, pro'cessie

proclaim, af(*or* ver')kondigen; uitroepen tot

proclamation, procla'matie

procrastinate, talmen

procure, (zich) ver'(*or* aan)schaffen

prod, (aan)porren

prodigal, ver'kwistend

prodigious, ge'weldig

prodigy, wonder *n*

produce, pro'dukten: produ'ceren, opleveren, voortbrengen; te voorschijn halen; aanvoeren; opvoeren; ver'lengen

producer, regis'seur; produ'cent

product, pro'dukt *n*, voortbrengsel *n*

production, pro'duktie

productive, produk'tief

profane, pro'faan : ont'heiligen

profess, be'weren, be'tuigen, be'lijden

profession, be'roep *n*; be'tuiging, be'lijdenis

professional, be'roeps(speler); vak'kundig

professor, pro'fessor

proffer, aanbieden

proficiency, be'kwaamheid

profile, pro'fiel *n*

profit, winst : zijn voordeel doen (met)

profitable, winst'gevend, voor'delig, nuttig

profiteer, o'weeër: woekerwinst maken

profound, diep('zinnig *or* gaand)

profuse, over'vloedig, over'dadig

profusion, overvloed

progeny, kroost *n*

programme, pro'gramme *n*

progress, voor'uitgang, voortgang; loop; vorderingen: vorderen, voor'uitgaan, vorderingen maken

progressive, progres'sief (per'soon)

prohibit, ver'bieden

prohibition, ver'bod *n*

prohibitive, schrik'wekkend hoog

project, plan *n*, onder'neming: uitspringen; slingeren; projec'teren; ont'werpen

projectile, projec'tiel *n*

projection, uitsteeksel *n*; pro'jectie

projector, pro'jectietoestel *n*

proletariat, proletari'aat *n*

prolific, zeer vruchtbaar

prologue, pro'loog; inleiding

prolong, ver'lengen, rekken

prolongued, lang'durig

promenade, prome'nade

prominence, be'lang *n*; ver'hoging, uitsteeksel *n*

prominent, voor'aanstaand; in het oog vallend; hooggelegen

promise, be'lofte: be'loven

promising, veelbe'lovend

promontory, voorgebergte *n*

promote, be'vorderen

promoter, oprichter

promotion, pro'motie; be'vordering

prompt, on'middellijk, stipt: nopen (tot); souf'fleren, voorzeggen

promulgate, afkondigen; ver'breiden

prone, ge'neigd: languit voor'over

prong, tand
pronoun, voornaamwoord n
pronounce, uitspreken; uit-spraak. doen
pronunciation, uitspraak
proof, be'wijs n; proef: be'-stand
prop, stut(ten); steunpilaar: zetten, (onder')steunen
propaganda, propa'ganda
propagate, zich voortplanten; ver'spreiden, propa'geren
propel, voortdrijven
propeller, schroef
propensity, ge'neigdheid
proper, juist; ge'past
properly, op de juiste ma'nier, netjes, goed; eigenlijk
property, eigendom n, bezit n; eigenschap
prophecy, voor'spelling
prophesy, voor'spellen
prophet, pro'feet
propitious, gunstig
proportion, (juiste) ver'houding; deel n: proportion'neren
proportions, pro'porties
proportional, even'redig
proposal, voorstel n; aanzoek n
propose, voorstellen; zich voor-nemen; een aanzoek doen
proposition, voorstel n; stelling; ge'val n
propound, opperen
proprietary, pa'tent-, merk-, eigendoms-; eigenaars-
proprietor, eigenaar
propriety, goede vorm
propulsion, stuwkracht
pros and cons, voor en tegen n
prosaic, pro'zaïsch
proscribe, ver'bieden; ver'ban-nen
prose, proza n
prosecute, ver'volgen; uitvoeren
prosecutor, aanklager
prospect, (voor')uitzicht n: zoek-en
prospective, eventu'eel; aan'-staande
prospector, pros'pector

prosper, ge'dijen
prosperity, voorspoed, welvaart
prosperous, voor'spoedig
prostitute, prostitu'ée
prostrate, voor'overliggend; ver'slagen: neerwerpen
protect, be'schermen
protection, be'scherming
protective, be'schermend
protectorate, protecto'raat n
protein, eiwit(stof) (n)
protest, pro'test('eren) (n)
Protestant, Protes'tant(s)
protestation, aan'houdende be'tuiging
prototype, prototype n
protract, ver'lengen, rekken
protracted, langge'rekt
protrude, (voor')uitsteken; zich opdringen
proud, trots (op); groot
prove, be'wijzen; blijken
proverb, spreekwoord n
proverbial, spreek'woordelijk
provide, voor'zien; zorgen
provided (that), mits
providence, (de) voor'zienigheid
provident, zorgzaam
province, pro'vincie; ge'bied n
provincial, provinci'aal; pro'vin-cie-
provision, voor'ziening; voor-waarde; voorzorg(smaatregel): provian'deren
provisions, levensmiddelen
provisional, voor'lopig
proviso, voorbehoud n
provocation, aanleiding
provocative, provo'cerend
provoke, (op)wekken, uitlokken; tergen
prow, voorsteven
prowess, dapperheid; vaardig-heid
prowl, rondsluipen
proximity, na'bijheid
proxy, volmacht; gevol'mach-tigde
prudence, voor'zichtigheid, be'-leid n
prudent, be'dachtzaam, ver'stan-dig
prudish, preuts

prune, pruime'dant: (be')snoeien
pry, snuffelen: (open)breken
psalm, psalm
pseudo(nym), pseudo('niem *n*)
psychiatrist, psychi'ater
psychic, spiri'tistisch
psychological, psycho'logisch
psychology, psycholo'gie
pub, kroeg
puberty, puber'teit
public, open'baar, pu'bliek (*n*): volk *n*
 in public, in het open'baar
publication, publi'katie
publicity, publici'teit
publish, uitgeven; be'kend maken
publisher, uitgever
pucker, rimpelen, zich samentrekken
pudding, pudding, toetje *n*
puddle, plas
puerile, kinderachtig
puff, wolkje *n*, stoot; soes: puffen; opblazen
pugilist, bokser
pugnacious, strijd'lustig
pull, ruk(ken); trek(ken) (aan)
 to pull up, uit(*or* op)trekken; stilhouden
pullet, jonge kip
pulley, ka'trol
pullover, slipover
pulp, vruchtvlees *n*; pap
pulpit, preekstoel
pulsate, kloppen; trillen
pulse, pols(slag)
pulverize, ver'brijzelen
pumice-stone, puimsteen
pump, pomp(en); uithoren
pun, woordspeling
punch, stomp(en); pons(en), drevel; punch: knippen
Punch-and-Judy, Jan Klaassen en Ka'trijn
punctilious, nauwge'zet
punctual, punctu'eel, stipt
punctuate, interpun'geren; onder'breken
puncture, lekke band, gaatje *n*: (door)prikken
pungent, scherp, prikkelend
punish, straffen

punishment, straf
punt, punter(en)
puny, nietig
pup, jong(e hond) (*n*)
pupil, leerling: pu'pil
puppet, mario'net; speelpop
purchase, (aan)koop; houvast *n*: (aan)kopen
pure, zuiver, rein; louter
purgatory, vagevuur *n*
purge, zuiveren
purify, zuiveren
Puritan, Puri'tein(s)
purity, zuiverheid, reinheid
purple, paars, purper (*n*)
purport, strekking: heten
purpose, doel *n*, be'doeling
purposely, on purpose, op'zettelijk
purr, spinnen; snorren
purse, beurs: samentrekken
pursue, (achter')volgen
pursuit, achter'volging: jacht; bezigheid
purveyor, leveran'cier
pus, pus
push, duw(en), zetje *n*: dringen
puss(y), poes(je *n*)
put, zetten, leggen; brengen; zeggen; doen
 to put down, neerzetten; onder'drukken; opschrijven; toeschrijven (aan)
 to put off, uitstellen; van zijn stuk brengen, afschrikken; uitdoen
 to put on, aantrekken
 to put out, uitsteken; uitdoen; blussen; lastig vallen
 to put up, ophangen; opsteken; (aan)bieden; maken, bouwen; ver'hogen; bergen, lo'geren; aanpraten
 to put up with, dulden
putrefy, ver'rotten
putrid, rot
putty, stopverf
puzzle, (een) raadsel (zijn) (*n*): piekeren
pygmy, dwerg
pyjamas, py'jama
pyramid, pira'mide

Q

quack, kwak(en): kwakzalver
quadrangle, binnenplein
quadrilateral, vierhoek(ig)
quadruped, vier'voetig (dier *n*)
quaff, met grote teugen drinken
quail, kwartel: (te'rug) sckrik-
  ken
quaint, typisch, eigen'aardig
quake, beven
Quaker, Kwaker
qualification, kwalifi'catie; re'-
  strictie
qualified, be'voegd
qualify, ge'schikt maken; de
  be'voegdheid   ver'werven;
  kwalifi'ceren
quality, kwali'teit; eigenschap
qualm, onbe'haaglijk ge'voel *n*;
  scru'pule
quandary, lastig par'ket *n*
quantity, (grote) hoe'veelheid;
  grootheid
quarantine, quaran'taine
quarrel, (reden tot) twist, ruzie:
  twisten
quarrelsome, twistziek
quarry, wild *n*, prooi; slachtoffer
  n: steengroeve: (uit)graven
quart, (approx.) liter
quarter, kwart('aal) *n*; windstreek;   wijk;   ge'nade: in
  vieren delen; inkwartieren
  quarter of an hour, kwar'tier *n*
quarters, kwar'tier(en) *n*; kring-
  en
quarterdeck, achterdek *n*
quarterly, drie'maandelijks
quartet, kwar'tet *n*
quartz, kwartz *n*
quasi, kwasi
quaver, trilling; achtste noot:
  trillen
quay, kaai, kade
queen, koning'in; vrouw
queer, raar: be'derven
quell, onder'drukken
quench, lessen; blussen
querulous, knorrig
query, vraag(teken *n*); twijfel:
  in twijfel trekken; een vraagteken zetten achter

quest, zoeken *n*
  in quest of, op zoek naar
question,   vraag;   kwestie;
  sprake; twijfel: onder'vragen;
  be'twijfelen
questionable, twijfelachtig
queue, rij: in de rij staan
quibble, spits'vondigheid: haar-
  kloven
quick, vlug
quicken,   ver'haasten;   sneller
  worden
quicksand, drijfzand *n*
quicksilver, kwikzilver *n*
quick-tempered, op'vliegend
quiet, rust(ig), stil; vrede
quieten, sussen, be'daren
quill, schacht; ganzepen
**quilt,   gewat'teerde   deken:
  wat'teren, doorstikken
quinine, ki'nine
quintessence, kwintessens
quip, geestigheid; steek
**quit,   ver'trekken   (uit);   op-
  houden
  to be quit of, af zijn van
quite, helemaal; verreweg; vrij:
  juist, ja
quits, kiet
quiver, peilkoker: trillen
quoit, worpring
quota, (even'redig) deel *n*
quotation, aanhaling(s-), ci'taat
  n: no'tering
quote, aanhalen

R

rabbit, ko'nijn *n*
rabble, ge'spuis *n*
rabid, dol
race, wedloop, wedren: ras *n*:
  racen; om het hardst lopen;
  rennen
racial, ras(sen)-
racing, wedrennen *n*
rack, rek *n*; pijnbank: folteren;
  afpijnigen
racket, racket *n*: herrie; afzette'rij
racketeer, afzetter
radiance, straling
radiant, stralend

radiate, (uit)stralen; straals-
gewijs uitlopen
radiator, radi'ator
radical, radi'caal
radio, radio(-)
radish, ra'dijs
radium, radium *n*
radius, straal; cirkel
raffle, ver'loting: ver'loten
raft, vlot *n*
rafter, dakspar
rag, lapje *n*, vod *n*; jool: keet
maken, te grazen nemen
ragamuffin, schooier
rag-and-bone man, voddenkoopman
rage, woede; rage: tieren
ragged, haveloos
raid, in(*or* over)val (doen)
rail, stang, spaak; rail; spoor
n: uitvaren (tegen)
railing(s), hek *n*
railway, spoorweg, spoorbaan
raiment, ge'waad *n*, tooi
rain, regen(en)
rainbow, regenboog
rainfall, regenval
rainy, regenachtig
raise, oplichten; ver'heffen;
ver'hogen; bij'eenbrengen, opbrengen; fokken; ver'wekken
raisin, ro'zijn
rake, hark(en); losbol: enfi'leren
rally, bij'eenkomst: (zich) ver'-
zamelen; bijkomen
ram, ram(men)
ramble, zwerftocht: zwerven;
zich slingeren; bazelen, afdwalen
ramp, ta'lud *n*; afzette'rij
rampant: to be —, woekeren;
hoogtij vieren
rampart, wal; bolwerk *n*
ramshackle, gammel
ranch, (vee)fokke'rij
rancid, ranzig
rancour, wrok
random, luk'raak
   at random, op goed ge'luk
range, ruimte, veld *n*, kring;
draagwijdte; baan; keten;
for'nuis *n*: vari'eren; zwerven
(over); (zich) opstellen

rank, ge'lid *n*; rang, stand: geil;
grof: be'horen (tot)
rankle, iemand dwars zitten
ransack, plunderen
ransom, losgeld *n*
rant, te keer gaan
rap, tik(ken): duit: gooien
rape, ver'krachting; roof: ver'-
krachten
rapid, snel
rapids, stroomversnelling
rapidity, snelheid
rapt, opgetogen, ver'rukt
rapture, ver'voering
rapturous, opgetogen, ver'rukkelijk
rare, zeldzaam; ijl
rarely, zelden
rarity, zeldzaamheid; ijlheid
rascal, schelm
rash, onbe'zonnen: uitslag
rasp, rasp(en)
raspberry, fram'boos
rat, rat; onderkruiper: overlopen
rate, koers, cijfer *n*, snelheid,
prijs; klas; plaatselijke be'lasting; ge'val *n*: schatten: be'rispen
rather, liever, eerder: nog'al:
nou en of!
ratify, be'krachtigen
ratio, ver'houding
ration, rant'soen ('eren) (*n*)
rational, ratio'neel, redelijk
rattle, rammelaar, ratel; ge'kletter *n*; rammelen, ratelen; van
streek brengen
raucous, schor, rauw
ravage, ver'woesting: teisteren
rave, raaskallen, razen, ijlen;
dwepen
raven, raaf
ravenous, uitgehongerd
ravine, ra'vijn *n*
ravishing, be'toverend
raw, rauw; ruw; groen; guur
   raw materials, grondstoffen
ray, straal: rog
rayon, kunstzijde
raze, uitwissen; slechten
razor, scheerapparaat(*or* mes) *n*
razor-blade, scheermesje *n*

re-, op'nieuw
reach, be'reik(en) (*n*); ge'-
deelte *n*: (zich) uitstrekken;
reiken; er (bij) komen
react, rea'geren
reaction, re'actie
reactionary, reactio'nair
read, (voor)lezen; zeggen, aanwijzen; stu'deren; opvatten
readily, ge'makkelijk; gaarne
readiness ge'reedheid; bereid'willigheid
reading, lezen *n*, lezing; stand;
interpre'tatie; lec'tuur: lees-
ready, klaar; be'reid('willig);
ge'makkelijk
ready-made, con'fectie, pasklaar
real, werkelijk, echt
realism, rea'lisme *n*
realist(ic), rea'list(isch)
reality, werkelijkheid
realization, be'sef *n*; ver'wezen-
lijking
realize, be'seffen; ver'wezenlijken; opbrengen
really, (in) werkelijk(heid)
realm, (konink)rijk *n*
reap, maaien; oogsten
reappear, op'nieuw ver'schijnen
rear, achter-: achterhoede,
achterkant
reason, rede(n): (be)rede'neren
(with)in reason, redelijk-
(erwijs)
 it stands to reason, het spreekt
van'zelf
reasonable, redelijk
reasoning, rede'nering
reassurance, ver'zekering
reassure, ver'zekeren; ge'ruststellen
rebate, korting
rebel, oproerling: in opstand
komen
rebellion, opstand
rebellious, op'standig
rebound, te'rugstoot: te'rug-
stuiten
rebuff, koude douche: voor het
hoofd stoten
rebuke, be'risping: be'rispen
recalcitrant, weer'spannig

recant, her'roepen; er van te'rugkomen
recapitulate, recapitu'leren
recapture, her'overen, op'nieuw
ge'vangennemen; weer op-
roepen
recede, te'rugwijken, te'ruglopen
receipt, re'cu *n*, kwi'tantie;
ont'vangst: kwi'teren
receive, ont'vangen
receiver, hoorn, ont'vangtoestel
n
recent, re'cent
recently, on'langs, in de laatste
tijd
receptacle, (ver'gaar)bak
reception, ont'vangst; re'ceptie
receptive, ont'vankelijk (voor)
recess, re'ces *n*; nis; schuil-
hoek
recipe, re'cept *n*
recipient, ont'vanger
reciprocal, weder'kerig; omge-
keerde *n*
reciprocate, be'antwoorden;
heen en weer gaan
recital, voordracht; opsomming
recite, voordragen; opsommen
reckless, roekeloos
reckon, (be')rekenen en: be'schouw-
en
reclaim, her'winnen, droogleggen, redden
recline, achter'over liggen
recluse, kluizenaar
recognition, (h)er'kenning:
waar'dering
recognizable, her'kenbaar
recognize, (h)er'kennen
recoil, te'rugloop: te'rugdeinzen;
te'ruglopen
recollect, zich her'inneren
recollection, her'innering
recommend, aanbevelen; aanraden
recommendation, aanbeveling:
ad'vies *n*
recompense, be'loning: be'-
lonen; schadeloosstellen
reconcile, ver'zoenen; over'eenbrengen
reconciliation, ver'zoening
reconnaissance, ver'kenning(s-)

reconnoitre, ver'kennen

reconstruct, weder opbouwen; reconstru'eren

reconstruction, weder'opbouw; recon'structie

record, offici'ele ver'melding; no'titie; (grammo'foon)plaat; re'cord n; repu'tatie: ongeëve'naard: optekenen; opnemen, te boek stellen

recount, nieuwe telling: ver'halen

recourse: to have — to, zijn toevlucht nemen tot

recover, te'rugkrijgen; inhalen; her'stellen

recovery, her'stel n

recreation, ont'spanning

recrimination, tegenbeschuldiging

recruit, re'kruut, nieuweling: rekru'teren

rectangle, rechthoek

rectangular, recht'hoekig

rectify, her'stellen

rector, dominee; rector

rectory, pasto'rie

recumbent, liggend

recuperate, her'stellen

recur, te'rugkeren

recurrence, her'haling

recurrent, steeds te'rugkerend

red(den), rood (maken or worden)

reddish, roodachtig

redeem, aflossen; ver'vullen; ver'lossen; ver'zachten

red-handed, op heter daad

red-hot, rood'gloeiend

redouble, ver'dubbelen

redoubtable, ge'ducht

redress, ver'goeding: weer goedmaken

reduce, ver'minderen; brengen

reduction, afname, ver'mindering; korting

redundant, over'bodig

re-echo, weer'galmen

reed, riet n

reef, rif n: reef n: reven

reek, stinken

reel, klos(je n): duizelen, wankelen

refer, ver'wijzen; zinspelen (op); be'trekking hebben (op); raadplegen

referee, scheidsrechter

reference, ver'wijzing; be'trekking; toespeling; ge'tuigschrift n: hand-

refine, raffi'neren

refined, geraffi'neerd; be'schaafd

refinement, raffi'nering; fi'nesse

refinery, raffinade'rij

reflect, te'rugkaatsen; weer'spiegelen; weergeven; nadenken

reflection, weer'spiegeling; spiegelbeeld n;

on reflection, bij nader inzien

reflector, re'flector

reflex, re'flex(-)

reform, ver'betering: ver'beteren; (zich) beteren

reformation, her'vorming; Refor'matie

refraction, breking

refractory, weer'barstig

refrain, re'frein n: zich ont'houden (van)

refresh, ver'kwikken; opfrissen

refreshing, ver'kwikkend; op'wekkend

refreshment, ver'kwikking, restau'ratie; con'sumptie

refrigerator, ijskast

refuge, toevlucht(soord n)

refugee, vluchteling

refund, te'rugbetaling: te'rugbetalen

refusal, weigering

refuse, vuilnis n: weigeren

refute, weer'leggen

regain, her'winnen; weer be'reiken

regal, koninklijk

regale, ont'halen

regard, aandacht; achting: be'schouwen; in acht nemen; be'treffen

regards, groeten

regardless of, ongeacht

regent, re'gent('es)

regime, re'gime n

regiment, regi'ment n; dres'seren

region, streek, ge'west *n,* ge'bied *n*

regional, ge'westelijk

register, re'gister *n* : registreren ; inschrijven ; aangeven, te kennen geven ; (laten) aantekenen

registration, regis'tratie

regression, achter'uitgang

regret, spijt : be'treuren

regretfully, met leedwezen

regrettable, betreurens'waardig

regular, ge'regeld, regel'matig, vast ; echt : be'roeps(sol'daat)

regularity, regelmaat

regulate, regelen

regulation, voorschrift *n,* be'paling *n* ; regeling

rehabilitation, rehabili'tatie

rehearsal, repe'titie

rehearse, repe'teren, instuderen

reign, re'gering ; be'wind *n*

reimburse, ver'goeden

rein, teugel : inhouden ; be'teugelen

reindeer, rendier(en) *n*

reinforce, ver'sterken

reinforcement, ver'sterking

reinstate, her'stellen

reiterate, her'halen

reject, afgekeurd voorwerp *n* ; afkeuren, van de hand wijzen

rejoice, ver'heugd zijn

rejoicing, vreugde(betoon *n*)

rejoin, zich weer voegen bij

rejoinder, re'pliek

rejuvenate, ver'jongen

relapse, instorting, te'rugval : weer instorten, weer ver'vallen

relate, ver'halen ; in ver'band brengen (met)

related, ver'want

relation, be'trekking, ver'houding ; fa'milielid *n*

relationship, ver'wantschap ; ver'houding

relative, fa'milielid *n* : be'trekkelijk ; respec'tief

relax, (zich) ont'spannen ; ver'slappen

relaxation, ont'spanning ; ver'slapping

relay, ploeg ; re'lais *n* : relay'eren ; weer leggen

release, vrijlating ; be'vrijding : vrij(*or* los)laten ; bevrijden ; vrijgeven

relegate, te'rugzetten ; ver'bannen

relent, zich laten ver'murwen

relentless, mee'dogenloos

relevant, van toepassing (op), toe'passelijk

reliable, be'trouwbaar

reliance, ver'trouwen *n*

relic, reli'kwie ; overblijfsel *n*

relief, ver'lichting ; opluchting ; hulp, aflossing(sploeg) ; reli'ëf *n* : extra

relieve, ver'lichten ; ont'lasten ; ont'zetten ; aflossen ; afwisselen

religion, godsdienst

religious, godsdienst-, gods'dienstig ; klooster- ; plichtsgetrouw

relinquish, opgeven ; afstand doen van

relish, smaak ; pi'kante lekker'nij : ge'nieten van

reluctance, tegenzin

reluctant, on'willig

rely, ver'trouwen(op)

remain, (over)blijven

remains, overblijfselen

remainder, rest

remark, opmerking : opmerken

remarkable, merk'waardig ; op'merkelijk

remedy, (hulp)middel *n* : ver'helpen

remember, zich her'inneren ; ont'houden, denken om ; de groeten doen van

remembrance, nagedachtenis

remind, her'inneren (aan)

reminder, (vriendelijke) aanmaning

reminiscent: to be — of, her'inneren aan

remiss, na'latig

remission, kwijtschelding

remit, overmaken ; kwijtschelden

remnant, res'tant *n*

remonstrate, protes'teren

remorse, wroeging

remorseless, onbarm'hartig

remote, afgelegen; ver; ge'ring
remotely, in de verte, enigs'zins
removal, ver'wijderen n;
ver'huizing
remove, ver'wijderen, afnemen,
uittrekken; afzetten
remuneration, ver'goeding
remunerative, winst'gevend
Renaissance, Renais'sance
rend, (ver')scheuren
render, geven; be'tuigen;
maken; ver'tolken; klaren
renegade, af'vallig(e)
renew, ver(or her)'nieuwen;
ver'lengen
renounce, afstand doen van;
ver'stoten
renovate, ver'nieuwen, opknappen
renown, ver'maardheid
renowned, ver'maard
rent, huur, pacht: scheur: huren,
pachten
rental, huur
renunciation, afstand doen n;
ver'werping, ver'loochening
reopen, her'openen; her'vatten
reorganize, reorgani'seren
repair, repar'atie; con'ditie:
her'stellen
reparation, schadeloosstelling
repartee, puntigheid, ge'vatheid
repast, maaltijd
repatriation, repatri'ëring
repay, te'rugbetalen
repeal, afschaffing: her'roepen,
afschaffen
repeat, her'haling: her'halen;
nazeggen, navertellen; opzeggen
repeated(ly), her'haald(elijk)
repel, te'rug(or af)slaan; afstoten
repellent, af'stotend
repent, be'rouw hebben
repentance, be'rouw n
repentant, be'rouwvol
repercussion, re'actie, te'rug-
slag
repertoire, reper'toire n
repetition, her'haling
replace, ver'vangen, ver'nieuw-
en; te'rugzetten
replacement, ver'vanging;
nieuwe

replenish, aan(or bij)vullen
replica, ko'pie
reply, antwoorden
report, ver'slag (n) (doen),
rap'port n, be'richt n; knal:
rappor'teren; (zich) melden
reporter, ver'slaggever
repose, rust(en)
repository, opslagplaats; schat-
kamer
reprehensible, laakbaar
represent, voorstellen; vertegen'woordigen
representation, voorstelling;
vertegen'woordiging
representative, vertegen'woor-
diger: representa'tief; typisch
repress, onder'drukken
reprieve, uitstel n, gratie
reprimand, be'risping: be'rispen
reprint, herdruk: her'drukken
reprisal, repre'saille
reproach, ver'wijt(en) (n);
schande
reprobate, onverlaat
reproduce, reprodu'ceren; (zich)
voortplanten
reproof, be'risping
reprove, be'rispen
reptile, rep'tiel n
republic, repu'bliek
republican, republi'kein(s)
repudiate, ver'werpen; niet
er'kennen; ver'stoten
repugnant, weerzin'wekkend
repulse, afslaan; afwijzen
repulsive, weerzin'wekkend
reputable, respec'tabel
reputation, (goede) naam
repute, aanzien n: houden voor
request, ver'zoek(en) (n), aanvraag: vragen om
require, nodig hebben; ver'lang-
en
requirement, be'hoefte, ver'eiste
n; eis
requisite, ver'eist(e n); be'hoefte
requisition, vordering: vorderen
requite, ver'gelden
rescind, intrekken
rescue, redding: redden
to come to the rescue, te hulp
komen

research, weten'schappelijk onderzoek *n*
esemblance, ge'lijkenis; over'eenkomst
esemble, ge'lijken (op)
esent, aanstoot nemen aan
esentful, ge'belgd
esentment, wrevel
eservation, voorbehoud *n*; reser'vatie
eserve, re'serve; reser'vaat *n*; gereser'veerdheid : be'waren, reser'veren
eserved, gereser'veerd; te'rughoudend
eservoir, reser'voir *n*
eside, woon'achtig zijn
esidence, woonplaats, woning; ver'blijf *n*
esident, inwoner; gast; resi'dent: inwonend
esidential, woon-
esidue, overschot *n*; resi'du *n*
esign, aftreden: neerleggen
  to resign oneself to, be'rusten in
esignation, ont'slag *n*; be'rusting
esilience, veerkracht
resin, hars
resist, zich ver'zetten, weerstand bieden; zich weer'houden (van); weer'staan
resistance, ver'zet *n*; weerstand(svermogen *n*)
resolute, vastbe'raden
resolution, be'sluit *n*, voornemen *n*; voorstel *n*; vastbe'radenheid
resolve, be'sluit(en) (*n*); vastbe'radenheid: (zich) oplossen
resonance, reso'nantie
resonant, reso'nerend
resort, (va'kantie)oord *n*; redmiddel *n*; zijn toevlucht nemen (tot)
resound, weer'galmen; weer'kaatsen
resource, (red)middel *n*, rijkdom, (hulp)bron
resourceful, vindingrijk
respect, eerbied; opzicht *n*; be'trekking: respec'teren, eer'biedigen

respectable, fat'soenlijk; respec'tabel
respectful, eer'biedig
respecting, aan'gaande
respective, respec'tief
respectively, respec'tievelijk
respiration, ademhaling
respite, ver'ademing; uitstel *n*
resplendent, glansrijk, schitterend
respond, rea'geren (op); be'antwoorden
response, antwoord *m*, weerklank; tegenzang
responsibility, verant'woordelijkheid
responsible, verant'woordelijk
responsive, ont'vankelijk (voor)
rest, rust (geven); steun: rest: (uit)rusten, liggen, leunen (met); be'rusten
restaurant, restau'rant *n*
restful, rustig, kal'merend
restitution, resti'tutie, ver'goeding
restive, on'rustig
restless, onge'durig, on'rustig, rusteloos
restoration, restau'ratie; her'stel *n*, te'ruggave
restore, restau'reren; her'stellen, te'ruggeven, terug'zetten
restrain, be'dwingen, in be'dwang houden
restrain, be'dwingen, in be'dwang houden
restrict, be'perken
restriction, be'perking; voorbehoud *n*
result, resul'taat *n*, uitslag, ge'volg *n*; uitkomst: uitlopen (op); komen
resume, her'vatten
resumption, her'vatting
resurrection, opstanding
retail, klein(handel), en de'tail
retailer, detail'list, leveran'cier
retain, (vast *or* ont')houden
retaliate, re'vanche nemen
retaliation, wraak
retard, tegen(*or* op)houden
reticent, terug'houdend
retina, retina

retinue, ge'volg *n*

retire, met pen'sioen gaan, aftreden; naar bed gaan; (zich) te'rugtrekken

retired, gepensio'neerd; afgelegen

retirement, ont'slag *n*; pensio'nering; afzondering

retiring, te'ruggetrokken

retort, vinnig (*or* ge'wiekst) antwoord(en) (*n*); re'tort

retrace, te'rugkeren op

retract, her'roepen

retreat, te'rug(*or* af)tocht; a'siel *n*: zich te'rugtrekken

retribution, ver'gelding

retrieve, te'rugvinden; her'stellen

retrograde, achter'uit

retrospect: in —, achter'af be'schouwd

return, te'rugkomst, te'rugkeer; te'rugbrengen(*or* geven *or* zenden) (*n*); opbrengst; rap'port *n*: re'tour-: te'ruggaan (*or* keren *or* komen)

  by return, per omgaande

  in return, in ruil

  many happy returns, nog vele jaren!

reunion, her'eniging; reü'nie

reunite, (zich) her'enigen

reveal, ont'hullen, open'baren; aan het licht brengen; kenbaar maken

revel, zich ver'lustigen; feestvieren

revelation, open'baring

revelry, pretmake'rij

revenge, wraak(zucht)

  to revenge oneself, to be revenged, zich wreken (op)

revenue, (rijks)inkomsten

reverberate, weer'galmen

reverberation, nagalm

revere, (ver')eren

reverence, eerbied; buiging

Reverend: The —, De Weleerwaarde Heer Ds., De Weleerwaarde Pater

reverent, eer'biedig

reverie, mijmering

reverse, omgekeerd(e *n*); tegendeel *n*; keerzijde; tegenslag,

nederlaag: omkeren; her'roepen; achter'uitrijden

reversion, te'rugkeer

revert, weer te'rugkeren; ver'vallen (in)

review, re'visie; te'rugblik; re'censie: op'nieuw in ogenschouw nemen; te'rugzien op; her'zien; recen'seren

revile, (be')schimpen

revise, nazien; her'zien

revision, repe'teren *n*; her'ziening

revival, opleving; weder'opvoering

revive, weer bijbrengen; (doen) bijkomen; weer opvoeren

revoke, her'roepen; niet be'kennen

revolt, opstand: in opstand komen; doen walgen

revolting, walgelijk

revolution, revo'lutie; omwenteling

revolutionary, revolution'nair

revolutionize, een ommekeer te'weegbrengen

revolve, (om)wentelen

revolver, re'volver

revulsion, ommekeer; walging

reward, be'loning: be'lonen

rhapsody, rapso'die

rhetoric, re'torica; reto'riek

rhetorical, re'torisch

rheumatic, reu'matisch

rheumatism, reuma'tiek

rhinoceros, ri'noceros

rhubarb, ra'barber

rhyme, rijm(pje *n*): rijmen

rhythm, ritme *n*

rhythmic, ritmisch

rib, rib(stuk *n*); ba'lein; nerf

ribald, liederlijk

ribbon, lint *n*; flard

rice, rijst

rich, rijk; machtig, extra fijn; warm

riches, rijkdom(men)

richly, rijkelijk

rickety, wankel

rid, af: afhelpen

  to get rid of, kwijt raken, ver'drijven

riddle, raadsel *n*: grove zeef: door'zeven

ride, rit(je *n*), tocht(je *n*): (paard)rijden

rider, ruiter, be'rijder

ridge, kam; nok; rug

ridicule, spot: be'spotten

ridiculous, be'lachelijk

rife, wijd ver'spreid

riff-raff, uitschot *n*

rifle, ge'weer *n*: plunderen

rift, scheur, kloof

rig, tui'gage; plunje: optuigen; in el'kaar draaien

rigging, tui'gage, want *n*

right, juist; goed; in orde; vlak, helemaal; pre'cies; recht (*n*); rechterzijde: rechtzetten

to be right, ge'lijk hebben

on the right, rechts

to the right, aan de rechterkant; rechts('af)

right away, on'middellijk

righteous, recht'schapen; (ge)recht'vaardig(d)

rightful, recht'matig

right-hand, rechter-

rightly, te'recht; goed

rigid, vast, stijf; star

rigmarole, ge'klets *n*

rigorous, zeer streng

rigour, strengheid

rim, rand, velg

rime, rijp

rind, korst, zwoerd *n*, schil

ring, ring; piste; kliek; tele'foontje *n*: luiden; bellen; weer'galmen

ringleader, belhamel

rink, baan

rinse, (om)spoelen

riot, oproer *n* (maken)

riotous, op'roerig; los'bandig

rip, scheur(en)

ripe, rijp; be'legen

ripen, rijp worden (*or* maken)

ripple, golfje *n*; lichte golfslag: kabbelen

rise, stijgen (*n*); stijging; opkomst; opslag; toename: opstaan; opstijgen; om'hooglopen; stijgen; opkomen

to give rise to, ver'oorzaken

risk, ge'vaar *n*, risico *n*: wagen, ris'keren

risky, ris'kant

rissole, cro'quet

rite, plechtigheid

ritual, ritu'eel (*n*)

rival, mededinger; mededingend: concur'reren met; wedijveren met

rivalry, wedijver; concur'rentie

river, ri'vier

riverside, oever

rivet, klinknagel: klinken

rivulet, beekje *n*

road, weg, straat

roadside, (aan de) kant van de weg, berm

roadway, rijweg

roam, dwalen

roar, ge'brul *n*, ge'raas *n*: brullen, bulderen; ronken

roast, ge'braden: braden

rob, be'roven

robber(y), rover('ij)

robe, toga, mantel

robin, roodborstje *n*

robust, fors

rock, rots, klip: schommelen; wiegen; schudden

rocket, ra'ket, vuurpijl

rocky, rotsachtig: wankel

rod, roe(de); 5 meter

rodent, knaagdier *n*

rogue, schelm

roguish, schalks

rôle, rol

roll, rol(len); roffel(en); lijst; broodje *n*; slingeren (*n*)

roller, rol, wals; zware golf

rollicking, uitgelaten, dol

Roman, Ro'mein(s); Rooms-(Katho'liek)

romance, liefdesgsechiedenis; ro'mance: fanta'seren

romantic, roman'tisch: ro'manticus

romp, stoeipartij: stoeien

roof, dak *n*; ge'welf *n*; ver'hemelte *n*

rook, roek

room, kamer; ruimte; aanleiding

roomy, ruim

roost, roest: op stok gaan
root, wortel (schieten); oorzaak: wortelen; omwroeten
 to root up (*or* **out**), uitroeien
rooted, vastgegroeid; ingeworteld
rope, touw *n*, koord *n*
rosary, rozenkrans
rose, roos
rosette, ro'zet
rostrum, spreekgestoelte *n*
rosy, roze, blozend; roos'kleurig
rot, ver'rotting; be'derf *n*; larie: (doen) ver'rotten
rotate, (doen) draaien
rotation, (om)wenteling; afwisseling
 in rotation, om beurten
rotten, (ver')rot; be'roerd; ge'meen
rotund, kort en dik
rouge, rouge
rough, ruw, on'effen; ruig; vaag; hard
roughly, onge'veer; in het klad
round, rond('om); om(-): ronde; reeks: omgaan
 to round off, afronden; afmaken, vervol'maken
roundabout, om-: draaimolen; circu'latieplein *n*
rouse, wakker maken; prikkelen
rout, wilde vlucht: op de vlucht drijven; snuffelen; opdiepen
route, route
routine, rou'tine: ge'bruikelijk
rove, zwerven
row, rij: herrie: roeien
rowdy, la'waaierig
royal, koninklijk; vorstelijk
royalty, vorstelijke per'sonen; oplagecommissie
rub, wrijven; schuren
 to rub out, uitstuffen
rubber, rubber; stuf *n*: robber
rubbish, afval, vuilnis *n*; rommel; klets
rubble, puin *n*
ruby, ro'bijn(rood)
rudder, roer(blad) *n*
ruddy, blozend
rude, onbe'leefd; grof

rudiment(ary), rudi'ment('air) (*n*)
rue, be'treuren
ruff, (plooi)kraag
ruffian, woesteling
ruffle, in der war brengen, rimpelen; ver'storen
rug, reisdeken; kleedje *n*
rugged, fors en hoekig; stoer
ruin, ru'ïne; ondergang: be'derven; ruï'neren
ruinous, ver'derfelijk; ruï'neus
rule, regel; heerschap'pij; lini'aal: be'slissen; be'heren, re'geren; lini'ëren
 as a rule, in de regel
ruler, re'geerder; lini'aal
ruling, be'slissing: re'gerend; heersend
rum, rum: raar
rumble, ge'rommel *n*: rommelen
ruminate, her'kauwen; be'peinzen
rummage, snuffelen
rumour, ge'rucht *n*
rumple, kreuken
rump-steak, biefstuk
run, wedloop; reis; ritje *n*; run; peri'ode: (hard)lopen; rennen; kruipen; raken; doorlopen; laten (vol)lopen; drijven
 in the long run, op de lange duur
 to run down, stil gaan staan; opsporen; over'rijden; uitgeput raken; afkammen
 to run into, tegenkomen; oprijden(*or* lopen) tegen
 to run out, aflopen; opraken
 to run out of, door . . . heen raken
 to run over, over'rijden; overlopen
 to run through, er door'brengen; door'steken; doorlezen
runaway, op hol ge'slagen
rung, sport
runner, hardloper; bode; loper
running, door'lopend: achter el'kaar
runway, groef; startbaan
rupture, breuk

rural, landelijk, platte'lands-
ruse, krijgslist
rush, drukte, haast; toeloop:
bies: rennen, vliegen; storten;
zich haasten
russet, roodbruin (n)
Russia, Rusland n
Russian, Rus(sisch (n))
rust, roest: (ver')roesten
rustic, boers; rus'tiek: platte'lander
rustle, ge'ritsel n: (doen) ritselen
rusty, roestig
rut, wagenspoor n; sleur
ruthless, mee'dogenloos
rye, rogge

S

sable, sabelbont n
sabotage, sabo'tage
sabre, sabel
sack, zak; plundering: (de) bons
(geven); plunderen
sacrament, sacra'ment n
sacred, heilig; ge'wijd
sacrifice, offer(ande) (n), op-
offering: (op)offeren
sacrilege, heiligschennis
sad, be'droefd; droevig
saddle, zadel(en) (n); opschepen
sadness, be'droefdheid
safe, veilig; zeker: brandkast;
vliegenkast
safeguard, waarborg(en)
safety, veiligheid
sag, doorbuigen; (af or door)zak-
ken
saga, sage
sagacious, schrander
sage, wijze: salie
sail, zeil(en) (n); ver'trekken,
varen
sailor, ma'troos, zeeman
saint, heilig(e); sint
sake: for the — of; ter wille
van; om . . . te
salad, sla
salary, sa'laris n
sale, (uit)verkoop, ver'koping
salesman, be'diende; handels-
reiziger

salient, op'vallend; treffend
saliva, speeksel n
sallow, ziekelijk (geel)
sally, uitval (doen)
salmon, zalm
saloon, sa'lon; bar; zaal
salt, zout (n): zouten
salutary, heilzaam
salutation, groet
salute, sa'luut n; salu'eren
salvage, berging; bergloon;
afval: bergen; redden
salvation, ver'lossing; zaligheid
salve, zalf: sussen; redden
salvo, salvo n
same, zelfde
all the same, deson'danks:
allemaal het'zelfde (or eender)
sample, monster n; staal(tje) n;
voorproefje n: keuren
sanatorium, sana'torium n; ziek-
enzaal
sanctify, heiligen
sanctimonious, schijn'heilig
sanction, sanctie: sanctio'neren
sanctity, heiligheid
sanctuary, sanctu'arium n; reser'vaat n; a'siel n
sand, zand n
sands, strand n
sandal, san'daal
sand-paper, schuurpapier n:
schuren
sandpit, zandgroeve; zandbak
sandwich, sandwich, be'legde
boterham
sandy, zandig, zand-
sane, ge'zond van geest, ver'standig
sanguine, opgewekt; blozend
sanitary, ge'zondheids-
sanitation, sani'tair n
sanity, ge'zond ver'stand n
sap, sap n: uitputten
sapling, jonge boom; jong'mens n
sapphire, saf'fier(blauw (n))
sarcasm, sar'casme n
sarcastic, sar'castisch
sardine, sar'dine
sardonic, smalend
sash, sjerp: schuifraamkozijn n
Satan, Satan
satchel, schooltas

satellite, satel'liet
satiate, (over)ver'zadigen
satin, sa'tijn(en) (*n*)
satire, sa'tire
satiric(cal), sa'tirisch
satirize, hekelen
satisfaction, vol'doening; ge'-
   noegdoening
satisfactorily, naar ge'noegen
satisfactory, be'vredigend
satisfy, vol'doen aan; be'vredig-
   en, te'vreden stellen
   to be satisfied with, te'vreden
   zijn over (*or* mēt)
saturate, ver'zadigen; door'trekken; door'weken
satyr, sater
sauce, saus; brutali'teit
saucepan, (steel)pan
saucer, schoteltje *n*
saucy, bru'taal; vlot
saunter, slenteren
sausage, worst(je *n*)
sausage-roll, sau'cijzebroodje *n*
savage, wild(e), woest
save, redden; sparen; voor'komen
savings, spaarpenningen
saviour, redder, heiland
savour, smaak: smaken (naar);
   ge'nieten van
savoury, smakelijk; pi'kant
   (schoteltje *n*)
saw, zaag: zagen
sawdust, zaagsel *n*
saxophone, saxo'foon
say, zeggenschap: (op)zeggen;
   luiden
   that is to say, dat wil zeggen
   it says . . . , er staat . . .
saying, ge'zegde *n*
scab, roofje *n*; schurft
scabbard, schede
scaffold, scha'vot *n*
scaffolding, stel'lage, steiger
scald, met kokend water be'gieten, met stoom branden; uitkoken
scale, schub; schilfer; ketelsteen:
   schaal; graadverdeling; (toon)-
   ladder: be'klimmen
scales, weegschaal
scallop, kammossel; schelp;
   schulp

scalp, scalp('eren)
scaly, ge'schubd; schilferig
scamp, rakker
scamper, rennen
scan, afzoeken; een vluchtige
   blik werpen in (*or* op); (zich
   laten) scan'deren
scandal, schan'daal *n*, schande;
   lasterpraat
scandalize, aanstoot geven
scandalous, schandelijk; lasterlijk
Scandinavian, Scandi'navisch;
   Scandi'naviër
scant, schraal; karig (zijn met)
scanty, spaarzaam, onvol'doende,
   dun
scapegoat, zondebok
scar, litteken *n* : rotswand
scarce, schaars
scarcely, nauwelijks
scarcity, schaarste
scare, schrik('barend be'richt *n*);
   bang maken
scarecrow, vogelverschrikker
scarf, das
scarlet, schar'laken (*n*)
   scarlet fever, roodvonk
scathing, bijtend
scatter, (zich) ver'strooien;
   uit'eendrijven
scavenger, opruimer; aasdier *n*;
   scharrelaar
scene, tafe'reel *n*; scène
scenery, decor *n*; landschap *n*,
   na'tuur(schoon *n*)
scenic, na'tuur-; toneel-
scent, geur, o'deur; reuk(zin);
   spoor *n*: ruiken; snuffelen
sceptic, scepticus
sceptical, sceptisch
sceptre, scepter
schedule, ta'bel; ceel; schema *n*
scheme, plan *n*; schema *n*:
   intri'geren
schism, scheuring
scholar, leerling; ge'leerde
scholarly, ge'leerd, weten'schappelijk
scholarship, ge'leerdheid;
   studiebeurs
school, school
schooling, schoolopleiding

schoolmaster, leraar

schoolroom, schoollokaal *n*

school-teacher, onder'wijzer-('es)

schooner, schoener

science, (na'tuur-)wetenschap

scientific, weten'schappelijk

scientist, ge'leerde

scintillate, fonkelen

scissors, schaar

scoff at, spotten met

scold, een uitbrander geven

scone, droog theegebak *n*

scoop, schoep, schep(pen); pri'meur

scooter, autoped

scope, be'stek *n*; vrij spel *n*

scorch, schroeien

score, stand, aantal punten *n*; twintig(tal *n*); parti'tuur: maken, be'halen; tellen; krassen

scorn, hoon: ver'smaden, het be'neden zich achten

scornful, minachtend

scorpion, schorpi'oen

Scot(ch), Schot(s)

scoundrel, schurk

scour, schuren: afzoeken

scourge, gesel(en)

scout, ver'kenner; padvinder. op zoek gaan

scowl, dreigend kijken

scraggy, mager

scramble, ge'jakker *n*; jachten (*n*): klauteren; zich ver'dringen

scrambled egg, roerei *n*

scrap, stukje *n*: kloppartij: oud: afdanken

scrapbook, plakboek *n*

scrape, knel: schrappen; schuren, krabben; schrapen

scratch, kras(sen), schram(men): krabben

scrawl, ge'krabbel *n*: krabbelen

scream, gil(len)

screech, ge'krijs *n*: krijsen

screen, scherm *n*; koorhek *n*: be'schermen, mas'keren

screw, schroef: schroeven

screwdriver, schroevedraaier

scribble, ge'krabbel *n*: krabbelen

scribe, schrijver, schriftgeleerde

script, schrift *n*; tekst

Scripture, Schrift

scroll, rol; krul

scrounge, (in)pikken; klaplopen

scrub, schrobben

scruple, scru'pule, ge'wetensbezwaar *n*

scrupulous, angst'vallig; nauwge'zet

scrutinize, nauw'keurig onder'zoeken

scrutiny, kritisch onderzoek *n*

scud, jagen

scuffle, handgemeen *n*

scullery, bijkeuken

sculptor, beeldhouwer

sculpture, beeldhouwkunst(*or* werk *n*): beeldhouwen

scum, schuim *n*

scurf, roos

scurry, ritsen

scurvy, scheurbuik: ge'meen

scuttle, bak: luik(gat) *n*: doen zinken: snellen

scythe, zeis: maaien

sea, zee

seafaring, zeevarend

seal, zeehond: zegel(en) (*n*): ver(*or* be)'zegelen, sluiten

sea-level, zeespiegel

sealing-wax, oogollak *n*

seam, naad; laag

seaman, zeeman, ma'troos

sear, ver'schroeien

search, zoeken; foui'lleren

in search of, op zoek naar

searching, onder'zoekend, diep'-gaand

searchlight, zoeklicht *n*

seashore, zeeoever

seaside, zee(oever)

season, sei'zoen *n*, tijd: kruiden; drogen

seasonal, sei'zoen-

seasoning, kruide'rij

seat, (zit)plaats; bank; zetel

seaweed, zeewier *n*

secede, zich afscheiden, zich te'rugtrekken

secluded, afgezonderd

seclusion, afzondering

second, tweede: se'conde: steunen

secondary, secun'dair; middelbaar

second-hand, tweede'hands; uit
de tweede hand

secondly, ten tweede

second-rate, tweede'rangs

secrecy, ge'heimhouding

secret, ge'heim (n); heimelijk;
ge'sloten

secretary, secre'taris, secreta'resse

secrete, afscheiden; ver'bergen,
ver'duisteren

secretive, ge'sloten

secretly, in het ge'heim

sect, sekte

section, (onder)deel n, afdeling;
sectie; doorsnee; para'graaf;
tra'ject n

sector, sector

secular, wereldlijk

secure, veilig; ver'zekerd;
vast(maken): zich ver'zekeren
van

security, veiligheid; waarborg;
ef'fect n

sedate, be'zadigd, waardig

sedative, pijnstillend (or
kal'merend) (middel n)

sedentary, zittend

sedge, zegge

sediment, be'zinksel n

sedition, opruiing

seduce, ver'leiden

see, (aarts)bisschopszetel, (aarts)-
bisdom n: (in)zien; ervoor
zorgen; ont'vangen, be'zoeken,
spreken, raadplegen; brengen
to see off, uitgeleide doen, wegbrengen
to see through, door'zien;
doorzetten
to see to, zorgen voor

seed, zaad n

seeing that, aange'zien

seek, zoeken; trachten

seem, (toe)schijnen

seemingly, ogen'schijnlijk

seemly, be'tamelijk

seep, sijpelen

seer, ziener

seesaw, wip

seethe, zieden; gisten

segment, seg'ment n, partje n

segregate, (zich) afzonderen

seize, pakken; nemen; aangrijpen

seizure, nemen n; be'slaglegging;
aanval

seldom, zelden

select, uitgelezen; chic: (uit)-
kiezen

selection, keus

self, zelf

self-assured, zelfbe'wust

self-centred, ego'centrisch

self-confidence, zelfvertrouwen n

self-conscious, ver'legen

self-contained, vrij; een'zelvig

self-control, zelfbeheersing

self-defence, zelfverdediging

self-denial, zelfverloochening

self-evident, vanzelf'sprekend

self-government, zelfbestuur n

self-interest, eigenbelang n

selfish, zelf'zuchtig

selfless, onbaat'zuchtig

self-pity, zelfbeklag n

self-preservation, zelfbehoud n

self-respect, zelfrespect n

self-righteous, eigenge'rechtigd

self-sacrifice, zelfopoffering

selfsame: the —, pre'cies de(or
het)'zelfde

self-satisfied, zelfvol'daan

self supporting: to be —, in
eigen be'hoefte kunnen
voor'zien

self-willed, eigen'zinnig

sell, ver'kopen

semblance, schijn, voorkomen n

semicircle, halve cirkel

semi-detached, twee onder één
dak

senate, se'naat

senator, se'nator

send, sturen, zenden
to send for, laten komen

senile, se'niel

senior, oudste, ouder

sensation, ge'voel n, ge'waarwording; sen'satie

sensational, opzien'barend; sen-
satio'neel

sense, zin(tuig n); ge'voel n;
ver'stand n: (aan)voelen

in a sense, in zekere zin
senses, ver'stand *n*
senseless, be'wusteloos; on'zinnig
sensible, ver'standig, praktisch
sensitive, ge'voelig (voor)
sensual, sensuous, zinnelijk
sentence, zin; vonnis *n* : ver'oordelen
sentiment, ge'voel(en) *n*
sentimental, sentimen'teel
sentinel, sentry, schildwacht
separate, af'zonderlijk : (af)scheiden
separation, scheiding
September, sep'tember
septic, septisch
sepulchre, graf *n*
sequel, ver'volg *n* ; ge'volg *n*
sequence, op'eenvolging, volgorde
seraph(im), sera'fijn(en)
serenade, sere'nade (brengen)
serene, kalm
serenity, vreedzaamheid
serf, lijfeigene
serge, serge
sergeant, ser'geant
serial, volg- : feuilleton *n*
series, serie, reeks op'eenvolging
serious, ernstig : ge'wichtig
seriously, ernstig, in alle ernst, au séri'eux
sermon, preek
serpent, slang
serrated, ge'karteld
serum, serum *n*
servant, be'diende; knecht, dienstmeisje *n* ; dienaar
serve, (be')dienen; opscheppen; ser'veren
service, dienst; strijdkracht; service; ser'vies *n*
serviceable, nuttig
servile, slaafs, kruipend
servitude, slaver'nij; dwangarbeid
session, zitting
set, (toe)stel *n* : vast, strak : zetten; vast worden
to set about, te werk gaan
to set against, ophitsen tegen; afwegen tegen

to set off, ver'trekken; af laten gaan
to set on fire, in brand steken
set-back, tegenslag
settee, bank
setting, zetting; (tijd en) plaats, om'geving
settle, regelen; zich vestigen; gaan zitten; ver'zakken
to settle down, tot rust komen
settlement, schikking; ver'effening; nederzetting
settler, kolo'nist
seven(teen)(th), zeven('tien)(de)
seventy, zeventig
sever, scheiden, ver'breken; doorsnijden
several, ver'scheiden; af'zonderlijk
severe, streng; ernstig; sober; hevig; zwaar
sew, naaien
sewage, ri'oolslijk *n*
sewer, ri'ool *n*
sewing, naaien *n*, naaiwerk *n*
sex, ge'slacht *n*
sexual, ge'slachts-, seksu'eel
shabby, haveloos; min
shack, keet
shackle, boci(en)
shade, schaduw, achtergrond; scherm *n*, kap; tint; tikje *n*, nu'ance: be'schutten; be'schaduwen
shadow, schaduw(en); zweem
shadowy, schaduwrijk; vaag
shady, lommerrijk; ver'dacht
shaft, schacht; straal; pijl
shaggy, ruig
shake, schudden (*n*)
shaky, on'vast, wankel
shale, leisteen
shall, zal, zullen
shallow, on'diep; opper'vlakkig
sham, namaak; schijn: voorwenden
shamble, schuifelen
shame, schaamte; schande: be'schaamd maken; te schande maken
a shame, jammer
shameful, schandelijk

shanty, keet
shape, ge'daante; vorm(en); zich ont'wikkelen
shapeless, vormeloos
shapely, goed ge'vormd
share, (aan)deel *n*; samen delen, ver'delen
shark, haai; oplichter
sharp, scherp; bijde'hand; pre'cies: kruis *n*
sharpen, slijpen
shatter, ver'brijzelen; ver'nietigen
shave, (zich) scheren
shaving, krul; scheren *n*
shawl, sjaal, omslagdoek
she, zij
sheaf, schoof; bundel
shear, scheren
shears, schaar
sheath, schede
shed, hok *n*, schuur(tje *n*): ver'gieten, storten; afwerpen; ver'spreiden
sheen, glans
sheep, schaap *n*, schapen
sheepish, schaapachtig
sheer, ragfijn; klinkklaar; loodrecht
sheet, laken *n*; vel *n*, plaat, vlak *n*: schoot
shelf, plank; platte rand
shell, schaal, schelp, schil(d *n*); huls; ge'raamte *n*: doppen; be'schieten
shellfish, schelpdier *n*
shelter, schutting, schuilplaats: be'schermen; schuilen
shelve, van zich afschuiven: glooien
shepherd, herder: ge'leiden
sheriff, drost
sherry, sherry
shield, schild *n*: be'schermen
shift, ploeg, werktijd: ver'schuiven
shilling, shilling
shimmer, glinsteren
shin, scheen
shindy, herrie
shine, glans: (laten) schijnen; glimmen; uitblinken
shingle, grint *n*

shiny, glimmend, blinkend
ship, schip *n*; in(*or* ver')schepen
shipbuilding, scheepsbouw
shipment, ver'scheping; zending
ship-owner, reder
shipping, scheepvaart, schepen
shipwreck, schipbreuk
  to be shipwrecked, schipbreuk lijden
shipyard, werf
shirk, zich ont'trekken aan
shirt, (over)hemd *n*
shiver, rilling: rillen
shoal, on'diepte: school
shock, schok (geven); shock: bos: aanstoot geven
shocking, aan'stotelijk; gruwelijk; schan'dalig
shoddy, prul-, snert-
shoe, schoen
shoot, uitloper: (dood)schieten; afschieten; storten
shop, winkel(en)
shopkeeper, winke'lier
shore, kust, oever: stut(ten)
short, kort; krap; bros
  to cut short, onder'breken
  in short, kort'om
  to run short, opraken
  to be short of, ge'brek hebben aan; te'kort komen
shortage, te'kort *n*
short-circuit, kortsluiting (ver'oorzaken)
shortcoming, te'kortkoming
shorten, (ver')korten
shorthand, stenogra'fie
short-lived, kort'stondig
shortly, (binnen)kort
shorts, korte broek
short - sighted, bij'ziend; kort'zichtig
short-tempered, prikkelbaar
shot, schot *n*; schroot *n*; poging; kiekje *n*; slag
shotgun, jachtgeweer *n*
should, moest(en); be'horen; zou(den); mocht(en)
shoulder, schouder(stuk *n*): op zich nemen
shout, schreeuw(en); brullen
shove, schuiven-
shovel, schop: scheppen

show, ver'toon *n*, schijn; ten'toonstelling, amuse'ments-voorstelling, schouwspel *n*, show: (ver')tonen; te zien zijn; laten zien; (be')wijzen; blijk geven van
  to show off, zich aanstellen; pronken
  to show up, aan de dag brengen; uitkomen

shower, bui; douche; regen; over'stelpen

shrapnel, gra'naatscherven

shred, flard; schijn

shrew, feeks

shrewd, schrander

shrick, gil(len)

shrill, schel

shrimp, gar'naal

shrine, schrijn; heilige plaats

shrink, (doen) krimpen; te'rugdeinzen (voor)

shrivel, (doen) ver'schrompelen

shroud, doodskleed *n*; sluier: staand want *n*: hullen

shrub, heester

shrubbery, heesterbosje *n*

shrug, ophalen

shudder, huiveren; schudden

shuttle, schuifelen, wassen

shun, schuwen

shunt, ran'geren

shut, dicht (doen); sluiten
  to shut up, (op)sluiten; zijn mond houden

shutter, luik *n*; sluiter

shuttle, schietspoel: pendel-

shy, ver'legen, schuw: schrikken: keilen

sick, ziek(en); misselijk; beu
  to be sick, overgeven

sickening, walgelijk; ver'velend

sickle, sikkel

sickly, ziekelijk; onge'zond

sickness, ziekte; misselijkheid

side, (zij)kant; zij(de); par'tij (kiezen)
  side by side, naast el'kaar

sideboard, buf'fet *n*

side-track, zijspoor *n*: van zijn onderwerp afbrengen *or* afdwalen;

sideways, zijdelings

siding, zijspoor *n*

sidle up to, schuchter be'naderen

siege, be'leg *n*

sieve, zeef: zeven

sift, zeven; ziften

sigh, zucht(en)

sight, ge'zicht *n*; beziens'waardigheid; vi'zier *n*: (in) zicht *n* (krijgen)
  at sight, op het eerste ge'zicht; van het blad
  to catch sight of, in het oog krijgen

sign, (uithang)bord *n*; wenk, teken *n*: (onder')tekenen; een teken geven

signal, sein(en) (*n*); een teken geven

signature, handtekening

signet(-ring), zegel(ring), (*n*)

significance, be'tekenis; be'lang *n*

significant, veelbe'tekenend; be'langrijk

signify, be'tekenen; te kennen geven

signpost, handwijzer

silence, stilte; stilzwijgen *n*: tot zwijgen brengen

silent, stil(zwijgend), zwijgzaam; stom
  to be silent, zwijgen

silently, in stilte, ge'ruisloos

silhouette, silhou'et

silk, zij(den)

silky, zijdeachtig

sill, vensterbank, drempel

silly, on'nozel, dwaas, flauw

silt, slib *n*: dichtslibben

silver, zilver(werk) *n*: zilveren

similar, ge'lijk, dergelijk

similarity, over'eenkomst

simile, verge'lijking

simmer, zachtjes (laten) sudderen; pruttelen; gisten

simper, meesmuilen

simple, een'voudig; enkel'voudig; simpel; on'nozel

simpleton, on'nozele hals

simplicity, eenvoud

simplify, vereen'voudigen

simply, een'voudig; ge'woonweg, al'leen

simulate, voorwenden; nabootsen

simultaneous, gelijk'tijdig

sin, zonde: zondigen

since, sinds('dien), na'dien; van'af: daar

sincere, op'recht

sincerity, op'rechtheid

sinecure, sine'cuur

sinew, pees

sinful, zondig

sing, zingen

singe, (af)schroeien; fri'seren

singer, zanger('es)

singing, zingen *n*; suizen *n*

single, enkel; eenpersoons-; onge'trouwd

  to single out, uitpikken

singly, af'zonderlijk; al'leen

singular, bij'zonder: enkelvoud *n*

sinister, si'nister

sink, gootsteen: (ver')zinken, ondergaan; tot zinken brengen

sinner, zondaar

sinuous, kronkelend

sip, teugje *n*: met teugjes drinken

siphon, hevel(en); si'fon

sir, mijnheer; sir

  Dear Sir, Mijne Heren, Zeer geachte Heer

sire, (voor)vader; sire

siren, si'rene

sister, zusje *n*; zuster

sit, (gaan) zitten; zitting houden; po'seren

  to sit down, gaan zitten

  to sit up, rech'top (gaan) zitten; opblijven

site, bouwgrond, ('bouw)ter'rein *n*; ligging

sitting-room, zitkamer

situated, ge'legen

situation, ligging; situ'atie; be'trekking

six(teen)(th), zes(tien)(de)

sixpence, kwartje *n*, halve shilling

sixty, zestig

sizable, flink

size, grootte, omvang; maat; lijmwater *n*

sizzle, sissen

skate, schaats(enrijden): vleet

skein, streng

skeleton, ske'let *n*; ge'raamte *n*

sketch, schets(en)

skewer, vleespen

ski, ski(ën)

skid, slippen

skilful, be'kwaam, knap

skill, be'kwaamheid, vaardigheid

skilled, ge'schoold

skim, afscheppen, afromen; scheren over; doorbladeren

skimp, zuinig zijn (met)

skin, huid; vel *n*; pels: villen

skinny, broodmager

skip, springen; overslaan

skipper, schipper

skirmish, scher'mutseling

skirt, rok; trekken (om)

skulk, lijntrekken; laf'hartig schuilen; sluipen

skull, schedel; doodskop

skunk, skunk

sky, lucht, hemel

skylark, veldleeuwerik; pret

sky-scraper, wolkenkrabber

slab, plak, plaat

slack, slap; laks; stil: gruis *n*

slacken, ver'slappen; laten vieren

slacks, lange broek

slag, slak

slake, lessen; blussen

slam, bons; slem *n*: dichtslaan

slander, (be')laster(en)

slanderous, lasterlijk

slang, slang *n*

slant, helling: hellen

slap, klap (geven): par'does: kwakken

slapdash, noncha'lant

slash, houw, jaap: (er'op los) maaien (*or* slaan); drastisch ver'minderen

slat, lat, reep

slate, lei(steen *n*): leien: ervan langs geven

slaughter, slachting: slachten; afmaken

slave, slaaf: zich afbeulen

slavery, slaver'nij

slavish, slaafs

slay, doodslaan

sledge, slede: voorhamer: sleeën

sleek, glanzig, glad

sleep, slaap: slapen
sleeper, slaper; slaapwagen;
dwarsligger
sleeping, slapen *n*; slapend:
slaap-
sleepless, slapeloos
sleepy, slaperig; doods; melig
sleet, natte sneeuw
sleeve, mouw
sleigh, arreslee
sleight of hand, goochela'rij
slender, slank, dun; karig, zwak,
klein
slice, snee(tje *n*): snijden
slick, vlot, glad
slide, glijbaan; glijkoker; plaatje
n: glijden
slight, ge'ring, licht; tenger:
klei'nering: klei'neren
slightly, iets; opper'vlakkig
slim, slank
slime, slijk *n*, slijm *n*
slimy, slijmerig
sling, slingerverband *n*; leng;
slinger(en); gooien
slink, sluipen
slip, sloop *n*; onderjurk; ver'gissing; strookje *n*; helling: (uit)-
glijden; wippen; uitschieten;
schuiven; laten glijden; aan(*or*
uit)doen; voor'bijgaan; ont'-
schieten
slipper, pan'toffel
slippery, glibberig, glad
slipshod, slordig
slit, spleet, scheur(en); snijden
slobber, kwijlen
slogan, leus
sloop, sloep
slop, morsen
slope, helling: hellen, schuin
lopen
sloppy, drassig; dun; slordig;
zoetelijk
slot, gleuf
sloth, luiheid; luiaard
slouch, slungelen, hangen
slough, moe'ras *n*: afgeworpen
vel *n*
slovenly, slonzig, slordig
slow, langzaam, traag; achter
   to slow down, ver'tragen,
   ophouden; vaart ver'minderen

slug, slak; hagelkorrel
sluggish, traag
sluice, sluis, ver'laat: spoelen
slum, slop, achterbuurt
slumber, sluimering: sluimeren
slump, ma'laise
slur, vlek, smet: in el'kaar laten
lopen
slush, half ge'smolten sneeuw;
bagger
slut, slet
sly, sluw
smack, klap, smak, pats: bijsmaak; zweem: een klap geven;
smakken met: zwemen naar
small, klein
smallpox, pokken
smart, vinnig; flink; bijde'hand,
handig; chic, keurig: zeer doen
smash, botsing; cata'strofe:
ver'pletteren,   stukslaan;
breken; botsen (tegen)
smattering, mondjevol *n*
smear, veeg: (be')smeren;
be'smeuren
smell, reuk, lucht: ruiken (naar);
rieken (naar)
smelt, smelten
smile, (glim)lach(en)
smirk, grijns (*or* grijnzen) van
vol'doening
smite, (hard) slaan; kwellen
smith, smid
smithereens, gruzele'menten
smithy, smidse
smock, kiel: smokken
smoke, rook: roken; walmen
smoky, rokerig
smooth, glad, vlak; kalm; vlot:
gladstrijken
smother, smoren;   stikken;
be'delven; doven
smoulder, smeulen
smudge, vlek(ken)
smug, zelf'ingenomen
smuggle, smokkelen
smut, roetdeeltje *n*; schunnig-
heden
snack, hapje *n*
snack-bar, cafe'taria
snag, uitsteeksel *n*; moeilijkheid
snail, huisjesslak
snake, slang

snap, klap, krak; drukknoop; kiekje *n*: knappen; happen; snauwen; pikken

snapshot, kiekje *n*

snare, (val)strik; (ver¹)strikken

snarl, grauw(en); snauw(en)

snatch, brokstuk *n*: grissen

sneak, klikspaan: klikken; sluipen; gappen

sneer, schimplach: be¹schimpen; smalen (op)

sneeze, niezen *(n)*

sniff, snuiven; de neus ophalen (voor); snuffelen; ruiken aan

snigger, grinniken

snip, snipper; knip(pen)

snipe, snip: ter¹sluiks één voor één neerschieten

snob, snob

snooze, dutje *n*: dutten

snore, snurken

snort, snuiven

snout, snuit

snow, sneeuw(en)

snowdrift, sneeuwbank

snowflake, sneeuwvlok

snowy, sneeuw-

snub, brute afwijzing: bits afwijzen

  snub nose, mopneus

snuff, snuif: snuiven: snuiten

snug, knus

snuggle, (zich) nestelen

so, zo: dus: ook

  or so, onge¹veer

  so that, zodat; opdat

soak, (door¹)weken; in de week zetten (*or* staan); (laten) trekken

  to soak up, (op)slorpen

soap, zeep

soap-suds, zeepsop *n*

soar, om¹hoogvliegen; de hoogte invliegen

sob, snik(ken)

sober, nuchter; sober: ont¹nuchteren

so-called, zoge¹naamd

soccer, voetbal *n*

sociable, soci¹aal; ge¹zellig

social, soci¹aal

socialism, socia¹lisme *n*

society, ver¹eniging; maatschap¹pij; ge¹zelschap *n*; deftige stand

sock, sok

socket, gat *n*, kas, holte

sod, zode

soda, soda

sodden, doornat

sofa, sofa

soft, zacht; week

soften, zacht maken (*or* worden); ver¹zachten

soggy, door¹weekt, drassig, klef

soil, grond, bodem: vuil maken

sojourn, ver¹toeven

solace, troost

solar, zonne-, zons-

solder, sol¹deersel *n*: sol¹deren

soldier, sol¹daat; mili¹tair

sole, enig: zool: tong

solely, al¹leen

solemn, ernstig; plechtig

solemnity, plechtigheid

solicit, ver¹zoeken om

solicitor, rechts¹kundig advi¹seur, procu¹reur

solicitous, be¹zorgd; ver¹langend

solid, vast (lichaam *n*); mas¹sief; stevig; soli¹dair

solidarity, saam¹horigheidsgevoel *n*

solidify, mas¹sief (doen) worden

soliloquy, al¹leenspraak

solitary, eenzaam

solitude, eenzaamheid

solo, solo

soluble, op¹losbaar

solution, oplossing

solve, oplossen

solvent, sol¹vent; oplossend: oplosmiddel *n*

sombre, somber

some, sommige; enige; (er) wat (van); een (of ander); onge¹veer

  some such, een dergelijk, zo'n

  some day, weleens

somebody, (een zeker) iemand

somehow, op de een of andere ma¹nier; hoe dan ook

someone, iemand

somersault, buiteling, salto mortale

something, iets

sometime, wel eens

sometimes, soms

somewhat, enigs¹zins; iets, wat

somewhere, crgcns; ccn plaats (waar)

son, zoon

sonata, so¹nate

song, lied *n*; appel en een ei

sonnet, son¹net *n*

sonorous, diepklinkend; weids

soon, spoedig, vroeg; lief

  as soon as, zo¹dra

  no sooner ... than, nauwelijks ... of

  I would sooner, ik zou liever

soot, roet *n*

soothe, sussen; ver¹zachten

soothsayer, waarzegger

sophisticated, mon¹dain

sophistication, ge¹kunsteldheid

soporific, slaap¹wekkend

sopping wet, drijfnat

soprano, so¹praan

sorcerer, tovenaar

sorcery, tovena¹rij

sordid, vuil; on¹smakelijk

sore, zeer; gepi¹keerd; teer: zere plek

sorrow, smart: treuren

sorrowful, droevig

sorry, treurig

  I am sorry, het spijt me

sort, soort: sor¹teren

soul, ziel; ster¹veling

soul-destroying, geest¹dodend

sound, ge¹luid *n*, klank: zeeëngte: degelijk, gaaf, ge¹zond, be¹-
  trouwbaar; flink, vast: (doen) klinken: peilen; polsen

sounding, klinkend: peiling

soup, soep

sour, zuur

source, bron

south, zuid(er-), zuiden(-) (*n*), naar het zuiden, ten zuiden van

southerly, zuidelijk

southern, zuidelijk, zuider-

souvenir, souve¹nir *n*

sovereign, vorst: soeve¹rein

sovereignty, soevereini¹teit

Soviet, Sovjet

sow, zeug: (be¹)zaaien

space, (tijd)ruimte; spatie: spati¹ëren, ver¹delen

spacious, ruim

spade, schop

span, spanwijdte; spanne

spangle, lovertje *n*: be¹zaaien

spaniel, spaniël

spank, voor zijn broek geven; patsen

spanner, moersleutel

spar, rondhout *n*: (oefenend) boksen; redetwisten

spare, vrij; re¹serve; schraal: (re¹serve)onderdeel *n*; sparen; missen; ont¹zien

spark, vonk(en); greintje *n*

sparkle, vonken schieten; fonkelen; tintelen; mous¹seren

sparrow, mus

sparse, dun(ge¹zaaid)

spasm, kramp(¹achtige be¹-
  weging); vlaag

spasmodic, kram¹pachtig; bij vlagen, intermit¹terend

spats, slobkousen

spate, stroom, vlaag, hoop

spatter, spatten; plassen (tegen)

spawn, kuit (schieten)

speak, spreken; uitdrukken

speaker, spreker; voorzitter

spear, speer

special, bij¹zonder, speci¹aal

specialist, specia¹list

specialize, speciali¹seren

specially, in het bij¹zonder, voor¹al

species, soort(en), ge¹slacht(en) *n*

specific, be¹paald; uit¹drukke-
  lijk; speci-fiek

specification, specifi¹catie

specify, specifi¹ceren; ver¹melden

specimen, proef; staaltje *n*

specious, schoonschijnend

speck, spikkel; vuiltje *n*

speckle, (be¹)spikkelen

spectacle, schouwspel *n*

spectacles, bril

spectacular, groots, grandi¹oos

spectator, toeschouwer

spectre, spook *n*; schim

spectrum, spectrum *n*

speculate, be¹spiegelingen houden; specu¹leren

speculation, be¹spiegeling; specu¹latie

speculator, specu¹lant

speech, (toe)spraak

speechless, sprakeloos
speed, vaart; snelheid; ver'snelling: snel rijden
speed(il)y, spoedig
spell, beurt; peri'ode: be'tovering: spellen; be'tekenen
spend, uitgeven; be'steden, doorbrengen; uitputten
spew, (uit)braken
sphere, bol; hemellichaam *n*; ge'bied *n*, sfeer
spherical, bol'vormig
spice, spece'rij
spicy, ge'kruid; pi'kant
spider, spin
spike, (ijzeren) punt; stekel
spill, fidibus: morsen; overlopen
spin, ritje *n*; vrille: spinnen; draaien
spinach, spi'nazie
spinal, ruggegraats-
spindle, klos; spil
spine, ruggegraat; stekel
spinney, bosje *n*
spinster, ongetrouwde vrouw
spiral, spi'raal(vormig)
spire, torenspits
spirit, geest; fut
  spirits, stemming; levenslust; sterke drank
spirited, vurig; geani'meerd
spiritual, geestelijk (lied *n*)
spit, spuug *n*: spit *n*; landtong: spuwen; druppelen
spite, kwaa'daardigheid: ergeren
spiteful, hatelijk
splash, spat: be'spatten; plassen; uit el'kaar spatten; natmaken
spleen, milt; gal
splendid, schitterend, prachtig
splendour, pracht
splice, splitsen; lassen
splint, spalk(en)
splinter, splinter
split, spleet; scheuring: splijten; splitsen; (ver')delen
splitting, barstend
splutter, sputteren
spoil, buit: be'derven; ver'wennen
spoil-sport, spelbreker
spoke, spaak; sport

spokesman, woordvoerder
sponge, spons; mos'covisch ge'bak *n*: sponzen; klaplopen
sponsor, borg en stichter; peet; op touw zetten
spontaneous, spon'taan; zelf
spool, spoel
spoon(ful), lepel
sporadic, spo'radisch
spore, spoor
sport, sport; grap, spot; fi'dele vent (*or* meid): spelen
sporting, sport-; spor'tief; aardig
sportsman, sportliefhebber
spot, vlek; stip(pelen); plek; scheutje *n*: in de gaten krijgen
spotless, smetteloos; brandschoon
spotlight, zoeklicht *n*
spouse, gade
spout, tuit; straal: spuiten
sprain, ver'stuiken
sprawl, uitgestrekt (gaan) liggen; wijd uit'eenlopen, zich wan'orderlijk ver'spreiden
spray, sproeiregen; sproeier: takje *n*: (be')sproeien
spread, wijdte; ont'haal *n*: (zich) (uit)spreiden; (zich) ver'spreiden; (be')smeren
spree, pretje *n*; braspartij
sprig, twijgje *n*
sprightly, opgewekt
spring, veer(kracht); lente; bron: springen; ont'staan(uit); (uit de grond) schieten
sprinkle, (be')sprenkelen, strooien
sprint, sprint(en)
sprout, spruit(en)
spruce, spar(rehout *n*): keurig: opknappen
spry, kwiek
spur, spoor; uitloper; prikkel: de sporen geven; aansporen
  on the spur of the moment, in de eerste opwelling
spurious, on'echt
spurn, ver'smaden
spurt, guts; vlaag: spuiten (met); spurten
sputter, sputteren, spatten

spy, spi'on; (be)spio'neren; be'speuren

squabble, ge'kibbel *n*: kibbelen

squad, troep

squadron, eska'dron *n*; es'kader *n*

squalid, vuil en ar'moedig

squall, (wind)vlaag: schreeuwen

squalor, vuile armoede

squander, ver'spillen

square, vierkant (*n*); plein *n*; kwa'draat *n*: recht('hoekig); quitte; eerlijk: in het kwa'draat brengen; afrekenen

squash, kwast: platdrukken, platgedrukt worden

squat, ge'drongen: neerhurken

squawk, krijsen

squeak, piepen

squeal, gillen

squeamish, overdreven ge'voelig

squeeze, ge'drang *n*: knijpen, uitpersen; bijstoppen; afpersen

squelch, ploeteren

squint, scheelkijken; pinkogen

squire, landjonker

squirm, zich in allerlei bochten wringen; in el'kaar kruipen

squirrel, eekhoorn

squirt, spuiten

stab, steek(wond): (door)steken

stability, stabili'teit

stabilize, stabili'seren

stable, stal(len): sta'biel, vast

stack, stapel: opstapelen

stadium, stadion *n*

staff, staf, stok

stag, mannetjeshert *n*

stage, e'tappe, stadium *n*; to'neel *n*; tra'ject *n*: ten to'nele brengen; op touw zetten

stage-coach, dili'gence

stagger, (doen) wankelen; ver'bijsteren; spreiden

stagnant, stilstaand

stagnation, stilstand; stremming

staid, be'zadigd

stain, (be')vlek(ken): smet; beits(en); kleurstof: afgeven; brandschilderen

stainless, smetteloos; roestvrij

stair, trede: trap-

staircase, stairs, trap

stake, paal: brandstapel; inzet(ten); staken

at stake, op het spel

stale, oud('bakken), ver'schaald, muf; suf

stalk, stengel: (be')sluipen

stall, stal(letje n); koorstoel: (laten) afslaan

stallion, hengst

stalwart, stoer

stamen, meeldraad

stamina, uithoudingsvermogen *n*

stammer, ge'stamel *n*: stamelen, stotteren

stamp, (post)zegel; stempel(en): fran'keren; stampen

stampede, pa'niek; stormloop: stormlopen

stand, standard, voet, stel *n*; tri'bune; plaats: (gaan *or* blijven) staan; liggen; zetten; ver'dragen, uitstaan; van kracht blijven; trak'teren; zijn

to stand back, achter'uitgaan; (van . . .) af liggen

to stand out, uitsteken; opvallen

standard, standaard; maatstaf; vaandel *n*

standardize, standaardi'seren

stand-by, re'serve, steun

standing, aanzien *n*: permanent; (stil)staand

standpoint, standpunt *n*

standstill, stilstand

stanza, vers *n*, strofe

staple, hoofd-: kram, niet

star, ster; ge'sternte *n*

starboard, stuurboord

starch, zetmeel *n*; stijfsel: stijven

stare, (aan)staren

stark, stapel-, spier-

starling, spreeuw

starry, sterren-

start, be'gin(nen) (*n*); start(en); schok: ver'trekken; aanzetten, aanslaan; opschrikken

startle, doen schrikken

startling, verbazing'wekkend; ont'stellend

starvation, ver'hongering
starve, (laten) ver'hongeren
state, staat, toestand; staatsie:
staats-: mededelen, uit'eenzetten, consta'teren
stated, ge'noemd; vastgesteld
stately, statig
statement, ver'klaring
statesman, staatsman
statesmanship, staatkunde
static, statisch
station, sta'tion *n*; stand-
(plaats): plaatsen
stationary, stilstaand; sta-
tio'nair
stationer, kan'toorboekhan-
del(aar)
stationery, schrijfbehoeften
statistic, sta'tistisch
statistics, statis'tiek(en)
statue, standbeeld *n*
stature, ge'stalte; ge'halte *n*
status, toestand; po'sitie
statute, landswet, sta'tuut *n*
staunch, trouw: stelpen
stave, duig; staaf: inslaan
  to stave off, afwenden
stay, ver'blijf *n*: stut: stag:
(ver')blijven; lo'geren
steadfast, stand'vastig
steady, stevig, vast; so'lide;
stand'vastig; kalm: vast-
houden
steak, lap
steal, stelen; sluipen
stealthy, heimelijk
steam, stoom: dampen; stomen
steamer, stoomboot; stomer
steed, ros *n*
steel, staal *n*: stalen
steep, steil; kras: (in)dom-
pelen
steeple, toren(spits)
steer, jonge os: sturen
steering-wheel, stuur *n*
stem, stengel, steel; (voor)-
steven: stuiten
stench, stank
stencil, stencil(en) (*n*)
stenographer, steno'graaf
step, stap(pen); pas; trede,
stoep
step-, stief-

step-ladder, trapleer
stereotyped, stereo'tiep
sterile, ste'riel; on'vruchtbaar
sterilize, sterili'seren
sterling, sterling: recht'schapen
stern, achtersteven: streng
stevedore, stuwa'door
stew, stoofschotel: stoven
steward, hofmeester; rentmeester; be'diende
stick, stok: plakken; (blijven)
steken; volhouden
sticky, kleverig
stiff, stijf, stroef; stevig; moeilijk
stiffen, stijver (*or* moeilijker)
maken
stifle, (ver')stikken; onder'drukken
stigma, brandmerk *n*
stile, overstap
still, stil(te): distil'leerketel: nog
(al'tijd): toch: kal'meren
stillness, stilte
stilt, stelt
stilted, hoog'dravend
stipend, be'zoldiging
stipulate, be'dingen
stipulation, voorwaarde
stir, ophef: (be')roeren, zich
ver'roeren; aanzetten
stirring, veelbe'wogen; op'windend
stirrup, stijgbeugel
stitch, steek, hechting: stikken,
hechten
stock, voorraad; ef'fecten; afkomst; boui'llon: standaard,
cou'rant: voor'zien(van), voorraad inslaan; in voorraad
hebben
stockade, palis'sade
stockbroker, e'ffectenmakelaar
stocking, kous
stodgy, onver'teerbaar; zwaar
stoic(al), stoï'cijns
stoke, stoken
stolid, stomp'zinnig
stomach, maag: ver'duwen
stone, (edel)steen; pit; 6·35
kilo: stenen: stenigen;
ont'pitten
stone-deaf, stokdoof

stony, steenachtig; steenhard; doods, koud

stool, kruk; stoelgang

stoop, ronde rug: bukken; zich ver'lagen

stop, oponthoud *n*; halte; re'gister: (dicht)stoppen; blijven (staan); stilstaan; ophouden (met); stopzetten; stelpen

 to put a stop to, een eind maken aan

stoppage, oponthoud *n*; opstopping

stopper, stop

storage, opslaan *n*; bergruimte: opslag-

store, warenhuis *n*; ba'zaar; voorraad; maga'zijn *n*: opslaan; opbergen

 to lay in a store of, inslaan

storeroom, bergruimte, pro'visiekamer

stork, ooievaar

storm, storm, (flinke) bui, onweer *n*: razen; stuiven; be'stormen

stormy, stormachtig, onweersachtig

story, ver'haal *n*, ge'schiedenis: ver'dieping

stout, ge'zet; stevig; flink: stout *n*

stove, kachel, for'nuis *n*

stow, stouwen; opbergen

stowaway, ver'stekeling

straddle, schrijlings staan (*or* zitten); spreiden over

straggle, zich ver'spreiden; achterblijven

straight, recht; eerlijk; in orde; puur

 straight away, di'rect

straighten, rechttrekken (*or* zetten); in orde brengen

straightforward, op'recht; een'voudig

strain, (in)spanning: toon: afkomst; trek: (over' *or* in)-spannen; (ver')rekken; afgieten

strained, ge'dwongen

strainer, ver'giet, zeefje *n*

straits, zee'ëngte, Straat; ver'legenheid

strand, streng: stranden

to be stranded, stranden; hulpeloos staan

strange, vreemd

stranger, vreemde; onbe'kende

strangle, worgen; onder'drukken

strap, riem, band: vastmaken (met een riem)

strapping, potig

stratagem, (krijgs)list

strategic, stra'tegisch

strategy, strate'gie

stratum, (aard)laag

straw, stro(otje) *n*; zier

strawberry, aardbei

stray, afgedwaald (dier *n*): (af)-dwalen

streak, streep; straal: strepen

stream, stroom: stromen

streamer, serpen'tine, wimpel

streamline(d), (ge')stroom-lijn(d)

street, straat

strength, kracht(en); sterkte; ge'halte *n*

strengthen, (ver')sterken

strenuous, inspannend

stress, aandrang, spanning; nadruk; klemtoon: de nadruk (*or* de klemtoon) leggen op

stretch, uitge'strektheid: (zich) (uit)rekken; spannen; uitsteken

 at a stretch, achter el'kaar

stretcher, bran'card

strew, strooien; be'zaaien

stricken, ge'troffen

strict, streng; pre'cies; strikt

stride, schrede: schrijden

strident, krassend

strife, twist, strijd

strike, staking: slaan; aansteken; (toe)schijnen, opkomen bij; treffen; staken; doorhalen

striking, treffend

string, touw *n*; snoer *n*; snaar; file; strijkinstrument *n*: (aan'een)rijgen

stringent, streng

strip, strook: (af)stropen; (zich) uitkleden; ont'doen; afhalen

stripe, streep: strepen

stripling, jonge borst

strive, streven (naar); worstelen

stroke, slag; haal; be'roerte; zet: strelen

stroll, wandeling: kuieren; trekken

strong, sterk

stronghold, bolwerk *n*

structure, struc'tuur, (ge')bouw (*n*); samenstelling

struggle, strijd; krachtsinspanning: vechten; strompelen

strum, trommelen

strut, stijl: trots stappen

stub, stomp, stronk, peukje *n*

stubble, stoppels

stubborn, hard'nekkig, hals'starrig

stud, knop; (boorde)knoopje *n*: stoete'rij: be'zaaien

student, onder'zoeker, leerling(-), stu'dent

studied, welover'wogen

studio, atel'ier *n*, studio

studious, leer'gierig

study, studie; stu'deerkamer: (be)stu'deren

stuff, stof, materi'aal *n*; goedje *n*; spul(len) *n*: volproppen; opzetten, vullen

stuffy, be'nauwd

stumble, struikelen, strompelen

stump, stomp, stronk: stommelen

stun, wezenloos slaan; ver'bluffen

stunt, stunt: be'lemmeren

stupefy, ver'stomd doen staan

stupendous, over'weldigend, machtig

stupid, dom, on'zinnig

stupor, ver'doving

sturdy, fors

stutter, stotteren

sty, hok *n*: strontje *n*

style, stijl

stylish, stijlvol; deftig

suave, minzaam

subconscious, onderbe'wust-(zijn *n*)

subdivision, onderverdeling; onderafdeling

subdue, onder'werpen; onder'drukken; dempen

subject, onderwerp *n*; vak *n*; onderdaan: onder'hevig (aan): onder'werpen; blootstellen (aan)

subjection, onder'werping; onder'worpenheid

subjective, subjec'tief

subjugate, onder'werpen

sublime, su'bliem

submarine, onder'zeeboot

submerge, over'stromen, ver'zwelgen

submission, onder'werping; onder'danigheid; be'wering

submissive, onder'danig

submit, (zich) onder'werpen; overleggen; zou(den) naar voren willen brengen; voorleggen

subordinate, onderge'schikt(e)

subscribe, tekenen voor; onder'schrijven; zich abon'neren (op)

subsequent, later

subservient, onderge'schikt; onder'danig

subside, zakken; afnemen; zinken

subsidiary, dochter-, bij('kom-stig)

subsidize, subsidiëren

subsidy, sub'sidie

subsist, be'staan; leven

subsistence, be'staan *n*

substance, stof; hoofdzaak; wezen *n*; sub'stantie

substantial, aan'zienlijk; so'lide

substantially, in wezen

substantiate, be'wijzen

substitute, plaatsver'vanger, surro'gaat (*n*): in de plaats stellen

substitution, substi'tutie

subterfuge, uitvlucht

subterranean, onderaards

subtle, sub'tiel, fijn, spits'vondig

subtract, aftrekken

suburb, voorstad

suburban, fo'renzen-, voorstadssucceed, slagen; (op)volgen

success, suc'ces n

successful, ge'slaagd; ge'lukkig

succession, op'eenvolging; suc'cessie

in succession, achter el'kaar

successive, opeen'volgend

successor, opvolger

succinct, kort en bondig

succulent, sappig

succumb, be'zwijken

such, zulk; zo('n); zo'danig

such as, zo'als; wat

suck, zuigen (op)

suckle, zogen

suction, zuiging: zuig-

sudden, plotseling

sue, ge'rechtelijk ver'volgen; smeken

suede, peau de suède

suet, niervet n

suffer, lijden; boeten

suffering, lijden n

suffice, vol'doende zijn

sufficient, vol'doende

suffocate, (doen) stikken

suffocation, ver'stikking

suffrage, kiesrecht n

sugar, suiker(en)

suggest, doen denken aan; voor- stellen; sugge'reren

suggestion, voorstel n; sug'- gestie; spoor n

suggestive, sugge'rerend; sug- ges'tief

suicide, zelfmoord

suit, pak n; kleur; huwelijks- aanzoek n: (aan)passen; ge'schikt zijn voor; schikken; goed staan(bij)

suitable, ge'schikt

suitcase, (hand)koffer

suite, ge'volg n; ameuble'ment n; aparte'menten

suitor, minnaar; eiser

sulk, mokken

sulky, gemelijk

sullen, stuurs; somber

sully, be'zoedelen

sulphur, zwavel

sultan, sultan

sultana, sul'tanarozijn

sultry, zwoel

sum, som

to sum up, samenvatten; op- sommen

summarize, resu'meren

summary, samenvatting: sum'mier

summer, zomer

summerhouse, tuinhuisje n

summit, top(punt n)

summon, ont'bieden, bij'een- roepen; ver'zamelen

summons, dagvaarding

sumptuous, weelderig

sun, zon(ne-)

sunbeam, zonnestraal

sunburn, zonnebrand

sunburnt, ver'brand

Sunday, Zondag

sundial, zonnewijzer

sundown, zons'ondergang

sundry, di'vers

sunken, blind; ingevallen

sunlight, zonlicht n

sunny, zonnig

sunrise, zons'opgang

sunset, zons'ondergang

sunshine, zonneschijn

sunstroke, zonnesteek

super, machtig

superb, groots, schitterend

supercilious, hoog'hartig

superficial, opper'vlakkig

superfluous, over'tollig

superhuman, boven'menselijk

superintend, toezicht houden op

superintendent, inspec'teur

superior, superi'eur, hoger; arro'gant

superlative, van de hoogste graad: superlatief

supernatural, bovenna'tuur- lijk(e n)

supersede, ver'vangen

superstition, bijgeloof n

superstitious, bijge'lovig

supervise, toezicht hebben op; survei'lleren

supervision, toezicht n

supper, (avond)eten n, avond- maal n, sou'per n

supplant, ver'dringen

supple, soepel, buigzaam

supplement, supple'ment *n*: aan-vullen
supplementary, aanvullend
suppliant, smekend: smekeling
supplication, smeekbede
supply, voorraad; voor'ziening: ver'schaffen; vol'doen(aan)
support, steun: (onder')steunen; onder'houden; staven
supporter, aanhanger, sup'porter
suppose, veronder'stellen
  I am not supposed to, ik mag (eigenlijk) niet
supposed, ver'meend; aan-genomen
supposing (that), stel dat
supposition, veronder'stelling
suppress, onder'drukken; ver'-bieden
. **supremacy**, oppermacht
supreme, opper-, uiterste
surcharge, toeslag
sure, zeker
  to make sure, contro'leren
surely, (toch) zeker
surety, borg
surf, branding
surface, oppervlak(te) (*n*), vlak *n*
surfeit, overdaad
surge, opwelling: golven, stor-ten; stuwen; zwellen
surgeon, chi'rurg
surgery, chirur'gie; spreekkamer
surly, nors
surmise, ver'moeden (*n*)
surmount, be'kronen; over'-winnen
surname, achternaam
surpass, over'treffen
surplice, koorhemd *n*
surplus, overschot *n*: over-('tollig)
surprise, ver'rassing, ver'bazing: ver'rassen; ver'wonderen, ver'-bazen
surprising, ver'wonderlijk, ver'-bazend
surrender, overgave: (zich) overgeven
surround, om'ringen, om'sing-elen
surroundings, om'geving
surveillance, toezicht *n*

survey, in'spectie; overzicht *n*; opmeting: inspec'teren; over'zien; opmeten
surveyor, ex'pert; opzichter; landmeter
survival, leven *n*, voortbestaan *n*; overblijfsel *n*
survive, over'leven; blijven be'staan
survivor, over'levende
susceptible, vatbaar, ge'voelig (voor)
suspect, ver'dacht(e): ver'moed-en; ver'denken
suspend, staken; schorsen; op-schorten
  to be suspended, hangen
suspenders, sokophouders; jar-re'telles
suspense, spanning
suspicion, ver'moeden *n*; achter-docht; ver'denking; schijntje *n*
suspicious, ver'dacht; achter'-dochtig
sustain, staande houden; voed-en; schragen; lijden
sustenance, voedsel *n*; onder-houd *n*
swab, zwabber(en): prop
swagger, zeilen; opscheppen
swallow, zwaluw: (door *or* in)slikken, ver'zwelgen
swamp, moe'ras *n*: over'spoelen; over'stelpen
swampy, moe'rassig
swan, zwaan
swank, opsnijde'rij: opsnijden
swap, (ver')ruilen
swarm, zwerm(en): wemelen
swarthy, donker
sway, heerschap'pij: schommelen ervan afbrengen
swear, zweren; vloeken
sweat, zweet *n*: zweten
sweater, trui
Swedish, Zweeds (*n*)
sweep, zwaai; schoorsteen-veger: (op)vegen; voeren; schrijden
sweeping, wijds; ver'strekkend
sweet, zoet; lief; fris: snoepje *n*; toespijs
sweeten, suiker doen in

sweetheart, liefje *n*, vrijer
swell, deining: (aan *or* op)zwellen; toenemen
swelling, zwelling, ver'dikking
swerve, zwenken
swift, snel: gierzwaluw
swill, draf: (uit)spoelen
swim, zwemmen; duizelen
swindle, oplichte'rij: oplichten
swine, zwijn(en) *n*
swing, zwaai(en); schommel; animo; swing: slingeren
swirl, (doen) warrelen
swish, ge'ruis *n*: ruisen
Swiss, Zwitser(s)
switch, schakelaar, wissel; teen: schakelen; overplaatsen
swoon, flauwte: be'zwijmen
swoop, zich storten
sword, zwaard *n*
syllable, lettergreep
symbol, sym'bool *n*
symbolic(al), sym'bolisch
symbolize, symboli'seren
symmetrical, sym'metrisch
symmetry, symme'trie
sympathetic, vol medeleven; wel'willend
sympathize, meevoelen
sympathy, sympa'thie
symphony, symfo'nie
symptom, symp'toom *n*
synagogue, syna'goge
synchronize, (doen) samenvallen; ge'lijkzetten
syncopate, synco'peren
syndicate, syndi'caat *n*
synod, sy'node
synonym(ous), syno'niem (*n*)
synopsis, sy'nopsis
syntax, syn'taxis
synthesis, syn'these
synthetic, syn'thetisch
syringe, spuit(je *n*): uitspuiten
syrup, stroop, si'roop
system, sys'teem *n*; stelsel *n*, net *n*; lichaam *n*
systematic, syste'matisch

T

tab, label; lus
table, tafel; ta'bel

table-spoon, eetlepel
tablet, ta'blet(je) *n*; ge'denkplaat
taboo, ta'boe (ver'klaren)
tabulate, classifi'ceren
tacit, stil'zwijgend
taciturn, zwijgzaam
tack, kopspijker; spoor *n*: rijgen; toevoegen; la'veren
tackle, tuig *n*; takel: aanpakken; tekkelen
tact(ful), tact(vol)
tactical, tac'tisch
tactics, tac'tiek
tactless, tactloos
taffeta, tafzij
tag, eti'ketje *n*; eindje *n*, bandje *n*
  to tag on to, zich aansluiten bij
tail, staart; pand: achter-
tailor, kleermaker
taint, smet: be'derven
take, (aan, in, mee *or* op)nemen; brengen; kosten
  to take down, opschrijven
  to take for, houden voor
  to take in, herbergen; innemen; in zich opnemen; beetnemen
  to take off, uittrekken; opstijgen: naäpen
  to take on, aannemen; op zich nemen
  taken aback, van zijn stuk ge'bracht
takings, ont'vangsten
talc(um), talk
tale, ver'haal *n*; praatje *n*
talent(ed), ta'lent(vol) (*n*)
talk, ge'sprek *n*; cause'rie; sprake; be'spreking: praten, spreken
  to talk over, be'spreken, be'praten
talkative, praatziek
tall, lang, hoog
tallow, talk
tally, eti'ket *n*: kloppen
talon, klauw
tame, tam: temmen
tamper with, knoeien met
tan, (geel)bruin: tanen; bruinen
tang, scherpe smaak
tangerine, manda'rijn

tangible, tastbaar

tangle, knoop, war: in de war raken (*or* maken)

tank, tank, bak

tankard, drinkkan

tannin, looizuur *n*

tantalize, tantali'seren

tantamount: to be — to, neerkomen op

tantrum, driftbui

tap, kraan: tik(ken), kloppen: (af)tappen

tape, band *n*

taper, waspit: taps toelopen

tapestry, tapisse'rie; wandtapijt *n*

tapioca, tapi'oca

tar, teer; pikbroek: teren

tardy, traag

target, schietschijf; mikpunt *n*, doel *n*

tariff, ta'rief *n*

tarnish, be'slaan, aantasten; be'zoedelen

tarpaulin, zeil(doek) *n*

tarry, (ver')toeven

tart, taart: slet; wrang

tartar, wijnsteen: driftkop: Tar'taar

task, taak

tassel, kwast(je *n*)

taste, smaak(je *n*), proefje *n*: proeven, smaken (naar)

tasteful, smaakvol

tasteless, smakeloos

tasty, smakelijk

tattered, haveloos

tatters, flarden

tattoo, taptoe: schouw(spel *n*): tatoe'ëren

taunt, schimpscheut: schimpen op

taut, strak

tavern, herberg

tawdry, op'zichtig, prullig

tawny, vaalgeel

tax, be'lasting: veel vergen van; be'schuldigen

to be taxed, be'lasting be'talen, onder'hevig zijn aan be'lasting

taxation, be'lasting

taxi, taxi(ën)

tea, thee

teach, onder'wijzen, les geven, leren

teacher, onder'wijzer('es), leraar, lera'res

teaching, onderwijs *n*, leer

team, elftal *n*; ploeg; span *n*

teamwork, samenspel *n*, samenwerking

tea-pot, theepot

tear, traan: scheur(en); vliegen

tease, plagen

teat, tepel; speen

technical, technisch, ambachts-

technicalities, tech'niek; formali'teiten

technically, technisch; strikt ge'nomen

technician, technicus

technique, tech'niek

tedious, ver'velend

teem, wemelen (van)

teetotaller, ge'heelonthouder

telegram, tele'gram *n*

telegraph, tele'graaf: tele-gra'feren

telephone, tele'foon: telefo'neren

telephone-box, tele'fooncel

telescope, teles'coop: in el'kaar schuiven

television, tele'visie

tell, (het) ver'tellen, (het) zeggen; onder'scheiden

telling, raak

temper, aard, hu'meur *n*; drift(bui); hardheid: ver'zachten; harden

temperament, aard; tempera'ment *n*

temperamental, tempera'mentvol, vol kuren

temperance, matigheid; ont'houding

temperate, ge'matigd, matig

temperature, tempera'tuur; ver'hoging

tempest, hevige storm

tempestuous, stormachtig, on'stuimig

temple, tempel: slaap

temporal, tijdelijk; wereldlijk

temporary, tijdelijk, voor'lopig

tempt, ver'leiden; lokken

temptation, ver'leiding; aan-vechting

tempting, ver'leidelijk

ten, tien

tenable, ver'dedigbaar

tenacious, vast'houdend; hard'nekkig

tenant, huurder, pachter

tend, ge'neigd zijn; lopen; over-hellen; (licht) kunnen: passen op

tendency, neiging

tender, mals; te(d)er; ge'voelig: of'ferte; be'taalmiddel *n*: ten-der: aanbieden

tendon, pees

tendril, rank

tenement, e'tagewoning

tenet, leerstuk *n*

tennis(-court), tennis(baan) (*n*)

tenor, te'nor; loop; strekking

tense, strak; ge'spannen, span-nend: tijd

tension, spanning

tent, tent

tentacle, voelhoorn; vangarm

tentative, bij wijze van proef-ballon

tenterhooks: on —, op hete kolen

tenth, tiende

tenuous, ijl, schraal

tenure, be'zit *n*; tijd

tepid, lauw

term, term('ijn); kwar'taal *n*: noemen

terms, be'woording(en); con'-dities; voet

terminal, eind('standig): pool-(klem)

terminate, (be')eindigen, af-lopen; opzeggen

terminology, terminolo'gie

terminus, eindstation(*or* punt) *n*

terrace, ter'ras *n*; huizenrij

terrestrial, aard-; land-

terrible, vreselijk, ver'schrik-kelijk

terrier, terrier

terrific, ge'weldig

terrify, schrik aanjagen

to be terrified, in doodsangst ver'keren, zich doodschrikken

territorial, territori'aal

territory, (grond)gebied *n*

terror, schrik, angst

terse, kort en bondig

test, proef(werk *n*), e'xamen *n*; be'proeving: testen, exami'-neren; op de proef stellen

testament, testa'ment *n*

testify, ge'tuigen (van); onder ede ver'klaren

testimonial, ge'tuigschrift *n*, ver'klaring

testimony, ge'tuigenis *n*

text, tekst

text-book, leerboek *n*

textile, tex'tiel

texture, weefsel *n*; samenstel *n*, bouw

than, dan

thank, (be')danken

thanks, be'dankt: dank

thankful, dankbaar

thankless, on'dankbaar

thanksgiving, dankzegging

that, dat; die; wat; daar-

thatch(ed roof), riet(en dak) *n*

thaw, dooi(en); (doen) ont'-dooien

the, de, het

the . . . the, hoe . . . hoe

theatre, schouwburg; to'neel *n*; ter'rein *n*; zaal

theatrical, to'neel-; thea'traal

thee, U

theft, diefstal

their, hun

theirs, (die *or* dat) van hun

them, hen, ze

theme, onderwerp *n*; thema *n*

themselves, zich(zelf), zelf

then, toen('malig); dan; boven'dien

by then, tegen die tijd

but then, maar . . . (dan ook)

then and there, on'middel-lijk

thence, van'daar; daaruit

theologian, theo'loog

theological, theo'logisch

theology, godge'leerdheid

theoretical, theo'retisch

theory, theo'rie

there, daar('heen); er

thereabouts, daar in de buurt; daarom'trent

therefore, daarom

thermometer, thermometer

these, deze; hier-

thesis, stelling; disser'tatie

they, zij

thick, dik; dicht

thicken, dikker worden; binden

thicket, struikgewas *n*

thickness, dikte; laag

thick-set, ge'drongen

thick-skinned, dik'huidig

thief, dief

thieve, stelen

thigh, dij

thimble, vingerhoed; dopmoer

thin, dun; mager; ijl: ver'dunnen

thine, de (*or* het) Uwe: Uw

thing, ding *n*
  a thing, iets
  the thing that, wat
  things, spullen; (de) dingen

think, denken (aan *or* over); nadenken; ge'loven; een i'dee hebben; vinden

thinnish, vrij dun

third, derde: terts

thirdly, ten derde

thirst, dorst(en); zucht (naar)

thirsty: to be —, dorst hebben; dorstig zijn

thirteen (th), dertien (de)

thirty, dertig

this, deze, dit; hier-

thistle, distel

thither, derwaarts

thong, riem

thorn, doorn

thorny, doornig; netelig

thorough, grondig; echt

those, die; de'genen; er; daarthou, gij

though, hoe'wel; al (. . . ook); (ja) maar, (en) toch
  as though, als'of

thought, i'dee *n*, ge'dachte; (na)denken *n*; at'tentie

thoughtful, in ge'dachten ver'zonken; at'tent

thoughtless, onbe'zonnen; onat'tent

thousand, duizend

thrash, afranselen; woelen

thread, garen *n*; draad: de draad steken door; zich (een weg) banen

threadbare, kaal; afgezaagd

threat, be'dreiging

threaten, dreigen met; be'dreigen

three, drie

thresh, dorsen

threshold, drempel

thrice, driemaal

thrift, zuinigheid

thrifty, spaarzaam

thrill, sen'satie: aangrijpen; ver'rukken

thrilling, aan'grijpend; (erg) op'windend

thrive, ge'dijen; bloeien

throat, keel

throb, bonzen, kloppen

throne, troon

throng, ge'drang *n*: (zich ver')dringen (op)

throttle, smoorklep: smoren

through, door('heen): doorgaand

throughout, door heel
  throughout the day, de hele dag door

throw, worp: werpen; (toe *or* af)gooien; gooien met

thrush, zanglijster

thrust, stoot, steek: stoten, steken; werpen

thud, plof

thug, ban'diet

thumb, duim: be'duimelen

thump, bons; stomp(en); bonken (op), bonzen (op)

thunder, donder(en (*n*)), onweer *n*

thunderbolt, dondersteen; bliksemstraal

thundercloud, onweerswolk

thunderous, daverend

thunder-storm, onweer(sbui) (*n*)

Thursday, donderdag

thus, (al')dus; zo

thwart, doft; dwarsbomen, ver'ijdelen

thy, Uw

tick, tik(ken); streepje *n*; ogenblikje *n*: teek: tijk: aftekenen

ticket, kaartje *n*

tickle, kietelen; jeuken; amu'seren

ticklish, kietelig; netelig

tidal, ge'tij-, vloed-

tide, ge'tij *n*. stroom: helpen

tidings, nieuws *n*

tidy, net(jes); flink: opruimen

tie, das; band; onbesliste wedstrijd: (vast)binden; strikken, knopen; ge'lijkstaan, ge'lijk aankomen

tier, rang, ver'dieping

tiger, tijger

tight, vast; dicht op el'kaar; strak; kachel

tighten, strakker aanhalen; ver'scherpen

tile, tegel; dakpan:· be'tegelen

till, tot(dat): geldlade: be'ploegen

 up till, tot (aan)

 not . . . till, pas

tilt, overhellen; kantelen; schuinhouden(*or* zetten)

 full tilt, met volle vaart

timber, timmerhout *n*; balk

time, (de) tijd; keer; ge'legenheid; maat, tempo *n*: de tijd opnemen van; uitrekenen

 at the same time, tege'lijkertijd: desondanks

 for the time being, voor'lopig

 in time, op tijd; op den duur; in de maat

timely, tijdig

timid, timorous, schuchter

tin, tin *n*; blik(ken) (*n*); bus, trommel

tinge, tint(en); tikje *n*

tingle, tintelen

tinker, ketellapper: prutsen

tinkle, tingelen

tinned, in blik

tinsel, klatergoud *n*

tint, tint(en)

tiny, heel klein

tip, punt, top:· (een) fooi (geven); wenk, foefje *n*: optillen, kantelen; storten

tipsy, aangeschoten

tiptoe : on —, op de tenen; in spanning

tire, band: ver'moeien; moe (*or* beu) worden

tired, moe; beu

tireless, onvermoeid

tiresome, ver'velend

tissue, weefsel *n*: vloei-

tit, mees

titbit, lekker hapje *n*

tithe, tiende

title, titel; aanspraak (op): be'titelen

titled, adellijk

titter, giechelen

to, naar; tot (aan); (om) te; in; aan: dicht

 to and fro, heen en weer

toad, pad

toadstool, paddestoel

toast, ge'roosterd brood *n*; toost: roosteren: drinken op

tobacco, ta'bak

tobacconist, si'garenhandelaar

toboggan, slee(ën)

today, van'daag; tegen'woordig

toddle, dribbelen

toe, teen

toffee, toffee

together, samen; tege'lijk

toil, arbeid: strik: zwoegen; zich slepen

toilet, toi'let *n*

token, (ken)teken *n*

tolerable, draaglijk; redelijk

tolerance, ver'draagzaamheid

tolerant, ver'draagzaam

tolerate, dulden

toll, tol: luiden

tomato, to'maat

tomb, graftombe

tombstone, grafsteen

tome, zwaar boekdeel *n*

tomorrow, morgen

tom-tom, tam'tam

ton, ton

tone, toon, klank; tint: harmoni'ëren

tongs, tang

tongue, tong; taal; klepel

tonic, ver'sterkend middel *n*

tonight, van'avond, van'nacht

tonnage, tonnenmaat
tonsil, a'mandel
too, ook (nog); (al) te
tool, ge'reedschap *n*, werktuig *n*
toot, ge'toeter *n*: toeteren
tooth, tand, kies
toothache, kiespijn
toothbrush, tandenborstel
tooth-paste, tandpasta
toothpick, tandestoker
top, top: tol: bovenste, bovenaan
topic, onderwerp *n*
topical, actu'eel
topography, topogra'fie
topple, tuimelen
topsy-turvy, op zijn kop
torch, zaklantaren; fakkel
torment, foltering: kwellen
tornado, wervelstorm
torpedo, tor'pedo: to.pe'deren
torrent, (berg)stroom; stortvloed
torrential, stort-
torrid, heet
torso, torso, romp
tortoise, schildpad
tortuous, kronkelend; draaiend
torture, foltering; kwelling: folteren; kwellen
toss, toss: opgooien; slingeren;
de lucht in gooien
tot, peuter; oorlam *n*
total, to'taal (*n*): be'dragen
totally, vol'komen
totter, wankelen
touch, aanraking; con'tact *n*;
tikje *n*; trekje *n*; aanslag:
(aan)raken; el'kaar raken;
(aan)roeren
touching, roerend
tough, taai; zuur; hard;
moeilijk: ruwe klant
tour, (rond)reis; rondtoer; (op)
tour'nee (zijn); (af)reizen
tourist, toe'rist
tournament, toer'nooi *n*
tourniquet, drukverband *n*
tousle, ver'fomfaaien
tow, sleeptouw *n*: slepen
toward(s), naar ... toe, in de
richting van; jegens; tegen
towel, handdoek

tower, toren: zich torenhoog
ver'heffen
town, stad
townhall, stad'huis *n*
toxic, ver'giftig
toy, (stuk) speelgoed *n*; speelbal:
spelen
trace, spoor *n*; tikje *n*: opsporen, vinden: overtrekken,
schetsen
tracery, tra'ceerwerk *n*
track, spoor *n*; pad *n*; baan:
opsporen
tract, uitge'strektheid, streek:
trak'taatje *n*
tractor, tractor
trade, handel(en); vak *n*; zaken:
handeldrijven
trade-mark, handelsmerk *n*
trader, handelaar; handels-
vaartuig *n*
tradesman, leveran'cier
trades-union, vakvereniging
tradition, tra'ditie
traditional, traditio'neel
traffic, ver'keer *n*; handel(en)
tragedy, treurspel *n*; trage'die
tragic, treurspel-; tragisch
trail, spoor *n*; nasleep; pad *n*:
(laten) slepen; kruipen; opsporen;
to trail off (*or* away), wegsterven
trailer, kruipplant; aanhangwagen
train, trein; sleep; ge'volg *n*;
reeks: opleiden; trainen:
(af)richten
trainer, trainer
training, opleiding; training
trait, trek
traitor(ous), ver'rader(lijk)
tram, tram
tramp, landloper; wilde boot;
wandeling: sjouwen; lopen;
trappen
trample, trappen
trance, trance; geestvervoering
tranquil, rustig
tranquillity, rust
transact, doen, sluiten
transaction, trans'actie; ver'-
richten *n*

transcend, te boven gaan
transcribe, overbrengen
transfer, overplaatsing; overdruk : overdragen, overbrengen,
over(*or* ver¹)plaatsen
transfigure, een andere ge¹-
daante geven
transfix, door¹steken: aan de
grond nagelen
transform, (ge¹heel) ver¹-
anderen ; transfor¹meren
transgress, over¹treden; te
buiten gaan
transient, kort¹stondig
transit : in —, onder¹weg
transition(al), overgang(s-)
transitory, ver¹gankelijk
translate, ver¹talen; omzetten
translation, ver¹taling
translucent, door¹schijnend
transmission, trans¹missie;
overbrengen *n*; gangwissel
transmit, overbrengen; uitzenden
transparent, door¹zichtig
transpire, blijken; zich voordoen
transplant, ver¹planten
transport, ver¹voer *n*, trans¹port
n : ver¹voeren
transpose, ver¹wisselen; trans-
po¹neren
transverse, dwars
trap, val(strik), hinderlaag;
sjees: in de val laten lopen;
opsluiten
trap-door, valluik *n*
trappings, sja¹brak; opschik
trash, prullen, prul¹laria
travail, barensnood
travel, reizen (*n*): zich voortplanten
traveller, reiziger
traverse, dwars: doortrekken
travesty, traves¹tie; aanfluiting
trawler, treiler
tray, blad *n*; bak
treacherous, ver¹raderlijk; vals
treachery, ver¹raad *n*
tread, tred(en); loopvlak *n*:
be¹treden; trappen
treason, landverraad *n*
treasure, schat(ten); ju¹weel *n*:

hoogschatten; angst¹vallig
be¹waren
treasurer, penningmeester
treasury, schatkist; minis¹terie
van fi¹nanciën *n*
treat, trak¹tatie, feestje *n*:
be¹handelen; trak¹teren
treatise, ver¹handeling
treatment, be¹handeling
treaty, ver¹drag *n*
treble, drie¹voudig: so¹praan:
verdrie¹voudigen
tree, boom; leest
trek, trek(ken)
trellis, latwerk *n*
tremble, beven
tremendous, e¹norm
tremor, trilling
trench, loopgraaf; voor
trenchant, snijdend; krachtig
trend, neiging; loop, richting
trepidation, schroom, beven *n*
trespass, op ver¹boden ter¹rein
zijn (*or* komen); be¹slag leggen
tress, lok
trestle, schraag
trial, ver¹hoor *n*; proef(neming);
be¹proeving; lastpost
triangle, driehoek; tri¹angel
triangular, drie¹hoekig
tribe, stam
tribulation, be¹proeving
tribunal, rechtbank; tribu¹naal
n
tributary, zijrivier; bij-
tribute, hulde(blijk *n*); schatting
trice, wip: trijsen, sjorren
trick, truc; kunstje *n*; streek;
slag: be¹driegen
trickle, straaltje *n*: sijpelen,
biggelen; druppelen
tricky, lastig, netelig
tricycle, driewieler
trifle, kleinigheid; klein beetje *n*;
fruit en cake met custard en
room: spotten
trifling, onbe¹duidend
trigger, trekker
trill, triller: trillend zingen
trim, net(jes): con¹ditie: bijwerken, bijknippen; gar¹neren

trimming, gar'nering, ver'siering
Trinity, Drie'ëenheid
trinket, kleinood *n*
trip, tocht(je *n*): (doen) struikelen; trippelen
to trip up, struikelen; zich in de
vingers snijden
tripe, pens
triple, drie'delig; drie'dubbel
tripod, drievoet
trite, afgezaagd
triumph, tri'omf: zegevieren
triumphal, tri'omf-
triumphant, zegevierend, triom'-
fantelijk
trivet, treeftje *n*
trivial, onbe'duidend
trolley, trolley; rolwagen(tje *n*),
ser'veerboy
trombone, trom'bone
troop, troep; pelo'ton *n*: zich
scharen; allen (tege'lijk) gaan
trooper, cavale'rist
trophy, zegeteken *n*
tropics, tropen
tropical, tropisch
trot, draf: draven
trouble, zorg; moeite (nemen):
hinderen; lastig vallen
troublesome, lastig
troublous, veelbewogen
trough, trog; dal *n*
troupe, troep
trousers, broek
trousseau, uitzet
trout, fo'rel(len)
trowel, troffel; schopje *n*
truant: to play —, spijbelen
truce, wapenstilstand
truck, vrachtauto; (goederen)-
wagen
trudge, sjokken
true, waar; echt; (ge')trouw;
zuiver
truism, afgezaagde waarheid
truly, heus
trump, troef: troeven
to trump up, ver'zinnen
trumpet, trom'pet(ten)
truncheon, stok
trundle, rollen
trunk, stam, romp; hutkoffer;
slurf: interlo'kaal

truss, bundel, spant: (vast)bin-
den
trust, ver'trouwen (op) (*n*);
be'waring; trust: hopen
trustee, execu'teur; gevol'-
machtigde
trustful, goed van ver'trouwen
trustworthy, be'trouwbaar
trusty, trouw
truth, waarheid
truthful, eerlijk
try, poging: pro'beren; be'-
proeven; op de proef stellen;
ver'horen
trying, moeilijk
tub, kuip, ton
tube, buis, slang; (binnen)band;
tube; onder'grondse
tuber, knol
tuberculosis, tubercu'lose
tuck, plooi: stoppen
Tuesday, dinsdag
tuft, bosje *n*
tug, ruk(ken); sleepboot: trekken
tuition, onderwijs *n*
tulip, tulp
tumble, tuimelen
tumbledown, bouw'vallig
tumbler, (limo'nade)glas *n*
tumor, tumor
tumult, tumult *n*
tumultuous, on'stuimig, ru'-
moerig; stormachtig
tune, wijsje *n*, melo'die: stemmen
tuneful, wcl'luidcnd
tunic, overgooier; tu'niek
tunnel, tunnel (maken)
turban, tulband
turbid, troebel
turbine, tur'bine
turbulent, woelig
turf, zode(n), gras *n*; rensport
turkey, kal'koen: Tur'kije *n*
turmoil, be'roering
turn, draai; bocht; ommekeer;
beurt; dienst; kunstje *n*:
(om)draaien; omslaan; om-
keren; worden; ver'anderen;
omzetten; wenden
to turn down, om'vouwen;
afwijzen

to turn out, uitdraaien; aantreden, opstaan; (er) uitzetten; produ'ceren; aflopen; blijken
to turn over, omslaan; (zich) omkeren; overdragen; over'denken
to turn to, overgaan op; zich wenden tot; aanpakken
to turn up, omslaan, optrekken; opdraaien; ver'schijnen
turnip, knol
turnover, omzet
turnpike, tolhek *n*
turpentine, terpen'tijn
turquoise, tur'koois
turret, torentje *n*; ge'schuttoren
turtle, zeeschildpad
tusk, slagtand
tussle, worsteling: worstelen
tut tut, nou nou
tutor, huisonderwijzer; pri'vé-leraar
twaddle, ge'wauwel *n* : wauwelen
twang, ping : tingelen
tweed, tweed
tweezers, pin'cet *n*
twelve, twaalf
twenty, twintig
twice, tweemaal
twiddle, draaien
twig, twijgje *n*
twilight, schemering
twin, tweeling
twine, twijn(en) : zich slingeren
twinge, steek
twinkle, fonkelen
twirl, (rond)draaien
twist, kromming; (ver')draaien; zich slingeren; ver'trekken
twitch, zenuwtrekking: trekken
twitter, tjilpen
two, twee
twofold, twee'voudig
type, type *n*; letter(type *n*): tikken
typewriter, schrijfmachine
typhoid, tyfus
typhoon, ty'foon
typical, typisch
typify, ty'peren
tyrannical, tiran'niek
tyranny, tiran'nie
tyrant, ti'ran

U

ubiquitous, alomheersend
udder, uier
ugly, lelijk
ulcer, zweer
ulterior, heimelijk, bij-
ultimate, laatste; uit'eindelijk; essen'tieel, grond-
ultimatum, ulti'matum *n*
ultra-violet, ultravio'let
umbrella, para'plu; tuinparasol
umpire, scheidsrechter
un-, on-
unable, niet in staat
unaccompanied, zonder bege'leiding; a-ca'pella
unaccountable, onver'klaarbaar
unaccustomed, niet ge'wend
unanimous, een'stemmig, eensge'zind
unassuming, be'scheiden
unattended, onbe'heerd
unauthorized, onbe'voegd
unavailing, ver'geefs
unavoidable, onver'mijdelijk
unaware, niet be'wust
unawares, onbe'wust; onver'hoeds
unbearable, on'draaglijk
unbelievable, onge'looflijk
unbound, niet ge'bonden
unbroken, onver'broken; on'afgebroken
unbutton, losknopen
uncalled-for, onge'vraagd; mis'plaatst
uncanny, griezelig, onge'looflijk, geheim'zinnig
uncertain, on'zeker
unchecked, onbe'lemmerd
uncle, oom
uncommon, onge'woon
uncompromising, on'buigzaam rotsvast
unconcerned, onver'schillig; onbe'kommerd
unconditional, onvoor'waardelijk
unconquerable, onover'winnelijk
unconscious, be'wusteloos; onbe'wust

uncontrollable, onbe'dwingbaar, onbe'daarlijk
uncork, ont'kurken
uncouth, lomp
uncover, ont'bloten; aan het licht brengen
unction, zalving, oliesel *n*
unctuous, zalvend
undaunted, onver'saagd
undecided, onbe'slist; in dubio
undeniable, ontegen'zeglijk, onbe'twistbaar
under, onder(-)
undercurrent, onderstroom; ver'borgen stroming
underdone, on'gaar
undergraduate, stu'dent
underground, onder de grond; onder'gronds(e)
undergrowth, kreupelhout *n*
underhand, onder'hands
underlying, grond-,
undermine, onder'mijnen
underneath, onder, be'neden: onderkant
understand, be'grijpen; horen; aannemen
understanding, be'grip *n*; ver'-standhouding: sympa'thiek
undertake, onder'nemen; op zich nemen
undertaker, be'grafenisonder-nemer
undertaking, onder'neming; be'-lofte
undertone, ge'dempte stem; grondkleur; ondergrond
underwear, ondergoed *n*
undesirable, onge'wenst
undo, los(*or* open)maken; onge'-daan maken
undoing, ondergang
undoubtedly, onge'twijfeld
undress, (zich) uitkleden
undue, over'matig
undulate, golven
unearth, opgraven; aan het licht brengen
unearthly, boven'aards; on'-mogelijk
uneasy, onge'rust, on'rustig
uneducated, onont'wikkeld
unemployed, werkloos

unemployment, werk'loosheid
unending, eindeloos
unequal, onge'lijk; niet opge-wassen (tegen)
unerring, on'feilbaar
uneven, on'effen; onge'lijk; on'-even
uneventful, onbe'wogen
unexpected(ly), onver'wacht(s), onvoor'zien
unfailing, nimmer falend; onuit'puttelijk; zeker
unfamiliar, onbe'kend; niet op de hoogte
unfasten, los(*or* open)maken
unfathomable, ondoor'gron-delijk
unfeeling, onge'voelig
unfetter, ont'ketenen
unfinished, onvol'tooid
unfit, onge'schikt
unfold, ont'vouwen, (zich) ont'-plooien
unforgettable, onver'getelijk
unforgivable, onver'geeflijk
unfortunately, jammer ge'noeg, he'laas
unfounded, onge'grond
unfurl, (zich) ont'plooien
ungainly, lomp, onbe'vallig
ungodly, goddeloos
ungovernable, on'tembaar
ungracious, on'hoffelijk
unhappiness, ver'driet *n*
unharmed, onge'deerd, onbe'-schadigd
unheard-of, onge'kend; onge'-hoord
unheeded, on'opgemerkt; onge'-merkt, ver'waarloosd
unholy, goddeloos; heidens
unicorn, eenhoorn
uniform, ge'lijk('matig): uni'-form
unify, ver'enigen
unimaginative, zonder fanta'sie
unimpaired, on'aangetast
uninformed, niet op de hoogte, on'wetend
uninhabitable, onbe'woonbaar
unintelligent, dom
unintelligible, onver'staanbaar, onbe'grijpelijk

uninvited, onge'nood

union, ver'eniging, unie; ver'-
bintenis

unique, u'niek

unison : in —, een'stemmig;
tege'lijk

unit, eenheid; afdeling

unite, (zich) ver'enigen

unity, eenheid; eensge'zindheid

universal, univer'seel; alge'-
meen

universe, heel'al n

university, universi'teit

unkempt, onver'zorgd

unkind, on'aardig

unknown, onbe'kend(e n)

unless, ten'zij

unlike, ver'schillend, anders dan
it is unlike him to forget, het
is niets voor hem het te ver'-
geten

unload, ont'laden, lossen

unlock, ont'sluiten

unmanageable, on'handelbaar

unmask, (zich) demas'keren;
ont'maskeren

unmistakable, onmis'kenbaar

unmitigated, onver'minderd;
onver'valst

unnerve, ont'zenuwen

unobtrusive, be'scheiden

unoccupied, onbe'zet; onbe'-
woond; niet bezig

unofficial, niet offi'cieel

unopposed, onbe'streden; zonder tegencandidaat

unpack, uitpakken

unpalatable, on'smakelijk; on'-
aangenaam

unparalleled, weergaloos

unpardonable, onver'geeflijk

unpleasant, on'aangenaam

unprecedented, onge'hoord

unpredictable, onbe'rekenbaar

unprincipled, ge'wetenloos

unprofitable, on'vruchtbaar

unquestionable, onbe'twistbaar

unquestionably, onge'twijfeld

unravel, ont'warren

unreasoned, onberede'neerd

unremitting, onver'droten

unreservedly, zonder voorbehoud

unrestrained, onbe'teugeld; onge'dwongen

unrivalled, ongeëve'naard

unruly, on'ordelijk, on'handelbaar

unsavoury, smakeloos; on'-
smakelijk; onver'kwikkelijk

unscathed, onge'deerd

unscrew, losschroeven

unscrupulous, ge'wetenloos

unselfish, onbaat'zuchtig

unsettled, on'zeker

unsightly, on'ooglijk

unsparing, kwistig, mild; mee'-
dogenloos

unspeakable, onbe'schrijf(e)lijk

unsuccessful, ver'geefs
to be unsuccessful, geen suc'-
ces hebben

unsuspicious, argeloos

untangle, ont'warren

untenable, on'houdbaar

unthinkable, on'denkbaar

untidy, slordig, wan'ordelijk

untie, losmaken

until, tot (dat)

untimely, on'tijdig; onge'legen

untiring, onver'moeid

unto, tot (aan)

untold, onver'teld; on'telbaar

untoward, on'gunstig

unused, onge'bruikt; niet ge'-
wend (aan)

unusual, onge'woon, onge'bruikelijk

unutterable, onuit'sprekelijk

unvaried, unvarying, onver'-
anderlijk

unveil, ont'hullen; ont'sluieren

unwarranted, ongerecht'vaardigd

unwavering, stand'vastig

unwieldy, log

unwind, afwinden; (zich) ont'-
rollen

unwittingly, onop'zettelijk, onbe'wust

unwonted, onge'woon

unwrap, uitpakken

unyielding, onver'zettelijk

up, (verder) op; (naar) boven;
om'hoog; over'eind: ver'-
streken

to be up to, in staat zijn; in de zin hebben, uitvoeren; zijn aan

upbraid, be'rispen

upbringing, opvoeding

upheaval, opschudding

uphill, de heuvel op, opwaarts; zwaar

uphold, hooghouden; steunen

upholstery, be'kleding

upkeep, onderhoud *n*

uplift, ver'heffen

upon, op

upper, boven(ste): bovenleer *n*

uppermost, hoogst; bovenst; op de voorgrond

upright, recht'op; op'recht

uprising, opstand

uproar, tu'mult *n*

uproarious, ru'moerig; storm- achtig

uproot, ont'wortelen; uitroeien

upset, om'verwerpen; in de war sturen; van streek maken

upshot, resul'taat *n*

upside down, onderste'boven

upstairs, (naar) boven

upstart, parve'nu(achtig); poen(ig)

upstream, stroom'opwaarts

up-to-date, mo'dern; op de hoogte

upturn, om'vergooien; opzetten

upward(s), opwaarts, naar boven; (en) hoger, (en) ouder

uranium, u'ranium *n*

urban, stedelijk, stads-, steeds

urbane, wel'levend

urchin, kwa'jongen

urge, (aan)drang: aanzetten; aandringen (op)

urgent, dringend

urn, urn

us, ons

usable, bruikbaar

usage, ge'bruik *n*; be'handeling

use, ge'bruik(en) *(n)*; toepas- sing; nut *n*: ver'bruiken

to be used to, ge'wend zijn (aan)

it used to be, het was vroeger

useful, nuttig, handig

useless, nutteloos

usher, ou'vreuse, plaatsaan- wijzer: leiden

usual, ge'bruikelijk, ge'woon

as usual, zoals ge'woonlijk

usually, ge'woonlijk

usurp, usur'peren

utensils, ge'rei

utility, nut(tigheids-) *(n)*

utilize, be'nutten

utmost, uiterste *(n)*, hoogste *(n)*

utter, vol'slagen: uiten

utterance, uiting; uitspraak

uttermost, uiterst

V

vacancy, vaca'ture, leemte

vacant, va'cant; onbe'woond; wezenloos

vacate, ont'ruimen

vacation, va'cantie

vaccinate, inenten

vaccine, lucht'ledig *n*

vacillate, weifelen

vacuum, lucht'ledig *n*

vacuum-cleaner, stofzuiger

vagabond, vagebond

vagary, gril

vagrant, ronddolend

vague, vaag

vain, ijdel: ver'geefs

in vain, tever'geefs

vale, dal *n*

valet, be'diende

valiant, koen

valid, (rechts')geldig

validity, deugdelijkheid; rechts- geldigheid

valise, va'lies *n*

valley, dal *n*

valour, koenheid

valuable, waardevol; kostbaar- (heid)

valuation, ta'xatie

value, waarde: ta'xeren; op hoge prijs stellen

valve, klep, ven'tiel *n*; lamp

van, (be'stel)wagen: voorhoede

vandalism, vanda'lisme *n*

vane, vaantje *n*; wiek, schoep

vanguard, voorhoede

vanilla, va'nille

vanish, (spoorloos) ver'dwijnen; uitsterven

vanity, ijdelheid

vanquish, over'winnen
vantage, voorsprong: gunstig
vapour, damp
variable, ver'anderlijk; ver'stelbaar
variation, afwisseling; ver'andering; vari'atie
variety, ver'scheidenheid, afwisseling; soort: varié'té n
various, ver'scheiden
varnish, ver'nis(sen) (n)
vary, vari'eren
vase, vaas
vassal, va'zal
vast, on'metelijk, kolos'saal
vastly, e'norm
vat, vat n
Vatican, Vati'caan n
vault, ge'welf n kluis: sprong:
springen
veal, kalfsvlees n
veer, draaien; vieren
vegetable, groente(-): plant'-
aardig
vegetarian, vege'tariër: vege'-
tarisch
vegetation, plantengroei
vehement, hevig
vehicle, voertuig n; drager
veil, sluier(en)
vein, ader; neiging, trek; stemming
velocity, snelheid
velvet, flu'weel n: flu'welen
venal, om'koopbaar
vendor, ver'koper
veneer, fi'neer(hout) n; ver'-
nisje n: fi'neren
venerable, eerbied'waardig; eer'-
waard
venerate, diep ver'eren
venereal, ge'slachts-
Venetian blind, jaloe'zie
vengeance, wraak
vengeful, wraak'gierig
venial, ver'geeflijk
venison, wildbraad n
venom(ous), ve'nijn(ig) (n)
vent, opening, luchtgaatje n;
uitweg: luchten
ventilate, venti'leren
ventilation, venti'latie
ventriloquist, buikspreker

venture, waagstuk n: (het)
wagen
venturesome, venturous,
stout'moedig
veracity, waarheid
verb, werkwoord n
verbal, in woorden; mondeling;
werk'woordelijk
verbatim, woordelijk
verbiage, omhaal
verbose, breed'sprakig
verdict, uitspraak; be'slissing
verge, rand: grenzen (aan)
verify, verifi'ëren
veritable, waar
vermilion, vermil'joen (n)
vermin, ongedierte n
vernacular, moedertaal
versatile, veel'zijdig
verse, poë'zie; cou'plet n
versed, be'dreven
version, ver'taling, lezing, be'-
werking
vertibrate, ge'werveld (dier n)
vertical, verti'caal: loodlijn
very, zeer, erg: pre'cies; al'leen
al
vespers, vesper
vessel, vaartuig n; vat n
vest, hemd n; vest n: (be')-
kleden
vestibule, vesti'bule
vestige, spoor n
vestment, (priester)ge'waad n
vestry, sacris'tie
veteran, vete'raan: er'varen
vet(erinary), veearts(e'nij)
veto, veto n: ver'werpen
vex, ergeren
vexation, ergernis
viaduct, via'duct n
vial, flesje n
vibrate, vi'breren
vibration, trilling ·
vicar, dominee, pas'toor
vice, ondeugd: bankschroef:
vice-
viceroy, onderkoning
vice versa, omgekeerd
vicinity, na'bijheid, buurt
vicious, boos'aardig; vici'eus
vicissitude, wissel'valligheid
victim, slachtoffer n

victor, over'winnaar

victorious, zegevierend

victory, over'winning

victual, provi'and innemen, provian'deren

   victuals, levensmiddelen

vie, wedijveren

view, uitzicht *n*, ge'zicht *n*;
mening: be'schouwen

   in view, in het ge'zicht; voor
ogen

   in view of, ge'zien

viewpoint, uitzichtpunt *n*;
ge'zichtspunt *n*

vigil, wacht, waken *n*, wake

vigilance, waakzaamheid

vigorous, krachtig, ener'giek

vigour, kracht, ener'gie

vile, af'schuwelijk

villa, villa

village, dorp *n*

villain, schurk

villainous, laag

vindicate, handhaven, recht'-
vaardigen, zuiveren (van
blaam)

vindictive, wraak'gierig

vine, wijnstok; wingerd

vinegar, a'zijn

vineyard, wijngaard

vintage, jaar *n*; wijnoogst

viola, altviool: vi'ooltje *n*

violate, schenden

violation, schennis

violence, ge'weld *n*

violent, hevig, heftig, geweld'-
dadig

violet, vi'ooltje *n*: vio'let

violin, vi'ool

violinist, vio'list

violoncello, violon'cel

viper, adder

virgin, maagd(elijk); onge'-
rept

virile, man'moedig, krachtig

virtual, eigenlijk

virtually, praktisch

virtue, deugd; ver'dienste

virtuous, deugdzaam

virulent, kwaad'aardig; ve'-
nijnig

visa, visum *n*

viscount, burggraaf

visibility, zicht *n*

visible, zichtbaar

visibly, zienderogen

vision, ge'zicht *n*; vérziende
blik; visi'oen *n*

visionary, dromer(ig); ingebeeld: ziener

visit, be'zoek(en) (*n*)

visitor, be'zoeker, gast

visual, ge'zichts-

vital, essen'tieel; vi'taal; fa'taal

vitality, vitali'teit

vitamin, vita'mine

vitiate, be'derven; on'geldig
maken

vivacious, levendig

vivid, hel(-); levendig

vocabulary, woordenlijst; woordenschat

vocal, stem-, zang-

vocation, roeping; be'roep *n*

vogue, zwang; populari'teit

voice, stem: uiten

void, on'geldig; ont'bloot: leegte

volatile, vluchtig; wispel'turig

volcano, vul'kaan

volley, regen, stroom; volley

volt(age), volt('age)

voluble, woordenrijk

volume, (boek)deel *n*; vo'lume
n, omvang; massa

voluminous, volumi'neus

voluntary, vrij'willig; wille'-
keurig; lief'dadigheids-

volunteer, vrij'williger: vrij'-
willig in dienst treden; aanbieden

voluptuous, wel'lustig; weelderig

vomit, (uit)braken

votary, liefhebber

vote, stem(recht *n*); motie:
stemmen; toestaan

voter, kiezer

vouch, instaan

vow, ge'lofte: plechtig be'-
loven

vowel, klinker

voyage, reis

vulgar, vul'gair, plat

vulgarity, platheid

vulnerable, kwetsbaar

vulture, gier

W

wad, prop; pakje *n*
waddle, waggelen
wade, waden
wafer, wafel; hostie
waft, drijven, zweven
wag, grappenmaker: kwispelen
wage, loon *n*: voeren
wager, weddenschap: wedden
om
wagon, wagen, wa'gon
waif, vondeling
wail, weeklagen; loeien
wainscot(ing), lambri'zering
waist, taille
waistcoat, vest *n*
wait, wachten; dienen
waiter, kelner
waiting-room, wachtkamer
waitress, kelner'in
waive, afstand doen van
wake, kielzog *n*; spoor *n*
  to wake up, wakker worden (*or*
  maken)
walk, wandeling, eind lopen *n*;
  loop; laan; sfeer: lopen, wandelen
  to go for a walk, gaan wandelen
wall, muur, wand, wal
wallet, (zak)porte'feuille
wallow, rollen; slingeren;
  zwelgen
wall-paper, be'hang(selpapier)
  n
walnut, walnoot; notehout(en)
  (*n*)
waltz, wals(en)
wan, bleek; flets
wand, toverstaf
wander, zwerven; dwalen
wane, afnemen (*n*)
wangle, klaarspelen; knoeien
  met
want, be'hoefte; ge'brek *n*,
  nood: willen (hebben); nodig
  hebben, moeten worden
wanton, bal'dadig; wild
war, oorlog: strijden
warble, kwelen
ward, pu'pil; zaal; stadswijk
  to ward off, afweren
warden, direc'teur

warder, ci'pier
wardrobe, klerenkast; garde'-
robe
wardroom, offi'cierskajuit
ware, waar, goed *n*
warehouse, pakhuis *n*
warlike, oorlogs'zuchtig
warm, warm: (ver')warmen
warmth, warmte
warn, waarschuwen
warning, waarschuwing
warp, kromtrekken; ver'-
draaien
warrant, be'vel *n*: waarborgen
warren, (ko'nijnen)berg *n*
warrior, krijgsman
wart, wrat
wartime, oorlogs(tijd)
wary, voor'zichtig
wash, was;ʼ golfslag: (zich)
wassen; spoelen
  to wash up, afwassen
washable, wasbaar
wash-basin, wastafel
washer, wasser; sluitring, leertje
n
washing, was(goed *n*): was-
wasp, wesp
wastage, ver'spilling
waste, ver'spilling: afval(-);
woest(e'nij): ver'spillen;
(weg)kwijnen
  to lay waste, ver'woesten
wasteful, ver'kwistend
wastepaper-basket, prullenmand
watch, wacht; hor'loge *n*: uitkijken; gadeslaan; opletten
watchful, waakzaam
watchman, waker
water, water (geven) (*n*);
wateren
water-colour, waterverf;
aqua'rel
watercourse, bedding
waterfall, waterval
watertight, waterproof, waterdicht
watery, water(acht)ig; regen-
wave, golf: wuiven (met);
watergolven, perma'nenten
waver, flikkeren; weifelen;
beven

wavy, golvend

wax, was(sen): wassen; worden

way, ma'nier, wijze; opzicht n; kant, weg, eind n; zin; vaart

by the way, tussen haakjes

to give way, toegeven; wegzakken

in a way, in zekere zin

to make one's way, zijn weg vinden; voor'uitkomen

wayfarer, reiziger, zwerver

waylay, aanranden; aanklampen

wayside, (aan de) kant van de weg

wayward, eigen'zinnig

we, wij

weak, zwak; slap

weaken, ver'zwakken; ver'slappen

weakling, zwakkeling

weakness, zwakte; zwak (punt) n

wealth, rijkdom; schat

wealthy, rijk

wean, spenen

weapon, wapen n

wear, dracht, kleding; slij'tage: dragen; slijten; zich houden

to wear out, (ver')slijten, afdragen; afmatten

weariness, ver'moeidheid

weary, moe

weather, weer n: ver'weren; door'staan

weather-beaten, door stormen ge'teisterd; ver'weerd

weathercock, weerhaantje n

weave, weeftrant: weven; (samen)vlechten

web, web n; weefsel n

wedding, huwelijk(splechtig-heid) (n)

wedge, wig: vastzetten

wee, heel klein

weed, onkruid n: wieden

weedy, vol onkruid; spichtig

week, (over een) week

weekend, weekend n

weekly, wekelijks, week-

weep, wenen

weeping, wenend; treur-

weigh, (af)wegen; drukken; lichten

weight, ge'wicht n

weighty, zwaar; ge'wichtig

weir, stuwdam

weird, griezelig, raar

welcome, welkom (n), ver'welkoming: ver'welkomen

weld, las(sen)

welfare, welzijn n: soci'aal, weten'schappelijk

well, goed; ver: wel: put, bron: wellen

as well, ook; even'goed; zo'wel

well-being, welzijn n

well-bred, wel'opgevoed

well-known, be'kend

well-nigh, nage'noeg

well-off, welge'steld; goed'af

well-read, be'lezen

wench, deern

west, West(en) (n), west(waards)

west of, ten westen van

westerly, westelijk, wester-

western, westers, westelijk

wet, nat (maken)

whak, mep: slaan

whale, walvis

wharf, kaai

what, wat (voor (een)), welk; waar-

what is the time? hoe laat is het?

what is it called? hoe heet het?

whatever, wat (or welk) dan ook; wat . . . toch

wheat, tarwe

wheedle, be'praten, aftroggelen

wheel, wiel, n, rad n: zwenken; duwen

wheelbarrow, kruiwagen

wheeze, piepen, hijgen

whelp, welp; kwa'jongen

when, wan'neer; (en) toen

whence, van'waar

whenever, wan'neer ook; telkens wan'neer

where, waar (naar toe)

whereabouts, waar onge'veer: ver'blijfplaats, ligging

whereas. ter'wijl

wherever, waar (. . . ook *or* toch); overal waar

wherewithal, middelen

whet, opwekken

whether, of

whew! oef!

whey (cheese), wei(kaas)

which, welk, wat; die, dat; wie

whiff, vleugje *n*, wolkje *n*

while, tijd: ter'wijl: hoe'wel
  to while away, ver'slijten

whilst, ter'wijl; alhoe'wel

whim(sical), gril(lig)

whimper, grienen, janken

whine, jengelen, janken

whinny, hinniken

whip, zweep: (met de zweep) slaan; wippen, schieten; kloppen

whir, ge'snor *n*: snorren

whirl, roes: dwarrelen; tollen, slingeren, stormen

whirlpool, draaikolk

whirlwind, wervelwind

whisk, klopper: (weg)wippen

whiskers, bakkebaarden; snor

whisky, whisky

whisper, ge'fluister *n*: fluisteren

whistle, fluit(je *n*): fluiten

whit, zier

white, wit; blank

whitewash, witkalk: witten

whither, werwaarts

Whitsun, Pinksteren

whittle down, ge'leidelijk ver'minderen

whiz, suizen

who, wie; die

whoever, wie . . . ook; al wie

whole, (ge')heel (*n*); vol'ledig
  on the whole, over het ge'heel ge'nomen

wholesale, groothandel: in-koops-; op grote schaal

wholesome, ge'zond

wholly, to'taal

whoop, kreet: schreeuwen

whooping-cough, kinkhoest

whore, hoer

whose, wiens, wier; van wie

why, waarom: wel

wick, pit, ka'toentje *n*

wicked, slecht; on'deugend; schan'dalig

wicker, rieten

wide, breed, wijd
  wide-awake, klaar wakker

widely, wijd en zijd; zeer

widen, (zich) ver'wijden

widespread, uitgestrekt; wijd ver'spreid

widow, weduwe

widower, weduwnaar

width, breedte, wijdte

wield, zwaaien; uitoefenen

wife, vrouw

wig, pruik

wiggle, wiebelen met

wild, wild: woest

wilderness, wildernis

wile, list: lokken

wilful, eigen'zinnig; moed'-willig

will, wil(len); testa'ment *n*: zal, zult, zullen; kunnen

willing, be'reid('willig), ge'willig

willow, wilg

wilt, ver'leppen

wily, slim, sluw

win, winnen, be'halen

wince, in'eenkrimpen, zijn ge'-zicht ver'trekken

winch, windas

wind, wind: blaas-: kronkelen; winden

windfall, afgewaaide vrucht; buitenkansje *n*

window, raam *n*

window-pane, ruit

window-sill, vensterbank

windscreen, voorruit

windward, loefzijde

windy, winderig

wine, wijn

wing, vleugel; cou'lisse; spat-bord *n*

wink, knipoogje *n*: knipogen

winner, winnaar

winning, winnend; in'nemend

winter, winter(-)

wintry, winters

wipe, (af)vegen

wire, (ijzer)draad (*n*); tele'-gram *n*

wire netting, kippegaas *n*

wireless, radio : draadloos
wisdom, wijsheid
wise, wijs, ver'standig : wijze
wish, ver'langen (*n*) ; wens(en) ;
 I wish that you were here, ik
 wou dat je hier was
 I wish to speak to him, ik zou
 hem willen spreken
wisp, bosje *n*, paar losse
 (haartjes) ; sliert
wistful, ver'langend, wee'moedig
wit, ver'nuft *n*, ver'stand *n* ;
 geest(igheid)
 at one's wits' end, ten einde
 raad
witch, heks
witchcraft, tovena'rij
with, met, bij ; van
withdraw, (zich) te'rugtrekken
wither, ver'welken ; ver'nietigen
withhold, ont'houden
within, binnen(in)
without, zonder ; buiten
withstand, weer'staan
witness, ge'tuige(nis *n*) : ge'-
 tuige zijn van ; ge'tuigen (van)
witticism, geestigheid
witty, geestig
wizard, tovenaar
wobble, wiebelen
woe, ellende : wee !
woeful, ramp'zalig
wolf, wolf : opschrokken
woman, vrouw ; mens *n*
womb, baarmoeder ; schoot
wonder, wonder *n* ; ver'wondering : (zich) ver'wondcren ;
 zich afvragen
wonderful, wonder'baarlijk ;
 prachtig
wont, ge'woon(te)
woo, het hof maken
wood, hout *n* ; bos *n*
wooded, be'bost
wooden, houten ; houterig
 woodland, bosland *n* : bos-
woodman, houthakker ; boswachter
woodwork, houtwerk *n* ; hout-
 be'werking
woody, bosrijk
wool(len), wol(len)
woolly, wollig

word, woord *n* ; be'richt *n*
wording, re'dactie
work, werk(en) (*n*) ; han'teren
worker, arbeider, werker
working, werking
workmanship, vakmanschap *n*
workshop, werkplaats
world(ly), wereld(s)
world-wide, over de hele wereld,
 wereld-
worm, wurm(en) ; kruipen ; indringen
worn-out, ver'sleten ; uitgeput
worry, zorg : (zich) be'zorgd
 maken ; lastig vallen
worse, erger, slechter
worship, aan'bidding ; gods-
 dienst(oefening) : aan'bidden ;
 ver'eren
worst, ergst, slechtst
worsted, kamgaren *n*
worth, waard(e)
worth while, worth doing
 (**seeing** *etc*), de moeite waard
worthless, waardeloos ; ver'achtelijk
worthy, (achtens')waardig,
 waard
would, zou(den) (willen) ;
 wilde(n) ; wou
would-be, zogenaamd ; ge'wild
wound, wond(en)
wrangle, kijven
wrap, sjaal, cape : wikkelen, inpakken ; hullen, ver'zinken
 to wrap round, omslaan
wrapping, ver'pakking
wrath(ful), toorn(ig)
wreak, koelen, oefenen
wreath, krans
wreck, wrak *n* : ver'nielen
wrench, ruk(ken) ; schroef-
 sleutel
wrest, ont'wringen, afpersen
wrestle, worstelen
wretch, stakker
wretched, el'lendig ; be'roerd
wriggle, draaien, wriemelen ; zich
 wringen
wring, (uit)wringen ; afdwingen ;
 omdraaien
wrinkle, rimpel(en)
wrist, pols

writ, (be'vel)schrift *n*, dagvaarding
write, schrijven
writer, schrijver
writhe, (zich ver')wringen
writing, (ge')schrift *n*, schrijven
n : schrijf-
wrong, ver'keerd ; on'juist ; niet
in orde : kwaad *n*, onrecht
(aandoen) (*n*)
  what is wrong ? wat man'keert
  eraan ? wat is er ?
  to go wrong, misgaan ; ver'-
  keerd gaan ; de'fect raken ; de
  ver'keerde weg opgaan
wrought iron, smeedijzer *n*
wry, zuur

X

X-ray, röntgenfoto : röntgenen

Y

yacht, jacht *n* : zeilen
yap, keffen ; snauwen
yard, plaats(je *n*), erf *n* : kleine
meter (91, 44 cm.) ; ra
yarn, garen *n* : ver'haal *n*
yawn, geeuw(en) ; gapen
ye, gij
yea, ja (zelfs)
year, jaar *n*
yearly, jaarlijks
yearn, vurig ver'langen (naar)
yeast, gist
yell, gil(len)
yellow, geel
yelp, janken

yes, ja
yesterday, gisteren
yet, nog ; al : toch
  as yet, tot nu toe
yew, taxus
yield, opbrengst : (zich) overgeven ; (be'z)wijken (voor) ;
opleveren
yoke, juk *n* ; schouder(*or* heup)-
stuk *n*
yokel, pummel
yolk, dooier
yonder, ginds
you, u ; jij, je, jou ; jullie
young, jong(en) (*n*) : jeugd
youngster, jongeman, jong
meisje *n*
your, uw ; je, jouw ; jullie
yours, (die *or* dat) van u, (die
or dat) van jou, (die *or* dat) van
jullie
yourself, (u')zelf, zich ; je ('zelf)
youth, jeugd ; jongeling
youthful, jeugdig

Z

zeal, vuur *n* ; ijver
zealot, dweper
zealous, ijverig ; vurig
zenith, zenit *n* ; toppunt *n*
zero, nul(punt *n*)
zest, animo
zigzag, zigzag
zinc, zink *n*
zip-fastener, ritssluiting
zodiac, dierenriem
zone, zone
zoo, dierentuin
zoological, zoö'logisch

TEACH YOURSELF BOOKS

DUTCH

H. Koolhoven

A course in the Dutch language, complete in one easy-to-follow volume.

One of the hurdles in learning any language is mastering its pronunciation: this is the first problem which this text overcomes. Chapter One deals as fully as possible with spoken Dutch, leading naturally to an examination of the technicalities of the language. Thirty chapters then introduce and practise, step by step, the various points of Dutch grammar, idiom and construction. Vocabulary is built up throughout the course and an extensive vocabulary is to be found at the end of the book.

A graded course, ideal for the beginner studying on his own or for students in the classroom.

Published in USA by
David McKay Company, Inc.

ISBN 0 340 05778 5

UNITED KINGDOM	60p
AUSTRALIA	$1.95*
NEW ZEALAND	$1.95

*recommended but not obligatory

TEACH YOURSELF BOOKS

GERMAN DICTIONARY

This dictionary provides the user with a comprehensive
vocabulary of working German and will be particularly useful to the student working through a basic course, such as
Teach Yourself German.

With over · 20,000 words in both sections, particular
emphasis has been placed on current usage, including slang
and idiom. The student will also find lists of principal strong
and irregular verbs and of commonly used abbreviations,
along with a concise German grammar.

Designed to be both practical and convenient, this dictionary
provides an invaluable aid to the study and reading of
German.

UNITED KINGDOM	60p
AUSTRALIA	$1.80*
NEW ZEALAND	$1.70

ISBN 0 340 05789 0   *recommended but not obligatory